VIRGINIANS AND THEIR HISTORIES

VIRGINIANS

AND THEIR HISTORIES

BRENT TARTER

University of Virginia Press

CHARLOTTESVILLE AND LONDON

in collaboration with the Library of Virginia

University of Virginia Press
in collaboration with the Library of Virginia
© 2020 Brent Tarter
Printed in the United States of America on acid-free paper

First published 2020

1 3 5 7 9 8 6 4 2

Library of Congress Cataloging-in-Publication Data
Names: Tarter, Brent, 1948– author.
Title: Virginians and their histories / Brent Tarter.
Description: Charlottesville : University of Virginia Press, 2020. | Includes
bibliographical references and index.
Identifiers: LCCN 2019050025 (print) | LCCN 2019050026 (ebook) | ISBN
9780813943923 (cloth) | ISBN 9780813943930 (ebook)
Subjects: LCSH: Virginia—History.
Classification: LCC F226 .T37 2020 (print) | LCC F226 (ebook) | DDC 975.5—dc23
LC record available at https://lccn.loc.gov/2019050025
LC ebook record available at https://lccn.loc.gov/2019050026

Cover art: Images from the collections of the Library of Virginia

CONTENTS

ACKNOWLEDGMENTS

THIS HISTORY OF VIRGINIA, published by the University of Virginia Press in collaboration with the Library of Virginia, began as a collaborative project of historians and editors at the Library of Virginia with me as coordinator. We planned to draw on our collective knowledge derived from our research in the primary sources of every decade of Virginia's English-language history and employ the insights of the best new scholarship to review and reinterpret the history of the people who have lived in the colony and state. Through a series of budget and staff reductions and reassignments of responsibilities the work eventually fell on me. Current and former Library of Virginia staff members who participated in the planning discussions, contributed information or memoranda on topics about which they had special knowledge, or read and commented on parts or all of one or more drafts are William Bland Whitley, Patricia D. Watkinson, Annie Gunter Tripp, Sandra G. Treadway, Emily J. Salmon, Gordon W. Poindexter, Jennifer Davis Mc-Daid, Jennifer R. Loux, Bill Leubke, Maria E. Kimberly, Gregg D. Kimball, Marianne E. Julienne, Emma Ito, Ann E. Henderson, Katharine E. Harbury, Donald W. Gunter, Catherine Fitzgerald Wyatt, John G. Deal, Edward D. C. Campbell Jr., Sara B. Bearss, and Barbara C. Batson, who also worked closely with me to select and procure the maps and illustrations. Professors John T. Kneebone, of Virginia Commonwealth University, and Kevin R. Hardwick, of James Madison University, read the entire text for the press and made insightful and well-informed suggestions. Christine Sisic, of the Library of Virginia, designed the jacket. My excellent friend and colleague the late Sara Bearss suggested the title.

VIRGINIANS AND THEIR HISTORIES

1

THE VIEW FROM CUMBERLAND GAP

FREDERICK JACKSON TURNER made an influential address to members of the American Historical Association in 1892. He invited them to imagine themselves standing at Cumberland Gap at the western tip of Virginia and watching American history march by. Turner said that they would first see deer and other wild animals wandering trails, then Indians pursuing their hunts through the woods, and after them the first European explorers and prospectors, then land speculators and settlers, and finally farmers and planters and entrepreneurs. Turner explained that as those people moved west through the eastern woodlands and across the Great Plains and the Rocky Mountains to the Pacific coast they created successive waves of frontier experiences that shaped the essence of American democratic culture.

The history of what became the United States and of what is now Virginia is not that simple, and it did not begin at Cumberland Gap or even at Jamestown in 1607 or at Plymouth Rock in 1620, where many of Turner's contemporary historians looked for the origins and meaning of American history. The narrative of rising democratic institutions and practices against a background of regional differences that shaped Turner's historical writing relegated American Indians to peripheral roles as victims of or obstacles to the triumphal progress of democratic civilization. It neglected women except as occasional agents of moral reform. It also marginalized the experiences and contributions to the nation's culture and economy of Africans and their descendants, some of whom first entered what became the United States even before the first immigrants landed at Plymouth Rock.

That master narrative was popular in the nineteenth and twentieth centuries and provided readers of American history and of Virginia's history a story of progress and achievement that was largely white and male. It was also largely political and military. It underestimated the importance of events in the historical experience that did not easily fit into themes of progress and democratic development. Progress and change—which were not always the same—came with pains and with losses, and at times the democratic narrative retreated rather than advanced.

Turner asked his audience to stand at Cumberland Gap and look west as American civilization and institutions moved from the Atlantic coast to the Pacific coast. If members of his audience had imagined themselves looking east from Cumberland Gap the view would have been different. They would have seen a relentless movement of people from another world who overspread the land where people had resided for countless generations. Newly arrived people pushed aside or killed people who were already there and largely replaced their culture and institutions with a radically different way of life for a radically different civilization. Seeing the events of the early years of the seventeenth century, what some scholars call the contact period, from the west allows you to see things differently than if viewing them from Jamestown or London. It is the same with all aspects of Virginia's history. Viewing them from different perspectives and in the light of insights not available to earlier writers requires us to interpret most parts of Virginia's colonial and commonwealth history differently from the way we used to understand them.

Writing the History of Virginians

The 1970s began what might be described as the golden age of historical scholarship on Virginia. Scores of original books and hundreds of articles in scholarly journals have explored aspects of the colony's and state's history that earlier writers had misunderstood, ignored, or dismissed as unimportant. Archaeologists, anthropologists, historians, economists, demographers, ethnographers, archivists, librarians, teachers, and smart people without formal academic credentials in any of those disciplines but with unsatisfied curiosities have enriched our understandings of many aspects of the history of Virginia and its peoples. Drawing on that scholarship permits us to reevaluate many events in Virginia history in the light of those new understandings and also to fill in some old and yawning gaps. That literature also requires us to reconsider what we thought we once knew about race relations, religious culture, economic changes, gender relations, and the lives of women and children that differed from the lives of the political and military leaders pre-1970s historical literature tended to emphasize. We can now understand more about Virginia's history and all of its peoples and construct a new narrative of how those people lived in the place now called Virginia.

Regional variety and cultural diversity are important themes in Virginia's history, as are interactions and conflicts—sometimes violent, sometimes not—between people of differing cultures. One of the most important of the many themes that appear and reappear through the centuries of Virginia's history is the relations between different races. From the early years of the seventeenth century Indians and descendants of Africans and Europeans have lived together and apart and interacted with one another in ways that fundamentally shaped how they all lived. Later immigrations from Scotland and Ireland, from Germany, from elsewhere in Europe, and still later from elsewhere in the United States, the Americas, and Asia changed the lives of the people who already lived in Virginia. Living in Virginia changed the lives of immigrants, too, although not always in the same way. It is necessary when contemplating any one of those encounters or populations to regard each in the contexts of what they shared and also of what they did not share with the others. Hence the title of this book, *Virginians and Their Histories.*

Virginia's history is all of their stories. To write about Virginians as a homogenous group, as some historians formerly did, excludes large portions of the population from consideration. Different groups of Virginians experienced their shared history in different ways. To state that Virginians believed something or experienced an event in a certain way is almost certainly to generalize inaccurately from one group to the whole. It is extremely difficult and almost always misleading to refer to Virginians as an undifferentiated population without regard to race, gender, or differences in wealth, social status, and geographic location.

English and later British imperial policies and commercial concerns shaped the context in which all the people in the colony of Virginia lived and regulated their political and economic lives. Some of those policies promoted and some inhibited the pace of European settlement. In many subtle ways the various peoples who lived in the colony produced a distinctive Virginia variant on English culture and government that in turn profoundly influenced how Indian, European, and African residents of Virginia and their descendants lived. Those dynamics changed when Virginia joined with the other colonies at the time of the American Revolution and after that with ratification of Constitution of the United States. The momentous events of the American Civil War upended virtually everything about how all Virginians lived. During the civil rights and women's movements of the twentieth century actions of Congress and federal courts forced important changes in Virginians' ways of life. National political events and national and international economic changes also influenced how Virginians lived. Few or none of the changes were within the power of any or all the people in Virginia to control or prevent.

The First People

Frederick Jackson Turner asked members of his audience to imagine themselves at a specific place, at Cumberland Gap, and also imagine themselves at a specific time. Cumberland Gap became important in the 1770s when explorers and families from mid-Atlantic colonies first began crossing the mountains at that place to enter Kentucky. By then, though, many generations of people to the east had created complex cultural relationships on the landscape between the mountains and the sea. If we image ourselves at Cumberland Gap and looking east across the landscape of Virginia and much further back in time we can begin to understand Virginia's long history afresh and look at all of it anew.

An imaginary observer standing at Cumberland Gap twenty thousand years ago and able to see around the curvature of the Earth could have watched the beginnings of an important human drama. Forested mountains and valleys stretched away from Cumberland Gap in every direction. To the south were the Great Smoky Mountains. To the west and northwest was the land later called Kentucky. Its mountains and deep valleys relaxed into rolling hills near the Ohio River, a broad avenue of transportation Indians used long before white explorers from England and France first viewed it in the seventeenth century. That land was western Virginia until 1792. To the north of Cumberland Gap was the land that in 1863 split off from Virginia and became West Virginia. It was also a large expanse of rugged mountains and valleys that stretched far north toward the headwaters of the Ohio River.

To the east and northeast of Cumberland Gap the imaginary viewer would see the landscape of what became the state of Virginia. It reached more than 400 miles east across high mountains and narrow valleys, across lower and gentler hills, across broad rivers and narrow streams, through forests and swamps, all the way to the Atlantic Ocean. Mountains stretched away northeast from Cumberland Gap in parallel rows with narrow valleys between them. Between the easternmost mountain ranges, the Allegheny and the Blue Ridge, was a broader valley later known as the Great Valley or the Valley of Virginia, a region so distinctive that Virginians gave its name capital letters. In the north of it the Shenandoah River and the South Branch of the Potomac River flowed northeastward. In the southwestern portion the upper tributaries of the Clinch and Holston Rivers flowed south and southwest into the Tennessee River Valley. The New River cut across the southwest-to-northeast ranges of mountains and valleys as it flowed north out of North Carolina and turned west and crossed the Valley of Virginia to become the Great Kanawha River along its way to the Ohio.

The imaginary observer might see some of the first human figures moving

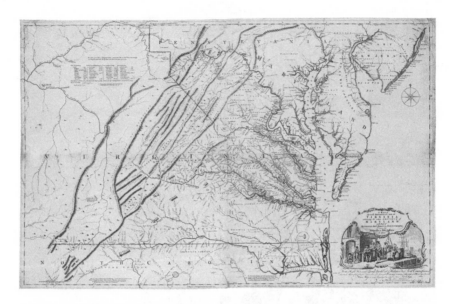

Joshua Fry and Peter Jefferson, *A Map of the Most Inhabited Part of Virginia* (4th state, London 1755), clearly shows the mountains and valleys northeast of Cumberland Gap, which is west of the edge of the map.

through the valleys of the mountains or might see distant smoke from the campfires of nomadic hunters and gatherers who stopped to sleep, hunt, or fish on the banks of eastern rivers or Chesapeake Bay. When and where those first people entered what is now Virginia is not known. Archaeological investigations at the Cactus Hill site in Sussex County in southeastern Virginia revealed that people were in Virginia between 20,000 and 15,000 BC.

Early human residents had many sources of animal and plant food available to them. Hunting, fishing, and foraging people moved and settled in families and dwelled at temporary campsites near streams at many locations within the present boundaries of Virginia. In the east they feasted on the rich supply of fish and shellfish from the waters near the bay. Moose, elk, deer, and bear were then common in much of the region. Fossil remains of mastodon and mammoth have been found in the valley of the North Fork of the Holston River near the modern town of Saltville in southwestern Virginia, and remains of a mastodon have been found near Yorktown in southeastern Virginia. By about 9500 BC people had established base camps in several places. Archaeologists have identified early camp or settlement sites at Flint Run, or Thunderbird, in Warren County in the northern part of Virginia, and at what is known as the Williamson Site in Dinwiddie County in the east-central part of Virginia. Indians quarried jasper (a quartz) at Flint Run and chert in Dinwiddie for

Artifacts from Werowocomoco

making tools and weapons. By 5,000 BC they were making axes using quartzite and basalt.

Late in the first millennium AD the people adopted the bow and arrow to replace the atlatl, or spear thrower, as their primary hunting weapon. When hunting deer and other large animals they surrounded an area and advanced toward the center to concentrate the animals. They sometimes set fire to the woods to force the game toward a place where the animals could more easily be killed. Early residents of what became Virginia also created elaborate pottery and ornaments of bone and shell that had artistic as well as utilitarian value. Surviving pieces of pottery and other goods indicate that considerable cultural variety existed in different places and at different times. People also engaged in long-distance trading along forest paths and rivers and developed trade routes that extended up and down the Atlantic coast and far inland to the northwest and southwest. Tribes in the Appalachian Mountains supplied sheet mica to the Hopewell Burial Mound people of the Ohio River Valley, and Indians in eastern Virginia acquired copper from people in the Great Lakes region.

It is not certain when people in the various regions of what became Virginia first adopted agriculture. About 2,500 BC they obtained squash and gourds from tribes to the southwest, and they later acquired corn and by about AD 1000 beans, as well. In order to raise crops in the forest Indians cut deep rings around tree trunks to sever the sapwood that carried water from the roots to the branches. The trees died, which allowed sunlight to reach the forest floor where the Indians planted their seeds and tended their crops. They also burned the underbrush to clear the land. Ash from the fires fertilized the soil. Land in such clearings could be cultivated for several years, after which people killed trees elsewhere and moved their fields. New forests then reclaimed abandoned fields. It was an efficient method of farming that modified the natural environment in ways different from how European methods of agriculture later altered the landscape.

People lived differently depending on where they lived and when they lived there. The geological regions within Virginia have always influenced how people have lived in its different parts. In the westernmost portion of what became Virginia is the high Appalachian Plateau, part of the Appalachian Mountain chain that extends southwest from the Gaspé Peninsula in Quebec to Alabama. Much of southern and eastern West Virginia as well as eastern Kentucky are part of the plateau. Within the present boundaries of Virginia the plateau includes Buchanan and Dickenson Counties, most of Wise County, the western portions of Russell, Scott, and Tazewell Counties, and the northwestern portion of Lee County.

The Allegheny Mountains along most of the current Virginia–West Virginia border are part of the Appalachian system. The Allegheny Mountains are a high and rugged mountain region with narrow and steep stream-eroded valleys that surmount horizontal or gently tilted sandstone and shale formations and coal beds. The coal underneath the mountains became the state's most important mineral resource late in the nineteenth century. During the early centuries of human habitation the mountains were probably the least densely populated region. The steep mountains and narrow valleys covered with mixed hardwood and conifer forests may have enticed hunter-gatherer people, but relatively few places appeared suitable for agriculture or long-term settlement. Cumberland Gap offered a relatively easy east–west crossing place.

In the valleys east of the Appalachian Mountains solution-weathering of limestone and dolomite formations in the area is responsible for the region's fertile soil and karst landscape of sinkholes, springs, and caves. Human habitation can be traced back to very early dates. The valleys provided natural routes for trade, migration, and invasion throughout human history, even though Indians may have used the region more as a pathway and as a shared seasonal hunting ground than as a place of long-term residence. For the early Indians as well as for the English- and German-speaking colonists of the eighteenth century the valleys of Virginia offered many advantages. The fertile soil supported populations of game that served as a source of food, and where the land was not too steep it was ideal for agriculture. Most of the landscape features of the region now have English names, but numerous places in the Shenandoah Valley and the Blue Ridge have German names. The loss of most of the Indian names graphically reflects the changes in the populations of human beings there since the seventeenth century.

Archaeological evidence of the existence of several large town sites in the southwestern valleys indicates that the people who lived there during the second millennium AD were numerous and were successful as farmers and hunters. They were culturally affiliated with the Mound Builders of the Ohio and Mississippi River Valleys. Remnants of their ceremonial mounds exist in several parts of southwestern Virginia, some of which were the objects of excavation or desecration during the nineteenth century. Ely Mound in Lee County was a very large oval about three hundred feet in circumference. A Mississippian town founded about AD 1500 and now known as the Crab Orchard Site in Tazewell County was excavated in the 1940s and again in the 1970s. The town was about four hundred feet across. Its residents constructed a palisade that surrounded and protected the town. They may have replaced it as many as three times during their long occupation of the site. The town was home to about four hundred people and had a large council house about sixty-five feet long and from thirty to forty feet wide. Archaeologists have studied another large palisaded town at Saltville. The existence of those large settlements indicates that the people who dwelled in the area and created the towns had developed complex and effective economic, cultural, and political systems. They could devote time and labor to creating and maintaining large-scale settlements and feeding the residents, indicating they no longer needed to devote all their energies entirely to subsistence hunting, fishing, or farming. The number of people who resided in the southern valleys at any given time is not known.

In the northern valleys and in the Potomac River watershed small populations gradually adopted agriculture and became more numerous during the first millennium AD as the climate warmed and permitted the cultivation of grain and other crops. When groups of people established annual settlements for agriculture they sometimes came into conflict with other groups who had traditionally used the region for seasonal hunting and fishing or for gathering nuts, berries, and other edible wild plants. In the lower portion of the Potomac River Valley a cooling of the climate known as the Little Ice Age, from the thirteenth through the sixteenth centuries, produced some significant shifts in settlement patterns. People moved to lower altitudes or lower latitudes where the game, fish, trees, and useful vegetation allowed them to continue their lifestyles with minimal disruption or adaptation to new conditions. Other Indians who had lived in what are now Maryland, Pennsylvania, and New York also shifted their hunting territories as their game moved southward or downward from higher elevations. Those population movements created new occasions for conflicts.

The eastern flank of the valleys is the Blue Ridge Mountain chain, a long, narrow range of steep mountains that extends from southern Pennsylvania to northern Georgia. It varies in width from about two miles at the Potomac River to more than fifty miles at the Virginia–North Carolina border. East of the Blue Ridge is the large Piedmont area of Virginia. Its name is derived from the Piedmont region of Italy and means foot of the mountains or foothills. In the south along the North Carolina border the Piedmont is more than two hundred miles wide; in the north it is much narrower. Near the Blue Ridge are isolated mountains and ridges with elevations as high as two thousand feet. The low relief of the Piedmont slopes gently eastward, but the rocks that make up and underlie it extend farther eastward deep beneath the adjoining Coastal Plain and the continental shelf. By the sixteenth century AD, a variety of people with different languages and cultural traditions resided in the Piedmont. The best known are the Siouan-speaking Tutelo, Saponi, Occaneechi, Monacan, and Manahoac. Some of them erected ceremonial mounds as residents of the western mountains and the Great Plains did. Thomas Jefferson made a study of one such mound in Albemarle County in the 1780s.

The eastern boundary of the Piedmont is the fall line where rivers pass over the margin of the Piedmont's hard, erosion-resistant rocks onto the Coastal Plain. The fall line exhibits some dramatic scenes like the Potomac River's Great Falls. At other sites, such as where the Rappahannock River crosses the fall line at Fredericksburg or where the James River crosses the fall line at Richmond, the rivers contain stretches of shallow, turbulent water that are not navigable. The roughly hundred-mile-wide Coastal Plain between the fall line and Chesapeake Bay is the least rugged region of Virginia. The topography is generally a low-relief terraced landscape with elevations ranging from two hundred feet inland to sea level along the Chesapeake Bay and Atlantic shorelines. The lower reaches of all of the rivers in the Coastal Plain are subject to tidal fluctuations, and the water there is mildly brackish. That region is often referred to as the Tidewater because the rivers and streams rise and fall twice daily as water piles up against the flowing tides in the bay.

Several broad rivers—two with native names, the Potomac and the Rappahannock, and two now with English names, the York and the James—flow east or southeast and empty into Chesapeake Bay and create fertile lowlands and bountiful wetlands. The strip of land between the Potomac and Rappahannock Rivers is traditionally referred to as the Northern Neck, and the strip between the Rappahannock and York Rivers as the Middle Peninsula. The land between the York and James Rivers has long been called merely the Peninsula. The region south of the James and Appomattox Rivers, east of the

Piedmont, and west of the coastal lowlands is often called the Southside. Each is a distinctive region to which Virginians have given capital letters.

A narrow peninsula borders the eastern portion of the bay. The Eastern Shore, as it is called, is almost surrounded by saltwater; the ocean is on its east and the less salty bay on the west. The narrow Eastern Shore is the southern part of the Delmarva Peninsula, which is wider north of the present Virginia-Maryland border. The Eastern Shore may have formed after the last Ice Age as dispersed coastal sediment coalesced around offshore shoals and barrier islands. Wave action and alongshore drift still transport sand along Virginia's coastline, building and reshaping the barrier islands. There are currently eighteen of them along the Eastern Shore and the barrier spit that extends southward from Virginia Beach into North Carolina.

With the melting of the last continental glacial ice the lower valleys of the Susquehanna River and its tributary rivers were drowned, which created the Chesapeake Bay and the wide lower regions of the Potomac, Rappahannock, York, and James Rivers. Although called a bay, the Chesapeake is by definition an estuary, a region where fresh river water interacts with salt ocean water. It is the largest estuary in the United States. It was—and is—an easy place to make a living. The land could easily sustain the low-intensity agriculture the Indians practiced. The rivers teemed with freshwater fish, including seasonal migrations of great swarms of herring and other anadromous fish that live at sea but return to fresh waters to breed, as well as large and succulent sturgeon. The bay had its own populations of fish that were adapted to its brackish waters, and millions of crabs and oysters seemed just waiting to be harvested. And during the winter when agriculture was impossible and crops harvested in the autumn grew scarce, an astonishing abundance of wintering waterfowl descended on the region from northern breeding sites. Early European visitors marveled at the large flocks of more than a dozen species of ducks, two species of geese, and two species of wild swans, all of which provided nourishment for residents of the bay area.

The many tidal inlets with habitable sites on the shore of the bay probably enticed some of the first human beings who visited the area to stay and make their homes. It is likely that the Coastal Plain has always been the most populous portion of Virginia. The abundant fish and shellfish of the rivers and bay, the turkeys, deer, bear, and other animals, and the fruits, nuts, vines, and other plants of the forests supported dozens of populations of people by the second millennium AD. They lived in semi-permanent towns and engaged in agriculture, fishing, and hunting, and in the wetlands near the bay gathered the starchy tuckahoe. The earliest English explorers of the Chesapeake Bay and lower Potomac River recorded the names of many of the groups or tribes who lived there and assigned their names to creeks, bays, peninsulas, or larger

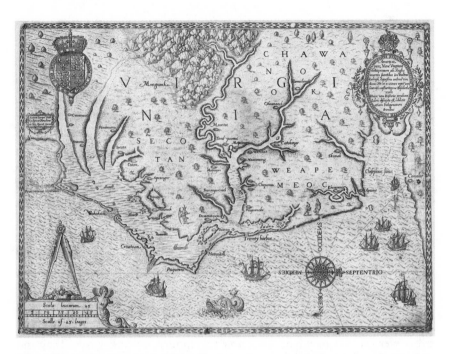

John White, *Americae pars, Nunc Virginia dicta,* 1590. As in most early Virginia maps, north is to the right, not the top.

regions that preserve evidence of Indian places of residence. The names of groups of people thereby became place names.

A long gradual warming trend reversed the effects of the Little Ice Age by the fifteenth and sixteenth centuries. Agriculture gained a firmer foothold in the lives of most or all the inhabitants of the Coastal Plain. The residents adopted seasonal lifestyles of hunting, fishing, planting, and harvesting and except during hunting and fishing seasons remained closer to the centers of their places of habitation. Protecting their separate worlds from outside encroachments became more important than during earlier and colder times when people had lived in smaller groups and moved more often. Agricultural settlement required people to organize themselves politically in order to wage occasional defensive or offensive warfare. They also had to develop diplomatic techniques and devise methods of negotiation with neighboring groups in order to avoid or to terminate conflicts. Large settlements also required coordination of economic activities and promoted the development of larger and more complex political leadership networks. In the lower Potomac River valley by the sixteenth century AD, some of the towns had formed leagues under the leadership of a paramount chief, or ruler, a process that almost certainly took place elsewhere in the region about that time.

The Powhatan of Tsenacomoco

The most numerous group of people in the region at that time was an Algonquian-speaking people who were culturally similar to other Eastern Woodland Indians. Known as the Powhatan, they resided in towns of the Coastal Plain and farmed the lowlands from the James River north to the Potomac. They raised tobacco, sunflowers, squash, beans, and maize (which the English called Indian corn), and they gathered the abundant food resources of the tidewater region. In addition to their agriculture their seasonal hunting, their fishing and foraging enabled them to support a complex and fairly stable society.

Powhatan society was a modified matrilineal one. Authority to rule descended through female lines. When a male ruler or chief died the next senior male descendant of his mother usually succeeded him, but some towns had women rulers. Through an initiation rite known as the *huskanaw* young men entered adulthood and assumed their roles as hunters or leaders. A *werowance* (whom the earliest English writers called chief or king) who could be either male or female (*werowansqua*) governed each town or tribe. Werowances may have been able to support multiple wives. They and priests may have been the only members of the society who were believed to enjoy an afterlife, but early English accounts of the religious beliefs of the sixteenth- and early seventeenth-century Indians in eastern Virginia are to some extent contradictory and unreliable and may have misinterpreted the substance and significance of Indians' beliefs and practices.

In the 1570s or 1580s, the chief Wahunsonacock consolidated about thirty Algonquian groups (among them the Rappahannock, Pamunkey, Mattaponi, and Appamattuck) to form an extended confederacy or chiefdom known as Tsenacomoco (pronounced Tsen-ah-kah-mah´-kah). The name has been translated as meaning densely inhabited land. Thirteen thousand or more people lived in an area that encompassed about six thousand square miles, mostly north of the James River and near the bay and the mouths of the other great rivers. As the paramount chief of the alliance Wahunsonacock was the *mamanatowick,* a revered spiritual and civil leader. He was also known as Powhatan.

At the beginning of the seventeenth century Wahunsonacock resided in the large town of Werowocomoco near a shallow bay on the north bank of the York River in what is now Gloucester County. Archaeological excavations at Werowocomoco revealed that it was the largest of the towns in the Chesapeake region and included the paramount chief's ceremonial house. Two long parallel trenches bisected the town. Their significance is unclear, but they may have featured in early religious ceremonies. The Powhatan made very effec-

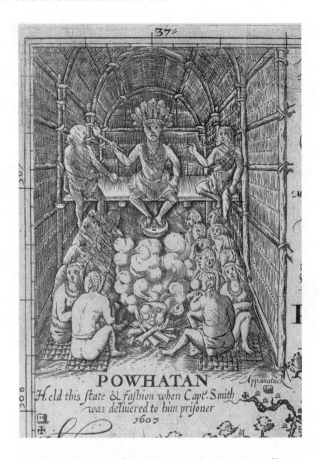

Powhatan in State, from John Smith, *The Generall Historie of Virginia, New England, and the Summer Isles* (London, 1624)

tive use of the natural resources of the area and were able to devote time and energy to other pursuits beyond subsistence farming, hunting, and fishing. Constructing a town on such a scale and providing sufficient food for its inhabitants required many people and much labor as well as skillful management of those resources. It is likely that Indians from throughout Tsenacomoco were as impressed by Werowocomoco and its leader as English visitors were beginning in 1607.

Engraved reproductions of paintings that John White made of residents of the Outer Banks of North Carolina in the 1580s may give a good idea of how some towns in Tsenacomoco appeared and how their residents lived. Early Englishmen such as Captain John Smith, William Strachey, and Alexander Whitaker wrote about the people of Tsenacomoco, their towns, and their

Archaeological investigation of Werowocomoco

cultural practices. Their accounts of the people and descriptions of the landscape contain variant spellings as a result of the writers' attempts to render into English the words they heard from the Indians. Their accounts sometimes disclose as much about English perspectives as about Powhatan lives. For example, Indian women worked the fields, harvested fruits and vegetables, and gathered tuckahoe from marshes, which contrasted with English agricultural practices that assigned such work to lower-class men. Indian men hunted and fished, which Englishmen of the time regarded as recreational activities reserved for men of privileged classes or as disreputable activities of poachers. Distribution of labor within Powhatan society appeared to English observers to be strange and uncivilized.

The earliest English observers and writers had all grown to maturity as subjects of Queen Elizabeth I and were comfortable with the idea that women of high status could rule their towns as werowansquas; but their general observations reinforced English perceptions of the Indians as uncivilized by English or European definitions. Englishmen probably misunderstood the decentralized nature of Powhatan political authority as can be seen by their application of hierarchical European terms such as king, queen, and emperor that inaccurately represented the realities of the cultural and political relationships among the people who lived in Tsenacomoco. Each town maintained a large measure of

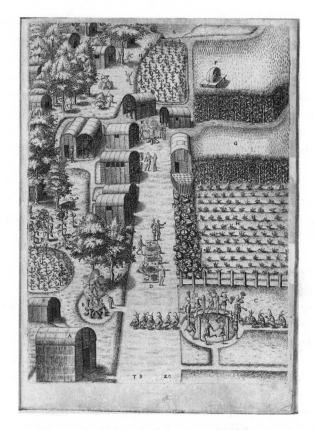

Village of Secotan, from Theodore de Bry, *Admiranda narratio* (Frankfurt, 1590)

independence. The paramount chief and local werowances reaffirmed their relationships through ritual exchanges, marriage alliances, and other cultural practices rather than primarily through coercion, as some early English writers appeared to believe. And not all tribes near the bay were part of the paramount chiefdom. The Chickahominy lived under the rule of religious leaders rather than political or military officers and maintained a large measure of independence from the Powhatan.

From Cumberland Gap the imaginary witness to history would have seen at the beginning of the seventeenth century that the Powhatan of Tsenacomoco were the most numerous and politically powerful people within view.

The First Europeans

From Cumberland Gap the imaginary observer could also have seen in the nearby valleys the first encounters between native residents of North America and people from Europe. Two members of Hernando de Soto's Spanish exploring party are believed to have entered what is now Lee County in southwestern Virginia in 1540. In 1567 another group of Spanish explorers attacked a Holstonia town at the site of the modern town of Saltville. Spain had long been interested in Bahía de Santa María and Ajacan, the Spanish names for Chesapeake Bay and Virginia. In 1570 they established a Jesuit mission on the south bank of the river later known as the York, but the Indians destroyed the mission in 1571. A year later Spanish troops from Florida retaliated and killed many Indians.

It is unlikely that people who lived near the ocean knew about the Spanish presence in the west or that people in the west were aware of Spanish visits to the bay. Some people in the east, however, had an opportunity to learn something about Spain. About 1560 a Spanish exploring party entered the bay and took a young man named Paquiquineo back to Spain, presented him to the king, baptized him, and gave him the name Don Luís de Velasco. After he had visited several Spanish colonies in the Caribbean and Mexico he returned with a party of Spaniards, resumed his life with his people, and may have taken part in extirpating the Jesuit mission.

Some eastern Indians definitely knew about the failed English attempt in the 1580s to establish a colony on the outer banks of what became North Carolina. They may also have learned something about England from reports that Manteo, one of the Indians who traveled there in the 1580s, brought back when he rejoined his family in the New World. Manteo astonished the English as Paquiquineo had astonished the Spanish by forsaking what Europeans regarded as their superior civilizations in favor of life with their families in what Europeans saw as a wilderness.

2

THE ENGLISH INVASION OF TSENACOMOCO

IT BEGAN IN THE TIME OF PLANTING as residents of the Chesapeake Bay area reckoned the changing of seasons and the passing of time. It began on April 26, 1607, as English people reckoned the changing of seasons and the passing of time.

Two people saw the beginnings of the invasion that permanently altered the landscape and history of the Chesapeake Bay region. One of them was a member of one of the tribes that dwelled near the coast and could have been male or female, child or adult. The other was a man or boy and probably English. We do not know the name of either, nor do we know precisely what they thought about what they saw. We know something about what they saw and what they and other people with them did, which allows us to understand in a general way what they may have thought.

The First Day

The first person who saw the beginning of the invasion from the land probably saw a ship's sail far out to sea as the sun rose behind it. That woman or girl, man or boy probably stood in the edge of the woods or on the beach near where the coastline bends from north-south to east-west at the south end of the great bay, at what the invaders called and modern maps identify as Cape Henry.

That person probably watched as the ship and two others slowly approached the coast. He or she probably knew that for many generations ships like the ones approaching had suddenly and without any warning appeared and then disappeared. Some remained for a short time and entered the bay. Some actually set ashore strangely attired hairy men who carried large, loud weapons that could wound or kill at a distance with tiny metal balls that invis-

ibly flew through the air much faster than the arrows of even the most powerful bowman.

He or she may possibly have known a little something about the missionary
settlement Spanish explorers had established two or three generations earlier
on the banks of one of the rivers that emptied into the bay. He or she probably
knew something about the settlement English men and women made in the
times of his or her parents or grandparents on a thin strip of sandy land now
called the Outer Banks of North Carolina. It would be safe to assume that the
Indian who first caught sight of the sails that spring day would have been surprised at the sight because it was unexpected, but because of what the people
there knew about the past he or she would most likely have assumed that just
another short-term visit from those strange people was about to begin. He or
she probably quickly informed family members, friends, and the tribe's leaders,
who later in the day approached the coast to see for themselves. Perhaps that
day or soon thereafter a tribal leader sent messengers farther inland to alert
other tribes nearby and farther away in Tsenacomoco.

The other person who was a first witness to the invasion was a man or boy
aboard one of the three ships, the *Susan Constant, Godspeed,* and *Discovery,*
the Virginia Company of London had sent to establish a trading and exploring
outpost on the east coast of North America. The man or boy who was the first
to catch sight of land as the sun rose behind him might have been a common
sailor standing watch before dawn, or he might have been a ship's officer or
even a passenger on deck peering keenly to the west as they approached the
coast. There were no women or girls aboard the three ships, only the 104 men
and boys who were passengers plus the crewmen and officers who worked the
lines, set the sails, and calculated latitude and estimated longitude as the three
ships followed the wind southwest from England to the Azores, west to the
islands of the Caribbean, then north and west to the place they called Virginia.
The ship's crew very likely included men from several parts of the British Isles
and also from elsewhere in Europe, the Mediterranean, or even Africa, as was
common at the time, so it is not certain that the first witness on the ship was
English. Whoever he was and wherever he was from he loudly called out the
landfall, and the other men and boys aboard the ships crowded to the rails to
get their first sight of the New World.

What that man or boy who first spotted the land knew and what the other
men and boys aboard the ships knew in greater or lesser detail was that they
were approaching a large landmass that differed in many ways from the island
they had left. They knew that it had its own populations of people who spoke
different languages than they and lived in what Englishmen and Europeans
early in the seventeenth century regarded as a very primitive manner. They
were what anthropologists later called Stone Age, or neolithic, people, who

although they had copper implements and adornments did not have bronze or iron tools or weapons.

The educated men aboard the ships certainly knew and many of the other men also probably knew that for a century or more sailing ships from different nations had coursed along that coast and sometimes landed briefly to explore the fringe of the mainland. The Spanish had been there several times, as had other Englishmen, some Frenchmen, and probably Dutchmen, too. They may not have known about the Spanish settlement, but they did know at least something about the earlier English expedition that had established the small, short-lived colony on the Carolina coast. From oral and published accounts the people on that expedition took back to England, from drawings they had made of the landscape and its inhabitants, and from printed reports about the Indians who traveled with them to England and back, some of the men on those ships in 1607 could have learned enough about the New World to have a reasonably good mental image of what they would see when they landed. They probably knew that the men, women, and children who did not return to England from that sandy settlement had mysteriously disappeared never to be seen again by any European eye. The men aboard the ships were probably as apprehensive about what would happen when they landed as they were excited about getting off their cramped ships and setting foot on firm, dry land. Would they meet hostile inhabitants on the beach? Would they meet a friendly welcome? They did not know.

One person saw ships approaching land from the sea; another aboard one of the ships first spied the land. In both cases, many more people quickly saw what they had seen, and before the day was done some Indians and some Englishmen had their first encounter. Englishman George Percy left a written account of what happened that day. "The six and twentieth of Aprill, about foure a clocke in the morning," he wrote, "wee descried the land of *Virginia:* the same day wee entered into the Bay of *Chesupioc* directly, without any let or hinderance; there wee landed and discovered a little way, but wee could find nothing worth the speaking of, but faire meddowes and goodly tall Trees, with such Fresh-waters running through the woods, as I was almost ravished at the first sight thereof. At night, when wee were going aboard, there came the Savages creeping upon all foure, from the Hills like Beares, with their Bowes in their mouthes, charged us very desperately in the faces, hurt Captaine *Gabrill Archer* in both his hands, and a sayler in two places of the body very dangerous. After they had spent their Arrowes, and felt the sharpnesses of our shot, they retired into the Woods with a great noise, and so left us."[1]

No Virginia Indian left a record of the events that survives, but from what they did we know that they reacted with anxious uncertainty. Like the first Englishmen who went ashore armed for self-defense, the Indians also appeared on the shore armed, probably also for self-defense. A smart little skirmish marked the end of the first day, but it is entirely likely that both parties had wished to avoid violence.

The Invaders

England and France embarked on colonization of the New World decades after Spain and Portugal established their first colonies in Africa, Asia, and in Central and South America. England's first settlements in the New World were small military and commercial outposts in a global contest for wealth and national greatness. The English hoped that their new outposts on the northeastern coast of North America would prevent the Spanish from expanding north of Florida into the Chesapeake region and the North Atlantic, where English explorers were searching for a northern water route to Asia. Virginia's founders embraced ideals of colonial promoters such as Richard Hakluyt, an Elizabethan clergyman and historian for whom exploration and colonization combined appealing motives of patriotism, piety, and profit. They hoped that Virginia could be a bulwark against Spanish colonial expansion, a base for missionary activities among the Indians, and a source of gold, silver, and raw materials England needed.

Sir Walter Ralegh, one of the sponsors of the first expeditions, had named the area Virginia to honor Elizabeth I, the Virgin Queen, during whose reign from 1558 to 1603 England began its colonial expansion. In the 1580s the English established a colony on the Outer Banks of North Carolina, but it failed, and the first settlers abandoned it.

Supporters of English colonization shared with other Europeans a conception of sovereignty and land ownership that led them to disregard claims indigenous populations asserted to control over the land where they and their ancestors had lived for hundreds or thousands of years. English charters and other documents specifically referred to land occupied by people who were not Christians as open to conquest and occupation by Englishmen, as if no people were there at all. Moreover, European and North American conceptions of people's relationship to the space in which they lived differed and set the stage for recurrent conflicts. English land law and European ideas about international relations embodied the principle of clear and known boundaries between areas treaties or deeds of sale assigned to different parties. Eastern Woodland Indians, however, understood occupation of land not by boundaries between tribes or nations but by centers of homelands with undefined regions between them open to all parties for use or transit. Those different conceptions of land use led to repeated disagreements, some of which were deadly, when the two populations with their very different notions of homeland occupied the same or adjacent areas.

In 1606 King James I issued a charter that authorized two groups of investors to form the Virginia Company and establish colonies in North America. Men from Bristol financed a settlement on the shore of Casco Bay in Maine, and men from London financed a settlement on the banks of what they called the James River in Virginia. The king appointed a council to direct the Virginia enterprise from England; and that council named a second council of settlers to manage affairs on the ground. The charter provided that Englishmen in Virginia should enjoy the same legal rights and privileges as Englishmen who remained at home.

The First Months

On April 26, 1607, the *Susan Constant, Godspeed,* and *Discovery* under the command of Captain Christopher Newport reached the Virginia coast at Cape Henry after an eighteen-week ocean voyage. They sailed west into the river they named for their king and explored for two weeks to ascertain the best place to establish their settlement. Parties of Englishmen went ashore at several places where werowances welcomed them with elaborate ceremonies intended to demonstrate the prosperity of the people and the number and strength of fighting-age men. Later in the month farther up the river Gabriel Archer visited what he called "Queene Apumatecs bower." Like George Percy's account of the first landing and other seventeenth-century texts, it helps to read it aloud and let the voice find the rhythms of early English syntax and smooth over antique spellings.

After Archer and his men arrived, he recalled, "we sawe the Queene of this Country cominge in self same fashion of state as Pawatah or Arahatec," two powerful werowances they had already met, "yea rather wth more majesty: she had an usher before her who brought her to the matt prepared under a faire mulbery tree, where she satt her Downe by her selfe. . . . she would permitt none to stand or sitt neere her: she is a fatt lustie manly woman." Archer regarded all that as a high comvpliment. The queen behaved exactly as he expected a royal person to behave. By her dress and bearing she clearly intended to display her superiority over both her own people and her visitors. She entertained the visitors and then, indicating that she already knew a good deal about the English and their armaments, she asked one of the men to fire his gun. At the loud report the werowansqua "shewed not neer the like feare as Arahatec though he be a goodly man."[2]

Captain Newport selected the site for the settlement in accordance with his instructions to protect the settlement from Spanish ships, which in the beginning the settlers feared more than they feared the Indians. On May 14 the men stepped ashore at the marshy peninsula they called James City, Jamestown, or James Island. The men were organized as a military expedition and

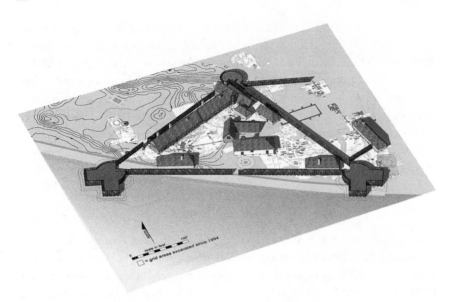

Conjectural reconstruction of Jamestown

expected to live off the country as any army occupying foreign soil did and as English armies had recently done in Ireland. They planned to purchase grain and other foodstuffs from the Indians or raid their towns if necessary.

The captain ordered the men to erect a fort. They completed the work speedily. "The fifteenth of June, we had built and finished our Fort," George Percy wrote, "which was triangle wise, having three Bulwarkes at every corner like a halfe Moone, and foure or five pieces of Artillerie mounted in them, we had made our selves sufficiently strong for these Savages, we had also sowne most of our corne on two Mountains," by which he meant dry ground away from the river. The corn "sprang a mans height from the ground, this Countrey is a fruitfull soile, bearing many goodly and fruitfull Trees, as Mulberries, Cherries, Walnuts, Cedars, Cypresse, Sassafras, and Vines in great abundance."[3]

The colony nearly failed, though, and many men died during the first year. Twentieth-century scholarship and archaeological excavations of the fort begun in the 1990s have largely discredited an old myth that depicted the first settlers as inexperienced English gentlemen who thought it was beneath their dignity to work and consequently starved. One reason for their troubles was a very severe and prolonged drought that began shortly before the English arrived. It sharply reducing the harvest throughout the area for several years and exposed the Powhatan as well as the English to hunger. The settlers were consequently unable to live off the resources of the Indians as they had

Jamestown archaeological site

planned. That increased the number and severity of the unavoidable conflicts between the two.

Powhatan's initial reaction to the arrival of Englishmen must have been mixed. English accounts of the period interpret Indian responses in a variety of ways. Some appeared welcoming, and Indians supplied Englishmen with provisions. Others appeared hostile. In reality, both were probably true at one time or place or another given different circumstances. As for Powhatan, he probably hoped to enlist the technologically advanced English as allies or to incorporate them into his chiefdom, but it is not clear whether he anticipated that they intended to remain for a long time or permanently. The longer they remained, though, the more cause he had to worry about the future.

The English also treated the Indians in a variety of ways that may have confused them as much as the differing attitudes of Indians confused the invaders. The English sometimes treated Indians as trading partners, sometimes as a source of needed foodstuffs, and at other times as objects of conversion to the Protestant Christianity of the Church of England. Several young English boys went to live with the Indians, learn their language, and act as interpreters; some Indian boys and girls, including Pocahontas, also known as Matoaca, one of Powhatan's many daughters, probably spent time with the settlers. The two populations slowly learned about each other, often employing children as interpreters. The difficulty of conversing across the language barrier and their differing cultural beliefs and practices inevitably led to misunderstandings and conflicts. When the English offered Powhatan a crown, however, and attempted to make him a dependent ruler under the authority of the king of England, he clearly understood the nature of the ceremony and resolutely refused to bow down as bidden when Englishmen forced the crown on him. Maintaining his dignity and his standing as paramount chief, Powhatan continued to bear himself as no man's inferior, whatever the English believed or however they acted, and he never condescended to enter an English settlement. In 1608 he sent one of his advisors, Namontack, to England as a diplomatic agent and ordered him to report back on the place where the invaders had come from in order for Powhatan to better understand what the English intended.

During its first two years Jamestown was a struggling outpost with unreliable direction and support from the Virginia Company of London and inept or divided leadership in Jamestown. Englishmen were not accustomed to the hot and humid summer weather and worked wearing wool garments or suits of metal armor. They may have suffered from innervating low-grade salt poisoning if they drank water from the river or from the well they dug a few paces inland. More than half of the men who landed in May died before the autumn. It used to be thought that the marshy peninsula with its brackish water and malaria-carrying mosquitoes were responsible, but some Englishmen may have developed resistance to malaria in England, and it is also unclear when malaria became widespread in eastern North America. It may be that poor nutrition and European diseases such as chickenpox, smallpox, and others afflicted the weakened settlers. Native North Americans had no immunity to those diseases, and several epidemics that may have resulted from introduction of foreign pathogens that sixteenth-century explorers had brought to the New World had already spread death throughout Tsenacomoco more than once.

George Percy kept a record of mortality during the first summer. It is a dismal list of almost daily deaths. "The sixt of August there died *John Asbie* of the Bloudie Flixe," meaning the bloody flux, or dysentery. "The ninth day died *George Flower* of the swelling. The tenth day died *William Bruster* Gentleman, of a wound given by the Savages, and was buried the eleventh day. The fourteenth day, *Jerome Alikock* Ancient, died of a wound, the same day *Francis Midwinter, Edward Moris* Corporall died suddenly. The fifteenth day, their died *Edward Browne* and *Stephen Galthorpe*. The sixteenth day, their died *Thomas Gower* Gentleman. The seventeenth day, their died *Thomas Mounslic*. The eighteenth day, there died *Robert Pennington,* and *John Martine* Gentleman. The nineteenth day, died *Drue Piggase* Gentleman. The two and twentieth day of August, there died Captaine *Bartholomew Gosnold* one of our Councell, he was honourably buried, having all the Ordnance in the Fort shot off with many vollies of small shot."[4]

Gosnold was one of the ablest and most experienced members of the gov-

Pocahontas saving John Smith, from John Smith, *The Generall Historie of Virginia, New England, and the Summer Isles* (London, 1624)

erning council. Only he among the men whose deaths Percy recorded received a military salute at his burial. Gosnold's death left only one other Englishman whose military experience and natural abilities made him a capable leader, Captain John Smith. After Smith became president of the governing council he established good trading relations with several Indian leaders and put the settlers to work by enforcing his rule that "he that will not worke shall not eate."[5]

During the first winter as Smith attempted to feed the men in the fort he made several brief excursions into the countryside. On one of them Powhatan's brother Opechancanough captured Smith and victoriously paraded him through the various Indian towns before presenting him to Powhatan at Werowocomoco. In a history Smith published in 1624 he related for the first time a story that became one of the most famous events in the founding of Virginia. After Powhatan and Smith conversed at length, the chief ordered his men to beat out the captain's brains with their clubs. Pocahontas, as Smith told the story, intervened and saved his life. Historians have debated ever since whether the event occurred at all or, if it did, what the significance of it might have been. Some writers characterized the story as a dramatic invention Smith created after all his English-speaking contemporaries in Virginia were dead and could not contradict him. Others believed that the event happened more

Virginia Discovered and Described by Captain John Smith, which Smith reproduced in 1624 in his *Generall Historie of Virginia* (8th state, from John Smith, *The Generall Historie of Virginia, New England, and the Summer Isles* ([London, 1624]).

or less as Smith described it and interpreted it as a ritual execution and rescue ceremony in which Powhatan made Smith subordinate to him and symbolically made the English subordinate to his chiefdom.

In 1608 Smith led two exploring expeditions up Chesapeake Bay and established trading relationships with other tribes as far north as the Potomac River. He recorded information about the bay and the people he encountered. The account of Smith's voyages and the map he later published contained the first detailed English-language descriptions of the area and its inhabitants. His party imposed English names on some of the places they visited in lieu of Indian names or because they did not know the Indians' names for those places. That was a subtle act of taking possession of the landscape, of the Indians' land, but the Indians did not see the map and therefore could not understand the long-term implications of that act.

After Smith was wounded in an accidental gunpowder explosion, he left Virginia in October 1609 and returned to England. He then embarked on a career as historian of the founding of the English empire. He published a long history of Virginia, which included excerpts from the writings of several other people; and he wrote a long account of a voyage he later made to the region he named New England. Smith's influential books drew on his knowledge of the mistakes and difficulties evident in the settlement of Jamestown and enabled later colonists to prepare and execute their plans with greater chances for success.

The First Decade

In 1609 the directors of the Virginia Company of London obtained from James I a new charter that allowed the company to appoint a military governor with absolute authority to manage the company's settlement more effectively. The king's original grant of 1606 had given the company control of an area that extended fifty miles north, south, and inland from the point of settlement. The company's 1609 charter granted the Virginia Company all of North America for two hundred miles north and south of the latitude of Point Comfort and west and northwest of the Atlantic coast to the Pacific Ocean, then known as the Great South Sea. The new boundaries embraced a large part of the area destined to become the United States.

English investors financed larger expeditions to Virginia after effective company propaganda stimulated hopes of rich returns for men and women who invested in the company. Inspired by dreams of converting Indians and

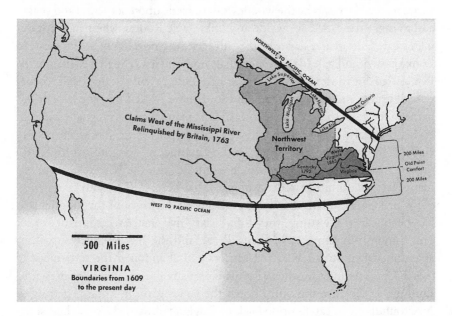

Map of Virginia Boundaries from 1609 to the Present Day illustrating boundary changes since the second charter of 1609.

eager for easy profits, investors pledged about £40,000 to the Virginia Company. In 1609 the company sent Sir Thomas Gates to Virginia with several shiploads of additional supplies and more colonists. The flagship that carried most of the supplies was wrecked on the island of Bermuda during a hurricane and did not reach Virginia until May 1610. Their experience on the island inspired William Shakespeare's play *The Tempest*.

The loss of the supply ship plunged the little colony into famine. In spite of the abundance of fish, shellfish, and waterfowl in the region, the winter of 1609–10 became known as the starving time. The men in Jamestown lacked effective leadership and suffered for it. George Percy's account of that winter is one of the most starkly grim narratives in all of American literature. Even as a small party of Englishmen lived comfortably and ate well at Kicoughtan, near Point Comfort a few miles downstream from Jamestown, men and women in the fort suffered terribly. Most of the inhabitants perished of starvation or disease.

Percy recalled, "some to satisfye their hunger have Robbed the store for the wch I Caused them to be executed Then haveing fedd upoun horses and other beastes as longe as they Lasted, we weare gladd to make shifte wth vermin as doggs Catts Ratts and myce." He quoted an old saying that "all was fishe thatt Came to Nett to satisfye Crewell hunger." People ate "Bootes shoes or any other leather some colde come by and those beinge Spente and devoured some weare inforced to searche the woodes and to feede upon Serpentts and snakes and to digge the earthe for wylde and unknowne Rootes, where many of our men weare Cutt of and slayne by the Salvages. And now famin beginneinge to Looke gastely and pale in every face, thatt notheinge was Spared to mainteyne Lyfe and to doe those things wch seame incredible, as to digge upp deade corpes outt of graves and to eate them. And some have Licked upp the Bloode wch hathe fallen from their weake fellowes." One man killed his pregnant wife, cut up her body, and survived for a time by cannibalism. Percy forced the man to confess "by torture haveing hunge by the Thumbes wth weightes att his feete a quarter of an howere before he wolde Confesse." For the "Crewell and unhumane factt" of cannibalism Percy ordered that he be put to death.[6]

When Gates and his men finally arrived in May without the supplies that had been lost in the storm, they found sixty-five emaciated survivors. After only a month in Jamestown, Gates, Percy, and the survivors gave up. They abandoned Jamestown as earlier settlers had abandoned the settlement in North Carolina and the other Virginia Company site on Casco Bay in Maine. On June 10 they left and sailed down the James River in hope of getting to Newfoundland to catch a ride back to England aboard ships of the fishing fleet. Before they reached the ocean they unexpectedly encountered a fleet of ships under the command of Governor Thomas West, baron De La Warr, entering the James River. He had brought new settlers and enough supplies to prevent Jamestown from becoming another failed colony.

Gates was an experienced army officer and veteran of military garrisons in the Low Countries. With De La Warr's approval he launched ferocious attacks on Indian towns to punish what the English regarded as misbehavior or brutality by the Indians, whom they frequently referred to as savages. The word *savage* derived from a French word that meant uncivilized, wild, or forest-dwelling, and did not in every instance denote cruel or barbarous behavior. The Englishmen's own actions, though, were often savage in that second meaning of the word. That August, Percy raided and burned the neighboring Paspeheah town. His soldiers killed most of the men and women and forced the werowansqua and her children into canoes to take them back to Jamestown. On their way the soldiers took jolly sport with her children by "Throweinge them overboard and shoeting owtt their Braynes in the water."[7] When the men reached Jamestown they prepared to burn the werowansqua, but Percy had seen enough brutality that day and quickly stabbed her to death with his sword before his men could kill her slowly in a fire.

Sir Thomas Dale arrived in 1611 in command of skilled, heavily armed military reinforcements. Gates, De La Warr, and Dale all issued directives during 1610 and 1611 that a company official compiled and published as a small book in the latter year entitled *Lawes Divine, Morall and Martiall.* The whole body of laws is often attributed to Dale alone and is sometimes called Dale's Laws, but in fact only the law martial that governed the soldiers was entirely of his composition, and it was a fairly standard military code for the time. The laws that Gates and De La Warr issued that regulated morality and religion were extraordinarily strict. They required severe punishment for many offenses, such as having a bodkin—a large needle—driven through the tongue for cursing or speaking disrespectfully of the clergy or company officials. The code imposed whippings and other severe physical punishment for gambling, failing to attend church, fornication, adultery, unnecessarily killing livestock, or stealing agricultural implements or other people's crops.

The list of crimes punished with death was long and included blasphemy, uttering treasonous words or words critical of the company, murder, sodomy, robbery, swearing, lying, trading with Indians without permission, stealing from Indians, cheating the company or the cape merchant (who operated the company's storehouse), trading with sailors without permission, and sending goods out of the colony without permission. It prescribed death for a third offence for several of the crimes punished for the first time with whipping, standing in the stocks or at the pillory, or having the tongue bored through or cut out.

Because Gates and De La Warr were absent from Virginia more than in

Sir Thomas Dale, attributed to Marcus
Gheeraerts the Younger, 1609–19

residence during the next five years, Dale was also acting governor as well as
commander of the military forces, and he enforced the entire strict code without quarter and against any and all offenders. When a man stole food out of
the common stock Dale had him tied to a tree and left him there to starve to
death as an example to the others. He executed or tortured men who failed
to obey orders, but he also ordered the construction of palisades as soon as he
arrived and directed the settlers to plant grain with which to feed themselves.

Dale was a skilled military commander and like Gates waged deadly war
on the people of Tsenacomoco and their neighbors. Within weeks of his arrival he burned the towns of the Nansemond and attacked the Appamattuck
towns below the falls of the James River. Later in the year he formed a new
settlement there and named it Henricus, after the king's eldest son Henry.
For almost a decade it rivaled Jamestown as a center of the colony's population. The men had originally worked company-owned land in common and
drawn rations from the company store, but Dale assigned settlers small plots
of ground on which they grew crops for their own support and profit. Dale's

Simon van de Passe, *Pocahontas*, 1616

brutal government succeeded, and by the time he returned to England in the spring of 1616, having been in charge of Virginia for more than half the time since its first settlement, the residents who survived produced enough food to be largely self-sufficient.

In the meantime Englishmen captured Powhatan's daughter Pocahontas and held her hostage in Jamestown for more than a year. During her captivity she accepted Christianity and in 1614 was baptized Lady Rebecca and married John Rolfe. Dale hoped the alliance would seal a peace and terminate several years of deadly low-intensity conflict between the settlers and the Indians. It is likely that Powhatan also regarded the marriage in much the same manner, as a diplomatic one. What Pocahontas thought is less certain. In 1616 she and John Rolfe sailed for England where early the next year she was presented to the king and queen at Court. As Pocahontas prepared to return to Virginia later that year she died and was buried at Gravesend in England. She was about twenty-two years old.

Tobacco

In 1614, the same year Rolfe married Pocahontas, he experimented with the West Indian plant *Nicotiana tabacum,* a milder form of tobacco than the Powhatan grew, and shipped Virginia's first marketable tobacco to England. In 1616 planters exported about twenty-three hundred pounds of tobacco, in 1618 twenty times that amount. The colony and the company had suddenly found a commodity that could make a profit. The company distributed ownership of tracts of land on the banks of the James River among its stockholders and issued charters for additional private settlements called hundreds or particular plantations, prototypes for later tobacco plantations.

The introduction of commercial tobacco production may be the most important event in Virginia's colonial history because of the many ramifications it had. Tobacco cultivation required many laborers, and between 1614 and 1622 hundreds of people traveled to Virginia as servants indentured to work (usually for seven years) to repay the costs of passage. An indentured servant possessed a written contract that specified the responsibilities of both master and servant. Each had a copy, and both were cut along an edge with identical jagged or wavy lines, indentations. Indenture agreements were legal contracts either party could enforce in court. Indentured servants hoped that if they survived they could become owners of their own farms.

The company also sent some German and Polish artisans and several Italian glassmakers to Virginia, but they were not very successful in establishing commercially successful enterprises. Late in the 1610s the company sent skilled workmen to the colony to produce iron from a vein of ore discovered near the mouth of Falling Creek in what later became Chesterfield County. It was the first ironworks established in North America. Some settlers engaged profitably in trading with Indians for furs, but most of them eagerly devoted themselves to growing profitable tobacco.

Tobacco made Jamestown a boomtown. The lure of quick wealth from tobacco production captured English imaginations on both sides of the Atlantic. The company gave one hundred acres of land to each settler with seven years' residence in Virginia (the records identified them as "ancient planters") and one hundred acres per share to investors who owned stock in the company. The company also offered fifty acres of land to any person who traveled to Virginia at his or her own expense or who paid for another person's passage. That became known as the headright system and was the basis of the colony's land policy for the rest of the century. It promoted increased immigration and rapid settlement.

Englishmen consequently began to regard Virginia as a place of opportunity and no longer as a place of starvation and privation. That is how a party of English religious separatists who had resided in the Netherlands since 1607 perceived Virginia when they asked for and received permission to settle in the colony's northern parts. They set sail in the summer of 1620, but storms drove their *Mayflower* north of their mark, and instead of settling in northern Virginia they landed in December at the place in Massachusetts Bay they called Plymouth.

The Second Decade

In 1616 when Powhatan had an opportunity to send one of his principal advisors to England he instructed the man to count the inhabitants there. That indicates that after a decade of English residence in Tsenacomoco, Powhatan was clearly worried about how many more might come. He probably never received a report from his agent. Dale returned to England at the same time. By then, the Virginia Company had terminated the military regime. The company appointed a civilian governor and an advisory Council of State to govern the colony. Company orders, called the Great Charter of 1618, authorized the election of representatives from each settlement to meet with Governor Sir George Yeardley and members of the Council of State to devise solutions for the problems of the rapidly developing colony. In 1619, free men at each of eleven settlements selected two representatives called burgesses to join the governor and council members in the General Assembly. In England the word *burgess* signified a man of sufficient social and economic respectability to be entitled to a role in municipal government.

The members of the General Assembly all met together in unicameral session in the church at Jamestown from July 30 to August 4. They took steps to guarantee settlers' rights to their land. They also ordered that the colony's ministers conduct religious services according to the practices of the Church of England and required every person to attend church twice every Sunday. By then a rudimentary organization of the Church of England had taken shape in the colony. During the following decades a more formal church structure evolved that at the parish level resembled that of the church in the mother country, but it operated in a distinctively Virginia environment and was adapted to local conditions and without the superintendence of a bishop.

The assembly of August 1619 was the origin of the oldest, continuously functioning representative legislature in the New World. The assembly evolved into one of the most important institutions in the colony and later furnished a model for representative government in the United States. Of symbolic importance, one of the first actions of the assembly was to endorse a request from the residents of Kichoughtan near Point Comfort that the company "change the savage name" of the place and "give that Incorporation a newe name."[8]

The company called it Elizabeth City to honor one of the king's daughters. The settlers had already begun taking possession of the country by imposing English names on the landscape, and that process accelerated in the 1620s as maps of the region executed later in the seventeenth century clearly demonstrate. Tsenacomoco was becoming Virginia.

English investors had learned valuable lessons from the near-disasters of the early years and later equipped their settlers well in hope of making a fast profit from tobacco cultivation. Very detailed records survive for the voyage to Virginia of the *Margaret* and thirty-five settlers in the autumn of 1619. The supplies included beads and other trade goods for commerce with the Indians; two Bibles and two Books of Common Prayer; twenty-four guns, three barrels of gunpowder, and sixteen swords; seeds for herb and vegetable gardens; bedding, several kinds of thread, and buttons; a quantity of copper, axes, nails, and two dozen hatchets; wooden bowls and other cooking and eating utensils; door locks, andirons, cheese, oatmeal, and many other items and staple provisions.

The *Margaret* reached Jamestown on December 4. Ten days later the secretary of the colony made a note of the arrival for the information of the investors back in England. On an unrecorded date the men sailed up the river to Berkeley Hundred, the site later of Berkeley Plantation in Charles City County. Their instructions required that "the day of our ships arrivall at the place assigned for plantacion in the land of Virginia shall be yearly and perputually keept holy as a day of thanksgiving to Almighty god."[9] Most of the men died, returned to England, or moved away within a year, and it is unlikely that enough men survived there to celebrate the anniversary of their arrival in December 1620. A misreading of the sponsors' instructions in the middle of the twentieth century created a legend that the men arrived at Berkeley Hundred on December 14 (the date of the secretary's notice) and immediately celebrated the first thanksgiving in North America. It is very likely that passengers on every ship who survived a voyage across the Atlantic Ocean going either direction gave thanks on arrival, but none established an annual commemoration of giving thanks.

An unknown number of English women traveled to Virginia after 1607, and some Indian women occasionally lived with the first settlers at the fort, but Virginia remained a largely male outpost for more than a decade. The Virginia Company's officers attributed some of the difficulties to the absence of women. A 1621 entry in the company's records explained that many of the men there were "enflamed wth a desire to returne for England" because without "the Comforts of Marriage" they "could not live contentedlie noe not in Paradize." The men, "uppon esteeminge Virginia, not as a place of habitation butt only of a short sojourninge: have applied themselves and their labours wholly to the raysinge of present profitt, and utterly neglected not onlie the staple Commodities, but even the verie necessities of Mans liffe."[10]

Company officers hoped the presence of more women would change everything and convert the unstable commercial and military outpost into a stable agricultural society. Between 1619 and 1621 they sent about 250 young Englishwomen to Virginia to marry the men who were already there. That did, indeed, change life for some of the men. They prospered under familiar patterns of family life that included women's cooking, sewing, and domestic manufacturing skills. In the following years an increasing number of women crossed the Atlantic with their fathers and husbands or later followed them to Virginia. Even more women immigrated during the first half of the seventeenth century as indentured servants who labored for a specified number of years in return for payment of their transportation expenses. All women and most men, whether bound or free, found that hard work was the norm for all except a very few of the wealthy elite, yet life in the New World appeared to offer young women and men greater economic mobility and perhaps more freedom than may have been possible for them within the constraints of society in England at the time.

A surviving record from September 1623 gives the names and occupations of nearly fifty men and boys who arrived in two ships that month. Nearly half of them came from the greater London area, but others came from as far away as Yorkshire. Ten of the men identified themselves as gentlemen, one was a student at Oxford University, and two were probably personal servants, but the others were all men qualified to do useful and important work. Seven were carpenters or joiners who did fine work such as furniture making, and one was a bricklayer. Others included two chandlers and one tallow chandler, skilled in making candles and soap; three haberdashers, a tailor, and a leather worker; two grocers; and one each who identified themselves as a goldsmith, a merchant, a vintner, and a cooper. Four of the immigrants were husbandmen who were skilled in farming or managing livestock.

During the 1610s the company shipped cattle and swine to Virginia, and settlers cultivated tobacco and grain intensively. The settlers initially adopted Indian methods of agriculture. They set fires to clear the ground of underbrush and cut rings around trees to kill them and allow sunlight to reach the forest floor. They used sticks, hoes, or other simple agricultural implements to scrape together small mounds of earth, as the Indians did, for sowing their seeds. By the 1620s, though, the English had cleared numerous large spaces near their settlements as they began to employ European methods of farming. The presence of European livestock, especially rooting swine, began to transform the landscape. Silting of streams from runoff from tilled fields probably began at that time and increased in severity later.

The profits industrious men made from planting and cultivating tobacco allowed for the development by the 1620s of a miniature stratified culture reminiscent of English culture but different in some significant ways. Government officials and men who controlled the labor of other people had to work less hard than other white men and could even engage in intellectual pursuits. John Pory, the secretary of the colony who served as Speaker of the 1619 assembly, ordered books from England to read during his leisure hours. Treasurer George Sandys, who resided in Jamestown from 1621 to 1625, had enough time on his hands when not keeping his accounts to complete much of a new translation into English of Ovid's *Metamorphosis,* which he published to considerable acclaim in London in 1626.

Within a few years tobacco had transformed Virginia and given it a future. The author of a 1620 promotional pamphlet entitled *A Declaration of the State of the Colony and Affaires in Virginia* boasted that "the Colony beginneth now to have the face and fashion of an orderly State, and such as is likely to grow and prosper."[11] The Virginia Company made plans to create a college at Henricus for the education of Indians and young Englishmen. Tobacco production increased the demand for labor in Virginia, and that drew Virginians into international commercial networks. English and Dutch merchant ships and others visited Virginia, brought people and supplies, and connected it with other parts of the North Atlantic world.

The First Recorded Africans

James I and many Englishmen thought that smoking tobacco was foul, unhealthy, and immoral, but for many white Virginians tobacco was very profitable. Tobacco cultivation was also very labor intensive. Much as planters in the Caribbean who used African laborers on their sugar plantations, tobacco planters in Virginia also began to exploit men, women, and children from Africa. A thriving international slave trade linked both sides of the Atlantic Ocean in an increasingly complex commercial web. Spanish, Portuguese, and Dutch traders dominated the trade, but English merchants and shippers also took part. Late in August 1619, according to John Rolfe, a ship with "20. and odd Negroes" aboard arrived at Point Comfort, downstream from Jamestown.[12] Men on the trading ship had forcibly removed the Africans from a Portuguese slave trading ship en route from Angola to the Caribbean. Rolfe's report of the event is the earliest-known clearly dated reference to persons of African origin in Virginia, but Rolfe did not state that they were the first Africans to arrive in the colony. It is possible that some had arrived earlier, and others certainly arrived not long afterward. An early enumeration of the residents of Virginia records the presence of several native Africans, but scholars have differed about whether the list was compiled before or after August 1619.[13]

Rolfe reported that Governor Yeardley and Abraham Peirsey—the cape merchant who was in charge of the company's stores—bought the Africans who arrived in August 1619, but it remains uncertain whether Yeardley and Peirsey regarded them as enslaved for life. None of the first Africans could have arrived with the papers of indenture white servants usually possessed, and without indentures African laborers remained extremely vulnerable to exploitation. Rolfe's letter can be interpreted to mean that Yeardley and Peirsey bought their labor, not their bodies. The status of African laborers in Virginia remained unclear for years. The words *slave* and *slavery* appear in Virginia documents from very early in the seventeenth century, although neither word appears in the laws of Virginia until the middle of the century. Englishmen and Europeans of the period were well aware of and probably participated in the widespread practice of enslaving people captured in warfare. The practice was quite common in the Mediterranean, in Africa, and among some tribes in the Americas. English-speaking men in Virginia probably did not imagine when they acquired some people of African birth in 1619 that they were taking the first step in creating a new labor regime that for nearly two and a half centuries dictated how people lived and worked in much of southeastern North America.

English statute and common law did not prohibit or regulate the holding of people in long-term or even lifetime servitude, but English law did prohibit the holding of Christians in slavery. Some Portuguese slave traders may have baptized people they purchased in Africa before shipping them to the New World. It is unlikely that English settlers in Virginia knew of those baptisms or regarded them as evidence of a genuine conversion to Christianity, which would have made it illegal under English law for planters to hold them in perpetual slavery. It is also entirely possible that by 1619 some English-speaking men in Virginia had enslaved some local natives. Scattered references in seventeenth-century Virginia court records, deeds, wills, private letters, and commercial agreements indicate that early settlers captured Indians during combat or purchased and held Indians in long-term servitude under conditions that probably resembled conditions under which they held people of African birth or descent.

The number of Africans imported into Virginia as part of the international slave trade remained small for the first twenty-five or thirty years after 1619. Some of the men and women who arrived in Virginia from Africa during that time are known to have become free. Some even acquired land and servants of their own, as did some indentured English immigrant servants.

Powhatan Counterattack

English settlements and tobacco plantations expanded beyond Jamestown and Point Comfort without Powhatan's expressed permission. The longer the settlers remained and the more numerous they became the more serious a potential threat they were to his chiefdom. Powhatan died in 1618 after more than a decade of English occupation of part of his Tsenacomoco. His brother Opitchapam succeeded him. Soon thereafter another younger brother, Opechancanough, became paramount chief. In 1622 he organized well-coordinated attacks on the English settlements, which his warriors carried out early in the morning of March 22. They killed more than three hundred colonists as far inland as the town of Henricus and at the ironworks on Falling Creek.

Opechancanough's warriors did not attack Jamestown. It is not clear whether they planned to attack the town. Several Indians gave advance warning to people in at least two settlements. One young Indian who lived with William Perry at Hog Island, across the river from Jamestown, informed Perry, who informed William Pace, who rowed across the river to alert the town. That warning may have allowed the residents to mount conspicuous defenses, which in turn could have persuaded the attackers to withdraw. None of the few surviving documents indicates whether Jamestown was an object of the attacks, but they clearly indicate that several Indians disclosed Opechancanough's plans. The name of only one of them is known. He may have been a trusted young man identified elsewhere as Chacrow. Copies of an original letter from the period spelled his name Chauco. When the story first appeared in print in William Stith's 1747 *The History and First Discovery and Settlement of Virginia* his name was spelled Chanco. He was probably not the Hog Island resident who informed Perry and Pace. Nevertheless, later writers carelessly conflated scattered fragments of information about Chacrow, Chauco, Perry, Pace, and the attack into an improbable and almost certainly incorrect legend that one young Christianized Indian name Chanco alone saved the entire English colony from extermination.

Later in 1622 Thomas Waterman, a company official who never traveled to Virginia, published a frightening account of what he described as a barbarous massacre; but in his semi-official *Declaration of the State of the Colony and Affaires in Virginia,* he portrayed it as a one-time aberration and predicted that peaceful and prosperous settlement would immediately resume. William Capps, who was in Virginia, though, wrote that the attack "burst the heart" of the survivors.[14]

3

ROYAL COLONY

IMMIGRATION FROM ENGLAND resumed soon after the Powhatan attack of March 1622, and some planters, shippers, and merchants profited from the tobacco trade; but the loss of many lives in the attack and the company's continuing inability to earn its shareholders a profit seriously undermined its credibility. Moreover, some of the company's leading officers were then out of royal favor. King James I appointed two commissions of investigation to advise him what to do about Virginia. One set of commissioners traveled to Virginia to report on conditions there, and the other set enabled the king to obtain a court ruling that provided him with justification for revoking the company's charter on May 24, 1624.

The king died the following year, and on May 13, 1625, King Charles I made Virginia England's first royal colony. He appointed a royal governor and members of the Council of State as the company had done and invested them with the same authorities the company's governor and council had exercised. The new king later created two additional advisory commissions to advise him how to govern Virginia and the other new English colonies, but neither of them persuaded him to issue a formal charter that specified the form of government for Virginia. For the most part the king paid little attention to the colony and gave it little support. He allowed Sir Francis Wyatt, the last company governor, to continue in office as the first royal governor until May 1626, when former governor Sir George Yeardley succeeded him. Yeardley died the following year. The institutions of government the company had established continued to function without significant alteration until after Sir John Harvey arrived as royal governor early in 1630, a full six years after the company ceased to exist.

Royal Government

The king was the original and sole source of political authority in the royal colony of Virginia. He could at any time change anything or everything.

Because he seldom issued specific directives concerning the colonial government, however, men in charge in Jamestown retained the rudimentary institutions of the company's government and developed them into more complex and sophisticated institutions. During the second quarter of the seventeenth century the basic institutions of government evolved under which colonists lived for the next 150 years; and some of those institutions continued to function with little change for another 75 years after the American Revolution. The king gave them legal and constitutional legitimacy by silently accepting or explicitly approving the innovations in government political leaders in Virginia developed.

The king (or the queen during the reign of Anne from 1702 to 1714) appointed the royal governor and a Council of State composed of about a dozen of the wealthiest and most prominent planters and merchants. The governor and the council jointly administered the colony's government. They sat together as the colony's principal court, known initially as the Quarter Court because it met four times a year and later as the General Court. The governor and members of the Council of State together with burgesses elected initially from the particular plantations and later as representatives of the counties formed the General Assembly. The governor, councilors, and burgesses all met together in one room as a unicameral legislature until 1643 when the burgesses began sitting separately and electing their own presiding officer, the Speaker of the House. The House of Burgesses, whose members were the only elected government officials in the colony, was composed of adult white men and represented the planters of Virginia.

Late in the seventeenth century the king appointed the first of several lieutenant governors for the colony. The colonial office of lieutenant governor is not the direct predecessor of the later office of lieutenant governor of the commonwealth. During the colonial period the man who had the royal appointment as lieutenant governor took office only in the event of the death of the governor or the governor's absence from Virginia. He then performed the duties of the governor's office and collected a part of the salary and other perquisites the governor was entitled to under terms each lieutenant governor negotiated with the governor whose work he performed. If both the governor and lieutenant governor died or were absent from the colony the senior member of the Council of State served as acting governor with the title president of the council.

Other institutions of government in Virginia superficially resembled their counterparts in England but always with important differences that local conditions in the colony dictated. As the population grew and spread up the rivers, along the coast of the bay, and on the Eastern Shore, governors delegated some civil authority and responsibility for local defense to military commanders at each of several principal settlements. Virginia had no ecclesiastical courts as in England to prove and record wills and oversee the estates of people after they died. The governor and council members initially performed those essential duties. The increase in and dispersal of the population eventually led the governor and General Assembly to assign those responsibilities to local officials. The evolution of county governments was a slow process that may have taken as long as two decades. By 1634, when the names of eight shires, or counties, first appear in extant records, men acting under the authority of the governor and council executed many of the essential functions of local government.

The governor appointed justices of the peace to serve on the county courts. At first called commissioners of the peace, the justices presided over the monthly meetings of the county courts, maintained order, and issued permits to operate inns or taverns. Being a judge of the county court was a prestigious responsibility and led to the formation in every county of a group of influential political leaders. Service as a justice of the peace made a man known and therefore more eligible to be elected to represent the county in the General Assembly. County courts evolved into courts of record where people recorded and enforced deeds and wills and resolved disputes about land and debts. Other important county officials were the county lieutenant who commanded the militia; the county clerk who kept the county's legal records; the surveyor who marked property boundaries and helped new settlers obtain land grants; the sheriff who collected the taxes and served summonses of the court; and the constable who made arrests and enforced the laws. Justices of the peace recommended men to fill vacancies on the county courts, and governors usually appointed those men, so in effect the county courts became self-perpetuating local governing bodies.

Most justices of the peace were prosperous tobacco planters without formal training in the law. In order that they would know how to conduct their business properly the General Assembly ordered in 1660 that all county courts obtain copies of several standard legal reference works. Among them were Michael Dalton's *The Countrey Justice, Conteyning the Practise of the Justices of the Peace out of Their Sessions* (a manual for justices of the peace in English counties, first published in 1618), and Henry Swinburne's *Briefe Treatise of Testaments and Last Wills* (the standard reference work on the settlement of estates, first published in 1591).

The king required that Virginia's laws and courts function as nearly as possible as English laws and courts. Relevant English common law and statute law adopted before 1607 along with laws the General Assembly passed governed how residents of Virginia lived. In the colony's courts officials dispensed with some of the complex writs and procedures of English law to allow for a speedier and simpler administration of justice. In the seventeenth century those courts understood that the rights of individual members of the society were best preserved if the good of the whole community was always kept foremost in mind. Individuals' rights were valued and protected only within a legal system that guaranteed that the English rule of law first secured peace and good order.

Circumstances in the colony often required legislators and judges to make innovations. For instance, during the seventeenth century white people in Virginia usually let their cattle and hogs run wild in the forest. Twice during the 1640s the planters in the General Assembly enacted laws that reversed English laws on that subject. English laws required owners of animals to fence them in or be liable for damages if their animals broke free and damaged another farmer's crops. In Virginia with its immense and thinly inhabited forests men and women let their livestock run at large. The assembly changed English law and required that farmers erect fences around their plots of cultivated land to keep other people's animals out or lose the right to sue for compensation if another person's livestock damaged their crops.

Parishes of the Church of England were also important institutions of local government. Throughout the seventeenth century most English-speaking white Virginians were active or nominal members of the Church of England. By the 1640s control of each parish rested in the hands of the vestry, a committee of laymen who administered the financial affairs of the local church and selected the minister. In the absence of a resident bishop in the colony vestries dominated Virginia's religious affairs more than parish officials did in England. Vestrymen and church officials had responsibility for care of orphans and the poor (and of public roads until the middle of the seventeenth century), presented evidence of immorality to grand juries, and kept records of births, baptisms, marriages, and deaths. In effect, Virginians converted an English institution of poor relief into a church governing body. The Church of England was the official, or established, church in Virginia from 1607 to 1786, meaning that the church was part of the government and the government was part of the church. Until the American Revolution all adult white men and heads of households paid taxes to erect churches, pay ministers, care for the poor and the orphaned, and support the other responsibilities of the Church of England.

In 1662 the General Assembly required parish churchwardens to assemble the people and in procession walk the property lines of all landowners. They jointly pointed out to everybody the landmarks of their property boundaries, and they renewed marks on boundary trees. If a difference of opinion arose the churchwardens brought up documents and called in two disinterested men to make a final determination. The law required churchwardens to conduct the processioning, or beating the bounds, as it was also called, every fourth year to refresh the marks and the memories. In 1705 a revised version of the law specified that after property lines had been marked three consecutive times without objection, the record of the landmarks could not be questioned in court. The Crown later invalidated that part of the law, but the assembly's enactment of it demonstrated how important the community's collective memory at the parish, or neighborhood, level had become. That the assembly gave parish officials instead of justices of the peace or county survey- ors the responsibility for protecting the rights of property owners and keeping the peace indicates how important the legislators believed the parishes of the Church of England were. Churchwardens and landowners processioned land every fourth year throughout the colonial period and in some instances well into the nineteenth century. So important were the church parishes that for a few years in the middle of the seventeenth century some of them paid the necessary expenses to send burgesses to the General Assembly, which seated them alongside the representatives of counties.

The Last Anglo-Powhatan War

An uneasy peace continued to exist between English colonists and Indians after 1622 as tobacco cultivation spread over the landscape of eastern Virginia. In 1634 the government erected a palisade across the peninsula between the James and York Rivers to protect some of the settlements from attack. Frag- mentary surviving records of the colonial government indicate that small- scale violent encounters frequently took place between English settlers and neighboring Indians, and from time to time fears of serious violence spread from place to place. From time to time, too, raiding parties of English-speaking Virginians burned Indian towns and destroyed or appropriated their crops.

Twenty-two years after the deadly 1622 attack Opechancanough launched a second brilliantly coordinated assault on the colonists' settlements. On April 17, 1644, his warriors killed about five hundred colonists in exposed settlements, a larger number than in 1622, but by 1644 English settlers num- bered about eight thousand. The assembly and Governor Sir William Berke- ley mounted an effective counterattack, soundly defeated Opechancanough's warriors, and captured the old chief. A Jamestown jailer later murdered Ope- chancanough, the last survivor among the English and Powhatan leaders who had witnessed the English invasion of Tsenacomoco in 1607.

The victors imposed a peace treaty on the Indians in 1646, and the para- mount chiefdom Powhatan had created ceased to exist. The treaty restricted Indians to land north of the York River and forced the local chiefs to acknowl- edge that they ruled their towns under the authority of the English king. The treaty required the chiefs in recognition of their subordinate status to present to the governor "twenty beaver skins at the goeing away of Geese yearely."[1] Those tribes became known as tributary tribes because the treaty required them to pay tribute to the government in the form of game. During the twentieth century chiefs of the Pamunkey and Mattaponi moved the presentation to the autumn. The treaty of 1646 is still in force between the state government and members of those tribes, some of whom live on land reserved to them by that treaty and remain exempt from the payment of some taxes.

The English Civil Wars

In 1642, the year Sir William Berkeley arrived in Virginia as governor, armies of the Crown and of Parliament began fighting the English Civil Wars. Parliament's armies won in 1646. Three years later they tried and executed King Charles I and proclaimed England a commonwealth, a realm without royalty. Berkeley was an ardent royalist, and he and the General Assembly declared allegiance to the late king's exiled son, Prince Charles. In 1652 Parliament sent a small fleet and three commissioners to secure the surrender of Virginia and of Maryland to the Puritan Commonwealth of England. Two of the commissioners were Samuel Mathews and Richard Bennett, prominent Virginia Puritans and politically influential planters since the company era. Berkeley and members of the assembly negotiated terms of surrender that permitted use of the Church of England's Book of Common Prayer for one year. Berkeley retired to his plantation at Green Spring, and other royalists also retained their property. The assembly amended the legal code to remove references to royal authority.

Lacking any detailed instructions from the Commonwealth of England the General Assembly met in April and May 1652 and decided to continue Virginia's existing form of government without other alterations. The burgesses appointed a new governor, and he, council members, and burgesses all agreed that "the right of election of all officers of this colony be and appertain to the Burgesses the representatives of the people." The elected burgesses repeated that assertion throughout the interregnum, the time between kings, when they annually appointed a governor and members of the Council of State.[2]

The burgesses chose a succession of three Puritan governors. Richard Bennett, of a prominent Virginia Puritan family, was governor from 1652 to 1655, when the assembly elected Edward Digges to succeed him. A son of a Puritan shareholder in the Virginia Company, Digges got along well with both royalists and parliamentarians and was a merchant and very successful producer of tobacco and silk on his Virginia plantation. In 1656 when Digges returned to

Sir Peter Lely, *Sir William Berkeley,*
ca. 1662

England on personal business the assembly elected another Puritan, the namesake son of Samuel Mathews, to replace him. Virginians with Puritan lean-
ings, such as William Claiborne, the secretary of the colony who supported
Parliament's commercial and religious policies, held most of the colony's high
offices from 1652 to 1660. But in most respects the change of government in
England had few important consequences to the people and government of
Virginia. The assembly functioned with fewer restrictions during the 1650s
than in any other decade, which firmly established it as the colony's legitimate
political authority.

One important unanticipated consequence followed the Virginia submis-
sion to Parliament. It brought the Chesapeake tobacco trade under the terms
of the English Navigation Act of 1651, which required that all colonial produce
be shipped to England in English ships and not be sent directly to any other
market. Advocates of cutting off direct commerce with the Netherlands had
won a major victory.

Early in 1660, after the sudden death of young Governor Samuel Mathews,
members of the General Assembly learned of the death of Lord Protector
Oliver Cromwell and the abdication of his son and successor, Richard Cromwell. Uncertain what to do members of the assembly asked Sir William Berkeley to resume the governorship. In March after careful negotiations Berkeley
agreed to serve "until such a command and comission come out of England
as shall be by the Assembly adjudged lawfull."[3] News of the restoration of the
monarchy in May 1660 reached Virginia by the autumn. Governor Berkeley
and the royalists in Virginia rejoiced. Justices of the peace in York County

purchased a large quantity of punch and cider for the people who assembled there and celebrated "the proclaiming of his sacred Majesty" Charles II to the sounds of blaring trumpets and booming cannon.[4]

The renewal of royal government brought few immediate benefits to Virginia. Charles II embraced the Commonwealth's mercantilist policy, and he signed the Navigation Act of 1660 that extended the restrictions on colonial commerce, including prohibition of direct sale of tobacco to merchants from the Netherlands. The navigation acts specifically empowered the General Court and the county courts in Virginia to conduct trials for infractions of the laws of Parliament.

According to an old tradition, Charles II was touched by the colony's loyalty to him at the time of his exile and gave Virginia the nickname the Old Dominion. It is more likely that the name refers to Virginia's status as England's oldest colony in North America and that it derives from Charles II's acknowledgment early in the 1660s of a gift of silk from "our auntient Collonie of Virginia," one of "our own Dominions."[5] In a law passed in 1699 the General Assembly referred to "this his majesties ancient and great colony and dominion of Virginia."[6]

Mid-Century Exploration

A young Puritan clergyman named Lionel Gatford published a book in 1657 after a visit to Virginia. He included in it one of the few passages that preserves a sample of Indian humor from seventeenth-century Virginia. "When the English complained to one of the neighbouring Indian Kings," Gatford recalled, "that some of his Indians had taken away some of their Hoggs; He assured them, that it was contrarie to his will and command." The chief told the Englishman that they should not complain because "the English had oftentimes killed and carried away divers of his Deer. And when the English replyed, that their hoggs were all marked" with slits or holes in their ears that identified which hogs belonged to whom, "so that the Indians might know them to be theirs," he answered, "Tis true, none of my deer are marked, and by that you may know them to be mine: and when you meet with any that are marked you may do with them what you please; for they are none of mine."[7]

Gatford did not indicate when or where the episode occurred or the tribal affiliation of the Indian. The reported exchange discloses important contrasting beliefs of Indian and English Virginians. Indians regarded the land and its resources as their common inheritance but sometimes acknowledged in theory but not always in practice that what Englishmen had brought with them from England was different. English Virginians regarded what they had brought from England as theirs and also that everything they found in

Virginia, including both land and deer and all other natural resources, were theirs too. Because of different beliefs about ownership of natural resources and places to live conflicts between the two populations remained a constant problem for generations after the invasion of Tsenacomoco began in 1607 and had overflowed onto land where other tribes resided.

Virginia's white population continued to grow and spread, and throughout the decades after the 1646 treaty isolated outbreaks of violence occurred where English and Indian populations lived in close proximity. A string of small defensive forts near the fall line erected after the treaty of 1646 evolved into trading posts where colonists and Indians engaged in licensed trade. The Indian trade involved furs and other items English-speaking men and women wanted, but it also involved traffic in human beings. Documents from the period demonstrate that people in Virginia held at least some native American people in slavery and that they purchased men and women from Indians tribes elsewhere. Expeditions to explore the backcountry probably had as one of their purposes the acquisition of additional enslaved laborers.

The trading forts served as bases from which colonists explored far beyond the first established settlements. Abraham Wood was one of seventeenth-century Virginia's principal explorers and traders. He lived for thirty years at one of the posts, Fort Henry, built on the site of present-day Petersburg, and organized or accompanied several expeditions into the interior. In 1650 Wood and Edward Bland led a few men from Fort Henry along the Blackwater River as far south as present-day Weldon, North Carolina. Bland published his descriptive journal of the expedition in London in 1651 with the title *The Discovery of New Brittaine.*

People had no clear idea of the continent's size and believed that the Pacific Ocean—the South Sea—was not far beyond the Blue Ridge Mountains. John Lederer, a German physician, led three expeditions to find a pass through the mountains to the ocean. On his second in 1670 he and a party of Henrico County militiamen explored as far as present-day Buckingham County. From there Lederer and a guide continued southward into North Carolina to the upper reaches of the Cape Fear River watershed. Later that same year Lederer led an expedition of ten Englishmen and five Indians northwest along the Rappahannock River until they reached the Blue Ridge, but they failed to find an easy pass across the mountains.

In September 1670 Wood sponsored the first recorded exploration of the trans-Allegheny region under Thomas Batte and Robert Hallom, or Hallam. (Reports of the expedition incorrectly spelled the surnames Batte as Battes and Hallom as Fallam.) They reached an area north of present-day Rocky Mount, Virginia. The next day an Indian guide led the party across the Blue Ridge Mountains, probably at Adney Gap. They followed the New River

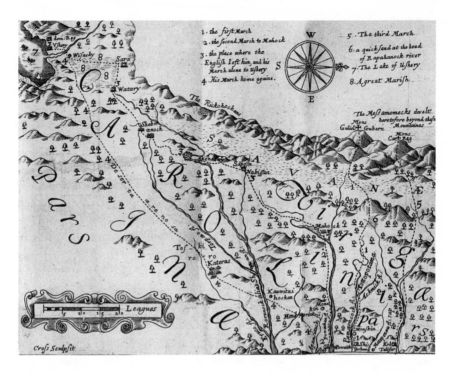

John Lederer, *A Map of the Whole Territory Traversed by John Lederer in His Three Marches* (London, 1672)

through the Allegheny Mountains near present-day Narrows, Virginia, and entered the Ohio River basin. It was an important event in the history of the American frontier. Near the present-day town of Matewan on the West Virginia–Kentucky boundary Batte and Hallom branded a tree with their initials and claimed the region for King Charles II of England. That same year at Sault Sainte Marie between Lakes Huron and Superior a party of French and Indians erected a wooden cross to establish a rival claim for King Louis XIV of France.

In 1673 Wood sent James Needham and Gabriel Arthur to find the South Sea. On their second attempt they reached as far as what is now northwestern Georgia. Needham then turned back toward Fort Henry for supplies but died on the return trip. Arthur accompanied Indian raiding parties into West Florida, South Carolina, and then north as far as the Ohio River before returning to Virginia in 1674. Those explorations gathered valuable information for future traders and settlers and also provided irrefutable evidence that the continent was far larger than anyone had imagined.

Information that exploration of the backcountry made available enticed

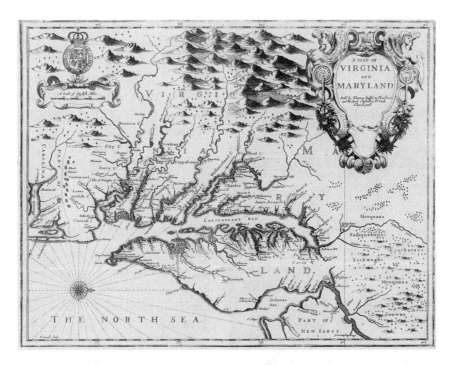

Francis Lamb, *Map of Virginia and Maryland* (1676) from John Speed, *The Theatre of the Empire of Great-Britain* (London, 1676)

immigrants and settlers in the eastern portion of Virginia to move to the frontiers west and north of established settlements. There they interacted with tribes of Indians who to that time had had only a few occasional contacts with English-speaking Virginians and who naturally resented intrusions into their homelands. That resulted in more fighting reminiscent of the hostilities that had marked the first decades of English settlement in Tsenacomoco. About that same time a band of northern Indians later known as the Westo moved through Virginia on their way south. During the final decades of the seventeenth century they participated in large-scale enslavement of members of other Indian tribes for sale to sugar planters in the Caribbean. As the Westo moved through Virginia they engaged in fights with both native Indians and colonists, which raised the level of fear among settlers on the frontier. Unverified reports suggest that several hundred settlers may have died in numerous small-scale encounters in the mid-1670s.

    In 1675 settlers in northern Virginia and the Doegs and Susquehannocks who lived across the Potomac River in Maryland also came into conflict, and a party of Virginia militiamen killed all the inhabitants of an Indian town.

Uneasy colonists on the exposed frontiers pressed for protection, but Governor Sir William Berkeley and the General Assembly were able to do little more than promise to erect a few small frontier posts that certainly could not have provided security for all the scattered outlying settlements. Taxes were already high as a result of the king's demand that the colony erect expensive (and ultimately useless) defensive works at Point Comfort and Jamestown during the Second and Third Anglo-Dutch Wars of 1665–67 and 1672–74. The taxes and a drought reduced income from tobacco planting in the middle of the decade and produced economic hardship that contributed to unrest throughout the colony.

Civil Unrest

Unrest among the population of lower-class white men and servants was widespread by the 1670s. On several occasions that unrest led to violence, as it had back in the autumn of 1663 when some of Oliver Cromwell's former soldiers and some indentured servants met secretly in a small house in Gloucester County to plot an insurrection. They planned to seize a local plantation and its store of arms and then recruit other servants from the countryside and march on Jamestown. They hoped to force the governor to negotiate their freedom or resettlement to another colony. An indentured conspirator named John Berkenhead disclosed the plan to his master, who arranged for the local magistrates to round up and try the others. Indicted for treason, they were all hanged except Berkenhead, who received his freedom and a large reward. The next session of the General Assembly passed a new law to restrict the movements of indentured servants. That was an unusual event, but small-scale episodes of servant unrest were commonplace in seventeenth-century Virginia as in England and in other colonies.

Early in January 1674 justices of the peace in Surry County arrested several poor artisans who assembled to complain about high taxes and attempted to prosecute them under an old English treason law. A 1670 Virginia law had deprived white men such as the protestors who were too poor to own property or pay taxes of the right to vote for members of the House of Burgesses (no men voted on who served on the county court); and required every person, even poor people, to pay a head tax, or poll-tax, in tobacco.

In pleas to the General Assembly in June 1676 and in complaints to royal commissioners of investigation early in 1677 white Virginians of the middling and lower classes from almost every county enumerated some very serious grievances. They complained that members of the House of Burgesses assembled too often and voted themselves excessively large expense accounts that taxpayers had to pay. Legislators left the frontiers defenseless against Indian raiding parties. Justices of the peace taxed people by the head, or poll, and did not tax land, which placed a proportionally heavier tax burden on poor people and landless artisans than on owners of large plantations. Some county courts went into secret session to set the annual tax levy, and justices of the peace told men who complained about the practice that how the court did its work was none of their business. Men in several counties demanded that ordinary residents be permitted to take part in setting the county tax rates. Some county clerks refused to let men see or obtain copies of official county records. Some sheriffs contrived to retain their offices for several consecutive years, which enlarged their local political influence and also increased their income because they collected fees for performing some of their tasks and kept a percentage of tax money they collected in lieu of a salary. Other men complained that parish vestrymen committed similar abuses and asked that members of vestries be elected at regularly scheduled intervals. Still other men complained that when a war with neighboring Indian tribes appeared imminent militia officers called their men into the field to erect forts and other buildings on their own property at public expense. The conduct of haughty, overbearing, entrenched local elites led to open revolt against some of the officials and practices of local institutions of the colonial government.

In 1675 when Virginians who lived near Indians were fearful and Virginians who resented the behavior of local government officials were angry, a spectacular flight of passenger pigeons, Halley's Comet, and a swarm of locusts all foretold trouble. Thomas Mathew, who then lived in the northern part of Virginia, later called them "ominous presages." Indians killed some of his farm laborers, and he and other people viewed the comet and the locusts as warnings of worse to come. The vast swarm of passenger pigeons was even more alarming. Mathew recalled, "This Sight put the old planters under the more portentous Apprehensions, because the like was Seen (as they said) in the year 1640 When th' Indians Committed the last Massacre, but not after, untill that present year 1675."[8] The "last Massacre" was actually Opechancanough's 1644 attack, but that Mathew remembered the date wrong was a minor matter in a culture in which people readily believed such ominous warnings. The first news of fighting between Indians and colonists in New England, known as King Philip's War, arrived early in 1676 as if to prove that the warnings were true and that Indians everywhere had begun a general assault on all the colonies.

Bacon's Rebellion

Bacon's Rebellion of 1676 was the largest and most violent uprising of white people in the history of the colony. It had several causes. One was the continuing warfare between settlers and Indians. In September 1675 Nathaniel Bacon (1647–76), a well-connected Henrico County planter who had recently arrived from England and had been appointed to a seat on the Council of State, seized several friendly Appomattock Indians in a dispute over ownership of some grain. Berkeley rebuked him for the "rash heady acction,"[9] but Bacon raised a force of volunteers and requested a commission from the governor to lead them against the Indians. The governor refused to endorse vigilante action, but Bacon defiantly led seventy men into battle and with the aid of the friendly Occaneechi Indians routed a band of Susquehannocks near the Roanoke River. Becoming suspicious of his allies, Bacon then attacked and killed many of them as well.

In the spring of 1676 Berkeley's long-successful policy of protecting Virginia's settlers and peaceful tribes from each other collapsed under the weight of angry men who feared for the safety of their families and farms. Frightened men rallied to the leadership of Nathaniel Bacon. In May, Berkeley proclaimed Bacon and his men to be in rebellion, and in June the governor arrested him in Jamestown, but the governor vacillated. Berkeley wished to maintain peace with the Indians and guarantee the continuation of the profitable trade in which he and other influential Virginia men were engaged; but he also knew that he had a responsibility to protect frontier settlers, some of whom were responsible for initiating fighting with the Indians. Uncertain what to do, Berkeley grumbled, "How miserable that man is that Governes a People wher six parts of seaven at least are Poore Endebted Discontented and Armed and to take away their Armes now the Indians are at our Throats were to rayse an Universall mutiny."[10]

The governor's well-connected and politically astute wife, Frances Culpeper Stephens Berkeley, sailed for London to explain the situation to the king and his ministers, and Berkeley called for a general election and summoned a new assembly to meet in Jamestown in June 1676. The legislators passed some significant reform laws that redressed most of the major grievances that had arisen in the counties. At that assembly session the governor and the rebel faced each other in a dramatic scene. Berkeley bared his chest and dared Bacon to shoot him. Bacon backed down, but he compelled members of the assembly to appoint him a general to command an army of a thousand men. Some people demanded that Bacon exterminate all the Indians, a proposal he endorsed, and the law that created his army allowed soldiers and officers to enslave for life the Indians they captured.

In August, Bacon issued two declarations against Berkeley and proclaimed himself a general "by the consent of the people."[11] Fear of Indian attacks prompted many white Virginians to support Bacon's rebellion against the governor. Bacon appealed for support from people in counties that were not

"Bacon Addressing His Men," a conjectural illustration
from Mary Tucker McGill, *History of Virginia, for the
Use of Schools* (Baltimore, 1873), 97

under immediate threat of Indian attacks by charging that high county taxes
and high-handed rule by local officials were a result of Berkeley's misgovern-
ment and that his local appointees abused their powers. Many poor Virginians
who had recently protested the behavior of their local justices of the peace or
militia officers eagerly responded to Bacon's charges. They joined his rebellious
band or signed oaths of allegiance to him. By August the colony was embroiled
in a full-scale civil war.

At one point when the two armed parties were facing each other outside Jamestown, Bacon placed a group of white women before his forces to
shield them from the governor's. The participation of women in the rebellion, whether voluntarily or involuntarily, was one of the many dramatic—
and to white male observers inexplicable—things about the events of 1676.
Armed parties of men on both sides rode about the colony plundering their
opponents' estates. Bacon's men ransacked and caused considerable damage to
Berkeley's plantation at Green Spring, near Jamestown. Bacon's rebels drove
Berkeley and his followers across Chesapeake Bay to the Eastern Shore at the
end of the summer, and Bacon's men burned Jamestown.

Bacon's army attacked several towns of Indians and chased Cockacoeske,
the queen of Pamunkey, and her family into the Dragon Swamp on the Middle
Peninsula. Curiously, for all his talk about dangerous Indians on the frontiers,
Bacon attacked only neighboring tribes who had treaties with the colony, and

none of them had taken part in the raids on the frontier. Bacon died of a fever late in October, and the revolt collapsed before the end of the year. Berkeley was old, tired, partially deaf, and by then very angry. He regained control of Virginia and began holding courts martial and hanging Bacon's principal lieutenants and confiscating their property. A royal regiment arrived in Virginia early in 1677 too late to assist the governor. The soldiers' requirements of food and lodging placed demands on Berkeley's government that it could not meet. Charles II also sent a three-member commission to investigate the causes of the rebellion and ordered the assembly to repeal all the reform laws enacted in June 1676. Knowing nothing of the circumstances under which the assembly had adopted the reform laws the king ignorantly assumed that Bacon had forced the legislators to pass them.

The king also recalled Berkeley to London and empowered one of the commissioners to succeed him as lieutenant governor. Until Berkeley departed late in April relations between him and the commissioners were strained. After the commissioners met with Berkeley at the governor's residence at Green Spring they prepared to get into the governor's carriage to ride down to the dock where their ship waited to take them to their lodgings. The colony's hangman suddenly mounted up in the postilion's place. The commissioners were astonished, and when they saw the governor's wife peeping out a window at them, they concluded that she had arranged for them to be publicly insulted in that manner. She denied that she was responsible, but they may have been correct. Sir William Berkeley then returned to England. Before he could report in person to the king the old governor died in July 1677 after nearly thirty-five years of loyal and generally effective service to the king and his Virginia subjects.

Aftermath of Bacon's Rebellion

On May 29, 1677, the royal commissioners concluded the Treaty of Middle Plantation with the Meherrin, Monacan, Nottoway, Pamunkey, Powhatan, and Saponi. It was the first treaty Indians had made with agents of the king rather than with the governor or General Assembly of Virginia. All the tribes avowed allegiance to Cockacoeske and to the king of England. In spite of her designation as chief of all the chiefs, that did not restore the old Powhatan paramount chiefdom, and her relationships with the other tribes were occasionally troubled. Thereafter each tribe or town maintained a separate relationship with the governor through its own interpreter or agent.

The rebellion and Berkeley's punishment of its leaders created lasting animosities among the colony's residents, as did the behavior of the royal commissioners. The governor's widow played a central role in that politically charged

Unidentified artist, *Frances Culpeper Stevens Berkeley Ludwell*, ca. 1660

atmosphere. Having gone to England when the rebellion was breaking out to explain the governor's actions to the king, she returned in time to witness her husband's final departure from Virginia. She became one of the leaders of what historians call the Green Spring Faction. Its members marshaled years of political experience to resist the Crown's policies to impose control on Virginia. The faction clashed with a succession of royal governors.

Just as the outbreak of Bacon's Rebellion had taken nearly everybody by surprise, the violence and widespread participation in it of people far removed from the dangerous frontiers surprised and puzzled the colony's officials. The presence of servants in the ranks of Bacon's rebels made the rebellion even more alarming to the leading planters. The women who vocally took part openly challenged the authority that the colony's public men believed that they alone should exercise. The colony's leading planters employed their social influence and their political power to strengthen their management of indentured and enslaved laborers and to restrict the ability of white women to challenge men's rights to control households and families.

Bacon's Rebellion interrupted the tobacco trade and severely reduced Charles II's customs revenue. That gave added weight to the proposals the king's brother, James, duke of York, had already made for consolidating royal control over all the American colonies. The Crown tightened its grip and sent Virginia a succession of firm-handed governors who challenged the accumulated powers of the General Assembly. During the next fifteen years royal governors and their resident lieutenant governors made the governor's office and the Council of State the dominant agents of royal authority in Virginia. Governors wrested from the House of Burgesses the power to appoint its clerk and reduced the independence of the lower house of the legislature. The Green Spring Faction delayed but could not prevent imposition of the new imperial policies, and by the 1690s the governor's widow and other members of the faction had all died or become reconciled to the new order. Except for the reduction in the influence of the General Assembly and an increase in the influence of the members of the governor's council, the other institutions of government in Virginia—the General Court, the county courts, the militia, and the parish vestries—remained largely untouched. They continued to provide the colony with competent administration of justice and religious guidance and enabled the colony's planters to develop the large-scale tobacco plantation system that dominated the economic, social, and political life of Virginia during the eighteenth century.

Historians have interpreted Bacon's Rebellion and its consequences in different ways. Some saw it as a rehearsal for the revolution that began exactly a century later in 1776 and characterized it as a democratic revolt against a despotic king and governor. Even though almost no evidence supports that interpretation, a plaque placed in the Capitol in Richmond in the 1920s celebrated Bacon as a champion of the common people. Other historians have focused on the war against the Indians. In part because the 1676 law allowed for the enslavement of captured Indians and in part because of the demands for exterminating them, they have seen the rebellion primarily as an escalation of Anglo-American expropriation of Indian land and territory. Another group of historians who focused on the participation of servants in Bacon's army characterized the rebellion as a consequence of social instability and ineffective institutions of government and social control. They suggested that the rebellion was one of the principal reasons why later in the seventeenth century planters began to shift from using unruly indentured servants on their plantations to importing larger numbers of men, women, and children from Africa.

No comparable large episodes of violence between groups of white Virginians erupted in the colony after Bacon's Rebellion, but wherever settlers and Indians lived in close proximity small-scale incidents continued to occur. Within the areas Englishmen had settled the population of Indians had dwindled since 1607 through disease, warfare, and loss of their lands. At the beginning of the eighteenth century the combined population of the eight tributary tribes of Indians, those who annually paid tribute under the terms of the treaties of 1646 and 1677 and who lived on tribal lands or reserves, was probably no more than about six hundred people.

At the end of the seventeenth century several tribes, notably the Meherin and Nottoway south of the James River and the Pamunkey north of the York River, complained to the governor that English people were trying to push them off their land and obtain ownership of the property to which the tribes were entitled. The written petition of the Nottoway in 1699, for instance, asked the governor "to consider of these things, and give such direction therein as he shall thinke fit; And to prevent any new Occasions of Difference with the English, they Desire that their lands may be ascertained by bounds, and that no English may be permitted to seat within those bounds."[12] In about 1705 or 1706 "Queen Ann and the Great Men of the Pamunkey Indians" asked the governor "to Order for the surveying & Patenting" of their land to protect them from encroaching Englishmen, "And that a Patent may be granted to us our. heirs & successrs. for the Remainder."[13] In those and other similar instances, governors issued orders that the Indians' lands be protected.

Benjamin Harrison, of Surry County, reported to the acting governor in 1709 about episodes of violence in southern Virginia and his attempts to prevent new fighting. "I have taken all the Care I Can to remedy all Complaints between the English and Indians," he wrote, "and truly think our people are as much or more to blame than the Indians: people Seats out Continually" — meaning that English settlers often settled on land where Indians had long lived—"wch Causes many Quarrils." Former government proclamations against such actions had not succeeded. Harrison concluded that unless public officials and settlers "pay more respect to the orders of the Govermt, I Cant See how it Can be Expected from the Indians."[14]

Indians almost always lost in the long run. The number of English in the colony was too great and continued to increase, and Indians had few or no effective means to defend their homelands. In 1705 the General Assembly expelled from Virginia most of the Nanziatico tribe, who lived in Richmond County, after some of its members were convicted of killing a white family. Making use of an old Virginia law that allowed the punishment of an entire Indian population for any member's killing of a white person, the assembly ordered that all the adults be sold into slavery in the West Indian colony of Antigua, and it distributed the children as slaves among various elite white families.

4

LIFE IN THE
SEVENTEENTH CENTURY

ETWEEN 1630 AND 1635 the white population of Virginia doubled
from about twenty-five hundred people to about five thousand. Imported livestock and the cultivation of cereal grains enabled Virginians to feed themselves within a few years after the starving time. In 1633 they
exported several thousand bushels of grain to colonists in New England. The
following year a visiting ship captain recorded what he saw and described
how well he ate. "This Countrey aboundeth in very great plentie," Thomas
Yong marveled, "insomuch as in ordinary planters houses of the better sort
we found tables furnished wth porke kidd chickens turkeyes young geese
Caponetts & such other foules as the season of the yeare affords, besides plentie of milk cheese butter & corne, wch latter almost every planter in the Countrey hath. . . . The swine here are excellent & I never tasted better in Italy or
Spain."[1] Governor Sir John Harvey in that same year reported that he had
planted pomegranates, oranges, lemons, and figs and intended to plant olives.
He and many other Virginians mistakenly believed that because Virginia was
on approximately the same latitude as the Mediterranean Sea those fruits
would grow in Virginia. Thomas Yong reported that the governor's political
rival, Samuel Mathews, also had a large and excellent garden.

Residents of Virginia during the seventeenth century lived very different
lives depending on when and where they lived, whether they were free, indentured servants, or enslaved, whether they were male or female, young or
old, and owned or controlled land. Differences also existed between educated
and uneducated people as well as between recent immigrants and members
of "ancient planter" families. As in England at the time, laws, traditions, and
social institutions reinforced hierarchical distinctions between social classes
and between the genders within each.

Political Life

Tobacco was the most important cash crop Virginians produced in the seventeenth century. Competition for control of the tobacco trade created the first political factions in the colony. Some former Virginia Company officials under the leadership of Samuel Mathews and William Claiborne enjoyed profitable relationships with some of London's most influential tobacco trading companies and repeatedly tried to revive the company in order to protect their interests. Other planters who had obtained high prices for their tobacco from Dutch trading firms opposed restricting the trade to English mercantile houses. From time to time the king proposed to control the trade himself even as he earned tax revenue from it.

Mathews and Claiborne were members of the influential Council of State. In the winter of 1634–35 they temporarily joined forces with burgesses who favored free trade to petition the king not to create a new monopoly under royal control. Governor Sir John Harvey refused to send the signed petition to the king. On April 28, 1635, Mathews and other powerful members of the Council arrested the governor, expelled him from office, and sent him to England under armed guard. The king reappointed Harvey and sent him back to Virginia to teach the Virginians who had the ultimate authority to govern the colony. Thereafter, however, royal governors succeeded only if they cooperated with and respected the political power of councilors and burgesses, joined them in seeking high prices for tobacco, and protected their landed estates.

Kings twice redrew the boundaries of Virginia. In 1634 Charles I issued a charter to create the colony of Maryland and included in it much of the northern portion of the territory Virginia claimed under the charter of 1609. The new colony included part of the Eastern Shore and all the land and water north of the low-water mark on south bank of the Potomac River as far west as the headwaters of that river. The Potomac River was, and is, in Maryland and the portion of Maryland that became the District of Columbia. From the 1630s to the 1670s conflicts occasionally took place between the government and inhabitants of Maryland and such Virginians as William Claiborne who claimed land north of the new charter boundary. Claiborne had established a large and profitable fur-trading outpost on Kent Island in Chesapeake Bay in 1631, well within the territory described in the first Virginia charters, but after 1634 the island was within the colony of Maryland. In 1663 Charles II issued a charter that granted a group of investors much of the land that eventually became North and South Carolina. The grants of 1634 and 1663 fixed the eastern portions of the northern and southern boundaries of Virginia at their present places.

Many of the men who rose to prominence began their careers in Virginia as participants in the trans-Atlantic tobacco trade and became permanent residents of Virginia and owners of land and laborers as a consequence of their success in that commerce. The General Assembly, which royal officials largely ignored for its first fifty years, developed into a miniature Parliament that made virtually all the laws that governed the colony. In 1643 Governor Sir William Berkeley allowed burgesses to begin meeting separately from members of the Council of State when the assembly met. By creating a bicameral — two-house — legislature Berkeley created a counterbalance to the powerful council Mathews and Claiborne, with their strong ties to British trading companies, had dominated. That allowed the assembly to pursue a free-trade policy and enabled tobacco planters to sell their tobacco in the high-priced markets in the Netherlands. The creation of a bicameral legislature in Virginia, as in several other colonies, was a political maneuver to solve a political problem, not an imitation of the structure of Parliament.

Race became the most important legal distinction between free and enslaved people and also between indentured and enslaved people. In the 1690s the General Assembly, in emulation of a recent act of Parliament, more precisely defined who was entitled to vote: free adult males who owned a minimum amount of land. It is very unlikely that any women or any Indians or African Virginians had voted or tried to vote during the seventeenth century, but that law effectively prohibited them from even trying and reinforced the importance of property ownership as a prerequisite for taking part in the government of the colony.

Virginian John Cotton described the capital city of Jamestown in the mid-1670s. His account is easier to understand when read aloud than silently. "The place on which the Towne is built, is a perfect Peninsulla," he wrote, "or tract of land allmost wholly incompast with water. Haveing, on the South side the River (Formerly Powhetan, now called James River) 3 miles brode, Incumpast on the North from the east point, with a deep creeke, rangeing in a cemicircle to the west, within 10 paces of the River; and there by a smalle Istmas, tacked to the continent. . . . It is Low ground, full of Marches and swamps, which makes the Aire especially in the Sumer, insalubrious & unhelty; It is not at all replenish'd with springs, of fresh water, & that which they have in ther wells, brackish, ill sented & penurious, and not gratefull to the stumack. . . . The Towne is built much about the middle of the South line, close upon the River, extending east and west, about 3 quarters of a Mile; in which is comprehended some 16 pair howses, most as the church built of Brick, faire and large; and in them about a dozen ffamillies (for all the howses are not inhabited) getting there liveings by keeping of ordinaries, at extraordinary rates."[2] The brick statehouse the assembly erected in Jamestown in the 1660s may have been the

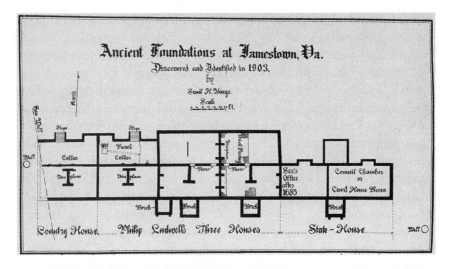

Samuel H. Yonge prepared this plan in 1903 after he excavated the foundations at the site of the Statehouse at Jamestown.

largest building in any seventeenth-century English colony. It symbolized how large and important the colony had become by then and also appeared to signal that its political and social institutions were secure and enduring.

Religious Life

Seventeenth-century archival records contain many references to churches in Virginia, but because most of the early buildings were earth-fast, frame structures, little archaeological evidence remains. Likewise, the scarcity of personal and family records for most early Virginians and the absence of a printing industry in the colony resulted in the survival of only a small body of documentary evidence from which historians could later assess the religious sensibilities of the colony's residents. Students of early American religious history often derived their understandings of religious beliefs from documents generated during religious controversies. The lack of such evidence from early Virginia may have suggested incorrectly that colonists did not take religious beliefs seriously, but it seems that members of the Church of England in Virginia did not engage in protracted, heated debates about fine points of theology and requirements for church membership as often or as intensely as in New England, where disputes created abundant evidence for scholarly examination.

Ministers of the Church of England in Virginia promoted a religious outlook that stressed faith and right behavior rather than strict uniformity of theological doctrine. So long as good order prevailed in the congregations and in the scattered parish communities differences of opinion about Scripture and liturgical practices may have incited little prolonged debate and created little evidence for scholarly analysis; but the presence of numerous churches, the activities of the parish vestries, the repeated actions of the Crown and the colony's governors to encourage religious observances, and the employment of religiously rooted language in public and private discourse all indicate that for Virginia's Protestants their religious beliefs were important to them.

During the first decades of the seventeenth century ministers were in short supply, and for long periods of time some residents lived without access to regular church services and the sacraments. It is not entirely clear what the unavailability of clergymen meant to those colonists, but parish clerks could officiate at some religious services. People with access to a copy of the Book of Common Prayer could read the daily lessons and prayers in their own households and bring up their children according to the teachings of the Church of England. In the 1650s the assembly twice offered a large cash bonus to clergymen who moved from England to Virginia and exempted their servants and slaves from taxation to encourage enough men to come and take charge of the colony's parishes. During the latter years of the seventeenth century and during the eighteenth the colony was reasonably well supplied with ordained ministers of the Church of England.

It is likely that many of the clergymen conducted schools and educated young Virginians in reading, writing, literature, mathematics, and the sciences (then known as natural philosophy), as well as in Protestant Christianity. During the decades after the dissolution of the Virginia Company the church and the colonists devoted less time and energy than before to efforts to convert the Indians to Christianity. No organization such as the company existed to provide leadership and resources for missionary work. The process by which Virginia's Indians became Christians, which most had done by the nineteenth century, is yet poorly understood.

Another thing that is not clear is how speedily the King James translation of the Bible, which was being prepared at the very time Jamestown was first settled, replaced the several earlier English translations the first colonists took with them to Virginia. The numerous references to Bibles in seventeenth-century documents seldom specify a particular translation or edition. The most common of the early English-language Bibles, called the Geneva Bible, contained numerous marginal commentaries, some with Calvinist or anti-Catholic language and some critical of monarchy. The Bible the king sponsored omitted those controversial commentaries. If the new translation replaced the Geneva Bible as the common English version in Virginia earlier rather than later in the seventeenth century, it may be that colonists found fewer rather than more occasions to debate fine points of Scripture and theology. The other important book for members of the Church of England was the Book of Common Prayer, often regarded as the second-most-likely book to be found in Protestant households. Its daily prayers for the king also reinforced the relationships between God and believers and also between the king and his subjects.

Religious persecution occasionally took place in seventeenth-century Virginia, which indicates that religious beliefs were indeed important to members of the Church of England who sought to protect themselves and their beliefs from the religious beliefs and practices of other people. Until the middle of the seventeenth century a significant proportion of white Virginians could be loosely characterized as Puritans. They were also members of the Church of England, but they disapproved in varying degrees of the formality of the church's liturgical worship service and a rigid reliance on the prescribed prayers and texts of the Book of Common Prayer. Puritans and the Virginians who employed the Book of Common Prayer by and large coexisted more-or-less peacefully most of the time because their differences of opinion were not often as serious as they grew to be in England by the 1640s.

The English Civil Wars that began in that decade between the king and the parliamentarians—between high churchmen and Puritan reformers—cast a shadow over Puritans who lived in Virginia. On several occasions during the 1640s the governor and the county courts attempted to prevent them from assembling. Some Puritans in the southeastern part of the colony moved to Maryland or dispersed to new settlements in the northern part of Virginia. After an initial attempt to suppress them the government abandoned the attempt to enforce strict religious uniformity in the interest of keeping the peace. During the 1650s while the Cromwellians were in control in England, Puritans were very influential in Virginia, but Virginians experienced much less of the severe religious contention that had led to civil wars in England.

Archaeological excavations of the 1607 fort site disclosed that a small number of Catholics lived at Jamestown during the first years of the colony. Italian glass workers and artisans from several other European countries no doubt included some Catholics. Whether they were at a disadvantage in that Protestant community as a result of their religious affiliation and beliefs is not known. By the middle of the seventeenth century a few Catholics resided unmolested on the banks of the Potomac River at the northern edge of settled Virginia. Margaret Brent, her brother Giles Brent, and their families found refuge in Virginia during the 1640s and 1650s after being driven from Maryland where Catholics had once been welcomed but had become a persecuted minority. They and their children and grandchildren became prosperous and respected planters, but they were never very numerous and posed no serious threat to the colony's Protestant culture. As a consequence of their respectable behavior and value to the community, during the brief reign of the Catholic king James II (1685–88) Virginians ignored English laws against Catholics taking part in public affairs, and some Catholics served as high-ranking militia officers and sat on the county courts. Catholic George Brent became a major in the Stafford County militia, was acting attorney general of the colony from the autumn of 1686 until the spring of 1688, and represented the county in the House of Burgesses in the latter year.

Members of the Society of Friends, commonly called Quakers, immigrated to Virginia beginning in the 1650s and suffered some harassment because of their beliefs and behavior. Quakers believed that Christians received religious inspiration directly from God and consequently rejected the need for ministers and the propriety of the liturgical worship service of the Church of England. They usually refused to obey laws that required everyone to attend the services of the established church. Believing in the equality of all believers Quakers permitted women to speak at meetings. Most members of the Church of England therefore viewed Quakers as potentially dangerous to the well-ordered, male-dominated, hierarchical society they believed was essential to peace, social stability, and preservation of the English Reformation. In the years immediately following the English Civil Wars when the colony's leaders were still worried about civil unrest, the governor and the General Assembly issued orders to prevent Quakers from meeting or to break up their meetings. Before the end of the seventeenth century, however, the colony's Quakers, who were more numerous than its Catholics, had become accepted as respectable planters and merchants and ceased to be perceived as an unsettling minority.

In the spring of 1691 the General Assembly met for the first time after the Glorious Revolution that deposed the Catholic king James II, placed William and Mary on the throne, and established a Protestant line of succession. Insofar as government and society in Virginia were concerned, that revolution had few serious, lasting consequences. One event is of interest, though. Arthur Allen, who had been Speaker of the House of Burgesses in 1686 and 1688, and another member-elect refused when the new assembly convened to take the required oath of loyalty to the new king and queen. Having taken oaths of loyalty to James II they conscientiously refused so long as he was still alive to take an oath to any other monarch. Their refusal was entirely on the religious grounds of their oaths to James II and not as a consequence of disloyalty to William and Mary or of opposition to the political results of the revolution in England. Allen reentered public service under no disabilities soon after the former king died in 1702. Oaths were more than mere formalities of taking office. They were solemn and public contracts with God and the king.

The revolution's replacement of Catholic James II with Protestants William and Mary was an act with important religious significance. Thereafter, all men who took a public office in Virginia had to take three interlocking oaths: one of allegiance to the Crown, one affirming the supremacy of the king (or queen) over all foreign princes (meaning the pope), and one disavowing belief in the Catholic doctrine of transubstantiation—in effect, one oath to the king (or queen), one oath to the Church of England, and one oath to the English Reformation.

Religious beliefs permeated the society, and people understood events of their lives from a religious perspective. An instructive episode occurred on the Eastern Shore in the spring of 1680. A young, unmarried woman gave birth to a child, and shortly thereafter the child died. The county court investigated the crime of fornication that produced the pregnancy and also investigated an allegation that someone had killed the illegitimate child. The court questioned the woman's mother about whether at the time of the woman's most extreme difficulty in labor she had demanded that the woman identify the father and withheld her assistance until the woman complied. That was a standard test for ascertaining paternity because people believed, and the courts acknowledged, that a person in imminent danger of dying could not lie and face the prospect of going directly to hell. The court needed to identify the father in order to make him pay the costs of raising the child so that the parish did not have to raise taxes to support the child.

The court also had the body of the child dug up and handed around so that people who were suspected of having a part in its death could fondle it. That was another standard test because people believed, and the courts acknowledged, that a murdered corpse would bleed or its wounds would change color if the murderer touched it. It was called trial by touch. Both of those legal tests assumed and required a firm foundation in religious belief, in hell, and in God's miracles. When the mother's stepfather handled the infant's corpse and witnesses saw bruised places grow "fresh & red so that blud was redy to come through the skin," they knew that they had identified the culprit. The stepfather went pale on the spot, and the court charged him with murder and with being the father of his stepdaughter's baby.[3] He fled and drowned while trying to escape.

The trial by water of persons accused of witchcraft rested on the same basis of religious belief. The best known of the Virginia witchcraft accusations occurred in Princess Anne County in 1706. After Grace Sherwood was accused several times of bewitching her neighbors the county court ordered several women to examine her privately to ascertain whether she possessed a third nipple (for suckling the devil) or any other evidences of being a witch, but the women at first refused to act. The court then ordered that Sherwood's hands and feet be tied and that she be lowered into consecrated water. That was another standard test to ascertain whether somebody was a witch because people believed, and the courts acknowledged, that consecrated water would not accept a witch, an agent of the Devil. If the person sank, he or she was innocent of the charge and would be hauled out, if lucky, before drowning. If the person floated, he or she was adjudged a witch. Grace Sherwood was adjudged a witch and ordered to be tried before the General Court in Williamsburg. The trial record is lost, but she was not convicted and executed for practicing witchcraft. She lived another thirty-four years. So far as surviving records show, no person was executed in Virginia for practicing witchcraft, and no widespread hysteria accompanied occasional accusations of witchcraft. The hesitant manner in which the residents and court of Princess Anne County Court investigated a series of charges against Grace Sherwood do not prove that residents of the colony disbelieved in witchcraft, merely that they found it difficult to prove that she injured any other person by practicing witchcraft.

Family Life

The white population of Virginia continued to increase in spite of high rates of death from disease, childbirth, and recurrent conflicts with Indians. Virginia's white population was about eight thousand in 1644, twenty-seven thousand in 1660, and forty-three thousand in 1680. Many of the inhabitants were young men who worked their own small tracts of land or were indentured servants who, if they lived long enough, could hope to acquire land after their periods of servitude ended. While working as servants, their labor contracts— their indentures—afforded them some legal protections against overwork or abuse. However, masters and mistresses often imposed significant limitations on their servants. Colonial laws allowed courts to add time to the service of an indentured servant who ran away to compensate the owner for the lost labor. Beginning in 1619 laws prohibited servants from marrying without permission of their masters or mistresses, and laws imposed more severe penalties on female servants than on male servants for some infractions. If a female servant became pregnant she would be punished for the crime of fornication along with the father, but the woman would also have time added to her service to compensate the owner for her lost work during or after childbirth.

Men outnumbered women in seventeenth-century Virginia, but women who survived childbirth tended to live longer than men. It is probable that relatively few couples lived long married lives together. It was common when a spouse died for the surviving spouse to remarry. Children often died in infancy or in childhood. White households and families in seventeenth- and eighteenth-century Virginia often consisted of a husband and wife, one or both of whom had previously been married, and either or both of whom might have children from previous marriages. Elderly or young unmarried relatives probably lived with them also, and orphaned children of relatives may have resided in many households. Indentured servants, hired laborers, enslaved laborers, and perhaps some other relatives may have also resided regularly in those households.

The uniting of prosperous families through marriage allowed some planters and merchants to become wealthy landowners. In part as a result of Virginia widows marrying ambitious immigrant men, many of the family names of the first generations of colonists disappeared during the second half of the seventeenth century. Other family names such as Randolph, Harrison, Dandridge, Custis, Carter, and Burwell, the names of families that played important leadership roles during the eighteenth century, replaced them.

English common law made women inferior to men in many respects. Women could not vote, and they could not enter into contracts without an adult man to serve as a legal "next friend." When a woman married, any property she possessed became her husband's property to do with as he pleased. Widows remained bound in many respects to the status of dependency that English law imposed on married women. Those legal traditions contributed to the consolidation of property in the hands of male members of emerging elite families because when they married a women, whether widowed or not, the men gained ownership of the property and could pass it along to his children.

The colony's leading planter families created a modified version of hierarchical English society and with it a measure of stability and order even as they competed vigorously with each other in the market for labor, for new land, and in contests for influential public offices. Their families furnished most members of the county courts, militia officers, parish vestrymen, and burgesses. The institutions of government and the church reinforced their social standing and authority. The ruling planter class shaped the economy and the colony's laws, took advantage of the headright system to acquire land, and controlled the patterns of settlement. Local officials such as the county clerk and county surveyor became powerful agents in facilitating the acquisition of large tracts of land by the families who had the most political influence. They and their families increased their wealth as a result. Other colonial officials did too, among them the surveyor general of the colony and the escheater general, who recovered land for the Crown if an owner died without an heir. The escheater general received a portion of the value of the property as his compensation. Land ownership, control of labor, social status, and political influence were all inextricably intertwined.

Historians have differed about when and how during the seventeenth century Virginia society gained the stability it exhibited in the eighteenth century. Some have emphasized or perhaps exaggerated the social chaos they perceived in the earliest years and believed that political and economic conditions did not create safe social and political stability until the final quarter of the seventeenth century. A larger number of later historians have argued persuasively that the early society was not so chaotic or anarchic as formerly believed and that both social and political institutions imposed a comfortable measure of stability and order on the society during the second quarter of the seventeenth century.

The language people used and the laws they adopted allow historians to understand some of their values. Men who made the laws used language that revealed much about their values. For example, the taxes vestries imposed for erecting churches, paying ministers, and caring for orphans and the poor and also the taxes county courts imposed for erecting courthouses and jails or arming the militia were charged at a rate of so much per able-bodied laborer. It was a head tax, or poll tax, on people who by their own labor or by the labor of their able-bodied servants, slaves, and children contributed to the colonial economy. Legislators did not normally tax white married women, which indicated that white men did not regard their domestic work in the household and for the family as valuable in the same way they valued production of food and tobacco in the fields. English and Virginia laws and the record books in the courthouses and parish offices identified a taxable person as a tithable, a term that originated in the church, not in the exchequer. In Virginia that word was applied until 1781 to every person who paid parish and county poll taxes. Some government officials continued to refer to taxable people as tithables well into the middle of the nineteenth century.

5

TOBACCO AND SLAVERY

THROUGHOUT THE SEVENTEENTH CENTURY royal officials in England and some influential Virginians attempted to diversify the colony's economy. They had more success than has often been realized because tobacco cultivation became the principal cash crop and overshadowed everything else. Governor Sir William Berkeley was especially eager to diversify the economy and conducted several demonstration projects on his property at Green Spring, near Jamestown. He produced potash in quantity, wine that he considered of high quality, and also silk. Edward Digges, of York County, who briefly served as governor during the 1650s, was a notably successful raiser of sweet-scented tobacco, but he also produced so much good-quality silk that he became famous in England for it and presented Virginia-made silk to King Charles II. The General Assembly awarded Digges a substantial bonus of £100 for his silk production, and he received a compliment in England in the form of laudatory verse in Samuel Hartlib's 1655 book, *The Reformed Virginian Silk-Worm*.

Tobacco

Tobacco production dominated the agricultural economy of the Chesapeake region for more than two centuries. Readily available land, a reliable demand for tobacco in England and Europe, and the profit for its producers kept the colony dependent on that one crop. In England in the seventeenth century the place name *Virginia* became a synonym for the word *tobacco*. Virginians used tobacco to purchase imported goods from England, to pay local tithes and taxes, and to acquire land and laborers to grow more of it. Tobacco and promissory notes payable in tobacco even served as Virginia's principal currency, with the value of nearly everything from servants to taxes expressed in pounds of tobacco. The plant was extremely important to the English, too.

Cartouche from Joshua Fry and Peter Jefferson, *A Map of the Most Inhabited Part of Virginia* (4th state, London 1755), showing barrels of tobacco being loaded aboard ship.

By the 1680s taxes on the tobacco trade furnished more than one-third of all the £2 million royal revenue.

Tobacco cultivation was very labor-intensive. Start-up costs were high on uncultivated land. Farmers usually employed Indian methods of cultivation by girding trees to kill them, burning the underbrush, and planting tobacco and other crops beneath the dead trees. They often harvested the timber and farmed among the stumps. A 1790s Benjamin Henry Latrobe watercolor of an overseer and several enslaved women shows that the practice endured through the eighteenth century. The painting also discloses that while the women were hoeing the ground, they were also burning the stumps, perhaps to prepare the soil for the plow, a farm implement just coming into widespread use then. Some planters continued planting tobacco in hills for many more years. Thomas Jefferson's plantation manager in Bedford County planted tobacco in hills through the 1810s.

Early in the season planters sowed tobacco seeds in specially prepared beds and tended them until the ground warmed sufficiently to transplant the seedlings into the fields. Throughout the long growing season workers had to weed the crop frequently, pluck damaging insects off the plants, and remove the lower leaves as the plants grew to force the best upper leaves to grow large and strong. At the end of the growing season workers pulled up the plants or cut them off at the base of the stem, hung the plants in covered barns to dry, and

Benjamin Henry Latrobe, *An Overseer Doing His Duty Near Fredericksburg, Virginia,* ca. 1798

then packed the leaves in large barrels called hogsheads for transport to the waterside and loading onto a ship for transportation to England. By then it was time to sow seeds from that year's crop for the next year's crop.

The rhythms of life for most Virginians followed the demands of their major cash crop. Virginians also raised livestock and grains, and many of them had orchards for producing fruits to be brewed into cider or distilled into brandy. Aside from producing necessary food and drink, work on the tobacco crop was an almost universal occupation. Most white families, whether owners of large plantations, farmers who worked their own small plots, or hired or indentured workers, spent much of their time producing Virginia's most important cash crop. Enslaved men, women, and children of African or American Indian descent did the same work for the benefit of their masters or owners.

In spite of the legal restrictions England's Navigation Acts of the 1660s imposed on sale of Virginia tobacco to merchants from the Netherlands, some Virginia planters and merchants managed to ship tobacco to Dutch markets. There, whether illegally imported directly into the Netherlands or legally shipped there through England, between the 1680s and 1710s Virginia tobacco commanded higher prices than tobacco from any other place. Items of Dutch manufacture discovered in archaeological excavations in eastern

William Tatham, *An Historical and Practical Essay on the Culture and Commerce of Tobacco* (London, 1800)

Virginia indicate that commerce between Virginia and the Netherlands remained brisk for decades. Some families who became famous and influential in Virginia, such as the Custis family, had commercial and kinship roots deep in trading networks based in Amsterdam and other cities of the Netherlands.

The prices Virginia planters received for their tobacco rose and fell unpredictably depending on the weather and changes in international markets. Good crops depressed the price per pound planters received, and although bad crops might drive up the price the reduced supply also sometimes reduced income. In 1682 farmers in Middlesex and several other counties went about

the countryside destroying tens of thousands of hills of tobacco plants to reduce the supply and thereby raise the price. Coming in the aftermath of Bacon's Rebellion the plant-cutting riot, as people called it, created a brief panic
in the colony's governing circles. Seventeenth-century governors negotiated
several times with Maryland for a joint reduction in the tobacco crop in order
to raise its price, but when the General Assembly passed laws to limit tobacco
production officials in Maryland refused to cooperate, or the Crown disallowed them.

Men and women who owned land near the lower reaches of the York River
were fortunate to be able to plant tobacco in soil that was better adapted to
tobacco cultivation than elsewhere in the Chesapeake region. A fine grade of
tobacco, called sweet-scented, thrived there but not elsewhere and gave planters in that region a competitive advantage over planters and small farmers elsewhere who grew a less-valuable strain of tobacco called Orinoco. Planters who
could grow sweet-scented tobacco became more prosperous and influential
more quickly than most planters in other regions of Virginia.

The Seventeenth-Century Slave Trade

Planters who raised sweet-scented tobacco were among the first to purchase
significant numbers of men, women, and children from Africa to labor in
their fields and begin the transition from reliance on English indentured servants to enslaved African laborers. As with planters in the lower regions of
the other major rivers, planters on the banks of the York River had their pick
of the best servants and slaves. Ship captains moved upstream to sell their cargoes of indentured servants or slaves, which left planters in the interior with
second or third choices in the labor market. Consequently, eastern planters, particularly planters of sweet-scented tobacco, grew wealthy sooner and
faster than other planters. They also exploited their socially and economically
privileged status to increase their political power. Together, those advantages
created economic and social distinctions between planters near the bay and
planters elsewhere.

King Charles II chartered the Royal African Company in 1672 and gave it
a monopoly on the transportation of enslaved Africans to English colonies in
the Caribbean and North America. English and colonial investors purchased
stock in the company and earned money from the profits of the shipping voyages. After the king abolished the company's monopoly in 1698 even more
investors participated in the slave trade, including Virginia merchants and
planters. Liverpool became the principal British port for the slave trade, but
men in the mainland colonies also engaged in the trade as owners of ships,
as investors in individual voyages, and as retailers of laborers to farmers and

planters who lived in the interiors of the colonies. Only a small portion of all of the millions of men, women, and children captured and sold into slavery in Africa wound up in North America. Most of them went to South America or to the island colonies where many of them were literally worked to death on sugar plantations and other enterprises dependent on cheap forced labor.

Africans or persons of African descent constituted only about 5 percent of Virginia's population when the king chartered the company. Some of them, such as Anthony Johnson of Northampton County, became successful free farmers, but others remained long-term servants or became lifetime slaves. Surviving depositions and court records demonstrate that some Africans labored for a limited number of years, as indentured servants did, but that planters sometimes refused to release them from service at the end of the term and forced those people into lifetime slavery.

Portuguese and Spanish traders introduced Catholicism into parts of West Africa during the sixteenth and seventeenth centuries, and references in Virginia county records suggest that some Africans arrived with Portuguese or Spanish names and perhaps with some knowledge of Christianity. The first name of Anthony Johnson might have originally been Antonio, and the surname of Emanuel Driggus, also of Northampton County, was probably Rodrigues. Islam was also introduced into West Africa before the seventeenth century, and the colony's bound labor force included some Islamic men and women. Sir William Berkeley is known to have owned three Islamic men. The governor offered them freedom if they converted to Christianity, and two of them did. Berkeley was so impressed by the third man's devotion to his religious beliefs that he freed him too.

The Law of Master and Slave

Africans who reached Virginia during the latter decades of the seventeenth century entered a thriving and growing colony that increasingly required additional laborers for the tobacco economy. Many centuries of English law defined relations between masters and servants in Virginia. Indentured servants worked under contracts planters could buy and sell. The contracts specified the responsibilities of the owners to provide food, shelter, and clothing until the term of the indenture expired and guaranteed remedies at law for indentured servants if their masters violated the terms of the contract or treated them harshly. Until the middle of the century it is likely that indentured white laborers made up more than half the English-speaking population of the colony.

Enslaved men, women, and children enjoyed few or none of the legal rights and protections English and colonial laws afforded to indentured servants.

The laws and practices of slavery evolved slowly in Virginia, but from the earliest years planters probably treated white indentured workers differently than they treated Indians and Africans. In September 1630 a court ordered that a white man be "soundly whipped, before an assembly of Negroes and others for abusing himself to the dishonor of God and shame of Christians, by defiling his body in lying with a negro."[1] The language of the order suggests that the white men who imposed the punishment regarded the offense as greater than would have been the case had he committed the deed with another white person. Laws that defined slavery often included references to Indians as well as to Africans.

By the middle of the seventeenth century colonial laws and practices regularly made distinctions between "servants" (usually meaning white indentured servants) and "Negroes" (usually meaning Africans serving for life). The July 1670 inventory of the estate of John Carter of Lancaster County, for example, listed more than thirty indentured servants, each with an English surname and a value based in part on how many months or years of service he or she then owed Carter's estate. The inventory also listed more than forty men and women of African birth or descent, none identified with a surname or with a record of how long his or her term of service had to run and each with a value significantly higher than the value of the short-term indentured servants. Carter and the men who appraised his estate clearly regarded all of his black laborers as enslaved for life.

Seventeenth-century laws regularly distinguished between free and unfree people, between people of African origin or descent and people of European or American Indian origin or descent. A 1640 order of the General Assembly concerning defense required "All persons except negroes to be provided with arms and amunition."[2] In order to make some common practices into enforceable laws or to solve particular problems the General Assembly, which tobacco planters in need of workers dominated, passed new laws to control laborers beginning in the 1660s. In 1661 the assembly recognized that there were two classes of runaway servants, indentured servants who could be punished for running away by having additional months or years added to their terms of service, and "negroes who are incapable of makeing satisfaction by addition of time."[3] That indicates that important portions of the colony's African laborers were by then being held in lifetime servitude.

A law the General Assembly passed in the following year arose in part from a case Elizabeth Key filed in the Northumberland County Court. She was the daughter of Thomas Key, a white man who had been a burgess in the 1630s, and one of his enslaved women of African origin or descent. Elizabeth Key claimed her freedom and won her case on the common law ground that the child of a free man was born free. But in 1662, because "some doubts have arrisen whether children got by any Englishman upon a negro woman should be slave or ffree," the General Assembly reversed English law and required "that all children borne in this country shalbe held bound or free only according to the condition of the mother." The member of the assembly who drafted the law may have owned an old English law book that described how descendants of villeins, medieval serfs, were tied to the land through the maternal line of descent. Thereafter all children of enslaved women automatically became the property of the woman's owner in the same way that puppies or calves became the property of the owners of dogs or cattle. The same law also imposed a double fine on "any christian" convicted of fornication "with a negro man or woman."[4] The assembly made another important distinction when it declared in 1668 that all black women, but not all white women, were taxable laborers.

English law prohibited holding Christians in lifetime slavery. When in 1667 a man named Fernando went to court to seek his freedom he stated that he was a Christian and had lived in England. The clerk of the court could not or would not read the baptismal certificate Fernando presented (it may have been in Portuguese), and the justices of the peace refused to proceed with the suit, which probably left him in slavery. In 1670 the General Assembly prohibited free blacks and Indians from purchasing the labor of "christian servants."[5] Twelve years later the assembly overturned the old English law by declaring that it was lawful for Virginians to hold in slavery persons who had converted to Christianity.

By many such gradual steps the condition of most black Virginians slipped into lifetime slavery, and planters' treatment of black enslaved Virginians became increasingly distinct from their treatment of white indentured servants or white hired laborers. In 1668, for instance, the General Assembly declared in An Act About the Casuall Killing of Slaves that it was not murder if a master killed a slave during the course of punishing or correcting "negroes," inasmuch as the lawmakers presumed that nothing "should induce any man to destroy his owne estate" on purpose.[6]

As early as the middle of the seventeenth century county courts began to reverse another ancient precept of English common law. The well-established doctrine of *caveat emptor*—buyer beware—governed commercial transactions. It was the responsibility of the purchaser to ascertain the quality of the merchandise he or she bought. If a person purchased a lame horse or a barrel of rotten corn the purchaser had no legal grounds for complaint against the seller. The tremendous demand for laborers in the colony and the ease with which physical defects of a servant or slave could be concealed from a prospective buyer led justices of the peace to place the burden instead on the seller. They required sellers of servants and slaves to disclose to buyers if a laborer was sick, lame, prone to diseases, feeble-minded, or pregnant. Any of those conditions could reduce the usefulness of the worker or depress the market price. The new rule of law became part of the common law of the colony. The General Court recognized it as such in the 1735 case *Waddill v. Chamberlayne* and refused to apply the old rule of *caveat emptor* in a case in which it clearly applied by the laws and precedents of English courts.

One by one the legal and social aspects of slavery and the plantation system coalesced. During the 1690s the General Assembly made two additional and important legal distinctions between white people and black people. In 1692 it ordered that enslaved people accused of crimes be tried in special local courts, called courts of oyer and terminer (literally, for hearing and deciding cases), in which all the ordinary rules of common law did not apply. Justices of the peace decided guilt or innocence without a jury. Defendants could not appeal a court ruling to a higher court. In contrast, the General Court in the capital tried before a jury all civil cases of consequence and all trials of white people accused of crimes. (An exception was piracy and crimes committed on the high seas, for which the governor convened special courts of admiralty until the Crown created a Virginia Court of Vice-Admiralty in 1698.)

At the same time, white Virginians exhibited ideas about persons of African descent that were different from their attitudes about persons of European and Native American descent. White Virginians regarded Europeans and Indians as more similar to each other than different but perceived Europeans and Africans as more different from each other than similar. In Virginia and elsewhere white residents of the colonies slowly developed a society based on enslaved labor and strong attitudes of racial differences and white superiority.

Despite Virginians' more favorable attitudes toward Indians, enslavement of Indians also increased during the final third of the seventeenth century. Early colonists had forced some Indians into slavery and later in the century captured or purchased Indians from tribes on the borders of the colony. In 1670 the General Assembly declared that Indians captured in war but of local origin or from the peripheries of settlement could be enslaved but only until age thirty. The law permitted Indians who were not Christians and had been imported by ship from other colonies to be enslaved for life. In the Carolinas and farther to the south, slave traders (including the Westo Indians, Spaniards, Englishmen, and Scotsmen) captured and offered Indians for sale. They sold between 30,000 and 50,000 Indians from the South Atlantic and western Gulf Coast to English colonies between the 1670s and 1715, mostly to the West Indian islands. The number of enslaved Indians that white Virginians purchased during that time is not known, but evidence suggests that the practice of enslaving and purchasing Indians increased in the colony during the final decades of the seventeenth century.

In 1705 as part of a comprehensive revision of all of the colony's laws the
General Assembly consolidated all legislation on the subject of slavery into
Virginia's first systematic slave code, something that could hardly have been
anticipated when the first Africans arrived in Virginia less than a century
before. The law clarified ambiguous provisions of earlier laws and made future
enslavement of Indians illegal. Uncertainties about how the old laws had applied to particular persons led many people to file suits for freedom in county
courts and in the General Court. Incomplete surviving archival records do
not indicate just how many such suits they filed, but they were numerous
enough (seven Indians filed suit in Henrico County between 1708 and 1712,
for instance) that in October 1711 the General Court had to adopt a standing
rule of procedure to govern all such cases. The rule stated that when people
held in slavery sued for their freedom the court would appoint legal counsel
for them and permit them to subpoena evidence in their favor. Even though
enslaved labor was by then essential to the economy of the colony, its slave-
owning leaders admitted that some illegal enslavement of Indians had taken
place and provided access to the courts for people who asserted a claim to
freedom based on illegal enslavement of a female Indian ancestor. Because an
owner might lose a valuable item of laboring property if an Indian or descendant of an African won a freedom suit, the court's rule required that the fact
of freedom be clearly proved and not merely asserted. Several hundred Virginians successfully sued for their freedom between 1705 and the American
Revolution.

Violence

Virginia's laws like the Act About the Casuall Killing of Slaves reflected the
fact that relations between masters and their servants and slaves were sometimes strained in Virginia, as elsewhere, and ultimately rested on the threat
of or the fact of violence. Several times during the seventeenth century justices of the peace or members of the Council of State investigated reports of
small-scale uprisings or plans for revolts. In the autumn of 1687, for example,
the governor received a report of "the Discovery of a Negro Plott, formed in
the Northern Neck for the Distroying and killing his Majt[ies] Subjects the Inhabitants thereof, with a designe of Carrying it through the whole Collony
of Virg[a]." The Middlesex County Court arrested and interrogated one of the
conspirators and reported to the governor and council. At the conclusion of
their own investigation, members of the Council of State publicly condemned
"the great freedome and Liberty that has beene by many Masters given to their
Negro Slaves for Walking on broad on Saterdays and Sundays and permitting
them to meete in great Numbers in makeing and holding of Funeralls for Dead

Negroes," which "gives them the Opportunityes under pretention of such pub-
lique meetings to Consult and advise for the Carrying on of their Evill &
Wicked purposes & Contrivances." The governor and council ordered "that a
Proclamacion doe forthwith Issue, requiring a Strickt observance of the Severall Laws of this Collony relateing to Negroes, and to require and Comand all
Masters of Families haveing any Negro Slaves, not to permitt them to hold or
make any Solemnity of Funeralls for any deceased Negroes."[7]

Hired laborers, indentured servants, and enslaved people were all subject
to requirements of English and Virginia laws, but enslaved laborers regularly
suffered more severe punishments than indentured servants. Masters often
punished enslaved people for infractions of orders, and few laws limited owners' ability to punish as they pleased. Sometimes, though, a planter sought
approval for inflicting a severe punishment. In September 1711 Christopher
Robinson of Middlesex County, member of a prominent and wealthy family
of planters and officeholders, took "his Negro boy Tom" to the county court
"for Lying out"—that is, running away from the plantation for a time—"and
doeing Severall Misdemeanors and praying that he might be adjudged to have
his two great Toes and a toe of Each foot next to them cutt of." The court
"Ordered that the said Christopher Robinson have liberty to cutt of the said
Toes accordingly."[8]

At a trial in April 1710 the General Court convicted two enslaved men,
"Salvadore an Indian and Scipio a Negro," of "high Treason," meaning rebellion. The court "Ordered that Salvadore be executed (according to the Sentence passed on him) at the Court house of Surry County on the first Tuesday
in May, and that his body be disposed of as follows . . . his head to be delivered
to the Sherif of James City County and by him sett up at the City of Williams-
burgh Two of his quarters likewise delivered to the s^d Sherif of James City one
whereof he is to cause to be sett up at the great guns in James City and the
other to deliver to the Sherif of New Kent County to be sett up in the most
publick place of the said County, and the other two quarters to be disposed of
and sett up as the Justices of the County of Surry shall think fitt to direct." The
court issued similar orders for Scipio's body and required the county courts
where they had lived to pay all the costs.[9]

County courts also executed enslaved people convicted of crimes and in
the cases of men charged with insurrection also ordered their bodies to be
dismembered. Orders preserved in court documents indicate that quartering
of convicted slaves, a punishment English law prescribed for traitors, was common enough that at one time or another residents of most Virginia counties
encountered rotting body parts stuck up on poles in public places to terrorize
enslaved people from rebelling against their condition.

County courts also had authority to issue writs that declared dangerous or runaway servants or slaves to be outlaws. Anyone could capture and return an outlawed person to jail dead or alive. In August 1736 three men proved to a justice of the peace in Goochland County that they had captured an outlawed slave named Hampton by presenting "the head of Hampton an outlaw'd Slave belonging to John Owen which said Slave . . . they could not take without Killing of him."[10]

Slavery in the Eighteenth Century

At the beginning of the eighteenth century the white population of the colony was approximately 58,000 and rapidly increasing. By 1750 the number of white and black Virginians together passed 250,000. The number of enslaved people of African origin increased from about 5,000 to more than 75,000 during that period. The prices of imported Africans fell during the 1730s and 1740s even as the prices planters received for their tobacco rose and credit became easier to obtain. That led to the period of greatest importation. The total number of people Virginians purchased is not known. Customs records document the importation of more than 70,000 men, women, and children between 1698 and 1775; but as Adam Smith pointed out in 1776 in his *Wealth of Nations* and as the editors of *The Trans-Atlantic Slave Trade Database* also pointed out more than two hundred years later, for numerous reasons customs house records were not always reliable. For the slave trade they probably underestimated the actual number by 20 percent or more. And for the years 1725–69, including some years during which importations were probably the largest, about one-fourth of all Virginia customs records do not even survive. The real number, including people whom shippers smuggled past the customs officers or bribed officers not to record, was certainly appreciably larger, probably far exceeding 100,000 people.

Planters who belonged to the colony's wealthiest families acquired large numbers of enslaved laborers to work in tobacco fields and perform the many diverse tasks required to run plantations and to care for the families of the owners. Other enslaved laborers lived and worked on small farms or plantations that also produced grains and garden crops. Conditions varied widely from one farm to another. In spite of the constant hard work, enslaved laborers probably did not die from overwork so often as in the early years of the colony or as they did on plantations in the Caribbean. The population increased naturally as well as by importation. Enslaved men and women had children, but their informal marriages and families had no legal standing or protection. When an owner moved or died one likely consequence was the separation of the members of an enslaved family.

Like indentured servants, some African laborers had a degree of local mobility, and they formed social and family networks with other people on nearby farms and plantations. The many contradictions inherent in the system gave rise to complex and ambiguous master-slave relations. Close contact between blacks and whites pervaded daily life and made it difficult for most masters to deny their slaves' humanity. Masters could give orders, inflict cruel punishments, and construct a worldview that cast their slaves as perpetual children contented in bondage. At the same time some of them formed deep, personal connections with their enslaved workers and respected the skilled work they performed.

Enslaved laborers did not run away in large enough numbers to cripple the system, but rumors of organized resistance spread through parts of the colony from time to time, and enslaved people responded to harsh or unfair treatment by engaging in work slowdowns, asserted their independence by cultivating meaningful relationships with one another, and by growing or making products for trade. Some enslaved people sold eggs or poultry to their owners or to neighbors, and they may also have acquired some items of personal property from their neighbors or from local shopkeepers. Threats of violence guaranteed white control, but individual households functioned best when patriarchal whites and enslaved blacks recognized that they were bound together by reciprocal obligations that, when met, allowed for a modicum of flexibility.

During and after the great rush of importations in the 1730s and 1740s people in the little towns and in the countryside heard a great variety of languages and dialects that reflected the many points of origin of enslaved laborers. Advertisements for runaways sometimes made reference to their being "outlandish," meaning not natives of the land. One such advertisement described a man as "a new Negro, and can't speak *English;* his Name is understood to be *Tom.*"[11] By the end of the eighteenth century most enslaved Virginians spoke a local dialect of Standard English. Trapped in servitude, they placed high value on forms of personal expressiveness that included dance (often accompanied by drum or banjo music), song, modes of dress, and hairstyles. Though African religious practices did not survive intact, beliefs in magic, spirits, and a supreme being were widespread and often influenced their practices and beliefs when they later became Christians. Enslaved people who resided in very small groups with small planters or on small farms may have preserved fewer African cultural, religious, and language heritages than did enslaved people who lived in larger slave communities on the large plantations where they could more easily keep their practices and memories alive among themselves. Transplanted Africans inventively combined elements of their native cultural and religious practices and beliefs with the version of English culture they encountered in the colony and began to forge a distinctly African American way of life.

The Political Economy of Tobacco

Tobacco remained the principal cash crop for most Virginia farmers and large-scale planters. In 1713, Lieutenant Governor Alexander Spotswood contrived a remedy for the depressed prices the colony's planters received for their tobacco and pushed through the General Assembly An Act for Preventing Frauds in Tobacco Payments, and for the Better Improving the Staple of Tobacco. It required county governments to erect public warehouses and required planters to deliver all their tobacco to the local warehouse for inspection. The act authorized the inspectors to destroy all the inferior tobacco (called trash tobacco) and to mark all hogsheads of tobacco according to the quality of the leaf inside. Spotswood and the sponsors of the law hoped to increase the price planters received for their good tobacco by reducing the overall quantity of tobacco shipped to Great Britain and by improving its overall quality.

Opponents of the law objected to the act in part because the lieutenant governor appointed inspectors at each of the numerous warehouses, which created a source of patronage and political influence some political leaders disliked. In 1715 the House of Burgesses passed a bill to repeal the law, but the Council, the upper house of the General Assembly, rejected the bill. Influential Virginia merchants and planters then transferred their attention to English merchants, with whose assistance they succeeded in 1717 in persuading the Crown to disallow, or veto, the law.

Perhaps coincidentally, perhaps as a consequence of the law, tobacco prices rose during the years when the inspection law was in force, but the market did not sustain the higher prices. In 1730 Lieutenant Governor William Gooch persuaded the assembly to pass a similar tobacco inspection law that had in its title the words "For Preventing Frauds in His Majesty's Customs," which may have made it proof against a royal veto. Like Spotswood's law, Gooch's law of 1730 was initially unpopular with many planters, but Gooch was a very skillful politician, and he wrote to and spoke with burgesses, merchants, and royal officials in England to explain the purposes and operations of the law. He also wrote and in 1732 published a pamphlet (and had it reprinted twice), the first political tract printed in Virginia, to persuade planters that the law would work to their advantage. Gooch's pamphlet was in the form of a dialog between Virginia planters.

Following the opening of the first tobacco warehouses mobs of people who feared that destruction of inferior tobacco would impoverish them burned the warehouses in Prince William, Northumberland, Lancaster, and King George Counties. The inspection law survived initial doubts about its utility and proved its value to the colony's tobacco planters and provided regular and

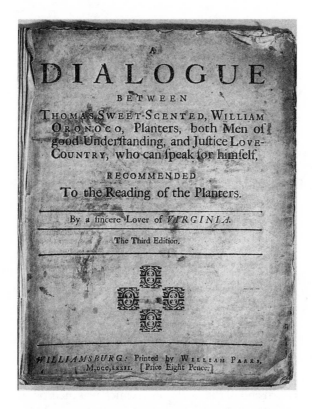

By a sincere Lover of Virginia, *A Dialogue between Thomas Sweet-Scented, William Oronoco, Planters, both Men of good Understanding, and Justice Love-Country, who can speak for himself, Recommended to the Reading of the Planters,* 3rd edition (Williamsburg, 1732)

reliable controls over the quality of the export crop. The destruction of trash tobacco contributed to keeping prices for Virginia-grown tobacco higher than tobacco grown in neighboring Maryland. Receipts, called tobacco notes, that the warehouses issued when planters deposited their tobacco in the warehouse circulated as a medium of exchange, like modern paper money.

6

LIFE IN THE EIGHTEENTH CENTURY

FIRE DESTROYED the colony's Statehouse in Jamestown on October 21, 1698. The following year members of the General Assembly moved the seat of government a few miles inland to Middle Plantation, which they renamed Williamsburg to honor the king. Governor Sir Francis Nicholson laid out the streets of the capital, and the assembly ordered the construction of a new brick Statehouse and a new brick palace for the governor's residence.

At the western end of the small town, which was incorporated as a city in 1722, were the new buildings of the College of William and Mary. James Blair, a clergyman and the bishop of London's commissary, or personal representative, in the colony, had procured a charter from the king and queen in 1693 to create a college for the education of the colony's young men and to prepare candidates for the ministry of the Church of England. Virginians raised more than £2,000 toward the establishment of the college, English benefactors contributed even more, and an English court awarded the college money seized from some convicted pirates. A school to educate Indians funded with private donations became a part of the College of William and Mary in 1697.

After the Jamestown fire, the General Assembly met in rooms at the college while the first Williamsburg Capitol was being constructed. Shortly after the Capitol was completed, the college caught fire. It was rebuilt on the same site. Its central building was later called the Wren Building, based on an undocumented belief that the noted English architect Sir Christopher Wren designed it.

Eighteenth-Century Virginians

In 1705, Robert Beverley published the first history of Virginia by a native of the colony. In the preface he wrote, "I am an *Indian*."[1] By that Beverley meant

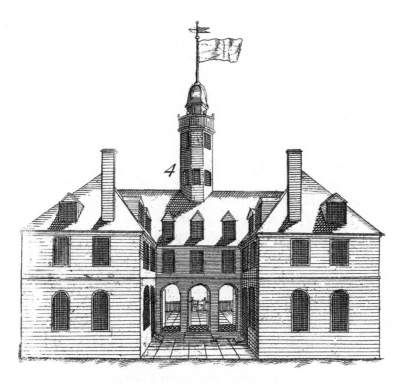

Capitol at Williamsburg from Bodleian Plate, ca. 1740

that he was a native Virginian and no longer, as people thought of themselves in the seventeenth century, English people living in Virginia.

Beverley's *History* was also the first book that provided a historical account of the entire seventeenth century as well as information about how the people of the colony lived at the beginning of the eighteenth, at the beginning of the colony's second century. Most white families then lived in frame dwellings roofed with shingles. Separate buildings for servants and enslaved laborers on some farms allowed landowners a measure of privacy and social distance from their labor force. That also gave workers and their families some small additional measure of privacy. Men and women continued to work in much the same way they had throughout the seventeenth century. Men labored in the tobacco and corn fields, looked after the cattle, chased down the wandering hogs, cut wood for heating and cooking, and performed much of the hard outdoor work on their farms. Many men did so even if they had hired laborers, indentured servants, or enslaved laborers to assist. Women cooked, cleaned, did washing, looked after the chickens and the dairy and churned butter, sometimes tended the vegetable garden, sewed and mended and perhaps spun and wove cloth; they brewed beer or pressed cider; they raised children and perhaps acted as nurses or midwives for their relatives and neighbors. Both men and women on the farms worked hard all day most days; hard physical labor was necessary to feed and clothe the members of the household and perhaps make a small profit with which to purchase necessities or other items they could not produce on their own property. Indentured servants and enslaved Virginians did the same kinds of labor but at the direction of and for the benefit of their masters or mistresses, not for themselves.

Beverley reported in 1705 that a few of the most prosperous planter families had recently built "large Brick Houses of many Rooms on a Floor, and several Stories high, as also some Stone-Houses" with large rooms and large glass windows "that they may be cool in Summer."[2] Within those large houses, many of which do not survive because they burned or were subsequently replaced with even larger ones, the elite families enjoyed a measure of leisure and culture that other white families did not. Even though the largest and most luxurious plantation houses in Virginia could not compare favorably to the great country houses of the English aristocrats, the mansions in Virginia were so much larger and more splendid than the houses of common people, servants, and slaves that the difference clearly set the great planter families apart from the rest of the society. On large plantations a cluster of outbuildings provided lodging for slaves. When a visitor in the 1680s approached a planter's residence, he wrote, "I thought I was entering a rather large village, but later on was told that all of it belonged to him."[3]

Those successful planter families were self-conscious about their status and adopted attitudes and exhibited behaviors they believed were suitable for a governing class. They, alone, had enough time and resources to spare that they could pay extended visits to each other, dine and dance in high style, purchase expensive imported clothing, and wager large sums of money on races between their best horses.

Sir Francis Nicholson learned the hard way that the elite of Virginia could hold its own even with a royal governor. He resided in Jamestown as lieutenant governor from 1690 to 1692 and returned as governor of the colony from 1698 to 1705. He was a man of learning and ability who during his two terms presiding over the government of Virginia encouraged the founding of the College of William and Mary and prepared the design for the new capital city of Williamsburg. Nicholson was also a man of short temper and accustomed to getting his way. His frustration and behavior when he did not led to several direct clashes with the Virginia elite and eventually to his dismissal as governor. Nicholson courted Lucy Burwell, the young daughter of a wealthy and influential planter. She refused his advances, but he continued to pursue her relentlessly. She enlisted her family to prevent her being married to a man she did not love, and her family enlisted others in her aid. Nicholson's public outbursts of temper over the failure of his courtship and his frequent passionate arguments with other Virginians so undermined his reputation in the colony that his improper conduct, together with disagreements about public policies, provided the colony's leading politicians with reasons to demand that the Crown replace him as governor. Nicholson had affronted the class mores of the Virginia elite and grossly violated their standards of morality and behavior. He paid the price, and they made their point. Dignity, self-mastery, and steady habits of command had become the hallmarks by which Virginia gentlemen and ladies judged who was qualified to hold responsible public offices and enjoy the respect and earn the deference that superior status gave them.

As the public stature of the great planters with their large estates and bands of enslaved workers increased, the status of white women in Virginia declined. Historians who have studied the condition of women during the latter years of the seventeenth century have discerned a clear reduction in the independence elite white women and women of the middling planter class could exercise in the increasingly patriarchal society. Women who were servants or were enslaved had almost no liberty and few resources with which to try to enforce their limited legal rights. The legal penalties for moral offences, such as fornication, had always been more severe for women than for men. A male servant who was convicted of fornication or fathering an illegitimate child would be punished according to law and perhaps made to pay the costs of bringing up the child; but a female servant who became pregnant might be punished for fornication and for having an illegitimate child and then have extra months or years added to the time of her servitude to compensate her master or mistress for the work time lost during pregnancy and after childbirth.

In many ways the attitudes and practices of the people who lived in Virginia began to diverge from those of people who stayed in England; and for working people of all kinds who owned little or no property the differences between Virginia and their places of origin may have seemed even greater. In some other respects Virginia's English-speaking population preserved practices that changed during the seventeenth and eighteenth centuries in old England and in New England. On the scattered plantations and small farms in Virginia women continued to have responsibility not only for feeding and clothing the family, including management of dairies and kitchen gardens, they also made cider from apples and other fruit to supply their families and laborers with drink. People of the time deemed consumption of water unhealthful if not mixed with alcohol, and most people drank cider, rum, or other alcoholic beverages daily at every meal. Elsewhere, commercial production of those drinks became a business that men managed, but in Virginia, where most men were busy in the fields, women retained that essential task as part of their routine household responsibilities. In that work and their other responsibilities women employed knowledge and skills in cookery and other domestic work they learned from their mothers and grandmothers.

White married women who could use the law to their advantage had more legal rights than other women. When a woman married, according to English common law, she ceased to have a legal existence separate from that of her husband. The law endowed the husband with all of his wife's property unless they negotiated a contract before they married that allowed her to retain ownership and control. The differences between the legal standing of free men and free women were most evident when a parent died. When a father died his will or the county court designated who would have legal responsibility for the children. Although mothers often received that responsibility the law did not require it or give mothers a preference. In the absence of a will the county court often appointed a responsible man as guardian of orphaned children. When a mother died, however, the county court took no notice because all the legal rights and responsibilities of parenthood remained as they had been before, with the father or male guardian. Even in widowhood women were often unable to enforce their legal rights and exercise their legal responsibilities alone and required the intervention of an adult white man to act for and assist them.

Perhaps most vulnerable were women whose husbands abused or abandoned them. The case of Susannah Sanders Cooper illustrates those vulnerabilities. Late in the 1710s her husband deserted her and their son and went to North Carolina. He illegally married twice there and also ran up debts. His creditors seized property Susannah had owned, which, because she were still legally married, had become her husband's property and was therefore liable for the payment of his debts. She was not legally entitled to own property in her own right or to protect what she had, but with the approval of her neighbors in New Kent County she nevertheless ran an ordinary that provided food and lodging for travelers and stableage for their horses.

Twenty years after Cooper's husband left she petitioned the General Assembly for passage of a special law to allow her to own and control her own property as if she were a *feme sole,* or unmarried woman. Sympathizing with her plight, the legislators passed a bill to protect what she had acquired in the event her husband returned and attempted to gain control of or sell what she had accumulated. The lieutenant governor submitted it to the Privy Council in London with a letter of support, but the king's ministers disallowed the bill ten years later rather than undermine the superior legal status of married men. Cooper was left to fend for herself. In spite of the decades of delay and the requirements of the law she successfully employed her skill and the sympathetic support of her neighbors and of Virginia political leaders to continue her independent career. Without her persistence in the face of adversity and without the support of influential local men she would have had little chance to avoid destitution, which was likely the fate of other women who had few or no legal resources to protect their interests and the welfare of their families.

Land and Labor

Land and labor and the ability to acquire them and control them remained, as during the colony's early years, the foundations on which fortunate families founded and enlarged great estates and gained access to public offices and with them the chance to increase their wealth and influence. In spite of occasional bad tobacco harvests or gluts in the market, the economy on the whole worked well for those fortunate families. For enslaved people and for free people with small land holdings it worked less well. Most of them had no voice in government decisions about taxes and other public policies that influenced how they lived.

It is no exaggeration to say that the form of government the leading men created during the seventeenth century and controlled during the eighteenth century was a government of the tobacco planters, by the tobacco planters, and for the tobacco planters. By the middle of the eighteenth century men who owned the minimum amount of property (a hundred acres of land or fifty acres of land and a house) in more than one county could vote everywhere they owned land; and because voting took place in each county on its court day, it was possible for a man to vote for members of the House of Burgesses in more than one county or to win election in a county in which he did not live. George Washington won election to the House of Burgesses for the first time in 1758 to represent Frederick County, where he owned land, rather than to represent Fairfax County, where he lived.

Almost all white and black Virginians lived on small farms. The colony was unlike England and New England, where towns were important centers of community life and regarded as essential for a well-ordered society. The churches, schools, merchants, and craftsmen in those towns met the religious, social, and material needs of the population. Officials in London and in Jamestown repeatedly and unsuccessfully tried to create towns in Virginia during the seventeenth century. In the early years of the eighteenth century, as the tobacco trade increased and spread, a few small landing sites evolved into busy small ports, such as Yorktown, Urbanna, and Norfolk; and by the middle of the century Richmond, Petersburg, Fredericksburg, and Alexandria, on the fall line, also became prosperous and important commercial centers. None of them had more than a few hundred inhabitants except Norfolk, which in 1736 received a charter as a self-governing borough with its own common council, board of aldermen, and mayor. By the mid-1770s it was by far the busiest port in Virginia and the colony's largest city, home to about six thousand people.

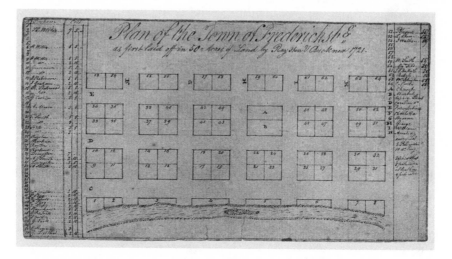

"Plan of the Town of Fredericksburg as first laid off in 50 Acres of Land by Royston & Buckner 1721"; pen and ink on paper

Williamsburg, the capital, was much smaller and the only other incorporated city in the colony.

Officials in the two incorporated cities, the members of the county courts, and the parish churchwardens were the government officers Virginians most often encountered. The clerks kept records of the governing bodies' proceedings, recorded deeds and wills, and issued marriage licenses. The courts regulated prices vendors charged in the markets and enforced colonial laws that established rates taverns and ordinaries could charge for lodging, food, drink, and care of horses. Sheriffs, clerks, and town officers received fees in lieu of a salary for the performance of their duties. When a person recorded a deed or filed estate papers with the court or obtained a marriage license, he or she paid the clerk a fee that was regulated by law. County clerks and surveyors were well positioned to take advantage of opportunities to acquire good land when it came available and also to earn substantial incomes from fees.

Justices of the peace received no compensation, but they annually selected a sheriff from among their members and often alternated the duty so that most judges served a term or two as sheriff, and sheriffs collected fees for serving writs and other legal services. Sheriffs also collected the taxes and retained a stated percentage of the tax receipts as a fee. Public office-holding, access to land and labor, and social standing and political influence were all intimately related and mutually reinforcing. Justices of the peace and vestrymen in effect selected their own replacements without any elections. The men who managed both institutions of local government in Virginia did so without the consent of the men and women whom they governed and with little oversight from royal officials in London or from colonial officials in Williamsburg.

Virginians and the Atlantic World

Even without European-style towns and cities, white Virginians during the seventeenth and eighteenth centuries shared much with people in other English-speaking colonies. Merchant ships regularly sailed up and down the Atlantic coast as well as to and from England and the Caribbean islands. They carried merchandise, passengers, and news and kept Virginia's residents informed about events in the rest of the world. Isaac Allerton was one such man. He was born about 1630 in Plymouth, Massachusetts, and was the son of a passenger on the *Mayflower* and an early graduate of Harvard College. He engaged in trade between New England, New Amsterdam, the West Indies, and Virginia. About 1660 he moved to Virginia, where he extended his interest into trading with the Indians. He married and became a justice of the peace in Westmoreland County and in 1675 was appointed to a prestigious seat on the Council of State. Other merchants, ship captains, and men like Allerton routinely did business throughout the colonies and kept residents of coastal Virginia supplied with merchandise and information. Although Virginia was initially a small English outpost far removed from what Englishmen regarded as civilization, some residents of Virginia had opportunities to interact in many ways with other residents of the North Atlantic coast.

Families who attended church or engaged in regular worship services or family devotions encountered reminders in their copies of the Book of Common Prayer of the close relationship of Virginia with England. The daily prayers included prayers for the health of the king and members of the royal family. The king was the head of the church, and the church was an integral part of their lives. When Virginians went to the courthouse to attend to legal business or meet with local merchants they listened to clerks reading royal proclamations and other public papers that also reinforced their understandings of the relationship between the colony and the mother country. Some of the wealthiest Virginia families sent their sons to school in England or, late in the colonial period, to the College of New Jersey (later renamed Princeton University) if they deemed the College of William and Mary inadequate.

Books and newspapers, most of them printed in England or Scotland but some in other colonies, circulated in eighteenth-century Virginia. In 1730 William Parks opened the first printing office in Virginia and six years later began to publish the colony's first newspaper. He printed the four-page weekly *Virginia Gazette* in Williamsburg and included advertisements for merchandise and runaway servants and slaves; reports of the arrival of ships; news from

Christ Church, Lancaster County, ca. 1930

Europe and the other colonies; proclamations, statutes, and other government documents; and increasingly the essays and poems that flowed from the pens of residents of Virginia.

In the final years of the seventeenth century and during the eighteenth century some wealthy and educated Virginians acquired notable private libraries. Printers and booksellers in Williamsburg offered a wide variety of reading material for sale. William Fitzhugh, the second William Byrd (1674–1744), and John Mercer all had large and excellent libraries that included practical works on law, medicine, and agriculture as well as books on religion, natural history, and novels and poetry. Attorneys and physicians had their own small collections of legal or medical texts and English-Latin dictionaries to assist them in their work. The College of William and Mary also had a select library available to professors and students.

Royal governors, members of the Council of State, burgesses, and influential attorneys assembled a reference library in the Capitol to enable them to exercise their responsibilities properly and in accordance with often-repeated instructions from England that the laws and courts of the colony resemble as nearly as possible the laws and legal practices of England. The reference library of law books, court reports, parliamentary records, and other historical reference works was available in the Capitol for the use of government officials and the colony's attorneys. The library also contained by the middle of the eighteenth century a substantial number of volumes of natural history and general reference, as well as maps and copies of the laws of some of the other English colonies. The contents of the library, so far as they are known, disclose what the leading men believed was important for the proper administration

Bookplate of the library of the Virginia Council of State

of the law and government of their colony. Their book collection and their political institutions indicate that they wanted Virginia to resemble a miniature England.

The legal code in Virginia developed into a sophisticated body of law. Legislators and judges still looked to England and consulted English law books, but their own laws and court records often guided their decisions. To provide a resource for judges of the county courts, George Webb compiled and in 1736 William Parks published a Virginia substitute for Michael Dalton's *Countrey Justice*, the standard guide for English justices of the peace that had been used in the colony for more than a century. Webb's *The Office and Authority of a Justice of Peace* was the first legal reference work compiled and published in Virginia. The very necessity for Webb to prepare a new manual for Virginia justices of the peace indicates how much Virginia laws and legal practices had come to differ from those of England, which made the old English manuals obsolete.

Some attorneys later stated that English laws passed after the settlement of the colony were not usually enforced in Virginia, but Webb's manual contained numerous references to post-1607 English laws and court decisions that were important to the judges in the colony's courts. When Richard Starke prepared a revised edition of *The Office and Authority of a Justice of Peace* for

Claytonia virginica, also known as eastern spring beauty,
grass-flower, or fairy spud. William P. C. Barton, *A Flora
of Virginia* (Philadelphia, 1821).

publication in 1774, he omitted a long section that dealt with prosecution
of people accused of practicing witchcraft. Parliament had repealed the early
seventeenth-century English witchcraft law after the publication of Webb's
guide, and Starke's omission of Webb's summary of the law of witchcraft indicates that Virginia's lawmakers and courts closely attended to post-1607 English laws when changes were relevant in the colony.

A few prominent Virginians earned international reputations for their
scientific work. During the 1680s and 1690s clergymen John Clayton (1656 or
1657–1725) and John Banister (ca. 1650–92) contributed botanical specimens
and essays on natural history to internationally respected English learned
societies. During the eighteenth century the second William Byrd (1674–
1744) and others participated in the compilation and international dissemi-
nation of information about the natural world. For several years in the 1720s
the naturalist Mark Catesby resided in Virginia, where he collected some of

the specimens for his celebrated *Natural History of Carolina, Florida, and the Bahama Islands* (1731–43). Clayton's eighteenth-century namesake kinsman, unusually referred to as John Clayton the botanist (1695–1773), lived in Gloucester County for more than fifty years and regularly corresponded with the leading naturalists in Europe. John Frederick Gronovius published Clayton's catalog of plants native to Virginia in two volumes as *Flora Virginica* (1739–43). The celebrated naturalist Linnaeus named a specimen Clayton sent him *Claytonia virginica*.

Surveyor John Mitchell published an important map of eastern North America, including Virginia, in 1755. Surveyors Joshua Fry and Peter Jefferson published an accurate map of the colony in 1753 and in a revised version in 1755; it became the most famous map of colonial Virginia. In 1770 another surveyor, John Henry, published the first map of the colony that showed county boundaries.

During the eighteenth century many of the wealthier white families sent some of their sons to England or Scotland for higher education or to reinforce family connections and commercial links with mercantile and political leaders in Great Britain. In both commerce and politics, family relationships were extremely important. The leading families were nearly all related to one other through marriage and created a Virginia cousinhood that was a counterpart

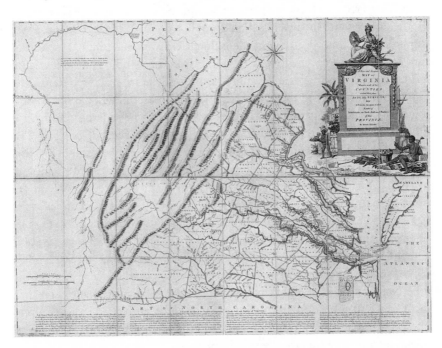

John Henry, *A New and Accurate Map of Virginia* (London, 1770)

of the English ruling class. Those close family relationships had enabled the planters to unite against Nicholson in the first decade of the century. During the second decade, Lieutenant Governor Alexander Spotswood found it difficult to make recommendations to the Crown for the appointment of new members to vacant seats on the Council of State because a majority of the sitting members were so closely related to each other and to the most eligible candidates that he feared a failure of justice if a significant case reached the General Court and too many of the members had to recuse themselves because of their family relationships.

Those close connections enabled a succession of members of some families—Robinson, Randolph, Lee, Harrison, Custis, Carter, Byrd, Burwell, and others—to hold influential government positions for several generations. The Randolphs are a good example. They were related by marriage to most of the other wealthy and powerful Virginia families. John Randolph, born in 1693, attended the College of William and Mary and studied law in London at Gray's Inn, one of the prestigious law courts. He was admitted to the bar and returned to Virginia, where Spotswood appointed him clerk of the House of Burgesses in 1718. Before going back to England in 1728 Randolph married into the Beverley family. As the colony's agent in the capital of the empire during another trip to England early in the 1730s he received a knighthood from King George II. As Sir John Randolph he was elected Speaker of the House of Burgesses in 1736 but died the following year. His eldest son, Peter Randolph, became a member of the influential Council of State. His second son, Peyton Randolph, who married a Harrison, also studied law in England, served twice as attorney general of Virginia, and was the last Speaker of the House of Burgesses and the first president of the Continental Congress. Peyton Randolph's younger brother John Randolph married into the wealthy and influential Jenings family, studied law in England, succeeded his brother as attorney general, and was one of the most prominent native Virginia loyalists at the time of the American Revolution. In turn, his son, Edmund Randolph, married a Nicholas and was the first attorney general of Virginia when it became an independent state. He was also governor of Virginia, a member of the Constitutional Convention of 1787 and of the ratification convention of 1788, the first attorney general of the United States in George Washington's cabinet, and the second secretary of state. Another Randolph served as governor of Virginia before the end of the eighteenth century and a third early in the nineteenth. Near relatives of the extended family were prominent in government, law, and education during and after the eighteenth century. Randolphs, like Lees, Harrisons, Carters, Burwells, and the other wealthiest and most influential families, were extensively intermarried.

Regional Diversity

The large colony contained within it a considerable variety of landscapes that affected how people in the different regions lived. Even the so-called necks of land between the great eastern rivers developed their own distinctive regional cultural characteristics. English Virginians, just like Indian Virginians, moved readily about the country on the many rivers and smaller streams that fed into Chesapeake Bay. Rather than being barriers between regions, the rivers were avenues of transportation. Nevertheless, late in the seventeenth century the General Assembly created several new long, narrow counties on the necks of land between the great rivers, even though people on one riverbank may have had more in common with and engaged in more business with people on the other side of the river than with people a few miles away on the other side of the neck. The most obvious difference between regions of eastern Virginia in the early decades was the distinction between the area where sweet-scented tobacco flourished and the larger area where planters grew Oronico tobacco.

The Northern Neck, the land in Virginia between the Rappahannock and Potomac Rivers, had its own character. While Charles II was in exile in Europe in 1649 following the execution of his father he granted the Northern Neck to several loyal court favorites. Soon after Charles II returned to the throne these patentees, or proprietors, renewed the grant, which he reconfirmed by a new charter dated May 8, 1669. As a consequence, although all the laws of Virginia had effect in that area, the charter transferred the privilege of granting and renting land there from the colonial governor and the Council of State to the proprietors. The proprietary descended in 1719 to the Fairfax family through the daughter of Thomas Culpeper, second baron Culpeper of Thoresway. He was an heir of one of the original patentees and was governor of Virginia from 1677 to 1683. From the creation of the Northern Neck Proprietary to the American Revolution a small number of influential men accumulated great wealth through the settlement, sale, and rental of land in that vast region. In part because he was agent for the proprietary for many years, Robert Carter (ca. 1664–1732) became the wealthiest man in Virginia and possibly the wealthiest man in the colonies. He was known during his lifetime and ever after as King Carter. So wealthy was King Carter that when his vast estates were divided among his several sons and sons-in-law after his death they all then became some of the wealthiest men in the colony, too.

Young men of established families and other white Virginians in search of new land and new opportunities moved to the west throughout the eighteenth century. Young men sought new land for themselves, and older families also moved west after years of tobacco growing reduced the fertility of their

Unidentified artist, *Robert "King" Carter,* ca. 1720; oil on canvas

farms. At the same time, immigration from the British Isles brought thousands of new settlers. As the population increased and tobacco planting spread farther into the Piedmont, the General Assembly created new counties where new groups of local leaders emerged to sit on county courts, serve on parish vestries, command militia companies, or represent their counties in the House of Burgesses. Until the middle of the eighteenth century the residents in the new counties tended to be tobacco planters and to replicate the economic and social conditions of the older tobacco counties. One exception was the settlement west of Richmond where a colony of Huguenots, French Protestant refugees, settled early in the eighteenth century, even though within a generation or two they, also, blended readily into the Anglo-Virginian society. The governor and Council of State exercised a considerable amount of discretion about how settlement of western areas took place and frequently granted to themselves and members of their own families large tracts of land that they planned to rent or sell to actual settlers.

West of the Blue Ridge Mountains a different settlement pattern created an entirely different culture. In 1715 Lieutenant Governor Alexander Spotswood led an expedition that found Swift Run Gap near the headwaters of a tributary of the Rapidan River. It offered a relatively easy passage across the mountains into the Shenandoah Valley. The fertile valley attracted thousands of immigrants. Within a few years Virginians began to purchase or rent land from some of the wealthy and well-connected eastern land speculators—William Beverley, the son of historian Robert Beverly, was one—who procured grants of large tracts of land there. Officials in England also promoted settlement of the western frontier of Virginia and encouraged immigration to the area from Scotland and Ireland. The British hoped that the settlers would serve as a buffer between the increasingly wealthy tobacco plantations in the east and the Indians who inhabited the western mountains and the Ohio Valley. Many of those immigrants entered the Valley from the north through Pennsylvania. Agents for the immigrants, among them men such as Benjamin Borden and James Patton, grew wealthy and became influential local community leaders in that way rather than through the traditional eastern way of planting tobacco and owning a large numbers of slaves.

Farmers in the west concentrated on grains and grazing more than on tobacco production, and on the average they owned smaller farms and fewer enslaved men, women, and children than in the east. In the western valleys a new set of prominent families arose, and although they intermarried as did the older leading families in eastern Virginia, in the west the family names were often distinguishably Scots-Irish in origin: Preston, Patton, McDowell, Floyd, Christian, Campbell, and Buchanan, to name a few. Many of them were Presbyterians rather than members of the Church of England as in the east. The Valley had fewer great plantations than the east and a less conspicuously stratified social structure. Numerous small market towns dotted the Valley, which gave it a different appearance and created a different set of social and economic relationships among the inhabitants than prevailed in the east.

During the third quarter of the eighteenth century a similar pattern of settlement spread southwest as far as the Holston and Clinch River watersheds in what is now southwestern Virginia. The busy commercial route known as the Great Wagon Road that followed old Indian trails stretched from south-central Pennsylvania through the valleys of western Virginia into the back-country of North Carolina and provided access for immigrants and avenues for commerce and commodities. As a consequence those regions of Virginia had closer cultural and commercial relationships with Philadelphia or towns along the Potomac River, such as Alexandria, than with Williamsburg or Norfolk.

In addition to the Scots-Irish settlers who may have been the majority in the western valleys, Germans and descendants of Germans (called Pennsylvania Dutch) also moved from or through Pennsylvania into the Shenandoah Valley and introduced a different language and different religious beliefs into Virginia. Most of them were Lutherans, but Mennonites, some Moravians, and members of other religious groups in the German Reformed tradition also lived in the mountains and valleys. They settled in small and loosely dispersed communities very unlike the scattered individual settlements east of the Blue Ridge. They erected houses and barns of native stone and in architectural styles different from the plantation architecture in the east.

So numerous were the German-speaking farmers, millers, and shopkeep-

Title page of the German-language compilation of Virginia tax laws printed in Philadelphia in 1795

ers during the second half of the eighteenth century that at the beginning of the American Revolution a regiment of infantry recruited in the Valley was referred to as the German Regiment. Its commander was John Peter Gabriel Muhlenberg. He was the son of German immigrants and both a Lutheran clergyman and an ordained minister of the Church of England. After the Revolution the state published an edition of Virginia tax laws in the German language for use in the northern Valley counties.

The Virginia countryside exhibited many evidences of enterprise and industry that contrasted with the agricultural plantation society for which the colony was most known. At the beginning of the eighteenth century Huguenot settlers west of the falls of the James River discovered deposits of coal in the banks of streams and began small-scale extraction of coal for local use. Later in the century enterprising landowners began pit mining on a larger scale and by the 1760s produced and marketed coal commercially. There are no surviving records to indicate how much coal they produced for consumption in Virginia, but customs records indicate that they exported more than 30,000 bushels of coal from the colony during the three-year-period that began in October 1763. Samuel Du-Val, who owned large pit mines in Henrico and Chesterfield Counties, may have been the best known of the mine owners. He advertised as far away as Rhode Island that his coal was as good as any imported from England. The availability of that coal and of nearby deposits of iron ore led to the development at the same time of an iron industry in central Virginia.

Elsewhere, woodcutters and charcoal burners provided fuel for ironworks in the Blue Ridge Mountains and the Shenandoah Valley. The Tayloe family was one of several planter families that also owned and operated ironworks and other industrial enterprises. The family's large ironworks in Prince William County constituted one of the largest enterprises of its kind in eighteenth-century Virginia. Not far to the west, Alexander Spotswood brought in Germans and created a large ironworks at the community called Germanna.

England's practice of sentencing criminals to serve their time as servants in the colonies rather than in prison meant that several thousand transported convicts resided and worked at any one time in eighteenth-century Virginia, much as indentured servants had during the seventeenth century. England sent thousands of thieves and other criminals to Virginia and Maryland, most of them to the counties in the Potomac River Valley. Even in a colony like Virginia where laborers were often in short supply, convicted thieves and other criminals were not a welcome addition to the labor force. It is possible that their presence in Virginia (temporary though it may have been for most of them) placed burdens on the parishes for relief of the poor and made the countryside less safe. In 1733 the attorney general successfully petitioned the Crown for an increase of his annual salary from £100 to £140 to compensate him for the extra work he did prosecuting transported convicts who were accused of committing new crimes in the colony.

Life for residents east of the mountains changed in numerous ways during the eighteenth century. In the northern counties of the colony where the land was not well suited to tobacco cultivation many farmers began to raise less tobacco and more grains and other crops for export or for domestic markets. In 1759 the General Assembly created a committee of prominent planters to correspond with English agricultural reformers and devise methods of diversifying the colony's economy and to reduce dependence on tobacco. The plan met with limited success, although George Washington and some other planters significantly diversified their commercial agriculture. Washington eventually constructed and operated a distillery, conducted a large commercial fishery in the Potomac River, and abandoned tobacco cultivation altogether in favor of less labor-intensive crops that provided a more regular income than tobacco.

One reason Washington stopped planting tobacco was that it kept him financially dependent on English merchants. When Washington became an adult most large planters in Virginia did business year after year with a specific English mercantile house. Each planter shipped his crop to the English merchant who in turn sold it on the international market, and with the money purchased and supplied the planter with manufactured goods or luxury items that could not be produced in the colony. Planters often had little or no negotiating leverage with the merchant who in effect was the planter's principal or only outlet for tobacco and also only source of credit.

The consignment system, as it was known, created mutually dependent but unequal relationships between colonial planters and English mercantile houses. Thomas Jefferson later complained that the system worked entirely to the advantage of English mercantile houses and to the disadvantage of tobacco planters. "A powerful engine for this purpose," Jefferson explained, portraying Virginia tobacco planters as unwitting victims of scheming English merchants, "was the giving good prices and credit to the planter, till they got him more immersed in debt than he could pay without selling his lands or slaves. They then reduced the prices given for his tobacco so that let his shipments be ever so great, and his demand of necessaries ever so œconomical, they never permitted him to clear off his debt. These debts had become hereditary from father to son for many generations, so that the planters were a species of property annexed to certain mercantile houses in London."[4]

Washington was unusual in completely abandoning tobacco cultivation before the American Revolution. The great demand for tobacco in Europe and the ability of Virginia planters to produce increasingly large quantities stimulated ingenious English and Scottish merchants to create an alternative to the consignment system. They sent resident agents, called factors, to Virginia to manage the western end of the trans-Atlantic tobacco trade. Those agents gradually replaced planters as middlemen between the small farmers and planters in Virginia and the great mercantile houses of London and Bristol. From the small port towns on the bay and major rivers, where the agents opened stores, the resident factors sent more agents into the countryside to purchase tobacco directly from producers and to sell merchandise imported from Great Britain. Taking only tobacco in payment for merchandise enabled the merchants to become in effect not only the sole suppliers for many of Virginia's inland planters but also their principal source of credit. The store system, as it was called, brought to Virginia a large number of enterprising young men from Scotland, where the merchants conducted the new system very successfully and engrossed a substantial portion of the tobacco trade that had once been centered in London and Bristol.

One consequence of the changed tobacco economy was a rapid rise in the standard of living for members of middle- and large-scale planter families who were able to import a wide array of merchandise. Simultaneously with the low cost of importing African laborers and the high price of tobacco, a building boom of great plantation houses began during the second quarter of the eighteenth century. Wealthy planters filled their mansions with stylish furniture and silver, imported elegant carriages, and dressed in the best English finery. Resident painters like Charles Bridges and itinerant artists like John Wollaston painted portraits of planters and merchants and their family members for display in their new great houses.

In 1766, John Wayles, Thomas Jefferson's future father-in-law, noted how much had recently changed where he lived on the banks of the James River above Jamestown. Twenty-five years earlier, he informed a Bristol trading firm, "£1000. due to a merch^t was looked upon as a Sum imense and never to be got over. Ten times that sum is now spoke of with Indifference & thought no great burthen on some Estates. Indeed in that series of time Property is become more Valuable & many Estates have increased more then tenfold, But then Luxury & expensive living have gone hand in hand with the increase of wealth. . . . All this is in great measure owing to the Cred^t which the Planters have had from England & which has enabled them to Improve their Estates to the pitch they are Arrivd at, tho' many are ignorant of the true Cause. In 1740. no man on this River made 100 hh^d of tobacco; now not less then six exceed that Number."[5] The abbreviation "hh^d" referred to a cask called a hogshead, which in the eighteenth century could hold as much as two thousand pounds of tobacco.

That led to more conspicuous differences between the planter families, who lived luxuriously in large brick mansions, and other Virginians, who had no fancy mansions, large herds of cattle and draft animals, or numerous enslaved laborers. Most white Virginians lived in smaller frame houses that were probably simply furnished and often crowded. When those farmers, servants, artisans, and their families joined the wealthier ladies and gentlemen at church or met them at the courthouse to transact business, they watched from the corners or galleries as the wealthy families took their seats in elegant pews in fine new brick churches, and the leading gentlemen took their seats behind the bar of stately new brick courthouses and literally looked down on the people whose lives they governed. The gentlemen and ladies thereby proclaiming their achievements and high social status

Most white Virginia families lived on their own small farms, worked for other farmers, or practiced artisanal crafts. Most black Virginians were enslaved and worked for their owners or were hired out to work for other white men or women, but a substantial number of free black people lived in some eastern counties, where they owned their own small farms or worked as craftsmen or as hired laborers for other farmers. Both white and black Virginians operated mills and worked as blacksmiths or at other tasks in most parts of the

Shirley Plantation, Charles City County, 1939

colony. In the countryside as well as in the small towns the economy required harness makers, blacksmiths, tanners, seamstresses, tailors, boot makers and cobblers, and woodcutters. Large planters hired plantation overseers, and men and women of both races worked in retail shops in the new, small towns, where they made or sold items of clothing or marketed fresh or salted foods from their farms or fisheries. County courts often apprenticed orphans or children of poor families to a shopkeeper or artisan to learn a trade.

In the counties that bordered Chesapeake Bay and the major navigable rivers many Virginians engaged in commercial fishing, worked on trading vessels, supplied food and fresh water for merchant ships, or built ships. Scattered references without many details indicate that Virginians built fishing vessels at many places around Chesapeake Bay. A visitor reported in 1765 that Norfolk was the only place in Virginia where ships of considerable size were constructed, which reveals that people built smaller vessels elsewhere. He also reported that Virginians shipped tall masts, cut from the forests of Virginia and North Carolina, out of Norfolk as far away as Havana, Cuba, and probably elsewhere. Construction of even a moderate-sized sailing vessel required many workmen: woodmen to cut and shape timbers; watermen and carters to transport heavy timbers and supplies to the construction site; skilled ship-

Hanover County Courthouse, 1933

wrights to direct the construction; unskilled laborers to do the heavy lifting; manufacturers of cordage, metal fittings, and perhaps suppliers of sailcloth.

Still other men were regularly employed making barrels and shipping crates, filling water casks, salting and packing meat, operating rope walks, baking ship biscuit, and supplying the provisions that all ships putting to sea required. Drovers regularly herded large numbers of swine from North Carolina and inland Virginia to Norfolk and the other ports to fill the provisioning needs of the shipping industry. It is possible that several thousand Virginians were employed in support of oceanic and coastal shipping during the eighteenth century, in addition to the men and boys who signed on as crew members and the other men and boys who worked in the domestic fishing fleets. Large warehouses stood on the waterfronts of Norfolk and of all of the smaller port towns. Those buildings, like plantation outbuildings, were so commonplace that people seldom mentioned them unless something out of the ordinary happened there or a storm damaged or destroyed them.

Hurricanes struck coastal Virginia from time to time, but only a few detailed descriptions survive. The *Maryland Gazette,* published in Annapolis, reported on a storm that hit Hampton Roads on October 7, 1749. The description of the damaged property indicates how substantial the commercial infrastructure of coastal Virginia was in the middle of the eighteenth century, especially in the vicinity of Norfolk where several new ships under construction were destroyed. Citing a ship captain who had been in Norfolk at the time of the storm, the paper reported, "Wind began to blow hard, and

Detail of Hampton Roads from Anthony Smith, *A New and Accurate Chart of the Bay of Chesapeake* (2d state, London, 1777)

about one or two in the Morning was very violent at N.E. with Rain, and still kept increasing; but the most violent of the Storm was from ten 'til two on Sunday. The Tide rose 15 Feet perpendicular higher than usual, forcing Ships and other Vessels ashore where the Water was never before known to flow; many of which are now so far from the Water, and some of them loaded, that it will cost as much as they are worth to get them afloat again, if it be practicable: Several new Ships were carried off the Stocks; all the Wharffs, and several Warehouses were carried away. A Warehouse of Col. *Tucker's*, 60 Feet by 30, having in it 90 Pipes of Wine and 40 Hogsheads of Rum on the lower Floor, and a Quantity of Corn and Oats in the Loft, was taken off it's Foundation, carried a Mile and a half from the Place where it stood, and landed upright on the other Side of the River, without any Damage to what was in it; this Warehouse passed by the *Hopewell,* the Eaves of it being about four Feet above Water, and touch'd her Quarter, without doing any Hurt. Wharffs with

Anchors, lying on them of 1000 *lb*. Weight, were seen floating on the Water, and were carried away bodily, Stones and Timber together; and the River was almost covered with Lumber, Masts, Yards, Rales, Casks, &c. And by a Letter from a Gentleman at *Norfolk* we are informed, that the Damage there amounts to upwards of 30,000 *l.* Some Gentlemen now at *Norfolk,* who were in *Jamaica* when the last great Hurricane happened there, which destroyed several Men of War, &c. say it was not so violent as this. The Tide kept continually fluxing, and run at a Rate of five Miles an Hour; it overflowed all their Streets, carried some small Craft near a Mile from the ordinary High Water Mark, and left some of them in Corn Fields."[6]

Severe floods also occasionally plagued Virginians. At the end of May 1771 heavy rains in the mountains produced what may have been the greatest flood in all of eastern Virginia's recorded history. Floodwaters far exceeded anything within memory. "From the Mountains, to the Falls," a Williamsburg newspaper reported, the flood swept away "almost every Thing valuable; and the Soil is so much injured that it is thought not to be of Half its former Value, and a great Part is entirely ruined.

"Old JOE, an honest and well known Negro Fellow at the Falls of James River, who is intimately acquainted with the Remains of an Indian Nation that has resided there for Ages, says that he was shown by their old Men the Marks of the greatest Fresh handed down to them by Tradition; and that, upon his carefully measure, it wanted near fifteen Feet of the late dreadful One." The report, though, is unclear whether the fifteen feet was a vertical measure of the depth of the water or a horizontal measure of how far the water flooded the shore.

The report continued, "In some Places, Trees, Carcases, &c. are matted together, from twelve to twenty Feet in Height; and, from the horrid Stench, there is no coming near enough to separate them. Happily, if, at this Season, we escape some contagious Disorder.—Miles in Length of Trees and Logs came driving down the River, and Nothing could withstand their Force. . . . There were no Rains to speak of at Richmond, and thereabouts, so that they must have fallen from the Mountains to about thirty or forty Miles above the Falls. From the first perceivable Rise of the River at that Place was about sixty Hours, and the Water sometimes rose at the rapid Rate of sixteen Inches an Hour.—Daily Accounts are received of the Loss of whole Families; and Houses came floating down, with People on them calling for Help, though none could be afforded. Accounts are already received of fifty odd People being drowned.

"A Letter from Fredericksburg says that several Houses and Mills have been swept away from that Place and Falmouth; that the highest Fresh in Rappahannock never came up to the Floors of the Warehouses, but that this rose as high as the Joists, whereby a large Quantity of Tobacco was floated out, nine Hundred Hogsheads from the Falmouth, or the lower Warehouses, and three Hundred from Dixon's, the upper Inspection. Much Salt, and other Goods lost; several Vessels driven from their Anchors; a Deal of valuable Land washed away; incredible Quantities of Trees and Fencing come down the River; only one Life lost."

The long newspaper report of the flood concluded, "A waggish Blade at Richmond, we are told, said it was his Opinion Old Nick had bored a whole through the Mountains, and let in the South Sea upon them."[7]

7

MID-CENTURY CHALLENGES

Oⁿ July 5, 1726, William Byrd (1674–1744) described to an English friend the good life he and a few other elite Virginia families enjoyed. "We abound is all kinds of provisions, without expence (I mean we who have plantations)," Byrd explained. "I have a large family of my own, and my doors are open to every body, yet I have no bills to pay, and half-a-crown will rest undisturbed in my pocket for many moons together. Like one of the patriarchs, I have my flocks and my herds, my bond-men, and bond-women, and every soart of trade amongst my own servants, so that I live in a kind of independance on every one, but Providence." He contentedly concluded, "we sit securely under our vines, and our fig-trees without any danger to our property."[1]

Byrd wrote exactly halfway, almost to the day, between Bacon's Rebellion of 1676 and the Declaration of Independence of 1776. His boasting of his "independance" indicated that he believed he was not inferior to anybody in social status and under no other person's influence; but in fact he was utterly dependent on free and enslaved workers to tend his gardens, farms, and live-stock to feed him and his family. He was also dependent on them to raise the tobacco that enabled him to rejoice in his fine mansion with its great library, to entertain his relatives and guests, and to have his own way in his house-hold, on his plantations, in his county, and for the most part in his colony. Seemingly secure in his wealth, status, and power, Byrd was also comfortable in his faith. Although a sinner who acknowledged his weaknesses, Byrd was sure of salvation as a good member of the Church of England. He could not have known it in 1726, but his elite class of Virginians would face new chal-lenges from within the colony and from outside the colony during the next half century.

The Challenge of the First Great Awakening

The first Great Awakening began in the middle of the eighteenth century and transformed the religious lives of many colonial Protestants. It introduced an enlarged element of Calvinism into the mix of religious traditions in Virginia. A distinguishing feature of the awakening was an intensification of the personal relationship people had with God. Many people whom the awakening touched asserted that they could be saved only through that personal relationship and a new birth of religious faith. Clergymen who were in the vanguard of the awakening departed from the cool and rational liturgical service of the Church of England and began to employ a more dramatic speaking style that appealed directly to the emotions of their congregations. Thousands of white Protestants responded favorably to their exhortations, and itinerant ministers moved about the colonies to spread the word, preaching and converting people to the new evangelical style of religious worship.

Evangelical ministers met both success and resistance in Virginia, where authorities for the most part governed in the spirit of the 1689 English Act of Toleration, which the General Assembly enacted as a Virginia law in 1699. English and Virginia laws allowed people freedom of religious belief but imposed some restrictions on the activities and religious services of men and women who dissented from the teachings and practices of the Church of England or attended alternative religious services. Virginia law required every person to pay taxes to support the Church of England, and those taxes supported no other church. The laws recognized as legal only marriage ceremonies clergymen of the Church of England performed. Governors and courts regulated or prohibited religious meetings of some dissenting sects and required licenses for dissenting ministers to conduct religious services. During the first half of the eighteenth century they routinely licensed resident Presbyterian and Lutheran clergymen to conduct regular religious services in their meetinghouses.

Unlicensed ministers who preached without approval or itinerant ministers who traveled about the countryside unaffiliated with any particular congregation appeared to be threats to public order and to the established church. In April 1747 Lieutenant Governor Sir William Gooch issued a proclamation against itinerant preachers whom he charged had "lately crept into this Colony" to corrupt "Faith and true Religion" and propagate what he denounced as "shocking Doctrines." The "Itinerant Preachers whether New-Light Men Moravians, or Methodists" were more than Gooch could tolerate, and he prohibited them "from Teaching Preaching or holding any Meeting in this Colony."[2]

Nevertheless, famed evangelist George Whitefield preached in Virginia, as did other evangelical ministers, and many members of the Church of En-

Unidentified artist, *Samuel Davies*

gland began to embrace the evangelicals. Presbyterians, Lutherans, and followers of the German Reformed tradition were then growing more numerous in
the northern and western regions, and some of them were in sympathy with
the evangelical movement. The best-known and most important leader of the
awakening in Virginia was Samuel Davies, who was minister to a Presbyterian
congregation at Pole Green in Hanover County from 1747 to 1758. His sermons at Pole Green Church and at other meetinghouses in central Virginia
drew many parishioners away from the services of the Church of England and
engaged them deeply in the awakening. Davies left Virginia after a decade to
succeed the colonies' greatest theologian, Jonathan Edwards, as president of
the College of New Jersey, now Princeton University. One young man who
attended Davies's church was Patrick Henry, who may have learned there how
to speak effectively and win the hearts of an audience, even though he remained a member of the Church of England.

Many African Americans and Virginia's Indian residents converted to
Protestant Christianity during and after the awakening. British organizations
such as the Society for the Propagation of the Gospel in Foreign Parts and the
Society for the Promotion of Christian Knowledge sent missionaries and religious literature to the colonies during the middle decades of the eighteenth
century. Some Presbyterian and Church of England clergymen conducted
schools for free and enslaved blacks in Virginia, but in many places they encountered opposition from planter families when they engaged in active conversion work among the enslaved population. Samuel Davies was particularly

industrious in converting African Americans to Christianity during the 1750s. Less is known about when or how Virginia Indians became Christians, but it is probable that many Indians and a large proportion of the colony's black residents were exposed to or converted to Christianity by the end of the eighteenth century. Baptist ministers were the most successful in appealing to African and Indian Virginians.

Members of the Church of England remained a large majority of white Virginians through the first three-quarters of the eighteenth century except in the western counties where Presbyterians formed a majority. In some Shenandoah Valley counties Presbyterians even sat on parish vestries because there were too few members of the Church of England in the area, and the social and governmental responsibilities of the parishes required responsible direction. Baptists were the fastest growing evangelical denomination in Virginia during the 1760s and 1770s. In almost all regions of Virginia east of the Blue Ridge, Baptist ministers formed congregations and drew members away from the Church of England. Some of the Baptists ministers refused to obtain licenses from the county court and complained when magistrates tried to monitor their sermons. The opposition some of those ministers faced produced strong and long-lasting resentment among Baptist converts.

A substantial portion of the political leaders of Virginia remained firmly committed to the teachings and institutions of the Church of England, and the awakening disturbed or alarmed them. As during the seventeenth century the Church of England and its parishes remained vitally important, central elements of the society and culture, and furnished its members with a religious outlook on the world that informed their sense of self. So important was the church to the colony that in order to support the church and its ministers properly and to attend to the religious and secular needs of the parishioners vestrymen levied higher taxes on the residents of their parishes than justices of the peace levied on people to run their counties. The awakening challenged a firmly established and vitally important part of Virginia's culture and government.

Early in the 1770s justices of the peace, sheriffs, and crowds of people in several areas east of the Blue Ridge Mountains mobbed Baptist meetings, threatened or beat Baptist ministers, and jailed Baptists who refused to seek licenses to preach. After one of several ministers who was jailed in Chesterfield County began to preach through the barred windows of the jail to people who gathered outside, the presiding judge of the county court, Archibald Cary, had a brick wall erected around the jail to stop the practice. The violent reaction of some Virginians to the preaching of the Baptists revealed that the magistrates and other men who beat, abused, jailed, or harassed Baptist ministers and congregations feared that the rapidly increasing sect posed a serious threat to their culture and way of life.

Baptists in eighteenth-century Virginia did not all agree with one another on a number of important theological points and about church government and the worship service. Most of them disapproved, as Puritans and Quakers had disapproved in the seventeenth century, of the hierarchical governance of the Church of England. Baptists often attempted to align the practices of their congregations with an approximation of the ancient church in the first years after Christ. Each congregation of Baptists was independent of all other religious bodies, and the members of each congregation governed the congregation and hired or dismissed ministers. Baptists had no select board of vestrymen who made decisions for the whole congregation as parish vestries did for the Church of England. Baptists also believed that a public confession of sins and public acceptance of a rebirth of religious belief were required for full membership in the church.

Each congregation was of very great spiritual as well as temporal importance to its members. Their commitment to saving souls led them, as early Puritans had also been led, to a shared commitment to godly living. Congregations intervened to settle disputes between church members, between members and their enslaved laborers who might also be members of the same or a different church, and even between husbands and wives. Church members often resolved personal or financial differences within their shared religious community rather than take them to secular court. They also improvised solutions to problems that the presence of enslaved men and women in the church created. In a few places Baptists even allowed enslaved men some participation in church governance. The congregations often recognized marriages between enslaved men and women, which the law did not, and generally permitted an enslaved person to remarry if a spouse had been sold away, as if the spouse were dead.

Those practices appeared dangerous to many members of the Church of England. An unidentified Caroline County official lectured Baptists who complained about licensing requirements and being imprisoned. "The private Opinions of Men are not the Objects of Law or Government," he explained; "while they keep those to themselves, they may enjoy them without Interruption from the civil Magistrate. But if they go about publickly preaching and inculcating their Errours, raising Factions tending to disturb the publick Peace, or utter Doctrines which in their Nature are subversive of all Religion or Morality, they become obnoxious" and subject to "civil Punishment."[3] He stated, in effect, that laws and judges decided which beliefs were "Errours" and which behaviors threatened "Religion or Morality." Full religious freedom did not exist in the colony, and oftentimes religious toleration was severely limited.

The Church of England had lost its hold on the religious loyalties of some Virginians. Historians once believed that the awakening succeeded in Virginia because there were too few Church of England clergymen in Virginia and too many of them were incompetent or immoral. In fact, ministers were more numerous and generally more capable than had been thought, and only a very few notorious instances of ineptitude or immoral conduct had left a false impression about the quality of the clergy. It may not have been so much the failure of the clergymen that the Church of England began losing its appeal as it was the success of the evangelical ministers and their message in exerting greater appeal.

Early in the 1770s some members of the Church of England considered appointing a bishop to administer its affairs in the colonies. The bishop of London had nominal jurisdiction over the church in the American colonies, but there was no resident bishop, and men had to travel to England to be ordained into the ministry. Whether the proposal for an American bishop was a direct consequence of the challenge the awakening posed is not clear, but theological disputes and other differences of opinion between ministers and vestries needed resolution, and in a few instances misbehaving ministers required discipline. Some people believed that an American bishop and ecclesiastical courts were necessary to administer the church effectively, but prominent burgesses and lay leaders of the Church of England in Virginia strongly opposed the plan. They argued that the church did not need and that Virginians did not want another agency of British control operating in the colony. Those Virginians feared that a resident bishop would undermine or destroy their ability to continue running their parishes as they pleased and as they had for almost a century and a half. The reaction in Virginia to the proposal to appoint an American bishop became entangled in questions of colonial versus imperial rights and powers as the American Revolution approached. In the end, the Church of England appointed no American bishop.

The Challenge of the Enlightenment

Readers of Virginia's newspapers (beginning in 1766 two printers each published a weekly *Virginia Gazette* in Williamsburg) and of pamphlets and books published during the middle decades of the eighteenth century would have been aware of the international intellectual ferment known as the Enlightenment. Of European origin, it took various forms associated with its intellectual origins in several countries, particularly in France, England, and

Scotland. The Enlightenment appealed to educated men and women who valued learning, logic, and the creative power of human reasoning. The Enlightenment emphasized the importance of rational thought and the acquisition of knowledge of the natural world as sources for understanding the human condition and for devising methods to improve it. The great compilations of information the French encyclopedists began to publish at that time reflected the rational purposes and methods and the optimistic spirit of the Enlightenment. Accurate knowledge and rational thought offered hope for human progress. Sympathetic members of the Council of State purchased some of the new encyclopedias for the library in the Capitol in Williamsburg.

On the one hand, the Enlightenment was compatible in several respects with the intellectual outlook of the Church of England, which stressed rationality in the interpretation of Scripture, and it was easy for some people who belonged to the church to embrace the Enlightenment. On the other hand, participation in the Enlightenment led some other people to question some fundamentally important tenets of Christianity, such as the virgin birth, the divinity of Jesus, and the doctrine of the Trinity. Some of them moved away from their Anglican intellectual outlook to a rationalism that disavowed the Trinity or even all the way to a less structured belief system termed deism that acknowledged the existence of a supreme being but did not acknowledge miracles or some other aspects of Protestant Christianity as the Church of England taught it.

Lieutenant Governor Francis Fauquier was a man of the Enlightenment and during his administration from 1758 to 1768 provided Virginians with a living example of its intellectual spirit. William Small who taught at the College of William and Mary during part of that time was also a man of the Enlightenment, who merged interests in the classics and the sciences (then called natural philosophy) in a way that appealed strongly to Thomas Jefferson, his star student. Jefferson was by no means alone among Virginians in embracing the Enlightenment spirit, but he more than any other Virginian of his time exemplified the Enlightenment's pursuit of knowledge and its optimistic confidence in improvement. He was an early Virginia member of the Enlightenment's foremost North American institution, the American Philosophical Society, which had its headquarters in Philadelphia, and of its Virginia counterpart, the aptly named Society for the Advancement of Useful Knowledge, which had its headquarters in Williamsburg.

The Great Awakening and the Enlightenment appealed to different Virginians for different reasons. One gave energy to faith and the emotions, the other to learning and reason. Their simultaneous appearance in Virginia during the second and third quarters of the eighteenth century undoubtedly modified and may have eroded some of the firm foundations of Virginia's old colonial culture based on hierarchy, conformity, and traditions that had made William Byrd comfortable in the 1720s.

The Challenge of War

During those same decades several prominent Virginians began transplanting that culture to the west. They joined with investors in other colonies and in England to form large syndicates, such as the Ohio Company and the Loyal Company, to acquire from the Crown large tracts of unsettled land west of the Allegheny Mountains. As speculators had earlier done in the Shenandoah Valley, the investors planned to sell or rent the land in small parcels to actual settlers.

That western region, though, was contested ground. Shawnee and other tribes inhabited the area, and fur traders based in New France also exploited the resources of the upper Ohio Valley. In the autumn of 1753 Lieutenant Governor Robert Dinwiddie sent a young militia officer, George Washington, to the northwest to demand that the French evacuate land Virginia claimed under its second and third royal charters. The following year Washington commanded a small party of Virginia militiamen on an expedition to seize strategic Fort Duquesne, which the French were building at the forks of the Ohio River, later the site of Pittsburgh. The French attacked the Virginians east of there at Fort Necessity in the Great Meadows and forced Washington to surrender on July 3, 1754. That began the Seven Years' War between France and Great Britain, known in North America as the French and Indian War.

The British recognized the critical importance of the forks of the Ohio River and in 1755 sent a regular army force under the command of Major General Edward Braddock to seize it. His army, augmented by colonial militiamen and including Washington, marched west from Alexandria to assault Fort Duquesne. On the morning of July 9, the French and their Indian allies attacked and defeated Braddock's combined command not far from the site of Fort Necessity. Braddock was mortally wounded, but Washington escaped unhurt and earned widespread credit for saving the remainder of the army. Almost overnight he became the most famous Virginian and for much of the war commanded a Virginia regiment stationed at the frontier town of Winchester. The colony created a second Virginia regiment under the command of the third William Byrd (1728–77) for service against the Cherokee on the southwestern frontier. Byrd established his headquarters at Fort Chiswell in what later became Wythe County.

The two regiments included many men who were conscripted (drafted) into service because voluntary enlistments did not furnish enough soldiers.

Charles Willson Peale, *George Washington as Colonel of the Virginia Regiment,* 1772

The conscription law was modeled on the act the General Assembly had passed in 1740 during a war between Great Britain and Spain, sometimes known as the War of Jenkins' Ear. The laws provided for the conscription of young white men who were not gainfully employed and owned no land, taking what burgesses undoubtedly regarded as a rootless and therefore potentially unruly class of people out of circulation and putting them in the army where they would be disciplined and made useful. In the beginning Washington had to hang several such men for disobedience and misbehavior before he successfully imposed military order on his regiment. Many of those drafted men later died of disease, and some of them died on the battlefield.

For several years residents of the Virginia frontier lived in constant fear of Indians who were allied with the French or were protecting their historic rights to hunt on land white settlers had occupied. Conflicts tended to be small and localized. Indian raiding parties swiftly descended on isolated farms or on small groups of settlers and as speedily withdrew. Families of victims of those raids in many instances killed any Indians they encountered, either from fear of new attacks or as retribution for past attacks. During the French and Indian War several small companies of soldiers, known as rangers, patrolled the violent border region, but they provided settlers little actual protection. The colony also erected a string of small forts in the Blue Ridge Mountains in hopes of being able to detect or repel Indians who moved close to the Piedmont, but they probably had little effect, either. The number of men, women, and children who died or were displaced during the war is not known for certain, but thousands of inhabitants of the region northwest of Winchester and in portions of the Valley of Virginia abandoned their homes and farms during the war in the face of or in fear of attacks.

The chronic, sporadic violence affected many people during the decades. A few instances gained wide notoriety. The case of Mary Draper Ingles became one of the most famous. At the end of July 1755, Shawnee raided the settlement at Draper's Meadow (near modern-day Radford), killed several members of Ingles's family, and took her, her children, and several other people hostage. After several harrowing months, the deaths of her children, and traveling with the Indians as far as the Ohio River, she escaped and eventually made her way back to her husband. Other western men, women, and children also spent time as captives of western Indians. Some returned, and some did not.

Dangers of life on the frontier were well known to the people who moved to the region and later became the raw materials for adventure stories, legends, and ballads. Well known at the time but less celebrated in the historical literature, some Virginians who escaped from slavery voluntarily joined Indians and lived the rest of their lives in the mountains and in the Ohio Valley.

In 1758 a combined force of British regulars and colonial militia under the command of Brigadier General James Forbes, and again including Washington, occupied Fort Duquesne. The British captured Quebec in 1759 and defeated a French fleet in the West Indies in 1762. By the Treaty of Paris signed on February 10, 1763, France relinquished its North American colonies to Great Britain, which then claimed the entire continent north of Florida and as far west as the Mississippi River, the border with New Spain.

Some surviving documents contain evidence of hardships survivors of the war later endured. During the colonial period Virginians who were in need had few public sources of assistance. They could appeal to a parish vestry for poor relief or to a county court for exemption from payment of taxes. They could also petition the General Assembly for passage of a special act to grant them financial relief. The formal third-person language of the petitions indicates that petitioners often had assistance from an attorney, a county clerk, or a justice of the peace in preparing their pleas. Several petitions submitted to the last session of the General Assembly of the colony in May 1774 preserve testimony of survivors of the French and Indian War.

The petition of Arthur Dent recounted that he "Served as a Private Soldier in the Virginia Regiment Commanded by Colo. Washington upwards of Seven years; that whilst he was in his Majesties Service he received three Different Wounds which has Disabled him in such a Manner as to render him Incapable of supporting himself, and that he is at this time Destitute of the Common Necessary's of Life." A committee of the House of Burgesses reviewed Dent's petition in May 1774 and recommended that he be allowed "£25 present Relief and £5 per Annum during Life." The onrushing events leading up to the American Revolution, however, led the royal governor to terminate the meeting of the assembly. The assembly never voted on the committee's recommendation, and Dent therefore received nothing.[4]

The same session of the House of Burgesses received a petition from Timothy Conway. He related that "at the Battle of the meadows under the Command of Colo. George Washington" he was wounded "through the wrist of his Right arm, which greatly endangered his Life, and was therefore discharged the Service." After shedding "several peices of Shatter'd Bone" from the wounded wrist he thought himself "so much Recovered, that he Could again serve his Country." Conway spent about eighteen months in a "Ranging Company" of scouts until the unit was disbanded. "He then inlisted again into the Virginia Regiment, and Continued in that service . . . till after General Forbeses Campaign, in the year 1758, The many hardships your Petitioner Suffered during that long and Painfull Service, Occasioned his wound to Break out into an ulcer which was thought incurable and was again discharged the service, and under these Circumstances, has never since Received the Smallest assistance, or support, from his Country . . . but being now under the weight of old age and unable to Labour for support of Life" he asked for relief. Like Dent and for the same reason, Conway received nothing.[5]

Neither did Jane Fraser, widow of "John Fraser formerly of the Province of Pensylvania." Her husband had been trading with Indians north of the Ohio River in June 1754 when news of war reached him, and he "thought it prudent to retire" to the east. On the way back he encountered Washington's men at Fort Necessity. Washington took some of Fraser's horses to assist in bringing up a company of reinforcements and supplies. After the surrender a few days later Fraser's "goods were taken & Plundered by the Enemy." Jane Fraser's petition for relief included a "particular account of which, taken the day before the sd. Engagemt. amounting to £2252.4." Her husband never sought compensation for his lost horses and goods, but after his death "two Merchts. in Philadelphia" pressed her for payment of "about seven hundred & fifty pounds, now due for the Purchase of part of the sd. goods, wch. she cannot discharge, without the total ruin of her self & seven young children."[6] The burgesses received her petition the day before the governor dissolved the assembly and did not even have time to review her documents.

Those petitions to the General Assembly and many other such documents are reminders that soldiers and sailors who died or were wounded in the service were not the only victims of war, that their families and civilians, like Jane Fraser and her seven children, were also victims then and for many years afterward.

Challenges from Great Britain

The British victory over the French ended foreign challenges to Virginia's western land claims, but in 1763 the British government issued a proclamation that prohibited settlement west of the mountains in hopes of reducing contacts between settlers and Indians and thereby preventing further clashes. The proclamation aroused resentment in Virginia and other colonies with western land, and in spite of it pioneering settlers crossed the Alleghenies and established farms and settlements in the areas that later became western Pennsylvania, Ohio, West Virginia, and Kentucky.

The relationship between Great Britain and the colonies changed in several fundamentally important ways as a result of the war. The stationing of a large army in the colonies increased the British debt and required new taxes. Parliament insisted on stricter enforcement of the trade and navigation acts that produced revenue for the royal treasury and that restricted colonial access to world markets. The British also strengthened enforcement of laws that prohibited colonists from producing or importing such vital commodities as salt as well as restrictions on manufacturing and other regulations that exemplified the constraints Parliament imposed on the colonists for the benefit of British manufacturers, merchants, and shippers. Those laws also generated revenue for the royal treasury. Until the French and Indian War residents of the colonies had successfully avoided some of those restrictions because of lax enforcement.

That long period of lax enforcement of imperial regulations is sometimes known in the historical literature because of its consequences as "salutary neglect." That neglect allowed residents of the colonies to develop their own institutions and practices, to pass laws they deemed necessary, and to mold their public institutions to meet their unique needs. While the king's ministers were preoccupied with other things those practices, nowhere more important than in the representative assemblies in each of the colonies, acquired legitimacy and constitutional status.

Virginia's political leaders were firmly committed to maintaining their status and ability to govern, but even as the awakening dramatically changed the culture of Virginia and the Enlightenment influenced its intellectual elite some of the leading public men in the colony engaged in unusual open discussions about political legitimacy, leadership, and public trust. In 1752 Lieutenant Governor Robert Dinwiddie precipitated the first debate by demanding a fee of one pistole (a Spanish coin then worth about £1 2s 6d in the colonies) for affixing his signature to land grants. Leading members of the General Assembly accused him of abusing his power by not seeking prior approval from the legislature, but Dinwiddie insisted that the king's royal commission authorized him to impose and collect the fee. Virginia's political leaders, however, argued that only the colonial assembly by virtue of its representing the taxpayers and its long-established legitimacy had the right to impose a new tax or fee. Landon Carter and other burgesses, including Richard Bland, who was a keen student of the colony's political and legal history, wrote several learned and forceful discourses in defense of the constitutional rights and powers of the assembly. Nevertheless, the king's Privy Council approved Dinwiddie's imposition of the fee. During the controversies about the pistole fee William Stith created the earliest known Virginia political slogan. He was a clergyman of the Church of England and president of the College of William and Mary. One day he deliberately offended Dinwiddie by raising his glass to toast "Liberty and Property and no Pistole."[7]

A few years later the same legislative leaders defended with equal insistence the assembly's passage in 1755 and 1758 of laws popularly known as Two-Penny Acts. Each specified that during a year of poor tobacco harvests, which raised the price of leaf tobacco, debts or other obligations payable in tobacco could be paid in cash at a rate approximating two pennies per pound of tobacco. The colony's clergymen stood to lose income because their salaries were legally set at 16,000 pounds of tobacco per year. At twopence per pound they received less money than 16,000 pounds of tobacco was then worth. They appealed to the Privy Council to have the king invalidate the second of the two laws. The clergymen succeeded by arguing that the act effectively amended the salary law that had already received royal assent and did not contain a clause suspending its operation until the king could approve or disapprove it.

Royal disallowances of bills the General Assembly passed and suspending clauses the king required on many bills often frustrated colonial legislators. Legislative leaders argued that the assembly had and should have constitutional authority to legislate for the good of the whole colony if an emergency did not allow time for the king to be consulted. Richard Bland, Landon Carter, and other Virginians took up their pens again. Grounding their reasoning in the colony's history they defended the legitimacy of the elected members of the General Assembly as the only body of men rightfully entitled to make key decisions affecting the people in the colony.

After the king disallowed the second Two-Penny Act a clergyman sued in the Hanover County Court in 1763 to recover the difference between what he had been paid in money and what he would have received had he been paid in tobacco. The opposing attorney, Patrick Henry, inflamed the jury with charges that the clergymen were rapacious and that the king had acted tyrannically in disallowing the law. The jury awarded the minister a mere one penny in damages, which effectively nullified the effect of the royal veto of the law. The Parsons' Cause, as it was known, earned Henry his first fame as an orator and convinced many people that if the king acted unjustly or violated colonists' constitutional rights, he forfeited his subjects' allegiance.

In that same year, the Seven Years' War concluded, and Great Britain tightened administration of the trade and navigation acts to increase revenue in order to pay off the large national war debt. In 1764 Parliament declared its intention to impose a stamp tax on the colonists, an unprecedented tax that had no relationship to the regulation of trade, which was the basis on which the British government had previously collected revenue in the colonies. The Stamp Act of 1765 established a system of excise taxes on numerous items of printed matter, among them newspapers, most types of legal documents such as deeds and marriage licenses, and even playing cards. The law required purchasers of the items and people who paid for licenses and other legal instruments to buy and affix a stamp to the paper as proof of payment of the tax.

The law imposed two burdens residents of the colonies found hard to bear. First, it required people to purchase the stamps with gold or silver and not with colonial paper money. Gold and silver were in very short supply, and as a practical matter many people would be unable to purchase stamps even if they were willing to comply with the law. And second, the law required that people charged with violating it be transported to Halifax, Nova Scotia, to be tried in a court of vice-admiralty without the benefit of a jury. Defendants would also have to pay the costs of transportation of witnesses to Halifax, which could make it financially impossible for people to defend themselves in the court.

Americans in every colony protested. They argued that because no American representatives sat in Parliament it therefore had no legitimate authority to tax the colonists directly; only the separate colonial assemblies elected in each colony could do that. Representatives of several colonies attended the Stamp Act Congress in Albany, New York, to coordinate colonial opposition to the tax and put pressure on English merchants to convince Parliament to repeal the act. Because the General Assembly was not in session to elect delegates to the Stamp Act Congress, Virginia was not represented, but it adopted its own resolutions against the Stamp Act and in December 1764 requested Parliament not to pass the bill and petitioned the king not to sign it. The two houses of Parliament passed and the king signed the bill in 1765.

At its next session of the General Assembly members of the House of Burgesses went much further. On May 29, 1765, the burgesses by a narrow margin adopted several strong resolutions that Patrick Henry introduced. The burgesses who opposed the resolutions did so not because they approved of the Stamp Act but because the resolutions directly challenged the authority of the king. Henry's resolutions denied that Parliament had a legitimate right to tax the colonies. In Henry's speech he charged that the king abused his royal power by signing Parliament's bills to tax the colonists. The Speaker of the House accused Henry of uttering treasonous words, and the following day the members repealed some of the resolutions; but Henry's resolutions put Virginia in the forefront of colonial resistance, the legislatures of several other colonies endorsed them, and newspapers up and down the coast reprinted them.

Two eyewitness accounts of Henry's dramatic speech survive. One is from Thomas Jefferson who was then a young law student in Williamsburg. In old age he briefly recalled listening to the eloquent speech and dramatic confrontation from the adjacent lobby. The other account was from a Scottish traveler who arrived in town after the debate had already begun and wrote about it in his journal. The journal records that as he approached the Capitol he passed three African Americans hanging from the gallows outside the jail. They had been convicted of robbery and hanged. "Shortly after I Came in" to the Capitol, the Scotsman wrote, "one of the members stood up and said he had read that in former times tarquin and Julus had their Brutus, Charles had his Cromwell, and he Did not Doubt but some good american would stand up, in favour of his Country, but (says he) in a more moderate manner, and was going to Continue, when the speaker of the house rose and Said, he, the last that stood up had spoke traison, and was sorey to see that not one of the members of the house was loyal Enough to stop him, before he had gone so far. upon which the Same member stood up again (his name is henery) and said that if he had afronted the speaker, or the house, he was ready to ask pardon, and he would shew his loyalty to his majesty King G. the third, at the Expence of the last Drop of his blood, but what he had said must be atributed to the Interest of his Countrys Dying liberty which he had at heart, and the heat of passion might have lead him to have said something more than he intended, but, again, if he said any thing wrong, he beged the speaker and the houses pardon. some other Members stood up and backed him, on which the afaire was droped."[8]

Burgess Richard Bland published a learned treatise to defend the constitutional rights of the colonial assemblies and to deny that Parliament had any constitutional right to tax the colonists. His *Inquiry into the Rights of the British Colonies* provided historical context for the Americans' belief that the colonial assemblies alone could justly tax residents of the colonies. Bland wrote that each colonial assembly was an equal colonial counterpart of Parliament. Bland's pamphlet and other newspaper and pamphlet literature helped educate the public about the great political and constitutional issues at stake. Men

Some enterprising manufacturers and merchants found
ways to make money from the political debates, and
women as well as men took part in the boycott of English goods. "Stamp Act" teapot; painted ceramic.

and women who may or may not have read the political tracts supported opposition to the Stamp Act. They refused to purchase British merchandise in
hopes of persuading merchants to pressure Parliament to repeal the law.

Justices of the peace in Northampton County "unanimously declared it
to be their opinion that the said act did not bind, affect, or concern the inhabitants of this colony, inasmuch as they conceive the same to be unconstitutional."[9] Justices of the peace in Westmoreland, Stafford, and Culpeper
Counties resigned rather than allow their courts to function using stamped
paper or to force the residents to purchase the hated stamps. People in several
Virginia communities publicly condemned Virginian George Mercer, who
was appointed distributor of stamps for Virginia, even before he arrived in
Williamsburg from England late in October 1765. The General Court was
then in session, and most of the colony's merchants and a great many attorneys,
burgesses, and county leaders were also in the city. They crowded around Mercer and demanded that he resign. Mercer arranged to have the stamps stowed
away for safekeeping aboard a royal warship and in fear and frustration finally
resigned his office. Without stamps the clerk of the General Court then refused to conduct any business.

Opposition to enforcement of the Stamp Act in Virginia was widespread
and strong, even though the short-term personal cost to many individual merchants and people with lawsuits pending in court may have been high. The
same was the case in most colonies. In response to coordinated pressure from
the colonial assemblies and from British and American merchants Parliament
repealed the Stamp Act in 1766. At the same time, Parliament passed and the

king signed An Act for the Better Securing the Dependency of His Majesty's Dominions in America upon the Crown and Parliament of Great Britain. The Declaratory Act, as it was commonly known, stated flatly that Parliament "had hath, and of right ought to have, full power and authority to make laws and statutes of sufficient force and validity to bind the colonies and people of America, subjects of the Crown of Great Britain, in all cases whatsoever."[10] In the general rejoicing in the colonies at the repeal of the Stamp Act most people overlooked the full importance of the Declaratory Act.

Challenges from Within

While burgesses and other Virginians were debating whether the king and Parliament had violated the constitutional rights of the colonists, two events in Virginia opened related debates about public trust and what constituted proper exercise of political authority. In the spring of 1766 several members of the Council of State, who were also judges of the General Court, posted bail for John Chiswell, who had been arrested and accused of murdering a man in a tavern. Those same council members would be the judges when Chiswell stood trial before the General Court. Chiswell was the wealthy and well-connected manager of the colony's lead mine at the southwestern fort that was named for him and where one of the Virginia regiments had been stationed during the French and Indian War. Some of the court's members had close business or family connections with Chiswell. Several men anonymously criticized them in the press for practicing favoritism and for releasing a man accused of murder when the colony's laws did not authorize bail in that circumstance.

Such bold public criticism of the colony's most elite officeholders was highly unusual. The council members felt insulted that their actions had even been questioned, much less condemned, and some of them informed the public that gentlemen in their station were entitled to respect and were immune to criticism. George Wythe, a rising lawyer of great ability and twice an acting attorney general of the colony, declared that even if Virginia's statutes did not authorize bail, the Court of King's Bench in England had exercised that power in similar cases. Therefore, he explained, judges of the General Court of Virginia were equally entitled to grant bail under the same circumstance. Likening the power of Virginia's highest court to the royal courts of Great Britain was not substantively different than asserting that the General Assembly was in effect the colonial counterpart of Parliament. Defenders of Virginia's political institutions and practices and of its vital interests developed an interpretation of their place in the British empire that gave each colony as well as England equal status among the British king's dominions.

Unidentified artist after John Wollaston, *John Robinson*

About the time the councilors let Chiswell out on bail, John Robinson
died. He was Chiswell's son-in-law, Speaker of the House of Burgesses, and
treasurer of the colony. Since late in the seventeenth century the General Assembly had usually appointed the Speaker of the House to the office of treasurer. The treasurer received and disbursed money the assembly raised by taxation and appropriated by law. Treasurers were allowed to keep a percentage of
the tax money they collected as a source of income to support the dignity of
the office of Speaker. The king's ministers had repeatedly instructed the colony's governors to separate the two offices in order to reduce the potential for
corruption or the accumulation of excessive political influence in the hands of
a person not directly responsible to the Crown. Soon after Robinson's death
an audit revealed that his accounts as treasurer were in arrears to the astonishing amount of more than £100,000. It was by far the largest financial scandal
in the colony's history.

Robinson had been a popular and respected statesman, the most skillful
and powerful political leader the colony had ever produced, but examination
of his accounts revealed that he may have augmented his political influence
by illegally lending large sums of public money to friends and political allies.
He also lent public money to some political adversaries, which led his admir-
ers to defend his actions as good for the cash-starved economy. Following
Robinson's death and ensuing scandal, Lieutenant Governor Francis Fauquier
was easily able to separate the offices of Speaker and treasurer.

The Robinson scandal left many white Virginians deeply disturbed. It disclosed that many of the most prominent families in Virginia were technically

insolvent. Everybody owed money to somebody—a British merchant, a local storekeeper, a neighbor, or a relative—and a great many people were consequently also creditors. So long as the networks of commerce functioned more or less smoothly and people did not start forcing payment of debts owed to them the credit system worked well enough. But the attempts of Robinson's executors to collect money he had lent from the public treasury exposed the inability of other men to pay. The scandal threatened to wreck the entire economy, and it did ruin several families and left other families nervous until the Revolution began. In fact, during the Revolution some loyalists (and some historians later) charged that avoidance of paying their debts to British merchants was one reason why Virginia's leading politicians almost all supported independence. Good twentieth-century scholarship demonstrated that avoidance of debt was not a primary reason Virginians supported independence, even though a good many of them used the war as an excuse to avoid payment for years or decades thereafter.

The almost simultaneous Chiswell episode and Robinson scandal coming in the immediate aftermath of the Stamp Act crisis almost certainly undermined to some extent the ability of the colony's most powerful families to command without question the confidence of the politically active white men who sat on the county courts and served in the House of Burgesses much in the same way perceived abuses of power by the king and Parliament undermined public confidence in and respect for royal government.

It was no accident that after Fauquier died in 1768 the king's ministers sent over the first full-fledged royal governor in more than sixty years. Between the death of Governor Edward Nott in August 1706 and Fauquier's death in March 1768 a succession of lieutenant governors had administered the government in Williamsburg. During that time absentee royal governors resided in England but drew large salaries and collected large fees from taxes imposed on colonists. The best-known eighteenth-century chief magistrates of the colony were all lieutenant governors: Alexander Spotswood, Sir William Gooch, Robert Dinwiddie, and Francis Fauquier. Lieutenant governors had the same authority as royal governors, but mounting tensions within the empire persuaded the king's minsters to send over a governor who was also a nobleman. The last two royal governors of Virginia, and the first to reside in Williamsburg since 1706, were Norborne Berkeley, baron de Botetourt, and John Murray, fourth earl of Dunmore.

8

INDEPENDENCE AND REVOLUTION

GEORGE WASHINGTON WROTE to a friend in July 1774 about an important disagreement they had. At the beginning of the summer Washington had taken part in calling a convention of representatives of Virginia's voters to coordinate with men in other colonies. Their objective was to restore the relationship between residents of the colonies and the government of Great Britain to the condition it had been before the Stamp Act of 1765. Many people, like Washington's friend, believed that the men who called the convention had acted rashly, that they should have instead petitioned the king and Parliament to refrain from passing any more laws to tax people in the colonies.

Washington believed further petitions would be ineffective. He asked his friend, "what further proofs are wanting to satisfy one of the design's of the Ministry than their own Acts; which are uniform, & plainly tending to the same point—nay, if I mistake not, avowedly to fix the Right of Taxation—what hope then from Petitioning, when they tell us that now, or never, is the time to fix the matter—shall we after this whine & cry for releif, when we have already tried it in vain?, or shall we supinely sit, and see one Provence after another fall a Sacrafice to Despotism?—If I was in any doubt as to the Right wch the Parliament of Great Britain had to Tax us without our Consents, I should most heartily coincide with you in opinion, that to Petition, & petition only, is the proper method to apply for relief; because we should then be asking a favour, & not claiming a Right wch by the Law of Nature & our Constitution we are, in my opinion, indubitably entitled to; I should even think it criminal to go further than this, under such an Idea; but none such I have, I think the Parliament of Great Britain hath no more Right to put their hands into my Pocket, without my consent, than I have to put my hands into you'rs, for money, and this being already urged to them in a firm, but decent manner by all the Colonies, what reason is there to expect any thing from their justice?"[1]

Imperial Crisis

Washington's brief summary of the political crisis in the British empire is one of the best and most concise statements of the colonists' main point. Writers of merit, including Virginians Richard Bland and Landon Carter, had explained in detail the relationship between Great Britain and its colonies—between the king and his colonial subjects—during the decade since the end of the French and Indian War. Even as Washington was writing his letter, Thomas Jefferson was preparing a pamphlet that explained that relationship yet again. Jefferson's *Summary View of the Rights of British America* traced Virginians' natural rights all the way back to an imagined Saxon past. Jefferson also argued, as Richard Bland already had, that the Englishmen who had settled the colonies took with them to America all their natural rights and that they had developed their own institutions of representative government without the assistance of Parliament, in which the colonies were not represented. Colonists owed loyalty to the king only, not to Parliament. Jefferson explained that the king had a unique constitutional relationship to the people of Great Britain and separate, unique constitutional relationships to the people of each overseas colony. Because each realm had its own law-making body—Parliament in Great Britain; the General Assembly in Virginia—the king violated the constitution of the colony when he cooperated with Parliament to tax or regulate residents of the colonies. As Washington wrote in the summer of 1774 and as most colonial Americans believed, the king and Parliament had gone too far, and it was time for Americans to assert and defend their constitutional rights.

Washington in his letter and Jefferson in his pamphlet explained what had led them at the beginning of the summer to call the controversial and unprecedented convention. Every two or three years after 1764, when Parliament first announced its intention to impose stamp duties on the colonists, a new tax or regulation provoked opposition in the colonies. The Townsend Acts, which Parliament passed in 1767, imposed new taxes on colonial trade, and the following year the House of Burgesses adopted resolutions in opposition to them. In 1769 when the burgesses passed another set of resolutions critical of Parliament, the royal governor, Norborne Berkeley, baron de Botetourt, summoned the assembly members to the Council chamber in the Capitol and dissolved the assembly. That meant that the legislature ceased to exist and that another election for another assembly would not be held until the governor or the king called one.

The continuing series of controversies about taxation of Americans who were not represented in Parliament took a dramatic turn in December 1773 when men in Boston threw a cargo of British East India Company tea into the harbor rather than allow collection of the tax on it. Parliament responded by passing the Coercive Acts to punish the city and to force all the colonies into obedience, but the terms of the Intolerable Acts, as they were known in America, stiffened colonial resolve. One of the laws closed the port of Boston to all commerce and punished the entire population until the city's residents compensated the company for the destroyed tea. Another law, the Massachusetts Government Act, actually revoked the royal charter of the colony and permitted the king to send a military governor to Massachusetts. Alert people throughout the colonies regarded the Massachusetts Government Act as a brazen interference by Parliament (and with the king's personal participation) that destroyed the ancient constitutional compact the people of Massachusetts had with the Crown.

News of the first of the Coercive Acts reached Williamsburg in May 1774. The General Assembly was then back in session. Members of the House of Burgesses ordered a day of fasting, humiliation, and prayer and denounced the Coercive Acts. Under instructions from the king, Governor John Murray, fourth earl of Dunmore, promptly dissolved the assembly before it could complete work on reenactment of some important Virginia laws. Some essential Virginia laws consequently expired. One was the law that set the fees public officials received for performing their duties, after which some county courts and clerks ceased to do business. The burgesses hoped to put enough pressure on Virginia and British merchants, who used the courts to collect money Virginia planters owed them, that they would in turn bring pressure on Parliament to repeal the obnoxious taxes. Another law that expired was the militia law, without which county militia officers could not legally train or muster their units into service in time of emergency. That left Virginians defenseless against Indians on the frontier, enslaved people who might rise up anywhere, and the governor's soldiers, sailors, and marines.

Following the dissolution of the assembly the burgesses reconvened as private gentlemen in Williamsburg's largest available room, at the Raleigh Tavern. There they summoned a convention to meet in Williamsburg in August and agreed to provide relief for the people of Boston. When news of the Massachusetts Government Act arrived a few days later the former burgesses began the process of calling the First Continental Congress to meet in Philadelphia in the autumn to coordinate colonial opposition to the unconstitutional acts of their king and his Parliament.

George Washington had been there and approved those steps, and he probably received criticism for doing so. Hence his letter of July explaining that humble petitions to the king and Parliament having failed it was time to claim "a Right wch by the Law of Nature & our Constitution we are, in my opinion, indubitably entitled to." Otherwise, as Washington wrote, the king and Parliament might revoke or destroy the constitutions of other colonies, and one by one they would "fall a Sacrafice to Despotism."

Dunmore's War of 1774

Later in the summer of 1774, because of the expiration of the militia law Governor Dunmore had to call for volunteers from several western counties to take the field and protect settlers from western tribes who resented the encroachment of settlers on land reserved to them under the terms of the Proclamation of 1763 and the several treaties they had negotiated with the king's agents. Dunmore personally led a party of volunteers to Fort Pitt, which was the English name for Fort Duquesne. Early in October he led them down the Ohio River to meet another party of volunteers under the command of Colonel Andrew Lewis who marched toward the river from the southeast. On October 10, 1774, Lewis's volunteers met and clashed with a large number of Shawnee and other Indians at Point Pleasant near the confluence of the Great Kanawha and Ohio Rivers. The Virginians beat back an attack led by the great Shawnee chief Cornstalk, who afterward negotiated a peace with Dunmore. The outcome of what later historians called Dunmore's War was that the Indians in the upper Ohio Valley in effect ceded to Virginia the land south of the Ohio River, what is now Kentucky and much of West Virginia.

William Ludwell Sheppard after Sir Joshua Reynolds, *John Murray, fourth Earl of Dunmore,* last royal governor of Virginia

Alternative of Williamsburg, a British engraving that portrayed Virginia leaders as forcing innocent men to take part in the boycott.

1775

The First Continental Congress was meeting in Philadelphia at that same time. Peyton Randolph, Speaker of the Virginia House of Burgesses, was its president. Virginia delegates George Washington, Edmund Pendleton, Richard Henry Lee, Patrick Henry, Benjamin Harrison, and Richard Bland were among the most influential members. Congress adopted a nonimportation association modeled on the one the Virginia Convention had enacted in August in hopes that economic pressure on British merchants would force Parliament to repeal the Coercive Acts. Many of the county courts in Virginia used the expiration of the fee bill as an excuse to close their doors to British creditors who sought to collect money from Virginia planters and merchants.

In 1774 and 1775 qualified voters elected a committee in almost every county to enforce the Continental and Virginia Associations. With the exception of an occasional special election for parish vestry positions, those were the first elections in Virginia in which men voted for local officials. County,

city, and town committees enforced the associations and branded shippers,
merchants, or customers who imported or purchased forbidden British goods
as enemies of American liberty. Sometime mobs acted on their own. In the
summer of 1775 when a quorum of the Isle of Wight County Committee
could not assemble to investigate charges against merchant Anthony Warwick, a mob locked him in the stocks and gave him a painful coat of hot tar
and feathers. "They then mounted him on a horse," a newspaper reported,
"and drove him out of town, through a shower of eggs, the smell of which . . .
seemed to have a material effect upon the delicate constitution of this *motleyed*
gentleman."[2]

The imperial crisis began to change the way Virginia politics worked. Until
the 1770s elections remained focused at the county level on the social standing
and character of men who were candidates for the House of Burgesses. Elections took place at irregular intervals, typically two to five years apart. There
were no political parties and no issues as later Virginians understood those
terms. Candidates provided food and drink to everybody who appeared at the
courthouse on election day, but the law prohibited candidates from making
promises to oppose or support any bill in the assembly, such as for changing a
county boundary, moving the courthouse, or authorizing a new ferry. Qualified voters made their choices in large part on what they knew about the characters and abilities of the men who sought election to the assembly. Voters cast
their votes orally for everybody to hear. It was a very public and personal form
of local politics in which reputation and honor were of primary importance.
Until the eve of the American Revolution candidates probably did not often
discuss such weighty matters as the proper relationship between the people
and government of the colony and their king and Parliament. Beginning in
1774 men and women in Virginia took a more active role in directing what
Thomas Jefferson in 1776 called "the course of human events."

Parliament showed no evidence of retreat during the winter of 1774–75,
and late in March 1775 Virginia's Second Revolutionary Convention met in
Richmond at Henrico Parish Church (renamed Saint John's Church fifty years
later) to elect delegates to the Second Continental Congress. During the convention Patrick Henry offered a resolution that the colony be put into a pos-
ture of defense. Without a militia law the colony could not defend itself from
Indians on the frontiers or if royal warships or troops landed in Virginia as
they had already done in Massachusetts. Moreover, rumors of insurrections of
slaves in several counties reminded all the colony's slave owners that without a
militia to put down an insurrection all white Virginians were in danger. Henry
proposed that the convention re-create the militia under its own authority
before it was too late. His proposal alarmed men who feared war. "Gentlemen
may cry 'Peace! Peace!'" Henry thundered at them, "but there is no peace. The

George B. Matthews after Thomas Sully, *Patrick Henry*

war is actually begun!"[3] By a narrow vote the convention passed Henry's resolution and created a committee with George Washington as chair to prepare
a plan for defense of the colony.

That same month Dunmore removed the gunpowder from the public
magazine in Williamsburg, an act that seemed to confirm fears that the British planned to disarm the colonies and subdue them by force. Henry had predicted that the next news from the north would bring word of clashing arms,
and in fact British troops and Massachusetts militiamen did begin the war
near Lexington and Concord on April 19, 1775.

The concluding words of Henry's March 1775 speech, "Give me liberty,
or give me death," became the watchword of Virginia patriots. The months
after Henry's speech and the outbreak of fighting in Massachusetts brought
about a radical transformation in Virginia and the other colonies. The Second Continental Congress convened in Philadelphia in May and met continuously through the remainder of 1775. In June it elected George Washington
commander-in-chief of the new Continental Army. That same month Dunmore fled Williamsburg with a small number of royal soldiers and established

By His Excellency the Right Honorable JOHN Earl of DUNMORE, His
Majesty's Lieutenant and Governor General of the Colony and Dominion of
Virginia, and Vice Admiral of the same.

A PROCLAMATION.

AS I have ever entertained Hopes that an Accommodation might have
taken Place between Great-Britain and this Colony, without being
compelled by my Duty to this most disagreeable but now absolutely-necessary
Step, rendered so by a Body of armed Men unlawfully assembled, firing on His
Majesty's Tenders, and the formation of an Army, and that Army now on
their March to attack His Majesty's Troops and destroy the well disposed Subjects of this Colony. To defeat such treasonable Purposes, and that all such
Traitors, and their Abettors, may be brought to Justice, and that the Peace, and
good Order of this Colony may be again restored, which the ordinary Course
of the Civil Law is unable to effect; I have thought fit to issue this my Proclamation, hereby declaring, that until the aforesaid good Purposes can be obtained, I do in Virtue of the Power and Authority to ME given, by His Majesty, determine to execute Martial Law, and cause the same to be executed
throughout this Colony: and to the end that Peace and good Order may the
sooner be restored, I do require every Person capable of bearing Arms, to resort
to His Majesty's STANDARD, or be looked upon as Traitors to His
Majesty's Crown and Government, and thereby become liable to the Penalty
the Law inflicts upon such Offences; such as forfeiture of Life, confiscation of
Lands, &c. &c. And I do hereby further declare all indented Servants, Negroes,
or others, (appertaining to Rebels,) free that are able and willing to bear Arms,
they joining His Majesty's Troops as soon as may be, for the more speedily
reducing this Colony to a proper Sense of their Duty, to His Majesty's
Crown and Dignity. I do further order, and require, all His Majesty's Leige
Subjects, to retain their Quitrents, or any other Taxes due or that may become
due, in their own Custody, till such Time as Peace may be again restored to this
at present most unhappy Country, or demanded of them for their former salutary Purposes, by Officers properly authorised to receive the same.

GIVEN under my Hand on board the Ship WILLIAM, off Norfolk,
the 7th Day of November, in the sixteenth Year of His Majesty's Reign.

DUNMORE.

(GOD save the KING.)

Proclamation of Governor Dunmore, November 7, 1775, offering freedom to slaves
who volunteered to fight for the king.

a military headquarters at Craney Island near Portsmouth. Virginia's Third Revolutionary Convention met in July and August and created a Committee of Safety to govern the colony and raised an army of two regiments to defend Virginia. The convention elected Patrick Henry colonel and commander-in-chief of Virginia's regiments.

On November 7, Dunmore issued a proclamation that offered freedom to slaves who ran away from their patriot owners and joined his army. He also recruited a small regiment of loyal white Virginians. Dunmore's little army of volunteers and regular royal soldiers charged Virginia soldiers and minute-men at the Great Bridge south of Norfolk on December 9, 1775, and suffered a stunning defeat. On New Year's Day royal warships shelled Norfolk, which started a fire. Drunken Virginia and North Carolina soldiers in the city lit fire to houses and shops of loyalists. The fire spread and burned much of Norfolk to the ground. Virginia officials concealed the role of the soldiers for several months and deliberately permitted the public to believe that Dunmore was responsible for everything. That added another grievance against the last and most unpopular of the royal governors of Virginia.

The shelling of Norfolk and resultant fire produced some of the first civilian casualties in the war for independence in Virginia. Norfolk resident Mary Webley later petitioned the General Assembly for relief. She informed the legislators that "on new Years Day last, while suckling her Child the youngest of three now dependent on her" she "had her Leg broken by a Cannon Ball from the Liverpool Man of War. That her Husband from the Loss of his right arm upwards of twenty Years since is scarcely able to maintain himself, That She hath at present no Ways or Means to procure Shelter or acquire Subsistence for herself and miserable little Children, her Husband and Self having had all their Effects totally destroyed in the Flames of Norfolk from whence they have been drove in most distresful Circumstances." The General Assembly awarded her £10.[4]

Independence

Virginia and the other colonies went to war with Great Britain as Patrick Henry had predicted. During the first months of 1776 residents of all the colonies had to choose to remain loyal to the king or not. Thomas Paine's brilliantly written pamphlet *Common Sense* condensed all the arguments against continued loyalty to the king into one persuasive case for independence. That and events on the battlefields of New England and mistaken ideas about who burned Norfolk persuaded many people that continued loyalty to the king was impossible. Dunmore's offer of freedom to escaped slaves convinced slave owners in Virginia that they had to seize control of the independence

John Toole after John Hesselius, *George Mason*

movement in Virginia in order to retain control of their colony. Reluctantly but in overwhelming numbers planters and politicians in Virginia made their choices, and in April voters elected delegates to the fifth and last of Virginia's Revolutionary Conventions.

The convention met in the Capitol in Williamsburg from May 6, through July 5, 1776. On May 15, the members voted unanimously to instruct the Virginia delegates in Congress to introduce a resolution for independence. In Philadelphia on June 7, Richard Henry Lee, the senior Virginia delegate, moved that Congress declare that the colonies "are, and, of right, ought to be, Free and Independent States."[5] On July 2, Congress passed Lee's motion and two days later explained its action to the world with the Declaration of Independence Thomas Jefferson composed.

On June 12, 1776, in Williamsburg the Virginia Convention adopted the Virginia Declaration of Rights, which George Mason had drafted. It spelled out the principles of representative government and guaranteed such fundamental liberties as freedom of the press and the right to a jury trial in both civil and criminal cases. The final clause, which the convention amended, transformed a recitation of the principles of the English Act of Toleration into a bold statement of religious freedom: "all men are equally entitled to the free exercise of religion, according to the dictates of conscience."[6] The Declaration of Rights was one of the most important state papers of 1776. It served as a model for other states and later for the United States Bill of Rights and for the French Declaration of the Rights of Man and Citizen, both written in 1789.

The language of liberty and equality with which men and women supported the American Revolution had lasting consequences in the politics of
the new nation. It is very unlikely that when George Mason wrote in his draft
for the Virginia Declaration of Rights in 1776, "That all men are born equally
free and independent, and have certain inherent natural rights," he intended
the language to be understood literally. The convention amended the language
before it adopted the declaration so as to exclude Virginia's enslaved population. The text as adopted stated that men did not surrender their natural rights
to life and liberty when they "enter into a state of Society." Enslaved Virginians not being members of the society or of the body politic did not therefore
have any personal right to life or liberty.[7]

Nor did Thomas Jefferson when he wrote in the Declaration of Independence that all men were created equal and entitled to life, liberty, and the
pursuit of happiness intend his language to apply to all people, or even to all
men. Mason and Jefferson were not writing about everybody. They were com-
posing state papers to justify a revolution and were writing to, for, and about
the political nation, which in Virginia included adult property-owning white
males, only. Nevertheless, much of Virginia's subsequent history and much
of American history can be interpreted as other people's attempts to make a
reality of the promises implied in Mason's and Jefferson's declarations—that
all people were equally entitled to life, liberty, and the pursuit of happiness—
all the rights of citizenship.

Virginia's first written constitution, which the convention unanimously
adopted on June 29, 1776, created a republic, or commonwealth, a government without royalty in which ultimate authority was exercised by a sovereign
people united for the common good, or common weal. To avoid any repetition
of abuses of executive authority, the Constitution of 1776 severely restricted
the powers of the executive branch of government. It denied the governor
power to veto bills, and it empowered the assembly to choose the governor
annually and an eight-member Council of State to advise the governor on
the exercise of his limited powers. In the event of the death, resignation, or
absence of the governor from the capital, the president of the Council of State
temporarily became acting governor with the title of lieutenant governor. The
new constitution also empowered the assembly to elect the attorney general,
treasurer, and all the state's judges and other officials. The convention elected
Patrick Henry the first governor of the independent Commonwealth of Virginia. He served three one-year terms. In 1779 the assembly elected Thomas
Jefferson to the first of two one-year terms.

Other than reduce the authority of the executive and augment the authority of the legislature the first written constitution of Virginia changed little in
how the government functioned. It left in place the county courts on which

justices of the peace (most of whom had no training in the law) exercised legislative, executive, and judicial responsibilities in their counties. The justices of the peace also decided who filled vacancies in their number, meaning that the county courts remained self-perpetuating bodies largely unbeholden to the citizens and under little supervision from the state. The new constitution also left in force the colonial law that limited the right to vote to adult white men who owned at least one hundred acres of land or fifty acres and a house or, in incorporated cities Williamsburg and Norfolk, a lot or part of a lot. Insofar as institutions and political practices were concerned independence did not by itself work a revolution in Virginia. Delegates in the convention and men in the counties chose independence in order to protect their ancient rights from the outside threats from the king and Parliament and also to protect their control over the colony from inside threats to their continued domination of society. They did not seek to begin a revolution to change Virginia.

Revolution

A revolution began in Virginia, anyway. During the first years of the war for independence most of the military action took place north of Maryland. During that time, the Virginia General Assembly considered a wide range of reforms. In October 1776 it created a five-member committee to revise the laws of the commonwealth. Thomas Jefferson was the most influential and creative member of the committee, which recommended simplifying the legal code and reducing the number of criminal offenses punishable by death. Completed in 1779, the committee's report also recommended abolishing primogeniture (by which in the absence of a will all inherited land passed to the eldest son) and entail (by which in a deed or will a person could permanently prevent heirs from disposing of or subdividing land). Primogeniture and entail had enabled owners of great landed estates to pass them along intact to later generations and to enlarge their protected holdings through strategic marriages. During the 1780s the General Assembly adopted most of the committee's bills, including the repeal of the laws of primogeniture and entail. The repeal of those laws set in train a slow and steady decline in the number and political influence of the great planter families that had dominated Virginia's public life since the seventeenth century.

The most important and famous bill in the report of the Committee of Revisers was the Act for Establishing Religious Freedom, usually referred to as the Statute for Religious Freedom. James Madison, a member of the House of Delegates from Orange County, guided it through the assembly in January 1786 while Jefferson was serving as minister to France. Clergymen and lay leaders of the Church of England, which transformed itself into the Protestant

George Catlin after Thomas Sully, *Thomas Jefferson*.
Jefferson was influential in many ways throughout his
long life.

Episcopal Church after the war, opposed adoption of the bill and instead endorsed a proposal, called the assessment, to tax all Virginians for the support
of *all* clergymen and teachers of Christianity.

Baptists with assistance from Presbyterians and some Lutherans enabled
Jefferson's bill to pass. Without the Baptists, in particular, Jefferson and Madison would not have been successful. Virginia's Baptists insisted that the state
government take no part in religious matters at all. In response to the persecution of their ministers early in the 1770s, Baptists skillfully organized petitioning campaigns to persuade the General Assembly to allow all Protestants full religious liberty. Their petitions linked the Revolution's language of
representative government and the war for political liberty with the specific

language of liberty in the Virginia Declaration of Rights and the Declaration of Independence.

One of the first and most eloquent petitions came from 162 men who met in Prince Edward County in September 1776. They stated that they "heartily approve and Chearfully submit ourselves to the form of Government adopted at your last Session: hoping that our united American States will long continue free and Independent. The last Article of the Bill of Rights we also esteem as the rising Sun of religious Liberty, to releave us from a long Night of ecclesiastic Bondage: And we do most earnestly request and expect that you would go on to complete what is so nobly begun; raise religious as well as civil Liberty to the Zenith of Glory, and make Virginia an Asylum for free enquiry, knowlege, and the virtuous of every Denomination. Justice to ourselves and Posterity, as well as a regard to the honour of the Common Wealth, makes it our indispensable Duty, in particular to intreat, That without Delay, You would pull down all Church E[s]tablishments; Abolish every Tax upon Conscience and private Judgment; and leave each Individual to rise or sink according to his Merit, and the general Laws of the Land. The whole amount of what we desire, is, That Our Honourable Legislature would blot out every Vestige of British Tyranny and Bondage, and define accurately between civil and ecclesiastic Authority; then leave our Lord Jesus Christ the Honour of being the Sole Lawgiver and Governor in his Church; and every one in the Things of Religion to stand or fall to Him; he being, in this respect the only rightful Master."[8]

The statute adopted in January 1786 is one of the most important bills the General Assembly ever enacted. The law transformed religious beliefs and institutions in Virginia into purely private and personal matters, and it knocked the legal props out from under the established Church of England. The explanatory opening clause is an eloquent assertion of the importance of religious and intellectual freedom: "Almighty God hath created the mind free," it began, "that all attempts to influence it by temporal punishments or burthens, or by civil incapacitations tend only to beget habits of hypocrisy and meanness, and are a departure from the plan of the holy author of our religion, who being Lord, both of body and mind yet chose not to propagate it by coercions . . . that TRUTH is great, and will prevail if left to herself, that she is the proper and sufficient antagonist to error, and has nothing to fear from the conflict, unless by human interposition disarmed of her natural weapons free argument and debate, errors ceasing to be dangerous when it is permitted freely to contradict them." The law declared "that no man shall be compelled to frequent or support any religious worship, place, or ministry whatsoever, nor shall be enforced, restrained, molested, or burthened in his body or goods, nor shall otherwise suffer on account of his religious opinions or belief, but

The original, enrolled parchment of the 1786 An Act for Establishing Religious Freedom has been in the archives of Virginia since its passage.

that all men shall be free to profess, and by argument to maintain, their opinions in matters of RELIGION, and that the same shall in no wise diminish, enlarge or affect their civil capacities." The statute declared, "the rights hereby asserted, are of the natural rights of mankind."[9]

The Speaker of the Senate of Virginia, whose signature on the bill along with that of the Speaker of the House of Delegates (Benjamin Harrison, a signer of the Declaration of Independence and a former governor) made it a law, was Archibald Cary, the man who had jailed and persecuted Baptist clergymen in Chesterfield County less than fifteen years earlier. Cary was the most famous antagonist of the Baptists during the years immediately prior to the American Revolution. It is ironic that his was one of the two signatures on the Act for Establishing Religious Freedom. (The clerks of the House and Senate also signed to authenticate it.) The few surviving letters from Cary do not disclose whether during the American Revolution he changed his opinions about Baptists or about whether the Church of England should remain the only official church in Virginia. Regardless of Cary's personal opinions, he had a constitutional duty and responsibility to sign and authenticate the official, enrolled bill, which made it a law.

Baptists thus prevailed in their campaign to disestablish the Church of England. They also helped create a new and more democratic political culture. Before that time individual people and groups in communities had often petitioned the assembly to pass laws of personal or local interest, such as moving the courthouse or establishing a new ferry, but Baptists enlisted thousands of people throughout Virginia in a concerted effort to change fundamentally important public policies. The Baptists' efforts on behalf of religious liberty and the gradual democratization of society and politics in Virginia went hand in hand. It may be a coincidence, but it may also be significant, that the first Jewish congregation to be established in Virginia was organized in Richmond just three years after the assembly adopted Jefferson's statute. Congregation Beth Shalome was one of the first six Jewish congregations in the United States. Catholics formed their first congregation in Virginia under the superintendence of a missionary priest in Alexandria in 1794, and within the next decade formed churches in Norfolk and Richmond.

The American Revolution altered life for nearly all Virginians. Even before independence thousands of men and women who might never before have taken part in politics read pamphlets and newspapers or debated the issues. Williamsburg and Norfolk were the only cities in Virginia where printers published newspapers, but Baltimore and Philadelphia papers circulated in the northern and western portions of Virginia. Newspapers and pamphlets got handed about in taverns and stores and on crowded courthouse lawns on court days. Many more people engaged in discussions about the momentous public issues than were able to subscribe to periodicals or even to read them. The rapid development of public support for Boston throughout Virginia in 1774 and 1775 indicates that a substantial portion of the white population was well informed and clearly understood the implications. Men and women joined the economic protest movement by refusing to purchase English goods and sometimes pressured their neighbors or family members to conform to the terms of the Continental Association.

Much else changed, too. It is possible, but not very probable, that a few property-owning widows or unmarried women may have voted for county tax commissioners in 1778 and for the three following years. Late in 1777 the General Assembly levied a tax on land and some items of personal property, to be collected in each of the succeeding six years. The law authorized "the freeholders and housekeepers of each county or corporation with this commonwealth" annually to elect tax commissioners to assess the value of the taxable property.[10] Richard Henry Lee thought that the inclusion of the words "and housekeepers" in the law extended the suffrage for that one purpose to unmarried and widowed women who were de facto heads of households, and perhaps also to male heads of households who owned less than the required minimum amount of land to vote for tax assessors.

We know what Lee thought from the published text of a letter (the original has long since disappeared) he wrote to his sister on March 17, 1778. Presuming that the text as first printed in an Alexandria newspaper in 1875 is correct, it indicates that Lee was responding to a complaint from his widowed sister, Hannah Lee Corbin. Her letter is lost, too, but she evidently believed that her property had been overvalued for taxation purposes and she may also have believed that, even more radically, she should not be taxed at all because she could not vote for members of the General Assembly. That violated the Revolution's principle of no taxation without representation.

Lee's published response has often been cited as evidence that Corbin insisted on the right to vote and that Lee agreed with her. Lee's reply, though, suggests that she may have asked for less and that he may have agreed to less. Lee wrote to his sister that under the 1777 law "commissioners are annually chosen by the freeholders and housekeepers, and in the choice of whom you have as legal a right to vote as any other person."[11] That is as far as he went in endorsing the right of women to vote, and his words disclose little about his beliefs and even less about her beliefs. No researcher has discovered any evidence that any women voted for tax commissioners before 1781, when the General Assembly changed the law and empowered county courts to appoint the commissioners.

Another widow, Ann Makemie Holden, of Accomack County on the Eastern Shore, may have gone further in 1787 when she deeded land to four male relatives who did not then own real estate and consequently could not vote. As enfranchised owners of the land she gave them, she required that they "Vote at the Annual Elections for the most Wise and Discreet men who have proved themselves real friends to the American Independance to represent the County of Accomack."[12] Holden died not long thereafter, and it is not clear from her words, as it might have become from her actions, whether she merely enfranchised four relatives or hoped through them to have four proxy votes in elections for members of the General Assembly.

White women supported the war effort in a variety of ways. In 1780 the wife of the commander-in-chief, Martha Dandridge Custis Washington, and the wife of the governor, Martha Wayles Skelton Jefferson, joined forces and inspired women from Alexandria to Williamsburg to raise thousands of dollars for the army through their churches and other community organizations. Other women wove homespun cloth as a substitute for boycotted or unavailable English textiles; they assisted with planting and harvesting crops in the absence of husbands-turned-soldiers; and they provided food and horses to fill army requisitions. Some women worked at the Westham Foundry in Richmond or the armory in Fredericksburg where they produced ammunition, and others attached themselves to military units and performed essential services such as washing, cooking, sewing, and nursing. One woman participated in actual combat. Anna Marie Lane, originally from New Hampshire, fought as a common soldier with her husband's unit at the Battle of Germantown, in Pennsylvania, in 1777 and was "disabled by a severe wound . . . from which she never recovered."[13] The General Assembly awarded her a pension as a disabled veteran nearly thirty years later, when she and her husband lived in Virginia, a pension exactly twice the value of the pension it awarded her husband, who was not wounded in battle.

The Revolution produced or hastened changes that were already taking place in Virginia. During the third quarter of the eighteenth century, for example, many large planters began to erect distilleries or produce cider on a large scale for sale to their neighbors. That began the process of transferring production of drink from women to men that had taken place in other colonies decades earlier. (George Washington, for example, erected a large distillery at Mount Vernon.) In the small new towns that appeared along the rivers and on the bay tavern keepers bought, manufactured, and sold drink in great quantities. Many of the tavern keepers were women even if their husbands were legal proprietors of the property and the tavern license. At some of those towns and also at the new country stores farther inland men sold alcoholic drinks to their customers, which created commercial markets for the male brewers and distillers who took advantage of that new market. The army's need for alcohol hastened the transfer of production from women in their individual households to large-scale commercial enterprises, which men owned and operated.

Beginning with the Revolution and continuing for several decades, the General Assembly gradually modified the state's court system. Until the final decades of the eighteenth century, county courts settled minor civil disputes and debt cases as well as tried enslaved people accused of crimes. All major criminal cases involving white people and all cases involving substantial amounts of money or property were tried at the Capitol. In the 1780s the assembly created district courts and appointed experienced attorneys to serve as judges. Those courts tried white people accused of crimes close to the residences of the parties involved, which allowed local juries rather than jury members recruited from the streets of Williamsburg or Richmond to hear and determine guilt and innocence. Except for minor local matters that justices of the peace continued to handle, local juries heard and decided all the important civil and criminal cases that arose in their communities. The assembly continued to make changes to the trial and appellate court systems all the way up to the Civil War. Studies of the state's courts reveal that those changes completed a professionalization of the administration of justice in Virginia that had been under way before the Revolution.

The War for Independence

At some times during the Revolutionary War as many as five to seven thousand Virginia men served in the Continental Army, and thousands more militiamen were in the field for brief service on several occasions. State legislatures had responsibility for recruiting men to serve in the Continental Army. Congress issued commissions to the officers, but the states paid and equipped the soldiers and hoped that Congress would later reimburse the state treasuries. It is likely that only a small proportion of Virginia soldiers served for the entire duration of the war. Men enlisted in the Continental Army for one- or two- or three-year terms depending on which of the many Virginia recruitment acts was in effect when they enlisted. For much of the war, in spite of the enthusiasm with which the initial volunteers had joined the army, the state had difficulty filling its quota of troops. The state offered bounties in the form of grants of western land where soldiers might settle after the war. Many veterans sold their bounty warrants for cash.

The enlistment and conscription acts met resistance or provoked complaints from the very beginning. That revealed that opposition to the war existed in many places or that some Virginians believed recruitment was done unfairly. As early as the first months of 1776 James Cleveland organized Loudoun County tenant farmers who threatened to withhold their rents until the revolutionary government met their demand that soldiers and officers all be paid the same salary. Under the original recruitment act colonels received 25 shillings per day and lieutenant colonels half that amount; majors received 10 shillings, captains 6, and lieutenants 4; but private soldiers received a mere 1 shilling and 4 pence, or a little more than 5 percent of what a colonel received and 22 percent of what a lieutenant received. Cleveland declared, "there is no inducement for a poor man to Fight, for he has nothing to defend."[14]

A few months later and more than 150 miles away more than two hundred men in Lunenburg County objected to the first recruitment act that allowed plantation overseers an exemption from service. "From this indulgence," they complained, "many persons are become Overseers that Otherways wou'd not, on purpose to Secure themselves from Fighting in defence of their Country as well as their own property . . . we look upon it to be extremly hard" that overseers could escape military service while other men might return from patriotic and dangerous military service to find their "Wives & Children dispers'd up & down the Country abeging, or at home aSlaving, and at the same time quite unable to help themselves to the Necessaries of life while the Overseers are aliving in ease & Affluence at the Expense of their Employers."[15]

The General Assembly received numerous such complaints throughout the war. Reluctance to enlist and opposition to conscription forced the General Assembly to offer ever-larger bounties during the war. By the autumn of 1780 discontent was widespread, and the state's legislators were almost out of ideas for encouraging recruitment. The House of Delegates even went so far as to give preliminary approval to a bill that would have required owners of a large number of enslaved people to provide one in every twenty to the state to be awarded to each new soldier who enlisted for the duration of the war. Members of the General Assembly who proposed the bill believed that wealthy planters were not bearing their part of the burden. The legislature did not pass the measure, which if enacted would have spread ownership of slaves to a larger number of Virginia farmers, but that the delegates even considered such a radical idea was a measure of the difficulty recruitment posed as the war dragged on and on without evident progress toward conclusion.

In 1780 in the vicinity of the state's lead mines in what became Wythe County—John Chiswell's old mine, where the Second Virginia regiment under command of Colonel William Byrd (1728–1777) had been stationed during the French and Indian War—British agents provoked an insurrection of Indians, loyalists, striking miners, and some loyalists' slaves who had been sent west to work in the mines. Several high-ranking militia officers who had charge of the mines put down the uprising so that the vital production of lead could be resumed. The officers rounded up suspects, conducted perfunctory military trials, and punished men at the whipping post or turned them over to angry mobs that plundered or seized their property. Two years later the General Assembly retroactively legitimized the actions of the officers and the mob actions. One of the militia colonels in charge was Charles Lynch. His leadership in the episode was the origin of the phrase "lynch law," which at first meant the extralegal punishment of people suspected of misdeeds.

Some Virginians who remained loyal to the king stayed in Virginia, sat out the war, and tried to avoid attracting attention to themselves. Members of several notable planter families, among them some Corbins, Byrds, and Wormeleys, who had been high-ranking officials in the royal government before the war, did just that. Ralph Wormeley, who had been a member of the Council of State, was arrested and detained early in the war. The state also arrested some very vocal opponents of independence and later confiscated their property along with much of the property of Virginians who left and returned to England or fought for the king.

When men went to war on either side, women remained home to tend the farm, mind the shop, raise the children, and perhaps oversee the work of hired or enslaved laborers. Men died of disease or were killed in battle, which left widows and orphaned children in difficult circumstances. Often lacking resources of their own or family members able to assist them they appealed to the General Assembly for relief or compensation. After John Hodges joined the army, his widow Martha informed the assembly in 1777, "he caught a cold that brought on a disorder which occasiond his death, leaving a Waggon & Team which is the principle support of your Petitioner & her children." But army officers twice commandeered the wagon and team, one of them damaged the wagon, and they compensated her at a much lower rate than the twenty shillings (one pound) per day at which she had been earning money with the wagon since her husband went away to fight and die for the country's independence. As Martha Hodges informed the legislators, she "Humbly concieves her Country to be justly indebted to her the Balance of £13.10.4."[16] Records do not indicate whether she received any or all of the compensation she believed she deserved and that she and her children definitely needed. She and they were among hundreds of other Virginians whose lives the war permanently altered.

Several thousand Virginia soldiers, most of whom were white men, fought in the Continental Army and took part in almost every major engagement. One of the most notable Virginia achievements was the expedition of militiamen George Rogers Clark led in the summer of 1778 to capture frontier outposts north of the Ohio River, which gave the United States military control of the whole territory east of the Mississippi River, north of Ohio River, and south of the Great Lakes, all of which were part of Virginia according to the royal charter of 1609. Colonel William Campbell, of Washington County, commanded militiamen from several Virginia counties and the Carolinas who won a major victory over the British at King's Mountain, South Carolina, on October 7, 1780.

Except for occasional coastal raids and fighting between loyalists and patriots at the state's lead mines little serious fighting occurred in Virginia until late in 1780. British armies under Generals Charles Cornwallis, William Phil-

lips, and Benedict Arnold twice swept through eastern Virginia the following year and destroyed supplies at Gosport near Portsmouth and threatened
Richmond. The General Assembly had moved the capital from Williamsburg
to Richmond in 1780 because Richmond was closer to the center of the state's
population and believed to be less vulnerable to the enemy. In 1781, though,
both Arnold and Lieutenant Colonel Banastre Tarleton reached Richmond.
They scattered the state's governing officials and burned part of the city as
well as military stores at Petersburg and Point of Fork. In one of those raids
almost all the archival records of the colony's executive department were lost
or destroyed and a large portion of the valuable library of the Council of State.

Benedict Arnold's army briefly occupied the Byrd family mansion, Westover, and plundered it of many valuable items. Mary Willing Byrd was head
of the household then. She was the widow of the third William Byrd who
had commanded a Virginia regiment during the French and Indian War but
remained loyal to the king in 1776. She was also the stepmother of several men
who remained loyal to the king and a relative of Arnold by marriage. Some
people therefore suspected her of aiding the enemy. In an impassioned appeal to Governor Thomas Jefferson she wrote, "no action of my life has been
inconsistent with the character of a virtuous American.... All my friends and
connexions are in America; my whole property is here—could I wish ill to
everything I have an interest in?"[17] Byrd succeeded in convincing the governor
of her patriotism and salvaged the remainder of the family's estate.

In the spring of 1781 Tarleton pursued the General Assembly as far west as
Charlottesville. Governor Thomas Jefferson barely escaped capture. His term
expired at that time, and because the assembly had not elected a new governor, the state was left for several days without any executive authority when it
needed an active commander-in-chief. The assembly retreated farther west, to
Staunton, but even then the British captured a few legislators in Charlottesville, including Daniel Boone who represented Fayette County in far western
Virginia.

Continental troops under the command of the General Marie Joseph Paul
Yves Roch Gilbert du Motier, Marquis de Lafayette, then forced Cornwallis
toward the Chesapeake Bay, and in July the British took up defensive positions near Yorktown. A French fleet under the command of Admiral Fran-
çois Joseph Paul de Grasse, comte de Grasse-Tilly, turned back a British fleet
at the Battle of the Capes on September 5, 1781, to prevent the British from
supplying or evacuating Cornwallis's force. Washington and the Continental Army, aided by the French troops of General Jean Baptiste Donatien de
Vimeur, comte de Rochambeau, marched from New England to Virginia and
forced Cornwallis to surrender his army on October 19, 1781. The Peace of
Paris between the Great Britain and the United States and its allies, France
and Spain, formally ended the war in 1783.

Liberty and Slavery

The language of the Declaration of Independence—that all men were created equal, that all were entitled to life, liberty, and the pursuit of happiness—did not produce freedom for the many enslaved Virginians. Nevertheless, during the Revolution and the following two decades the General Assembly passed laws to make it easier for owners of slaves to free them. The number of Virginians who gained their freedom during that period is not known. A few planters freed large numbers of slaves. Robert Carter, of Westmoreland County, freed more than five hundred men, women, and children in 1791 after he converted to evangelical Christianity and joined the Baptist Church. When George Washington wrote his will later in the decade he directed that his slaves be freed after his widow's death. Washington hoped, in vain as it turned out, that other Americans would follow his example. Under the terms of the 1796 will of Richard Randolph, his widow provided about 350 acres of land for about ninety of the enslaved men, women, and children he freed. For several generations those families and their descendants lived in freedom at the place they called Israel Hill, near Farmville. Most emancipations, however, probably involved one or two enslaved people or small groups.

Some African Virginians who served in the army during the war received the liberty for which they had fought. The most famous of them was "James (a slave belonging to Will: Armistead)." In 1786 he petitioned the General Assembly for his freedom based on his wartime service. He recalled that "perswaded of the just right which all mankind have to Freedom, notwithstanding his own state of bondage, with an honest desire to serve this Country in its defence thereof, did, during the ravages of Lord Cornwallis thro' this state, by the permission of his Master, enter into the service of the Marquiss Lafeyette: That during the time of his serving the Marquiss he often at the peril of his life found means to frequent the British Camp; by which means he kept open a channel of the most useful communications to the army of the state: That at different times your petitioner conveyed inclosures, from the Marquiss into the Enemies lines, of the most secret & important kind; the possession of which if discovered on him would have most certainly endangered the life of your petitioner: That he undertook & performed all commands with chearfulness & fidelity, in Opposition to the persuasion & example of many thousands of his unfortunate condition."[18] With his petition he submitted an affidavit from General Lafayette. In January 1787 the General Assembly passed a special law to free James, who then adopted the name James Lafayette.

Some African Americans fought for the king. In the autumn of 1775 Dunmore recruited a regiment of Virginia loyalists, many of whom never returned to Virginia or returned only long after the war. He also recruited a regiment

James Lafayette

of black Virginians—called Lord Dunmore's Ethiopian Corps—who joined him after his November 1775 proclamation that offered freedom to enslaved men who joined the British. More black Virginians received their freedom by fighting for the king against the United States than by fighting for the independence of the new United States. Most later settled in New Brunswick in Canada or chose to try life in Africa. They were proud of their service to the king and pleased to have become free.

Peter Anderson, formerly of Norfolk, related in a petition to the War Office in London about 1783 that he had "serv'd under Capt. John Fordyce in the 24 Regiment of Grenideers Listed under Lord Dunmore & was Always ready & willing when call'd for & was at the Battle at the great Bridge in Virginea when 350 Grenideers & 100 Blacks fought 1600 Americans where he was taken & in great Danger of His Life when he got out of the Garrett Window & Lost his all 4 Beds & Furniture 20 Head of Hogs 4 Chests of Cloaths he was six Months in Prison & six Months in the Woods" before he was able to return to the king's army. "I am A free Man," he boasted, "& willing to serve His Majesty again But having Nothing to Subsist on he hopes your Honor's will allow Him some Support His Age is 38 Years."[19] Records leave it unclear what, if any, compensation Anderson received.

In 1787 Shadrack Furman also submitted a petition to the British government. Because he could not write he dictated his petition and signed it with his mark. Furman declared that he was "a free black man and lived in Acamack County in America at the Commencement of the late Troubles in very good Circumstances and on Account of his Attachment to the British Government rendered himself inimical to the rebels. That the rebels getting Information of his entertaining some of the British Troops in his House and otherwise supplying them with provisions when they first came into Virginia, they on the first of January 1781 burnt destroyed or carried away" almost £150 worth of his property.

Furman's sufferings had scarcely begun. "Shortly afterwards," he continued, "in order to extort Intelligence from petitioner respecting the British Troops he was Seized by the rebels and after dangerously wounding him in divers parts, the Marks of which pet^r can still shew, they stripped tied up and gave him 500 Lashes and then left him almost dead in the Field by reason of which your Honors petitioner lost his Eye Sight, and the use of one of his Legs by a stroke of an Axe they gave him, and his Health is otherwise so much impaired from the wounds in his Head received from them, that he is sometimes bereft of reason."

But that was not all: "That soon after the aforesaid ill Treatment & as soon as your pet^r got a little strength and dreading further ill usage from the Rebels pet^r went on Board of a privateer," a private ship fitted out to act as a warship, which Furman boarded at Tangier Island in Chesapeake Bay. Furman "Joined the British army and . . . rendered himself as useful as possible until his Situation from the aforesaid ill Treatment rendered it necessary to send him to Head Quarters under the Care of the General Doctors." Furman and his wife eventually went to England to seek compensation for his lost property and relief to support themselves. Reduced, as he told authorities, "from a comfortable Situation in Life . . . to the lower Ebb of poverty and Distress on account of his Loyalty and Attachmt. to His majesty," he asked "that some provision or support may be Granted to your pet^r and wife who are now entirely depending on the Charity of the public having neither Friends Credit or Money."[20] It is also unclear what Furman and his wife received in compensation or relief.

Unfortunately, hundreds of men, women, and children died in the attempt to join the British or perished in overcrowded camps or ships after they reached the British lines. It is an irony of history that British naval officers dumped into Chesapeake Bay bodies of African Americans who died aboard their ships in search of freedom, much as officers of slave-trading ships dumped the bodies of African natives into shark-infested waters of the Atlantic Ocean en route to lifetime slavery in the New World.

Twenty years after the first men tried to join Dunmore the sad evidences of their fate could still be seen. In 1796 a visitor to the Elizabeth River near Norfolk wrote, "Many Waggon loads of the bones of Men women and Children, stripped of the flesh by Vultures and Hawks which abound here, covered the sand for a most considerable length. . . . The hopes of getting on board the English fleet collected them at the mouth of the Chesapeak bay, they were left behind in thousands and perished. Children died sucking the breasts of their dead mothers, and Women feeding upon the corpses of their starved children. The remnants of decaying rags still point to the skeletons of many of these miserable victims."[21]

After the War

Some of the most famous leaders of the American Revolution were Virginians. George Washington commanded the Continental Army until he resigned in December 1783, and other Virginians, such as Colonel George Rogers Clark and Colonel Henry "Light Horse Harry" Lee, had distinguished careers in the field. Among the most able Virginia delegates to Congress during and after the war were Thomas Jefferson, Richard Henry Lee, and James Madison. Other Virginians, including William Lee and Arthur Lee, undertook diplomatic missions to Europe, and young men with bright and long futures, such as John Marshall and James Monroe, entered public service as army officers and moved into law and politics during and after the war. The practical political skill those and other Virginia leaders displayed on the national stage was in part a consequence of the extraordinary school of statecraft the institutions of government had become in Virginia by the time the Revolution began.

In the 1780s the General Assembly asked Thomas Jefferson, then United States minister to France, to do several things. One was to commission a statue of George Washington for the new state Capitol in Richmond. Jefferson contracted with the greatest sculptor of the age, Jean-Antoine Houdon, to carve a full-length marble statue of Washington, whom many people regarded as the greatest man of the age. Houdon traveled to Virginia to make a plaster cast of Washington's face in order to render the statue lifelike. It has stood in the

Jean Antoine-Houdon, *George Washington*

Lawrence Sully, *A South West View of the Capitol at Richmond Virginia,* engraving by Alexander Lawson, published in *Virginia & North Carolina Almanack* (Petersburg, 1802)

state capital since the 1790s. Jefferson also had Houdon execute two marble busts of Lafayette, one of which the state government presented to France to commemorate the French general's valuable assistance in the war for independence. The other copy is in the Capitol in Richmond. The General Assembly also made Lafayette a naturalized citizen of Virginia.

The General Assembly also asked Jefferson to prepare a design for the new state Capitol building. Jefferson chose as his inspiration the Maison Carrée, in Nimes, France. He believed that the Roman temple was generally regarded as the best example of architecture from the ancient world, and the early Roman republic was one of the earliest examples of the republican form of government. Jefferson hoped that introducing the classical architectural example of the ancient Romans to the new United States would inspire his countrymen to improve the quality of public buildings. The new Capitol did, indeed, influence public architecture in the United States. Columned porticoes on classic temple designs became commonplace as courthouses and statehouses and later as post offices and other public buildings.

9

VIRGINIANS AND THE NEW NATION

E ARLY IN THE 1770S Daniel Boone led the first large parties of settlers along the Wilderness Road through Cumberland Gap into Kentucky. The westward movement of white Virginians continued throughout the Revolutionary War and increased after the war. Between 1776 and 1792 the General Assembly created ten counties west of the Big Sandy River. That river became part of the eastern boundary of Kentucky when the new state of that name, encompassing more than 40,000 square miles, entered the Union as the fifteenth state in 1792.

The passage of white Americans, some of whom took their enslaved black laborers with them, into the west led to conflicts between settlers and Indian residents of the area. The Cherokee and other southern tribes had never agreed that Virginians could settle the land south of the Ohio River and resisted the migration and sometimes attacked the western settlements. In the region of western North Carolina that became eastern Tennessee one Indian resisted so effectively early in the 1790s that government officials in Richmond singled him out for death. His name appears in government documents as Captain Benge, Bench, Benje, and Benjie. In April 1794 a Virginia militia lieutenant killed and scalped him. The lieutenant's commanding officer sent the scalp to Richmond as proof that Benge was dead and recommended that the General Assembly reward the lieutenant with a fancy new rifle. Scalping of Indians was probably not common, but from time to time during the seventeenth and eighteenth centuries frontier men had sent Indian scalps to Jamestown, Williamsburg, or Richmond in exactly the same way men presented crow skins or wolf ears to county courts to collect bounties for destroying what they regarded as harmful animals. Captain Benge's life became legendary in southwestern Virginia, and reports persisted as late as the 1920s that his scalp was still on display in the state Capitol in Richmond. It cannot now be found.

The Constitution and Bill of Rights

During the war for independence Congress drafted the Articles of Confederation, a constitution that delegated a few specific powers to Congress and placed virtually no restrictions on the states. The states did not ratify the articles until 1781 because several states without claims to large tracts of western land first insisted that residents of all states share the revenue to be derived from the sale and settlement of the west and have equal access to land there. Virginia deeded its land north of the Ohio River to the nation. In the Ordinance of 1785, which Thomas Jefferson drafted, Congress provided that the territory be surveyed into one-square-mile sections, or townships. Two years later Congress passed the Northwest Ordinance, which provided for the administration of the northwestern territory, established procedures for the formation of new states, and prohibited the introduction of slavery there.

In the years immediately after the end of the war the Articles of Confederation appeared to be inadequate in the face of the problems that confronted the new nation. The new government was too weak to force the British to evacuate posts in the Ohio River Valley or to guarantee westerners commercial access to the Mississippi River. Congress also lacked authority to enforce the Treaty of Paris provisions that authorized British merchants to collect debts many Americans, including a large number of Virginians, had contracted with British mercantile firms prior to the Revolution. Laws in some states blocked access to the courts to agents of British creditors, and the consequence was prolonged litigation and some stagnation of commerce.

Congress also had its own financial problems. It had a national war debt to pay off and no authority to raise taxes. Congress could only request state legislatures to provide revenue to the national treasury but could not require them to pay. Some state governments either refused or were unable to contribute their quotas of money to the support of the national government, which ruined the national credit. Many political leaders believed that state regulation of commerce impeded the development of a robust national economy, and some feared that state laws for the relief of debtors hampered economic progress and further injured the public credit.

Virginia men took the lead in the movement to strengthen the national government. In 1786 the General Assembly called a conference to meet in Annapolis to discuss commercial matters with Maryland. That gathering in turn recommended that a national convention meet in Philadelphia in the summer of 1787. George Washington, who was elected president of the convention, headed Virginia's distinguished delegation, which included Governor Edmund Randolph, George Wythe, George Mason, James Madison, James McClurg, and John Blair. Wythe and McClurg left the convention early and took little part in the deliberations. Randolph presented the Virginia Plan for a new central government, which was largely the work of Madison and became the basis of the convention's debate and the general outline of the Constitution's structure.

The stronger national government the convention proposed to the states in 1787 awakened fears of centralization among many patriots of the revolutionary generation who believed that it imposed too many restraints on democracy in the states. Patrick Henry and George Mason led opposition to ratification of the Constitution in Virginia. During debates at the ratification convention in Richmond in June 1788 delegates from the western counties worried that the Constitution might permit eastern states to bargain away the rights of westerners to use the Mississippi River and the seaport of New Orleans in order to gain concessions of value to New England merchants and commercial fishermen. Much of the convention debate focused on the enlarged powers the Constitution granted to Congress and the provisions that placed limits on the powers of state governments. Skeptics also viewed with suspicion the provision for an independent judiciary and a powerful chief executive. Both renewed fears of excessive governmental power that had brought on the Revolution.

George Mason criticized the document, as he had in Philadelphia, because it lacked a bill of rights. Randolph, like Mason, had refused to sign the Constitution when the convention adopted it in Philadelphia and, until shortly before the Virginia ratification convention met, favored holding a second national convention to revise it before it was ratified. At the opening of the Virginia convention, though, Randolph announced his support for ratification. Members of the Virginia Convention searchingly examined the document during nearly a month of debate and on June 25, 1788, voted 89 to 79 to ratify it. Two days later the convention proposed a long list of amendments to protect individual rights and reduce the power of the new national government.

Shortly before the delegates voted to ratify the constitution Patrick Henry announced, "If I shall be in the minority, I shall have those painful sensations, which arise from a conviction of being overpowered in a good cause. Yet I will be a peaceable citizen!" He concluded, "I shall therefore patiently wait in expectation of seeing that Government changed so as to be compatible with the safety, liberty and happiness of the people."[1] After the convention adjourned Mason summoned a meeting of opponents of the Constitution to make plans for the future. Henry declined to take part, and former governor Benjamin Harrison, a signer of the Declaration of Independence, got up and left the meeting when he heard that Mason wanted to organize opposition to the new constitution. Having lost, Harrison explained, they should "submit as good citizens, until those destructive consequences to their liberty should appear, which the minority apprehended, in which however he hoped they would be mistaken."[2] The acquiesce of Henry and Harrison in the will of the elected majority expressed the essence of the national commitment to representative government men had fought to preserve during the Revolutionary War.

Madison won election to the House of Representatives of the First Congress, which met in the spring of 1789. There he drafted amendments in the form of a bill of rights to protect Americans from possible abuses of power by the new federal government. He drew on the Virginia Declaration of Rights and included provisions several state ratification conventions had suggested, including those the Virginia Convention had proposed. The amendments Congress submitted to the states for ratification on September 25, 1789, did not include any changes to weaken the authority of Congress or of the national government. Ratification of the Bill of Rights, which action by the General Assembly of Virginia completed on December 15, 1791, put the handiwork of Virginia's statesmen into the Constitution of the United States. The Bill of Rights quieted the fears of some opponents of the Constitution, but it did not reconcile everybody to the new form of government because it did not significantly weaken the taxing power of Congress or remedy what some men like Mason continued to believe were fundamental flaws in its structure.

James Madison mastered the art of legislative government during his service in the House of Delegates and in the Continental Congress during the Revolutionary War. During four terms in the House of Representatives while George Washington was president, Madison became the country's first great legislative leader. The effective style of representative government that had matured in the colony of Virginia provided the basic model for both the structure of the new national government and the manner in which it operated under the Constitution.

Virginia Politics in the New Nation

Virginia was the largest and most populous state in the new United States. The first national census, taken in 1790, disclosed that Virginia had 821,287 residents, of whom 315,057 were enslaved. It had the largest number of white people, the largest number of free black people, and the largest number of enslaved people in the country. The large size and population of Virginia and the prominent role Virginia's statesmen played in the new nation made it one of the most influential states. Virginian George Washington served two terms as the first president of the United States, from 1789 to 1797. Thomas Jefferson was secretary of state from 1790 to the end of 1793, and Edmund Randolph was attorney general from 1790 until he succeeded Jefferson as secretary of state from January 1794 to August 1795.

Early in the 1790s Congress decided to locate the new national capital

The original parchment copy of the Bill of Rights Congress sent to Virginia for ratification. It bears the authenticating signatures of the clerks of the House of Representatives and the Senate as well as the signature of Frederick Augustus Conrad Muhlenberg, Speaker of the House, and John Adams, vice president of the United States and president of the Senate.

city on the banks of the Potomac River. Washington was enthusiastic about placing the capital near his own residence at Mount Vernon. He had become deeply engaged in creating a company to construct a canal around the falls of the Potomac to link the western country to the sea via that river. Maryland and Virginia ceded to the United States land to be known as the District of

Columbia, to which the government offices moved early in 1800. The Virginia portion of the district, called Alexandria County, became part of Virginia again in 1846. In 1920 the General Assembly renamed it Arlington County.

Jefferson and Madison organized the first national political party, or faction, initially known as the Anti-Federalist and later as the Republican or Jeffersonian Republican Party. They opposed policies Secretary of the Treasury Alexander Hamilton proposed early in the 1790s, and that President Washington endorsed, for the federal government to pay off the war debts of the states and create a national bank to assist in the collection of revenue and financing the debt. People who were in general agreement with Hamilton came to be called Federalists. Virginia state politics became entangled in that national politics at an early date. In December 1792 the twenty Virginia members of the electoral college met in Richmond to vote for president and vice president. All of them voted to reelect President George Washington as anticipated. According to a story that later reached Vice President John Adams, the electors then "held debates and made Phillippicks" and sang the French revolutionary anthem "Marseilles." Six electors who had been expected to vote for Adams for vice president changed their minds and voted with the other fourteen men for Governor George Clinton, of New York, who was more sympathetic than Adams to the French Revolution and less sympathetic to the British.[3]

Two years later Washington called out militia to put down the Whiskey Rebellion in western Pennsylvania, where men refused to pay a new federal tax on the distillation of alcohol. Militia units from Virginia went into the field under the command of Governor Henry "Light Horse Harry" Lee. The General Assembly, which had a majority of Republicans, then replaced the absent Federalist governor with a Republican, Robert Brooke. The Whiskey Rebellion was the first serious challenge to the authority of the new federal government, and it spilled over into the western regions of Virginia and other states too. By the time Washington voluntarily retired from the presidency in March 1797 the Constitution and the new federal government were firmly established and widely regarded as legitimate, but new issues and a new national political landscape meant that Virginia state politics functioned in a new world of American partisan politics.

In 1798 the threat of war with France prompted Congress to pass the Alien and Sedition Acts to curtail criticism of the government and allow the president to deport undesirable foreigners. Alarmed at the potential threat to civil liberties the acts presented, Jefferson and Madison attempted to mobilize national public opinion by means of similar resolutions they drafted and the legislatures of Kentucky and Virginia adopted. Jefferson's Kentucky Resolutions declared that a state could obstruct the enforcement of an act of Congress the state government regarded as unconstitutional. That appeared to threaten the continued existence of government under the new Constitution. No other state legislature endorsed the Kentucky Resolutions or even the less emphatic Virginia Resolutions Madison drafted, which did not go so far as to insist that a state government could nullify enforcement of unconstitutional federal laws. In the 1790s no court or authority has yet determined how to establish whether a law was unconstitutional or how to make it inoperative.

The Jeffersonian Republicans then mounted an election campaign in 1800 that resulted in the defeat of many Federalist members of Congress and of President John Adams when he ran for reelection. Jefferson and vice presidential candidate Aaron Burr tied for the most electoral votes. The House of Representatives after a long series of ballots eventually broke the tie and selected Jefferson as the nation's third president. He took office for the first of two consecutive four-year terms on March 4, 1801. That peaceful change of principal government officers as the result of an election and without resistance from the defeated candidate was another triumph for the new Constitution and for practical representative government.

Virginia's political leaders differed among themselves during the decades after ratification of the Constitution about how properly to interpret it. The influence and example of men like Patrick Henry and George Mason, who feared the potential of a powerful national government to sacrifice local and state interests for regional or national goals, exercised a strong influence in Virginia. Many men who had supported ratification of the Constitution, including Madison and Jefferson, shared some of the same apprehensions after they became alarmed at Hamilton's plans for a powerful and vigorous federal government. They all believed that the language of the Constitution should be very strictly interpreted and that the federal government should not exercise any responsibilities the Constitution did not specifically grant to it.

Jefferson's distant relative John Randolph of Roanoke emerged early in the nineteenth century as one of the firmest supporters of that point of view in Congress. He even became a critic of Jefferson and Madison because he believed that they adopted a too lenient attitude on the question of strict application of the Constitution and leaned in favor of allowing too much influence to the national government. Randolph and other strict constructionist, states' rights men became known as Tertium Quids, third things who were neither Federalists nor Jeffersonian Republicans.

The most powerful early statements of their philosophy came from the pen of John Taylor, known as John Taylor of Caroline because he lived in Caroline County, to distinguish him from other Virginians of the same name who lived elsewhere. Taylor developed the intellectual justification for states' rights, limited government, and strict, literal interpretation of the language of the Constitution. His influential *Defence of the Measures of the Administration of Thomas Jefferson,* published in 1804, and his even more important *Construction Construed, and Constitutions Vindicated,* published in 1820, established him as one of the foremost thinkers in the emerging states' rights tradition. Taylor was also a keen student of southern agriculture. His collection of newspaper essays on agricultural reform and political economy appeared in book form in 1813 with the title *Arator; Being a Series of Agricultural Essays, Practical and Political, in Sixty-one Numbers.* It was reprinted in an enlarged edition several times.

Taylor's opposition to a strong national government was based in large part on his opposition to the emerging national economy that relied on banks, credit, and paper money and received stimulation from government activities, such as funding the national debt through creation of a national bank, support of an army and navy, and building roads. He stated his objections to all of them in his last major publication, *Tyranny Unmasked,* in 1824. In all his writings Taylor described the nation's emerging political economy as permitting an immoral collusion of government and financiers that would inevitably destroy the agricultural republic of which he was a prominent member in Virginia.

Taylor and many other Virginians condemned innovative actions of the federal government and believed that government intervention in the lives of people to be actually or potentially tyrannical. At the same time, though, the state government in Virginia under its Constitution of 1776, which imposed almost no limitations on the state's government or the General Assembly, was deeply engaged in guiding and managing the economic life of the state and the people in its communities. For example, in 1779 the General Assembly passed the first state laws to incorporate new cities and towns. Prior to the American Revolution only the king or the king's deputy, the royal governor or lieutenant governor, could issue charters to incorporate towns or cities or educational institutions, such as the College of William and Mary. When assembly members incorporated the towns of Alexandria and Winchester in 1779 they could point to no clause in the state constitution that granted the assembly that authority. The assembly, instead, acted as the sovereign governing power in Virginia. Each new town received a charter the assembly enacted as a state law. The assembly incorporated the towns of Fredericksburg and Richmond in 1782, Petersburg in 1784, Lynchburg in 1786, and Charlottesville and Staunton in 1801. The assembly also chartered Hampden-Sydney College in 1783. After the Revolution, promoters of every plan for a commercial venture such as a canal, toll road, ferry, institution of higher learning, bank, or eleemosynary institution had to apply to the General Assembly for a special act of incorporation. In granting or denying those applications the assembly played an important part in guiding the future development of the state — not unlike the role Hamilton had proposed the federal government play.

The state government regularly intervened in and regulated local and personal matters that affected everybody in Virginia. In 1796, to select a legislative session at random, the General Assembly passed a law to impose limits on descendants of the Fairfax family who inherited the Northern Neck Proprietary, and it passed separate acts concerning the inherited land or property of two other people. It passed separate laws to allow a Lutheran congregation in Shenandoah County to hold a lottery to raise money to complete construction of a new church, and additional lotteries to permit the town of Norfolk to raise money to pave its streets, to aid in rebuilding houses lost in a Lynchburg fire, to erect a new bridge in Petersburg, to pay for construction of a new building for the New London Academy, to clear obstructions from the Roanoke River, to erect a new house on the glebe land in Gloucester County, and to repair the road between Winchester and Romney. The assembly passed a state law that altered the date for the meeting of the court of hustings in Alexandria, another to allow the town to tax its residents for paving the streets, and another to annex a small piece of property to the town. It passed an act to allow trustees in five towns to permit lot owners an additional period of time in which to construct buildings before the lots reverted to the town for resale, and another act to provide for the replacement of dead or departed trustees of one town who had been appointed by name in previous statutes. The assembly passed two other laws to regulate the sale of lots in two other towns. It passed a law to add part of Bath County to Pendleton County, another to carve Brooke County out of Ohio County, and another to alter the boundary line between Botetourt and Montgomery Counties. It passed a law to create a district court to serve three counties. It passed separate laws to alter regular monthly court days in Southampton, Powhatan, Mecklenburg, Frederick, and Campbell Counties and in the city of Williamsburg, the town of Winchester, and the borough of Norfolk. It passed a law to create a town in Halifax County and another to create a town in Botetourt County. It passed a law to authorize the operation of fifteen new ferries in the state and another law to permit a sixteenth. It passed an act to allow eighteen named counties to offer bounties for the killing of squirrels or crows. It passed a law to authorize investors to cut a canal through the Dismal Swamp, a law to allow the Potomac Company to purchase slaves to improve the navigation of that river, and three other acts to facilitate removal of obstructions to navigation of the Appomattox River, Quantico Creek, and Pigg River. It passed two laws to provide for repairing specific sections of public road. It passed an act to provide for compensating people for tobacco lost when a public warehouse burned. It chartered Liberty Hall Academy (a Rockbridge County school that grew into Washington and Lee University), and it passed two laws to create a charity school in Fredericksburg and a law to establish a library company in Loudoun County. The assembly passed a law to grant citizenship to three named men, and another law to keep Mary Boush on the role of state pensioners. The General Assembly of Virginia micromanaged the state and its residents long before the invention of the word *micromanage*.

Second Great Awakening

The second Great Awakening began in Virginia late in the eighteenth century and continued well into the nineteenth. It was in many respects a continuation of the first awakening and produced some very visible changes in public behavior and expectations. The urgency participants in the awakening felt to save their souls and the souls of other people took many forms. After Methodists formally separated from the Church of England in the 1780s they held huge, protracted camp meetings at which preaching and baptism quickened the spirits of thousands of people. Members of many Protestant denominations attended the meetings, at which several clergymen sometimes took part. The sermons' emphasis on conversion and on moral reform, whether at camp meetings or in small congregations, discouraged gambling, dueling, drinking, theatrical performances, and other forms of popular entertainment evangelicals believed were inherently sinful or exercised a morally corrupting effect on people. They also frowned on such frivolities as fine dress and other ostentatious displays of wealth or personal pride. During that time white gentlemen, for example, adopted somber dark clothing in place of the fancier dress of the colonial gentry. Modesty in dress and behavior thereafter became one of the hallmarks of cultured society.

Religious leaders persuaded the General Assembly to outlaw dueling in 1810. The preamble of the law described dueling as "the result of ignorance and barbarism, justified neither by the precepts of morality nor by the dictates of reason."[4] The new law required all men to take an oath that they had never engaged in a duel before they could serve in any civil or military office. The law also declared that insulting language gentlemen regarded as a sufficient occasion for a duel should instead be prosecuted in a court of law. The statute could be interpreted both as a moral reform measure and as a repudiation of what upper-class gentlemen undoubtedly regarded as their own socially acceptable means of defending their honor from insult.

Religious beliefs had many influences on personal behavior and public policy. Beginning in the 1790s Baptists pressured the General Assembly to confiscate the glebe lands of the Episcopal Church, which inherited them from its colonial predecessor, the Church of England. The colonial government had provided glebes, which usually consisted of a house and small plantation, to parishes and ministers at public expense for the support of the minister.

Beginning in the 1790s and continuing for about three decades, Baptists and other men persuaded the General Assembly to confiscate glebes when parish pulpits became vacant and to transfer the property to the county overseers of the poor, who inherited the colonial church's responsibility to care for orphans and paupers. The confiscation of the glebes reveals how deep and long-lasting was the resentment Baptists felt about the behavior of the Church of England before the Revolution. By the time of the confiscation of the glebes the Church of England had transformed itself into the Protestant Episcopal Church, a largely evangelical denomination.

Thomas Campbell and his son, Alexander Campbell, immigrated to western Pennsylvania early in the nineteenth century and then to northwestern Virginia. They were Presbyterians who soon affiliated with Baptists and led a revival movement during the 1810s and 1820s that formed the Disciples of Christ, one of the most successful Protestant denominations founded in the United States. From his church in Brooke County, where in 1840 he created Bethany College, the younger Campbell wrote and traveled constantly for decades and proselytized and made converts. His published works, including the periodicals *Christian Baptist* and its successor, the *Millennial Harbinger,* fill more than sixty volumes. The Campbellites, as the Disciples were often then known, was one of the fastest-growing evangelical denominations in the United States during the second quarter of the nineteenth century.

The 1786 Act for Establishing Religious Freedom allowed different denominations to flourish without hindrance in Virginia, but individual churches and the denominational organizations—diocese, presbytery, conference, convention—functioned under severe legal limitations. After the General Assembly by law briefly incorporated the Protestant Episcopal Church in the 1780s legislators refused to pass any other act that incorporated a denomination, a congregation, or a religious body. Lawmakers and judges interpreted Jefferson's statute very strictly to mean that the assembly could not grant independent legal existence to any religious institution or group. The unintended consequence was that churches, congregations, and denominations could not legally receive bequests, buy or sell church buildings, acquire land to enlarge cemeteries, or create and operate educational institutions, seminaries, or even societies to provide relief for the families of deceased or infirm elderly clergymen. Without legal authority to manage their own properties individual churches and church organizations often had to apply to the General Assembly for special laws that allowed trustees to act for them and accept bequests or buy or sell church buildings, and they often had to go into court to enforce their limited rights to their property.

Even though Jefferson's statute appeared to remove religious matters from the jurisdiction of the state—and it did allow a wide latitude for religious diversity—in fact the legislature and the courts frequently intervened in church matters at the request of individual congregations or groups of churches who required relief in their legally precarious situations. A general law enacted in 1842 eased the situation of the churches to allow them to create boards of trustees to manage their property and institutions, but the legislature enacted no special or general incorporation laws for churches during the nineteenth century. Virginia may have been the only state that did not afford religious congregations or denominations that measure of legal independence. In 1851 the third state constitutional convention inserted into the new constitution a prohibition against any incorporation of any religious body or society.

On the night of December 26, 1811, a theater in Richmond caught fire during the performance of a play, and seventy-two people died, including the recently elected governor, George William Smith. Part of the problem was that the doors through which people tried to escape opened inward, and in the push the frightened theatergoers could not open the doors. The fire and deaths produced a national debate about the morality of the theater as an institution. It should have, but did not, stimulate a national debate about safety in large public buildings. Leading members of Richmond's society did not turn against play-going as a consequence, but rather than rebuild the theater they united to commemorate the dead and erected a church on the site. They intended that Monumental Church serve both the Episcopalian and Presbyterian congregations in the city. The local Episcopal Church was in disrepair, and the Presbyterians had no church of their own, but after an initial period of sharing Monumental Church, the Presbyterians constructed their own church, and the old Henrico Parish Church was repaired and was renamed Saint John's Episcopal Church. Monumental Church became another Episcopal church with its own congregation. And within a short time residents of Richmond erected the first of several new theaters downtown.

Two of the principal clergymen in Richmond, Episcopalian John Buchanan and Presbyterian John D. Blair, were good friends who cooperated closely and preached on alternate Sundays in the Capitol or in the only church to which they occasionally had access. As in many other towns and cities in Virginia early in the nineteenth century Richmond also had several Baptist and Methodist congregations. In 1820 the population of Catholics in Virginia was large enough that the pope created the Diocese of Richmond to serve their needs. Protestants, Catholics, and Jews in Richmond offered people elsewhere in Virginia an example of religious diversity and generally peaceful toleration. Late in the 1810s, Presbyterian clergymen and lay leaders united in successful opposition to Thomas Jefferson's desire to appoint Thomas Cooper, a distinguished chemist and a Unitarian, to the faculty of the new University of Virginia. They believed that Cooper's religious beliefs disqualified him from educating the state's young men.

Monumental Church, Richmond

However much life for Virginia's residents resembled life for other Americans, nineteenth-century developments in the state took place within a distinctive Virginian context that in some ways mirrored the political debates about the proper roles of the state and national government. For example, family connections remained very important throughout Virginia. When domestic discord disrupted a white family, other family members and residents of the local community usually tried to act as mediators or provided support to men, women, and children whose lives were affected. Some marital conflicts divided families and their communities bitterly. If family and community efforts could not resolve differences during the decades between the beginning and the middle of the nineteenth century, members of broken families had to appeal to the General Assembly for a special law to divorce a husband and wife. That was a very public and often embarrassing process. Sally Campbell Preston McDowell, daughter of Virginia governor James McDowell, was one of the most prominent women who suffered through the private personal anguish and humiliating public scrutiny. She described the protracted process as the great catastrophe of her life.

The assembly was extremely reluctant to grant divorces except in instances of proved adultery or extraordinary physical abuse. Grounding its law and practice in the old ecclesiastical law of the Church of England, Virginia's legislators, lawyers, and judges prolonged well into the nineteenth century a set of values and legal processes that most of the other states abandoned soon after the Revolution. Virginia was one of the last states to permit applications for divorce to be handled entirely in the courts in order to keep family difficulties from being exposed in very public politics.

The War of 1812

Two events of 1807 focused attention on Virginia. During the spring and summer of that year former vice president Aaron Burr stood trial in Richmond for treason for allegedly attempting to separate the western states from the United States and join them to Spain. Chief Justice John Marshall presided over the proceedings. Before the conclusion of the trial, in which Burr was acquitted, the British man-of-war *Leopard* fired on and boarded an American navy ship, the *Chesapeake,* near the Virginia Capes. The British removed and impressed into the British navy several sailors who were serving on the *Chesapeake.* The episode did not lead directly to war, but President Thomas Jefferson and his successor, James Madison, who took office in March 1809, were preoccupied during the ensuing years with deteriorating relations with both Great Britain and France. The two European powers were at war with each other during the second series of Napoleonic Wars.

In June 1812 diplomacy failed and Congress declared war on Great Britain. The war was very unpopular in New England for many reasons, one of which was that it prevented shippers and merchants from earning a living, but the war created unanticipated difficulties for all the states and generated opposition in most of them. The United States had only a very small army, which meant that the state militias had the primary responsibility to defend the country. Virginia's location on the Atlantic coast at the mouth of Chesapeake Bay made it especially vulnerable and required the governor to mobilize the militia. As in some of the other states, the militia in Virginia was poorly prepared. Many companies lacked enough guns, and the state's military bureaucracy consisted of the governor, an overage adjutant general who seldom went from his plantation to Richmond, and an overworked deputy adjutant general. They struggled to find enough muskets and rifles and to obtain tents and other equipment. Throughout the war, which lasted until January 1815, Governor James Barbour and Virginia's members of Congress stayed in frequent contact with President James Madison and Secretary of State James Monroe (who was a former governor of Virginia and for part of the time also secretary of war) and with the professional army and navy officers assigned to Virginia to defend the coastline and the people of Virginia.

Most of the work of defending Virginia fell on the militia, and men from nearly every county in the state served on active duty at some time during the war. Late in 1812, General Joel Leftwich led several companies into north-central Ohio to prepare the way for a planned attack on the British in Canada. Militia terms of service in the field were usually short, and in spite of their hard marching and work to erect an advance fortification, the Virginians returned home before the campaign actually began. In the east, Virginia militiamen served in all the counties on Chesapeake Bay and also along the York, Rappahannock, Potomac, and James Rivers to guard against anticipated British movements up those rivers. As in the west, rotation of assignments as militia companies' terms of service expired hampered coordination and impeded sustained successful operations. Moreover, when militia and regular army units operated together frictions sometimes occurred because regular army officers refused to serve under the command of higher-ranking militia officers.

The American navy was also small and primarily intended for coastal defense, but it was too weak to protect the entire Atlantic coastline. One of the navy's finest ships, the *Constellation,* remained in Norfolk harbor for much of the war while a much superior British fleet sailed almost unimpeded throughout the lower reaches of Chesapeake Bay. The *Constellation* was too valuable to risk but too small to challenge the British. To protect the *Constellation* and the crucial harbor and cities of Norfolk and Portsmouth the governor ordered several hundred militiamen to the area, where during the course of the war several thousand men served at one time or another. On June 22, 1813, the British attacked and attempted to land on Craney Island, at the mouth of the harbor north of Portsmouth, as a prelude to attacking Norfolk and Portsmouth. Outnumbered Virginia militiamen with only a few cannon directed such accurate and deadly fire at the British landing barges that the British withdrew and never again attempted a major assault on Norfolk harbor.

A few days later the British attacked Hampton, across Hampton Roads from Craney Island, and scattered unprepared Virginia militiamen and then plundered the little city. According to widespread reports they also committed rapes and other war crimes against the city's civilian residents. The poor performance of the militia at Hampton detracted from the remarkable victory other militiamen had won a few days earlier at Craney Island.

The British fortified Tangier Island in Chesapeake Bay and in 1814 mounted a major campaign in Maryland. About four thousand Virginia militiamen assisted Maryland militia and United States Army units. The British nevertheless captured and burned Washington, D.C., and nearly reached Baltimore. When a small unit of British entered the city of Alexandria late in August during that campaign officials of the undefended city surrendered, another singularly embarrassing event that Virginia's civil and military leaders deeply regretted but that most other Americans never even noticed because of the much more dramatic burning of the national capital.

The experience of the war led the Virginia General Assembly at its October 1814 session to revise the state's militia laws, but the assembly could do little to remedy the problems the militia and the state government faced. The federal government was inadequately prepared to supply the militia or pay them promptly when the president called state militia into national service. Those responsibilities fell back on the governor and other state officials. When militiamen were called to duty, that left residents in most of the state's counties fearful of slave uprisings. More than 40 percent of Virginians lived in slavery at the time of the war, and in many of the state's eastern counties enslaved people were a majority of the population. About 3,400 enslaved Virginians and Marylanders ran off and sought refuge with the British or joined the British in their fight against the United States just as a larger number had during the American Revolution.

The war demonstrated how inadequate the nation's army was. Madison eventually replaced all the generals who were in service when the war began with younger and in some instances more able men. One young Virginian from Petersburg, Winfield Scott, rose rapidly to the rank of general by leading a series of successful campaigns in the northern states. The navy, too, had some successes. Western militiamen and volunteers under the command of General Andrew Jackson, of Tennessee, defeated a British invasion force near New Orleans in January 1815, the most impressive American military achievement of the war, one that ironically took place shortly after British and American diplomats signed a peace treaty in the Netherlands.

10

LIFE IN THE FIRST HALF OF THE NINETEENTH CENTURY

DECADES OF TOBACCO CULTIVATION and erosion depleted the soil in many parts of eastern Virginia by the nineteenth century, which prompted thousands of white Virginians to move to new land in western states. They often took their enslaved laborers with them. As George Washington and some other men had done before the Revolution, many large planters and small farmers shifted production from tobacco to other cash crops or experimented with different farming techniques. Many of them, as Washington had also done, read widely in the literature of agricultural reform and soil chemistry. John Alexander Binns, of Loudoun County, conducted some of the first and most successful experiments in scientific agriculture. Beginning in the 1780s he applied gypsum (hydrous calcium sulfate known then as plaster of paris) to his fields and almost immediately doubled his wheat production. He imported and ground gypsum from France and Nova Scotia and kept detailed records of the results. Binns also planted clover and other legumes, which fixed essential nitrogen from the atmosphere and enriched the soil. He compared crop yields from treated and untreated fields and published the results of his experiments in 1803. Skeptical critics refused to believe that his soil treatments had produced such high yields so in 1804 Binns issued a new edition that included affidavits from respectable planters that verified his claims.

Binns's work anticipated by more than a generation the famous experiments Edmund Ruffin conducted in Prince George County. Ruffin experimented on a much larger scale than Binns and with a wider variety of fertilizing agents, including guano he imported from South America. Ruffin's 1832 book, *Essay on Calcerous Manures,* described his use of calcium as a soil amendment to reduce acidity and increase fertility. The reports of his experiments, which he published in the *Farmers' Register,* a Virginia magazine, and elsewhere earned him wide respect as one of the South's most innovative and important agricultural reformers. Ruffin was deeply disappointed that most Virginia planters did not adopt his reforms. Throughout the first half of the nineteenth century other Virginia farmers often lamented in their private letters and in public their inability to make consistently good profits from their plantations.

Mechanization of agricultural work began during the decades between the American Revolution and the American Civil War. During the final years of the eighteenth century and the first years of the nineteenth farmers adopted plows and changed methods of cultivation, especially in the grain-growing regions of Virginia. Thomas Jefferson won an international prize for designing a plow moldboard that eased the passage of the plow through the soil. Agricultural reformers such as Thomas Mann Randolph, who served as governor from 1819 to 1822 and was a son-in-law of Jefferson, introduced contour plowing to reduce soil erosion, which the new methods of cultivation had accelerated. Cyrus McCormick, with the assistance of his enslaved man Jo Anderson, developed one of the first successful grain-harvesting machines while living in Rockbridge County. McCormick moved to Chicago in the 1840s, where he produced reapers in great quantity before, during, and after the Civil War. Factories in Virginia produced and sold plows and other agricultural implements. Magazines such as the *Southern Planter,* which was founded in Virginia in 1814, regularly carried illustrated advertisements for farm machinery manufacturers in Virginia produced during the nineteenth century.

Indians who resided in eastern Virginia faced the same economic difficulties as white and black farmers, and many of them also moved, although less often than white Virginians to the west. Individual members of all tribes sought employment away from their families and often melted into the general population. In other instances they lived in such small groups that, as in the

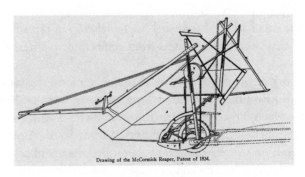

Drawing of the McCormick Reaper, Patent of 1834.

McCormick reaper

case of the Rappahannocks, extant documents seldom mentioned them, as if they had ceased to exist. Insofar as most white Virginians were aware, the descendants of the first Virginians really had disappeared. Most members of most tribes retained their tribal identities or affiliations, however, and the Mattaponi and Pamunkey preserved the remnant of their land and an unbroken tribal organization.

The state appointed white trustees for each tribe and placed management of the land in the trustees' hands. Some of the reservation lands the tribes acquired during the seventeenth and early eighteenth centuries were of poor quality or of inadequate size to be profitable. Most of the tribes sold parts of their land or entirely relinquished their property. By the middle of the nineteenth century only the Mattaponi and Pamunkey retained their original land, but early in the 1840s the Pamunkey had to enlist the help of the General Assembly to prevent local white men from encroaching on their reservation.

Internal Improvements

Roads were terrible at the beginning of the nineteenth century. An 1817 newspaper article quoted a traveler as exclaiming, "The Lord deliver me from the roads of Virginia. . . . The situation of the Commonwealth's highways calls aloud for the attention of the Legislature; they are in the most disgraceful situation; the finger of scorn is continually pointed from the hand of the stranger to the roads. It is humiliating to a Virginian to hear the strictures by strangers in passing through the Commonwealth."[1]

In part to stimulate agricultural prosperity, but also to adapt the state to the emerging national market economy, enterprising Virginians embarked on many small- and large-scale commercial and industrial projects during the first decades of the nineteenth century. The General Assembly took an active role in directing and supporting improvements in the state's transportation networks, projects that at the time were collectively called internal improvements. In 1784 the General Assembly chartered two companies to free the James and Potomac Rivers of obstructions to navigation and to construct locks and operate canals, but the work proceeded slowly because of engineering difficulties and high cost. In 1812 the assembly appointed commissioners, with Chief Justice John Marshall as chair, to complete the survey of a route to link the Atlantic Ocean and Ohio River with canals and a road. The commission produced a detailed plan, complete with cost estimates, for making the James River navigable for barge traffic as far west as the Allegheny Mountains. From that point a road across the mountains would connect the eastern river to the Great Kanawha River that emptied into the Ohio River at Point Pleasant. As Marshall explained in his final report on the project at the end of the year, the

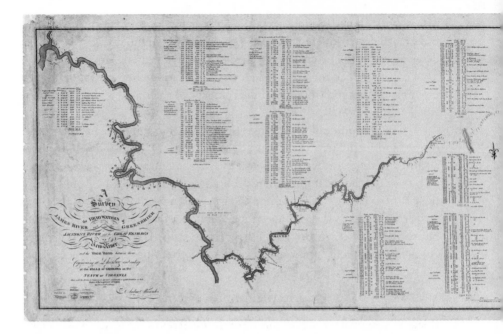

Andrew Alexander, *A Survey of the Headwaters of James River and the Greenbrier, Jackson's River and the Great Kenhawa or New River,* 1812

canals and road would draw the rapidly increasing agricultural productions of the populous Ohio Valley states directly through the center of Virginia, enrich all the regions through which it passed, and make the cities of eastern Virginia the nation's principal seaports. Imported manufactured goods could be transported to the west through the same ports, rivers, canals, and roads and further enrich Virginia and increase the state's importance in the new nation.

Marshall's vision was similar to the one Washington had entertained for the Potomac River. Both were bold and truly national projects that would have placed Virginia in a position to play a central role in the nation's economic future. Work on both canals proceeded slowly, though, because of engineering challenges and difficulty raising adequate capital. Long before the James River and Kanawha Canal was in operation as far inland as Lynchburg, New Yorkers completed the Erie Canal to connect the Hudson River to the Great Lakes. New York then stood better positioned than any other eastern city to become the nation's greatest city and draw to it commerce and economic influence that might otherwise have flowed toward Virginia's seaports.

In 1816 the General Assembly created the Board of Public Works to stimulate canal and turnpike construction projects and to provide capital. The state purchased up to 40 percent of the stock of each new company, and one or

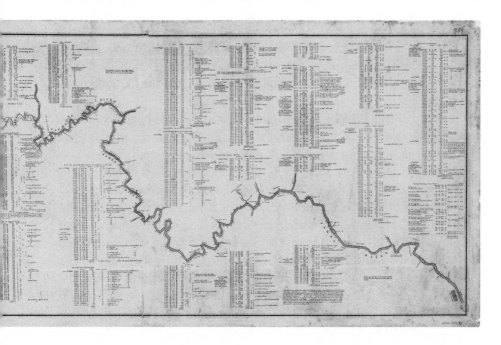

more representatives of the state government usually sat on the companies' boards of directors. Beginning in the 1830s the General Assembly chartered railroad companies to construct lines to link the state's major cities and rivers as well as a line from Petersburg south into North Carolina to connect the inland Virginia port with the large agricultural region of southern Virginia and north-central North Carolina. A competing rail line from Norfolk and Portsmouth also reached into North Carolina, and other lines linked Richmond by various routes to Fredericksburg and eventually Washington, D.C. More railroad companies may have failed financially than succeeded, though, and for many years the Virginia communities that the railroads served enjoyed rudimentary passenger and mail service only because the first roadbeds and steam engines were inadequate to the transportation of much heavy freight. In October 1832 the first steam locomotives to operate in Virginia began running up and down part of the track south of Petersburg toward Weldon, North Carolina. They reached a remarkably high speed of eighteen or twenty miles per hour. It was one of the first functioning steam railroads in the South.

Across the Potomac River in Maryland construction of the Baltimore and Ohio Railroad began in 1828 and strengthened links between the Maryland port city and northwestern Virginia. The railroad reached the Potomac River opposite Harpers Ferry in 1834, long before work on the canal made the river navigable that far upstream. Following construction of a bridge across the river two years later the railroad was extended westward to Martinsburg in 1842 and all the way to Wheeling, west of Pittsburgh, in 1852. More than two hundred miles of Baltimore and Ohio track was in Virginia. Before the end of the 1850s, the Northwestern Virginia Railroad connected the Baltimore and Ohio at Grafton to the Ohio River at Parkersburg.

Railroads in neighboring Pennsylvania and the National Road, a wide and well-graded road that connected Philadelphia to Wheeling as early as 1818, gave residents in the northwestern counties of Virginia much easier access to northern cities and markets than to the cities and markets of eastern and southern Virginia. In the 1840s residents of Wheeling watched as engineers constructed what was then the world's longest suspension bridge across the Ohio River. The bridge tumbled into the river not long after it was completed, but engineers soon replaced it with a new bridge that was better designed and constructed and that continued in use for decades. By then, steamboats transported people and freight up and down the Ohio River and most of the state's other rivers, as well as began to take from sailing ships an appreciable amount of coastal freight and passenger traffic. Railroads, canals, turnpikes (or toll roads) and other internal improvement projects employed both free and enslaved men for construction, maintenance, and operation of the new large-scale enterprises.

In May 1835 under the breathless headline "Something Extraordinary" a Norfolk newspaper reported that the steamboat *Thomas Jefferson* had left Norfolk "on Monday morning at six o'clock, for Richmond, with passengers, and returned in season to leave here again next morning (yesterday) at the same hour! This is the first demonstration that has been given of the practicability of going from Norfolk to Richmond and returning on the same day. . . . The distance between Norfolk and Richmond, by water, is computed at 150 miles, and as the Thomas Jefferson stopped six hours in the 24 which intervened between her time of leaving here on Monday and Tuesday mornings, she run 300 miles in 18 hours; very nearly equal to 17 miles an hour."[2]

The introduction of steam engines expedited commerce but also created new problems. In March 1829 the *Norfolk and Portsmouth Herald* reported on one of the dangers. "For the first time since the introduction of steam boats in our waters," the paper informed its readers sadly, "we have the painful task of recording the circumstance of the *explosion of a boiler,* with its appalling consequences." The boiler on the steamboat *Potomac* in route from Richmond to Norfolk exploded without warning, "shockingly scalding" a white man, a free black man, and an enslaved black man who were working together in the boiler room. The enslaved man died the next day, and the other two appeared to be mortally wounded. "Austin White, 1st steward, a slave of Mr. John Cocke, of Portsmouth, who was in the forward cabin, was also dreadfully injured, principally by inhaling the scalding steam which filled the cabin, but may possibly recover."[3]

Industrialization

Industrialization accompanied the transportation revolution. Water-powered mills along the state's rivers and streams ground wheat and corn, banks began doing business in some of the eastern cities, and commerce flourished at the ports of Alexandria, Fredericksburg, Norfolk, Petersburg, and Richmond. Huge new flour mills in Richmond drew on the increasing production of wheat in eastern Virginia and supplied markets as far away as Argentina.

Some of Virginia's economic achievements were impressive, and its industries nearly always employed slave labor. Several profitable gold-mining companies operated in the Piedmont beginning in the 1840s; a thriving salt industry developed near Charleston in the Kanawha River Valley; and in northwestern Virginia the city of Wheeling became a major iron-producing center. Comparisons of economic development policies and of the coal and iron industries of Virginia and Pennsylvania indicate that Virginians had more difficulty raising adequate capital than the Pennsylvanians in part because the General Assembly protected the interests of slave-owning planters in Virginia rather than adequately encouraged the development of industrial and transportation projects. A devotion to plantation interests rather than the unsuitability of slave labor in industrial settings may have been among the reasons why Virginia, one of the leading coal- and iron-producing states in the country at the beginning of the nineteenth century, was no longer as significant by the middle of the century.

During much of the nineteenth century Richmond residents lived in an almost permanent cloud of dense coal smoke. Coal from the nearby pit mines in Henrico and Chesterfield Counties supplied fuel for household heating and cooking as well as for many industrial purposes. A visitor early in the 1820s complained, "The atmosphere is impregn[a]ted with the dense murky effluvia of coal-smoke, which begrimes the pores of the skin, and affects respiration."[4] It was much the same in every industrial city. In April 1861 the *Atlantic Monthly* published an unsigned short story entitled "Life in the Iron-Mills" by Wheeling resident Rebecca Blaine Harding (later better known by her married name, Rebecca Harding Davis). It is a gritty story of life in the city's iron mills and vividly described the coal smoke that enveloped the industrial city. The smoke, she wrote with echoes of Dickens, "rolls sullenly in slow folds from the great chimneys of the iron-foundries, and settles down in black, slimy pools on the muddy streets. Smoke on the wharves, smoke on the dingy boats, on the yellow river,—clinging in a coating of greasy soot to the house-front,

Edward Beyer's 1852 *View from Gambles Hill* depicts the factories and mills on the
north bank of the James River in Richmond as well as part of the canal and a railroad.
In many ways nineteenth-century Virginia cities resembled nineteenth-century
cities elsewhere in the United States.

the two faded poplars, the faces of the passers-by. The long train of mules,
dragging masses of pig-iron through the narrow street, have a foul vapor hanging to their reeking sides."[5]

Railroads and steamships contributed to the smoke by burning great quantities of wood and charcoal, as did iron furnaces and other industrial enterprises elsewhere. The demand for firewood required hundreds or thousands
of men (both free and enslaved) to cut and haul timber to docks, wharves,
railroad stations, and foundries. Construction of canals and railroads together
with the development of iron, coal, salt, and other industries during the first
half of the nineteenth century created a variety of job opportunities (mostly
hard physical labor) for free men and provided owners of enslaved laborers
with new sources of profit from leasing or selling their surplus slaves to the
new companies. Those industries also gave Virginia's cities and small towns a
new importance as the state became less dependent on tobacco growing and
developed a more diversified agricultural and manufacturing economy. Large-
scale tobacco manufacturing facilities in Richmond, Petersburg, Lynchburg,
and Danville prepared tobacco for export to international markets and made
owners of the factories wealthy and respected community leaders. So, too,
with flour milling, which in Richmond led to the construction of several very
large brick mills, one of them reportedly the largest industrial building in the
country at the time it was built. Before the first large textile mill to be built in

Virginia was erected in 1828 in Danville, several small textile mills in and near Petersburg began employing women as operatives. Those mills remained in business until the twentieth century.

Urbanization

Those cities, as well as in the ports of Norfolk and Portsmouth, and the smaller eastern cities of Winchester, Staunton, Harrisonburg, and Fredericksburg and the western cities of Wheeling, Parkersburg, and Clarksburg, though still comparatively small, grew into important regional commercial and civic centers. Each boasted one or more newspapers in which local men wrote about the politics and economics of change. Virginia was not as urbanized as some states, but by the middle of the nineteenth century the state had a lively urban culture. People moved from the countryside into urban environments that became much more varied than had previously existed anywhere in the state or in most other southern states.

The variety of religious denominations, the presence of private schools and academies, the existence in some cities of theaters and banks and even colleges exposed residents of the cities to a variety of lifestyles and cultural institutions quite different from what was available on the farm, in the small towns, or elsewhere in the South. Richmond was one of the largest industrial cities in the South and beginning in the middle of the century had a German-language newspaper. The proportion of foreign-born residents of Richmond in 1860 was very nearly the same as the national average. The residents of that city, and perhaps other Virginia cities, too, lived in a varied culture that in many ways resembled urban centers elsewhere.

In some portions of the countryside immigrants were also conspicuous. For example, engineers who directed the digging of a tunnel under the crest of the Blue Ridge Mountains in the 1850s for a railroad line to connect Charlottesville and Staunton brought in Irish laborers to do the work. Owners of enslaved men often refused to lease their valuable men to work in such a dangerous place. The register of births for Augusta County documents that a large number of Irish women lived at the camp where Irish laborers worked. Some of them and their children no doubt remained in Virginia after the project was completed.

The descendants of the Germans who had first moved into the Valley a century earlier still often used their native language. The brothers Ambrose and Solomon Henkel established a printing business in the Shenandoah Valley town of New Market in 1806 and published in both English and German. So did the later Valley partnership of Ephraim Reubush and Aldine Kieffer. They also printed songbooks for shape-note singing, a simplified form of musical

Ambrose Henkel, *Das Grosse Buch A-B-C* (New Market, 1817), was one of many German-language publications produced in the Shenandoah Valley during the first half of the nineteenth century. This elementary work for teaching children to read indicates that parents there continued to have their children learn German.

notation that was popular during much of the nineteenth century in small rural churches where few members of the congregation could read music.

In Virginia's cities, evidences of bourgeois culture began to appear well before the middle of the century, including musical societies, debating clubs, and fraternal and social societies. The white residents of those cities lived lives in many ways similar to those of residents of northern or midwestern towns and less like other inhabitants of the rural South. Merchants, ministers, journalists, and educators traveled between the cities and corresponded with their counterparts elsewhere, which involved them in the emergence of an urban American middle class. At the same time those urban dwellers often maintained contact with families in the countryside, which kept alive Virginia traditions and practices and gave each city its own individual Virginia character. Residents of the country and small towns who were ambitious to make names for themselves often perceived moving to the city as a step up into a larger world with greater opportunities for advancement and recognition of success.

Both men and women lived different lives in the cities than in the country. Professional men such as lawyers, doctors, clergymen, and teachers probably earned better livings in the cities than in the country. Young or single women also had access to employment opportunities in the nineteenth-century cities where families hired governesses, teachers, and companions for their children. For most women, though, hard factory work, manual labor, or domestic work such as cooking, cleaning, washing, and other household labor was the common lot for all but a few women who were members of prosperous white families and could purchase or hire domestic servants. That was the case on plantations as well as in the smaller towns and larger cities.

Some white women in the cities and small towns owned millinery shops, ran dressmaking and other businesses, and managed their own financial affairs. Because Virginia had no married women's property act until 1877, a married woman surrendered all her property and the right to its management and profits when she married unless she executed a premarital agreement. Unlike the women who lived on scattered farms in the country, women who lived in Virginia's cities were often conspicuous participants in civic and commercial affairs in spite of the legal and social constraints society placed on women during the nineteenth century. A great many Virginia women adroitly created or took advantage of opportunities to associate for purposes they deemed important. Through churches and benevolent societies they often provided their towns and cities with valuable public services such as orphanages and schools.

For wealthy white Virginians, whether living in cities or on plantations, the nineteenth century created new ways to interact with each other and reinforce their shared sense of community. Ladies and gentlemen often visited some of the natural springs in Virginia's mountains and valleys to drink or bathe in the mineral waters that supposedly had medicinal value. Entrepreneurs constructed elegant hotels and advertised widely that their waters and resorts were healthful and cultivated places for ladies and gentlemen who wished to escape the summer heat and unhealthy conditions that often prevailed in crowded cities. A spa society renewed itself each season at the Virginia resorts. Other wealthy Virginians traveled to New England or the Finger Lakes region of New York where fashionable hotels competed with elegant

Edward Beyer's 1852 illustration of Red Sulphur Springs in Monroe County, in the Allegheny Mountains (and now part of West Virginia) shows elegantly dressed ladies and gentlemen strolling the manicured grounds of the extensive resort.

seaside resorts in Rhode Island for the business of the elite of New England and mid-Atlantic society.

White women of Virginia during the first decades of the nineteenth century often assumed the responsibilities of what twentieth-century historians called republican motherhood. The social mores of the time deemed women the special repositories of virtue and religion and endowed them with the corresponding responsibility to prepare their sons for responsible roles in public leadership. Taking charge of education and morality, those women often shunned public roles in favor of private, family, or church-related activities in pursuit of the ideal family life. The ideals of middle- and upper-class American family life in the nineteenth century dictated the almost constant attendance of wives and mothers in the home and often subordinated the personalities and desires of the women to the desires and reputations of their husbands. It was during that period that American women began to identify themselves, and were identified in public, by their husbands' names, as Mrs. David Campbell or Mrs. Governor Campbell, rather than by their own names, such as Mrs. Maria Campbell, as had been the case in the eighteenth century. Women who wanted or needed to read a treatise on the role of cultured ladies in nineteenth-century American society could read popular books by native

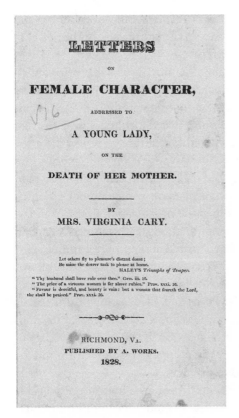

Title page of Virginia Randolph Cary's *Letters on Female Character* (Richmond, 1828); it appeared again in a second and enlarged edition in 1830.

residents of Virginia. Mary Randolph's *The Virginia Housewife* (1824) and Virginia Randolph Cary's *Letters on Female Character* (1828) were among the first and most influential statements of the ideals of the time.

White women formed majorities in most of the churches in Virginia, conspicuous evidence of the leadership responsibilities they shouldered and were expected to exercise in matters of morality. Women also took part in the new enterprise of foreign missionary work. Most of the major Protestant denominations in Virginia created missionary societies during the nineteenth century, raised money, and dispatched missionaries to Asia or Africa to carry the message of evangelical Christianity to people of other cultures. They also opened and ran churches, schools, and orphanages there. The number of Virginia missionaries was probably small, but the number of Virginians who supported their work was large, and both missionaries and their supporters found satisfaction and spiritual enrichment from taking part in the attempt to spread Christianity to other peoples. The same impulses also led to the construction in the cities and towns of Virginia of new churches large enough to accommodate congregations that were growing in size. The resources that individual congregations expended in the construction and maintenance of churches and synagogues is evidence of their importance in the culture and of the power of religious beliefs in the general population.

Many of the schools, orphanages, and other institutions that provided assistance to members of working-class families began as charitable organizations that white women's organizations or churches created. A Virginia expression of a larger national reform impulse that flourished during the first half of the nineteenth century, such community institutions provided for the poor and for orphans and extended into social work the religious motivations of the era. Temperance organizations and other reform groups flourished in Virginia as elsewhere, often under the auspices of women's groups. Baptist clergymen founded the state's first temperance organization in 1826, but laymen and women of most Protestant denominations readily joined the moral reform movement. White men often participated in the same reforming spirit as members of fraternal organizations such as the Freemasons, Odd Fellows, and Sons of Temperance, which provided fellowship as well as opportunities to improve communities. During the 1840s and 1850s many of those male organizations gradually took control of the schools and other organizations that women's groups had founded, which reduced the number and variety of ways in which women could take part in directing the spirit of reform and the content and context of community improvement.

White women could not vote, run for office, or even hold any responsible position in public administration because they could not enter into contracts or post bonds to guarantee their performance of their responsibilities. They nevertheless often exercised considerable influence in Virginia politics. As the acknowledged custodians of the culture's moral virtues, they both privately and publicly influenced political discussions and the political behavior of their adult male relatives. During the 1840s political parties and candidates began to appeal directly to Virginia's women in hopes they would persuade their husbands, fathers, and sons to vote for a particular candidate or party. When Massachusetts Senator Daniel Webster campaigned in Richmond in 1844 the local Whig women invited him to address their meeting, and he knew that it was worth his while to do so. The Whigs, who often characterized themselves as the nation's moral reform party, made the first appeals to Virginia women, but Democrats soon emulated the Whigs. By the middle of the 1840s, possibly even earlier, women frequently attended political rallies, and political candidates regularly addressed women as politically influential citizens, even though they could not vote.

Conditions in cities stimulated both men women to advocate measures to improve the quality of life. Urban areas with dense concentrations of people were loud, smelly, and often unhealthy. Many urban residents kept cows or

Grand Mass Meeting at
Wytheville.

**The Democracy of Wythe, invite their brethren gene-
rally, whig and democrat, but especially the citizens of
the glorious South-western Congressional District, to
meet them in council on the 31st inst,. at Wytheville.**

To the Ladies, aye the Ladies, a cordial invitation is extended.

The undersigned a committee appointed for that purpose, having tendered the above general invitation, venture to assure their whig and democratic friends of every condition and wherever they be, that a Welcome, a Virginia welcome shall be theirs.

They assure them, that great pains have been taken to have before them, intellectual and impressive speakers. Speakers, who will not only meet the great political questions of the day with argument and scrutiny, but with power and eloquence. Our speakers shall tell you the GLORIOUS news from Pennsylvania and Georgia. They shall tell you, of the proud democracy of Delaware, and Maryland, and Ohio, and New Jersey—in a word, they will tell of the GULF STREAM, how the GREAT DEMOCRATIC tide is swelling, and surging, and rising, and rolling over the land. They will tell you, that from the farthest Eastern extreme in Maine, to the far off Western boundary of Louisiana, from the Atlantic to the rocky mountains, all is well! ALL IS WELL!! They will tell you too, of the LONE STAR They will tell you of Texas and her gallant sons. They will tell you of their bravery, their daring, their devotion to liberty. They will tell you of the Texian-man's descent, that he is "bone of our bone, and flesh of our flesh." They will tell you, of his fond recollection of the Stars & Stripes, the flag of the father land—they will tell you of their sacrifices—of Goliad and the Alamo—of Fanning and of Crockett.

You shall also hear of the candidates for the Presidency of these United States—of the virtuous and talented Polk, of his many political conflicts, his generous and manly bearing. They will tell you of the "great embodiment of whiggery," Mr. Clay—they will tell you of his daring ambition, his CONTEMPT for the will of constituents, the sovereign people,—they will remind you of John Randolph, of Humphrey Marshall and of the murdered Cilley.

Will you come? Aye will you—come in your strength. You shall see banners borne, and flags streaming—you shall hear the drum. Music, soul-stirring music shall fall upon your ear—and roused in the spirit you can march from the encampment to the polls, and with the millions of the Democracy, deposit your vote for POLK & DALLAS, and proclaim to the world that Texas and Oregon were ours, are ours, and shall be ours, and that no Tyrants strength, nor Traitors betrayal can wrest them from us.

The committee have received the welcome intelligence, from COL L. C. HAYNES, one of the democratic electors for Tennessee, that he will be present. If you love eloquence, and wit, and anecdotes well told, come and hear Col. Haynes of Tennessee. Many of the subscribers have heard him, and these unhesitatingly say to one and all, his is the manner, the matter and the language of eloquence.

J P Mathews,	James L Yost.	John Grayson,
I J Leftwich,	Robert Crockett,	Michael Cassell,
John B Straw,	Michael Jackson,	David H. Stuart,
Daniel Brown,	Alex. S Mathews,	George Walton,
James H Piper,	James Fullen,	John Jackson,
Robert Kent,	Ashur Bailey,	Wm. Peirce,
John Hendrick,	B. R. Floyd,	A. C. Moore,
Alexander Peirce,	Ephraim Ward,	Allen T. Crockett,
Robert Raper,	James T Gleaves,	Casper Yost,
John Sanders,	F. K. Rich.	Michael Brown,
B. F. Aker,	John H. Allen,	Christopher Brown,
Harold Smyth,	John H. Johnson,	Jacob Gose,
John Stailey,	John Stuart,	George Stuart,
James K. Johnson,	David Graham,	Thomas Jackson.

Wytheville, Va., October 21, 1844.

This 1844 broadside invited women as well as men from southwestern Virginia to attend a Democratic Party rally in Wytheville.

chickens. Those animals and the many horses and mules used to transport goods and people generated large quantities of waste. People sometimes emptied chamber pots directly into the streets. A person who signed himself or herself A Friend to Cleanliness published a complaint in a Norfolk newspaper in 1795. He or she began, "I have been in many Cities, Towns, and Villages in the course of my peregrinations, but never passed through so dirty or filthy a town as NORFOLK."[6] Five years later citizens of the city who evidently had no faith in the city's common council petitioned the General Assembly to require regulations to protect public health. "It is generally considered," they complained, "that the stench arising from the docks in this Borough, at low tide, from the quantity of filth, dead animals and other nausious matters, thrown into them, are great causes of Sickness."[7] Much the same could have been said—and often was—about other towns and cities.

Cities could be dangerous. Fires that began in houses with wooden chimneys could spread rapidly and destroy the homes and businesses of other people. Cities made people vulnerable to contagious diseases that like fires spread more quickly there than in rural areas. A yellow fever epidemic that hit Norfolk and vicinity in the summer of 1855 killed about 2,300 people. It was the most deadly of the many outbreaks of contagious disease in nineteenth-century Virginia.

The Myth of Decline

In spite of the many industrial enterprises and transportation projects in operation or under construction during the second quarter of the eighteenth century, some influential Virginians worried that the position of leadership the state had enjoyed during and after the American Revolution had slipped away. Beginning with the essays William Wirt published in collected editions under the titles *Letters of the British Spy* in 1803 and *The Old Bachelor* in 1814, the state's intellectuals lamented for five decades what they referred to as the decline of Virginia. The state did not appear to be as influential in national councils as it had been at the time of the founding of the nation, even though the state remained the most populous in the country until 1820. Three consecutive Virginians were president from 1801 to 1825, Thomas Jefferson, James Madison, and James Monroe. At least one native or resident of Virginia ran for president in every election but one before 1856, and John Marshall was chief justice of the United States from 1801 until his death in 1835. Nevertheless, economic development elsewhere appeared to proceed faster than in Virginia, and political leaders such as Andrew Jackson and Henry Clay in the West, John C. Calhoun in the South, and Daniel Webster in the North seized leadership roles in national politics. Influential Virginians in Congress were often on the defensive or in opposition to national policies such as Clay's American System, which proposed to employ the energies of the federal government in pursuit of national economic growth. Hard economic times that followed financial crises that began in 1819 and in 1837 afflicted most Virginians and appeared to confirm the discouraging reports about Virginia's status. Thousands of white Virginians and their families left the state, and many of them took enslaved Virginians with them.

The literature of decline exaggerated the reality. Other states appeared to be outpacing Virginia, but during that same time Virginians created many and substantial commercial and industrial enterprises. Soil exhaustion, financial problems, and the lure of open land led many thousands of Virginians to move to other states and territories in the West. Statistics compiled after the 1850 census indicate that nearly 400,000 white natives of Virginia then lived in other states, about as many as remained in Virginia. As those Virginians moved away into the western states and territories, the state lost many potential leaders. Between the American Revolution and the Civil War thirty-one men served as governor of Virginia and nine as acting governor, but at least seventy-seven natives of Virginia served as governors of other states during that same time. An uncounted but much larger number of men born in Virginia became legislators, judges, congressmen, mayors, bankers, doctors, educators, newspaper editors, clergymen, and businessmen in other states during those decades.

Even as the literature of decline flourished, the *Southern Literary Messenger,* a monthly magazine of history and literature founded in Richmond in 1834, gained a national reputation. Its most distinguished editor was Edgar Allan Poe, who published trenchant criticism and original poetry in the *Messenger* and elsewhere during the years he lived in Richmond. The city became one of the principal publishing centers in the South. The success of the *Southern Literary Messenger* and the abundance of published sermons, religious tracts, and other writings of Virginians were evidence of how important a significant portion of the public believed literature and religion to be. That work and much more of lesser note supported printing offices in most of the state's larger cities and towns. Many Virginians wrote for publication, and they and other Virginians were able through the expanding postal system to purchase or subscribe to newspapers and periodical publications from other parts of the country.

Some of the most notable Virginia writers reflected some of the principal concerns of the residents of the state during the first half of the nineteenth century and may have reinforced the sense of decline. Historian John Daly Burk began a four-volume history of Virginia in 1804. He interpreted the whole of the colony's history as a preparation for the American Revolution, and he wrote about Bacon's Rebellion of 1676 as a rehearsal for the democratic reforms of the revolutionaries. About the same time, residents of Surry County renamed the brick house of the Allen family Bacon's Castle. A few adherents of Nathaniel Bacon had holed up there after their leader died. The people at the beginning of the nineteenth century who applied the name to the Jacobean brick house may or may not have known the details of the rebellion, but they were clearly struck by the fact that exactly one century elapsed between Bacon's Rebellion and the American Revolution. The new historical literature and the 1807 celebration of the two-hundredth anniversary of the establishment of the colony linked them together. Burk's biographer and successor as principal historian of colonial and revolutionary Virginia, Charles Campbell, of Petersburg, published a one-volume history in 1847 and an enlarged edition in 1860. Campbell's histories also portrayed the colonial and Revolutionary leaders of Virginia in a heroic way.

Biographies of some of the great Virginians of the Revolution reinforced the heroic interpretation. Mason Locke Weems published an extremely popular and highly fictionalized biography of George Washington in 1800, and Chief Justice John Marshall published a five-volume biography of Washington between 1804 and 1807. William Wirt published the first of many editions of his influential biography of Patrick Henry in 1817. Those books on some of the great founders may have provided authors of essays and books on the decline of Virginia a heroic backdrop against which to lament the condition of Virginia in the early decades of the nineteenth century. Those writers wrote as if they believed the state should be able in every generation to produce men comparable to the unusually great leaders of the American Revolution.

The theme of decline was a central element in what was called the Virginia Novel that became a popular literary genre during the second quarter of the nineteenth century. Maryland writer John Pendleton Kennedy may be said to have created it with his 1832 novel, *Swallow Barn; or, A Sojourn in Old Virginia.* Two years later William A. Caruthers published *Cavaliers of Virginia* and in 1845 *Knights of the Horse-Shoe,* the second a fictionalized account of Alexander Spotswood's 1715 expedition to the crest of the Blue Ridge Mountains. Those books, Nathaniel Beverley Tucker's 1836 novel, *George Balcombe,* and many others portrayed Virginians of the past in a romanticized and heroic mode and characterized contemporary Virginians as valiant, honorable, and stylized personifications of a lost glorious past. John Esten Cooke wrote novels and verse in the same vein from the 1850s until his death in the 1880s and during the latter years of his life wrote histories and fiction about the Civil War. His large body of work extended into the latter years of the century the cohesive themes of former greatness as inspiration in times of decline or trial.

The literature white Virginians wrote and read was part of a larger body of popular American literature in which the romanticism was a central element. To a lesser extent the writings of those Virginians were also part of an emerging body of distinctively southern literature. Martinsburg writer and illustrator David Hunter Strother, who worked under the pseudonym Porte Crayon, produced distinctively Virginia literature and images and linked the romanticism and Americanism of the historians and novelists with an emerging southern and Virginian literature. A cousin of John Pendleton Kennedy, he illustrated a new edition of *Swallow Barn* early in the 1850s and published *Virginia Illustrated* in 1857. He was a popular and well-paid illustrator for several national publications before and after the Civil War.

Many artists lived or worked in Virginia and fit easily within the national literary culture and the genre of romanticism. Resident and itinerant painters did portraits for prosperous Virginia families. By the middle of the century daguerreotype artists and early photographers also satisfied the demand for individual or family portraits. The sculptor Alexander Galt, of Norfolk, trained under distinguished artists in New York and in Italy and during a short life of thirty-five years executed notable busts of several Virginians. John Gadsby Chapman, born in Alexandria, spent much of his long and distinguished career in Italy, but before he left the United States he painted romanticized and allegorical works of Pocahontas and Captain John Smith and a huge mural for the Rotunda of the United States Capitol. His *Baptism of Pocahontas* epitomized the heroic and romantic interpretation of Virginia's early history that was a frequent subject of Virginians' pens and paintbrushes.

In Virginia, as elsewhere in the South and other parts of the United States, the works of Scottish writer Sir Walter Scott became extremely popular because their romanticism appealed to the sense of latter-day chivalry of the state's white upper classes. Place names derived from Scott's novels dot the railroad line between Portsmouth and Petersburg, later part of the Norfolk and Western. According to legend, the wife of the railroad's founding engineer was so enamored of Scott that when the track was laid during the 1850s she gave the new communities along the railroad names from Scott's novels—Zuni, Ivor, Waverly, and New Bohemia. During that same decade Virginia newspapers often printed long accounts of gentlemen reenacting medieval jousting tournaments. An extremely fine bust of Scott by the noted British sculptor Sir Francis Leggatt Chantrey was a prized possession of a Richmond family, who donated it to the state in 1904.

Education

One signal failing of Virginia and of every other southern state during the period between the Revolution and the Civil War was an unwillingness or inability to establish an effective system of public education. New England states pioneered in public education, but the southern states did not follow the example. The General Assembly authorized each county and city to form a board of school trustees and operate schools, but the state provided little money and few incentives, and in many or most of the counties the local authorities made little effort and did not raise enough money to support good schools and teachers. The result was that there were few schools available for most children, and those that existed were poor and poorly supported.

In 1854 residents of Halifax County complained to the General Assembly about the sorrowful consequences of the feeble efforts the state had made to educate its children. "The parent must be degraded, before the child can be instructed," they explained. "The man must prove himself a pauper, before his offspring can be admitted to the school room. In a country like ours, where labour is so abundantly rewarded, and where the evils of extreme poverty are generally so easily escaped, by industry and care, pauperism is oftener the badge of idleness and of vice, than of misfortune, and no citizen of decent pride will wear this badge of degradation, so long as he can conceal it from the eyes of his acquaintances. The poor parent, too often ignorant of the blessings of learning, erects a barrier of pride against the progress of his child. He refuses as a gift, what he would gladly use as a right." The petitioners published their long complaint in a pamphlet for wide distribution, but it had little effect on the state's political leaders.[8]

Prosperous families hired tutors or sent their children to private academies. Hundreds of small institutes and academies in the state offered challenging academic curricula for families who could afford it. They increasingly perceived the education of upper-class women during the early years of the nineteenth century as an essential part of a democratic society that relied on mothers to raise virtuous and responsible sons and citizens. By the 1850s several of the schools, such as the Female Collegiate Institute in Buckingham County, began to refer to themselves as colleges, which suggests the advanced educational level to which some of the women's academies aspired.

By contrast, the state supported several institutions of higher education where sons of families that were prosperous enough to educate their children could gain additional advantages. The University of Virginia, which the General Assembly chartered in 1819, held its first classes five years later in Charlottesville in the remarkable buildings Thomas Jefferson designed and earned a reputation as a distinguished institution of higher education. One of its most famous faculty members was William Holmes McGuffey, whose *Eclectic Readers,* first published in 1836, taught children to read for decades with simple moral lessons. Hampden-Sydney College, in Prince Edward County, a Presbyterian school begun at the time of the Revolution, had both

Buckingham Female Collegiate Institute

a medical school and a theological seminary affiliated with it for a time. Washington College, in Lexington, which evolved from an academy founded before the Revolution, was also a successful and respected Presbyterian institution of higher education. The Virginia Baptist Education Society, founded in 1830, took over an academy in Powhatan County that two years later moved to a site near Richmond, the origins of what developed into the University of Richmond. Also in 1830, Methodists opened Randolph-Macon College, and nine years later the state created Virginia Military Institute. The College of William and Mary, which had fallen on hard times after the Revolution, remained small, but it rebounded early in the nineteenth century.

Political Philosophies for the State and Nation

Despite its small size, the College of William and Mary exercised an influence in the South disproportionate to its size during the second quarter of the nineteenth century. Law professor Nathaniel Beverley Tucker taught two generations of students at William and Mary and was one of the most influential proponents of strict, states' rights interpretation of the Constitution. Tucker was the intellectual successor of John Randolph of Roanoke and John Taylor of Caroline, both of whom had served in Congress at the beginning of the century and spoke and wrote powerfully against interpreting the Constitution as Alexander Hamilton, Henry Clay, and John Marshall interpreted it. Tucker indirectly influenced public policy and decades of debates on public policy in Virginia and elsewhere in the South, where his former law students participated in politics, served on local and state courts, and won election to legislatures and Congress.

Thomas Ritchie, long-time editor of the *Richmond Enquirer,* also supported a strict states' rights interpretation of the Constitution as the Tertium Quids had at the beginning of the nineteenth century. His newspaper was often the public voice of a powerful group of Virginia Democrats, sometimes referred to as the Richmond Junto, that succeeded John Randolph of Roanoke and John Taylor of Caroline as leaders of the dominant states' rights wing of the Democratic Party. Against expansive interpretations of the powers of the national government, they placed Virginia in the forefront of political opposition to some of the nation's most famous statesmen. The *Richmond Enquirer* was probably the most influential Democratic newspaper in the South during the half century before the American Civil War. Editors of the *Richmond Whig* offered an alternative interpretation, and for three decades before the American Civil War it was also one of the most influential newspapers in the southern states.

Spencer Roane was the leading intellectual on the Virginia Supreme Court of Appeals for twenty years late in the eighteenth century and the early in the nineteenth. He employed his position as an interpreter of the law and the constitutions of the state and nation to contest the brilliant decisions Chief Justice John Marshall delivered in the Supreme Court of the United States. Roane and Marshall stood at opposite ends of the American political continuum. Their remarkable writings explored and explained differing visions

Cephas Thompson, *Spencer Roane,* ca. 1809

Henry Inman, *John Marshall*, 1832

of American society, American law, and American development, the one local or sectional, the other national. So important were the theoretical legal and constitutional writings of Roane and Marshall and several other talented men that it might have seemed at times in the early years of the nineteenth century that no one in Virginia wrote about anything else but law and politics. In expounding political philosophies for the nation, those white Virginia men were influential leaders who in no way exemplified the Virginia that was supposed to be in decline.

The actions of three of the Virginia-born presidents of the United States illustrate the tensions that existed within the debates about the proper relationship between the states and the national government and whether the Constitution should be interpreted strictly. The three were known for believing that the Constitution be construed literally and that the national government should be restrained in its influence and growth, but each acted in ways that revealed a willingness to depart from some core principals to meet national objectives. Thomas Jefferson (president from 1801 to 1809) quietly urged his supporters to support ratification of the treaty by which the United States purchased Louisiana from France in 1803 and silently ignore the serious constitutional objections they entertained about whether the Constitution authorized acquisition of new territory. James Madison (president from 1809 to 1817) had as a member of Congress in the 1790s urged President George Washington to veto the bill that established the Bank of the United States because the Constitution did not grant Congress the authority to issue charters of incorporation, but after the War of 1812 Madison recommended

William Hart, *John Tyler*, 1841

that Congress reestablish the bank. Experience had convinced him that the bank was a necessary and proper institution in aid of the government. John Tyler (president from 1841 to 1845) had opposed Andrew Jackson's exercise of strong executive power in the 1830s, but he vetoed several important bills Congress passed because he disagreed with their purposes, not because he believed they were unconstitutional, which he had originally believed was the only valid reason a president could veto a bill. Tyler also undertook several foreign policy initiatives that significantly enlarged the influence of the executive branch of government, and he engineered the congressional annexation of Texas in 1845 that many strict constructionists believed was of doubtful constitutionality.

11

SLAVE STATE

THE ONCE-POPULAR IMAGE of the nineteenth-century South as a place of large and gracious plantations was a reality for very few Virginians. Most white Virginia families and free black families lived on small farms or in towns and worked for themselves or for others. Historians of the American South and some economic historians once believed that the institution of slavery put Virginia and other southern states at an economic disadvantage in competition with free states that relied on free labor; but industrial slavery was often profitable in the southern states.

Freedom and Slavery

During and after the American Revolution all states north of Maryland provided for the gradual abolition of slavery, usually by requiring that no person born after a certain date could be held in slavery or that all enslaved persons became free at a specified date or age. Congress also prohibited the introduction of slavery into the area north of the Ohio River. The moral dilemma the institution of slavery posed in a country dedicated to liberty was painful to many white Virginians. Some white Baptists and Methodists in Virginia, as well as Quakers and Mennonites, declared that slavery was an immoral system and that its existence violated the principles of Christianity and the ideals of liberty enunciated during the American Revolution. Many Baptists and Methodists nevertheless accepted slavery by the early years of the nineteenth century, although they often readily allowed both free and enslaved blacks into their congregations and in a few instances even allowed black men some role in church governance. Proposals for the abolition of slavery in Virginia in the aftermath of the American Revolution coincided with a temporary relaxation in the laws governing emancipation, but no general emancipation plans, such as those adopted in some northern states, made it through the General Assembly. The assembly did prohibit the importation of Africans and slaves from other states, which did not necessarily indicate that legislators wanted to abolish slavery, only abolish the loathsome international slave trade. That law inconvenienced some planters who lived near a state boundary and could therefore not move their enslaved property from a plantation in North Carolina or Maryland to another in Virginia, so the assembly eventually had to modify the law.

White Virginians who proposed plans to abolish slavery early in the nineteenth century usually coupled emancipation with colonization of the freed people to some place outside of Virginia. The expense of compensating owners of enslaved people and the difficulty and expense of colonizing freed people made those proposals financially and politically impossible to implement, and the General Assembly did not adopt any of them.

Some white Virginians left the state because of slavery. Either they could not compete with owners of slaves in raising tobacco or other cash crops, they had moral or religious objections to slavery, or they did not want to raise their children to be dependent on slave labor. Southampton County Baptist minister David Barrow actually published a pamphlet in February 1798 to explain to his congregation and neighbors why he was leaving Virginia for Kentucky. He cited numerous reasons for abandoning the slave-owning economy in which he had always lived. "I cannot comfortably support my family," he explained, "educate my children, and attend so much to public calls, as I have done, with my means in this poor country, without falling into the line of speculation, or that of holding slaves." He went on, "I wish that all masters, or owners of slaves, may consider how inconsistently they act, with a Republican Government, and whether in this particular, they are *doing as they would others should do to them!*"[1]

The institution of slavery had entrapped some of Virginia's Indians as well as tens of thousands of African Americans. Enslavement of Indians had been illegal in Virginia since 1705, but a number of Virginia Indians that cannot now be accurately estimated remained enslaved. Some of them sued for their freedom during the interval, and those who could establish their descent from illegally enslaved Indian women were entitled to their freedom, as were the descendants of the women who won such suits. Each person who claimed to be illegally enslaved had to file a separate suit and go through a long and complex legal process. County courts provided counsel and allowed claimants to gather evidence and subpoena witnesses in their behalf. Some of the freedom cases involving descendants of Indians revealed remarkable family histories. In 1820 Rachel Findlay, of Wythe County, won a protracted lawsuit in the Powhatan County Court. She was the daughter of a woman who in 1773 had won her freedom as the descendant of an illegally enslaved Indian woman, but their owner nevertheless sold her to a man in southwestern Virginia. Findlay lived in slavery for four more decades. In 1813 she filed a freedom suit, but it took her seven years to obtain her freedom. With the assistance of some judges, lawyers, and family members and against the resistance of other judges she won freedom for herself and for as many of her descendants as could be identified and found.

Some other cases had tragic endings. Members of the enslaved Gibson family filed suit in Lynchburg while the Findlay case was working its way through the court system and produced genealogical charts to document their descent from an illegally enslaved woman of mixed African and European ancestry. Their court-appointed attorney had a stroke in 1819 or 1820, and because he did not bring the suit back into court their case consequently lapsed. They and all of their descendants remained in slavery.

Most enslaved and free black Virginians enjoyed almost none of the benefits of the American Revolution. In spite of the insistence the state's political leaders maintained during the after the Revolution that trial by jury be protected by the Declaration of Rights and later by the Constitution and the Bill of Rights, they did not extend that right to the state's enslaved population. They retained the local courts of oyer and terminer established in the 1690s as the courts that tried enslaved people accused of crimes. Justices of the peace continued to decide guilt or innocence without a jury and without all the procedural protections of the common law. Verdicts and procedural rulings in those courts could not be appealed, which denied to enslaved defendants a legal protection guaranteed to all white defendants. The only hope a man or woman had of rectifying a miscarriage of justice after a conviction was to apply to the governor for a pardon, or in the case of a death sentence for a commutation to transportation out of the country.

Free African Americans in Virginia occupied a middle status between free white people and enslaved black people. Many free persons of color, as the laws and records often defined them, worked as hired laborers, but some owned their own farms or small businesses. A very small proportion, probably less than 2 percent of them, owned one or more enslaved people, who in most instances were probably close family members. Twentieth-century archaeological excavations of the site of Archibald Batte's home and store at Bermuda Hundred, in Chesterfield County, provided additional evidence about the lives and families of free African Americans in nineteenth-century Virginia. They lived much like lower-class white people, although they had fewer legal rights than those white people. After Batte died in 1830 and his widow died in 1832, their son moved to Pittsburgh, Pennsylvania, where laws and social customs did not impose as many restrictions on him and his family.

Free black Virginians, if convicted of certain crimes or of failure to pay taxes, could be enslaved. As a result, the state government actually purchased and sold enslaved people. A freed person who failed to leave the state within a year (after 1806), failed to pay taxes, or was convicted of any of a number of crimes could be sold into slavery. In each of those cases the state sold a person and kept the purchase price. Enslaved people convicted of capital crimes were either hanged or deported from the country. In both of those cases the state compensated the owner by purchasing the slave at a fair market value using taxpayers' money. The state then sold the convict to a slave trader who by law was supposed to sell the person outside the limits of the United States. Again, the state kept the purchase price. By the 1850s traders had no convenient nations to which to transport enslaved convicts and surreptitiously sold them to unsuspecting white people in southern and southwestern states. The money the state received in each of those sales went into the Literary Fund that had been established early in the century to support public school systems counties chose to establish for their poor white residents. Every year for decades the state received thousands of dollars for selling human beings, and owners of human beings received thousands of taxpayers' dollars.

Black Virginians could not give testimony in court against white people, although white people could give testimony against black people. The double standard was based on understandings of who was trustworthy and who was not and also for the protection of the rights of owners of enslaved people. The death in 1806 of George Wythe, a signer of the Declaration of Independence and one of the state's most learned and respected judges, brought that double standard into high relief. Wythe's distant relative, who stood to inherit a significant part of the estate, was accused of poisoning him, but the only person who could give evidence against him was an African American. Because African Americans were not permitted to testify against the white man, no one was held legally responsible or even tried for Wythe's death.

Allegations published in 1803 that Thomas Jefferson was the father of several of the children of Sally Hemings, one of his enslaved women, exposed to public examination a private aspect of slavery that most white people preferred not to acknowledge. Debate about the accuracy of that allegation continued for two centuries, but there was never any doubt that enslaved women were peculiarly vulnerable to sexual exploitation. The presence of enslaved people of mixed-race ancestry on plantations and in towns throughout Virginia made that fact unavoidably obvious. Critics of slavery often singled out sexual exploitation and the existence of mixed-race slaves as one of the inevitable and most deplorable consequences of slavery. What none of Virginia's political leaders acknowledged publicly was that by holding mixed-race people in slavery they were also were holding in slavery people of European as well as of American Indian ancestry.

At the same time, though, a small number of Virginia men and women—

Unidentified artist, *Virginian Luxuries,* ca. 1825

including black, white, and Indian Virginians—were involved in affectionate interracial relationships that members of white society sometimes condoned. Even within the harsh regime of slavery, a great deal of local variation existed that permitted some people to live outside some of the constraints.

Gabriel's Conspiracy of 1800 and Its Aftermath

In the summer of 1800 Gabriel, an enslaved blacksmith who lived in Hanover County, organized the largest conspiracy against slavery in Virginia history. The conspirators planned to seize the state Capitol and a store of arms in Richmond at the end of August and bargain for the emancipation of all the state's enslaved people. Two men disclosed the plan to authorities, and a flash flood prevented the conspirators from assembling and putting their plan into effect. The militia arrested all the principal men, and a court of oyer and terminer convicted and hanged twenty-six of them and sentenced several others to be sold out of the country. The trials disclosed that the conspirators fully understood the revolutionary language of freedom. Gabriel intended, in imitation of Patrick Henry's famous 1775 speech, to raise over the Capitol a banner that read "death or liberty."[2]

Two years later reports of another conspiracy planned for southeastern Virginia at Easter 1802 generated new alarms. In 1806 the General Assembly placed more restrictions on emancipations and required every freed slave to leave the state within one year or be reenslaved. Severe as that law appeared on its face, in practice it did not always operate with full effect. Some freed people who enjoyed a measure of local respect and were gainfully employed and not likely to commit crimes or become a charge on the city or county relief roles received permission from county courts or special acts of assembly to remain in Virginia. Many more remained without obtaining legal permission because their neighbors did not object.

After the discovery of Gabriel's conspiracy the General Assembly required every city and county clerk to maintain an accurate register of all free persons of color, as they were then called. It is not evident how scrupulously city and county clerks enforced the laws that regulated the behavior of free blacks. In some places and at some times enforcement may have remained lax. At times of alarm about rumored uprisings county officials and militia officers sometimes disarmed free blacks, ordered the feared slave patrols to be more vigilant, or resumed enforcement of the restrictive laws. Rumors of revolts by enslaved people appeared often enough in private correspondence, newspapers, county government records, and letters to the governor that it is likely that fear of an insurrection gripped most communities at one time or another. The strict or lax enforcement of laws concerning free blacks offers a crude measure of how frequently those fears were aroused.

The slave patrols that periodically rode about the countryside at night to control the behavior of the enslaved population naturally generated resentment among African Americans because of the ability of the patrollers to harass or inflict corporal punishment on them without legal restraint. Law and custom required enslaved men and women to have written passes from their owners or overseers to be off their plantations at night or to travel long distances. Patrollers also sometimes harassed free African Americans, too. The enforcement of those regulations, like the laws respecting free blacks, may have been inconsistent, but the possibility of abuse was constant for free blacks as well as for enslaved men and women. It is also possible that the patrollers who owned no slaves of their own had limited inhibitions about abusing people who were the property of other men and women or that their ability to take part in controlling the black population gave them a shared sense of commitment to the slave system.

In December 1815 the General Assembly received two petitions from recently freed women that dramatically exposed the effects on families the existence of slavery imposed on many black Virginians. Nancy, of Loudoun County, had recently become free by the terms of her owner's will. The law required her to leave the state within a year, but according to the will her three

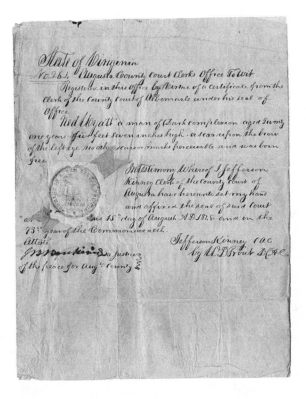

Registration in Augusta County of Ned Wyatt on August 15, 1848. The registration described Wyatt as "a man of Dark complexion aged Twenty one years five feet seven inches high, a scar upon the brow of the left eye no other scars or marks perceivable and was born free." Such descriptions were important for identifying free people, who had to carry their free papers, as they were called, with them.

children remained in slavery until they reached adulthood. Nancy asked the assembly to pass a law to allow her to remain in Virginia with her children because being forced to abandon them "will be almost as severe as the loss of life."[3] The petition of Lucinda, of King George County, related that she had become free under the terms of the will of her owner, but the will required that all the freed slaves be taken out of Virginia. Lucinda petitioned to be reenslaved and sold to her husband's owner. The "benefits and privileges to be derived from freedom, dear and flattering as they are," she stated, "could not induce her to be separated from her husband."[4] Legislative records indicate that neither Nancy nor Lucinda received legislative relief and should by law have been sold back into slavery or required to leave their Virginia families.

American Colonization Society

In 1816 Americans from throughout the country founded the American Society for Colonizing the Free People of Color of the United States (usually known as the American Colonization Society). It included many famous Virginians among its members and officers. The society planned to assist free people in colonizing the west coast of Africa. Opponents of slavery often embraced the society's objectives in hopes of gradually reducing or eliminating slavery from Virginia. Other society leaders and members appear to have been less inclined to abolish slavery than to rid the state of free blacks, whom they viewed as a dangerous influence on the enslaved population. Differences of motivation among the society's members may have reduced its effectiveness, but some African Virginians took advantage of the offer. One of the first parties left Virginia in January 1821 under the leadership of Lott Cary, of Richmond, a man who had worked his way out of slavery and acted as the political and spiritual leader of the emigrants. They colonized the region of West Africa that in 1847 became the independent nation of Liberia. The settlers named the capital of the new country Monrovia, for James Monroe, who was president of the United States when the first black Virginians emigrated. The first president of Liberia was Joseph Jenkins Roberts, a Norfolk native and Petersburg merchant before he moved to Liberia.

The experiences of the Virginians who colonized West Africa beginning in the 1820s were curiously similar to the experiences of the Englishmen who first

Joseph Jenkins Roberts

colonized Virginia more than two centuries earlier. They struggled because of inadequate support from their sponsors; they established their settlements on land they claimed as their own even though other people already lived there; they exploited local people as sources of labor and food; and they introduced foreign agricultural practices, modes of commerce, and religion. It is ironic that the African Virginians carried to Africa and introduced there Virginian ideals and practices of government, society, and commerce that led them to behave overbearingly toward the native African people, even as white elites in Virginia had behaved overbearingly toward Indians in the seventeenth century and toward Africans and their descendants then and afterward.

Nat Turner's Rebellion of 1831 and the Slavery Debate of 1832

The bloodiest revolt against slavery in Virginia occurred in August 1831. Enslaved men in Southampton County seized weapons and horses and killed nearly sixty white people before local militia quelled the rebellion and in turn killed an unknown number of enslaved people, most of whom had taken no part in the rebellion. The leader of the rebellion was an unordained preacher, Nat Turner. He was eventually captured, convicted, and hanged. While in jail he told his life story and explained his motivation to a white lawyer. No one knows for certain whether the lawyer modified what Turner told him before he published the statement as *The Confessions of Nat Turner* that autumn. By portraying Turner as an impractical religious zealot the *Confessions* created the impression that the Southampton County revolt was merely the consequence of a delusional man's actions and not a serious threat to the society based on enslaved labor.

Nevertheless, the brutal reality of the rebellion and its aftermath made the many other rumors of slave rebellion that circulated elsewhere in Virginia's localities more frightening. In January 1832 at the next session of the General Assembly members of the House of Delegates debated the place of slavery in Virginia society. Several delegates condemned slavery during their speeches, and some made expensive suggestions for gradually eliminating slavery and transporting the freed slaves to Africa or elsewhere, but they did not consider immediate abolition of slavery a practical alternative. The delegates terminated the debate for fear that continued discussion of abolishing slavery might incite more revolts.

In the aftermath of the rebellion the General Assembly tightened the laws to control free blacks as well as enslaved men, women, and children. The new laws required that trials of free blacks be conducted in courts of oyer and terminer without juries as were trials of enslaved men and women. They included a new but ineffective method to deport all free blacks from Virginia. They

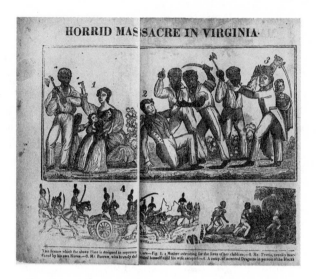

This engraving entitled *Horrid Massacre* was published
not long after Nat Turner's 1831 rebellion and no doubt
added to the fears of white people elsewhere who worried
about rebellions in their own vicinity.

made it illegal for African Virginians to preach even in their own churches. In
spite of the clear words of the Act for Establishing Religions Freedom, white
men in the General Assembly closely regulated and restricted the religious
freedom of all of the state's black men, women, and children. By the time of
Nat Turner's rebellion African Americans in most of the larger towns and
cities in Virginia had founded their own churches. Their churches in Petersburg, Richmond, Manchester, and Norfolk were large and thriving, and First
African Baptist Church in Richmond had one of the largest congregations of
any church in the state. The 1832 law imposed white supervising clergymen
on black congregations. Another law made it illegal for anybody to assemble
enslaved people in a school in order to educate them. It did not, as was often
said, make it illegal for anybody to educate any African American. It was more
in the nature of a law against assembling groups of people for that purpose,
and individual men and women continued to educate some of their enslaved
men, women, and children.

All people who lived through the insurrection in Southampton County
retained vivid memories of what happened. White people and owners of slaves
elsewhere recalled the event later when rumors of insurrections circulated or
enslaved people acted in ways that aroused white people's suspicions. Black
Virginians remembered, too. One enslaved man in King and Queen County

recalled more than fifteen years later how he had to hide the books with which he was learning to read. "We poor colored people," he remembered, "could not sleep at nights for the guns and swords being stuck in at our windows and doors to know who was here and what their business was and if they had a pass port and so forth and at that time a colored person was not be seen with a book in his hand . . . many a poor fellow burned his books for fear."[5]

A few months after the General Assembly's debates about slavery Professor Thomas R. Dew, of the College of William and Mary, published *Review of the Debate in the Virginia Legislature.* It instantly became one of the most influential books about slavery. Dew departed from the argument that Virginians had often advanced that defended the institution of slavery as an unavoidable inheritance of history or as a necessary evil. He portrayed slavery as a naturally occurring labor system, one that history, law, and the Bible all condoned. Dew's 1832 book was one of the first to propose that slavery was the proper condition for African Americans, which fundamentally altered the context and content of the following generation's debates about slavery.

The Slave Economy

Slavery was generally a profitable labor system for most owners during the first decades of the nineteenth century. The state's farmers and planters continued to work their land with enslaved laborers, and builders and operators of turnpikes and canals, mills and ferries, railroads, and the coal mines near Richmond, the saltworks in the Kanawha Valley, and the iron manufacturing industry in Virginia also profitably exploited slavery. In 1847 after white operatives at the Tredegar ironworks in Richmond went on strike, the management of the state's largest industrial operation replaced them with enslaved laborers who could not strike and who could be more strictly controlled. The companies that constructed and operated the state's first steam railroads often purchased or hired slaves to do construction work and other manual labor. Drivers of freight wagons and the skilled boatmen who transported heavy freight on the state's rivers and canals included white men and black men, free men and enslaved men.

The institution of slavery was also well adapted to Virginia's cities. Prosperous white city residents usually owned a few slaves to cook, clean, and manage their households. Many others who could not afford or did not wish to purchase slaves participated in the slave economy in much the same way by leasing domestic workers from their owners. Owners of slaves usually leased their laborers on one-year contracts. The week between Christmas and the New Year was the traditional time for executing those contracts, meaning that in the middle of the winter enslaved laborers from the countryside often moved into town. Laborers who then resided in town might return to the country or change masters and perhaps places of residence in the city.

Owners of tobacco factories and mills purchased or hired enslaved laborers just as owners of plantations, canals, and railroads did. Particularly in the cases of slaves hired from country plantations to work in urban mills, those African Virginians lived in dramatically different ways than their country counterparts. Rather than reside in small cabins on farms, they often boarded in residences they selected in the city, which gave them a greater range of choices in where and how they lived. City councils in some of the cities outlawed the practice of slaves residing in housing of their own choosing without the direct supervision of their owners or the manufacturers who hired them; but it appears that there were few practical alternatives, and the practice, though often illegal, was quite common. In the cities and perhaps in the smaller towns enslaved people may have lived under looser supervision than was the case in the country, but in the cities and towns they were liable to being arrested by night watchmen or punished in a mayor's court that without a trial or a jury could order enslaved people, free blacks, or even poor white people locked up or punished at a whipping post.

Among the opportunities life in the city provided to some enslaved Virginians was access to more means to escape from slavery than rural residents ordinarily had. Hundreds or thousands of them annually ran away from their owners. Some unknown proportion returned voluntarily or were captured and returned involuntarily. Others made successful escapes on their own or, more likely, with the aid of other African Americans or of white people who were willing to break the law to assist escaping slaves. In 1827 a writer for a Norfolk newspaper deplored the ease with which enslaved people escaped to freedom with the assistance of steamboat crews. He began by stating that although "intercourse between our town and other towns of our country has been much increased within the last few years; the benefits resulting from which are not unattended by great and serious disadvantages. . . . I allude to the transportation of persons of color, more particularly by the Baltimore and Philadelphia lines. . . . This is an offence punishable by our laws" to the extent of "a fine of *five hundred dollars, imprisonment in the Penitentiary for four years,* and *double the value of the slave carried away.*"[6] The problem grew worse, and in 1856 the General Assembly passed a law to require inspection of ships leaving Virginia ports. The revealing title of the law was An Act Providing Additional Protection for the Slave Property of Citizens of This Commonwealth.

The most famous of the many Virginians who escaped from slavery were Henry Brown and Anthony Burns. With the help of friends Brown had himself shipped in a box by railroad from Richmond to Philadelphia in 1849, and Burns escaped from Richmond by boat five years later. Brown accepted for

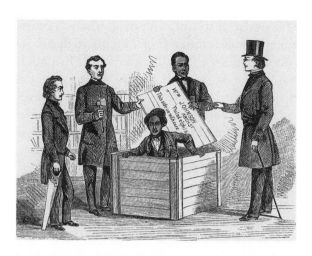

Resurrection of Henry Box Brown, 1849

himself the middle name Box and as Henry Box Brown toured New England as part of an antislavery campaign before he fled to England after passage of the Fugitive Slave Act of 1850. Under the terms of that law he was subject to being seized and returned to slavery in Virginia. Burns suffered that very fate. Arrested in Boston, he found himself forcibly returned to Richmond and locked in the cells of one of the local slave trader's holding pens, called slave jails. Both men gave accounts of their lives in slavery and their escapes to abolitionists who assisted them in publishing autobiographies. Other men who escaped from slavery also contributed to an extensive antislavery literature. Perhaps because of the difficulties of traveling with children, fewer women than men attempted to escape from slavery or succeeded in doing so.

Living conditions of enslaved men and women in Virginia may have been, as apologists for slavery often asserted, less horrible than in the cotton- and sugar-producing states of the lower South; but conditions in which some enslaved people lived should not be characterized as better than others, only as less horrible. However vulnerable enslaved people might appear when on trial before courts of oyer and terminer, the laws and legal practices of Virginia afforded them some protection against arbitrary conviction. It is likely that in most instances they were regarded as innocent until proved guilty, as was the case with white defendants. In some instances attorneys on their own or by appointment of the court represented enslaved defendants during trials. That application of the rule of law could work to the advantage of enslaved people and could be interpreted on the one hand as evidence of the comparative mildness of the slavery regime in Virginia. On the other hand, it had been a practice since the colonial days, and it continued into the 1860s, for the government to reimburse the owner of an enslaved person who was convicted and sentenced to death or to exile (called transportation), so that the owner did not suffer financially from the misdeeds of the criminal. That can be interpreted as evidence that the slavery regime in Virginia strongly favored the interests of the owners and that it was protection of the financial investment in the enslaved person that led courts to accord legal protections to slaves accused of crimes. It was important for financial as well as for legal and moral reasons to convict only a guilty person.

Enslaved people knew that they were in constant jeopardy of being sold or of having their families broken up. Witnesses who described the heartbreaking scene of grief-stricken slaves at Montpellier, in Orange County, at the end of June 1836 for the burial of former president James Madison may have misinterpreted it. Many of the plantation and household workers had been the property of the Madison family for generations, since Madison's grandfather purchased their African ancestors from a slave-trading ship almost a century earlier and moved them to the foothills of the Blue Ridge Mountains. White witnesses noticed the obvious emotions and the many tears enslaved women, men, and children shed and interpreted the grief as evidence of a sincere love for their owner. That may have been true, but the enslaved residents of Montpelier also knew that Madison's death meant that most of them would soon be sold to raise money to pay his creditors and to give Madison's widow and her financially inept son revenue on which to live. The tears were for themselves and members of their own families who were soon sold and dispersed, many of them never to see their parents, spouses, children, brothers, or sisters again. Even though many men and women who sold or freed slaves stipulated that family members not be divided, they could not control what later happened to those people. Divided families may have been the rule rather than the exception for most enslaved Virginians.

Separation of family members even led some Virginians who had gained their freedom to request that they be reenslaved. In the 1850s the General Assembly passed a law to ease the unusual process. Some historians later viewed that law as a particularly vile attempt to reenslave the state's free black population, but in fact it was the result of petitions several freed people, as Nancy and Lucinda had done in 1815, prepared and sent to the legislature or to local courts asking that they be reenslaved. The principal reason was that they generally had to leave the state and therefore their families after they became free. They asked for reenslavement in order to remain with their families. Reenslavement did not, as some apologists for slavery believed, prove that African Americans benefitted from slavery and preferred slavery to the responsibilities of freedom and caring for themselves.

Free black Virginians lived in a legal environment different from slavery but also different from white Virginians. Because many free persons of color were of mixed-race ancestry, racial distinctions were extremely important. For example, laws prohibited African Americans and Indians from testifying against white people in court, but white people could testify against either. An episode that occurred in Richmond in 1858 highlighted the difficulties of some of those men and women. William Ferguson was charged with assaulting a free black man. Ferguson was the son of prosperous free mixed-race parents who had obtained a certificate from the city's Court of Hustings the previous year which declared that because each member of the family was of less than one-fourth African ancestry, they were all therefore legally "not negros."[7] The man Ferguson was accused of assaulting and two other free black men appeared in the Richmond Mayor's Court to testify against him. The mayor, sitting as judge, ruled that just because Ferguson was not legally black according to the judgment of the Court of Hustings, that did not make him legally white. The mayor allowed the three black men to testify against Ferguson, and he was convicted and fined. In effect the state's laws allowed Ferguson to be classified differently for different purposes. In 1860, though, Ferguson identified himself to the census enumerator as white, as did his sister who married a white cousin.

Domestic Slave Trade

Financial panics of 1819 and 1837 forced many Virginia slave owners to leave Virginia and take some or all of their slaves with them. In order to pay their debts, some planters sold slaves to other planters or to traders who took them to slave markets in Alexandria, Richmond, or Norfolk for transshipment to the lucrative slave markets in Memphis and New Orleans. Those movements and sales also broke up Virginia families and imposed hardships on family members who remained, as well as exposed those who left to difficult trips to distant states and to hard lives there. Other Virginia planters who owned more slaves than they could profitably use on their plantations leased or sold laborers to augment their incomes and reduce their expenses, often with the same dire consequences for the enslaved families. Records of the iron, salt, and tobacco industries in Virginia indicate that in all of Virginia's industrial regions a significant portion of the laboring force consisted of enslaved laborers leased from owners who lived elsewhere.

The slave-trading house of Franklin and Armfeld in Alexandria, the largest in Virginia from 1828 to 1835, purchased large numbers of men, women, and children from people in Virginia, Maryland, and the District of Columbia for sale farther south. Several large slave-trading firms operated elsewhere in Virginia then and later. Among the large slave-trading operations in Richmond

HECTOR DAVIS,

Auctioneer & Commission Merchant

For Sale of Negroes,

FRANKLIN STREET,

RICHMOND, VA.

Sells Negroes both publicly and privately, and pledges his best efforts to obtain the highest market prices.
He has a safe and commodious jail, where he will board all Negroes intended for his sales at 30 cents per day.

This advertisement of Richmond slave trader Hector Davis is fairly typical of the time.

some of the best known at the middle of the century were those of Bacon Tait, Silas Omohundro, Robert Lumpkin, and Hector Davis. Those businesses and their owners were not necessarily social outcasts as they were later portrayed. They were successful, necessary, and respected members of the business communities of their cities because they provided useful services in the disposition of unwanted surplus slave property and also served as middlemen in the important slave-hiring process. Early in 1860, Hector Davis and several other Richmond slave traders chartered a bank to assist them finance their businesses. They called it the Traders Bank of Richmond. The major slave-trading houses sent thousands of men, women, and children to ports for exportation or along the state's roads. In Richmond, and perhaps elsewhere, some owners of slave-trading houses won election to public office.

The Richmond traders Omohundro, Lumpkin, and Davis are known to have had several children with enslaved women whom they may have regarded as their wives, and Tait had children with a free African American woman. All four had long-term, familylike relationships with those women, and they provided for their children and resettled them in free states, where many of their descendants eventually passed as white. Those mixed-race families exhibited some of the most sensitive and difficult-to-understand dynamics of life in a society in which slavery was central to everything, particularly in the cases of Corinne Omohundro and Mary Lumpkin. They both took an active part in operating their husbands' slave jails where people waited to be bought or sold. They made certain that on the day of a sale the people to be sold were clean and well-dressed so as to bring a high price. Historians have struggled to learn how those women understood their lives: they were enslaved; they were mothers of enslaved children; they may have been wives without the legal rights free wives enjoyed; they daily witnessed and participated in the separation of other people's children from their parents and saw them sold to strangers for transportation elsewhere; they probably knew that their own children could be seized and sold if their owners/husbands could not pay their debts. It may require the imaginative insights of a genius like Shakespeare or Kafka to understand those women in their peculiar but not unique circumstances.

For other people engaged in the domestic slave trade simple greed and a disregard for human suffering may explain how they attempted to profit from misery on a vast scale. The drivers who conducted coffles of slaves from their places of residence to the distant southwest are a prime case in point. They were probably much less respectable than the urban businessmen/traders. They were engaged in a conspicuously distasteful part of the slave economy. A British visitor told of encountering a gang of enslaved people being transported from the Alexandria slave-trading house of Franklin and Armfeld to Louisiana. He saw them in September 1834 near the New River not far from Christiansburg, Virginia.

"Just as we reached New River, in the early gray of the morning, we came up with a singular spectacle," George W. Featherstonhaugh wrote, "the most striking one of the kind I have ever witnessed. It was a camp of negro slave-drivers, just packing up to start; they had about three hundred slaves with them, who had bivouacked the preceding night *in chains* in the woods; these they were conducting to Natchez, upon the Mississippi river, to work upon the sugar plantations in Louisiana . . . they had a caravan of nine waggons and single-horse carriages, for the purpose of conducting the white people, and any of the blacks that should fall lame, to which they were now putting the horses to pursue their march. The female slaves were, some of them, sitting on logs of wood, whilst others were standing, and a great many little black children were warming themselves at the fires of the bivouac. In front of them all, and prepared for the march, stood, in double files, about two hundred male slaves, *manacled and chained to each other.* I had never seen so revolting a sight before! Black men in fetters, torn from the lands where they were born, from the ties they had formed, and from the comparatively easy condition which agricultural labour affords, and driven by white men, with liberty and equality in their mouths, to a distant and unhealthy country, to perish in the sugar-mills of Louisiana, where the duration of life for a sugar-mill slave does not exceed seven years! To make this spectacle still more disgusting and hideous, some of the principal white slave-drivers, who were tolerably well dressed, and had broad-brimmed white hats on, *with black crape round them,* were standing near, laughing and smoking cigars."[8]

Henry Clay Bruce, who grew up in slavery in Prince Edward County, recalled many years later seeing gangs of slaves being regularly driven along the road from Richmond to the lower South. "Usually," he wrote, "the slave men were hand-cuffed together with long chains between them extending the whole length of the gang which contained as many as forty, sometimes, or

Joseph Diss deBar, *Off to Old Kentuck* (1847), depicts
a gang of slaves being marched off for sale in a distant
state.

twenty on each side of the chain marching in line. The women and small boys
were allowed to walk unchained in the line while the children and the lame
and those who were sick rode in wagons. The entire caravan would be under
the charge of the owner and a guard of four or five poor white men armed each
with a rawhide whip, with which to urge the gang along and to keep them in
line or at least in the road."[9]

During the half century before the American Civil War, it is likely that
the business of buying and selling slaves was the most important commercial
enterprise in Virginia. After the 1820s traders exported as many as 8,000 to
10,000 Virginians to the southern and southwestern states each year, a much
larger total number than Virginia's planters had imported from Africa during
the century prior to the American Revolution. Nearly all of those men and
women and children had already been bought or sold at least once before

they reached any of the largest slave trading firms in Alexandria or Richmond, where they were then sold again, often resulting in the permanent separation of husbands and wives and of parents and children.

Revenue from the sale of people far exceeded the amount of money Virginians received for selling tobacco and flour, the two other most valuable commodities exported from the state. According to treasury department records, in 1860 Virginians exported processed and leaf tobacco worth $3,078,362 and flour worth $2,029,315. Those were the most lucrative exports to foreign countries, followed by staves for manufacturing barrels and crates, grains, ground meal and flour, and cotton. Economic historian Frederic Brancroft estimated in his pioneering 1931 book, *Slave Trading in the Old South,* that during the 1850s the annual average exportation of enslaved people from Virginia was at least 8,000, and he calculated that an average of more than 9,000 people were sold out of Virginia every year during the period 1830–60. Ulrich B. Phillips estimated in his *American Negro Slavery* in 1929 that prime field hands in Virginia brought about $1,200 each in 1860, nearly double the price in 1850. Taking Bancroft's numbers as likely conservative and discounting Phillips's prices as representing prime field hands only, still the value of Virginia slave exports in 1860 could have been in the range of $6 to $8 million, which surpassed the combined value of the state's top five agricultural export products.

Fredricka Bremer Visits Virginia

The state's denial to enslaved and free African Americans of legal rights white Virginians highly prized for themselves was only one of many internal contradictions the institution of slavery created. Indeed, slavery required white Virginians to hold some mutually contradictory beliefs about civil and human rights, freedom of speech and religion, and even about families and how people should treat each other. To some extent the pervasive institution and the constant humiliations slavery imposed on the state's most vulnerable people could become invisible to other people through routine.

Visitors to the state often saw the institution of slavery more clearly than people who lived with it every day and benefitted from or became inured to its brutalities and consequences. In the middle of the nineteenth century, for instance, Swedish social critic Fredrika Bremer published a two-volume account of her travels through the United States. She recalled being horrified at what she saw of slavery in Richmond. Her frank account of her visit to the city at the middle of the century is worth quoting at length.

"I have to-day, in company with an estimable German gentleman, resident at Richmond, visited some of the negro jails, that is, those places of imprisonment in which negroes are in part punished, and in part confined for sale. I saw in one of these jails, a tall, strong-limbed negro, sitting silent and gloomy, with his right-hand wrapped in a cloth. I asked if he were ill.

"'No,' replied his loquacious keeper, 'but he is a very bad rascal. His master, who lives higher up the river, has parted him from his wife and children, to sell him down South, as he wanted to punish him, and now the scoundrel, to be revenged upon his master, and to make himself fetch a less sum of money, has cut off the fingers of his right hand! The rascal asked me to lend him an ax to knock the nails into his shoes with, and I lent it him without suspecting any bad intention, and now has the fellow gone and maimed himself for life!'"

Bremer went on, "In another prison, we saw a pretty little white boy of about seven years of age sitting among some tall negro girls. The child had light hair, the most lovely light-brown eyes, and cheeks as red as roses; he was, nevertheless, the child of a slave mother, and was to be sold as a slave. His price was three hundred and fifty dollars. The negro girls seemed very fond of the white boy, and he was left in their charge, but whether that was for his good or not is difficult to say. No motherly Christian mother visited either this innocent imprisoned boy, or the negro girls. They were left to a heathenish life and the darkness of the prison."

She continued her tour of the city's slave market. "In another 'jail' were kept the so-called 'fancy-girls,' for fancy purchasers. They were handsome fair mulattoes, some of them almost white girls" whom traders sold to men who purchased them for sex partners. The fancy trade, as it was called, was no secret, and it was a big business. Some of the women who belonged to traders knowingly participated in the fancy trade and may possibly have begun life-long relationships with their owners/husbands in that same manner.

The birthday of the nation impressed and puzzled Bremer. "Yesterday, the 4th of July," she wrote, "the great day of America, was celebrated, as usual, by speech-making and processions, and drinking of toasts, and publicly reading of the Declaration of Independence. It was read in the African church of the city; but why they selected the negro church of all others for the reading of the declaration of freedom, which is so diametrically opposed to the institution of slavery, I can not comprehend, when the burlesque of the whole thing must be so evident to every one."[10] In truth, the city's and state's white elites often rented First African Baptist Church in Richmond for celebrations or political rallies for the simple reason that it was the largest hall in town. The irony of white men celebrating liberty in a church where most of the congregation was enslaved struck Bremer forcefully; but for white men and women who lived all their lives in the midst of slavery they could not see what she could not avoid seeing.

12

DIVIDED STATE IN
A DIVIDED NATION

ONSTITUTIONAL CONVENTIONS MET in Virginia in the winters of 1829–30 and 1850–51. Delegates to both conventions discussed at great length their ideas about representative government and disagreed with one another on several fundamentally important practical issues of law and politics. For the most part their differences arose from the wide variety of circumstances in which residents of Virginia lived during the first half of the nineteenth century, especially from the uneven distribution of slavery in the state.

Constitutional Convention of 1829–1830

The Constitutional Convention that met in Richmond from October 5, 1829, to January 15, 1830, featured some of the most distinguished public debates on American politics after ratification of the Constitution of the United States. Its members included venerable founders of the nation such as James Madison, James Monroe, and John Marshall, leading statesmen of the early years of the nineteenth century such as John Randolph of Roanoke and Philip Pendleton Barbour, and rising young leaders, among them future president John Tyler. They met to revise the Constitution of 1776 and in the process debated the nature of representative government as well as practical questions such as the organization of the executive and judicial branches of government. The debates were often learned and eloquent and attracted national attention. The artist George Catlin painted the scene in the chamber of the House of Delegates in the Capitol and was able to paint each delegate's face from life.

Western Virginians had argued for years that the Constitution of 1776 denied them some of the elementary rights of American citizenship their ancestors had fought for during the American Revolution. The old require-

George Catlin, *Virginia Convention of 1829–1830,* ca. 1830. Catlin painted the scene in the chamber of the House of Delegates and was able to paint the faces of the members from life.

ment that men own land in order to vote disfranchised a large number of adult white men, and the apportionment of representation in the General Assembly was heavily weighted toward the eastern counties. As a result, people in eastern Virginia, who on average owned more slaves than people who lived elsewhere, had an disproportionately large representation in the General Assembly and shaped public policies favorable to slave owners and unfavorable to everybody else.

Eastern men who owned too little property to vote joined western men in demanding that the convention grant universal white manhood suffrage. From the capital city the convention received a long and eloquent appeal in the form of a petition from men who identified themselves as "*the Non-Freeholders of the City of Richmond.*" Drafted by Attorney General John Robertson and adopted at a public meeting in the city, it quoted from the Virginia Declaration of Rights and referred to the writings of Thomas Jefferson to argue for removing what the petitioners called distinctions "between the privileged and the proscribed classes" in Virginia. "Experience has but too clearly evinced," their long plea began, "what, indeed, reason had always foretold, by how frail a tenure they hold every other right, who are denied this, the highest prerogative of freemen.... Comprising a very large part, probably a majority of male citizens of mature age, they have been passed by, like aliens or slaves, as if destitute of interest, or unworthy of a voice, in measures involving their future political destiny: whilst the freeholders, sole possessors, under the existing Constitution, of the elective franchise, have, upon the strength of that possession alone, asserted and maintained in themselves the exclusive power of new-modelling the fundamental laws of the State: in other words, have seized upon the sovereign authority."[1]

At almost the same time a person writing under the name VIRGINIA FREEWOMAN argued, as Hannah Lee Corbin may have when she wrote to her brother during the American Revolution, that women who owned property deserved the vote for the same reasons that men who owned property were allowed to vote. "You say, we have not intellect enough to vote, and assist in the government," VIRGINIA FREEWOMAN addressed members of the convention in a public letter. "Where are the proofs of your superiority? You keep us in ignorance—and then you boast of your superior attainments. You make us embroider for you; thrum upon the guitar or piano; draw sketches of your lordly faces; convert us into spinsters and seamstresses, to make your garments; but you exclude us from your best schools. You prevent us from cultivating science, studying politics, improving our understandings; and then you insist upon our ignorance as the evidence of our mental Incapacity.... You boast too, of your superior independence of mind. You say, that you alone can exercise the right of suffrage, firmly and freely. Indeed! and what say the disfranchised non-freeholders to this arrogant assumption—and what ought *we* to say to it?—That it is not founded on truth."[2] A majority of adult white Virginia men and virtually all African American and American Indian men in Virginia could truthfully have made the same argument VIRGINIA FREEWOMAN made.

Convention delegates changed the property qualification for the suffrage to allow adult white men to vote if they owned land worth at least $25—which was a substantial amount of money in those days—or were householders who paid taxes. That expanded the number of men who could vote by about 15 or 20 percent, but it still left nearly half the white men in the state unable to vote. The delegates did not even consider VIRGINIA FREEWOMAN's revolutionary idea of allowing women to vote. Opponents of democratic reform prevailed by a narrow margin on nearly all important issues. The delegates awarded a few more seats in the General Assembly to the west but included two clauses that gave voters east of the Blue Ridge permanent majorities in both houses of the assembly. That Great Gerrymander, as it should be called, clearly protected the rights and interests of the declining minority of men who owned slaves and lived in the eastern part of the state from any potential threat that the majority of men who did not own slaves might pose.

The convention made the 1786 Act for Establishing Religious Freedom part of the constitution, but the delegates did not adopt the most important democratic reform proposals that had provided the impetus for holding the convention. A majority of the delegates refused to enlarge the number of public offices to be filled through popular election. Unwilling, yet, to allow democracy to expand as far and as fast in Virginia as it was then expanding in most other states, the majority of the convention members proposed and the state's restricted electorate ratified a new constitution that changed or re-formed very little. It left in place most governmental institutions and political practices that Virginians had created during the seventeenth century for a hierarchical society of tobacco planters.

The new constitution did make a few changes. It increased the governor's term of office from one year to three with no eligibility for a second consecutive term, but it did not enlarge the power of the governor's office or grant the governor authority to veto bills. Governors before and after the adoption of the new constitution made recommendations to the General Assembly on matters of public policy, but lacking any veto threat they were not particularly influential in shaping legislation. Newspapers seldom even mentioned it when a new governor was sworn into office, and before the 1860s no new governor of Virginia made an inaugural address. The assembly remained the most potent political institution in Virginia. It had the sole authority to grant or deny requests for divorces and to grant or withhold requests for new or amended municipal and corporate charters. People who wished to open a bank, build a turnpike, operate a toll bridge or ferry, open a college, or sell stock to create or enlarge a business or factory all had to apply to the General Assembly at its annual session. People who did not have strong political connections or an influential local delegation in the assembly had little chance to succeed. The General Assembly consequently exercised a strong, sometimes controlling, influence on the character and pace of economic, social, and political change in Virginia.

Regional Diversity

Differences between the regions of the state were clearly evident during the Convention of 1829–30, and they increased afterward. As Charles Henry Ambler, the first historian of sectionalism in the state, wrote early in the twentieth century, old Virginia could be viewed as consisting of two large, unequal inclined planes that sloped away from the mountains in the center, one toward the Atlantic Ocean, the other toward the Ohio River. That clear mental

image rested directly on the geography of Virginia and reflected Virginians'
nineteenth-century perceptions. The division of Virginia into two states in
1863 seemed to prove that the mountains had always divided the people of
the state into two distinct populations. However, it is more illuminating to
view the regional diversity and its political and constitutional consequences
by looking not at the mountains but at the watercourses.

The Ohio River formed the northwestern boundary of Virginia, which
was then an Ohio Valley state as much as and in the same way it was a southern
state and also a mid-Atlantic state. The river was a boundary only for legal and
political purposes in that it separated the slave state of Virginia from the free
state of Ohio, but the river did not so much separate the people who lived on
either side into otherwise distinct cultures with different economic interests
or political values. Virginians in the first two ranges of counties south of the
Ohio River lived in very much the same world as Ohioans who lived north
of it. Those Virginians, though, lived in a very different world than any other
Virginians inhabited. The many steamboats that navigated the Ohio River
together with the National Road and the Baltimore and Ohio Railroad reinforced the commercial, cultural, and political linkage of the Ohio Valley
region of Virginia with the ports of Baltimore and Philadelphia and with the
free states of Ohio and Pennsylvania. Those and other factors also separated
them from the portion of Virginia east of the Allegheny Mountains. As a man
in the northwestern city of Clarksburg explained in 1861, "it must be recol-
lected that our intercourse is almost entirely with the West and the North,
we have none with The Central and eastern portions of Virginia. We are not
slaveholders, many of us are of Northern birth. We read almost exclusively
Northern newspapers and books, and listen to Northern preachers."[3]

Most Virginians in the sparsely populated counties on the western slope
of the Allegheny Mountains east and south of the Ohio River counties had
no easy commercial connections to that western river or to eastern Virginia.
Slavery was of little consequence there, manufacturing and extractive industries had not yet developed extensively, and large-scale commercial agriculture
was much less evident than in most of the remainder of the state. Virginians
who lived in that region shared relatively little with their Ohio Valley neighbors to the west or with slaveholders farther east or south.

The counties in the upper watershed of the Tennessee River where rivers
and streams flowed southward out of Virginia into Tennessee were part of a
larger economic and cultural region that was in the midst of major changes
in the middle of the nineteenth century. The region that is now southwestern
Virginia (with the exception of the westernmost counties) gained access to
commercial markets to the east, north, and south in the 1850s with the completion of the Virginia-Tennessee Railroad between Lynchburg and Goodson,

which was later renamed Bristol, on the state border. Railroads and canals linked the people in that area through Lynchburg to eastern Virginia and the commerce of the Atlantic world; and railroads south of Bristol linked southwestern Virginians to the waterways of the Tennessee Valley and ultimately to the lower regions of the Ohio and Mississippi Rivers. Reliance on slave labor and the population of enslaved people in the area increased notably after completion of the railroad. White people whose region the new railroad was then transforming were coming to share much more with men in eastern Virginia than with nearer men in the western Virginia mountains. The consequences of that transformation became very conspicuous during the 1850s and during and after the secession crisis.

In eastern Virginia the landscape took its shape and character from the great bay of Chesapeake and its tributaries. The two Eastern Shore counties between the bay and the ocean were physically detached from the rest of Virginia and throughout the nineteenth century were more nearly commercial and cultural appendages of Maryland than integral parts of old Virginia. In 1861 some men there even contemplated joining their two counties to Maryland.

The density of the enslaved population was greater throughout the region than anywhere else in Virginia. The rural eastern and southeastern counties more nearly resembled the lower South than did any other parts of the state. At mid-century more than 40 percent of Virginians in almost every county east of the Blue Ridge and south of the Rappahannock River lived in slavery. In eighteen of the fifty-six counties more than 50 percent of the population was enslaved in 1860, in another twelve more than 60 percent, and in two others more than 70 percent. The white farmers and planters in southeastern Virginia consequently more often identified their interests with those of cotton planters in the Carolinas and Georgia than with the values of other Virginians elsewhere.

Between the eastward-flowing rivers and the westward-flowing rivers was the northward-flowing Shenandoah River, which squeezed itself between the Blue Ridge Mountains to the east and the Allegheny Mountains to the west. The North and South Branches of the Potomac River drained the eastern slope of the Allegheny Mountains immediately to the west of the counties in the Shenandoah Valley. Through the Valley of Virginia stretched the long and busy Valley Road, and by the middle of the century several new railroads augmented commercial and cultural connections between the Valley of Virginia and Baltimore and Philadelphia. Slavery had always been of somewhat less importance in the Shenandoah Valley than to the east of the Blue Ridge but of more importance than to the west. In some of the counties Quakers, Mennonites, and members of some religious denominations in the German Reformed tradition strongly disapproved of slavery. By the 1850s, though, slavery had become an integral part of life that influenced how everybody lived, even people who owned or rented no enslaved laborers or opposed slavery. The Valley's historic commercial connections with Baltimore and Philadelphia, not with Richmond or Norfolk, gave it a social and political orientation, except on issues relating to slavery, that more nearly resembled the outlook of people in the Ohio Valley than in most other regions of Virginia.

Early nineteenth-century Virginians often spoke of a divided Virginia with the Blue Ridge Mountains separating east from west. But as the events of the secession crisis and the formation of West Virginia during the 1860s demonstrated, by mid-century the long Valley west of the Blue Ridge had come to have more in common with eastern Virginia than with western Virginia. The real line of demarcation between east and west was the Allegheny Mountain range, not the Blue Ridge.

Politics in the Divided State

The decades after ratification of the state's second constitution brought rapid changes to Virginia. Railroad construction, industrialization, urbanization, and a large increase in the population of the region west of the Blue Ridge transformed the state in many ways. National events influenced what those changes meant to the people of Virginia. Early in the 1830s the Whig Party formed to unite people who opposed President Andrew Jackson's administration. Like Virginia's Tertium Quids, Jackson disapproved of interpreting the constitution to allow an expanded role for the federal government in directing or promoting national economic development. He vetoed a bill to recharter the Bank of the United States. But he took a strong nationalist stand against South Carolina after that state claimed the right to nullify a tariff law Congress passed that raised costs southern farmers paid for imported merchandise. Virginians, like political leaders elsewhere in the United States, divided into Democrats who generally agreed with Jackson and Whigs who did not.

Democrats and Whigs battled each other during political campaigns and during sessions of the General Assembly. Both parties rewarded their supporters with jobs in the post office or in the small state bureaucracy. For some as yet unexplained reason, even though members of the General Assembly voted along partisan lines for the appointment of clerks, doorkeepers, sergeants at arms, and other functionaries of the legislature, they did not treat the extremely influential office of Speaker of the House of Delegates as a partisan position. When the Speakership became vacant the two parties strove to place one of their own in the office, but after a man was elected Speaker he was usually reelected without serious opposition as long as he was willing to serve.

The curiously nonpartisan character of the Speaker's office was an anomaly in that age of intense partisanship.

There was no solid South in the nineteenth century, and unlike some decades in the twentieth century no one-party politics in Virginia. Politically, the state was competitive, although Democrats had a slight advantage over Whigs. Democratic Party candidates won every presidential election in Virginia from the 1820s through 1856, although often by very small margins. Perhaps the divided nature of the Whig Party in the state prevented it from more effectively campaigning for the party's presidential candidates. Some Virginia Whigs eagerly embraced the national improvement agenda that Henry Clay called the American System. They hoped to employ the power of the national government to stimulate economic development. Other Virginia Whigs remained opposed to that expansive vision of the proper role for the national government and became Whigs largely because of their opposition to a strong presidency as evidenced by Andrew Jackson's administration.

Native Virginia Whigs William Henry Harrison, who won the presidency in 1840, and Zachary Taylor, who won in 1848, both lived in other states for most of their lives, but they came closer to carrying Virginia when they ran for president than any other Whig candidates, including even the popular and respected Henry Clay, of Kentucky, who was also a native of Virginia and was a candidate for president three times. One of the states' rights Whigs, John Tyler, was elected vice president in 1840 and succeeded to the presidency in April 1841 when Harrison died. Tyler's administration was unhappy and generally unsuccessful in large part because he was often at odds with the national leaders of his own Whig Party.

White women often took an active part in partisan politics, and political campaign events became popular public occasions in which men, women, and children all participated. Lucy Maria Johnson Barbour, widow of Governor James Barbour, formed a statewide organization of women in 1844 to raise money to erect a statue of Henry Clay in Richmond. Although initially criticized publicly for projecting herself too visibly into politics, Barbour and her association of Whig women persisted. The unveiling in Capitol Square in April 1860 of a life-size marble statue of Henry Clay attracted national attention. The statue was one of the most visible and lasting monuments to women's political activity during the 1840s and 1850s.

The dedication in February 1858 in Capitol Square in Richmond of a monumental bronze equestrian statue of George Washington, which was eventually surrounded by statues of other Virginia revolutionary leaders, reinforced national unity in Virginia and emphasized Virginia's role in the founding of the United States. So, too, did the action of many white American women, including some from Virginia, who in their roles as republican mothers founded

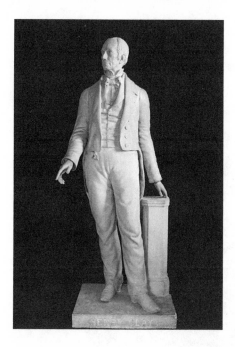

Joel Tanner Hart, *Henry Clay,* 1860

the Mount Vernon Ladies' Association of the Union in 1853. The association was the first large-scale, national historic preservation organization. It pioneered in the acquisition, preservation, and interpretation for American citizens of a uniquely important American historical site. The association's board included members from every state, and like the Virginia Whig women who had raised money for the statue of Henry Clay, the association emphasized patriotism and national unity during a time of increasingly divisive sectional politics.

In the intense partisanship of the 1830s and 1840s leaders of both parties in Virginia came out in favor of abolishing the property qualification for the suffrage in favor of universal white manhood suffrage. In part that was a straightforward attempt to gain votes, but it also reflected an emerging change in political philosophy in the country and the state. A large portion of the population came to believe that their legacy of political liberty from the American Revolution should be a political culture that permitted all free adult men to vote and to have a chance to run for public office. Called Jacksonian Democracy, the concept led almost every state in the country except Virginia to abolish property qualifications for voting by 1850.

Congressional annexation of the independent Republic of Texas in March 1845 and the admission of Texas as a new slave state exacerbated sectional differences within the United States and led to war between the United States

This 1858 photograph of what at the time was called
Virginia's Washington Monument was taken shortly
after the dedication

and Mexico in 1846. Several companies of Virginia militia mustered into service under the overall command of the senior general in the U.S. Army, Winfield Scott, a Petersburg native who had gained fame during the War of 1812.
Another native Virginia officer, Robert E. Lee, distinguished himself during
the army's march from the Gulf Coast to Mexico City. Militiamen and officers
as well as regular army soldiers and officers from throughout the country saw
action together in Mexico, little knowing that in a few years they would face
one another on battlefields in a civil war.

The treaty that concluded the war with Mexico awarded to the United
States a large portion of North America, including the area that became the
states of California, Nevada, Utah, Arizona, and New Mexico and large parts
of what became Colorado and Wyoming. The fate of that large western area
led to a major political crisis in the nation. Men and women in some northern
and midwestern states disapproved of allowing slavery into the western territories, but political leaders in most of the slave states insisted on the right
of slave owners to move with their slave property into the southwest and into

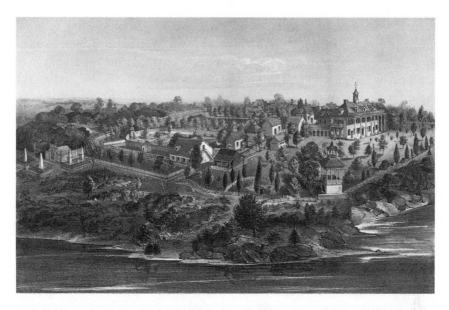

This 1858 idealized lithograph entitled *Mount Vernon, Home of George Washington* was printed five years after the founding of the Mount Vernon Ladies' Association of the Union.

the Great Plains, which the United States had acquired from France in 1803. Some Virginians hoped to reduce their reliance on slavery in that way, but others wanted to create new slave states and thereby preserve the balance in Congress between the free and slave states. The set of laws Congress adopted in 1850, collectively known as the Compromise of 1850, appeared to resolve the resulting political crisis but did not answer the main question whether slavery was to be permitted in the west.

One very important part of the Compromise of 1850 was the Fugitive Slave Act, which Virginia senator James Murray Mason sponsored. He was a grandson of George Mason, who had drafted the Virginia Declaration of Rights in 1776 and opposed ratification of the Constitution in 1788 because he feared a too-strong federal government. In 1850 Senator Mason and most legislators from the slave states insisted that a strong Fugitive Slave Act was necessary to protect the rights of owners of enslaved men, women, and children. Several state legislatures in free states had enacted what they called personal liberty laws that prohibited state officials from assisting in the capture and return to slavery of people who escaped into a free state. The federal government then had no agency that could enforce the Constitution's provisions for the return of runaways. The law of 1850 permitted southerners to pursue runaways into free states and seize them and return them to slave states without interference from state authorities—even without a judicial proceeding to prove that a person who claimed ownership had legally owned the person in question. It is one of the ironies of Virginia's history that Mason, the grandson of a founding father who disapproved of a strong federal government, led the fight for passage of the bill that increased the power of the federal government to prevent legislators in free states from exercising what they believed was their state's right to protect African Americans within their jurisdictions from slave catchers.

Constitutional Convention of 1850–1851

While the dramatic legislative debates in Washington about the provisions of the Compromise of 1850 were concluding, Virginia voters elected members of the second state constitutional convention of the nineteenth century. A mere two decades after the Convention of 1829–30, population growth and political changes in the western part of Virginia and demands that originated largely in that region for reforming the state constitution led to the convention, which met in Richmond between October 14, 1850, and August 1, 1851. The debates in that convention were more contentious and less formally intellectual than in the Convention of 1829–30. Advocates of democratic reform clashed repeatedly with opponents of extending political democracy.

Unlike in the 1829–30 convention, reformers won several major victories in the state's third constitutional convention. The delegates agreed to abolish the property qualification for voting and adopted universal white manhood suffrage. Convention members created the new office of lieutenant governor to serve as president of the Senate and become governor in the event of the governor's death or resignation. The office was not identical to the colonial office of the same name or of the office of that name under the Constitution of 1776. They allowed voters for the first time to elect such local officers as justices of the peace and sheriffs and also the governor, lieutenant governor (a new office the constitution created), and attorney general as well as all the state's judges, including judges of the Supreme Court of Appeals. Most states had adopted most or all those reforms by 1850, but in Virginia the struggle to extend democracy was difficult and protracted.

Many political leaders in the eastern portion of the state resisted the increase of political influence of Virginia's non-slave-owners, both in the east and especially in the west, where ownership of slaves was comparatively uncommon. It is unlikely that all eastern slave owners believed that all westerners or men who owned no slaves were secret abolitionists, but eastern delegates feared that the influence in the General Assembly of a larger number of men who did not own slaves might lessen the state government's commitment to the institution of slavery or place high taxes on slave property that would work to the disadvantage of owners of enslaved people. The Constitution of 1851 revised and disguised the Great Gerrymander of 1830 to provide western Virginians a small majority of seats in the House of Delegates but guaranteed eastern Virginians a permanent majority of seats in the Senate. The decreasing minority of voters in the east could thereby make the Senate an impregnable fortress for the protection of slavery.

Taxation of slaves was an issue of fundamental importance on which eastern and western delegates to the Convention of 1850–51 differed. The state collected taxes on land, based on its assessed value, and on many items of personal property, including slaves. Laws set the tax rates on items of personal property at a flat rate or based the tax on the value of the property. The new constitution placed a maximum value of $300 for the taxation of enslaved adults. That cap allowed men and women who owned large numbers of slaves to pay a proportionately smaller amount of taxes on their personal property than the majority of white men and women in the state who owned few or no slaves. The rapid rise in the monetary value of enslaved people during the 1850s as a result of increased demand in the southwestern states subsequently made the cap a serious grievance in western Virginia.

Universal white manhood suffrage and the popular election of more public officials brought about numerous changes in Virginia's political culture. Many white men who had not voted and could not hold office before 1851 entered public life. Richmond bricklayer Martin Meredith Lipscomb exemplified the new generation of political leaders who emerged at that time. Born in 1823, he ran for mayor of Richmond in 1853 and lost, but in 1854 he campaigned among the working classes and won election as city sergeant, the office in the city comparable to that of sheriff in a county. The city's veteran traditional political leaders were visibly unnerved when working men invaded the world of public service that had always been reserved for gentlemen. As they had feared, Lipscomb and many others like him made Virginia's political culture more egalitarian and democratic. Lipscomb spoke to working men in bars and on the streets, which before that time no candidates had ever even considered doing. "We have shown," he told one crowd, "that the 'humble mechanic' can raise his head with the proudest, and ask at your hands that suffrage which every citizen in our free country has a right to ask." Lipscomb remained active in Richmond city politics until shortly before his death fifty years after his first run for public office. He almost always took the side of reformers and working-class white men. After the Civil War he championed the rights of African Americans to vote.[4] Lipscomb and men like him upset established political apple carts in ways that had been impossible before adoption of the Constitution of 1851.

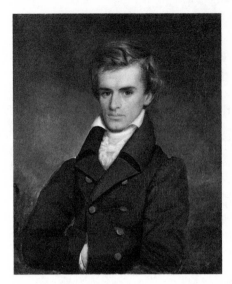

John Gadsby Chapman, *Henry Alexander Wise*

Henry Alexander Wise was another such man. A native of the Eastern
Shore and grandson of prominent political leaders, he had served in the House
of Representatives during the 1830s and 1840s, was ambassador to Brazil from
1844 to 1847, and was a delegate to the Convention of 1850–51. Wise advocated public education and the interests of working people. He was one of
the few eastern members who openly approved of universal white manhood
suffrage and spoke repeatedly of his role in the convention later in the decade
when he ran for governor. He also advocated public education and industrial
development and tried to reduce the state's reliance on slavery. Wise won election as governor of Virginia in 1855 in part because he appealed to working-
class men. He was a brigadier general in the Confederate Army from 1861
to 1865.

During the decade following the Convention of 1850–51, the state substantially increased its support for and investment in internal improvements. It
did so for several reasons. Improved roads, canals, and railroads would make it
easier for farmers and manufacturers to market their products and do business
in an emerging national marketplace. Construction of public works such as
railroads stimulated the economy, and those avenues of transportation could
make the countryside more prosperous and the cities through which they
passed more prosperous, too. The activities of the Board of Public Works increased during the decade chiefly because of the construction of railroads. The
board continued to purchase stock in new railroad companies. The General
Assembly issued charters to new railroad companies and had to issue bonds to
borrow the money to invest in and stimulate the new companies. By the be-

ginning of 1861, Virginia had more than 1,800 miles of railroads in operation, more than any other southern state except Tennessee.

In the process, the state created a public debt of almost $34 million. It was by far the largest public debt in any southern or Ohio Valley state. It was, in fact, the third largest public debt in the United States, after only Pennsylvania and New York. Per capita, the Virginia debt was actually much larger than either; and because about 30 percent of all Virginians lived in slavery and paid no taxes, the debt was even greater per taxpayer. At the time the debt did not appear to present a potential problem for the state. Its creation reflected an overall public confidence of the state's business and political leaders that Virginia and Virginians would prosper as full participants in the increasingly sophisticated national and international economies. Railroads were the key to that national and state prosperity, and the taxes and dividends they paid to the state treasury could contribute toward paying off the debt. Little did they know at the end of the decade how big a problem that debt would create at the end of the next decade.

Slavery and Sectionalism in State and Nation

By the middle of the century divisive issues relating to slavery had become increasingly important within both the state and the nation. The generations of Virginians who had grown up during the American Revolution or in its afterglow had died, and with them died some of the antislavery beliefs that enabled people early in the nineteenth century to advocate the gradual abolition of slavery or to emancipate some or all of their slaves. The generation of Virginians who came of age during the second quarter of the century had very different ideas about slavery. Instead of agonizing about whether slavery contradicted Christianity or the principles of the nation founded on liberty, a majority of white Virginians evidently adopted pro-slavery ideas. One powerful statement of that new ideology came from John Brown Baldwin. A son of a judge of the Virginia Supreme Court of Appeals, Baldwin was born in 1820 and became a distinguished attorney in Staunton. He spoke early in 1861 about his beliefs and about how public opinion in the South had changed. "I have always entertained the opinion that African slavery, as it exists in Virginia, is a right and a good thing," he proclaimed, "on every ground, moral, social, religious, political and economical—a blessing alike to the master and the slave—a blessing to the non-slaveholder and the slaveholder."

Baldwin went on to explain how things had changed since his childhood. "I can remember myself when slavery, and the evil and the sin of slavery rested upon the minds and conscience of the South like an incubus. I can recollect, sir, when it was only spoken of by Northern men to denounce it, and by South-

ern men to offer up a feeble apology for its existence. That was the condition
of the public opinion of the South upon this question when I first recollect it.
What is it now? Sir, since the day when the Reformation of the Church was
proclaimed by the Reformers" in the times of Martin Luther and John Calvin,
"there never has occurred so wonderful, so thorough a revolution in public
opinion in any country on any subject as has occurred in the opinion of the
people of the South on the subject of slavery. Instead of its being looked upon
now as a curse or a crime it is not only defended, but justified, aye, and approved by the South as a system of servitude between an inferior and a superior
race, conferring benefits and blessings upon them both. Sir, the conscience of
the South is easy. The South stands self-acquitted on this subject of our greatest institution and our greatest blessing."[5]

It is worthwhile to pause and notice that Baldwin spoke about the South
and about southerners when he actually meant a large portion of the white
people in the slave-holding states. That was typical of the time. That character-
ization of the attitudes of some people in the state and region made it appear
that residents of Virginia and the other states were all of one mind, which was
not the case anywhere. It certainly was not the case for enslaved men, women,
and children in those states. And that overly broad generalization has also had
misleading consequences when it has been repeated in thoughtless historical
accounts that in effect ignored and left all dissenters out of the story and incorrectly portrayed the old South as merely the embodiment of its elite white
men. That was the case for other comments in other decades, too, not just for
Baldwin on the eve of the Civil War.

The state government took an active role in protecting the institution of
slavery and the interests of slave owners and also in suppressing discussion
about slavery. The Constitution of 1851 included for the first time a prohibition on the legislative abolition of slavery and restricted owners' abilities to
free their own enslaved property. The 1848 revision of the law Of Offences
against Public Policy made it a crime punishable by one to five years in the
state penitentiary for "Any free person who shall write, print, or cause to be
written or printed, any book, pamphlet, or other writing, with intent to advise or incite persons of colour within this commonwealth to rebel or make
insurrection, or denying the rights of masters to property in their slaves." In
addition to making it illegal to criticize the ownership of human beings, the
law also made it a criminal offence for any federal postmaster to deliver any
such writing to any person in Virginia or fail "to have such book, pamphlet
or other writing burned in his presence."[6]

The nation's Protestant churches wrestled with the issue of slavery during
the 1840s and 1850s. Baptists and Methodists, the most numerous Protestant
denominations, divided into northern and southern factions during the sec-

ond quarter of the nineteenth century. A large proportion of clergymen of those denominations in the states where slavery remained a profitable and essential institution preached an interpretation of Scripture that legitimized slavery. The Bible contained many explicit references to slavery as practiced in ancient times and no specific condemnations. By the end of the 1850s few southern clergymen preached or wrote in opposition to slavery. Several prominent Virginia ministers contributed to the argument that Christian masters and mistresses who took care of the physical and spiritual welfare of enslaved people were to be commended for doing God's work and not condemned for owning slaves.

A less literal interpretation of Scripture than prevailed in the South appealed to many clergymen and antislavery leaders in the North. All northern ministers did not speak out against slavery, but many did. Clergymen in northern states by the middle of the nineteenth century increasingly focused on actions of owners of slaves that were inconsistent with Christian behavior. They mentioned sexual exploitation and the fancy trade; separation of family members; the terrorism of slave patrols; the violation of human rights that the slave trade created; and the routine brutalities and degradations the institution of slavery imposed on enslaved people. Those clergymen argued that ownership of slaves was therefore contrary to the teachings of the Bible.

Public criticism of slavery died away in Virginia during the second quarter of the nineteenth century as most white people, like John Brown Baldwin, accepted the arguments of clergymen and political leaders that slavery was both a positive good for white society and also for the enslaved people. Virginian George Fitzhugh advanced one of the strongest defenses of slavery in two controversial books, *Sociology for the South; or, The Failure of Free Society,* published in 1854, and *Cannibals All! or, Slaves without Masters,* published in 1857. Fitzhugh compared slave labor with free labor regimes in the United States and in Europe and concluded that owners of southern slaves treated them better than northern capitalists treated their paid factory workers. Fitzhugh's books, which could be interpreted to argue that slavery was the preferred system to organize all labor, including even white working people, went beyond the most widely accepted pro-slavery arguments, which usually rested on a belief in the inherent inferiority of Africans and of people of African descent.

Two native white Virginia writers, Mary Henderson Eastman and Martha Haines Butt, published novels in the 1850s to counteract the influence of Harriett Beecher Stowe's 1852 antislavery novel *Uncle Tom's Cabin.* Eastman's 1852 *Aunt Phillis's Cabin; or, Southern Life as It Is* and Butt's 1853 *Antifanaticism: A Tale of the South* both pronounced slavery a good Christian institution and a beneficial one for the South. That placed them squarely in opposition to the increasing hostility to slavery. They dared, and few southern men are known

Martha Haines Butt of Norfolk was an aspiring writer whose 1853 novel, *Antifanaticism: A Tale of the South,* was only one of her published books, but it was the only one with a political message. Her portrait appeared in the national magazine *Frank Leslie's Illustrated News* on January 14, 1860.

to have objected, to take a public part in the most divisive moral and political debate in the country.

That is not to say that slavery became universally accepted. Mary Berkeley Minor Blackford, of Fredericksburg and Lynchburg, was one persistent critic of slavery, but other than supporting the work of the American Colonization Society she kept her criticisms confined to her journal and discussions with family and friends. She, like many other women of the time, was reluctant to discuss controversial matters of politics and policy in a public venue. Some other opponents of slavery spoke out boldly, but the most notable of them did so outside Virginia. Moncure Daniel Conway was born into a slave-owning family of planters in Stafford County in 1832 and acquired from his mother an early dislike for slavery. After studying for the ministry in New England he emerged as a severe critic of slavery. Estranged from the society of his birth, he lived much of his life in northern states and in Europe, but he often wrote about Virginia. As an abolitionist late in the 1850s and a Unitarian minister and well-respected intellectual, Conway appeared to have become the opposite of the typical Virginia gentleman in values and behavior.

The Politics of Sectional Division

The national disintegration of the Whig Party in the middle of the 1850s had many repercussions in Virginia, particularly after the formation in the Northeast and Midwest of the Republican Party, whose members were widely regarded as opposed to slavery. In fact, many members of the new party were not so much opposed to slavery as they were opposed to the spread of slavery outside the southeastern states. Some Virginia Whigs joined the Democrats, but others tried to maintain their independence as a state party without a national counterpart. In many northern states the short-lived American Party (also known as the Know-Nothing Party) appealed to former Whigs by charging that Catholic immigrants who often voted for Democratic Party candidates were dangerous to American freedoms. In Virginia, the Know-Nothing Party made fewer such charges, perhaps because Catholics were less numerous and anti-Catholicism less pronounced, but for a brief time in the mid-1850s they won some elections by appealing to Whigs without a party of their own and to Democrats.

The 1855 gubernatorial campaign pitted the Democrats against the Know-Nothings. It was only the second statewide election for governor in Virginia history. Henry A. Wise was the Democratic Party candidate. Know-Nothings, Whigs, and Democrats who disliked their own controversial and unpredictable nominee united as the Opposition in an unsuccessful attempt to defeat Wise. During that campaign and others of the 1850s, Democratic candidates and newspapers often insinuated that because some northern Know-Nothing leaders were well-known opponents of slavery, Know-Nothing candidates in Virginia were not to be trusted. Some Virginian Know-Nothing candidates sought to defend their reputations as loyal slave owners by proclaiming that they were slave owners by the deliberate purchase of slaves, not by the accident of birth into a slave-owning family. When Democratic congressman John Letcher, who as a young man had questioned the propriety of slavery, was preparing to run for governor in 1859, he had to reclaim his place among the politically worthy before he could campaign with any chance of success. He published a letter boasting that he was "the owner of slave property, by purchase, and not by inheritance," that he fully approved of slavery and deliberately chose to own slaves.[7]

The 1850s was a decade of increasingly tense national division on the subject of slavery and whether it should be allowed to expand into the western territories. In 1854 Congress passed the Kansas-Nebraska Act to provide for the settlement of portions of the Great Plains and set the terms under which residents there could apply for statehood. The act repealed the portion of the Missouri Compromise of 1820 that prohibited slavery in the territory north of $36° 30'$ north latitude (the southern border of the state of Missouri, which was in effect a westward extension of the southern border of Virginia). That alarmed men and women who opposed the spread of slavery into the territories and the potential creation of additional slave states. That same year former Whigs and others founded the Republican Party, which quickly attracted the loyalties of many opponents of the extension of slavery and within two years also gained the loyalty of many northern Know-Nothings.

In an attempt to settle the political and legal questions the rapid settlement of the Plains and the anticipated application of residents there for statehood created, the Supreme Court in March 1857 ruled in *Dred Scott v. Sandford* that Congress had exceeded its constitutional authority in 1820 by excluding slavery from the western territory. The Supreme Court in effect stated that Congress had a constitutional responsibility to protect the property rights of slave owners in the territories. The court also declared that African Americans were not and could not be citizens entitled to all the protections of the law. That decision further enflamed sectional tensions. Violence erupted in Kansas between supporters and opponents of a draft state constitution that permitted slavery. One particularly strong-minded abolitionist, John Brown, and his sons killed several supporters of slavery in Kansas. People in Virginia closely followed the increasingly divisive national debates and took sides.

People in the nation also closely followed another court case that was never settled and therefore did not have the consequences people who opposed slavery feared. In 1852 Jonathan Lemon and Julia Stewart Lemon left their home in Bath County, Virginia, en route to a new life in Texas. They and their eight enslaved men, women, and children traveled by boat to New York, where they planned to transfer to a steamship for the trip to Texas. However, antislavery activists in New York separated the Lemons from their slaves and declared them free because New York law prohibited slavery. With financial support the General Assembly of Virginia provided, the Lemons sued for the recovery of what they regarded as their property. For reasons that are not clear, the General Assembly discontinued its financial support, and the case eventually lapsed in the New York court system. Jonathan and Julia Lemon returned to Virginia and lived there the remainder of their lives.

The Lemons' New York lawsuit, had it got into federal court, could have produced a second judicial ruling of comparable importance to *Dred Scott v. Sandford*. Federal judges might have ruled that all states had a constitutional responsibility to protect people's right to own slaves. That could have nationalized slavery as opponents of slavery feared and stated at the time. They cited the court case as one of many instances in which what they called the "slave power" endangered free labor and representative government in the United States in general and even in the free states.

Presidential Election of 1860

On the night of October 16, 1859, John Brown and eighteen other men crossed the Potomac River from Maryland into Virginia and the next day seized the United States arsenal at Harpers Ferry. Brown intended to arm local slaves and begin a war to end slavery. Governor Wise dispatched state militiamen to the scene, and on the eighteenth, after a brief skirmish, Colonel Robert E.

David Hunter Strother pen sketch of
John Brown, 1859

Lee and his aide Lieutenant J.E.B. Stuart, in command of a company of marines, captured Brown and his men. The state charged Brown with treason
against the Commonwealth of Virginia. He was convicted at a trial in Charles
Town and was hanged on December 2, 1859. Brown's raid convinced many
southerners that northern extremists were intent on the violent destruction
of southern society.

Brown's raid embarrassed leaders of the new Republican Party. Most of
them disapproved of slavery or of allowing slavery into the West, but few were
active abolitionists, and almost none were willing to tolerate inciting enslaved
people to rebellion. As a consequence of Brown's raid, Republican leaders
changed their plans to hold the 1860 national convention in the northwestern Virginia city of Wheeling and moved it to Chicago.

In 1860 Americans selected a new president from among four candidates.
The Republican Party nominated Abraham Lincoln, of Illinois, a known opponent of slavery. The Democratic Party split into two factions. One nominated Senator Stephen A. Douglas, of Illinois, and the other Vice President
John C. Breckinridge, of Kentucky. A new party that called itself the Constitutional Union Party nominated John Bell, a former Whig and Know-
Nothing from Tennessee. What may have been the most important difference
among the candidates concerned slavery and the western territories—that is
to say, the future of slavery in the United States. Lincoln and the Republicans
strongly opposed the expansion of slavery, and Breckinridge and most southern Democrats strongly opposed any restrictions on the expansion of slavery.
Douglas endorsed the concept of popular sovereignty to allow residents of

territories to decide for themselves whether to permit slavery. Popular sovereignty was unpopular with most Democrats in the slave states because it could produce territorial laws or draft state constitutions that prohibited slavery; and it was unpopular with some Democrats and all Republicans in the free states because it could produce territorial laws or draft state constitutions that protected slavery. Bell merely endorsed preservation of the Union and took no stand on any other national issues.

Lincoln was extremely unpopular in most of Virginia and in the other slave states. Virginia's small Republican Party had its headquarters in Wheeling, where the editor of the Wheeling *Daily Intelligencer,* Archibald W. Campbell, was also the party's founding chair and a delegate to the 1860 national convention. Other than in the Ohio Valley counties and in some Shenandoah Valley and Potomac River counties almost nobody planed to vote for Lincoln. One exception was in the Aquia region of Prince William County. In July 1860 a large number of Lincoln supporters there planned to erect a flagpole and fly a Lincoln banner. Other people in the area threatened them with violence if they did. The Lincoln supporters then appealed to the state adjutant general and to the governor for protection. The governor ordered that a company of the county militia march to Aquia, but the militiamen did not protect the Republicans; they protected the men who chopped down the flagpole and then chopped it up into souvenirs.

Nearly every state allowed or required men to vote by ballot by 1860, but voting in Virginia remained by voice vote. All voters announced out loud who they voted for, and the men who conducted the election noted how they voted and often kept lists of who voted for whom. In presidential elections, voters could also hand in ballots, or tickets, that listed the names of the candidates for president and vice president and the names of the candidates for presidential elector; but voters still had to announce aloud who they voted for, and each voter had to sign the back of the ticket. Archibald Campbell's Wheeling *Daily Intelligencer* printed and sold Republican presidential tickets.

Where opposition to Lincoln was strong, which was nearly everywhere, it took a brave man to vote for the Republican candidate. Shortly before the election the governor received a letter from one such apprehensive man. "As the Presidential election is approaching," John M. Smith wrote from the mountains in Giles County, "I would like to Know from you what is to prevent me from Voting for Lincoln. as he is the man I prefer. the reason of this letter is that there is a great deal of threatning on the part of Slave holders in regard to poor men exerciseing the elective franchise and as I am a law abideng citizen and has paid my taxes to the commonwealth of Virginia every year and performed all the duties and complied with all the obligations imposed on me I think it hard if I should be prevented from exerciseing the wright of

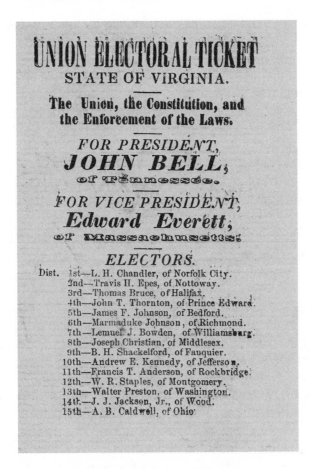

1860 Union Party electoral ticket

suffrage that other men do in selecting any one of the four candidates before the people for the office of President of the United states as my choice. . . . I wish merely to have the privilege of casting my vote for the man I prefer and nothing more."[8] Official election returns record no vote cast for Lincoln in Giles County.

In 1860 Virginia was entitled to fifteen electoral votes. Most Virginia Democrats voted for Breckinridge in November 1860, but Douglas won a significant number of votes in the cities and the Shenandoah Valley. Bell did well in the areas of the state where Whigs had traditionally been strong, in the cities and many of the most prosperous plantation counties, including traditional Whig strongholds in the Shenandoah Valley. The election in Virginia was more a traditional partisan contest between former Whigs (Bell was a former Whig congressman and Know-Nothing senator) and two Democrats than it was a prelude to a vote on preservation of the Union. In fact, Breckinridge won the largest number of votes in the counties that later became West Virginia and remained in the Union, and Bell won the largest number in the other counties and cities. Abraham Lincoln received 1,929 votes in Virginia, most of them in the Ohio Valley counties and in the northwestern city of Wheeling, but he also received votes in some counties in the Shenandoah Valley and in the upper part of the Potomac River Valley. Fifty-five men voted for Lincoln in Prince William County and four in Portsmouth.

The 1860 presidential election was the closest in Virginia's history. The incomplete file of official returns preserved in the state's archives contain discrepancies between the number of votes candidates received in some counties and the totals as later printed in newspapers and almanacs. What are probably the most accurate totals, published in the *Richmond Daily Enquirer* on December 24, 1860, show that Bell received 74,701 votes (44.65%), Breckinridge 74,379 (44.46%), Douglas 16,292 (9.74%), and Lincoln 1,929 (1.15%). Because some election officials misspelled the names of some candidates for presidential elector on the official reports, the state's attorney general required that those votes be tabulated as if cast for other men, with the result that the secretary of the commonwealth and governor certified the election of nine Bell electors and six Breckinridge electors.

The six Breckinridge electors all resigned, even though the state's constitution and laws did not require all the state's electoral votes to be awarded to the candidate who received the largest number of votes. Bell therefore received all fifteen of Virginia's electoral votes. He also received the electoral votes of two other border slave states, Kentucky and Tennessee. Lincoln received no electoral votes in any of the slave states, but he won so many in the free states that he received a majority of all of the electoral votes and won election to the presidency.

13

CIVIL WAR AND
EMANCIPATION

THE ELECTION OF Abraham Lincoln to the presidency in November 1860 provoked men in South Carolina to secede from the United States on December 20. Conventions in Mississippi, Alabama, Florida, Georgia, and Louisiana all voted to secede in January, and Texas quickly followed. On February 4, 1861, representatives of the seven states met in Montgomery, Alabama, and created the Confederate States of America. They formed a provisional government and a few days later swore in Jefferson Davis as president.

The Virginia Convention of 1861

In response to the secession crisis, the General Assembly of Virginia called for the election of delegates to a state convention. The eyes of both North and South were on Virginia. With the largest population of enslaved people in any of the states, almost half a million, Virginia was also strategically placed between the lower South and the free states. Many people believed that Maryland and North Carolina and perhaps some of the other slave states that remained in the Union until the spring (Missouri, Arkansas, Kentucky, Tennessee, and Delaware) would follow Virginia's lead. Influential political leaders in Virginia and in the other upper South slave states hoped to use their central position within the old Union to restore it. Unlike in the lower South states that seceded early in 1861 after Lincoln's election, those states remained in the Union for five and a half more months.

A large majority of the delegates elected on February 4, 1861, opposed secession. The only voters in the state who elected a significant number of men who favored speedy secession were in the counties south of the Rappahannock River and east of the Blue Ridge. A large majority of the state's enslaved

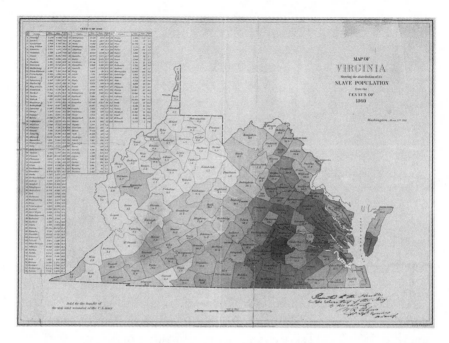

Henry S. Graham, *Map of Virginia Showing the Distribution of Its Slave Population from the Census of 1860* (1861). Printed in Philadelphia, this and other state and regional maps showing the uneven distribution of slavery in the South were sold to raise money for wounded and ill soldiers of the United States Army.

population lived in that region. In nearly every county at least 40 percent of the inhabitants were enslaved, and in most more than half. In the counties of Amelia and Nottoway more than 70 percent of the entire population lived in slavery. Opponents of secession won in nearly all of the state's cities and most of its counties. The surprised editor of the *Abingdon Democrat,* who believed that secession was necessary, concluded, "the *immediate* secession candidates have been badly whipped—in fact, have been almost annihilated,—and the gentlemen representing the '*wait-a-bit*' ticket triumphantly elected."[1]

The editor was correct. The 152 delegates who convened in Richmond on February 13 opposed secession by a margin of at least two to one. In spite of spirited pro-secession resolutions adopted in many of the state's counties and cities, the opponents of secession won a tremendous victory in February; the men they elected to act for the state during the crisis overwhelmingly opposed secession.

The Virginia state convention was unlike any of the other state conventions that met and acted quickly. The Virginia convention remained in session from February 13 until May 1. It was the only state convention that tried to save the Union rather than leave it. In the beginning the delegates delayed taking any action while former president John Tyler presided over a conference that met in Washington, D.C. to try to find a compromise that would resolve the sectional crisis by bringing the states that had seceded back into the Union on terms free states could accept. The failure of that conference, together with a generally unfavorable reaction in Virginia to Lincoln's inaugural address on March 4, discouraged opponents of secession in the state, but on April 4, the convention defeated by 90 to 45 a motion to recommend secession to the voters.

The debates were largely about preserving the Union, not whether to retain or abolish slavery. None of the delegates spoke against slavery. In fact, many of the opponents of secession argued that slavery in Virginia was safer with Virginia in the Union than out of it. If Virginia seceded, owners of enslaved men and women would lose the right to take their slave property into the western territories of the United States. That would bottle slavery up in the southeastern states where a surplus of laborers would doom slavery economically. Furthermore, without the protection of the Fugitive Slave Act slave owners in the border states would lose the assistance of the federal government in recovering runaways. George William Brent, a delegate from Alexandria, predicted accurately that if Virginia seceded and civil war began, Virginia would be the main battleground, and under that circumstance it would be impossible for the state to preserve slavery. "I regard secession," he warned the other delegates, "as the doom of slavery in the border States."[2]

Advocates of secession argued that Virginia and the other upper South slave states would be in a permanent minority if the lower South slave states remained out of the Union and the upper South states remained in the Union. Hanover County's George W. Richardson, an early advocate of secession, explained the advantages he believed Virginia would gain by seceding from the United States and joining the Confederacy. "The Constitution of the Confederate States," he explained, "will be administered by a Southern Congress, a Southern President, with a Southern Cabinet, and construed by Southern Judges, all looking to the interest of Southern slaveholders; and not by a Northern free soil executive and abolition Congress, and a supreme Court to be abolitionized as rapidly as death shall remove the remainder of the venerable States rights Judges who now grace its bench."[3]

Opponents of secession succeeded in keeping Virginia in the Union until the middle of April, but they failed to find a solution to the national crisis. Supporters of secession held numerous public meetings during the winter and spring and adopted spirited resolutions to demand immediate secession. So far as is known most of the public meetings that issued declarations in favor of secession during the spring of 1861 were composed entirely of men; but in

March 1861 a large number of white women met in Essex County, in eastern Virginia, and issued a long declaration to the women of Virginia. They "*Resolved,* That we endeavor by every means in our power to imbue with the spirit of immediate secession all our countrymen who come within the range of our influence; assuring them if war be the consequence of this—the only honorable course for Virginians to pursue—they will ever find us ready and willing to cooperate with them to the utmost limit of our power, and that we shall consider it a glorious privilege to share in any privation that may befall them on the road to independence, considering it far preferable to endure the calamities of the most bloody and disastrous war, than to submit tamely to the yoke of insulting adversaries."

The women proposed to purchase "a flag bearing the device of our native State, and present it to the Essex Cavalry, with our most earnest prayers to the God of our Washington, that the slumbering spirit of Virginia chivalry may be roused by the sight of its glorious motto"—*sic semper tyrannis,* thus always to tyrants—"and that we may yet behold the radiant Goddess of Southern Freedom standing triumphantly over the prostrate form of Northern despotism."[4] Meetings of women in Petersburg and in Gloucester County adopted and published resolutions in support of the Essex County women.

Women who favored secession often harassed members of the convention in Richmond who opposed but did not change their minds. In frustration, early in April several prominent men, including former governor Henry A. Wise, who was a member of the convention, issued a call for what they called a spontaneous southern rights convention. They hoped to force the elected convention to vote for secession or perhaps even seize control of the government and secede in spite of the convention and the known wishes of Governor John Letcher, who opposed secession.

On April 12, South Carolinians fired on Fort Sumter in Charleston Harbor. Three days later Lincoln called for 75,000 militiamen to put down the rebellion and protect government installations. He called for three regiments from Virginia, a total of 2,340 officers and soldiers, but Letcher refused to comply. When news of the events in Charleston and of Lincoln's proclamation reached Richmond, many men who had opposed secession in order to avoid starting a civil war changed their minds. Wise, in the meantime, issued private orders without any legal authorization for Virginia militia companies to seize the federal arsenal at Harpers Ferry and the United States Navy Yard at Norfolk.

The delegates no longer had to decide whether secession was legal or wise or in Virginia's interest. War had begun, and the decision they had to make was which side to take. On April 17 during the final debates Wise dramatically pulled out a large horse pistol, placed it on his desk in the Capitol, and dared any convention members who opposed taking immediate action to assassinate him. By a margin of 88 to 55 the delegates voted to submit an Ordinance of Secession to the voters for ratification in May.

As the editor of the *Lynchburg Daily Virginian* explained, "the President's infamous Proclamation, indicating a purpose to subjugate the Southern States . . . did the business in Virginia, not the attack on Fort Sumter. It was this that swept away the last refuge of the Union men in Virginia. They could not maintain their ground in the face of the Proclamation breathing nothing but vengeance, subjugation and war."[5] Still, secession passed the convention by only an 8-to-5 margin. Some of the delegates who voted against secession on April 17 later changed their votes, and they and most of the others remained in Richmond to create an army to defend the state and take the initial steps to make Virginia one of the Confederate States of America. Pending ratification of the Ordinance of Secession in a popular referendum scheduled for May 23, the convention negotiated a diplomatic agreement with Alexander Hamilton Stephens, vice president of the Confederacy, to permit the independent state government to act in concert with the Confederacy.

Three days after the convention voted to remove Virginia from the Union, it created a three-member advisory council to assist the governor in preparing the state's defenses. The convention voted to offer command of the state's defense forces to Colonel Robert E. Lee. The delegates did not know that Lee had recently declined an offer he received through an intermediary from his mentor and fellow Virginian, General Winfield Scott, to command the United States Army. Lee resigned from the army rather than have to obey orders to coerce the seceded states. On April 23, 1861, he accepted the Virginia appointment and became commander of the state's new army. In accepting his commission as a major general of Virginia's defense forces, Lee stated that he had vowed never again to draw his sword except in defense of his country, by which he meant Virginia. Members of the convention recalled the words of George Washington's will in which he bequeathed his battle swords to a nephew with an instruction not to draw it except in the defense of his country. If the United States could no longer be held together except by force, insofar as Lee was concerned it was no longer worth preserving.

The Virginia convention then accepted an offer from the provisional Confederate government, and late in May, Richmond became the capital of the Confederacy. On May 23, the state's eligible men voted to ratify the Ordinance of Secession. Voters in eastern and central Virginia overwhelmingly approved the ordinance. East of the mountains and in most of the mountain counties opposition to secession almost completely dissolved in the face of war. A majority of men in the Ohio Valley counties of Virginia voted against secession, as did some significant numbers of men in the upper region of the Potomac

The ceremonial copy of the Virginia Ordinance of Secession was prepared by a German immigrant, William Flegenheimer, and signed during the second session of the convention in June 1861. A few delegates who were elected to replace members who died or resigned to enter the army signed during the third session in November, even though they had not been in the convention when it adopted the text of the ordinance on April 17, 1861.

David Hunter Strother, "The Village Magnates," shows three gentlemen discussing the proposed Ordinance of Secession, which is posted on the wall behind them, while a crouching African American, presumably enslaved, quietly watches and listens from behind the fence.

Valley. In the panhandle town of New Martinsville in May women sang revised lyrics of *Yankee Doodle* that proclaimed secessionists as traitors to the United States. In nearby Hancock County women presented an American flag to volunteers who marched off to defend the United States, much as the women of Essex County had presented a Virginia flag to the militia of that county in March. In both regions Virginians identified themselves as the true heirs of the American Revolution. In Hancock County the women told the soldiers that "in time to come we expect to be able to point to you proudly and say, they are our countrymen and they are Virginians!"[6]

On May 23, the state's voters also elected members of the General Assembly and in some northern and northwestern counties voters elected members of the United States House of Representatives in spite of the governor's proclamation to prohibit men from voting for members of Congress. On that same day they also voted whether to ratify the first amendment ever proposed to a Virginia constitution. A week after the convention voted to secede it submitted to the voters a constitutional amendment to remove the $300 limit on the taxation of slaves. Delegates from the western counties had argued for that change during the debates about secession, and enough eastern members reluctantly decided that it was a sacrifice worth making to grant a demand of the westerners and stop the bitter sectional debate that divided the convention. The state's voters ratified the amendment, although several thousand voters in the eastern counties where the densest populations of slaves resided voted against it.

Restoring Virginia to the Union

The constitutional amendment did not work as intended. Soon after the April 17 vote on secession many of the western opponents of secession left Richmond—some fearing for their lives—and returned home. John Snyder Carlile called a mass meeting in his hometown of Clarksburg, and the members of the meeting in turn called for a convention of loyal men from throughout Virginia to meet in Wheeling in May. That convention then issued a formal call for a second convention to meet in June to take steps to restore Virginia to the Union.

The declaration of the May convention that Carlile drafted denounced secession as treason. "Why should the people of North Western Virginia allow themselves to be dragged into the rebellion inaugurated by ambitious and heartless men," he asked, "who have banded themselves together to destroy a government formed for you by your patriot fathers, and which has secured to you all the liberties consistent with the nature of man, and has, for near three-fourths of a century, sheltered you in sunshine and in storm, made you the admiration of the civilized world, and conferred upon you a title more honored, respected and revered, than that of King or Potentate—the title of an American citizen.... We will, in the strength of our cause, resolutely and determinedly stand by our rights and our liberties secured to us by the struggles of our Revolutionary Fathers, and the authors of the Constitution under which we have grown and prospered beyond all precedent in the world's history. We will maintain, protect and defend that Constitution and the Union with all our strength, and with all our powers, ever remembering"—he quoted Thomas Jefferson—"that Resistance to tyrants is obedience to God."[7]

The June convention in Wheeling, following the unprecedented actions of the Richmond convention, took its own unprecedented action. It declared that Governor Letcher and the other state officers in Richmond had forfeited their offices by cooperating with the rebellion. The convention elected Francis H. Pierpont (who changed the spelling of his name to Pierpoint about that time) governor and also elected a new lieutenant governor and attorney general. On June 20, Pierpont took office as governor of Virginia by appointment of the Wheeling convention and delivered an inaugural address to the convention. It was the first inaugural address any governor of Virginia had ever made. "We have been driven into the position we occupy to-day, by the usurpers at the South," he told the convention. "We representing the loyal citizens of Virginia, have been bound to assume the position we have assumed to-day, for the protection of ourselves, our wives, our children, and our property. We, I repeat, have been *driven* to assume this position; and now we are but recurring to the great fundamental principle of our fathers, that to the loyal people of a State belong the law-making power of that State. The loyal people are entitled to the government and governmental authority of the State. And, fellow-citizens, it is the assumption of this authority upon which we are now about to enter."[8]

On July 4, President Lincoln recognized Pierpont's government as the legitimate government of all the loyal people of Virginia. That was the first act of the federal government to reconstruct the union of states. Pierpont had the famous phrase from one of Daniel Webster's speeches, "Liberty and Union," added to the seal of the commonwealth of Virginia, a visual repudiation of secessionist beliefs that liberty for white men was no longer possible in the United States. Several men represented the Virginia that the convention had restored to the Union in the United States House of Representatives from 1861 to 1863 and three in the United States Senate from 1861 to 1864.

Another convention of delegates from northwestern Virginia met in

The seal of the Restored Government of Virginia reproduced the seal designed in 1776 but added to it three words from Daniel Webster's famous 1830 speech, "Liberty and Union, Now and Forever, One and Inseparable."

Wheeling in the autumn of 1861 and drafted a constitution in order to apply for admission to the United States as a separate state. They initially planned to name the new state Kanawha, but during the long sectional controversies of the previous decades westerners had taken pride in being identified as western Virginians, so they voted to name the new state West Virginia. The constitution those midwestern Virginians wrote was radically different than the Virginia Constitution of 1851. It required that all voting be by secret ballot rather than by public voice vote. It provided that seats in the legislature of the new state be reapportioned following each federal census in order that legislators represent their constituents and not regions or other interests such as slave property, as had been the case with the Virginia Constitutions of 1830 and 1851. It required that all taxes be assessed based on the market value of land and items of personal property. It prohibited the state from creating a public debt of the kind that Virginia incurred for promoting construction of canals, toll roads, and railroads. It abolished the old county court system and created democratic local governments similar to New England townships. It placed limits on the tenures of county sheriffs and limited their political power. And it created the first free public school system in any southern state.

Before Congress admitted the new state to the Union it required that the draft constitution be amended to abolish slavery. As amended and ratified the West Virginia Constitution of 1863 declared that all children born in the state after July 4 of that year be free; that enslaved persons ten years of age or younger on that date be freed at age twenty-one; and that enslaved persons between the ages of ten and twenty-one on that date be freed at age twenty-five. However, it left all adult enslaved Virginians who lived in West Virginia as of July 4, 1863, enslaved for life.

Virginia had two governments between 1861 and 1865, one that was part of the Confederate States of America and had its capital in Richmond, and the other that was part of the United States of America and from 1861 to 1863 had its capital in Wheeling and from 1863 to 1865 in Alexandria. It was called the Restored Government because it was the government of Virginia that loyal men had restored to the Union. During the early years of the Civil War elected senators and delegates served in its General Assembly from the counties of Prince William, Loudoun, Fairfax, and Alexandria in northeastern Virginia, from the counties of Northampton and Accomack on the Eastern Shore, and from the counties of Princess Anne, Norfolk, and Elizabeth City and the city of Norfolk in southeastern Virginia.

The government of the Confederate state of Virginia in Richmond refused to acknowledge the loss of the western counties and allowed men who claimed to represent some of those counties to serve in the General Assembly. Several men from the counties of West Virginia also served in the Confederate

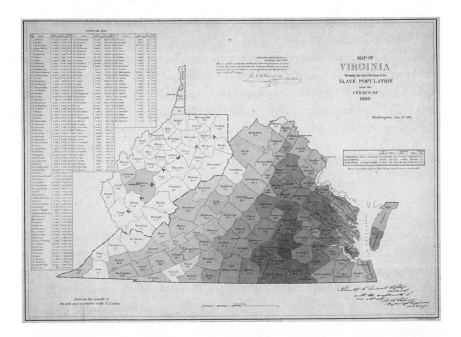

This modified version of the 1861 *Map of Virginia Showing the Distribution of Its Slave Population from the Census of 1860* was probably printed late in 1861 before the constitutional convention in Wheeling decided that the new state would be called West Virginia, not Kanawha. The boundary line indicates roughly the separation between the counties with representatives in the convention and the counties without.

Congress. The people of western Virginia were deeply divided about the war both before and after the formation of the new state of West Virginia. Both armies raised regiments there, and in some places virtual anarchy prevailed as unauthorized war parties terrorized the countryside. In Nicholas County, civil government virtually ceased to function by September 1861. Families as well as communities divided into warring factions. In Upshur County, the brothers Albert and John W. Reger recruited and trained two companies of volunteers, Albert's to fight for the Confederate States, John's for the United States.

A substantial number of Virginians throughout the state remained loyal to the United States even when some close relatives supported the Confederacy. For example, Philip St. George Cooke was a career army officer who remained in the United States Army and during the war became a brigadier general. One of his sons-in-law commanded a New York regiment during the war, but two others served in the Confederate Army. His own son, John Rogers Cooke, became a brigadier general in the Confederate Army. The two generals of the opposing armies did not reconcile until late in the 1880s. The Southampton County family of George Henry Thomas in effect disowned him. A professional soldier and officer in the United States Army when the war began, Thomas declined an offer to command the Virginia artillery and became one of the most distinguished and successful of all the general officers in the United States Army during the Civil War. He commanded armies in the Tennessee Valley and on the Atlanta campaign and earned the nickname Rock of Chickamauga for his tenacious stand at the heights of that name near Chattanooga in September 1863.

War

A majority of the men who volunteered for the Virginia defense forces in the spring of 1861 or later enlisted in the army of the Confederacy did not own many slaves, and most owned none. It is likely that in the very beginning most of them, like Robert E. Lee, thought first about defending Virginia from the United States, but a southern patriotism quickly took hold, and the officers and soldiers knew that they were fighting to preserve a way of life for all of the region's white people—a way of life that was based on slave labor.

The fighting in Virginia began on May 1, 1861, near Fairfax Court House, where a member of the Virginia Convention, John Quincy Marr, was killed while commanding a company of Fauquier County men. A month later, in Barbour County in western Virginia, men from Indiana and Ohio, marching east, encountered men from Virginia, marching west, both seeking to control the northwestern counties of the state. Early in the morning of June 3, they met near the covered bridge at Philippi, and the Union men routed the Confederates, who fled the scene, giving the battle a nickname, Philippi Races. Lee and other Virginia commanders, including Wise who became a Confederate brigadier general, labored hard during the remainder of the year to keep United States forces from taking control of the northwestern counties, but the Confederates suffered a second defeat at the Battle of Cheat Mountain early in September. The most famous of the early large-scale engagements of the war took place in northeastern Virginia, where United States and Confederate forces clashed on July 21, at Bull Run, near Manassas Junction. General Thomas J. Jackson, a former instructor at Virginia Military Institute, earned fame and a nickname, Stonewall, in that battle and became for a time the most famous Confederate officer.

In many ways the Civil War was different from any previous wars in which Americans fought. Both United States and Confederate States armies used railroads to transport troops and supplies. When they were available both employed modern repeating rifles rather than muzzle-loading or single-shot

Viewing the battlefield from a tethered balloon

arms. Both armies used tethered balloons to detect enemy forces and direct artillery fire. The telegraph allowed commanders and government officers to communicate rapidly with each other, and new photographic techniques allowed for reproduction of field maps using sunlight. It was the first war to be extensively recorded in photographs.

Naval warfare changed just as dramatically. In the spring of 1861 Virginia forces seized the United States Navy Yard and its facilities in Norfolk harbor. They refloated the USS *Merrimack*, which navy men scuttled when the yard was first attacked, and refitted it with iron armor produced at the Tredegar ironworks in Richmond. Rechristened the CSS *Virginia*, it was one of the first two completely armored warships in the world. On March 8, 1862, it steamed out into Hampton Roads and easily sank the USS *Cumberland*. The following day the *Virginia* encountered the only other ironclad warship, the strange and innovative USS *Monitor*. The two ships exchanged hundreds of rounds of heavy cannon fire at close range without either seriously damaging the other. The battle between the *Monitor* and the *Merrimack*, as it was almost always called, was an epoch-making moment in naval warfare. Two months later when the United States Army entered Norfolk, the Confederates burned their own ironclad to prevent the United States from repossessing it.

The war lasted much longer and was much more bloody than anybody on either side anticipated in the spring of 1861. Virginia was the main battleground of the Civil War in the east. The United States Army stationed its forces in northeastern Virginia in an arc that allowed them to protect Washington, D.C., and such strategic spots as Hampton Roads and Harpers Ferry, and to occupy the fertile Shenandoah Valley. Stonewall Jackson's Confederate brigade performed almost miraculous marches up and down the Shenandoah Valley during the second half of 1861 and in 1862, meeting and repulsing a succession of United States Army incursions into Virginia.

J. O. Davidson, "The *Monitor* and *Merrimac,* First Fight between Ironclads," 1866; published by L. Prang & Co., Boston

During the initial year of the war the Virginia forces and the Confederate Army conducted a largely defensive campaign in response to United States attacks in the northwest and the northeast. In the summer of 1862, General George B. McClellan slowly marched a very large force from Hampton Roads in the southeast through Williamsburg and almost to the outskirts of Richmond in an attempt to capture the Confederate capital. In a series of running engagements known as the Seven Days at the end of June, Confederate defenders of Richmond forced McClellan to withdraw. At that time, Jefferson Davis named Robert E. Lee commander of the Confederate Army in Virginia. Lee immediately renamed his command the Army of Northern Virginia.

The grand strategy of the United States was to split the Confederacy by controlling the Mississippi River and to disrupt the eastern states by blockading the coast and capturing Richmond. In twenty-six major battles and more than four hundred smaller engagements, more men fought and died in Virginia than in any other state. For almost four years, Lee and such capable field commanders as Jackson, J. E. B. Stuart, and Jubal A. Early repelled attempts to take Richmond and envelop Virginia. After Lee assumed command, he adopted a more aggressive strategy and invaded Maryland and threatened Washington. Defeated at Antietam Creek, near Sharpsburg, in September 1862, Lee withdrew into northern Virginia, where he fended off several attacks. Casualties at Antietam had been appalling, with dead and wounded men scattered over acres of battlefield. As the war wore on, the death toll became even worse. At the Battle of Fredericksburg in December 1862, Lee's army lost about 5,000 men killed, wounded, or captured and inflicted more than 12,000 casualties on the United States Army.

At Chancellorsville, near Fredericksburg, in May 1863, in another series of fierce battles Confederates defeated the United States Army, but a friendly fire accident mortally wounded Lee's greatest field commander, Stonewall Jackson. Lee nevertheless boldly planned another invasion of the North, and at the beginning of July 1863 near Gettysburg, Pennsylvania, he fought and lost one of the greatest battles of the Civil War before he again withdrew to Virginia. The United States captured Vicksburg, Mississippi, that same week, which secured the Mississippi River for the United States and accomplished the goal of splitting the Confederacy. In hindsight that made July 1863 seem to be the turning point in the war.

Of all the many heroic actions of Virginia's troops, none so caught the public imagination as the Battle of New Market, on May 15, 1864, when young cadets from Virginia Military Institute marched into battle and many of them died during one of the several incursions into the Shenandoah Valley.

Off the Battlefield and at Home

Tens of thousands of Virginia men, old and young and almost all white, fought in the Confederate Army, and thousands of them were killed or died in overcrowded and unclean hospitals or prison camps, and many more were wounded. The death toll was staggering and unparalleled in North America. A few white women also fought for the Confederacy, concealing their identities and dressing as soldiers. Other women, such as Belle Boyd, became famous as espionage agents and provided vital information to Confederate armies.

Virginians who were not in the army or navy struggled with consequences of the war. By the end of 1861 inflation was rampant, and prices of basic food-stuffs doubled, even quadrupled. Everything seemed to be in short supply. Without sufficient sources of medicine both the army and the civilian population were nearly helpless in the face of outbreaks of pneumonia, scarlet fever, and smallpox. Regiments from other southern states and civilians who accompanied them filled Virginia's cities to overflowing. Conditions were so bad that a large crowd of frustrated Richmond residents, most of them white women, erupted on April 2, 1863, in what became known as the Richmond Bread Riot.

It was no doubt a relief to hard-pressed civilians in the spring of 1864 when the General Assembly suspended the collection of property and license taxes for one year. State officials had so successfully managed their meager resources or shifted expenses to the Confederate government that a surplus accumulated in the state treasury. The auditor of public accounts, Jonathan McCally Bennett, received credit for that remarkable achievement. He was from Weston, in Gilmer County, and after the war returned to his home in what had become West Virginia.

Hardship faced almost every family in Virginia. Most white families had one or more men away fighting in the army. With so many men in military service white women in Virginia managed plantations, family farms, and businesses or did jobs and accepted responsibilities previously closed to them. They worked as hospital orderlies, government clerks, teachers, even munitions workers. Forty women died when a Richmond ammunition factory where they worked blew up in March 1863. Within weeks the plant reopened, and a full complement of other women took their places. Sally Tompkins opened a private hospital that had one of the best survival rates in Richmond, but because it was a private and not a military hospital she could not receive public compensation for caring for wounded soldiers. The Confederate secretary of war gave her the rank of captain so that her excellent hospital could receive government assistance to continue its successful work.

While soldiers were off fighting and dying on the battlefields or suffering in prisoner of war camps or in wretched hospitals, their family members at home tried as best they could to get along without them. In the absence of husbands, fathers, brothers, and sons, the women, children, and old men took care of farms, tilled vegetable gardens, cared for livestock, or operated small businesses. Some of the children even tried to attend school in areas where contending armies did not appear and wreak havoc on the countryside. From their homes they could often see or hear horrifying sights and sounds of warfare. Both large armies and small scouting or foraging parties swarmed over Virginia's farmland in search of enemies or foodstuffs. Sometimes they acted violently toward the civilians and wantonly destroyed property of no military value.

For a majority of Virginians, that was their Civil War experience, not comradeship, heroism, or sacrifice on a battlefield. Women anxiously waited for their husbands or sweethearts or sons to come home or learned how to cope if they did not. Children grew up without seeing their fathers or having their protection when cavalry galloped onto their property or soldiers marched through scavenging for provisions. All those civilians carried for the remainder of their lives memories of those long days and longer nights. Their memories of the war in which they did not fight but in which they, too, suffered, influenced them long after the war was over. In some instances they had more difficulty reconciling themselves to the outcome of the war than some of the men who fought in it.

Unionism during the War

A large majority of white Virginians had opposed secession until April 1861, but people in a large majority in the counties that remained part of Virginia actively supported the Confederacy after the state seceded. Irish and German immigrants who had recently settled in Virginia as well as northern merchants and businessmen in Virginia's towns and cities faced difficult choices when the war began or struggled with competing loyalties. Some white Virginians who remained loyal to the United States during the war were imprisoned or harassed. John Minor Botts, a former Whig congressman and an outspoken opponent of secession, spent time in a Confederate prison for his refusal to renounce his beliefs. The number of other white Virginians who remained loyal to the United States is impossible to calculate. Claims for lost property some of them filed with the United States government after the war indicate that several thousand people shared the sentiments of Botts, and some of them shared his fate.

Some of them escaped detection. Samuel Ruth, for one, was superintendent of a section of the Richmond, Fredericksburg, and Potomac Railroad that stretched from Richmond north almost as far as Fredericksburg. He used his position to create minor delays and obstructions of traffic that impeded Confederate troop and supply movements. The delays Ruth caused were enough to give serious trouble to the Confederates but not enough to get him arrested for sabotage or espionage.

The most remarkable of all the Unionists was Richmond resident Elizabeth Van Lew, who often visited prisoners of war in the city and helped many of them escape. She directed one of the most successful espionage operations that provided vital information about the Confederate government and military movements. One of her formerly enslaved women, known as Mary Richards or Mary Elizabeth Bowser, worked as a household servant in the residence of President Jefferson Davis and conveyed vital military and political information through intermediaries to Van Lew, who relayed it to United States Army officers. Long after the war Virginians created a legend that Van Lew had escaped detection by pretending to be mentally deranged (hence, references to her as Crazy Bet), but there is no evidence that she ever did so, and her wartime writings and behavior clearly show her to have been a shrewd and careful person.

State and Confederate officials sought to impose control on the often chaotic conditions the war created. Early in the war, military officers, often with the approval of local, state, or Confederate government officials, imposed martial law or employed military force to control or prohibit the manufacture and sale of alcohol in the vicinity of military encampments. Throughout the war,

Elizabeth Van Lew

especially in the vicinity of Richmond, men of northern birth, with known Union sympathies, or who were suspected of having Union sympathies were incarcerated under the authority of the Confederate Department of War. The department appointed several distinguished Virginia attorneys, among them former state attorney general Sidney Smith Baxter, to act as habeas corpus commissioners to determine what to do about the men who were arrested. The commissioners acted for the most part without legal authorization or staff, and as a consequence some men languished in jail for many months without recourse to courts, without an opportunity to prove their allegiance to the Confederacy, or any other means of relief.

Lemuel Babcock, of Charles City County, was one such man. He was arrested in part because of his northern birth. Babcock owned a few slaves and had run a lumber business in the county since the 1840s, and he joined the Home Guard in 1862. Nevertheless, he was arrested in 1862 on suspicion of being an abolitionist and again in 1864, but both times he was released for lack of evidence. The experience led him to become a member of Van Lew's espionage network, and he was arrested again in 1865 but escaped from the train that was carrying him and others from Richmond to Danville when the Confederate government evacuated the capital of the Confederacy.

The Bowden family, of Williamsburg, also suffered as a consequence of the conspicuous loyalism of its adult men. Lemuel Jackson Bowden had been a Democratic member of the House of Delegates during the 1840s and 1850s and represented the city and several surrounding counties in the Constitutional Convention of 1850–51. His brother, Henry Moseley Bowden, had also been active in Democratic Party politics and contracted to provide food and other supplies to the mental hospital in Williamsburg, where his wife was a matron. Because of their conspicuous and unpopular Unionism, the brothers and their families had to flee their hometown in 1862. Lemuel Bowden briefly represented Restored Virginia in the United States Senate until his death early in January 1864, and Henry Bowden moved to Norfolk, where under the protection of the United States Army he emerged as a leading Republican reformer and later served in the Constitutional Convention of 1867–68. Both men's sons also became influential Republicans: Lemuel's son Thomas Russell Bowden was the Republican attorney general of the Restored Government of Virginia from 1863 to 1869, and Henry's son George Edwin Bowden became a Republican member of Congress in the 1880s and an important party leader in Virginia until his death early in the twentieth century. Henry's daughter married a United States Army officer who represented a Virginia district in the House of Representatives after the war. The transformation of the members of that states' rights Democratic family into radical Republicans was a direct result of their experiences during and after the secession crisis. Theirs was such an unpopular choice in Williamsburg that for more than a century afterward their names scarcely appeared in any context in the local history literature.

Many other people endured similar difficulties, especially if they lived in strategically important parts of the state. Men who lived on the Pamunkey and Mattaponi reservations appealed to the governor for relief in the autumn of 1861 when the King William County Court ordered them and local free blacks to Yorktown to work on fortifications. The men stated that they were Indians and not free African Americans and were therefore not legally required to obey the order. The governor agreed, but a committee of the Senate of Virginia reported the following spring that its members and the county court regarded all the men as mixed-race free black men and therefore eligible to be impressed into service. As before and afterward, the vulnerable legal status of Virginia's Indians exposed them to potential violations of their rights that colonial treaties and state laws should have secured to them. For their self-protection, some Virginia Indians managed to travel to Canada where they sat out the war.

Most Pamunkey men and women on the reservation remained loyal to the United States throughout the war. Confederate authorities arrested several Pamunkey men and imprisoned them in Richmond for their well-known loyalty. When able, the men assisted the United States Army as guides and river pilots. One of them, Terrill Bradby, related afterward that "in May 1862 I entered the Federal service & remained in it till the close of the war," even though his wife and family suffered abuse from local Confederates. When the war began, Bradby recalled, "my sympathies were with the Union cause. I had been a sailor for years out of Northern ports, as a great many of our people were. We had 14 Pilots in the Union service & not a man in that of the rebels. I had never voted. We had never been taxed. I entered the Union Service the first chance I got & stuck to it till the end.... I always wanted to see the Union preserved & the secessionists put down, & I fully & frequently risked my life in the Union Cause."[9] When soldiers in the United States Army camped at the Pamunkey reservation, Bradby's cousin, Caroline Bradby Cook, whose husband died in 1861, welcomed them and cooked and washed for them, even while they systematically dismantled her fences and burned the wood in their campfires.

Counties in southwestern Virginia may have been home to a larger proportion of loyalists or lukewarm supporters of the Confederacy than any other region away from the Ohio Valley. Nearby eastern Tennessee was the most important stronghold of Unionism in the entire Confederacy, and late in the war in neighboring North Carolina, Unionists organized the Heroes of America. They undoubtedly had members or sympathizers in the mountains and valleys of southwestern Virginia. That area was contested ground, too. Both sides fought for control of the strategic Virginia-Tennessee Railroad, the Cumberland Gap, and the vital salt works at Saltville. Throughout the war the counties of southwestern Virginia experienced both military and civilian violence as contending forces moved back and forth through the mountains and across the valleys.

Emancipation

Many thousands of the half-million enslaved Virginians unwillingly worked in a variety of war-related tasks in aid of the Confederacy such as constructing fortifications, cleaning military hospitals, and caring for horses and mules at military encampments. In the beginning the state paid owners of slaves the same rent per day it paid owners of horses. Some men with special skills toiled as blacksmiths, shoemakers, and coal miners. As some of the opponents of secession had predicted, however, warfare immediately began to undermine the institution of slavery. As one man later said, "I was free to all intents after the 27th day of May 1861, when my master went off" to enter the Virginia army.[10] So many men impressed to work on military fortifications ran away that by the end of the war the number of enslaved men in some Virginia counties had fallen significantly.

When enslaved Virginians safely could, they seized the opportunity the war offered to free themselves, usually by crossing through military lines into

This record documents the payment of rent for the services of enslaved men who worked on fortifications at Gloucester Point in April 1861.

territory the United States Army controlled. In the beginning they met a mixed reception because army officers were uncertain whether to treat them as refugees to be cared for or as escaped slave property to be confiscated or returned. Army officers and politicians at first referred to them as contraband of war, a term originally applied to captured merchandise and goods on civilian ships, which indicates that in the early years of the war many northern men still regarded enslaved people as a form of property. The families who were fortunate enough to reach Hampton and similar safe sites eagerly embraced their first opportunities to attend schools, which the army, some northern churches, and other charitable organizations established. The army even created a school for escapees at Arlington, Robert E. Lee's mansion across the Potomac River from Washington.

The United States government began the war with no policy about enslaved people who escaped to the protection of its army. The thousands of men, women, and children who fled eventually forced the government to act. On January 1, 1863, Abraham Lincoln issued the Emancipation Proclamation

This photograph shows a party of people who fled to freedom at Cumberland Landing.

and declared free the enslaved property of people living in states or parts of states that were in rebellion against the authority of the United States government. The nature of the Civil War then began to change. United States soldiers began to fight not only to save the Union but also to end slavery because they came to believe it had been the cause of the war. In increasing numbers African Americans took a major part in deciding the outcome and enlisted in the several regiments of United States Colored Troops recruited in Virginia. They fought with great gallantry and success both to save the Union and to secure freedom for themselves and for others. At Fort Harrison near Richmond in September 1864, four Virginians and several other African Americans from other states earned medals of honor for bravery. At least 5,723 black Virginians, and probably many more, served in the United States Army during the war.

The Restored Government of Virginia abolished slavery. After Pierpont moved the capital from Wheeling to Alexandria in the summer of 1863 he, too, decided that slavery had to be abolished. The Emancipation Proclamation did not apply within some portions of the Virginia he governed, which left civil and military officials with conflicting responsibilities about how to act when families that sought to escape slavery entered their jurisdiction. Moreover, many legislative and judicial districts specified in the Constitution of 1851 were no longer in Virginia, and the constitution provided no means of amending it to bring the districts into conformity with the new reality. That autumn Pierpont recommended that the loyal state of Virginia hold a convention and write a new constitution. Pierpont suggested that it abolish slavery in Virginia and seek compensation from the federal government for owners who thereby lost valuable property.

FREEDOM TO SLAVES!

Whereas, the President of the United States did, on the first day of the present month issue his *Proclamation* declaring "that, *all persons held as Slaves in certain designated States, and parts of States, are, and henceforward shall be free,*" and that the Executive Government of the United States, including the Military and naval authorities thereof, would recognize and mantain the freedom of said persons. *And Whereas,* the County of Frodrick is included in the teritory designated by the Proclamation of the President, in which the *Slaves should become free,* I therefore hereby notify the citizens of the city of Winchester, and of said County, of said Proclamation, and of my intention to maintain and enforce the same,

I expect all citizens to yield a ready compliance with the Proclamation of the Chief Executive, and I admonish all persons disposed to resist its peaceful enforcement, that upon manifesting such disposition by acts, they will be regarded as rebels in arms against the lawful authority of the Federal Government and dealt with accordingly.

All persons liberated by said Proclamation are admonished to abstain from all violence, and immediatly betake themselves to useful occupations.

The officers of this command are admonished and ordered to act in accordance with said proclamation and to yield their ready co-operation in its enforcement.

R. H. Milroy,
Brig. Gen'l Commanding.

Jan. 5th, 1863.

This June 5, 1863, "Freedom to Slaves" broadside announced the enforcement of the Emancipation Proclamation in Winchester and Frederick County.

The convention was small, with only seventeen members elected from the counties of Loudoun and Fairfax and the city of Alexandria in northeastern Virginia, the counties of Northampton and Accomack on the Eastern Shore, and the counties of Warwick, Princess Anne, Norfolk, New Kent, James City, Elizabeth City, and Charles City and the cities of Williamsburg and Norfolk and the town of Portsmouth, all in southeastern Virginia. They met in the federal courthouse in Alexandria from February 13, through April 11, 1864. With only one dissenting vote the convention on March 10 adopted a provision that declared that "Slavery and involuntary servitude (except for crime) is hereby abolished and prohibited in the State forever." Men rang church bells in the city to celebrate, and newspapers throughout the United States reported the event. Incomplete records and a lack of in-depth research leaves it unclear

Company E, 4th U.S. Colored Troops. The regiment was one of four composed of African American men who all voluntarily enlisted.

what, if anything, the Restored Government or the counties and cities did to enforce the abolition of slavery. Some owners undoubtedly complied, but others may not have. Whether, when, or how approximately 50,000 enslaved Virginians in the cities and counties represented in the convention gained their freedom as a result of the Constitution of 1864 is not known.

The new constitution also disfranchised all men who had taken part in the army of "the so-called confederate government, or under any rebellious State government."[11] Otherwise, the Constitution of 1864 was not so radical a departure from previous Virginia constitutions as the new West Virginia Constitution was. For the remainder of the war, the government in Alexandria administered areas of Virginia where the United States Army was in control—in the vicinity of Alexandria, on the Eastern Shore, and in and around Norfolk and Hampton Roads. Almost all histories of the American Civil War refer to those areas as occupied territory, but it would be just as accurate to refer to them as territory the United States Army liberated. Following the defeat of the Confederacy in April 1865 and the simultaneous collapse of the Virginia state government that had its capital in Richmond, the Constitution of 1864 served as the constitution for the government of what remained Virginia until the end of the decade.

Charles Magnus, *Bird's Eye View of Alexandria,* 1863. Alexandria with its Potomac River port and its railroad connections to various parts of Virginia was not only the capital of the Restored Government of Virginia from the summer of 1863 to the summer of 1865, but also a vitally important military asset of the United States government.

End of the War

After Ulysses S. Grant assumed command of the United States Army in 1864 the tide of battle began slowly to turn against the Confederacy. Backed by the North's greater population and industrial and agricultural resources, Grant sent General Philip Henry Sheridan into the Shenandoah Valley to lay waste to what was then and thereafter known as the breadbasket of the Confederacy. Grant personally took command of the army in the field and began relentlessly hammering Lee's Army of Northern Virginia. At the Battle of the Wilderness, near Fredericksburg, in May of that year Grant forced Lee to withdraw. Unlike his predecessors Grant did not pause after the ferocious and bloody fighting but pressed south in one deadly battle after another. At Cold Harbor, in Hanover County, at the end of May the fighting was some of the most intense of the war in the east. Grant persisted with a series of bloody battles that carried his army to the James River east of Richmond in the middle of June.

Grant then threw his army across the river and laid siege to Petersburg. Lee fortified the city with all the troops he could spare from the defensive lines at Richmond. Grant's repeated attacks failed to break through the Confederate lines. Even a huge explosion that miners set off on July 30, 1864, after they tunneled under a Confederate fortification failed to open a gap in the Confederate defenses. That Battle of the Crater resulted in the deaths of hundreds of United States soldiers, some of them African Americans, without making any difference.

The people of Petersburg and the people of Vicksburg, Mississippi, shared a unique experience for inhabitants of North America, life under protracted military siege. Petersburg was under siege for almost ten months. Confederate defenders resided in besieged Petersburg and on its outskirts, and wounded soldiers and civilians crowded into houses and public buildings that served as hospitals. The United States Army shelled the defenders and the city almost constantly. The defensive lines were so close to the residential and business sections of Petersburg that a near miss of a military target often struck a civilian structure. Warehouses, churches, private houses, places of business, and Petersburg's citizens took direct hits. Fires and falling walls killed residents throughout the siege as the sound of artillery boomed all around.

People who did not or could not move away eventually became used to the noise and danger. One Sunday early in 1865 during the service at Second Presbyterian Church a large shell struck the building but did not explode. The minister was a former artillery officer, and he knew precisely what to do. The congregation followed him outdoors and watched as he calmly pried the defective shell out of the wall of the church. He extracted the powder and later gave it to local boys for use during the next autumn's hunting season. A Confederate officer on duty in Petersburg wrote, "Twas truly surprising how utterly indifferent the women and children had become to passing shells. As I rode along, a huge one bursted about a hundred yards from two ladies who were crossing the street. I expected to see them faint, scream, run, at least dodge, but no, they only looked at it and went on without even quickening their pace."[12]

During the siege Lee's army dwindled in size as a result of soldiers being killed, wounded, or captured, and quite a few men left the camps and went home for personal or family reasons. So severe was the shortage of soldiers by the beginning of 1865 that Lee and Jefferson Davis reluctantly asked the Confederate Congress to authorize recruitment of African Americans with a promise of freedom for slaves who fought for the Confederacy. That controversial request, which Congress granted, indicated how depleted the Army of Northern Virginia had become. Very few, if any, black Virginians responded to the offer during the brief interval between its adoption and the end of the war.

On April 2, 1865, Lee realized that he could no longer hold Petersburg and withdrew his army west through the valley of the Appomattox River. Later that day the Confederate government and the Virginia state government abandoned Richmond. Jefferson Davis retreated to Danville and tried to reform his government there. Officials of the state government dispersed, and the government disintegrated. Government under the Constitution of 1851 was in a very real sense one of the last casualties of the Civil War.

The United States Army, including companies of United States Colored Troops, entered Richmond, the capital of the Confederacy, on April 3, to find that much of city was on fire. Retreating Confederate officers and state officials had ordered that valuable supplies and stores of cotton be burned in order that they not fall into Union hands. High wind whipped up the flames, which spread through much of the city's business district. The fire burned the state courthouse and consumed nearly all of the pre-1865 colonial and state judicial records and the original archival records of several counties that had sent their record books to Richmond for safekeeping. The Capitol remained unguarded for several days thereafter, and soldiers, officers, and other souvenir hunters carried away books, works of art, and historic records, including one of the original signed parchments of the Virginia Ordinance of Secession. It was finally returned to the state at the end of 1929.

Abraham Lincoln visited the still-smoking city the next day after the army liberated/occupied it. Jubilant freed people greeted him and escorted him to

One of numerous drawings and engravings (there are no photographs) of jubilant freed people escorting Abraham Lincoln through the streets of Richmond. Paul Fleury Mottelay, ed., *The Soldier in Our Civil War a Pictorial History of the Conflict, 1861–1865, Illustrating the Valor of the Soldier as Displayed on the Battle-Field* (New York, 1886).

the state Capitol, which had also served as the Capitol of the Confederacy, and to the mansion a few blocks away where Jefferson Davis had resided. The flag of the United States flew over the Capitol of Virginia again—and not just any flag. Soon after the Convention of 1861 had voted to secede fourteen-year-old Richard Gill Forrester quietly took possession of the United States flag that had then flown over the state Capitol. The descendant of a free black woman and a prominent Jewish merchant, Forrester saved the flag for four years. In April 1865 when the Confederate government and army evacuated Richmond and the United States Army entered the city, he carried the flag back to the Capitol so that it could fly again above the Capitol of Virginia.

Grant's army, meanwhile, rushed in pursuit of Lee's retreating Confederates, and on April 9, Lee surrendered the Army of Northern Virginia at Appomattox Court House. Some Confederate units escaped south into the Carolinas, and Davis tried to re-form his government at Danville before fleeing southward, too. By the time Davis was finally captured, the other Confederate army units had surrendered, and the bloodiest war in North America was finally over.

14

CONSTRUCTING
A NEW VIRGINIA

T
HE PERIOD AFTER the Civil War has always been called Reconstruction, but that is one of the most imprecise words in the literature of American history. It compresses many separate events into one and incorrectly suggests uniformity across time and place. Consequently, the word has meant different things to different people under different circumstances.

What specialists in the period have referred to as presidential reconstruction began in July 1861 when Abraham Lincoln recognized the Restored Government of Virginia as the legitimate government of the loyal people to begin reconstructing the union of states. With that large objective in view, Presidents Lincoln and Andrew Johnson implemented different policies for different places until March 1867, when Congress passed over Johnson's veto An Act for the More Efficient Government of the Rebel States, often referred to as the First Reconstruction Act. Congress began to construct new southern governments and societies on the basis of free labor and equal rights. One feature of what has been called congressional reconstruction was military supervision of civil government in states of the former Confederacy, which was often referred to inaccurately as military rule or military reconstruction. Because the federal government often had to send federal marshals or troops to protect Republican and African American voters from violence on election day during those and later years, some people misidentified that phase of reform as military rule.

Some writers have used the vague term Reconstruction to refer only to the period of congressional reconstruction, which in Virginia ended in January 1870, but other people have employed the term to cover the period up to or through 1876, after Congress passed the last of the post–Civil War civil rights acts and ceased trying to construct a new inclusive, egalitarian, and democratic South.

Late nineteenth- and early twentieth-century white people often characterized the years after the Civil War as a time of widespread corruption and domination of state and local governments by rapacious northerners (called carpetbaggers), their unscrupulous local accomplices (called scalawags), and illiterate and easily manipulated former slaves. That was a serious distortion of a complex reality. It incorrectly implied that most or all the white men who held public office were carpetbaggers or scalawags and that all the black men were easily corrupted. It left out of the narrative the experiences of most people, both black and white.

Moreover, the experiences of people in each state differed. Government officials in most places in the South were neither more nor less corrupt than elsewhere in the United States, and in fact Virginia suffered less political corruption than some other states. Several men of northern birth occupied important offices in the state's government during and after the period, but some native white Virginians adapted their lives and political allegiances to the radically changed politics after the end of the slave labor system. At no time did immigrants from northern states or freedmen dominate government in Virginia. Some of the achievements of former slaves and of black people who had been free before the war were remarkable, considering the disadvantages under which they labored and the impediments they often faced.

Virginians did not all share the same vision of the state's post-emancipation future. Setting aside the conflicting and sometimes misleading or erroneous connotations the word *reconstruction* carries, we can see Virginians more clearly during those years if we view them as maneuvering in a wholly changed political environment to construct a new Virginia in a free labor economy without slavery—either with or without full civil and political rights for African Americans.

Freed People

The most important unanswered question in April 1865 when the Confederacy collapsed, the army began to enforce the Emancipation Proclamation throughout Virginia, and the Constitution of 1864 with its prohibition on slavery became effective everywhere in the state was what the end of slavery would mean for the freed people. Political leaders in Virginia and in Washington debated the implications of the emancipation of almost half a million Virginians, but freed men and women had no need to debate among themselves. They knew.

On April 4, 1865, the day after the United States Army liberated/occupied Richmond, African American members of the Colored Monitor Union Club met in Norfolk. Their purpose was to obtain all the rights of citizenship, including "the right of *universal* suffrage to *all* loyal men, without distinction of color, and to memorialize the Congress of the United States to allow the *colored* citizens the *equal* right of franchise with other citizens."[1] When some residents of Norfolk called for an election of members of the General Assembly from the city, members of the club boldly resolved to vote. At their summons more than a thousand African American men assembled in the Bute Street Methodist Church on May 25. They sent small delegations to each of the four polling places in the city to ascertain whether election officials would receive their votes. Officials in three of the wards refused, but in the city's Second Ward they agreed to record the votes of black men on separate tally sheets designated as votes of men whose legal qualifications were in doubt. In small groups 354 men went to the Second Ward and voted for white candidates who pledged themselves to support African American suffrage. Election officials accepted but did not report their votes. The 712 residents of the other three wards at the church unanimously recorded their votes on their own tally sheets for the same candidates. None of the victors applied to the assembly in June to take his seat, so legislators did not have to rule that the votes were illegal, inasmuch as the Virginia Constitution of 1864 specifically limited voting to adult white males.

Members of the Colored Monitor Union Club reassembled on June 5, at the Catharine Street Baptist Church, and adopted a long "Address from the Colored Citizens of Norfolk, Va., to the People of the United States." They claimed full rights of American citizenship. The long and impassioned address to their "*Fellow Citizens*" began, "We do not come before the people of the United States asking an impossibility; we simply ask that a Christian and enlightened people shall, at once, concede to us the full enjoyment of those privileges of full citizenship, which, not only, are our undoubted right, but are indispensable to that elevation and prosperity of our people, which must be the desire of every patriot."[2]

In the spring and summer of 1865 black men formed political organizations in several Virginia cities and insisted that their state and federal governments protect all their rights as free citizens. In Richmond early in June, for instance, a very large public meeting drew up a long resolution and appended to it evidence of abuse African Americans had suffered since April, some of it at the hands of United States Army officers and soldiers. The meeting appointed a committee to present the address and complaints to the president of the United States. Andrew Johnson received the men politely in Washington but did little or nothing to ameliorate their situation.

Those first political actions of African Americans brought to public attention some very able leaders. Thomas Bayne may have drafted the addresses of the Union Monitor Club. He had escaped from slavery in Norfolk, settled in New England, become a dentist, and returned to Virginia during the winter of 1864–65 to preside over several of the club's meetings in the spring. If not Bayne, the author may have been Joseph T. Wilson, a Virginia native and wounded veteran of the United States Army with a distinguished career ahead of him as a newspaper editor, Republican Party activist, and historian of emancipation and of the United States Colored Troops.

The Richmond man who took charge of preparing the address to the president and who led the delegation to Washington was Fields Cook, who quickly emerged as an influential leader in the large and vibrant African American community that had Richmond as its center. Born into slavery in King William County about 1817, he moved to Richmond with the permission of his owner about 1834 and obtained his freedom by 1850. About that time he wrote a long autobiography. His manuscript is preserved in the Library of Congress and is one of the few extant extended compositions by an enslaved Virginian. Cook acquired property and influence in Richmond after he received his freedom and became a Baptist minister. His intelligence, literacy, and influence as a clergyman enabled him to speak with eloquence for the large African American community when he led the delegation to the White House in mid-June 1865. Cook later served on a federal grand jury, took part in organizing the workingmen of Richmond, and actively supported radical reformers in the state's Republican Party. In 1870 he moved to Alexandria and became pastor of the Third Baptist Church and later of Ebenezer Baptist Church. Until Cook died in 1897 he continued to play an active part in politics and in support of full citizenship rights for African Americans. His lifetime of achievements made him stand out among his contemporaries as unusually successful, and his accomplishments also provided an example of the possibilities that freedom made available to Virginians who had once been enslaved.

More than sixty African American men, under the leadership of Cook and Bayne, met in Alexandria early in August 1865 in the Colored State Convention, the first statewide convention of black Virginians ever. "We claim, then, as citizens of this State," one of their several declarations insisted, that "the laws of the Commonwealth shall give to all men equal protection; that each and every man may appeal to the law for his equal rights without regard to the color of his skin; and we believe this can only be done by extending to us the elective franchise, which we believe to be our inalienable right as freemen, and which the Declaration of Independence guarantees to all free citizens of this Government and which is the privilege of the nation. We claim the right of suffrage."[3]

At the same time, some white Republicans, including both native Virginians who had remained loyal to the United States and other men who settled in the state during or immediately after the war, realized that they would remain a permanent minority party if they did not enfranchise black men and make a political alliance with them. They formed the Virginia Union Association in order, among other things, to "secure the elective franchise to our colored population, as soon as it can be safely done" so that Virginia could have a government by people who had always been loyal to the United States and not by former Confederates.[4]

Some freed people remained where they had lived before the war, but many men, women, and some children left their former owners in search of work or family members from whom the domestic slave trade had separated them. The attempts of formerly enslaved people to unite with family members began even before the war ended and continued for many years afterward. They placed advertisements in newspapers, dictated or wrote letters that they mailed to family members or former owners. Some wrote to county sheriffs or to the governor. On May 21, 1865, Stephen Flemming wrote to the governor of Virginia from New Orleans to try to learn about his family. "About 16 years ago," he began, "I was Sold as a Slave, from the State of Virginia, Bowling green, near Fredericksburg, in to the State of Louisiana I left behind Me a wife, and 5 living Children I never heard from her Since, and I wish her to Know (if she is alive) where I am, and for her to write to me, in order to determine for the future. . . . My Wife's Name was Polly Roy before she was married to me." Flemming named each of his children and also mentioned "a baby in Arms." He asked the governor to "make me a happy Man" by helping him reestablish contact with his wife and children. "P.S. I belonged to Jessee Terril of Caroline County from my birth until I leff."[5] Surviving Virginia records do not indicate whether Flemming succeeded in his quest. Some men and women like him found their relatives, but thousands of people were unable to reunite with their family members.

Early in 1866 the General Assembly passed a law to allow men and women who had been enslaved to register marriages they had entered into before emancipation and make their marriages legal and their acknowledged children legitimate. The law also declared that marriages between African Americans were thereafter to be regarded under the law as equally protecting their families the same as earlier laws had always protected the families of white Virginians.

The army's Bureau of Refugees, Freedmen, and Abandoned Lands, commonly referred to as the Freedmen's Bureau, sent agents to most Virginia cities and counties to protect freed men, women, and children who had to enter into labor contracts to obtain work to support their families. The agents faced many obstacles that former owners threw up to the negotiation and enforcement of labor contracts. Agents also intervened to protect freed people from violence or exploitation. Congress empowered the agents to adjudicate disputes that would otherwise have wound up in local courts, and agents sometimes disarmed civilians in hopes of preventing violence. Nevertheless, white-on-black violence took place in scores of communities. In May 1866 people burned three African American churches in Petersburg, and bureau agents reported seventy-two episodes of serious violence against freed people from April through July that year and ninety in the year 1868.

The bureau also created the state's first public school system—exclusively for African Americans. A majority of the teachers were African American, but some were white, and some who moved to Virginia to teach remained in the state after the Freedmen's Bureau ceased operating schools in 1869. The bureau spent more than $200,000 on Virginia schools, which enrolled nearly 33,000 students. Missionaries from churches and other philanthropic organizations sent teachers to Virginia during and after the war to establish schools. One of the schools they created, known initially as the Richmond Theological School for Freedmen, opened in 1865 in the notorious slave jail of Robert Lumpkin. It later merged with Wayland Seminary, in Washington, D.C., and with Hartshorn Memorial College for women in Richmond and Storer College in Harpers Ferry, West Virginia, to became Virginia Union University, the oldest historically black institution of higher learning in the state.

"Misses Cooke's School Room, Freedmen's Bureau, Richmond, Va."; engraving from *Frank Leslie's Illustrated Newspaper,* November 17, 1866

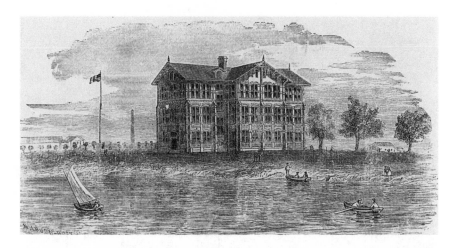

Hampton Institute, Hampton

The most important and famous of the educational institutions founded in Virginia during that time was Hampton Normal and Agricultural Institute, renamed Hampton University in the twentieth century. It opened in 1868 at the site of a school that educated refugees from slavery during the war. Its founder was Samuel Chapman Armstrong, a former United States Army general and committed educational reformer. The institute admitted both men and women, offered basic courses in English, the humanities, and the sciences, and prepared African Americans to teach in the new schools. Hampton Institute had an influence far beyond Virginia. It was a nationally recognized example of successful education of African Americans. Armstrong was able to sustain northern philanthropic support for the school for several decades, and its graduates educated several generations of black Virginians and Americans in many other states. The example of one of its first graduates, Virginia native Booker T. Washington, who served for many years as superintendent of Tuskegee Institute, in Alabama, also contributed to the enduring influence of similar trade- and teacher-training colleges elsewhere in the South. One was Christiansburg Institute in the town of Christiansburg in western Virginia. Organized in 1885 as an academically demanding school, it later became an industrial school for African Americans.

Another important institutional change that took place with the end of the Civil War was the formation of independent African American churches throughout Virginia. Some large black congregations had existed before the Civil War, but most free black and enslaved Virginia Christians attended churches organized and run by white members and with white ministers. After Nat Turner's Rebellion of 1831 the General Assembly made it illegal for black

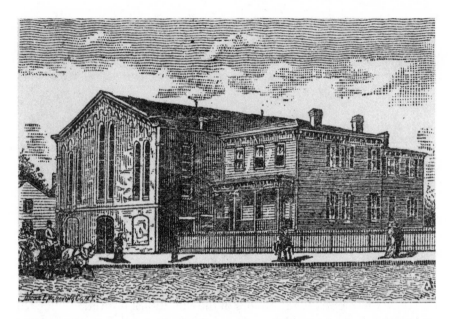

African Methodist Episcopal Church parsonage, Portsmouth, from Edward Pol-
lock, comp., *Sketch Book of Portsmouth, Va., Its People and Its Trade* (Portsmouth,
1886), 157

ministers to preach to black congregations, and many black churches, including even First African Baptist in Richmond, the largest in the state, had white
clergymen affiliated with them to supervise religious instruction. Indeed, one
of the first complaints that the delegation of Richmond men made to Andrew
Johnson in June 1865 was about the harmful effects that the old laws had on
their free exercise of religion. African Americans quickly formed independent
congregations after the war to have their own places of worship. That was their
desire nearly everywhere, but in the changed circumstances after emancipation
some white congregations in effect expelled black church members, which
began a long period of racial segregation in religious worship in Virginia.

Despite the efforts of the Freedmen's Bureau, one consequence of the inex-
perience of freed people in the market for free labor was that they sometimes
became trapped into long-term labor agreements that resembled peonage. The
vulnerability of rural African Americans led some of them to became financially dependent on landowning employers through the sharecropping system.
Sharecroppers (both black and white) worked land that other people owned
and paid a stated portion (a share, usually a half) of the annual crop directly
to the landowner. In a year of poor crops that could leave farmers and their
families insufficient income to support themselves and their dependents. Bor-

rowing against a future crop was often an easy way for sharecropping families to meet immediate needs, but that could lead to long-term indebtedness and an inability to negotiate new agreements or even to move to another farm, county, or state. The sharecropping system was not always profitable for landowners, either, if tenants failed to produce good crops. The system probably retarded recovery of the South's agricultural economy.

The federal government did not, and never intended to, confiscate the property of Confederates and distribute it to the freed people, but rumors that former slaves were each to receive forty acres of land and a mule led to disappointment when that did not happen. Nevertheless, thousands of freed people managed through hard work and frugality to purchase farms for themselves. At the end of the century a larger proportion of African American farmers owned their own farms in Virginia than in any other state. In Lousia County, for example, about 39 percent of African Americans owned farmland by 1900. Even though the average black family's farm was smaller than the average white family's, owners of land, even if they were relatively poor, were able to escape some of the constraints that faced all African Americans, whether formerly enslaved or formerly free, during the final decades of the nineteenth century.

Many African Americans who had been free before the Civil War were able to flourish in the new conditions after the war because they already had experience in operating their own small businesses or managing their own farms, or as responsible officers in churches. In some of the new African American churches as well as in the many self-help institutions, such as burial societies that acted as simple insurance providers, people who had been free before the war assumed leadership roles out of proportion to their numbers. Black ministers, in particular, became influential community leaders, not only because of their special responsibilities for guiding the religious and moral lives of their communities but also because their churches became social and sometimes political centers for African Americans.

White Man's Government

Soon after Robert E. Lee surrendered the Army of Northern Virginia on April 9, 1865, Governor Francis H. Pierpont moved the government offices from Alexandria to Richmond and began governing the whole state under the Constitution of 1864. Virginia and the other states of the former Confederacy faced the enormous task of recovering from the war. Because more battles had been fought in Virginia than in any other state, Virginia emerged from the war in worse condition than most of the other states. Virginia's once-formidable industrial base had been severely damaged, and its railroads were

Photograph of the burned district of Richmond, 1865

dilapidated after the strains of wartime. Several cities and principal towns suffered major damage, and almost the entire business district of Richmond had burned. The state's agrarian economy was also devastated, and economic and social disruption were so severe that even six months after the war about twenty-five thousand Virginians survived only on rations the United States Army distributed. Hundreds of thousands of people—African Americans, returning soldiers, and refugees—were without employment or shelter. Even worse, more than sixteen thousand Virginians died fighting in the two armies. Add deaths in prisons and from disease and perhaps as many as thirty thousand Virginians had died in the war.

Pierpont called the General Assembly into special session in Richmond in June 1865. It scheduled a general election for October to elect members of the United States House of Representatives and both houses of the General Assembly from all of the counties that remained in Virginia. It also removed some of the restrictions on voting by civilians who had not actually fought for the Confederacy. The assembly's loosening of the restrictions imposed by the Constitution of 1864 on voting by men who had supported the Confederacy was part of Pierpont's attempt to resume peaceable civilian government in the state speedily.

Both the governor and the president adopted lenient attitudes toward men who had taken part in the Confederate government or its army. Johnson began removing political disabilities at a fast rate. Hundreds of white Virginians who had not held high military or civilian office applied for and received presidential pardons. Pierpont endorsed many of the applications, which allowed men who had previously served in state and local government to act as justices of the peace, sheriffs, and in other essential roles, as well as be eligible to serve in the General Assembly.

People interpreted the results of the October 1865 general election according to their own perspectives. Some observers remarked that the proportion of opponents of secession elected to Congress suggested that the state's voters were reconciled to the outcome of the war and the abolition of slavery. Other observers, including African Americans, complained that the number of experienced politicians from prewar days and veterans of Confederate government and military service who were elected to the General Assembly returned too much power to members of the old regime. Congress refused to seat senators or representatives from any states of the former Confederacy at that time.

During the General Assembly session in the winter of 1865–66, legislators adopted the Cohabitation Act to legalize African Americans' marriages. They also passed a vagrancy law that imposed strict controls over the public activities and laboring conditions of freed people and granted broad powers to employers to dictate and enforce terms of employment. The law was aimed at freed people who did not have permanent employment or had left their former owners to search for family members. It empowered law enforcement officials to jail people who did not have jobs or refused to work at prevailing wages, which employers deliberately set at very low rates. Under some circumstances law enforcement officials could hire out men and women to work much as hired slaves had worked, or required them to wear a ball and chain as if they were convicted felons. The vagrancy law illustrated how much had yet to change. White legislators believed that they should continue to regulate the behavior of black people in the same manner they had placed limitations on the liberty of free blacks before the war. It is not clear that the white legislators ever even asked themselves whether they should continue to govern all black Virginians in ways that they never governed any white Virginians. General Alfred H. Terry, the military commander in Virginia, prohibited enforcement of the act. "The ultimate effect of the statute," he announced less than two weeks after its passage, "will be to reduce the freedmen to a condition of servitude worse than that from which they have been emancipated—a condition which will be slavery in all but its name."[6]

A large majority of white Virginia men with political experience disapproved of the transformations the United States Congress ordered. After they had obtained pardons and could resume participation in politics, they organized in opposition to the radical reforms Republicans advocated. In December 1867 at a large convention in Richmond they organized the Conservative Party to conserve, or preserve, as much as possible of the state's venerable old political traditions. In instructions the party circulated for enrolling Virginians in the Conservative Party its leaders appealed to white Virginians to oppose "negro suffrage, negro office-holding, and negro equality generally." In short, the Conservative Party's agenda was that Virginia's government should be "and ever shall be, *a white man's government.*"[7]

First Military District

The Virginia vagrancy act and many other actions of governments of states of the former Confederacy convinced radical Republican reformers in Congress that they had to take charge of the situation to guarantee that the end of slavery produced real freedom and not just slavery in another form. In March 1867 Congress passed An Act for the More Efficient Government of the Rebel States, usually referred to as the First Reconstruction Act. It created six military districts and placed a general in command of each and with authority to supervise civilian governments and if necessary replace government officials or take cases out of state courts to try them under federal authority. Virginia became the First Military District. The officers who supervised civilian government in Virginia were Major General John M. Schofield from March 13, 1867, until June 2, 1868; Major General George Stoneman from June 2, 1868, to March 31, 1869; Brigadier General Alexander S. Webb from April 2, to April 19, 1869; and Brigadier General Edward Richard Sprigg Canby from April 20, 1869, to January 26, 1870.

For the most part the generals intervened in state and local government fairly seldom and allowed government under the Constitution of 1864 to function so long as its officials did not impose unwarranted restrictions on freed men, women, and children. In 1868, however, under new orders, the generals dismissed most of the elected and appointed government officials in Virginia and replaced them. It was actions such as that which gave rise to the term military rule that inaccurately characterized the years after the end of the war. During that time the federal government regarded the governor and other officials as provisional appointees of the army to be retained or dismissed at the general's pleasure; but the military did not actually rule the state, and the state's constitution and laws remained in effect.

It was a difficult time of adjustments and also of some significant accomplishments in the radically new conditions the defeat of the Confederacy and the abolition of slavery produced. Everyone had to adapt to changed conditions and adopt new ideas about the relationships between white people and black people, between people who owned property and people who did not, between people who worked for themselves and people who worked for others. Lifelong habits of thought and action were hard to change. Examples of the persistence of old processes of thought are extremely numerous. To cite one extreme example, Thomas Salem Bocock had been a member of the United States House of Representatives and late in the Civil War the last Speaker of the Confederate States House of Representatives. Soon after the Army of Northern Virginia surrendered a few miles from his residence in Appomattox County, he exchanged some supplies with a neighbor for a few slaves. Bocock clearly did not yet perceive the import of all the remarkable changes that were beginning to take place. Those enslaved people no longer had any legal monetary value, but he acted as if they were still property. In 1867 the tax collector in Cumberland County placed the letters *fn,* for "free Negro" beside the names of African Americans, as he and his predecessors had done before the Civil War—as if there were any other kind in 1867. The man who compiled the index or the man who set the type for the journal of the December 1870 session of the Senate of Virginia revealed that he, too, had not yet abandoned old ways of thinking. Just as he might have done ten or fifty years earlier, he included an entry for "Free Negroes."[8]

Constitutional Convention of 1867–1868

As part of its new and more radical plan for reshaping the states of the former Confederacy, Congress required early in 1867 that those states adopt new constitutions. Virginia's government was functioning under the Constitution of 1864 that had abolished slavery and not under the old Constitution of 1851, but General Schofield called for a referendum on whether to have a convention, and an election to choose members if the referendum passed. Congress required that African American men be allowed to take part in the election and also be candidates. During the weeks and months preceding the voting African Americans held conventions in the state's cities, towns, and counties to organize for the first time politically and to nominate candidates for the convention. The army conducted the election on October 22, 1867, and tabulated votes of white and black voters on separate lists. A significant number of registered white voters refused to take part, and African Americans actually cast more votes than white men. The vote broke sharply along racial lines, with 92,507 African American voters providing a large portion of the 107,342 votes for holding the convention and white voters all but 638 of the 61,887 votes against. Moreover, almost all black men voted for candidates who favored

The First Vote. Once believed to be a scene in Richmond, this generic illustration was on the cover of *Harper's Weekly* on November 16, 1867, which contained articles on elections in several states of the former Confederacy.

radical reforms, and most white voters opposed those candidates. Having voters approve the convention gave it a legitimacy in addition to the authority of the acts of Congress under which it was conducted.

The convention met in Richmond from December 3, 1867 to April 17, 1868. Two dozen African American men won election to the convention. They were the first black officeholders in Virginia's history. They and 33 white men of northern or foreign birth and a smaller number of native white Virginians committed to reform constituted a majority of the 105-member convention. They elected John Curtis Underwood as president. An abolitionist native of New York who had resided in Virginia before the Civil War, Underwood held a minor post in the federal government during the first part of the war and later, by appointment of Abraham Lincoln, was a federal judge with his office in Alexandria. As a consequence of Underwood's notoriety, the convention and the constitution that it adopted came to be known by his name, which suggested that he dominated the convention or dictated the terms of the constitution it wrote. Calling the convention and the constitution by his name seriously misrepresented the many valuable contributions of white Republicans and African American members.

The convention delegates wrote a new constitution that differed significantly from its predecessors. They added to the state's Bill of Rights, which to that time had been called the Declaration of Rights, language adapted from the West Virginia Constitution of 1863 and from the Virginia Constitution of 1864 that disavowed secession, acknowledged the supremacy of the Constitution of the United States and the laws of Congress over the states, and prohibited slavery in Virginia. Those provisions endorsed the outcome of the

This illustration of the Constitutional Convention appeared in the February 15, 1868, issue of the national magazine *Frank Leslie's Illustrated Weekly*. It clearly shows the biracial membership of the convention but also shows the gallery crammed with African American men observing the convention in session. The convention admitted African Americans to the galleries but required that men and women sit in separate sections.

Civil War. The delegates also added a new Section 20 to the Bill of Rights. It read, "That all citizens of the State are hereby declared to possess equal civil and political rights and public privileges."[9]

The new constitution replaced the old county court system with a more democratic form of county government that resembled that of the New England township. That was the origin of the modern county supervisor form of government. The constitution authorized the election of more categories of local officials and required that local judges be persons learned in the law, not merely members of prominent families. The new constitution for the first time empowered the governor to veto bills the General Assembly passed, but it allowed the assembly by a two-thirds vote of both houses to override a veto. That significantly increased the importance of the office of governor and his influence in the legislative process. Another first was a provision to allow for amendment of the state constitution.

One of the most important innovations in the new constitution required the General Assembly to establish and support a statewide system of free public schools for all children. Thomas Bayne, who had won election as a delegate from Norfolk, tried to persuade the other delegates to require that the public schools be racially integrated, but they voted down his proposal. Bayne's speech in the convention on January 20, 1868, in favor of granting all men the right to vote reflected the beliefs of most African American men at that time about their place in the new American nation. Paraphrasing Thomas Jefferson and specifically citing the Declaration of Independence, Bayne stated that all men were created equal in the eyes of God, and that no men had the right to deprive any other men of their God-given rights. "Has a man the right to live?" Bayne asked the other delegates. "Was he born a freeman? Did God make man a slave? I say, no. If God never made man a slave, man was born free, and had a right to liberty. That is the principle of the Declaration of Independence. . . . I rejoice to-day that it is my privilege to stand on this floor and say that we are now beginning to live where we can recognize God as the great giver of all good gifts, and among them, the right of suffrage."[10] African American delegates in the Convention of 1867–68 enthusiastically supported establishment of the public school system and the extension of political rights to freedmen.

The delegates did not seriously consider granting women the right to vote, even though Underwood made a speech from the floor of the convention that endorsed woman suffrage. One provision to expand women's rights the delegates might have included in the new constitution but did not was a guarantee that married women could own and sell property independent of their husbands. Several southern constitutional conventions added such provisions to their constitutions, or state legislatures added them to their statute books. Those conventions and legislatures acted to protect the financial security of children and grandchildren of men who died during or as a consequence of the war. The acts prevented a widow's subsequent marriage from giving her new husband full legal power to sell or waste estates intended for the children and grandchildren of families with property. It is not clear why the Virginia convention did not consider including a similar provision in the new state constitution.

The convention did include a section to protect from foreclosure $2,000 worth of the property whereon a family lived. It was called a homestead exemption and was fairly common in the mid-nineteenth century. Perhaps the convention delegates believed that it was ample protection for the financial security of the descendants of Confederate soldiers. A decade later, in 1877, the General Assembly passed a Married Women's Property Act. By then every other state in the country had secured to married women the right to buy, sell, and control their own property and to protect their children's futures.

A few white men and women endorsed other radical ideas, including woman suffrage. Anna Whitehead Bodeker, of Richmond, wrote letters to the editor endorsing votes for women and in 1870 founded the Virginia State Woman Suffrage Association, which had the support of a small number of prominent white men and women in the state, including John C. Underwood and his wife. Bodeker invited Susan B. Anthony and other national advocates of women's rights to speak in Richmond and in 1871 appeared at a polling place and prepared to vote. The election judge refused to allow her to cast a ballot, but she succeeding in putting in the ballot box a slip of paper that declared that the Fourteenth Amendment made her a citizen of the United States and that as a citizen she had the right to vote. Bodeker's suffrage association soon lapsed into inactivity.

Even without woman suffrage, the constitution the convention voted to submit to a ratification referendum was much too radical for many white Virginians. The grant of the vote to African Americans, alone, was enough to generate widespread opposition. The disfranchisement of almost all former Confederates generated equally intense opposition, even among some African Americans. General Schofield refused to schedule the required ratification referendum. In April 1868 he replaced Pierpont in the governor's office with a radical, Republican Henry H. Wells. A year of political drift followed. The General Assembly did not meet between the spring of 1867 and October 1869, and army officers continued to supervise the state government and through it of most city and county government offices, too.

By the summer of 1869 the generals had removed from office most state and local officeholders and replaced them with men who had little or no involvement in the government of the Confederacy or the state government that met in Richmond during the war. That included the members of the Virginia Supreme Court of Appeals. From June 1869 until February 1870 a United States Army officer and two retired army officers, all with legal training or judicial experience, formed the highest appellate court in Virginia. Their successors, whom the General Assembly elected in 1870, and the General Assembly both validated the rulings the military appointees had handed down. Thereafter, though, the court's own records and histories of Virginia incorrectly referred to the court under those three judges as a military court of appeals, as if it were not the actual state court of appeals but an oppressive court martial forced on the civilian citizens of Virginia. State judges later overturned none of the official actions of those judges, prosecutors, local officials, legislators, or administrators simply because army generals had appointed them.

The prominence of black Virginians, men of northern origins, and native-born political outsiders in the leadership of the state's new Republican Party, together with the provisions of the new constitution, reinforced the determination of many experienced white political leaders to regain control of state government. Wells offended nearly all factions of the Republican Party and even drove some of the moderate Republicans into league with the Conservatives, which set the stage for Alexander Hugh Holmes Stuart, a former Whig congressman and cabinet officer from Staunton, to negotiate a compromise among the state's Conservative leaders, key Republicans in Congress, and President-Elect Ulysses S. Grant. The Conservatives offered to accept the proposed state constitution, including suffrage and equal political rights for African Americans, provided that the sections that disfranchised former Confederates and barred them from public office be put separately before the electorate for ratification. On July 6, 1869, in the second election in which African Americans voted in Virginia, the voters overwhelmingly approved the new Constitution and rejected the restrictive provisions on former Confederates.

Radical Republicans prepared for the 1869 general election by nominating a slate of radical candidates, with Wells as the candidate for governor and an African American physician, Joseph Dennis Harris, for lieutenant governor. To present a united opposition to the radicals, Conservatives endorsed a ticket of moderate Republicans with Gilbert C. Walker as the candidate for governor and Republicans who had remained loyal to the United States during the war as candidates for lieutenant governor and attorney general. Walker was a New York lawyer who had settled in Norfolk five years earlier and become a banker and manufacturer. Walker defeated Wells in the general election, and Conservatives won majorities in both houses of the General Assembly.

On October 8, the assembly met to ratify the Fourteenth and Fifteenth Amendments to the Constitution, which Congress required before it admitted members to either House from the former Confederate states. The Fourteenth Amendment made all persons born in the United States citizens, prohibited states from denying anybody life, liberty, or property without due process of law, required them to afford all residents the equal protection of the laws, and invalidated all public debts incurred in support of the Confederacy; and the Fifteenth Amendment prohibited states from denying the vote to men on account of race, color, or previous condition of servitude. On January 26, 1870, Grant signed an act of Congress that allowed Virginia's senators and representatives to take their seats in Congress, which terminated the army's authority to supervise civilian government in the state.

The law did not, as many people stated, readmit Virginia to the Union. Only Confederates had ever maintained that their states had been out of the Union. The United States government had always maintained that those states remained in the Union while disloyal men in them made war against the United States. That was the rationale for supervising governments in the former Confederacy, to bring those governments and the residents of those states back into their proper relationship to the Union.

Ratification and implementation of the Constitution of 1869 and ratification of the Thirteenth, Fourteenth, and Fifteenth Amendments to the Constitution of the United States completed the most thorough constitutional revolution in the state's history that had been begun with the Constitution of 1851. Virginians thereafter lived in a completely reformed political system. Between 1850 and 1870 slavery was abolished, and half a million Virginians became citizens, although women did not obtain all the rights of citizenship. All adult men—not merely white men who owned land—gained a constitutionally protected right to vote and hold public office. Voting by ballot replaced voice voting. Legislators represented their constituents, not a vested property interest. The old undemocratic county court system gave way to democratically elected local governments. All the state's courts for the first time were supposed to have judges with proper legal training. Governors became important political leaders and exercised influence with the legislature for the first time. Elections of governors became one of the centerpieces of partisan politics. All citizens could hope to send their children to a free public school. Private enterprise would have to develop a transportation infrastructure for the state without direct public financial assistance, or the state would have to do the work itself. The federal government became empowered to guarantee equal citizenship rights and voting rights, anything in state constitutions and laws to the contrary notwithstanding. In short, the elite white male oligarchic government of Virginia created in the early decades of the seventeenth century for a hierarchical society of tobacco planters had been entirely swept away. In its place men of all races and classes had equal opportunities to participate in politics and government.

Adapting Virginia to the new realities of free labor and black voting had just begun. Within months a tragedy occurred in Richmond that arose from the changes that were then taking place. Two men claimed to be mayor of Richmond, one under a military appointment and the other under appointment of the city council. When the Virginia Supreme Court of Appeals assembled on April 27, 1870, to hand down its decision in the lawsuit to determine who was entitled to the office, so many people crowded into the court room in the Capitol that the floor gave way and crashed into the chamber of the House of Delegates below. The Capitol Disaster, as it quickly came to be known, killed about sixty people and wounded dozens more.

The First Public School System

Thirty African American men won election to serve in the Senate and House of Delegates during the 1869–71 sessions of the General Assembly. The first black legislators in Virginia's history, they were a minority but an important minority. Those sessions of the assembly set the stage for the political struggles

William Henry Ruffner

of the ensuing decade. The assembly passed a bill in 1870 to establish the state's first public school system as the new state constitution required. The legislators elected William Henry Ruffner to be superintendent of public instruction. He and University of Virginia law professor John B. Minor drafted the bill the General Assembly adopted with some modifications. It authorized the state board of education, consisting of the superintendent, the governor, and the attorney general, to appoint a superintendent of schools for each county and city and to provide for purchase or construction of schools, employment of teachers, and acquisition of textbooks. Ruffner also developed a uniform curriculum. Sometimes compared with Horace Mann who was credited with creating the nation's first free public school systems in New England, Ruffner was the essential educational leader in Virginia during the 1870s, even though public funding for the new school system never reached the level he believed necessary. Ruffner's background as a Presbyterian clergyman and one-time critic of slavery made him controversial, and his support for educating African American children as well as white children also made the public school system controversial.

African Americans in the General Assembly supported Ruffner's bill in 1870, but they disapproved of its requirement for racial segregation of the schools. Two members of the Senate unsuccessfully introduced amendments

This framed collection of photographs of members of the House of Delegates in 1871 provides the only likenesses of some of the first African Americans to serve in the General Assembly. The person who prepared the group portraits segregated the African Americans on the bottom line. Within a few years legislative officials ceased including African American senators and delegates in official portraits entirely.

to the bill to prohibit racial segregation, and later a member of the House of Delegates made a motion to delete the requirement. That motion also failed, and then most of the African American delegates voted against passage of the bill as their only means of objecting to what they believed was a denial of rights of equal citizenship they and their children gained with the abolition of slavery and ratification of the Fourteenth Amendment.

The public schools founded in 1870 constituted the first statewide system of public education in Virginia. Even though the General Assembly never appropriated adequate money for the schools, they immediately became very popular. Both white and African American families eagerly sent their children to the schools in hopes that education would improve their chances for success in the new Virginia. The need for public education was great. The state then had 2,024 schools (including public schools in a few cities) but only about

7 that offered education above the elementary level. Fewer than 60,000 white people and only about 11,000 black people had attended any school in Virginia the previous year, when the Freedmen's Bureau schools closed. About 44 percent of all people in the state older than ten could not read. One of four white Virginians older than ten and nine of ten black Virginians older than ten could not write.

Indians on Virginia's reservations, caught in between as they had often been before, also thirsted for education but did not immediately benefit from the new public school system. They appealed to the governor and the General Assembly for the establishment of schools for their children. The federal government and the Freedmen's Bureau assumed no responsibility for them, and state officials, although offering polite encouragement, initially did little to assist the Mattaponi and Pamunkey to create their own school systems. The tribes were intent on maintaining their tax-exempt status, based on the treaties of 1646 and 1677, and were therefore reluctant to take part in the new public school system that was financed with state and local taxation.

Ruffner was a tireless advocate for public education, even though many prosperous white Virginians initially resented having their tax money appropriated for the education of poor black and white children. Ruffner argued that paying for good public education was the best investment Virginians could then make. "The money raised for the purpose is all expended within the State," he explained, "it goes directly back to the pockets of the people. . . . By such expenditure as this the State is not poorer, but far richer. It is like an expenditure for clover seed by a farmer, which makes a return far greater than the outlay. And the State which refuses to educate its children on the score of economy, pursues just the destructive policy of the farmer who will not expend enough to procure proper seeds, manures, implements and labor, but pursues what he calls the cheap system of farming, which ends in the utter impoverishment of the land and its owner." Ruffner continued, "But let the invigorating influence of education permeate her masses, and by the force of her awakened energies she will bear her burden lightly, and gather strength as she goes."[11]

The Postwar Economy

Legislators in the 1869–71 sessions also sought to rebuild the state's devastated economy, but the damage done during the war was great, and the abolition of slavery eliminated an important source of property tax revenue, which left the government few resources with which to stimulate economic activity. Some immediate challenges may have been beyond the government's ability to meet. "Our Society has for one of its objects the arousing of our people to the importance of increasing the skill of our labor and enlarging the variety of our products," explained William T. Sutherland, a prominent Danville tobacco trader, in his 1869 address as president of the State Agricultural Society. "So long as we buy our horses, mules and bacon from the West, and so long as almost every article used on our farms or about our houses, from a threshing machine to an axe-helve, and from a dress coat to a tooth-pick, comes from New England, we may expect to groan under the evils of poverty, which we will doubtless be always ready to attribute to our bad luck rather than to our bad management."[12]

Virginians in all walks of life faced economic and social changes to all aspects of their lives during the decades after the Civil War. Two Virginians transformed hardship into personal prosperity with pickled cucumbers. One was Samuel Ballton, who was born into slavery in Westmoreland County in 1838. During the Civil War his owner leased him to work on a railroad. He escaped and joined the United States Army. After the war Ballton moved to New York and lived at Greenlawn on Long Island, where he raised cucumbers and became a very successful businessman. Long before he died in April 1917 he was widely known as the Pickle King of Greenlawn. The other was Ellen Tompkins Kidd, a white Richmond woman born before the Civil War. She helped her family during the decades after the war, as did many other women, by selling items she made at home. Because many women sewed to raise extra money, that income was often called pin money. Kidd made and sold pickles under the name Pin Money Pickles. She sometimes went aboard trains that stopped in the city and sold her pickles in the dining car. She opened a large pickling plant in the city and eventually sold pickles to restaurants and other businesses throughout the United States. Kidd was a wealthy and internationally respected businesswoman when she died 1934.

Ballton and Kidd were successful in their pickle businesses because they created and sold products in regional markets that were expanding in importance and becoming national markets. The new commercial world in which they operated was still based on agriculture, but it was unlike the production and marketing of commodities when small farmers and great planters in Virginia produced tobacco, corn, and wheat as their principal cash crops. Markets and commercial agriculture both changed significantly during the nineteenth century and with profound effects on people who had been engaged principally in the plantation economy. The abolition of slavery required planters to hire farm workers and pay wages or to lease their land or enter into relationships with sharecroppers. When possible, farmers substituted machinery for farm laborers, but a simultaneous concentration on large-scale production of commercial crops increased the vulnerability of individual farmers and planters to diseases or pests that destroyed their crops.

The abolition of slavery required white ladies and gentlemen who had been accustomed to having servants do their cooking and cleaning, their plowing and harvesting, their milking and washing, to hire people to do that work or do it themselves. Work that people who regarded themselves as superior and refined would never have done before the end of slavery became work they had to do afterward. Those changes in responsibilities and the rhythms of life undermined the social status of planters and their families and allowed business and professional people to gain a larger measure of respectability as the most successful men and women to emulate.

In part as a consequence of the changing economy of farm life, men and women of ambition often moved to towns and cities to engage in business, to teach school, or to enter one of the learned professions. Business colleges opened in many of the state's cities and towns to train young men in modern business practices, and by the end of the nineteenth century to train young women for clerical and secretarial work. Women dominated the teaching profession in the new public schools of Virginia. That was true to a certain extent among African American women as well as among white women. Thousands of Virginians both white and black left the state in search of employment or enlarged opportunities elsewhere.

Taking advantage of resources the federal government obtained through the sale of public lands, Hampton Institute became the state's first land-grant college. In 1872 the General Assembly created the Virginia Agricultural and Mechanical Institute (later Virginia Polytechnic Institute and State University), at Blacksburg, the state's principal land-grant college for white men. Its original purpose was to educate young men in modern agricultural science for the new market economy. The institute also contributed in other important ways to the economic and scientific progress of Virginia. Engineering became a very important component of the curriculum, which was no coincidence. Rebuilding the state's railroads required skilled professional engineers.

Rebuilding the railroads also required an especially large amount of money, a fact that brought several large southern railway lines under the control of northern financiers. Railroad investors were able to reorganize and consolidate some of the Virginia lines, but during the long national recession that followed the financial Panic of 1873, northern syndicates purchased controlling interests in most of the major Virginia railroads. Among the most important southern railway systems formed during those years were the Chesapeake and Ohio, the Norfolk and Western, and the Southern, all of which traced their beginnings to antebellum Virginia.

Industrial, agricultural, and commercial progress depended in large part on railroads. When the Norfolk and Western laid rails west from Radford in 1883 it opened up the Pocahontas coalfields on the Virginia–West Virginia border and made it possible for mining companies to ship coal directly to the port of Norfolk. The parallel extension of Chesapeake and Ohio lines north of the James River promoted the rapid growth of Newport News at the line's eastern terminus. Many communities along their tracks prospered,

View of Virginia Polytechnic Institute, later Virginia Tech

but none more so than Big Lick. Renamed Roanoke in 1882, the city became an important railroad center, and by the end of the century the Norfolk and Western operated the South's largest locomotive-manufacturing plant there. Other industries developed in different regions of Virginia. Richmond, long a center for the manufacture and sale of tobacco products, became a national leader in the production of cigarettes after 1876, and Danville expanded its flourishing textile industry and drew on the cotton and wool produced in the southeastern states.

The coalfields that opened in southwestern Virginia and elsewhere in Appalachia during the final decades of the nineteenth century produced a new phenomenon, the company town. The good coal seams were in areas remote from population centers, and coal companies responded by building residential communities at or near the mineshafts. They rented or sold small houses to the miners and their families and often built schools, churches, stores, and recreational facilities such as baseball fields. Those company towns earned evil reputations for several reasons, not least the practice of some companies that paid wages not in cash but in company scrip, which could be redeemed only at the company bank or store. That and the inability of most mining families to travel to neighboring or distant towns for supplies meant that the families of coal miners sometimes became enmeshed in a debt dependency not unlike that in which sharecroppers found themselves. Nevertheless, thousands of poor farmers from many parts of the South and some from Europe flocked to the coal mines in search of work. Some of them worked for several months or years, sent money home, and then returned to their old homes. Others moved their families to the coalfields and created new communities in the mountains of Appalachia. Railroad and timber companies and some manufacturing companies also erected company towns that resembled those in the coalfields.

Many of the new industries, in addition to railroads, employed complex machinery and exposed working men and women to new dangers. Stories about injuries and deaths of railroad workmen and factory workers appeared frequently in the state's newspapers. Roanoke newspapers reported eight deaths or serious injuries of railroad workers between March and August 1890. On a Sunday night in Lynchburg, according to one of the reports, the body of a brakeman was found near a railroad bridge. "His head was severed from his body and rolled from the trestle down the embankment to the edge of the river, where it was found by those who discovered the body. His right arm was cut off at the shoulder, and the body otherwise mangled. The dead man's lantern was found near him, shattered into fragments." The brakeman had been "married about three weeks ago. His body was taken to Clifton Forge where his family resides."[13]

Conditions in the mines were even more dangerous and during the ensuing decades cost thousands of men their lives and devastated their families; but men could often find paying work in the mines when they could not find work elsewhere. On March 13, 1884, the first large Virginia mining disaster occurred in the Pocahontas field in Tazewell County. A telegraphic dispatch printed in the state's newspapers the next day described the scene: "The destruction at the mine is terrible and complete. There were 100 men in the mine at the time of the explosion, not one of whom is believed to have escaped. Those who were not killed outright by the terrible force of the explosion most likely perished from after-damp," meaning gasses that suffocated survivors. "The cause of the explosion is not yet definitely ascertained, as the entrances to the mine are all full of bad air, but the presumption is that one of the miners struck a fissure filled with gas."

The report continued, "Several parties ventured into the mines this morning, but could not long endure the foul atmosphere. A number of bodies were discovered horribly mangled—some of them with the heads torn from the trunks, and others with limbs all gone, presenting an appalling spectacle. The work of destruction was not confined entirely to the interior of the mines, but houses 200 or 300 feet distant were overturned, and in several instances entirely demolished. The large ventilator of the Southwest Virginia Improvement Company," which pumped fresh air through the mine, "was blown to atoms, and the mines cannot be entered until another is constructed for the purpose of freeing the atmosphere of the suffocating fumes. This work is now progressing speedily. A large force is engaged on the outside of the mines constructing coffins and perfecting other arrangements for the interment of the dead miners, most of whom are foreigners."[14]

15

THREE LOST CAUSES

Robert E. Lee died on October 12, 1870, in Lexington, where he had been president of Washington College since the autumn of 1865. By the time of the Battle of Gettysburg, Lee had come to personify the Confederate cause. His ability and character made him the perfect symbol for all that former Confederates wished to see that was good in the old South. That he acquiesced in the outcome of the war and accepted a college presidency in order to prepare the next generation of southern white men for shouldering their responsibilities provided a powerful example in both the North and the South for people who favored rapid reconciliation. Lee died during a week of major floods that destroyed some of the antebellum canal networks. The two events appeared to sweep away the old Virginia.

Following Lee's death, Edward Virginius Valentine, a Richmond sculptor who was trained in Europe and had a very successful career in the United States, created one of the state's most important sculptures for Lee's burial site at the chapel at Washington College, which was renamed Washington and Lee University. Valentine's full-length marble of a recumbent Lee, as if sleeping and not dead, became a powerful icon. No other man and no other piece of art came so much to represent what Virginia's former Confederates cherished in their past.

The Lost Cause

Most white Virginians, in addition to navigating the troubled waters of political and social change, had to deal with grief, anger, and disappointment at the outcome of the war that had been lost—the Lost Cause, they called it. Evidence of the war's devastation could be seen nearly everywhere during the months and years after April 1865, not only in burned buildings but also in the faces of the people and literally on their bodies. Men with missing arms or legs lived in virtually every community. Other men suffered from permanently

Edward Virginius Valentine, *Recumbent Lee,* in the chapel at Washington and Lee University.

injured health as a consequence of their wartime experiences. Widows with children and few means of taking care of them were also everywhere, as were grieving men and women whose husbands, fathers, brothers, sons, or grandsons had been killed or had died during the war. The agricultural economy may have begun to recover fairly soon after the fighting was over and the soldiers returned home, but adapting to all of the changes that the war produced took much longer.

Families and local institutions such as churches and fraternal societies rather than the state government assumed responsibility for assisting men who were disabled during the war and for their families, widows, and orphans. Some local governments had assisted soldiers' families during the war, and in many communities churches and fraternal organizations such as Freemasons provided work or other assistance to help families through the financial hard times after the war. The state government appropriated money to purchase artificial arms and legs for men who lost limbs and beginning in the 1880s also provided limited pension and survivor benefits for veterans and their widows.

One of the conspicuous ways in which white Virginians dealt with the human toll the war took was to memorialize the dead. Numerous women's organizations took the initiative in caring for the cemeteries in which the Confederate dead were buried. In the process they created the annual observance known in various parts of the South at the time as Decoration Day, Confederate Memorial Day, or finally Memorial Day. In the spring of each year veterans and their descendants, widows, daughters, and other women who

Memorial obelisk in Hollywood Cemetery, Richmond, at the site of the reburial of Confederate soldiers and officers killed at Gettysburg.

felt the loss, and younger generations of white Virginia men and women attempted to gain strength by concentrating on the virtues and sacrifices of the men who fought and died.

The many civic commemorations emphasized sacrifice, heroism, and comradeship on the battlefield and in effect reinterpreted the meaning of the Civil War to deemphasize its political causes and consequences. During the following decades, nearly every county and city erected a monument to its Confederate soldiers or its most famous officers, which filled the civic landscape with conspicuous reminders of the Lost Cause. The best known and one of the largest of the memorial projects involved the disinterment in 1872 of more than two thousand Confederate dead from the battleground at Gettysburg, Pennsylvania, for reburial in Hollywood Cemetery in Richmond, which became one of the South's principal shrines to the sacrifices of Confederates.

Keeping alive the memories of the cause that had been lost, and that survivors had to reconcile themselves to, took many forms. Former Confederate soldiers formed the United Confederate Veterans in 1889 to keep alive their shared experiences, and their descendants created other societies, including the United Daughters of the Confederacy in 1894 and the Sons of Confederate Veterans in 1896, which carried the message of the Lost Cause to new generations of Virginians. Many popular writers contributed to the same vision of the past. So-called plantation novels, which romanticized life in the antebellum South, as well as biographies and stirring accounts of the war reinforced the Lost Cause interpretation of the war and eventually convinced many northern readers that the soldiers of the Confederacy had not been guilty of treason or of fighting to preserve slavery.

Hard feeling resulting from the war and its aftermath persisted for decades in Virginia and had conspicuous political overtones. For example, following the death in Bedford County in November 1872 of a member of the Constitutional Convention of 1867–68, a writer for a Lynchburg newspaper composed a bitter obituary notice. "Mr. G. C. Curtis, a prominent Radical politician of Bedford," it read, "died at his home in that county on Friday last, of consumption.—Mr. Curtis was a native of New York, and came to Virginia soon after the war. He was a bitter Radical, and always ready to adopt the most extreme party measures.... Probably no man has ever died in any community less regretted than the deceased."[1]

Even as white Virginians mourned their losses in the war, black Virginians celebrated their freedom. Freed people assembled annually to mark the anniversary of emancipation. In some communities they did so at the beginning of the new year, the date of the Emancipation Proclamation; some celebrated in April, either on the date of Richmond's liberation/occupation or when Lee surrendered; and others later chose other days, often the nineteenth of June, on which date in 1865 the army in Texas freed some of the last enslaved people. Annual emancipation commemorations continued to be important events in many African American communities for decades, in some places as late as the middle of the twentieth century. For African Virginians, the Civil War was not about sacrifice or loss. It was about freedom for themselves and their families. Its outcome was a cause for celebration, not for lamentation.

Lamentation was the central theme in much of the literature white Virginia writers published during the decades after the Civil War. In some ways, their histories, novels, and short stories were an extension of the literature of decline from the years before the war. Memoirs of Civil War service, regimental histories, and biographies of Confederate heroes were popular works. Finding much to admire in a society that was lost and in acts of military valor, writers and readers gave themselves solace by trying to hold onto what was valuable to them in the past and in their shared sense of loss. Historians, authors of textbooks, and popular writers produced shelves of books on those themes for decades. John Esten Cooke thrived as a successful writer after the war as much as he had before. Jubal Early and other former Confederates industriously publicized a Confederate version of Civil War history that by the end of the nineteenth century convinced many Americans that Confederate soldiers had fought to preserve their homes and their way of life and states' rights, not to preserve slavery or to destroy the Union. In some respects, the Virginians who wrote about the Civil War promoted a reconciliation of northern men with former Confederates rather than of the defeated Confederates with victorious northerners.

Scores of white women in the upper South during the latter part of the nineteenth century, many of them Virginians, employed their pens in order to understand new realities of life in the changed South. Some writers were com-

John Adams Elder, *Appomattox* (1887), depicts an unnamed Confederate soldier as if in thoughtful mourning for the cause lost at Appomattox Court House. This was one of many powerful visual icons of the Lost Cause.

mercially successful and some were not, but readers who shared perspectives and anxieties did not have to look far in search of abundant reading material. Those women wrote about and their readers read about virtues and values lost or endangered, the difficulties of preserving family honor and traditions when the family had been economically ruined or had lost valued members, and how in a new society they could find their own places of dignity and value.

Near the end of her 1867 book *Richmond during the War,* Sarah Ann Brock reflected on the effects that the war and its conclusion had on her and other members of the once-prosperous white society of which she had been a member. "There was no one so obscure or humble, so far remote in the wilds and mountain fastnesses of our country," she wrote, "but that he shared in the common distress, and there was no table so bountifully supplied, no wardrobe so faultlessly elegant in its appointments, that did not show the effect of the war. If within our homes we had comforts and elegances, we had only to step out on our streets to meet here a soldier with one leg, there one with one arm, another who had lost an eye, another with a horrid scar, that told a tale of battle; or on our passage through a certain quarter of our city where government work was given out to the indigent, we would see hundreds of poor women in waiting for the coarse sewing from which they earned the pittance that saved them from hunger; or we might pass government offices and see numbers of the most refined and elegant daughters of former ease and luxury, accustomed from their birth to seek only their own enjoyment, in daily toil at the desk of clerk, by which they earned a livelihood."[2]

Even more white men than women wrote about the same subjects. Among the most popular Virginia writers in the immediate aftermath of the Civil War was the humorist George William Bagby, who began publishing in the 1850s. His works, mostly short stories and lectures, combined humor and pathos with an affectionate backward look at days gone by. Often writing in imitation of the spoken dialect of poor white people, he poked fun at pompous characters and also gave dignity to simple, direct ideas and pleasures. Funny in the same style as his contemporary humor writers in other states, Bagby helped people look at the past with appreciation for its values and at the postwar present in the same way, which eased the difficult task white Virginians and other southerners had during the 1870s and 1880s of adapting their lives to radically changed circumstances.

Of all the Virginia writers of the period, Thomas Nelson Page, born in Hanover County in 1853, was probably the most popular and successful. He wrote voluminously for decades, well into the twentieth century. His works included fiction, poetry, and history. Regarded in many quarters as an early realist writer because of his detailed descriptions of southern people and life, his works also resonated with themes from the earlier literature and often had a thick overlay of romantic nostalgia. Page did a major disservice to understanding the old Virginia, though, when in his 1904 book, *The Negro: The Southerner's Problem,* he wrote that in 1832 the General Assembly had come within one vote of abolishing slavery. For generations that misstatement misled many serious readers into believing that the state's late-antebellum political leaders were not as committed to slavery as a social and economic system as in fact they had been—and that the Civil War had therefore not been fought to protect slavery but to protect abstract states' rights. However hard some white Virginians tried to hold onto parts of the pre–Civil War past, the cause for which their men had fought was definitely lost.

The Rise and Fall of the Readjusters

As some Virginians looked backward nostalgically, most Virginians of every age, race, class, and place of residence had to live in the new social and economic environment the abolition of slavery created, and they had to look forward. That included adjusting to citizenship for African Americans and a biracial politics. The state's new system of public schools appeared to offer a means of escaping some of the limitations of nineteenth-century life for poor and middle-class families of both races, but in spite of the promise of a better future through education many parents soon saw the schools and their children's prospects decline.

The state's public debt left over from the prewar years threatened adequate appropriations for the schools. The state inherited a large and growing debt from the prewar years, much of it incurred for the construction of railroads the war had ruined. Because neither state government (the Confederate state government in Richmond nor the Restored state government in Wheeling and Alexandria) paid any significant amount of interest on the debt during the war, accumulated interest raised the outstanding principal from about $34 million in 1861 to about $45.6 million at the end of the decade. Bankers, lawyers, businessmen, and many political leaders feared that if the state government did not honor its obligation and pay its debt people in Virginia would be unable to borrow the capital they needed from northern or foreign investors to rebuild the economy. At the same time the increasing size of the debt and the loss of tax revenue on enslaved property made paying the debt increasingly difficult. They were in a dilemma: they needed to do two expensive things, pay the debt and revive the economy; but to do either required simultaneous success at doing the other, and both required money.

In 1871 the General Assembly passed what was called the Funding Act of 1871. It provided for issuing new state bonds to cover two-thirds of the principal, in hopes West Virginia, under the terms of its Constitution of 1863, would pay the other third. The law required owners of the old bonds to exchange them for new bonds that matured in thirty-four years and paid 6 percent annual interest. The interest rate was about standard for public securities at the time. To make the bonds attractive to investors the assembly allowed creditors at the time of the exchange to accept what were called coupon bonds. Each bond had attached to it sixty-eight coupons that the owner could detach at six-month intervals to collect half the annual interest then due. The bond owner could either present the coupon at the state treasury and collect the interest, use the coupon to pay part of his or her taxes, or sell the coupon at less than face value to a broker who would collect the interest and make a profit based on the difference between the price he paid and the interest he received.

The debt was about nine times annual state revenue in 1870, and payment of interest ate up about half the state budget. The Funding Act of 1871 required that so much tax revenue be paid to northern and foreign bond speculators that too little remained in the state treasury to finance the schools properly. Moreover, because people could pay taxes with the interest-bearing coupons tax collection did not bring nearly enough money into the treasury. Every dollar in taxes paid with a coupon was a dollar the state could not spend on teacher salaries, book purchases, or other vital government services. In 1872 legislators over the governor's veto repealed the clause in the law that permitted payment of taxes with coupons, but the Virginia Supreme Court of Appeals declared the repeal statute unconstitutional.

Legislators could not or would not increase taxes or create new sources of revenue, and as a consequence the Funding Act of 1871 crippled the state government and threatened more than a decade of budget deficits. Legislators shifted money intended for the schools to debt service. Moreover, the resulting economic uncertainty undermined efforts of the state's business leaders to redevelop the prewar economy based on large-scale commercial agriculture and industry. The old plantation economy had ceased to be the driving force in Virginia before the Civil War, and in the years immediately afterward the weakened industrial economy languished in the prolonged recession that followed the financial panic of 1873. Plans to construct a new Virginia could as easily fail as succeed.

An alternative to full payment of the state debt, which seemed an impossible task, and repudiation, which might ruin the state's credit, was a reduction in the interest rate, repudiation of part of the debt, and a good-faith effort to pay the balance. Advocates of adjusting, or readjusting, payment of the debt came to be called Readjusters, and adherents to the policy adopted in 1871 were called Funders. For more than a decade the two factions battled each other on the campaign trails, in the General Assembly, and in state and federal courts. Dissatisfaction with the Funders mounted as the schools and other public services deteriorated, and Virginians suffered during the recession that followed the Panic of 1873.

The leader of the Readjusters was William Mahone, of Petersburg, a slightly built, bearded man of inexhaustible energy and ambition who had commanded Confederate forces at the Battle of the Crater and created what became the Norfolk and Western Railroad. Mahone forged a coalition of politicians of both parties, farmers, small businessmen, African Americans who opposed the reduction of school appropriations, and others disenchanted with the consequences of the Funders' policies. The Readjusters' promises to save the public schools and Mahone's organizing skills together produced victories at the polls. In 1879 Readjusters won majorities in both houses of the General Assembly, and the next year the assembly elected Mahone to the United States Senate. In 1881 after African American Republicans made an alliance with the Readjusters, the Readjuster candidate for governor, William E. Cameron, of Petersburg, defeated the Funder John Warwick Daniel, a Conservative from Lynchburg, which gave Readjusters complete control over state government.

Readjusters enjoyed broad appeal among white and black parents who wished their children to receive educations that would allow them to succeed in the future. Some Funders remained opposed to public education, and their comments helped Readjuster candidates. In 1878 when legislators were debating a bill to increase the amount of money for the schools John Warwick Daniel opposed it in the Senate of Virginia as a reprehensible scheme to cheat the state's creditors. "He said," according to a newspaper report Daniel later confirmed, "he would rather see a bonfire made of every free school in the State, and a bonfire then made of his own house, than that this bill" or any others to reduce payment of interest on the debt should pass.[3]

After the assembly passed the bill, Governor Frederick William Mackey Holliday vetoed it. His veto message expressed an elite view of Virginia's society that only a small proportion of prosperous families like his enjoyed. "Our fathers did not need free schools to make them what they were," he lectured the legislators. "Happy this generation could it rival them in those virtues that go to make up the glory of a commonwealth! They would not have tolerated them on the soil of Virginia had they to be established by the denial of their honest debts. . . . Public free schools are not a necessity. The world, for hundreds of years, grew in wealth, culture, and refinement, without them. They are a luxury, adding when skilfully conducted, it may be, to the beauty and power of a state, but to be paid for, like any other luxury, by the people who wish their benefits."[4] What Holliday meant was that if poor white and black parents wanted their children educated they should pay for it themselves, the same way wealthy people paid to educate their children.

Daniel's and Holliday's comments alienated a great many white men and women and contributed to the success of Readjuster candidates who offered voters a choice: have their tax money sent to out-of-state and foreign bond speculators or spent for the benefit of all their children. Early in the 1880s several Readjusters won election to the House of Representatives, too, including from districts with large white majorities, such as the Ninth Congressional District in southwestern Virginia and in the Valley of Virginia. White and black Virginians supported the Readjusters, even though black support was what attracted the most attention.

In 1882 the Readjuster majorities in the General Assembly passed the Riddleberger Act, named for Harrison Holt Riddleberger, a member of the Senate from Harrisonburg and after 1883 Mahone's colleague in the United States Senate. The act replaced the existing 6 percent bonds with new bonds that paid 3 percent interest and matured in fifty years. The total face value of the new bonds was approximately one-third less than the 1871 bonds, and the law declared that coupons on the new bonds could not be used to pay taxes. The Readjusters appointed auditors who enforced the tax laws strictly, and the government collected hundreds of thousands of dollars in delinquent taxes. Readjusters also reduced taxes on farms and small businesses and raised taxes on corporations and corporate property. By the simple reform of requiring state assessors to determine the taxable value of railroads rather than permitting railroad company officials to make their own appraisals, the Readjusters greatly increased tax revenue. Their policies relieved heavily burdened tax-

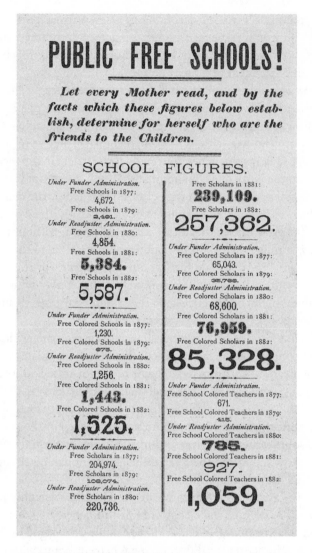

PUBLIC FREE SCHOOLS!

Let every Mother read, and by the facts which these figures below establish, determine for herself who are the friends to the Children.

SCHOOL FIGURES.

Under Funder Administration.
Free Schools in 1877:
4,672.
Free Schools in 1879:
2,491.
Under Readjuster Administration.
Free Schools in 1880:
4,854.
Free Schools in 1881:
5,384.
Free Schools in 1882:
5,587.

Under Funder Administration.
Free Colored Schools in 1877:
1,230.
Free Colored Schools in 1879:
675.
Under Readjuster Administration.
Free Colored Schools in 1880:
1,256.
Free Colored Schools in 1881:
1,443.
Free Colored Schools in 1882:
1,525.

Under Funder Administration.
Free Scholars in 1877:
204,974.
Free Scholars in 1879:
108,074.
Under Readjuster Administration.
Free Scholars in 1880:
220,736.

Free Scholars in 1881:
239,109.
Free Scholars in 1882:
257,362.

Under Funder Administration.
Free Colored Scholars in 1877:
65,043.
Free Colored Scholars in 1879:
35,766.
Under Readjuster Administration.
Free Colored Scholars in 1880:
68,600.
Free Colored Scholars in 1881:
76,959.
Free Colored Scholars in 1882:
85,328.

Under Funder Administration.
Free School Colored Teachers in 1877:
671.
Free School Colored Teachers in 1879:
415.
Under Readjuster Administration.
Free School Colored Teachers in 1880:
785.
Free School Colored Teachers in 1881:
927.
Free School Colored Teachers in 1882:
1,059.

Public Free Schools! Note the clever way in which the typesetter emphasized differences between Funder and Readjuster support for African American schools with different fonts and type sizes.

payers and replenished the state treasury. Within two years a $1.5 million surplus replaced the Funders' deficit. An undated campaign leaflet evidently printed in 1883 and addressed to mothers informed them that Readjusters had appropriated more money and hired more teachers for African American schools than Funders had. The purpose of the leaflet was to encourage African

American mothers to make sure their enfranchised husbands and other male relatives voted for Readjuster candidates.

Readjusters enacted several measures African Americans supported, including a law to abolish public whipping, a painful and humiliating form of punishment left over from slavery times. They also passed a constitutional amendment to repeal a recent amendment Conservatives had forced on the state that required payment of a poll tax as a prerequisite for voting, which made it prohibitively expensive for some poor African Americans to register to vote. The Readjusters replaced members of the governing boards of the Medical College of Virginia and the University of Virginia in order to improve the faculties and curricula of both schools, and they installed a Readjuster as president of Virginia Agricultural and Mechanical Institute. In 1882 they founded Virginia Normal and Collegiate Institute near Petersburg, the country's first publicly supported college for African Americans, to prepare men and women to be teachers in the schools. It was renamed Virginia State University in the twentieth century. The Readjuster majority in the General Assembly also established the first state mental hospital for African Americans, later known as Central State Hospital. As evidence of the party's strong support for the new public school system, the Readjuster superintendent of public instruction replaced most of the city and county school superintendents Ruffner and the Conservatives had appointed. Some of the new superintendents appear to have been more sympathetic to the educational needs of black students.

Governor Cameron's message to the General Assembly in December 1883, midway through his one four-year term as governor, expressed the essence of the Readjusters' beliefs about the importance of public education. "The condition of the public free school system should engage the active interest of every citizen of this commonwealth," he informed the legislators. "There is no individual and no element of our population but should rejoice to know that the state in the past two years has been able almost to double the facilities for free education . . . the executive of the commonwealth knows no higher duty than to contribute all in his power to furnish the means for teaching all the people to understand their rights, to know the limits of their privileges, and to feel and perform the full measure of their duties. To whose whom we have armed with the powers and responsibilities of citizenship, present or future, a high obligation exists. To call human beings into the front of the battle of life and deny them or obstruct them in the means which are essential to their intelligent use of freedom would be as gross an abuse as to call men into real war and fail to put into their hands the weapons with which to make them soldiers. It is to be hoped that these views will meet with no opposition in Virginia, and that all persons of all classes will agree that our best policy, as our highest duty, dictates the free education of all the children of all classes of our people."[5]

Cameron, Readjuster politicians, and voters who elected them held a radically different set of beliefs than Daniel, Holliday, and Funder leaders who placed their faith in elite white Virginians and offered little or no hope to poor white or black Virginians who together formed a large majority of the state's population.

The biracial political coalition in a state of the former Confederacy attracted national attention. Not since federal government supervision of state governments ceased had African Americans anywhere in the South had such a prominent political role. In spite of imposition of a poll tax as a prerequisite for suffrage, African Americans nevertheless reentered political life to support the Readjusters and repeal the poll tax. The number of African American men who ran with Republican and Readjuster support and won election to the assembly increased during the peak years of the Readjusters. People elsewhere took notice as Virginians experimented with a constructing a completely new political culture to replace that of the old South.

Early in 1882 William Mahone, who joined the Republicans when he took his seat in the United States Senate, received an invitation to deliver the main address in Boston on Washington's Birthday. That by itself indicated the importance of the Readjuster coalition. Mahone was their leader, but he was also a former brigadier general in the army of the Confederacy, so it was remarkable that the Bostonians invited him at all. He did not attend the celebration, but he sent a long letter that was read on the occasion and also printed in several Virginia newspapers. "Our people have just declared popular education to be among the most sacred duties and trusts of representative government," Mahone wrote, "and are bravely executing that honorable decree. With valuable and beneficient results we are rapidly guaranteeing a priceless ballot to all entitled to it under the American theory. Conspicuous among the achievements of the advanced thought that places Virginia in full alignment with the highest American civilization is the prompt justice with which she deals with an element of population which has been the fruitful source of passionate disputation. Virginia has closed the long strife, which Mr. Jefferson foresaw and dreaded as he would dread 'the fire-bell at night,' over the status of the colored man.... In Virginia he is at last in the full panoply of acknowledged citizenship."[6]

Mahone's explanation of Readjuster policies as in keeping with "the American theory" and "the highest American civilization" rather than with traditional Virginia values indicated how much he and other Readjusters had become committed to constructing a new Virginia political culture with African Americans as full (even though not always fully equal) partners. His

William Mahone

public statements together with the reforms the Readjusters pushed through the assembly that spring convinced many white Virginians that he had gone entirely too far and that it was time for traditional white political leaders to unite and crush the biracial coalition that in their eyes had become as threatening as the radical Republican reformers had been in the 1860s.

The threat to traditional elite white government was very real. Between the 1867 election and the 1890s, almost a hundred African American men won election to the Constitutional Convention, the House of Delegates, and the Senate of Virginia. The careers of some of them during the decades after the Civil War illustrate both the possibilities for success they enjoyed as well as the limitations the times imposed on them. Men who had been born free or who had escaped from slavery, like Thomas Bayne, were among the first political leaders to achieve success and gain influence. In the 1869 and 1870 sessions of the assembly, the first in which African Americans served, Ballard T. Edwards, of Manchester, in Chesterfield County, proposed half a dozen measures intended to protect vulnerable freedpeople. Born free in 1828 and a successful brick mason and leader in his Baptist church, Edwards introduced bills to protect free people and their rights: to limit the number of hours men could be forced to work so that working people could go to night school and get an education; to forbid railroad and steamboat companies from making distinctions among passengers and customers based on race; to reduce the toll on the bridge between Manchester and Richmond that many of his neighbors crossed daily to go to and from work and to erect a toll-free bridge; and to regulate the practice of paying wages in company scrip rather than in cash, which, as in the coal mining towns, threatened to bind employees in long-term debt to employers. The white majority in the assembly did not pass any of Edwards's proposals, but he and other black assembly members during the next two decades strove to protect their political and economic rights and the new public school system.

Among the best known and most successful African American political leaders in Virginia was Peter Jacob Carter. He was born into slavery in Northampton County on the Eastern Shore in 1845, joined the United States Army during the Civil War, and returned to Virginia afterward able to read and write. He soon entered politics and was elected in 1871 to the first of four consecutive two-year terms in the House of Delegates. Carter quickly emerged as one of the leading African American Republicans in Virginia. He spoke throughout the far-flung First Congressional District in eastern Virginia during election campaigns and often presided at district and state party conventions. Well known and respected, he was an able leader. Even though he lacked any formal higher education, he served a term on the board of the new Virginia Normal and Collegiate Institute. Carter died, perhaps of appendicitis or possibly as a result of poisoning, in 1886, widely recognized at the time as a major political figure in eastern Virginia.

Among the more obscure men who entered politics during the decades after the Civil War was Johnson Collins, who was also born into slavery in 1847. He had a rudimentary education and worked as a laborer in Brunswick County after the Civil War. In 1879 with Republican and Readjuster backing he won election to the House of Delegates, where he served one two-year term and supported the reform program of the Readjusters. He did not seek reelection, but in 1880 he proudly identified himself to the census enumerator as a member of the legislature. Later in the decade he moved to Washington, D.C., where for about twenty years he earned a very modest living as a watchman. Collins died in Washington, virtually unnoticed, in 1906.

The contrast between Carter's and Collins's lives reveals the possibilities and limitations African Americans confronted between the end of the Civil War and the beginning of the twentieth century. In business, on the farm, in the professions, in their households, and also in politics, men and women who had an education or experience in managing their own affairs or as officers of church congregations or other organizations were much more likely to prosper and succeed. People like Johnson Collins competed with less chance to succeed.

Much the same could be said about white men and women as about black men and women, but such generalizations do not always hold true, and they obscure the significant accomplishments of many talented Virginians. The lives of two women serve as good examples. Rosa Dixon Bowser was born in Amelia County early in 1855, probably into slavery. After freedom came in

1865 her family moved to Richmond and joined First African Baptist Church. She taught in the Sunday school there and in 1873 graduated from high school and became a public school teacher. She married another teacher in 1879, but he died two years later. Bowser organized African American teachers in Richmond, leading to the founding of the Virginia State Teachers Association, one of the first of Virginia's statewide professional associations of African Americans. She served two years as president of the association and also held high office in several other state and national organizations, some of them strictly for women and some for both women and men. In 1896 she was an unsuccessful candidate for the presidency of the National Association of Colored Women.

Lucy Goode Brooks, like Bowser, was also born into slavery, in 1818, and as an adult lived in Richmond, where she married and had several children. She and her husband had to enlist the help of white men to purchase and eventually free some of their children, but one daughter was sold and carried away to Tennessee. After the Civil War, Brooks's husband became a successful businessman. She persuaded the Ladies Sewing Circle for Charitable Work to join with the local Cedar Creek Meeting of the Society of Friends to establish an orphanage for African American children. The orphanage survived into the twentieth century, and in 1984 the renamed Friends' Association for Children created the Lucy Brooks Foundation as its fundraising agency. Her sons Albert Brooks (named for the husband of Queen Victoria) and Robert Peel Brooks (named for a British prime minister) became prominent business and social leaders in Richmond's African American community. Like many of their white contemporaries and like Rosa Dixon Bowser, the members of the Brooks family had successful careers in a city, which offered opportunities for joining together with neighbors to pursue community objectives, opportunities probably not available on farms or in small towns

Many of the most important achievements of Virginia's late nineteenth-century women, black and white, were in the field of education. They also founded and ran orphanages, served as missionaries overseas or helped raise money to support missionary work, and worked in factories and in clerical jobs at banks and other businesses. Among African Americans, such organizations as the Grand Fountain United Order of True Reformers united men and women in a variety of mutually reinforcing activities. The True Reformers supported the temperance movement that sought to reduce consumption of alcohol and the resultant problems. It also served as an insurance provider and eventually spun off a bank and a newspaper in Richmond. William Washington Browne, the order's director, became nationally famous, and for a time its insurance company was one of the largest black businesses in the United States.

Politics of White Supremacy

The Conservative Party had dissolved with the success of the Readjusters. In preparation for the 1883 legislative elections its leaders revived it in the form of a new state Democratic Party with an avowedly white supremacist platform. In order to entice white men who had supported the Readjusters away from the biracial party, the Democratic state convention that year accepted the Readjuster refinancing of the debt and pledged to support the public school system. Shortly before the election a street brawl in Danville between white and black men captured statewide attention in large part because Democratic Party propagandists portrayed it as a race war and blamed the Readjusters. Democrats won control of both houses of the General Assembly that year and two years later elected former Confederate general Fitzhugh Lee to the governorship. African American men resumed voting for Republican candidates who seldom won election except in western Virginia, but with African American support Republicans remained a political threat to Democrats.

Political debate about the state debt subsided by the mid-1880s, but Democratic legislators and governors repeatedly passed laws to prevent payment of taxes with coupons from the old bonds that were still in circulation. The methods they employed were controversial and led to numerous court cases to challenge their legality. At least eighty-five cases reached the Virginia Supreme Court of Appeals during the 1870s, 1880s, and early in the 1890s, and twenty-nine reached the Supreme Court of the United States. In spite of federal court rulings that most of the laws violated the contract clause of the Constitution of the United States, the assembly and the state's judges repeatedly evaded those rulings. Litigation continued until 1892 when the state finally reached an agreement with its creditors. The General Assembly passed the Olcott Act, which satisfied creditors by issuing new one-hundred-year bonds (at 2 percent interest for the first decade and 3 percent thereafter) to pay off the debt.

Only the question of West Virginia's share remained. Following a long series of lawsuits that Virginia filed against West Virginia in the Supreme Court of the United States, the West Virginia Legislature agreed in 1919 to pay a portion of the third of the principal that Virginia had always maintained was that state's proper debt. Virginians paid taxes until 1944, and West Virginians paid taxes until 1939 to retire the public debt created before the Civil War for construction of railroads that had almost all been abandoned, destroyed, or rebuilt by the 1870s.

During the 1880s the Democratic Party candidates campaigned regularly on white-supremacist platforms, and the number and influence of the African American candidates and legislators rapidly declined. One black Virginian, John Mercer Langston, won election to the House of Representatives late in

John Mercer Langston

the period. He was born into slavery in Virginia in 1829, but by virtue of his intelligence and the education he received in Ohio he became the first president of Virginia Normal and Collegiate Institute. In 1888 Langston ran for Congress as one of two Republican candidates from his district. Many white Republicans, at William Mahone's urging, voted for a white Republican, and that allowed the Democratic candidate to claim victory. Corruption at the polling places was so bad that Langston challenged the result. The Republican majority in the House of Representatives disallowed so many fraudulent Democratic ballots that Langston became the first African American from Virginia to serve in Congress. He served only part of one term. Before the next election so many white Republicans had become convinced that cooperation with African Americans was politically risky that he did not win nomination to a second term.

Twice during the latter years of the nineteenth century Democrats rewrote election laws to make it more difficult for African Americans to vote or to win elections. In 1884 after they won majorities in both houses the General Assembly passed over Governor Cameron's veto a new election law usually referred to as the Anderson-McCormick Act. It created new three-member electoral boards for each county and city and authorized the assembly to elect all the board members. That gave the Democratic Party majority in the assembly a monopoly on voter registration and the conduct of elections, and they used it to their partisan advantage.

The constitutional requirement for voting by ballot instead of voice vote introduced in 1864 had not insulated voters from intimidation or guaranteed fairness at polling places. Candidates printed ballots with their own names on them, or political parties printed ballots with the names of all party nominees on them. Voters took ballots to the polling places and either deposited them in the ballot box or handed them to an officer of election who placed them in the box. Ballots were not secret. Candidates or parties often printed ballots on different sizes or different colors of paper. Everyone could see how every voter voted.

In his 1950 autobiography public health pioneer Bathurst Browne Bagby recalled the tricks Democratic election officers had used to defeat Republicans in his native King and Queen County at that time. "There were many methods of stuffing the ballot box," he explained. "It was usually placed from ten to twenty feet from the door, where the voter stood. A judge of the election would take the Republican ticket in his left hand, from the voter, but put in the box a Democratic ticket, which he had concealed in his right hand. Another common trick was to put a handful of Democratic tickets in the ballot box, when the Republican judge was taking a drink of water or liquor, or had turned his back. Sometimes, when the judge would go to dinner or to the toilet, a duplicate box, filled with Democratic tickets, would be substituted for the original box. Then sometimes the Democrats would have two tickets printed, a large one that most people voted, and which was shown around, and a very small one which the Republicans never saw until the ballot box was opened at night. The old reliables would fold three or four of these small tickets into such a small package that the size was no larger than a regular ticket. When the ballot box was opened, all seemed very much surprised that it contained many more tickets than voters. Of course, this trick was pulled off in the Republican precincts. The officials either had to throw out the whole vote in that precinct or blind-fold a judge and get him to draw out the excessive number of tickers. My Uncle Atwood Walker was always one of the judges of the elections at Stevensville, and was the one that they always blind-folded. It is said that he had such a keen sense of touch that he nearly always drew out a Republican ticket."[7]

Because the Anderson-McCormick Act fostered new forms of political corruption the assembly changed election laws again ten years later. The 1894 Walton Act introduced the secret, or Australian, ballot. The state printed ballots with all the names of all the candidates for every office, and voters marked them at the polling place. That meant, without specifically requiring as much, that voters be able to read, and illiteracy among African Americans remained much higher in the 1890s than among white Virginians. The law authorized election officials to assist blind voters, who could not be certain that election officials marked their ballots as instructed. The new system was secret, but like the old it was susceptible to corruption. The law required each voter to draw a line "through three-fourths of the length of the name" of every candidate he wished to vote against.[8] That provided Democratic vote counters ample leeway to decide that a voter had not quite drawn a legal line through enough of a Democratic candidate's name, which disqualified the ballot a Republican had cast; or that a voter had just barely drawn a legal line through a Republican candidate's name, which allowed it to count and be counted for a Democrat.

Officials who conducted elections employed other methods to influence the outcome of elections. They sometimes required African Americans or known Republicans to stand in separate lines from white Democrats and allowed all the Democrats to vote first or made certain that lines of African Americans moved so slowly that many men were unable to vote before the polls closed. Counters of votes also sometimes cheated, altered official returns, destroyed ballots, or stuffed ballot boxes. Party workers of both parties sometimes resorted to public intimidation of voters, bribery, or violence to win elections. The cause of African American participation in public life as full citizens and influential voters was thereby as lost as the cause of the dead Confederacy.

The Third Lost Cause

In large part because of the obstacles to African American voting the number of black Virginia men able to win election declined to almost zero by the end of the century. That is one of the reasons why in the 1890s when African Americans, poor white farmers, Republicans, and others combined forces in the People's Party (or Populist Party, as it was usually known), the reformers had almost no success in Virginia. That can be most easily seen in the history of the Colored Farmers' Alliance and Cooperative Union of Virginia. It was the last of several nineteenth-century agrarian movements, most of which were racially segregated. It was also probably the largest organization of African Americans in nineteenth-century Virginia other than the loose associations of Baptist churches; and it was also one of the shortest-lived. Its rise and fall is instructive.

Farmers were the largest group of working people in Virginia through the end of the nineteenth century. Their economic fortunes rose and fell as a consequence of national economic changes as well as changing local markets and unpredictable weather. During the 1870s and 1880s American farmers created numerous national, state, and regional organizations to promote agricultural prosperity. Some organizations were self-help associations like the Grange (or Patrons of Husbandry), and some like the Greenback Party were openly political and advocated currency inflation to raise agricultural prices. The Farmers' Alliance movement was both. The shared political objectives of the racially segregated white and "colored" alliances included currency inflation through resumption of the coinage of silver; regulation or even public ownership of railroads; regulation or abolition of national banks; direct election of United States senators; a graduated federal income tax; and political reforms to reduce what members of the alliances often characterized as corrupt close relationships between politicians, bankers, railroads, and big businesses such as fertilizer manufacturers and tobacco companies. They also promoted a subtreasury plan to have the federal government establish small banks throughout the country to lend money to farmers who put up their land or crops as collateral.

Tobacco farmers appeared particularly vulnerable in Virginia. They sold their crops in a less competitive market as tobacco manufacturing became consolidated in the hands of a small number of large firms. The creation of the American Tobacco Company in 1890 restricted producers' options even further. Tobacco growers, most of them white, in southern Virginia participated in the formation of the Tobacco Growers' Protective Association of Virginia and North Carolina in 1903. It tried to reduce the influence of tobacco warehouse operators and enable farmers to bargain with buyers more effectively.

Some large-scale Virginia planters took part in the more radical Farmers' Alliance movement during the 1880s and 1890s. Elsewhere in the South and in the Great Plains the alliance movement recruited large numbers of farmers and enjoyed significant political success in pursuit of regulation of warehouse operators, railroads, and currency reform. In Virginia, the alliance movement had less success in recruiting small and middle-sized farmers. Movement leaders scarcely even tried. Large-scale commercial farmers such as Robert Beverley, of Fauquier County, assumed the leadership of the alliance movement and supported its major reform efforts. The alliance's political party, the Populist Party nominated James B. Weaver of Iowa for president and former Virginia attorney general James G. Field for vice president in 1892. But in statewide elections during the 1890s, the party had little success. A significant portion of the state's dominant Democratic Party endorsed some of the Populists' national objectives, such as currency inflation, but they did not promote a reform agenda in the state legislature. Populist leaders in Virginia did not recruit black Virginia farmers, who were relatively inconspicuous in the state's alliance movement, unlike black farmers elsewhere in the South who were deeply involved in the political upheavals of the 1890s. That was in part because the number of African American voters in the state was decreasing during that decade, but it was also a consequence of the biracial Readjuster movement in the 1880s, after which few white political leaders of any political party in Virginia were willing to form an alliance with black Virginia voters.

Hundreds or thousands of African American farmers in Virginia joined the Colored Farmers' Alliance movement, which a white minister, Richard M. Humphreys, founded in Texas in the 1880s. It grew rapidly in the cotton-raising regions of the South. In the tobacco-growing region of Virginia, where the alliance apparently recruited most of its members, both African American and white farmers perceived the growth of large tobacco manufacturing firms like the American Tobacco Company as serious threats to their economic independence. The large firms attempted to control the prices they paid farmers for leaf tobacco and left farmers who refused to accept the low prices without any market. To counter those large businesses, the alliances established exchanges where farmers could purchase seed, fertilizer, and equipment at wholesale prices and try to form joint marketing agreements to deal with cotton buyers and tobacco manufacturers. One of the exchanges was in Norfolk, where a white alliance official, Joseph J. Rogers, managed it.

Alliance leaders encouraged farmers of both races to develop a cross-racial class consciousness for united action. The president of the national Colored Alliance hired men or persuaded volunteers to act as organizers and lecturers to educate farm owners and agricultural laborers about the alliance and to recruit members. Organizational records of the national and state alliances unfortunately do not survive to document the work of the organizers or to provide verification of membership claims. By the spring of 1890 Humphreys had secured the services of William H. Warwick to serve as state organizer and lecturer in Virginia. An African American about twenty-seven or twenty-eight years old, Warwick lived in Boydton, in Mecklenburg County. By that October, according to one account, about ten thousand Virginia farmers had joined the Colored Farmers' Alliance. Rogers reported that Virginia had alliances in twenty-five counties.

Representatives from alliances in about a dozen counties founded the Colored Farmers' Alliance and Cooperative Union of Virginia in August 1890. "The object of the organization," according to a newspaper account of the meeting, "is to create a market for what the farmers produce and to obtain at cheaper rates what they purchase. They expect to accomplish this by uniting together and establishing exchanges throughout the State at which they can buy and sell at wholesale prices."[9] The founders elected Rogers superintendent, or president, of the state alliance and director of the exchange in Norfolk; they appointed a state board of directors; and they elected Warwick organizer and lecturer for the states of Virginia, Maryland, and West Virginia.

The white Southern Farmers' Alliance had recently scored significant victories in elections in several states because Democrats endorsed their proposals. Some of those Democrats, though, also promoted racial segregation and discrimination and endorsed plans to disfranchise African American voters. Several very influential white Virginia Democrats embraced some alliance proposals, but in the aftermath of the Readjuster movement they were openly hostile toward African American participation in politics. Leaders of the white Virginia Farmers' Alliance were for the most part Democrats engaged in large-scale commercial agriculture, and they had little interest in poor African American farmers who for the most part owned or worked on small farms. They had little interest even in organizing poor white farmers as political allies.

The Colored Farmers' Alliance in Virginia apparently flourished during 1891, but few records survive to document the work of its leaders or the number of its members. By one unverified account it had enrolled twenty thousand members in forty-two counties. In the state convention that year the delegates elected Warwick state superintendent and adopted a resolution that in effect declared independence from both the racially exclusive Virginia Farmers' Alliance and the state's Democratic Party. Members of the Colored Alliance, it stated, understood "that our salvation rests in neither of the old political parties and are no longer slaves to either, but are organizing to protect ourselves and thus free the toiling masses of our race from the deadly fangs of monopoly, and rings, and trust companies."[10]

Soon after the convention adjourned Humphreys and Rogers denied Warwick access to alliance membership lists, so he could not collect dues. The exchange ceased to function, and without support of the national organization the state alliance had to struggle along on its own. Warwick was unable to salvage it, even though he announced that if necessary the Colored Alliance would pursue its own agenda. Black and white farmers shared the same economic problems, he explained, and "we are willing to act together with our white brethren and the people all over this country to bring about these reforms. We are one common people with a common interest in the same country, and we are here to stay. And no people better realize the need of unity of purpose and action to suppress the outrages perpetrated upon white and colored alike by class legislation, ballot-box stuffing, lynch law mobs, than the colored people. And we feel safe to say we voice the honest sentiment of every good and thinking colored man in this country when we say they stand ready to act with any party that will go to work to remedy these evils."[11]

Warwick attended and was elected assistant secretary of the conference in St. Louis in February 1892 that founded the People's Party. He also attended the national convention of the People's Party in Omaha that summer when it nominated candidates for president and vice president. African Americans did not participate meaningfully in the 1892 Virginia campaign of the People's Party, not even Warwick. So strong had been the backlash among opponents of the biracial Readjuster Party that political cooperation between the races, as occurred in neighboring North Carolina in the 1890s, was no longer possible in Virginia. Their cause was lost, too, like the cause of the Confederacy in the 1860s and the cause of the Readjusters in the 1870s and 1880s.

16

JIM CROW VIRGINIA

The song "Jump Jim Crow" was a well-known nineteenth-century tune. Performers at minstrel shows and in early vaudeville acts often sang it or danced to its sprightly rhythm. The words of "Jump Jim Crow" were full of negative stereotypes of African Americans as impulsive, ignorant, comically credulous, irresponsible, unreliable, and dishonest. The new regime of racial segregation based on white supremacy that emerged in the United States during the decades after the abolition of slavery was known almost from the beginning as Jim Crow.

Racial Segregation

Even as residents of Virginia participated in the changes that nearly all Americans faced during the final decades of the nineteenth century, the state remained southern in many ways and was unique in others. Before freedom, the laws and practices of slavery assured white domination and the legal subordination of free blacks, who could not enjoy all the civil rights white people possessed. After freedom, many influential leaders of white society continued to perceive and to treat black Virginians as socially inferior. In some places, for example, rigid social codes or local laws required that if black and white people met on a sidewalk, the black person had to step aside and let the white person pass—perhaps even have to step into a muddy street.

When possible, black Virginians took advantage of opportunities freedom brought. The Constitution of 1869 for the first time allowed—required—African Americans to serve in the state militia. Black militia companies, which would have been unimaginable before the Civil War, formed in several cities and drilled as part of the state's militia system. The state constructed an armory for black militia units in Richmond. When the Spanish-American War broke out in 1898 the governor mobilized the Virginia militia, including several companies of African Americans formed into the all-black 6th Virginia

Major Joseph H. Johnson (*seated, second from right*) and members of the 6th Virginia Volunteers

Volunteers under the command of Major Joseph H. Johnson. The experience of those soldiers was intensely disappointing. The governor placed white regular army officers in command of the regiment in place of the able and respected black militia officers already in place. When the regiment went to Georgia for training and then to Florida in preparation for taking part in the invasion of Cuba, the soldiers suffered disgraceful treatment at the hands of local citizens and also United States Army officers. The unit did not make it to Cuba before the war ended, and the men returned to Virginia deeply disillusioned. That episode sharply exhibited the limits on full citizenship white Americans imposed on African Americans.

Virginia was fully American, but many of its white citizens retained their identification with the Confederacy or the old South. Early in 1890 the Confederate Memorial Literary Society opened a museum in the house in downtown Richmond that had served as the residence of Jefferson Davis during the Civil War. In May of that year the state erected a large, dignified equestrian statue of Robert E. Lee that people hauled ceremoniously through the streets of Richmond and placed at the edge of a cornfield. The fashionable residential neighborhood developers soon constructed there had Monument Avenue running through its center. During the ensuing four decades monumental statues of Jefferson Davis, J.E.B. Stuart, Stonewall Jackson, and Matthew Fontaine Maury were installed in what became one of the country's most famous outdoor tributes to the Confederacy. Nobody in Virginia ever erected a comparable monument to the abolition of slavery.

Jim Crow laws and social customs affected nearly all aspects of life. For example, when the state and federal governments jointly hosted a major international celebration at Norfolk in 1907 to commemorate the three hundredth anniversary of the settlement of Jamestown, some of the most popular features of the six-month fair were a reenactment of the battle of the *Monitor* and the *Merrimack* and exhibitions that featured Civil War land battles. The main avenue on the fairground was called the Warpath. The fair was more a celebration of modern America with former Confederates and former Confederate states as full partners than it was a commemoration of the founding of the colony. The men and women who visited the fair in 1907 were the children and grandchildren of people who had lived through or taken part in the Civil War, which was even then a very real memory for their families.

Black Virginians, too, had memories of the Civil War and a history to present at the 1907 exposition. With a separate grant of money from the federal government and little encouragement from the state, a committee of black men erected a large museum on the fairground to exhibit images and artifacts of African American history. The so-called Negro Building, which was one of the largest on the fairground, included an elaborate set of tableaux by artist Meta Warrick Fuller that traced the history of African Americans into, through, and out of slavery. The men who organized the exhibitions also published a companion book, *The Industrial History of the Negro Race of the United States,* that celebrated the achievements of the state's black population during the four decades since the abolition of slavery. Elsewhere at the fair the achievements of white people predominated. The fair's organizers left Virginia Indians, as usual, almost invisible.

Meta Warrick Fuller, *Landing of First Twenty Slaves at Jamestown.* Fuller's dioramas were photographed and reproduced as illustrations in Giles B. Jackson and D. Webster Davis, *The Industrial History of the Negro Race of the United States* (Richmond, 1908).

Considerable variety probably existed from place to place in Virginia in how well African Americans lived during the decades after emancipation. Black laboring men and women routinely received lower pay than white people or had to take jobs with more difficult or dangerous working conditions. At the yards of the Newport News Shipbuilding and Dry Dock Company white supervisors relegated black men to low-paying, unskilled jobs. When the company conducted safety tests on the davits that raised and lowered lifeboats, supervisors filled the boats with black men rather than risk white men or heavy equipment in the dangerous tests. Company officials thought that was amusing and included a photograph of one such test in a company history they published in the middle of the twentieth century.

White Virginians and black Virginians drew farther apart physically during the decades after the end of slavery, more so in cities and towns than in the countryside. Enslaved domestic servants had often lived with or quite close to the people they served and who owned them, but after freedom black Virginians often chose to live with their own families and to travel back and forth to their places of work. In towns and cities a significant portion of African American women worked in domestic service, doing the cooking, cleaning, washing, and other chores in the houses of middle-class or wealthy white families. African American men often did hard manual labor. New patterns of residential segregation emerged in the state's towns and cities. During the twentieth century some cities adopted ordinances to require racially segregated neighborhoods. Insurance and real estate companies refused to insure or market houses in areas reserved for one race to members of another. And courts enforced restrictive covenants some white people added to deeds of sale to prevent sale of their property to people who were not white.

As racial segregation became more common, African American men aroused suspicion if white people found them in neighborhoods where no black people lived. Many black men worked for delivery companies or did maintenance or construction work that required them to enter mostly white portions of the towns, which put them in jeopardy. While Jim Crow segregation was developing lynchings became more common in the southern states and even elsewhere in the country. An African American man found in a place where white people believed he did not belong was vulnerable to violence, even to being lynched on some occasions. Lynchings were less common in Virginia than in many southern states, perhaps a reflection of a traditional white Virginia insistence on employing legal processes to settle disputes and punish crimes. But black Virginians were certainly not immune from lynching and other forms of violence and intimidation. At least eighty-six men were victims of lynching in Virginia from the 1880s to the 1930s. Even sympathetic white Virginians tolerated dual systems of justice and morality for white people and black people.

John Mitchell Jr.

During the 1890s, John Mitchell Jr., of Richmond, emerged as the state's most eloquent spokesmen for African Americans. As editor and principal owner of the *Richmond Planet,* an influential weekly newspaper of wide circulation, Mitchell boldly crusaded against lynching and other forms of racial discrimination and injustice. A journalist of national reputation, he was courageous in challenging the views and practices that predominated among the state's white society and political leadership. He was also a successful businessman and financially secure enough to employ the power of his paper to its full extent. That he published the *Planet* for four decades was a tribute to his persistence and his business ability. Most white Virginians probably remained unaware that a black Virginian owned and published a newspaper at all. Had they read the *Planet* many of them would have been outraged at Mitchell's denunciations of their values and actions.

If white Virginians knew little or nothing about Mitchell before 1904, they certainly learned about him then. The Virginia Passenger and Power Company began to require African Americans to ride in the back seats of its streetcars in Petersburg, Richmond, and Manchester, which before its annexation to Richmond in 1910 was a separate city south of the James River. Mitchell organized a boycott, and for almost a year domestic workers and laborers walked to and from work rather than acquiesce in the insulting segregation rule. Streetcar companies in other Virginia cities also required segregation on cars and busses, and people organized boycotts in Portsmouth,

Norfolk, Newport News, Lynchburg, and Berkeley, a suburb of Norfolk. Stories on them appeared in African American newspapers nationwide. The boycotts were an important mass protest against Jim Crow, but none of the Virginia boycotts succeeded in forcing public transportation companies to change their policies. Indeed, in 1906 the General Assembly passed a state law that required racially segregated seating in all public transportation vehicles.

One decade earlier, in 1896, the Supreme Court of the United States in the landmark case *Plessy v. Ferguson* had ruled that states or localities could require racially segregated seating in railroad cars and other means of public transportation. The judges declared that such racial segregation did not violate any person's right to equal treatment under the law—equal protection of the laws—which the Fourteenth Amendment prohibited states from infringing. So long as states provided substantially equal treatment racial segregation was therefore constitutional. The doctrine of separate but equal allowed enforced racial segregation in most public spheres in the South, even though in public transportation, public schools, access to public places, and in many other ways state and local governments enforced separation but almost never provided genuine equality. In *Plessy v. Ferguson* the Supreme Court gave Jim Crow constitutional protection.

The Segregated Economy

The segregated society meant a segregated economy. African American men, as well as many white men, were often engaged in hard physical or manual work, but many African Americans owned businesses in Virginia during those years. African American business women and men operated successfully in a racially segregated society and economy, but even the most successful of them remained vulnerable to Jim Crow laws and customs. Prominent white political leaders boasted that race relations in the state were better than elsewhere in the South, which in some respects may have been true, but many of the state's African Americans would have disagreed. Thousands of black men and women moved to northern or midwestern states during the early decades of the twentieth century to escape Jim Crow and in hopes of finding better jobs, working conditions, and housing for their families and schools for their children.

One consequence of racial segregation was the development in most cities and towns of an African American professional class. Black commercial neighborhoods with grocery stores and other businesses that African American men and women owned and operated existed in virtually every city and town. Black doctors and dentists, black-owned insurance companies, burial societies, savings and loan associations, and banks provided services to African American customers that they could not always obtain from white-owned businesses. Those business people together with teachers, clergymen, and journalists like Mitchell provided vital services to their communities as well as important leadership and inspirational role models, even if they remained largely invisible to their professional white counterparts.

People's Building and Loan Association of Hampton was one such successful black business that served its community. Enterprising black physicians and successful black businessmen founded and financed Whittaker Memorial Hospital in Newport News and the Burrell Memorial Hospital in Roanoke. After Dr. Dana O. Baldwin returned to Virginia following his service in World War I, he settled in Martinsville and founded Saint Mary's (later Memorial) Hospital. The African American business community he developed in his neighborhood included shops, a theater, a drugstore, and several other businesses and was known for decades as Baldwin's Corner.

The most famous African American business leader early in the twentieth century was Maggie Lena Mitchell Walker. She was the daughter of a Richmond woman who had been born into slavery. Her mother worked for Elizabeth Van Lew, the white Richmond woman who aided prisoners of war during the Civil War and operated a successful espionage ring for the United States Army. Before she married Armstead Walker in 1886, Mitchell was educated in the city's new public schools, attended Richmond's Colored Normal School, and taught school while taking courses in business and accounting. She was a member of the First African Baptist Church from a young age, and her deep religious faith was evident in many aspects of her life and works.

In 1881, she joined the Independent Order of St. Luke, a mutual benefit society, and was secretary of her chapter by the time she graduated from high school. In 1890 Walker became the order's Right Worthy Grand Chief. She organized events, attended conferences, and began a juvenile department for the community's children. Nine years later when the organization was facing severe financial and membership problems Walker won election to its highest office, Right Worthy Grand Secretary. Under her leadership the order recovered and founded a newspaper and a department store. On November 2, 1903, it opened St. Luke Penny Savings Bank. Walker was president of the bank from its founding until 1930. She was the first black woman bank president in the United States. Her bank later merged with two other African American banks in Richmond and became the Consolidated Bank and Trust.

Walker took part in numerous philanthropic and community-enrichment organizations and was a founder and first president of the Richmond Council of Colored Women. She cared deeply about children and developed programs to teach hygiene and health, thrift and generosity, and the importance of education. She also created a college loan fund. Walker's work was far-reaching, and she aided several African American health and educational programs out-

Maggie Lena Mitchell Walker

side of Richmond. She also was a founder of the Richmond branch of the National Association for the Advancement of Colored People (NAACP) and several other important African American associations. And she sponsored voter-registration drives when the Nineteenth Amendment granted women the vote in 1920. Walker's powerfully uplifting oratorical style endeared her to audiences, and she was a popular public speaker and nationally recognized business leader. She was well read and much admired both as a successful business leader and as a role model for African Americans in Richmond and elsewhere. A high school in Richmond is named for her, and her residence in the city's Jackson Ward is a national historic site.

Thousands of other African American men and women succeeded in business or in the professions according to the same standards white men and women valued, but African Americans faced unique barriers and challenges because of racial prejudice. An example is Thomas Calhoun Walker (no relation to Maggie Walker), who was born into slavery in Gloucester County in 1862 and became an attorney. Late in the nineteenth century he had to defend his right to practice his profession when he appeared in a court in a county where he had no friends to sponsor his admission to practice in the court. The local commonwealth's attorney objected to his taking part in a trial, but Walker obtained the judge's permission to represent his client. He made an eloquent speech that appealed to values and standards of justice white English-speaking people had created. "I have qualified in the courts of Gloucester

County," Walker told the judge. "I have read and studied the same books that the commonwealth attorney has studied, not one of which I wrote. These books were all written by eminent judges and lawyers of the white race and it is their conception of the dignity and righteousness of the law which, presumably, we all wish to see prevail in the state of Virginia."[1]

Walker was one of very few African American lawyers in Virginia and one of even fewer who lived and practiced outside a city. He helped children obtain educations and served the African American community in many ways through the 1930s. He succeeded in large part because he refused to challenge white expectations openly and often worked behind the scenes to evade or undermine some of the worst features of racial segregation and discrimination. People who did not know Walker well sometimes regarded him as an Uncle Tom who conformed to white people's expectations by being deferential and speaking and acting humbly. By not antagonizing influential white lawyers and public officials Walker may have been able to accomplish more than if he had been confrontational, like editor John Mitchell. Unlike Mitchell, Walker had to function in a profession dominated by some of the state's most powerful white men, and he found ways to succeed within the constraints those men imposed on people like him.

However influential and respected members of the professional class of African American men and women were in their segregated communities, they could never hope to gain a comparable respect from white society. Among the many unwritten rules of Jim Crow was that African Americans of all classes addressed white Virginians of all classes respectfully with courtesy titles such as Mr., Mrs., Miss, Dr., Sir, or Ma'm. Black people often even appended Mr. or Miss to white children when addressing them by their given names. But white people, including children, seldom or never addressed African Americans by their surnames and almost never with courtesy titles. A black clergyman might earn the right to be referred to as Reverend, a college teacher as Professor, or a physician as Doctor, but otherwise most white people heaped on most black people the same humiliating language of inferiority they had during slavery days by calling them by their given names and ignoring their surnames. Maggie Walker once counted it a singular quiet victory that at a meeting in the governor's office one of the secretaries actually addressed her as Mrs. Walker rather than as Maggie.

Disfranchisement

Throughout the decade and a half between the overthrow of the Readjusters and the beginning of the twentieth century politicians who believed in white supremacy rewrote election laws and blatantly interfered in the conduct of elections to reduce the likelihood that African Americans or Republicans could win elections.

Even many of the white leaders of the state's Republican Party gave up their old alliance with black voters, which made it virtually impossible by the end of the nineteenth century for Republican candidates to win election anywhere in Virginia east of the mountains. In some portions of western Virginia Republicans were numerous enough to win local and legislative elections. Democrats often employed violence, intimidation, and vote buying to win elections, and they sometimes threatened black men with loss of their jobs if they voted for Republicans or if they voted at all. Ballot box corruption was widespread and well known during the final two decades of the nineteenth century. Members of both political parties engaged in illegal intimidation or vote buying. Newspapers reported violence at almost every election. Corruption or allegations of corruption produced one or more challenges to the outcome of a congressional election nearly every year during the 1880s and 1890s.

In 1900 enough of the state's Democratic Party leaders were intent on writing the party's dominance and white supremacy into the state constitution that in the face of opposition from some powerful party leaders they were able to put through the General Assembly a law to hold a constitutional convention. Recent hard-fought election campaigns had been expensive, corrupt, and occasionally violent. Other Democrats wanted to streamline the state's judicial system, introduce other reforms such as primary elections to nominate candidates for public office to reduce the influence of political party leaders who dominated party conventions, or regulate the politically powerful railroads.

In 1901 when many eastern Republicans evidently refused to take part the voters elected eighty-eight Democrats and twelve Republicans (one ran as an independent), all but one from western and southwestern Virginia, to the convention that met in Richmond in two sessions between June 12, 1901, and June 26, 1902. The convention adopted suffrage restrictions that Carter Glass, of Lynchburg, prepared. They were similar to the ones introduced in several other southern states that denied the vote to blacks without appearing to violate the letter of the Fifteenth Amendment to the Constitution of the United States.

The suffrage article consisted of twenty-one separate sections and was by itself longer than the whole Constitution of 1776. Every one of its sections described who could not vote or contained procedures for making it difficult or impossible to vote. The article had two main parts. The first applied only to the first election to be held after adoption of the constitution. It limited the vote to war veterans and their adult sons and to property owners who had paid at least $1 in property taxes during the previous year or who could give a reasonable explanation of any portion of the new state constitution. The second specified that after January 1, 1904, any male at least twenty-one-years old and who met a residency requirement could register to vote if he had paid a $1.50 poll tax for each of the preceding three years, completed the registration application in his own handwriting and without assistance, and also satisfactorily answered any questions the registrar asked concerning his qualifications. That operated as a literacy test and also empowered registrars to decide for themselves who did and who did not give satisfactory answers to questions about the constitution or qualifications to register.

The cumulative feature of the poll tax requirement was specifically intended to make it more difficult for African Americans, many of whom were poor, to qualify. The poll tax was the only state tax the government did not attempt to collect. People had to pay it voluntarily and many months before registration opened if they wished to qualify to register and vote. The $1.50 poll tax seems small, but at the time when the average annual income of an African American farmer in the South was only a few hundred dollars a year, the cumulative $4.50 for three years could have been 1 percent or more of annual income. Then about six months before the election they had to register; but Democratic Party registrars imposed many obstacles on Republicans and African Americans. Registrars might tell an applicant at the courthouse that his records were at home, or at home that his records were at the courthouse. The wide leeway registrars had in deciding who was qualified allowed them to refuse registration to a great many men. Registrars, without authority of law, often asked applicants difficult or irrelevant questions in order to disqualify them from voting.

As Dr. Bagby's relation of stuffing ballot boxes indicated, people who wished to deprive African Americans of the vote did not conceal their purposes or methods. Many of them bragged about their ingenuity in contriving means to reach that end. During the constitutional convention Democrat Alfred P. Thom, a corporate lawyer from Norfolk, explained, "I do not expect an understanding clause to be administered with any degree of friendship by the white man to the suffrage of the black man. I expect the examination with which the black man will be confronted, to be inspired by the same spirit that inspires every man upon this floor and in this convention. I would not expect an impartial administration of the clause. I would not expect for the white man a rigid examination. The people of Virginia do not stand impartially between the suffrage of the white man and the suffrage of the black man. . . . We do not come here prompted by an impartial purpose in reference to negro suffrage. We come here to sweep the field of expedients for the purpose of finding some constitutional method of ridding ourselves of it forever."[2]

Republican Alfred P. Gillespie, of Tazewell County in southwestern Virginia, may not have been a friend of African American voting, but he denounced the dishonesty of the provisions by which white Democrats intended to deprive African Americans of the vote. "I have been taught to believe," he charged, "that where a man was guilty of a fraud, or of cheating another man, the man who committed the fraud should be punished, that a man who steals a vote should be punished. . . . The remedy suggested here is to punish the man who has been injured. It is now proposed to right a wrong by punishing those who have been defrauded of their votes to the extent of destroying their right of suffrage; in other words, the negro vote of this Commonwealth must be destroyed to prevent the Democratic election officers from stealing their votes, for it seems that, as long as there is a negro vote to be stolen, there will be a Democratic election officer ready to steal it."[3]

In closing the debate on disfranchisement Carter Glass noted proudly that the new constitution would disfranchise nearly all African American men in Virginia by making a "fine" distinction between disfranchising them because of their race, color, or previous condition of servitude—which the Fifteenth Amendment prohibited—and instead by the racist means of "legislating against the characteristics of the black race."[4] Those characteristics included being thriftless, dishonest, ignorant, and irresponsible, as he and many other white people in Jim Crow Virginia believed they understood the naturally inferior character of African Americans.

A separate section of the suffrage article provided an extra measure of safety for white supremacy. It empowered the General Assembly to impose a property qualification for voting in local elections in a county, city, or a political subdivision. It may never have been used, but the convention inserted it into the constitution as an available emergency measure to disfranchise African American men in communities where black majorities might otherwise elect public officials. In a very few magisterial districts African Americans won election as justices of the peace early in the twentieth century, but by then the office of justice of the peace was no longer an important one. A black petty magistrate posed no danger to any white citizens.

In addition to intense debates in the convention about the most effective means to disfranchise black voters, the delegates also disagreed about the implications of some proposals, such as literacy tests, which could disfranchise a large number of white voters. During those debates it became evident that a significant number of delegates believed that it was worth the price to disfranchise some white voters as a means to the end of disfranchising most black voters; and some delegates believed that disfranchising poor or illiterate white voters was also a good thing to do, to rid politics of the influence of people who had little or no property or education. Together, delegates who held one or the other of those views formed a substantial majority of convention members.

Other provisions of the Constitution of 1902 and the election laws adopted during the next session of the General Assembly gave the Democratic majority in the assembly the power to appoint and supervise most of the registrars and polling-place officers. In addition to voluntarily paying the poll tax, men who wished to vote had to fill out a registration application unaided, and some registrars provided no form, which meant that applicants had to know in advance exactly what to include on the application and what to omit. Often, being a reliable Democrat was enough to satisfy a registrar, but being a Republican or an African American or even a Democrat believed to possess unsatisfactory political opinions was enough to allow the registrar to find or invent a reason to deny the application.

Those provisions worked as intended in part because illiteracy remained high in many parts of Virginia, especially for African Americans, even three decades after the founding of the public school system, a function of inadequate appropriations for public schools. The new registration procedures prevented most uneducated people, especially if they were Republicans or African Americans, from registering to vote. In southwestern Virginia where hundreds of white men lost the ability to vote, journalist and local historian William C. Pendleton recalled, "It was painful and pitiful to see the horror and dread visible on the faces of the illiterate poor white men who were waiting to take their turn before the inquisition. They had seen some of their neighbors and friends turned away because they were unable to answer satisfactorily the questions put to them by the registrars; and it required much earnest persuasion to induce them to pass through the hateful ordeal. This was horrible to behold, but it was still more horrible to see the marks of humiliation and despair that were stamped upon the faces of honest but poor white men who had been refused registration and who had been robbed of their citizenship without cause. We saw them as they came from the presence of the registrars with bowed heads and agonized faces" and sometimes with tears in their eyes.[5]

The disfranchisement of white as well as black men because they had not been able to obtain an education is reminiscent of the complaint VIRGINIA FREEWOMAN made in her public letter to members of the Constitutional Convention of 1829–30. She had then accused Virginia's political leaders of denying women an education and then denying them the vote on the grounds of their ignorance. As Pendleton wrote about the disfranchisement of poorly educated white men in 1902, the new state constitution deprived them of the vote they had enjoyed since the middle of the nineteenth century in part because the state had not provided adequate public schools in rural parts of southwestern Virginia.

The suffrage article of the new constitution was an almost total rejection of the democratic reforms embodied in the Virginia Constitutions of 1851, 1864, and 1869 as well as the political changes imposed on Virginia after the Civil War and that Readjusters adopted afterward. Only voting by ballot, the popular election of some local officials, and the public school system remained intact from the democratic reforms of the constitutional revolution of 1850–70. Unlike in most of the other southern states that disfranchised black voters, in Virginia the new constitution also disfranchised a large number of white voters. Registration and voting dropped drastically as a result. The number of white voters fell by almost 50 percent, and the number of black men who still voted fell by about 90 percent. In the 1900 president election 264,357 Virginia men voted; in 1904 a mere 130,842. The Republican vote fell from 43.8 percent to 35.2 percent. Together those figures represented a significant triumph for both partisanship and white supremacy.

One of the last and most controversial acts of the convention delegates was to proclaim the constitution in effect as the Conventions of 1776 and 1864 had done without submitting it to the voters. Men who were going to lose the right to vote had no chance to reject the constitution that disfranchised them. The new Constitution of Virginia took effect without a referendum on July 10, 1902. The state's governor, lieutenant governor, attorney general, legislators, local officials, and judges immediately began performing their duties in accordance with the new constitution. When the legality of the convention's proclamation of the constitution was challenged in court, the Virginia Supreme Court of Appeals adduced in 1903 in *Taylor v. Commonwealth* the almost universal acceptance of the constitution by the state's public officials as authority for rejecting the challenge. Two men appealed to the Supreme Court of the United States to block elections scheduled to be held under the new state constitution because the people had not ratified it, but the Supreme Court did not decide the case until 1904, long after the scheduled elections. The Supreme Court then declared in *Jones v. Montague* and *Selden v. Montague* that "the thing sought to be prohibited has been done and cannot be undone by any order of the court."[6]

The Politics of White Supremacy

After the Constitution of 1902 went into effect, the Democratic Party was in effective control of politics everywhere in Virginia except in the southwestern counties and some counties in the Blue Ridge Mountains and Shenandoah Valley. Republicans in those areas held on tenaciously and offered a progressive alternative to the socially and economically conservative Democrats. The Ninth Congressional District in southwestern Virginia was a Republican stronghold from the 1890s until the 1920s. It was known as the Fighting Ninth for the fiercely competitive partisanship that persisted there long after Democrats had succeeded in overwhelming Republicans nearly everywhere else in Virginia. Southwestern Virginia had a different and more democratic political character than the rest of the state. Campbell Slemp, of Wise County, who had been the white Readjuster-Republican candidate for lieutenant governor in 1885, skillfully directed the district's Republican campaigns for years and represented the district in Congress from 1903 to 1907. His son, Campbell Bascom Slemp, then succeeded him and won reelection without interruption until he retired in 1923. He then became chief of the White House staff of President Calvin Coolidge. For two decades with his base of political power in southwestern Virginia, C. Bascom Slemp was one of the most influential Republicans in the entire South.

The Virginia Republican Party had by then also become largely a white man's party, as lily white, as was said, as the Democratic Party. At the 1921 Republican Party state convention white delegates refused to seat almost all the African Americans who had won election to it. In protest, John Mitchell Jr. assembled a "lily black" ticket of Republican candidates for statewide offices. He was the candidate for governor and Richmond banker Maggie Walker the candidate for superintendent of public instruction. The quixotic campaign received little attention from the white press, Mitchell went on vacation and did not even campaign, and the ticket received but few votes. The most influential black journalist in Virginia by then was not Mitchell but Plummer Bernard Young, editor of the weekly Norfolk *Journal and Guide*. He opposed Mitchell's confrontational approach to political and civil rights issues and vacillated between endorsing Republican and Democratic presidential candidates throughout the 1920s and 1930s. Many black Virginians during the latter decade found the national candidates and policies of the Democratic Party more attractive than those of the Republican Party.

The imposition of strict racial segregation that began during the latter decades of the nineteenth century continued during the first decades of the twentieth century. Early in the 1920s two Richmond men founded the Anglo-Saxon Clubs of America to promote racial segregation and the preservation of white supremacy. Classical pianist and composer John Powell and a self-proclaimed expert on racial distinctions, Earnest Sevier Cox, campaigned for new laws to protect what they called the purity of Anglo-Saxon blood. "Civilization issues from the white race," Cox wrote in an influential article, "and in preserving the white race we preserve civilization. . . . There is no doubt but that the blood of the negro is prepotent when mixed with the blood of any other race. Negro race traits and predispositions revert in mixbreeds far removed from the pure negro. This is but the expression of a well-known biologic law, and arises from the fact that the negro is the most primitive and generalized type of man."[7] What Cox wrote was an incorrect summary of what was then regarded as the best-available science, but many white Americans believed him, anyway.

Shortly thereafter an incident took place at Hampton Institute that materially aided their campaign. Mary Copeland arrived for a program late and had to sit with African Americans rather than in the section reserved for white visitors, which was fully occupied. Her husband, Walter Scott Copeland, was editor of the two daily newspapers in Newport News, and he published strong editorials that condemned his wife's treatment and joined with Powell and Cox in a campaign that succeed in 1924 when the General Assembly passed the Act to Preserve Racial Integrity. It amended a 1910 law that had declared: "Every person having one-sixteenth or more of negro blood shall be deemed a colored person."[8] The new law defined as "white" only people with "no trace whatsoever of any blood other than Caucasian."[9] That classified a much larger number of mixed-race people as "colored" than ever before. The law subjected all people who were not white by its definition to all the discriminatory racial segregation laws. In 1926 the assembly passed one of the country's toughest laws to prohibit racially integrated public meetings of the kind that had angered Mary Copeland's husband.

Predictably, both laws outraged John Mitchell. People described the Act to Preserve Racial Integrity as imposing what they called a "one-drop" rule, that is defining as "colored" every person who had as much as one drop of blood of African ancestry. If one drop of African blood made a person black, Mitchell asked, why did not one drop of European blood not make a person white? That would classify a large number of people of mixed-race ancestry as white rather than as "colored." Mitchell exposed the unfair, racist reasoning as entirely indefensible.[10]

Walter Ashby Plecker, director of the state bureau of vital statistics, maintained relentlessly and vehemently that there were no Indians in Virginia who were not also descended from African Americans. By the one-drop rule he and the state government classified members of all of the Indian tribes in Virginia as "colored" and subjected them to racial segregation and discrimination. Pamunkey chief George Major Cook denounced Plecker's interpretation and application of the Racial Integrity Act. As a young boy he and his mother, Caroline Bradby Cook, had watched without objection as soldiers of the United States Army dismantled her fences and burned the wood in their campfires. "The Pamunkeys will never, no never, submit to be classed as negroid," the chief declared. "The Pamunkeys are a proud and noble race and rather than submit to a loathsome, humiliating, negroid classification, they would prefer to be banished to the wilds of Siberia, there to be hid from the great spirit sunshine, and let their bodies rot in the mines."[11] In addition to pleading for the separate racial integrity of his tribe, he also insisted that no Virginia Indians had any African ancestry, which was probably incorrect. In Cook's public statements on race he appeared to harbor deep prejudices against African Americans. Like other twentieth-century Virginians, Cook and members of other Virginia tribes may not have been free of the racial prejudices of the time, however strongly they protested being victims of such prejudices. The General Assembly ignored Cook, and it did nothing to redress the Indians' grievances. The assembly later amended the Racial Integrity Act to declare white descendants of Pocahontas legally white, to redress one of their grievances.

The Rappahannock tried unsuccessfully to create a separate school system for Indians rather than continue the poorly supported Indian school or condemn their children to attend the inferior segregated schools for black students. Eventually, the state offered to pay for high school education of Indians at schools in Kansas and Oklahoma rather than spend tax money to improve their schools in Virginia.

Few white politicians or journalists championed the rights of the state's African American or Indian populations. One white Norfolk journalist was unusually sensitive to racial and ethnic discrimination. Louis I. Jaffé was editor of the Norfolk *Virginian-Pilot* from the 1920s through the 1940s. The son of Jewish immigrants, he had suffered from discrimination. In 1927 he fairly

Louis I. Jaffé

exploded in outrage about the attempt of city councilmen in another city to force an old black janitor out of his job at a public library in order to install a white man in his place at a larger salary. "What exhibition of rapaciousness, race prejudice and political spoliation could be cheaper, commoner or meaner?" Jaffé exclaimed. "These are the little tyrannies and petty skulduggeries that make bitter the relations between the races and mock the strivings of the more enlightened Southern elements for a better and fairer racial adjustment."[12] Few or no white journalists repeated or endorsed what Jaffé wrote, but P. B. Young reprinted part of the article in the Norfolk *Journal and Guide* the following week and praised the sentiment.

It is important to note Jaffé's use of the words *cheaper, commoner,* and *meaner.* He deliberately selected those words to brand the actions of those white men as beneath the proper standards "more enlightened" white men prized. Which is to say, he branded the behavior of those men as conduct that only inferior men would engage in, and mocked the pretensions of white Virginians. Perhaps the best journalist in Virginia during the first half of the twentieth century, Jaffé won the Pulitzer Prize for his June 22, 1928, editorial, "An Unspeakable Act of Savagery," a powerful condemnation of lynching.

During the first decades of the twentieth century, which should be regarded as the low-water mark of race relations and racial equity in Virginia, white public officials in many cities and counties erected monuments to Confederate soldiers. Ostensibly, those monuments honored men who died fighting for Virginia, but nobody doubted that the monuments were also official proclamations of white supremacy. White Virginians were in charge, and African Americans were not. The humiliations and restrictions of Jim Crow drove many thousands of people out of Virginia. They left family members and the places where they had lived for decades or even centuries, much as people had immigrated to the colony centuries earlier to escape intolerable or dead-end conditions to seek a better future elsewhere. Jim Crow annoyed, perplexed, or angered many more people; but it also spurred to action some of the people who grew up during those decades and later fought racial discrimination and segregation during the civil rights movement. As the great Virginia civil rights attorney Samuel Wilbur Tucker recalled late in life, "I got involved in the Civil Rights movement on June 18, 1913, in Alexandria," because on that day, he explained, "I was born black."[13]

17

PROGRESSIVE VIRGINIANS

T HE SEVERE REDUCTION of the suffrage embodied in the Constitution of 1902 and the enabling laws passed to implement it were deliberate attempts to turn back the clock on the democratic reforms of the constitutional revolution of 1850–70. White supremacists who wished to eliminate black men from public life promoted their objective using the language of progress. They called it "reforming the ballot box" and "purifying the electorate." Their language was in tune with important national trends to reform and improve many aspects of life in the increasingly industrialized and urbanized country. Collectively the social, political, and economic reforms were called Progressivism. White middle- and upper-class women, most of whom lived in cities or large towns, provided most of the leadership and ideas for the Progressive movement in Virginia.

Progressivism and Its Origins

A dramatic development boom took place in the Valley of Virginia in the years immediately after 1888, when the Shenandoah Valley Railroad first provided an unbroken rail link between the Pennsylvania Railroad at Hagerstown, Maryland, and the Norfolk and Western Railroad at Roanoke. The new line had been planned to stimulate economic development of the Valley, and a speculative boom followed its completion. Towns like Buena Vista and Basic City (later Waynesboro) grew rapidly, and promoters sold optimistic investors property and houses that in some instances were not yet built. Promotional literature for Buena Vista depicted a thriving industrial city even though many of the roads and structures illustrated in the brochures did not yet exist. When the speculative bubble burst, a great many people lost money, businesses, and homes. If there were winners in the scramble for dollars it was some of the attorneys whose services were required before and during as well as after the boom. William Alexander Anderson erected one of the largest private resi-

One of the Valley boom promotional publications ca. 1890 depicted Buena Vista as a thriving and busy city, but the factories and residences it included had not been built and never were.

dences in Lexington, in part with legal fees he collected during the years surrounding the Valley boom. Anderson was president of the Virginia State Bar Association in 1900 and the following year won election to the first of two consecutive four-years terms as attorney general of Virginia.

Prolonged economic depressions in the 1870s and 1890s and the formation of a national labor movement affected Americans everywhere. The nation was rapidly industrializing, and the consequences directly influenced all producers and consumers. Many Virginians took advantage of new economic opportunities, and many faced new economic challenges. It was a recognition of the extent to which Virginians fully participated in the new national economy that the first large national labor union, the Knights of Labor, held its 1886 national convention in Richmond. The meeting was remarkable in that black and white delegates participated equally.

The rise of the organized labor movement was in part a consequence of the many new and hazardous industrial and manufacturing processes. Men and women who worked in mines, mills, and factories banded together to pressure employers for safer working conditions as well as for increased pay and shorter hours. Accidents could kill people or leave them seriously injured and throw their families into poverty. The state government responded, much as governments did elsewhere in the United States, and created an industrial commission and bureaucratic agencies to monitor workplace safety. Virginia's commissioner of labor and industry annually reported on workplace accidents and made recommendations for improvement, but the state government did not often impose strict regulations or safety requirements.

Residents of the cities and towns lived through different kinds of pressures than farmers as a result of economic change. Virginia's cities were the best indicators of the extent to which the state participated in the same national economic changes that the rest of the nation experienced. Owners and officers of banks, factories, railroads, and construction firms, to name only a few of the more thriving businesses, prospered during the 1880s and 1890s, as could readily be seen in nearly every Virginia town and city. Large private houses in a variety of exuberant styles (including Gothic, Queen Anne, and Richardsonian Romanesque) erected in the state's cities during the final decade of the nineteenth century and the first decade of the twentieth testify to the success many Virginia business leaders enjoyed.

Photographs taken of Virginia's towns and cities at that time show prosperous business and commercial districts with telephone and electric wires high above the streets, linking residents and businesses with the most modern technology and changing the ways in which people lived and communicated with one another. Those photographs and maps of Virginia's cities show little essential difference between how Virginians lived in their cities and how other Americans lived in theirs. In 1888 Richmond installed the first commercially successful electric streetcar system in the United States to provide inexpensive and reliable transportation for working men and women. It also gave them convenient access to such new urban amenities as city parks.

The experience of the city of Roanoke was in some respects atypical, but it illustrated many of the conditions in Virginia's cities at the end of the nineteenth century. After the Roanoke County town of Big Lick became an important railroad center and was renamed Roanoke early in the 1880s, its population rapidly increased, from about 1,000 residents in 1882 to about 35,000 by 1910. That made Roanoke a big city by contemporary southern standards. The Norfolk and Western Railroad erected a very large locomotive manufacturing factory and servicing facility in Roanoke. Owners of ironworks and other related industries also constructed factories, and residential housing for the many people who moved there looking for employment. So rapid was the industrial growth of Roanoke that it acquired the nickname of the Magic City, and somebody even quipped that Roanoke grew so fast that it was the only place in the country where people could catch bullfrogs by electric light.

Poor and inadequate housing was a constant problem for the city's rapidly increasing population of working people. Laborers often lived in ramshackle neighborhoods that stood in stark contrast to the large and elegant houses where bankers, lawyers, railroad executives, and industrialists resided.

This early twentieth-century photograph of a Norfolk street scene could have been taken in almost any American city. In this instance, the photographer was one of Virginia's finest artists with the camera, Harry C. Mann.

The contrast between the city's achievements and the price of those achievements could be seen in the Hotel Roanoke, built by railroad executives early in the 1880s. It included well-appointed public spaces and private rooms and a large and excellent restaurant that became popular with travelers and prosperous local residents. The hotel's owners boasted that the rooms had tastefully designed water closets. The drains from the water closets emptied into the city's first sewer line, but the sewer emptied directly into Lick Creek near the railroad tracks close to the center of the city and the residences of its working people.

In 1893 a crowd of white Roanoke residents lynched Thomas Smith, a black man suspected of assaulting a young white woman. The city's police force and the local militia were unwilling or unable to protect Smith, and the mob hanged him from a tree near downtown and shot his body full of bullets. Witnesses and participants refused to identify anybody who took part in the lynching, and none of the killers was punished. Roanoke's rising reputation with northern financiers suffered as a consequence of the lynching. The city's businessmen and political leaders worked to repair the damage done to the image of the emerging modern industrial community. Eleven years later, however, a race riot in Roanoke revealed that social and economic problems and racial prejudice persisted to the detriment of the overall health of the city and especially of the welfare of its black working class.

Alcohol was one of several obvious problems. Roanoke women founded a chapter of the Woman's Christian Temperance Union early in the 1890s, and some of the city's clergymen advocated prohibiting the sale of alcohol. Early in the 1890s a group of white Roanoke women organized the Ladies Union Benevolent Society to provide assistance to unemployed workers and their families. Women's clubs were a new phenomenon in middle- and upper-class urban communities and throughout the country were in the forefront of what was sometimes called the municipal housekeeping movement. Some clubs began as literary societies or social groups and evolved into community service organizations that participated in local politics and engaged in many kinds of civic improvement work.

In 1906, Willie Walker Caldwell and other veterans of civic improvement projects in Roanoke organized the Woman's Civic Betterment Club of Roanoke. It raised money to build parks, playgrounds, and schools. It established a public library, lobbied for stricter food and beverage inspections at the city market, and paid for a sanitation study of the city. Their work and the stains on the city's reputation that the lynching and race riot created led the city to commission a professional planner to develop means of making Roanoke more physically attractive and at the same time control saloons and reduce municipal corruption. The city government did not implement the planner's proposals, however, and urban development continued, with all the attendant problems that rapid and unplanned urban growth often created.

Men and women in other Virginia cities and towns advocated similar changes, and most cities created public health bureaus or other civic agencies in response. In hindsight, some of their actions seem very inadequate. For instance, at the beginning of the twentieth century the cities of Newport News and Hampton both installed municipal sewer systems, then a popular urban improvement. But like the system in Roanoke it did not transport wastewater to a treatment plant but emptied it into local creeks, which, in turn, flowed over lucrative oyster beds and made the oysters there unsafe for consumption. Local health authorities had power to prohibit sale of oysters harvested from those beds, but nobody had authority to prevent the discharge of sewage into the creeks. In Hampton all the sewers emptied into Hampton Creek. "It further appears," a judge wrote in the 1910s, "that long prior to the construction" of the sewer system, "there were, and still are, private sewers and overhanging closets which emptied into these waters, including the county poorhouse, the normal school with eleven hundred negro and Indian pupils and teachers, and the National Soldiers' Home, with over three thousand inmates; and that such sewers and closets have continuously and do now drain and empty directly into Hampton creek, and are not connected with any city sewer."[1] The stench was often unbearable and always unavoidable, and the danger to public health should have been obvious. However, nobody had authority to force a change.

The Constitution of 1902

The Constitutional Convention of 1901–2 included some new provisions that appeared consistent with the Progressive impulse; others simply continued or froze into place longstanding Virginia political institutions and practices. The constitution's articles on city and county government implicitly recognized the unique Virginia system of separation of cities and counties that had been evolving slowly without design for more than a century. Unlike in every other state, each city and county in Virginia was a distinct political entity. No city was legally in a county, even if a county entirely surrounded it. Every city and its neighboring county or counties were as legally separate as the neighboring counties were from each other. The constitution specified that cities of different sizes were to be governed under different general laws, and it specified that only the General Assembly could enact amendments to city charters. That provision gave constitutional sanction to a legislative practice that had begun soon after the American Revolution and that prevented citizens from changing the form or function of their own local governments.

The Constitution of 1902 included the essence of the 1870 school law that expressly prohibited the education of white and black children in the same schools. It also placed authority to appoint local school boards in the hands of city councils and county boards of supervisors. Voters and parents therefore had little direct influence on school boards and local school policies. The provisions for public education in the new constitution could have been even worse for African Americans. Convention members declined to adopt proposals that revenue collected from white taxpayers be spent exclusively on schools for white children and that revenue collected from black taxpayers be spent exclusively on schools for black children. Because African American families paid less in taxes per capita than white families—the convention collected data to prove it—the constitution could have provided less to African American students per capita than to white students. As it happened, though, without constitutional sanction some school boards often did just that, anyway.

The constitution authorized the General Assembly to permit primary elections to nominate candidates for public office and created a reformed and more professional county court system. The new constitution also created the

State Corporation Commission composed of three members, initially called judges. In Virginia as in most other states railroads had come to be perceived as sources of political corruption. During the second half of the nineteenth century railroads were among the most important of all businesses and corporations. They obtained many benefits from governments at all levels and amassed large sums of money with which to influence lawmakers. Railroads routinely gave public officials free passes to curry favor with them. Many people suspected that railroad interests actually dictated the actions of legislators and judges; and because most of Virginia's railroads had come under the control of large syndicates with headquarters outside the state, both the state's vital transportation network and its government appeared to be subject to outside influence. With their virtual monopolies on most routes, railroads were able to raise passenger rates at will and to impose discriminatory freight rates. All those practices and circumstances brought railroads and railroad lawyers under suspicion. The General Assembly's appointment of railroad lawyer Thomas Staples Martin to the United States Senate in 1894 was widely believed to have happened because railroads bribed legislators to elect him.

The constitution empowered the State Corporation Commission to grant charters of incorporation to businesses, to regulate their conduct, to protect the rights and the interests of investors in those businesses, and to regulate freight and passenger rates on public carriers. The commission also had authority to set rates electric power companies and other public utilities charged for their services. The convention delegate who was the principal creator of the commission, Allen Caperton Braxton, of Staunton, argued that requiring responsible corporate behavior would reduce potential dangers posed by more radical reformers, such as socialists. The constitution endowed the judges of the commission with legislative, executive, and judicial powers to such an extent that the commission soon came to be regarded as a fourth branch of the state government. The constitution made the commission a court of law and required it to afford citizens and corporations due process of law. That immunized the commission from legal challenges that had made it difficult for legislators in other states to regulate corporations, which had often successfully complained to federal courts that regulations deprived them of their property without due process of law. The State Corporation Commission attracted favorable attention from reformers throughout the nation. It was one of the most original and effective state governmental agencies in the nation early in the twentieth century.

Virginia Progressives

In the age of Jim Crow many of the nation's leaders were anxious about the future of Anglo-American society. During the first two decades of the twentieth century immigration from southern and eastern Europe dramatically increased. That prompted calls for restrictions on Catholics, Slavs, and other people who were not from western Europe, which had supplied the United States with most of its white population during the previous centuries. Congress and several states strengthened racially motivated restrictions on immigration from China and Japan during those years, too, which were also the years during which racial segregation on railroads and streetcars, in public education, and other forms of racial discrimination and separation were being written into national and state laws.

Some prominent members of Virginia's leading business and industrial families influenced public debates on the values of American society through heritage organizations they founded or in which they held responsible offices. Two may be singled out as representative in character even though they were more influential than the others. The Daughters of the American Revolution (DAR), created in Washington, D.C., in 1890, and under the effective direction for many years of Virginia native Mary Virginia Ellet Cabell, provided an opportunity for elite white women to help shape the national education agenda through its local chapters and members. Their political and social views were often in sympathy with the national trend toward excluding African Americans and new immigrants from a full place in American society. The Association for the Preservation of Virginia Antiquities (APVA), organized in 1888 and for its first half century run largely by elite white women, also helped shape the public debate by its emphasis on the sacrifices and contributions of the white men who had founded the colony of Virginia in the seventeenth century. The unease of the leaders of the APVA with the democratic impulse at the end of the nineteenth century was evident in their selection of sites to be commemorated and preserved and in the way in which they interpreted the colony's history to the citizens of the state.

The same could be said of Mary Tucker Magill and Rose Mortimer Ellzey MacDonald, authors of some of the most popular histories of Virginia used as textbooks in the state's schools during the first decades of the twentieth century. Those books portrayed Virginia's history in a flattering light. They minimized the importance of slavery and concentrated on the achievements and virtues of the state's founders and of its Revolutionary and Civil War heroes. Some of the textbooks published during the final years of the nineteenth century and the first years of the twentieth century simply ended with the Civil War, as if that marked the end of what had been admirable about Virginia's past.

When Virginians looked to the future at the beginning of the twentieth century, they saw what many other Americans saw, a state and a country in which mechanization, industrialization, urbanization, and social change were all increasing. To meet some of those changes Virginians formed private associations or appealed to local, state, or federal governments for action. Women established clubs and organizations to aid children and the poor, and they called attention to problems in public health. Women formed the Instructive Visiting Nurse Association in 1901. It was one of many organizations that undertook to improve the sanitary conditions in which the state's poorest residents lived. Its members worked to provide health care for children whose parents could not afford to take them to private physicians. Such organizations led to the creation in most cities and some counties of public health agencies and to the formation of the state department of health in 1908. The General Assembly granted it only rudimentary regulatory authority, but it collected valuable statistics, sent agents to poor communities that had no public health programs, and in several other ways for the first time in Virginia made state and local governments active partners with the people in improving public health and reducing disease.

Tuberculosis provides one example. Throughout the nineteenth century, the disease (known then as consumption) was one of the most common causes of death in the United States. In 1882 scientists discovered the bacterial cause of the illness, *Mycobacterium tuberculosis*. Medical researchers then learned that the disease could be prevented, or could be cured if detected early. Many states, including Virginia, took measures to prevent its spread. They mounted educational campaigns and passed laws to curb drinking from common cups, coughing and sneezing without using a handkerchief, and even chewing the ends of pencils. In the 1920s the Virginia Tuberculosis Association and the State Board of Health cooperated in educational efforts to reduce the spread of tuberculosis, and the General Assembly passed a law against spitting in public places. Railroads and courthouses provided spittoons and posted placards that condemned spitting. The state created and operated the Catawba Sanatorium in Roanoke, the Blue Ridge Sanatorium in Charlottesville, and the Piedmont Sanatorium for African Americans in Burkeville. Doctors and nurses at those asylums treated patients with a controlled regimen of rest, supervised exercise, nutritious food, and fresh air. By the middle of the twentieth century the dread specter of tuberculosis had largely disappeared from Virginia.

Public education attracted the attention of Progressives because of the relatively poor quality of public schools in many parts of the state, particularly in the rural counties in southern and southwestern Virginia. The public health movement mobilized largely white and female reformers aided by a few white physicians. Educational reform differed by including both men and women, both white and black, and even people who in other circumstances were not usually regarded as reformers. Prominent Richmond clubwomen Lila Meade

Valentine (a founder of the Instructive Visiting Nurse Association) and Mary-Cooke Branch Munford founded the Richmond Educational Association in 1900, and Munford undertook a decades-long but unsuccessful campaign to allow women to enroll as undergraduates at the University of Virginia. In 1905 educational reformers mounted a successful statewide fundraising effort known as the May Campaign, which inspired a network of fifty local education associations, most under the leadership of white women, that worked tirelessly to improve Virginia's public schools.

The General Assembly created several normal colleges (teacher training schools) for white women. The first, founded in Farmville in 1884, later became Longwood University. In 1908 the assembly founded two more, one at Harrisonburg (later James Madison University) and the other at Fredericksburg (later the University of Mary Washington), and in 1919 it established the fourth at Radford (later Radford University). The assembly made education of white male and female teachers a priority at the College of William and Mary and of black men and women teachers at Virginia Normal and Collegiate Institute (later Virginia State University) and at Hampton Normal and Agricultural Institute (later Hampton University), too. Most of the teachers educated in those schools were women. White men who received their educations at the older and more prestigious universities filled most of the administrative positions in the state's public schools for white students, and black men who had attended Virginia State, Hampton, or one of the numerous black colleges in neighboring states or the District of Columbia directed public schools for black students.

Black and white educational reformers worked on parallel paths to improve schools and teacher training in the segregated public school system. A strong belief in the value of education led black and white women in some places to forge alliances that benefited students of both races in spite of strong prejudices in white society against such cooperative endeavors across racial lines. White Virginians did not block national philanthropic organizations such as the Julius Rosenwald Fund and the Anna T. Jeanes Foundation that provided money to improve schools and schooling for black Virginians.

In spite of the work of educational reformers during the first decades of the twentieth century, many communities had very poor public schools, and many school-age people had no access to an adequate education. The Episcopal Church, among other institutions, tried to assist and sent missionaries to the mountain counties of Virginia. In a report from Franklin County in 1926 one of the educational missionaries wrote, "Our day school runs ten months in the year—eight months for the winter term, and two in summer, July and August. At this time we gather in many children who have wandered off to the pitiful little public schools around here, and are what I call derelicts in education. The State is doing what it can, but it is hard to work out the educational plan in an isolated, illiterate community. One hope of ours is to help form public opinion so that public schools can function normally. One mountain man said to me, 'You-all have showed us what a school ought to be. We never knew before.'"[2]

The state supplied limited support for a few small elementary schools for Indians, but as was the case with many of the schools for African Americans, they offered only a rudimentary elementary curriculum. Members of the Mattaponi and Pamunkey tribes attempted to improve the schools. On several occasions during the 1910s they also appealed to the governor for assistance in protecting their treaty rights, as when local officials illegally tried to collect taxes on fishing nets in violation of the treaties or to regulate their hunting and fishing rights. In 1916 and 1917, agents of the Chesapeake Pulp and Paper Company stored harvested timber without authorization on a Mattaponi wharf for later shipment by water to the paper mill in West Point. The Mattaponi demanded action from the governor and attorney general to force the paper company to stop trespassing on reservation land, and the company backed down. Governors and legislators often expressed sympathy when they met with or corresponded with Mattaponi or Pamunkey leaders, but in fact the state government furnished little assistance. The attitude of some white officials toward the state's Indians was reflected in the practices of early twentieth-century secretaries or administrative assistants in the governor's office who often filed routine correspondence in folders they callously mislabeled "Indian Problems."

The Progressive impulse, with educational reform at its center, also included campaigns against child labor and for public health initiatives, consumer protection laws, and an eight-hour workday. It carried Andrew Jackson Montague into the Virginia governor's office in 1902 against the wishes of the older pro-business Democratic Party leaders. His accomplishments were modest compared with the records of Progressive governors in other states; but he and his successors, Claude Augustus Swanson (1906–10) and William Hodges Mann (1910–14), persuaded the General Assembly to make modest increases in appropriations for public schools. Political leaders in Virginia were generally lukewarm about Progressivism or openly hostile.

The state's congressional delegation was often divided on reform legislation enacted during the administrations of Presidents Theodore Roosevelt and Virginia native Woodrow Wilson. Representative Carter Glass, who entered Congress after fashioning the restrictive suffrage provisions of the 1902 constitution, took part in one of the first important reforms of Wilson's administration. His role in passing the 1913 Federal Reserve Act, which created the nation's first central banking system, earned widespread praise and gained him a reputation as an expert on banking. Glass was secretary of the treasury from December 1918 to January 1920, when he succeeded Thomas Staples Martin in the United States Senate.

During the Progressive period Virginia took small, incremental steps rather than long, dramatic strides in the direction of state intervention in social and economic affairs. Still, the steps were important breaks with the past. The state offices created for monitoring labor and public health concerns were small and did a better job of accumulating information than in promoting change. During the first decades of the twentieth century when members of the General Assembly and public health or public education officials discussed needs and new proposals, they couched their discussions in language that clearly indicated a reluctance to move far or fast or to lose control of the process. Political and professional leaders revealed in their discussions and also in the policies they adopted that they urgently desired to avoid disturbing the racial and social hierarchies. Maintaining the state government's control over local governments and over experimentation had a higher priority for many of them than the desire for change. As a result, providing health services to the poor and assisting unmarried women during pregnancy remained a private or family concern or, as in some of the larger cities, a social service function of churches.

One successful experiment in public administration was an exception to the general rule and proceeded without impediment from the state government. In 1908 the city of Staunton appointed a professional city manager with full responsibility for administration of the city government. The city council set policy, but professional managers and specialists directed the work of city departments. It quickly proved to be a very successful municipal reform that gained nationwide acceptance. Moreover, with legislative approval, beginning late in the 1920s and 1930s a few cities established juvenile and domestic relations courts that provided assistance and improved supervision for young people who got into trouble. In most respects, though, the General Assembly acted to preserve the status quo, and its members insisted on elite white supervision of reforms. In 1922 the assembly established a state board of motion picture censors. For more than forty years thereafter a small group of white men and women viewed and approved or disapproved every commercial film scheduled to be shown in Virginia and ordered deletion of scenes that violated their personal standards of morality or perceptions of appropriate race relations.

Woman Suffrage

One of the most important national reform campaigns in which Virginians took part was for woman suffrage. Orra Gray Langhorne, of Lynchburg, revived the woman suffrage issue during the 1890s, but the association she founded and led was short-lived. In 1909 a dedicated group that included writers Ellen Glasgow, Mary Johnston, and Kate Langley Bosher, artists Adèle Clark and Nora Houston, and educational reformer Lila Meade Valentine founded the Equal Suffrage League of Virginia. Within its first few months and under the able direction of Valentine, the league joined with the National American Woman Suffrage Association and began a public campaign to educate Virginians about women's roles and voting. Virginia's suffragists argued that women as taxpayers and citizens deserved and needed the vote and that their influence in politics would improve the quality of government at all levels. Many of the league's leaders were also active in educational or public health reform movements, and they emphasized the importance of those reforms to women and families and the responsible roles that women should play in the political arena in support of issues relating to families and children.

The campaign for woman suffrage in Virginia was chiefly the work of elite white urban women. They created their statewide campaign through contacts they had with members of church organizations and missionary societies, educational and public health reform groups, and other collaborative projects. Several new organizations of professional women also enabled suffragists to identify other supporters of woman suffrage in other communities. The Equal Suffrage League grew steadily and by 1916 was the largest organization of women in Virginia to that time—perhaps the largest nonmilitary organization of Virginians of any kind. By 1919 it had about 175 chapters and more than 20,000 members. Valentine even persuaded a group of Richmond businessmen to form the Men's Equal Suffrage League of Virginia.

Virginia suffragists employed many techniques to enlist women to their cause. They made speeches (often from decorated automobiles), rented booths at fairs, and distributed "Votes for Women" buttons. They canvassed house to house, passed out leaflets, and spoke in public to educate Virginia's citizens and legislators and to win their support for woman suffrage. Mary Johnston visited women's colleges to rally faculty and students to the cause, addressed members of both houses of the General Assembly in 1914, as well as legislators in Tennessee and at the National Governor's Conference. For a few months in 1914, the league published a monthly newspaper, the *Virginia Suffrage News.* In Richmond, where the league held meetings in Capitol Square and on Broad Street in downtown, Adèle Clark sometimes set up her easel and started painting to entice curious spectators to suffrage speeches. "It reached the point," she later recalled, "where I couldn't see a fireplug without beginning, 'Ladies and gentlemen.'"[3]

Opponents of woman suffrage, including both women and men, formed their own opposition organization. They argued that most Virginia women

Officers and supporters of the Equal Suffrage League of Virginia in Capitol Square in Richmond during one of many rallies held in support of votes for women.

had no interest in voting and that woman suffrage would open the door for black women to vote and undermine white supremacy and the state's Constitution of 1902. In 1915 Attorney General John Garland Pollard—he and his sister Mary Pollard Clarke both favored woman suffrage—privately advised Valentine that the section in the state constitution that permitted the assembly to impose a property qualification on poor voters in black-majority counties would prevent African Americans from winning any elections in the state. African American woman in Virginia discussed woman suffrage among themselves and very often advocated votes for all women. Because they knew that white opponents of woman suffrage regarded all African American voters as dangerous, those black women seldom spoke out in public in ways that attracted the attention of white people.

The Equal Suffrage League initially focused on winning support in the General Assembly for a voting-rights amendment to the state constitution, but the all-male legislature defeated proposals for a woman suffrage amendment in 1912, 1914, and 1916. Some suffragists grew impatient with the slow pace of reform and broke ranks. They joined the more militant Congressional Union (later the National Woman's Party), which pressured Congress to propose a woman suffrage amendment to the United States Constitution. During World War I, the National Woman's Party demonstrated in Washington, D.C., and Pauline Adams, a former president of the Equal Suffrage League branch in Norfolk, was among the protestors arrested during those demonstrations and jailed in the federal detention center in Lorton.

Suffrage advocates in Virginia took heart in 1918 when Great Britain granted women the vote and celebrated the following year when Virginia native Nancy Langhorne Astor, Viscountess Astor, was the first woman to take a seat in the House of Commons. Repeated disappointment marked their efforts to persuade Virginia's General Assembly to propose an amendment to the state constitution. During World War I the Equal Suffrage League changed tactics and endorsed a proposed federal amendment, even though the league's leaders firmly (and correctly) believed that a mere half century after the Civil War the state's political leaders would not agree to an amendment to the Constitution that forced the southern states to do anything. To demonstrate to members of the legislature how many Virginians had converted to the cause of woman suffrage, the league's leaders sought endorsements from as many Virginians as possible.

They succeeded in that goal, although almost nobody at the time noticed, and the success has never caught the attention of historians. What attracted the most attention were two actions of the General Assembly in March 1920. Both houses of the assembly by large margins voted down the proposed Nineteenth Amendment, but both houses also recognized that the amendment might soon win ratification. The legislators passed a bill to allow women to register and vote, provided they paid their poll tax for that year, but only if enough states ratified the amendment. What escaped widespread notice was that the General Assembly at almost the same time proposed an amendment to the state constitution that deleted the word *male* from the list of limitations on the suffrage. It passed both houses by fairly comfortable majorities. Before amendments to the state constitution could take effect, the assembly had to pass them twice with an election of members of the House of Delegates between the legislative actions. That meant that voters would not have a chance to ratify it until November 1922. By then the question was moot because the Nineteenth Amendment granted Virginia women the vote in August 1920. The General Assembly did not submit the amendment it passed in 1920 to the voters in 1922.

In 1927 the state's voters ratified an amendment to the state constitution that exempted wives and widows of military servicemen from payment of the poll tax as a prerequisite for registration, which constitutionally recognized woman suffrage in the state. A major constitutional revision voters ratified in 1928 eliminated the word *male* from the constitution and brought the state constitution into conformity with the national constitution. Members of the General Assembly of Virginia withheld ratification of the Nineteenth Amendment until 1952. A story that circulated at the time explained that the daughter of a member of the House of Delegates told her father that she had learned in school that Virginia had not ratified the amendment and asked why. At the next session of the assembly he and a large number of legislators introduced a motion to ratify the amendment, and it passed both houses of the assembly by large majorities.

In 1921 the Republican Party state convention nominated Lynchburg suffragist Elizabeth Dabney Langhorne Lewis Otey for superintendent of public instruction, the first woman a major political party ever nominated for statewide office in Virginia. A small number of women ran unsuccessful for the General Assembly that year, and in 1923 Democrats Sarah Lee Fain, of Norfolk, and Helen Moore Timmons Henderson, of Dickinson County, won election to the House of Delegates. They were the first women members of the Virginia legislature. Fain won reelection twice, but Henderson died shortly after being nominated for a second term. Sally Cook Booker, a teacher in Henry County, won election to the first of two terms in 1925; and in 1927 Nancy Melvina Caldwell, a teacher in Galax on the border between Carroll and Grayson Counties, and Henderson's daughter, Helen Ruth Henderson, both won election to one term in the House of Delegates. Emma Lee White won election to the House of Delegates from the district of Mathews and Gloucester Counties in 1929 and 1931. No other women succeeded in winning election to the General Assembly until after World War II, and no woman won election to the Senate until the 1979.

Prohibition

A reform movement that deeply engaged many Virginia men and women of both parties was the nationwide campaign to limit or prohibit the manufacture, sale, and consumption of alcohol. The Virginia branch of the Woman's Christian Temperance Union, founded in 1882, promoted temperance rather than outright prohibition, but the male-dominated Anti-Saloon League, founded in 1901, sought an end to all sale and consumption of alcohol. Prohibitionists made steady progress in Virginia, and by early in the twentieth century some counties or magisterial districts within counties had outlawed alcohol. The Anti-Saloon League, under the able leadership of Virginia Methodist minister James Cannon, campaigned effectively for years, and in 1914 the assembly passed the first of a series of statutes that outlawed the manufacture and sale of alcohol and created a state prohibition control department independent of the regular law enforcement agencies. When the Eighteenth

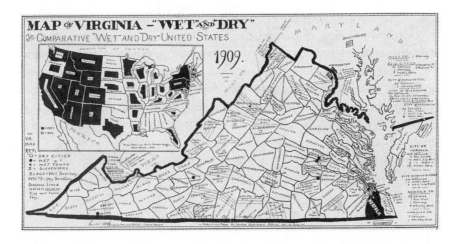

This 1909 map shows which counties and cities in Virginia had prohibited the manufacture and sale of alcoholic drinks and which had not. The legend states that diagonal lines "indicate *comparatively wet* territory."

Amendment became part of the Constitution in 1919, the whole United States became dry.

Throughout the years of statewide prohibition from 1914 to 1919 as well as national Prohibition from 1919 to 1933, the state was officially dry, but Virginians were not without alcohol. Since colonial times people had brewed their own beer and ale, distilled brandy and whiskey, and made their own wine. At the time of the Whiskey Rebellion of 1794 some of them had participated in resistance to federal taxes imposed on their products. In the twentieth century, alcohol distilled from corn—known as whiskey, moonshine, white lightning, panther sweat, and other names—was a popular drink in many parts of the state. Virginia newspapers were filled during Prohibition with stories of distillers, bootleggers, and speakeasies and the attempts law enforcement officials made to put them out of business. A fairly typical newspaper story described a scene in Alexandria in 1921. "Police headquarters," it reported, "has been one of the show places in Alexandria the last few days. One of the cells, usually reserved for devotees of John Barleycorn, has recently been devoted to storage of the 1921 crop of 'corn likker.' More than 100 gallons of potential cheer are stored in this one barred cell, and the bottles, fruit jars and other receptacles have been the cynosure of many admiring eyes during the last few days."[4]

Federal agents from the Bureau of Internal Revenue (revenuers) raided distilleries before and after Prohibition to break up stills that produced alcohol on which the distillers had paid no tax. Moonshining continued in many places after the repeal of Prohibition in 1933. Franklin County gained fame as one of the principal centers for the distillation of corn liquor, even though state enforcement records clearly documented extensive illegal distilling in virtually every county and city in the state. Thirty-four residents of Franklin County, including the commonwealth's attorney and several other local, state, and federal officials, stood trial in federal court from April to July 1935 in what was called the Great Moonshine Conspiracy Trial. All but the commonwealth's attorney and two deputy sheriffs were convicted on charges they had produced and sold more than a million gallons of unlicensed whiskey and deprived the federal government of $5.5 million in excise taxes.

Eugenics

The so-called racial integrity campaign that led to the passage of the 1924 Act for Preserving Racial Integrity was part of the larger, nationwide eugenics movement, another manifestation of the fears of some white Americans that new immigrants and African Americans posed a threat to Anglo-American culture. Respected members of the University of Virginia faculty served as officers and leaders in national organizations devoted to protecting western European culture through scientific means. What some of those men wrote and said was not significantly different from what John Powell and Earnest Sevier Cox wrote and said about African Americans. Indeed, the men and women who made scientific racism popular drew on some of the best scientific literature then available, which appeared to sanction their belief in a hierarchy of racial types with distinctive cultural practices.

The same literature also appeared to support conclusions about the hereditary nature of intellectual capacity and of susceptibility to insanity, alcoholism, or other physical or medical conditions that landed some people in mental hospitals, jails, or poorhouses. States and localities throughout the country adopted and enforced laws against interracial marriage, and in Virginia and elsewhere some state officials also employed the power of the state to prevent people whom they believed to be undesirable from having children. The state forced residents of Virginia's mental hospitals and people deemed mentally or morally defective to undergo surgical sterilization for the purpose of improving the genetic stock of the state and nation. In that respect, the eugenics movement was fully within the larger Progressive tradition.

Uncertain about the constitutionality of the 1924 Virginia law that allowed the procedure, Virginia officials arranged to have a case brought in federal court to settle the question. It was in every sense a contrived case. The attorney assigned to represent the defendant, Carrie Elizabeth Buck, worked in league with the physicians and attorneys for the Virginia State Colony for

Epileptics and Feebleminded, in Lynchburg, to generate a verdict and a court record that would place directly before federal courts the power of the state to protect its people from the dangers posed by a supposedly increasing population of morally degenerate and socially unfit people. The local court declared that Buck was feebleminded, and that her mother also was, on the grounds that neither she nor her mother was married. They declared her infant daughter, who was conceived as a consequence of rape, socially unfit.

The case *Buck v. Bell* went to the Supreme Court of the United States, where Associate Justice Oliver Wendell Holmes, following the reasoning of the doctors and their attorneys and relying on their unproved diagnosis of Carrie Buck as feebleminded, upheld the state's power to decide who was socially unfit and to prevent those people from having children. Holmes famously wrote, "three generations of imbeciles are enough."[5] During the next five decades Virginia sterilized more than 8,300 people in the state's public institutions. Other states, acting under the latitude of *Buck v. Bell,* may have surgically sterilized as many as 50,000 people.

During the 1920s and 1930s German scientists and members of the National Socialist Party—the Nazis—closely followed the American eugenics movement. Virginia laws and practices did not directly inspire their later extermination of Jews and other people they deemed inferior, but American scientists, including several Virginians, provided the Germans with models to emulate. The example of the Holocaust of the 1940s later doomed forced sterilization in the United States and related attempts to improve the species through biological manipulation.

The Literary World

The decades of significant changes in the Progressive era coincided with a flourishing literary culture in Virginia. The Civil War and colonial Virginia furnished the settings for some of the work of one of the state's most successful novelists, Mary Johnston. Her works sold well nationally and earned her credit as a superior prose stylist between the 1880s and her death in 1936. Investing the landscape of Virginia with almost mystical qualities, Johnston refrained from excessive romanticism in setting the historical stages for her characters. Nevertheless, the past and the Civil War were powerful forces in her fiction, which was popular both because it was well suited to the time and because it was excellent literature. Johnston was also a forward-looking woman who took a leading role in the campaign for woman suffrage. Her 1913 novel *Hagar* was a powerful early feminist statement.

Johnston's near contemporary, Ellen Glasgow, also wrote about the long shadow that Virginia's history cast over its residents. Glasgow was a keen stu-

dent of psychology and wrote about hopes and dreams and about disappoint-
ments and failures of men and women in a world of unending uncertainty.
Even though she never married, some of her finest novels, the 1913 *Virginia*
and the 1925 *Barren Ground,* explored the relationships of married people
and how the different expectations of men and women and the social roles
expected of women complicated their lives. Glasgow's work was the finest
fiction written in Virginia in the first half of the twentieth century—some
people say ever. She received the Pulitzer Prize for literature in 1942 for her
autobiography, *In This Our Life,* her last book, although it might be that she
received the prize late in life for the whole of the distinguished body of work
that she had produced.

One of the most famous Virginia writers during the first half of the twentieth century was James Branch Cabell, of Richmond. His 1919 novel *Jurgen*
was condemned in New York as indecent. Like much of Cabell's writing, it for-
sook reality and presentism for imaginary landscapes and mythical represen-
tations. The complex family and human relationships in the fictional land of
Poictesme in the volumes of *Biography of the Life of Manuel* (1927–30) nevertheless appear as reflections of the upper-class white culture of Cabell's own
Virginia. Cabell's first wife, Rebecca Priscilla Bradley Shepherd Cabell, was
deeply involved in the patriotic and preservation societies of the 1920s and
1930s. The Cabells were part of a literary group in Richmond that attracted national notoriety. H. L. Mencken, of Baltimore, and other critics in New York
and elsewhere praised the *Reviewer,* the monthly periodical that the Cabells'
associates published during the first half of the 1920s. One of the editors was
Margaret Waller Freeman, who became Cabell's second wife. The *Reviewer's*
principal editor was Emily Tapscott Clark, who had her own separate and
successful literary career in the 1920s and 1930s. In 1927 she published *Stuffed
Peacocks,* a set of thinly disguised character sketches of Richmond's social and
literary elite that exhibited her keen powers of observation and description
and left the objects of her criticism perplexed or angry.

One of the men Clark wrote about in *Stuffed Peacocks* was Douglas South-
all Freeman, who edited the Richmond *News Leader* from 1915 until he retired in 1949. Freeman received the Pulitzer Prize in 1935 for his four-volume
biography of Robert E. Lee, and early in the next decade he published three
volumes on Lee's major subordinate commanders, *Lee's Lieutenants.* He also
began a seven-volume biography of George Washington that his assistants
completed after his death, which earned him a second Pulitzer Prize. During the two world wars of the twentieth century, Freeman wrote about military events in Europe and the Pacific for his Richmond newspaper by drawing
analogies from Civil War battles and maneuvers in Virginia. He believed that
readers of his newspaper knew all about Civil War campaigns and that if he
explained the world wars to them through Civil War analogies they would

thereby understand the major conflicts of the twentieth century. For Freeman, the events of the Civil War were still living memories.

For other Virginia writers early in the twentieth century, the Civil War was of less critical importance. John Fox, a resident of Big Stone Gap in southwestern Virginia, published *The Little Shepherd of Kingdom Come* in 1903, a popular novel set in the Civil War but with the unusual twist for a Virginia writer in that its central character joined the United States Army rather than the Confederate States Army. Fox's 1908 *Trail of the Lonesome Pine* focused on a romance between a northern engineer and a young woman who lived in the mountains of southwestern Virginia. Its themes include the adjustments people who lived in that part of Virginia had to make in dealing with economic and social changes that industrialization and mining brought to their Appalachian culture. It was made into two films, and an outdoor stage drama based on the novel became a popular regional theater piece in southwestern Virginia in the 1960s and continues to this day.

Fox's near-contemporary and near-neighbor Frank Monroe Beverly was a sometime newspaper editor and publisher and also a noted poet who celebrated the beauty and culture of the Appalachian region. James Taylor Adams, a generation younger than they, also wrote for the local press but was most noted for compiling and preserving folklore and music from Wise County, where he lived, and elsewhere in Appalachia. Beverly and Adams were less well known than Fox, but like him, and very unlike Freeman, they found their cultural roots in the white residents of the mountains and valleys rather than in the great events of the American Revolution or the Civil War.

Unlike them all, poet Anne Spencer, of Lynchburg, published in national periodicals associated with the Harlem Renaissance, a flourishing of African American artistic, literary, and musical burst of creativity with its center in New York during the 1920s. She was a victim and a critic of the South's racial segregation policies and a founder of the Lynchburg chapter of the National Association for the Advancement of Colored People (NAACP). She and her husband entertained some of the country's leading African American intellectuals in their Lynchburg home. In her poetry, Spencer expressed her innermost beliefs in lines that showed a keen appreciation of the early works of the Brownings and of African American poet Paul Laurence Dunbar. Spencer's ability earned her, among her contemporaries who knew her work, a reputation as an extremely fine poet. By the latter years of the twentieth century she was regarded as one of the finest poets of twentieth-century Virginia.

Virginia Roots Music

Progressives' contemporaries sought to preserve some distinctive elements of Virginia's folk culture. James Taylor Adams was one of many collectors of Appalachian folklore and music. The Hampton Folk-Lore Society was founded in 1893 and the Virginia Folk-Lore Society in 1913. Both organizations and many individual people sought out works of art, furniture, and musical instruments. The legends, stories, and songs of Virginia's peoples with differing cultural heritages exhibited distinctive regional variations. Early in the twentieth century, University of Virginia professor Arthur Kyle Davis collected an abundance of folklore material and deposited it in the university's library. The materials Davis and the others collected include some of the most valuable resources for studying Appalachian culture.

Following the development of commercially successful audio recording technology, collectors also made recordings of ballads, sacred music, and instrumental music. In addition to collecting folklore, Davis recorded 325 aluminum audio disks of folksongs and ballads in the 1930s. A national market already existed for gospel and choral music as a consequence of the popularity since the final years of the nineteenth century of such touring musical ensembles as the Hampton Institute Singers. Beginning in the 1920s, radio broadcasts stimulated interest in music in a much wider public beyond the collectors and academics. Commercial recording companies sent agents into many parts of Virginia and elsewhere in the South to make field recordings of people playing and singing their favorite music. In southeastern Virginia an ensemble tradition, called gospel quartet singing (even though many groups contained more than four members) was very popular in African American churches. The style derived in large part from sacred music in black churches, but it had a broad appeal, and commercial recording companies recorded a number of Virginia quartet groups during the 1920s and 1930s. Roscoe Lewis, of Hampton Institute, made about 200 recordings in the Hampton Roads area.

The best known of the many field-recording sessions took place in Bristol in July 1927. It was not the first or the only such recording session, as has sometimes been supposed, nor was it the birth of country music, as has also been said. The dozens of musicians from southwestern Virginia, West Virginia, Tennessee, Kentucky, and the Carolinas who sang and played for the Victor record company did not then and there create a new musical style. The commercial recording of their music, though, made it widely available, and the men and women who purchased the records made from the Bristol recording session found and enjoyed an expressive music that drew on many sources. European and African elements and musical styles had evolved for generations to create a style that was distinctive to the region but relatively unknown to most other Americans before the twentieth century. The wide appeal the recordings enjoyed reflected the music's origins. The songs were about the good and bad times of people's lives, how they worked hard in the mines or fields, how they danced and drank, how they loved and lost, perse-

Maybelle Addington Carter, Alvin Pleasant Carter, Sara Dougherty Carter (*from left to right*)

vered and despaired. In much of the music the conspicuous religious faith that made it possible for people to endure hard times was on or just beneath the surface. The most commercially successful of the musicians who were recorded at Bristol in 1927 were Alvin Pleasant Carter, Sara Dougherty Carter, and Maybelle Addington Carter, from Scott County. Their compelling music, in which other members of their family also performed, influenced popular musical tastes in the United States for the remainder of the twentieth century.

Agents of the Library of Congress's Archive of American Folk-Song sought out and recorded blues, gospel, and old-time music in Virginia. At the Virginia state penitentiary in 1936 they recorded work songs, minstrel music, spirituals, and blues to capture and preserve versions of folk music that they believed had not been influenced, or tainted, by broadcast or recorded music. In fact, though, musicians had always borrowed from and learned from one other. By the 1930s it is unlikely that anyone could have found any performers whose music did not draw on the music of other people. The wide distribution of recorded music and its availability on radio created a national ideal of what the music should sound like. Agents for commercial recording companies may have been predisposed to record music that sounded like what they sought rather than to seek further for other musical expressions that might have been influenced differently or perhaps less by records and radio broadcasts. Even the Library of Congress's recordings exhibit a melding of styles that recording and broadcast technology had influenced.

The popularity of folk- and old-time music in the Piedmont and southwestern Virginia led to the creation of several annual folk music festivals, the first in 1928. The White Top Folk Festival, begun in Grayson County on August 15, 1931, was the largest and most influential. John Powell, the classical pianist and composer from Richmond, John A. Blakemore, a wealthy businessman from near Abingdon, and Annabel Morris Buchanan, a folklorist who then lived in Marion, sponsored the first festival at which writers and folklorists joined musicians to enjoy and learn from each other's compositions and performances. More than 10,000 people attended the festival in 1937, where more than 300 people performed. Eleanor Roosevelt, the wife of the president, made a well-publicized appearance at the 1933 festival.

Audio recordings and radio (and television later) introduced Virginians to aspects of the rest of the world they had not had easy contact with before the middle of the twentieth century, but by the same means people elsewhere learned about Virginia. The popularity after the 1920s and 1930s of Virginia's roots music owed much to the then-relatively new technology of radio. During the 1930s a Richmond radio station with a particularly powerful signal broadcast a program that featured vaudeville-like acts and much traditional music. The title of the show was the *Corn Cob Pipe Club*. It had a large, nationwide audience. A regular listener in Seattle, Washington, three thousand miles away, wrote a letter to the station in March 1934 and addressed the envelope with line drawings of an ear of corn, a pipe, and a club and the word Richmond. Letter carriers knew where to deliver the letter, which remains in the station's archive. After World War II the same radio station broadcast to a national audience a weekly program of popular music titled *The Old Dominion Barn Dance*.

18

TWO WORLD WARS AND THE GREAT DEPRESSION

RESIDENTS OF VIRGINIA had always interacted with people elsewhere in North America and the world. People and events elsewhere influenced Virginians' lives in many ways. That was more so the case in the twentieth century than ever before. The two world wars and the prolonged depression between them arose from circumstances entirely beyond the abilities of Virginians to influence, and these events profoundly changed the lives of all Virginians.

World War I

While Americans were debating the merits of the many Progressive proposals to reform American society the United States entered World War I in the spring of 1917. The governor appointed a Council of Defense to coordinate the state government's mobilization. About 78,500 Virginians served in the armed services and support units during the year and a half America was in the war. About one-third of them were black men who served in racially segregated units, mostly in support services. Many of the soldiers and members of the Virginia guard served as elements of the army's 111th Field Artillery and 116th Infantry Regiments and others in the 29th, 42d, and 80th Divisions. Approximately 3,700 Virginians lost their lives from all causes during the war.

Virginia men were subject to conscription for military service for the first time since the Civil War. Of the men who served in the army, navy, and marines more than 58,000 (roughly three-quarters) were drafted. When draft boards called up members of several Indian tribes, they refused to report and explained that as tributary Indians and in effect wards of the state they were not subject to the national draft. Pamunkey Chief George Major Cook (son of Caroline Cook, whose fences United States Army soldiers burned for fuel during the Civil War) requested the governor, and through him the adjutant general of the army, to rule on the question. The governor and the army agreed that Virginia's Indians were exempt from being drafted. Their rights protected, Indians then voluntarily enlisted.

More than 260,000 members of the American Expeditionary Force passed through Newport News in route to Europe, and more than 440,000 returned through the port to the United States. The federal government expanded naval facilities in southeastern Virginia, and thousands of civilians moved there in search of jobs in support of the war effort or to work at the busy shipyard at Newport News and the navy installations at Norfolk and Portsmouth. Throughout the state, civilians faced new forms of government control over their daily lives, such as rationing of gasoline and coal to conserve fuels for the war, and forgoing meat one day a week to make more available for service-men. For each federal program and for many of the state's enforcement efforts, men and women worked for food or fuel regulation agencies; local boards administered the draft system; and local citizens bought and sold war bonds, collected scrap materials for the army and navy, registered resident aliens and probably kept watch over their behavior, and worked to keep up morale. In Christiansburg people gathered in the town square once or twice a week to sing patriotic songs.

One Virginian, Sargent Earl D. Gregory, of Chase City, earned the Medal of Honor at Bois-de-Consenvoye, north of Verdun, France. On October 8, 1918, as a member of Headquarters Company, 116th Infantry, 29th Division. Shouting "I will get them," Gregory "seized a rifle and a trench-mortar shell, which he used as a hand grenade, left his detachment of the trench-mortar platoon, and advancing ahead of the infantry, captured a machinegun and 3 of the enemy. Advancing still farther from the machinegun nest, he captured a 7.5-centimeter mountain howitzer and, entering a dugout in the immediate vicinity, single-handedly captured 19 of the enemy."[1]

Public expressions of patriotism during the war led in many parts of the country to harassment of German Americans and of people who opposed government policy or even appeared to support it inadequately. After Leon Whipple, a journalism professor at the University of Virginia, proclaimed his pacifism and stated that wars did not solve problems, the university's board of visitors terminated his faculty appointment.

The armistice on November 11, 1918, concluded the fighting in Europe, and American soldiers and sailors returned to the United States to be discharged and return to civilian life. The mass movement of servicemen and also of physi-cians and nurses no doubt accelerated the spread during the winter of 1918–19 of a particularly virulent strain of influenza known at the time as the Spanish

Sgt. Earl D. Gregory

flu. It may have killed between 50 and 100 million people worldwide, even more than died in Europe during the war. Virginia was not spared. In the autumn of 1918 the directors of the state fair closed it when the contagious disease first appeared, and the state health department recommended that county fairs close, also. A fair that remained open in Doswell produced what the state health commissioner later described as "disastrous consequences."[2] The commissioner estimated that nearly 16,000 people died in the state during the epidemic, but it is likely that the number was much greater than his preliminary statistics revealed. If the epidemic had a positive consequence it was a heightened awareness of the value of sanitation and public health programs in Virginia.

The thousands of Virginia men and some Virginia women who went to Europe during the war brought back with them impressions of an outside world they had not known. Other Americans who passed through or were stationed in Virginia during the war saw clearly how much the state resembled the rest of the United States in some ways, and how much, in some other ways, it was different. Members of a California guard unit in training at Camp Lee, near Petersburg, during the spring and summer of 1918 were shocked when they attended a Memorial Day event in Richmond and saw Confederate flags flying nearly everywhere with scarcely an American flag to be seen. It had never occurred to the Californians that in Virginia it was still Confederate Memorial Day.

The Roaring Twenties

Following a brief recession after the end of World War I, most sectors of Virginia's economy prospered through much of the 1920s—the Roaring Twenties, as the decade came to be known. The variety of new businesses in Virginia during the first decades of the twentieth century reflected the increased diversity in the American economy as a whole. Factories in Lynchburg and Richmond manufactured and sold automobiles. Manganese mines in the Blue Ridge and Shenandoah Valley supplied ore for a metal much in demand in industrial America. Large paper mills at West Point and Hopewell took advantage of the ready availability of softwood timber in Virginia; and a thriving furniture manufacturing industry in the counties near Martinsville took advantage of the hardwood timber in the mountains. Coal mining and timber harvesting in southwestern Virginia provided jobs for thousands of people. Where the land was cleared cattle grazing increased in importance. On the Eastern Shore where commercial fishing had been a mainstay of the economy for generations, farmers also raised fruits and vegetables for shipment to markets in Norfolk, Washington, Baltimore, and cities farther north. Railroad connections between the Eastern Shore counties and the northern cities made possible a rapid increase in truck farming and also provided access to markets for the watermen who harvested fish and shellfish from Chesapeake Bay and the Atlantic Ocean. Those thriving businesses employed many people, both black and white, during the 1920s. So did the expanded shipyards in the Hampton Roads cities and the new chemical industry at Hopewell, known as City Point during the Civil War, which became an important munitions manufacturing site during World War I.

People who lived near Chesapeake Bay or the navigable portions of the eastern rivers continued as in the past to have contact more often with Baltimore merchants than with Fredericksburg, Norfolk, or Richmond merchants. Several enterprising Baltimore steamship companies ran regularly scheduled overnight ferries between the Maryland city and landings in many places in eastern Virginia. They furnished customers with merchandise, delivered Baltimore newspapers, and took their produce to market or enabled them to travel to Baltimore for shopping. During the early years of the twentieth century as in the past, parts of the Northern Neck and the Eastern Shore remained as much or more an extension of Maryland than as parts of Virginia. There was a Baltimore Store near Talleysville, in New Kent County, only a few miles from Richmond.

The decade after World War I was one of so much change that it is as if twentieth-century Virginia really emerged in the 1920s. Women gained the right to vote and won election to public office for the first time. The General

Assembly adopted the Racial Integrity Act and the public meetings law that required racial segregation. The assembly also passed and the Supreme Court affirmed the law for surgical sterilization of people the state deemed unfit to breed. Harry Flood Byrd became the dominant political leader in the Democratic Party and the state. His "pay-as-you-go" system of financing highway construction and reorganization of the state government bureaucracy foreshadowed the next forty years of public policy choices Virginians made.

The Byrd Organization

The white male leaders of the Democratic Party were opposed to extending the reforms of the Progressive period, although one young party leader, Harry Flood Byrd, earned a reputation as a progressive governor. A successful businessman, owner and publisher of the Winchester and Harrisonburg newspapers, and owner of some of the state's largest apple orchards, he won election to the Senate of Virginia in 1915 and became chair of the Democratic Party's state central committee in 1922.

Byrd made his reputation in the General Assembly as an advocate for construction of a state system of public highways, which he believed was necessary for the economic development of Virginia. The state's political leaders all agreed on the objective but disagreed about how to finance road construction. Byrd organized a successful campaign in 1923 to defeat a referendum proposal to issue revenue bonds for road construction. Advocates of bonds had asserted that borrowing money would enable road construction to proceed more speedily than if construction were to be paid for from current revenue derived from taxes on gasoline, tires, and licenses, the pay-as-you-go program that Byrd favored. Winning the referendum helped make Byrd the most important political leader in Virginia even before he became governor. The requirement to pay for construction from current revenue enabled Byrd and party leaders who agreed with him to keep the state government committed to low taxes, minimal public services, and white supremacy.

Byrd won election as governor in 1925, and during the next four years he made many changes in state government. He called his plans the "Program of Progress." He revamped the state's executive budget system that had been created in 1918, increased the governor's control over the budget and the executive departments, placed agency heads under direct supervision of the governor, and simplified the state bureaucracy, all of which produced efficiency and saved money. Byrd also persuaded the voters to amend the state constitution to reduce the number of elected state officials and make the treasurer, superintendent of public instruction, and secretary of the commonwealth appointive.

Byrd's reputation as a progressive (small p) governor derived from his re-

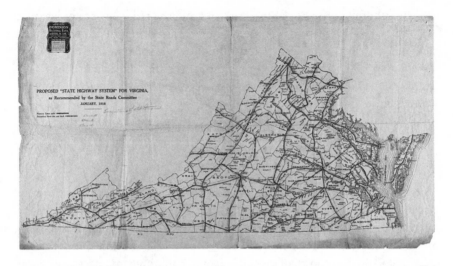

The first plan for a statewide system of public highways in 1918 to be constructed at public expense. *Journal of the Senate,* 1918 sess.

form of the state government, not from a commitment to a large comprehensive agenda of economic and social reform. In fact, Byrd's first executive order as governor was that state employees work an eight-hour day, which in many industrial settings would have been regarded as a welcomed reform, but prior to Byrd's administration state employees had worked a seven-hour day. One effect of his making the office of governor a much stronger one was that he and his successors, many of whom he helped select, could effectively resist efforts to expand expensive public services.

Byrd commissioned a national consulting firm to study the state government and assist him to prepare his plan for bureaucratic reorganization. The firm also studied the organization and functioning of local government and recommended sweeping changes to what the consultants regarded as an inefficient and bloated system. "In fact," the report concluded, "there is nothing to commend the present form of county government in Virginia. In many of the counties it is grossly political, careless, wasteful, and thoroughly inefficient. It has been that way for years, but still it exists and seems to flourish."[3] Byrd and his principal advisors quietly buried that part of the report, which if implemented would have destroyed the local party apparatus, known as courthouse rings, through which the party's state leaders controlled local politicians and local government.

Members of the Byrd organization used agencies of state and local government for political purposes. In 1922, for example, when Byrd was organizing the defeat of Republican Congressman C. Bascom Slemp in southwestern

Virginia, he arranged for the auditor of public accounts to send examiners from Richmond to each county in the district that had an elected Republican treasurer. The auditors seized records of poll tax payment to guarantee that Republican treasurers could not do what Republicans had accused Democratic county treasurers of doing: add names of reliable voters to the tax lists after the deadline for payment of the poll tax had passed. Members of both parties engaged in deceitful or even illegal practices, such as paying poll taxes of poor people or casting votes for people who did not show up at the polls in person.

The clerks of court, sheriffs, treasurers, voter registrars, and other local elected officials usually cooperated in the interest of winning elections. Politicians regarded the office of clerk of court (successor office of the colonial county clerk) as the most desirable and influential political post, not because of the intrinsic influence of the clerk but because the office had become the traditional leadership post of the courthouse rings. In some counties, the office and its political influence appeared to be almost hereditary. Members of one family held the office in Franklin County from the 1850s to the 1940s, three consecutive generations held the office in Charles City County, four in Brunswick County, and five in Goochland County. Such commitment and continuity enabled local political organizations to function effectively and overwhelm opposition for long periods of time.

During the 1920s and 1930s the Democratic Party state committee sometimes assessed local and state officials a portion of their salaries to finance political campaigns and to pay poll taxes. Local officeholders were always vulnerable to political pressure from the state bureaucracy because, as in the colonial period, some officials collected fees rather than salaries for performing their jobs. The State Fee Commission regulated their fees and also the salaries of the salaried local officials. In 1934 Byrd's closest political friend and ally, Everett Randolph Combs, became chair of the powerful commission, which was renamed the State Compensation Board. Combs had risen to political prominence as clerk of court in the southwestern county of Russell and was the chair of the Democratic Party in the Ninth District in 1922 when he and Byrd directed the campaign that wrested the district's congressional seat away from Slemp and the Republicans.

A study made in the 1940s found that elected officials and employees could often provide enough votes, given the small size of the electorate, to control the outcomes of Democratic Party primaries, which in most areas of the state guaranteed victory in the general election. The party's state leadership, in effective control of most of the local governments and party apparatus in the state, operated one of the most formidable and long-lasting political machines in the United States. Beginning with John Strode Barbour's successful refashioning of the party in its campaigns against the Readjusters in 1883 and 1885, the party organization dominated Virginia's politics and government for eighty years, for half that time, until Byrd's death in 1966, under Byrd's leadership.

Supporters of the Byrd organization opposed most or all of the changes Progressives advocated and prevented the state from achieving as robust a Progressive reform agenda as in many other states, including most southern states. Nearly every Progressive proposal required new government agencies and an expansion of the power of government into the personal and professional lives of the people. New government agencies not only reduced freedom of activity for some business owners, but also cost money and required increased taxation to pay for them. Whether in the form of schools, public health programs, regulation of commerce, reduction of or elimination of the ability of people to consume alcohol, or even maintenance of racial segregation, government at all levels during the Progressive era grew in size, authority, and expense. Business leaders like Byrd disliked bigger and more expensive government and blocked efforts of supporters of many Progressive reforms from achieving all they desired.

In 1927 public health pioneer Dr. Bathurst Browne Bagby complained about the consequences of the Byrd organization's emphasis on keeping tax rates as low as possible. Bagby was the man who bragged about how his uncle and other men had cheated Republicans and African Americans at the polls in the nineteenth century. After becoming a noted public health advocate in both Virginia and Georgia, Bagby called attention to some of the implications of focusing too much on the tax rates on prosperous people and not enough on the welfare of all the people. "In reading the discussions on taxes," Bagby wrote in a letter to a Richmond newspaper, "I am carried back to the 'good old days' when taxes were low. I remember the roads of sand or mud, when it took a day to go from Tappahannock to Bowler's and back, a distance of fourteen miles.... I remember the dilapidated one-room school that ran only five months in the year, and was often conducted by a teacher whose chief qualification was that she was a near relative of a school trustee.... Yes, they were the 'good old days' of low taxes and lower service, of larger ignorance and blacker misery."[4]

Republicans seriously challenged Democrats twice during the 1920s, once successfully, and both times with unwelcome assistance. In 1925 the Democrats nominated John Michael Purcell for state treasurer. Purcell was the first Catholic to run for state office on a major party ticket in Virginia, and he was the target of what the Norfolk *Virginian-Pilot* described as a statewide campaign of political knifing. The Ku Klux Klan and other anti-Catholic organizations and individuals opposed Purcell so effectively that his poorly known opponent came closer to winning election than any other Republican candidate.

Prejudice against Catholics was neither a new nor a temporary phenomenon. That same year, anti-Catholic prejudice erupted in Richmond when a Catholic organization erected a statue of Christopher Columbus in one of the city parks. Three years later, anti-Catholicism and strongly held opinions on Prohibition allowed Republican presidential candidate Herbert Hoover to defeat Democratic nominee Alfred E. Smith in Virginia. Smith was the governor of New York, an outspoken opponent of Prohibition, and the first Catholic to run for president on a major party ticket, and he was also a victim of religious prejudice in Virginia and elsewhere in the South.

Those elections took place in the context of an extended public debate in Virginia about religion, public education, and church-state relations. As in many other political controversies, candidates and voters exhibited strongly held moral views. In 1925 the General Assembly considered bills to require Bible reading in the state's public schools. With support from some of the state's most prominent Methodists, including Bishop James Cannon, and other Protestant leaders, the proposal attracted wide attention. Two Richmond men with national reputations directed the opposition: George W. McDaniel, pastor of the city's First Baptist Church, and Edward Nathan Calisch, rabbi of the city's Congregation Beth Ahaba. They successfully appealed to the tradition of separation of church and state in Virginia begun with Jefferson's 1786 Act for Establishing Religious Freedom and argued that state involvement in religious affairs was unconstitutional in Virginia and also unwise. Compulsory Bible reading in the state's public schools did not become law, even though for several decades thereafter many school districts allowed or encouraged teachers to read from and teach the Bible in public school classrooms.

In 1929, the year following Hoover's defeat of Smith in Virginia, the Democratic Party faced a coalition of Republicans and ardent Democratic supporters of Prohibition. Byrd and his closest advisors generally cared less about Prohibition than about protecting the policies they implemented during the 1920s. They selected an improbable candidate for governor, John Garland Pollard, who was not a member of the Byrd organization's inner circle. He had been attorney general in the 1910s and a critic of the organization's leadership in that decade. In 1929 he was dean of the school of government and law at the College of William and Mary and a widely respected Baptist lay leader and supporter of Prohibition. Pollard easily won election in 1929, and the first serious challenge to Byrd's party leadership dissolved.

Byrd and the party's inner circle had to maneuver behind Pollard's back in 1933, though, when Congress submitted to the states a constitutional amendment to end nationwide Prohibition. Pollard refused to call the General Assembly into special session to expedite ratification of a measure he disapproved of, so Byrd's legislative lieutenants made use of a provision of the state constitution to have the assembly call itself into special session and pass enabling legislation for the requisite ratification convention. That body ratified the amendment on behalf of the state. Byrd thus managed to remove a once-divisive political issue from the gubernatorial campaign of 1933. His chosen candidate, George Campbell Peery, easily won the Democratic Party nomination and the general election. When Prohibition ended, the General Assembly created the Alcoholic Beverage Control board to regulate the legalized industry and granted it a statewide monopoly on the sale of all alcohol except beer and wine. It was another of the many ironies of Virginia history that the Byrd organization, whose leaders consisted of men and women who disapproved of strong government and championed the freedom of businessmen and women to operate as they pleased, nevertheless created a state monopoly on the distribution and sale of alcohol.

The Depression of the 1930s

The economic collapse that followed the stock market crash of October 1929 together with the worst drought to hit the state in several generations crippled the Virginia economy. About 50,000 people who worked for salaries or by the hour lost their jobs in 1930, and the value of goods manufactured in the state fell from $897 million that year to $817 million in the next and continued to fall as the unemployment rate continued to rise. By the inauguration of President Franklin D. Roosevelt in March 1933 the Great Depression affected nearly every Virginian. Most of the state's banks failed or were in financial difficulty by then. When a bank failed at that time its depositors lost all of their money. Without money to pay rent or mortgages, people lost their homes; without money to repay loans, people lost their farms or businesses; without work, people went hungry everywhere in Virginia.

Demand for manufactured goods and services and also for coal, timber, and other raw materials all fell, which threw miners and factory workers out of jobs. People who were able to keep their jobs, such as public employees, often had their salaries reduced. In some industries labor unions engaged in intense efforts to protect jobs and prevent wage reductions, but business conditions were bad, many businessmen were suspicious of or hostile toward organized labor, and the consequences for union members and other working people were often bleak. In 1937 at a synthetic fiber plant in Covington workers struck in hopes of obtaining better pay and more job security. The governor intervened and broke the strike. He called out the militia and invoked the state's antilynching law, which made it a crime for groups of people to assemble for an unlawful purpose. The governor declared that the striking workers' picket line was an illegal barrier that prevented men who were not on strike from going to work.

The attitude of influential state government officials toward organized labor was unfriendly; nevertheless many thousands of men and women who worked for railroads, in mills, mines, and shipyards, and in other manufacturing industries were union members. National labor unions made repeated attempts to increase the number and proportion of southern workers in the organized labor movement, but the efforts met with mixed success in Virginia. In 1930, textile workers in Danville took part in a nationwide strike for better wages, but they did not take part in a second national strike in 1934. Coal miners went on strike in 1933 and demanded to be paid better, to be paid for the time that it took them to travel to and from the coal seams deep in the mountains, and for improved safety in the mines. The strike did not achieve its goals, but federal legislation and rulings of federal courts eventually redressed some of the miners' grievances. Among the Virginians who participated eagerly in the organized labor movement was Lucy Randolph Mason who, as her name indicates, was descended from and related to some of the distinguished planter families of colonial Virginia; but Mason was a champion of working people, and she traveled throughout the South during the 1920s and 1930s to ameliorate the conditions of working men and women and promote organization of unions affiliated with the Congress of Industrial Organizations (CIO), the more radical of the two national labor organizations.

The federal government responded to the economic crisis of the 1930s with a wide and unprecedented variety of assistance agencies. One of the first federal agencies created in March 1933 was the Federal Emergency Relief Administration. In June, its state division, the Virginia Emergency Relief Administration, began sending federal aid to the more than 80,000 unemployed Virginians who were on relief. Under the direction of William A. Smith, a Petersburg civil engineer, the agency employed approximately 45,000 people on more than 2,500 work-relief projects. One such program, the Women's Work Division, under the direction of educator Ella Agnew, found or created paying work for women with few workplace skills. Some of them worked as cooks, others cleaned government offices, and some staffed child-care centers. In Portsmouth and Norfolk women joined rat-catching patrols to reduce the chance of epidemic disease.

One of the largest of the New Deal programs, the Public Works Administration (PWA), invested approximately $117.3 million in 740 federal projects and 350 local ones in Virginia. In one three-year period the state's schools received $11.8 million from the PWA, of which $1.75 million was for the state's predominantly rural African American school districts where schools were decidedly inferior to the schools of white students. The PWA financed many

The smiles on the faces of these eager children leave no doubt about their enthusiasm for the bookmobiles that supplied their schools and communities with books they could freely borrow.

other programs, including a housing project in Altavista, a waste-treatment plant in Staunton, harbor improvements in Newport News, and additions to the Veterans Administration Hospital in Roanoke. PWA money paid for construction of several buildings at the College of William and Mary, Mary Washington College, and Virginia Polytechnic Institute. Substantial federal assistance helped pay for the new Alderman Library at the University of Virginia and a new building for the Virginia State Library in Richmond. During the 1930s, a demonstration libraries project, also under New Deal sponsorship, provided the first rudimentary public library services and access to bookmobiles in many rural communities of Virginia.

The popular Civilian Conservation Corps (CCC), founded in March 1933, opened its first camp in the nation the following month near Luray in the George Washington National Forest. Between 1933 and 1942, the CCC spent $109 million in Virginia. It employed 107,210 men in more than eighty Virginia camps. The CCC provided men with paying work. That enabled young men to send money home to their families and to learn job skills and work habits that stood them in good stead when the labor market later improved. As one CCC worker explained, "I've found myself at last, I know exactly what I want to do more than anything else in the world. I want to be a dentist. It took me a dickens of a time to get my bearings, but I've got myself in hand at last. I might never have found out what I wanted to do, if daddy and mama had'nt agreed for me to go into a C.C.C. Camp."[5]

Creating enduring facilities that benefited all Virginians, men in CCC camps built 986 bridges, strung 2,128 miles of telephone line, stocked waterways with 1.3 million fish, planted 15.2 million trees, and developed the state's park system; the first six state parks opened in 1936. The CCC and most other New Deal programs were racially segregated in Virginia. An African American CCC camp created Seashore State Park (later renamed First Landing State Park and Natural Area) on the south bank of Chesapeake Bay. The federal government also developed Virginia's first state park for African Americans, Twin Lakes State Park in Prince Edward County, which opened in 1939.

The federal Works Progress Administration (WPA), created in 1935, funded locally sponsored projects and was specifically intended to provide temporary wages for people who were out of work. In 1938 the WPA hired unemployed farmworkers who created the Norfolk Botanical Gardens. Black and white women worked together in Petersburg to landscape and plant trees and flowers in Lee Park in the city. In the process they compiled a valuable and impressive reference catalog of local indigenous plants. The Virginia WPA wage ranged from $21 to $75 per month and unlike many other federal programs also assisted unemployed professional men and women. One WPA program, the Virginia Writers' Project, began in November 1935 under the imaginative and very able direction of Eudora Ramsay Richardson. The WPA sponsored the publication of histories of several Virginia counties and produced two noteworthy books in 1940: *Virginia: A Guide to the Old Dominion,* a volume in the American Guide series, and *The Negro in Virginia,* which Hampton Institute professor Roscoe Lewis compiled, although he did not get credit for his work on the title page. *The Negro in Virginia* was a notable contribution to scholarship and was a better history of Virginia's African Americans than any book then available was of Virginia's white or Indian residents.

The WPA enhanced the cultural landscape of Virginia, too. It hired out-of-work artists to create public art, such as murals for post offices and other public buildings. It also sponsored art centers for both white and black Virginians, and it employed writers to produce educational radio programs. One of the best known of all the arts projects in Virginia was the Barter Theater, in Abingdon, which the WPA supported. In hard times when working people had little money for entertainment, the theater accepted payment in kind, such as chickens, for admission to its plays. At the Barter Theater, southwestern Virginians were treated to performances featuring some actors who later gained international fame, among them Ernest Borgnine, Patricia Neal, and Gregory Peck. In eight years, the WPA employed as many as 95,000 Virginians and paid approximately $66 million in wages.

Some New Deal programs that provided work for unemployed people sought to preserve aspects of the state's culture but in fact imposed a set of

Leslie Garland Bolling carving *Queen-of-Dreams,* ca. 1937

stereotypes on it. Planning for the creation of Shenandoah National Park in Virginia and the Great Smoky Mountains National Park in North Carolina and Tennessee began before the Depression. The development of Shenandoah National Park and the Blue Ridge Parkway, a scenic highway between the two national parks, involved modifications of a mountain landscape to fit a particular perception of how the Appalachian countryside should look. The state government forced people who owned and worked the land in the proposed park and in the immediate vicinity of the parkway to sell their land to the government and move away from their homes. Construction crews often removed evidence of their habitations and created pastoral vistas or farm sites that conveyed the impression that the people who had lived in the mountains were quaint or simple relics of the past.

The Politics of the New Deal

As a government study described the Appalachian portion of the southern states during the 1930s, the South appeared to be the nation's number-one economic problem. In solving the region's economic problems, Virginia's state government was a reluctant or hesitant partner with the federal government. Unlike in the other southern states, Virginia's political traditions, with the obstacles that it placed on participation in the political process, had hindered development of a vigorous competitive political culture that enabled advocates of farmers and working people to elect an appreciable number of public officials who supported social or economic changes. Even more so than during the Progressive period at the beginning of the twentieth century, during the 1930s the state's Democratic Party leaders resisted large-scale change. That placed them at odds not only with the party's national leadership but also with a significant portion of the party's southern leaders. Both of Virginia's senators (Harry Flood Byrd and Carter Glass) and all but two of its congressmen opposed almost all the New Deal reforms and relief agencies. Only Congressman John W. Flannagan, who represented southwestern Virginia's Ninth Congressional District, and one-term Congressman Norman R. Hamilton, of Portsmouth, consistently supported the New Deal. The state's first two Depression governors, John Garland Pollard and George Campbell Peery, concentrated on cutting and balancing the state's budget and were unsympathetic to or skeptical about the wisdom or ability of the federal government to ameliorate conditions during the Depression. As a consequence of the state's political leadership being hostile to New Deal reforms, Virginia was the last of all the states to adopt legislation to allow its citizens to participate in the social security system, which ultimately became one of the most important of the federal government programs of the 1930s.

Some other new federal government agencies required no corresponding state government action and were instrumental in transforming the lives of thousands of Virginians. The Federal Deposit Insurance Corporation (FDIC) guaranteed the security of money people deposited in participating banks, which after the great bank failures at the beginning of the 1930s provided significant security to all Americans. One of the most transformative of the new agencies was the Rural Electrification Administration (REA). Electric power companies did not often provide service in rural areas because the companies doubted that they could recover the costs of stringing long lines to scattered farms. With assistance from the REA, people of those areas formed electric cooperative companies to provide the first electricity to rural households. The availability of electricity meant that those Virginians could have access to what other Virginians already enjoyed—electric lights, radios, and phonographs. Among the most important benefits electricity provided to rural families was the ability to install reliable electric pumps in their wells so that they could have indoor plumbing for the first time.

The New Deal's efforts during the 1930s to stabilize the fluctuating prices of staple agricultural products and reduce or end the boom-and-bust risks of southern farming involved limiting production of tobacco, cotton, and some other crops. Until the Supreme Court declared the law unconstitutional in

1934, the first Agricultural Adjustment Administration set maximum allowances of acreage that individual farmers could plant. It also controlled marketing of some of the state's most commercially valuable agricultural products. The second Agricultural Adjustment Administration continued the programs, and for decades thereafter the federal government was deeply involved in regulating the lives and business affairs of Virginia's farmers.

Harry Byrd and the men who composed the leadership of the Democratic Party were on the whole more conservative than most other members of the party in the state or nationally, and they opposed the New Deal more vigorously than Democratic voters in the state did. Roosevelt won large majorities in Virginia when he ran for reelection in 1936 and again in 1940 when he ran for a third term as president. Differences of opinion about the New Deal within the party contributed to the election of James H. Price as governor in 1937. Price had been a loyal supporter of Byrd in the General Assembly in the 1920s. He served two terms as lieutenant governor in the 1930s, and many Democrats believed that he had earned the nomination for governor in 1937. Byrd opposed him and tried without success to field a strong opposition candidate, but Price was a popular man and won the nomination and the general election. When in office, he replaced several of Byrd's supporters in key offices in the bureaucracy with men more sympathetic to the New Deal or men who resented Byrd's control over the party. Price and Roosevelt tried to wrest the federal patronage away from Byrd and Glass because of their relentless and public opposition to the New Deal, but the attempt failed, and Byrd remained in firm control of the party. He gave his quiet blessing—"the nod," as insiders referred to it—to anti–New Deal Congressman Colgate W. Darden for governor in 1941. Byrd gave only perfunctory support to Roosevelt's presidential candidacy in 1940 and 1944 but never thereafter endorsed a Democratic Party nominee for president.

Historic Tourism

Independent of the federal government's agencies to improve the state economy, John D. Rockefeller Jr. contributed to the development of the important new tourism industry in Virginia. At the urging of Williamsburg clergyman William Archer Rutherfoord Goodwin, Rockefeller began to acquire property in Williamsburg in the 1920s, and during the 1930s financed the restoration and reconstruction of several private residences and public buildings in the old colonial capital. The innovative outdoor living history museum became a popular tourist attraction, and work on restoration continued for decades. The restored colonial capital was midway along what became the Colonial National Historical Park, a scenic motorway that linked Jamestown where the first colonists landed in 1607 and Yorktown where the British surrendered in 1781.

About the same time Rockefeller began to purchase property in Williamsburg, the state government embarked on a campaign to make the Virginia's many historic sites into tourist destinations. The State Commission on Conservation and Development (after 1938 the Virginia Conservation Commission) clearly foresaw that the family automobile was to be the most popular means of vacation travel. Between 1927 and 1941 the commission installed nearly 1,000 historical markers along the state's highways to mark the sites of important events, the birthplaces of great Americans, and the founding of counties and cities, churches and businesses. The historians who selected the sites to mark and who wrote the texts of the markers omitted most of the important events in the history of Virginia's African Americans. The markers that they placed at sites associated with Virginia's Indians often explicitly described Indians as making savage attacks on innocent frontier settlers, but they did not often mark sites where colonists attacked or killed Indians. The state highway historical marker program, one of the first on a large scale in the country, initially taught the state's motorists a heroic, white, male version of history with the events of the American Revolution and the American Civil War at its center.

After World War II tourism continued to grow and became one of the state's largest industries. The Colonial Williamsburg Foundation continued to renovate old structures and build new replicas of old buildings and to expand its interpretive programs. The educational museum the state constructed at Jamestown in 1957 to commemorate the anniversary of the first English settlement in Virginia was another innovative outdoor public education project that allowed visitors to gain a sense of what the landscape, buildings, and people of Virginia looked like and how they lived 350 years earlier. In many Virginia cities and towns preservationists and local historians also saved historic buildings or created museums for educational and tourism purposes. The work in Richmond between 1930s and the 1960s of preservationists Elisabeth Scott Bocock, Louise F. Catterall, and Mary Wingfield Scott contributed much to the evolving national concept of adaptive reuse of historic buildings.

World War II

The relief agencies and economic reforms of the New Deal, even though they offered assistance to thousands of Virginians during the 1930s, did not end the Great Depression. World events beyond the control of Virginians or even of the United States did that. The war that began in Europe in 1939 led to a revival of the American economy, as Great Britain and the allies purchased agricultural products and war supplies from the United States. Construction of naval ships stimulated the economies of Virginia and other states where firms like the Newport News Shipbuilding and Dry Dock Company hired thousands of men and women to build warships and transport vessels.

For most Americans, the war in Europe probably seemed at first a distant thing, reminiscent of World War I but not immediately threatening. On the Atlantic coast, however, near the major port cities, German submarines patrolled within sight of land and torpedoed and sank merchant ships leaving American ports for Europe. Virginians near the mouth of Chesapeake Bay could sometimes see burning freighters from the beach, and early in 1942 Germans laid mines in the mouth of the bay. All along the coast, the War and Navy Departments constructed heavily fortified observation posts and coastal defenses before the United States entered the war. Navy pilots trained at bases in eastern Virginia and bombed islands in the Chesapeake Bay to test new naval warfare tactics. The navy also used the islands for target practice with the huge new rifled guns the navy developed for the next generations of warships. In May 1940 the governor of Virginia appointed a state defense council, and by the summer of 1942 nearly 250,000 men and women were enrolled in one or more of the many civil defense organizations that supported the war effort by collecting scrap metal, staffing air raid warning posts, and later working at United Service Organization (USO) hospitality sites for troops going off to war.

The Japanese attack on Pearl Harbor on December 7, 1941, propelled the United States into the world war and led to further increases in manufacturing, mining, and other industries that hired men and women in great numbers. That stimulated the national economy and brought both the country and Virginia out of the Depression. The shipyards at Newport News built more than four hundred ships—totaling approximately three and a half million tons—during the war. Nearly 1.7 million men and women passed through the sprawling Hampton Roads Port of Embarkation during the war years. Other military installations in Virginia also expanded rapidly to meet wartime needs, and they employed additional civilians in the process. Chemical factories in Hopewell and Radford produced explosives, synthetic materials, and other essential war supplies. The munitions plant at Radford employed as many as 20,000 people at one time. The war redistributed the working population of Virginia and created new concentrations of industrial and manufacturing jobs. The war also put the Northern Virginia appendages of the District of Columbia and the region around Norfolk and Newport News on a trajectory of rapid growth and change that continued for the remainder of the twentieth century.

The population of the suburbs of Washington, D.C., had already grown as

Photographer at work at the Port of Embarkation in
Newport News documenting the movement of service
members en route to war.

a consequence of the expansion of the federal government during the 1930s,
and the war stimulated even more growth. In 1941–43 the Navy and War Departments constructed a new headquarters, the Pentagon, in Arlington. At the
time it had the largest floor space of any building in the world. Its construction heralded the beginning of a tremendous building boom and population
expansion in and around the nation's capital. The naval base at Norfolk and the
shipbuilding yards in Hampton Roads drew people from southern Virginia
and North Carolina to the region, rapidly increasing the population. With
that rapid increase in population came new pressures on the localities.

Norfolk gained an unenviable reputation as the country's worst war city.
The extraordinarily rapid growth of operations at the navy base and the nearby
shipyards created demands for housing and related public and social services
local people could not immediately meet and also stimulated an equally rapid
increase in the number of saloons and brothels. Vice and corruption infected
the city government and police department, and during the war the state had

to take over operation of law enforcement in the city because of the widespread problems wartime conditions created.

The United States reinstituted military conscription even before the Japanese attack. As in World War I, locally appointed draft boards oversaw the registration and induction of young men into the armed forces. The Selective Service System, which administered the draft, set racial quotas for draftees based on the proportion of the races in the population. For each state, it employed racial classifications the state had established. The Racial Integrity Act of 1924 and Walter Plecker's administration of the Bureau of Vital Statistics had effectively classified the Indians of Virginia as "colored," so the army assigned them to racially segregated all-black units in the armed services. On behalf of members of their tribes, chiefs of the Chickahominy and Pamunkey demanded that Virginia Indians not be assigned to black units but be permitted to serve as Indians alongside white Americans. They persisted throughout the war in their challenges to being classified as "colored." Several Monocans refused to be inducted when drafted as Negroes, but a sympathetic federal judge dismissed charges against them in 1943. Three Rappahannock men were imprisoned when they refused to be inducted as "colored," but they were later released and assigned to hospital duty as if they had been conscientious objectors.

Black Virginia soldiers and sailors served in racially segregated units in all branches of the armed forces. Some of them performed menial or support tasks, but several men from Virginia flew fighter planes with the celebrated Tuskegee Airmen. Their success changed the minds of some white people who had been skeptical that black men were capable of flying sophisticated aircraft. At home, black men and women continued to work and live in racially segregated conditions, but they devised their own goals for the war, referred to as the Double-V campaign: V for victory over the enemies abroad, and V for victory over racial segregation at home.

More than 300,000 Virginians served in the armed forces during World War II, including Virginia National Guard units mustered into federal service and assigned to the 116th Infantry and 111th Field Artillery, both part of the 29th Division. Virginians served in all theaters of the war. On D-Day, June 6, 1944, the 116th Infantry, with companies from Bedford, Harrisonburg, Lynchburg, and Roanoke, participated in the invasion of France. Forty of the soldiers were from Bedford, and nineteen of them died on Omaha Beach, and three died later in the Normandy campaign. The National D-Day Memorial at Bedford, dedicated in 2001, honors those men and all others who died in the invasion of Europe. Approximately 12,000 Virginia men and women died in military or auxiliary wartime service. Eight Virginians earned medals of honor during the war.

This poster promoted the sale of war bonds to African Americans by emphasizing the heroism and service of the Tuskegee Airmen.

The federal government recruited a large number of women, many of them Virginians, to do secret code-breaking work in Washington and at Arlington Hall, near the Pentagon. They worked on breaking the secret diplomatic, army, and naval codes of the Germans and Japanese and even of the Soviet Union, which was an ally during World War II but a potential adversary afterward. Many of the women were mathematicians or schoolteachers before the war. Their work was essential to the war effort but remained a highly classified secret for decades afterward, until long after many of the women were dead. At the same time, other women who worked at an army base in Pennsylvania did the complex calculations to plot trajectories for long-range artillery; and another group of women worked at a navy base in Maryland to calculate the trajectories of the new naval rifles. And at Langley Field, in Hampton, Virginia, another group of women mathematicians did the complex calculations neces-

This 1943 poster heralds the service of members of the Women's Army Auxiliary Corps.

sary for the country's aircraft manufacturers to design wings, propellers, and airplane fuselages for faster and more agile warplanes. Unlike at the military and naval facilities, the facility in Hampton hired African American as well as white women. Because of the nature of their work the white male officers referred to them as computers.

As during World War I, civilian Virginians worked extra hours to support their families and the war effort. They also faced restrictions on their personal freedom and could buy limited supplies of gasoline, tires, meat, and some other foodstuffs only with federal ration coupons. Because so many men were serving in the armed and naval forces, women took civilian jobs not usually open to them before the war. At defense plants women assembled munitions

V-J (Victory in Japan) Day in Hampton Roads

and sewed and packed and labored at jobs that the war created or that before the war had been the exclusive preserve of men. In spite of the demand for skilled labor, white women in Virginia made few lasting gains in employment as a result of the war. Employers usually paid women less than men, and when the war was over the jobs disappeared or men returned to claim them. Black women had fewer new opportunities than white women or lost them sooner.

The surrender of Germany in May 1945 and of Japan in September led to widespread celebrations in Virginia. During the following winter the rapid demobilization of the armed forces, the shutting down of many war industries, and the end of price and wage controls produced a brief but severe economic slowdown. The union movement, which had suffered from bad press during the war, particularly as a consequence of a wartime strike the United Mine Workers threatened in 1943, remained under fire after the war. In Virginia, when unionized employees of the Virginia Electric and Power Company went on strike in 1946, Governor William M. Tuck made use of a little-known provision of the state's militia law and placed the striking workmen on active duty in the unorganized militia, of which the governor was commander-in-chief.

Tuck ordered them back to work and broke the strike. The next session of the General Assembly passed a Right to Work Law that outlawed labor contracts that required all the people working for a company to be union members.

Thousands of soldiers, sailors, airmen, and marines returned home to Virginia and took advantage of the G.I. Bill of Rights, through which they obtained low-interest loans to buy houses. It also helped them continue or complete their educations. Many men who fought in the war might never have been able to afford to go to college without the G.I. Bill, and thousands of returning servicemen crowded into classrooms in Virginia's colleges and universities.

19

CIVIL RIGHTS

THE CAMPAIGN TO dismantle the racial segregation and discrimination of Jim Crow began long before the 1950s when the Supreme Court of the United States declared unconstitutional state laws that required racial segregation in public schools. People everywhere began to take notice. The movement continued long after the 1960s when Congress passed several landmark civil rights acts and federal courts invalidated the poll tax and state laws against interracial marriage. The civil rights movement involved people in protests and street demonstrations, in acts of civil disobedience and terms in jail, in public debates and political campaigns, and in courtrooms. To an extent perhaps unprecedented in American history the success of the civil rights movement was as a consequence of legal battles. African Americans fought to persuade other Americans that institutional racism violated some of the fundamental moral and legal principles of the country. Making the moral argument they invoked the language of the Declaration of Independence that all men were created equal and were entitled to life, liberty, and the pursuit of happiness. Making the legal argument they relied on the Fourteenth Amendment to the Constitution that granted Congress authority to guarantee that states provide all people equal protection of the laws and not deprive any people of life, liberty, or property without due process of law.

Religious and civic leaders, political activists, journalists, and lawyers provided leadership in the movement, but of equal or greater importance were the thousands of students, teachers, and parents who directly attacked Jim Crow, especially in public education. More of the critically important court cases of the civil rights movement arose in Virginia than in any other state. And advocates were fortunate that some of the ablest and most persistent civil rights lawyers in the country practiced in Virginia. More than in any other state, the civil rights movement in Virginia was a courtroom drama.

Gaining Momentum

The Double V of the African American community during World War II—victory against the nation's enemies overseas and victory against discrimination at home—was not an innovative goal. Black veterans returning from World War I had been similarly energized. The streetcar boycotts of the first decade of the twentieth century were the most conspicuous but not the only means by which people opposed Jim Crow. In 1939 Samuel Tucker, destined for a distinguished career as a civil rights attorney, began the Virginia campaign for equal access for African Americans to public facilities. After the public library in Arlington County refused him service because he was black he staged one of the country's first sit-ins. He and several friends entered the library and refused to leave. Their sit-in did not force the county to desegregate the library, but Tucker pioneered a technique that other civil rights activists used with great success in the 1950s and 1960s.

Also in 1939, Norfolk science teacher Aline Elizabeth Black filed suit in federal court to force the school district to pay black teachers on the same scale as white teachers. The school board fired her for initiating the court case. Another teacher, Melvin O. Alston, pursued the legal action and won a judgment in federal court that the Norfolk school board had to grant equal pay to black and white teachers with equal qualifications and experience. The ruling did not apply to other cities and counties, and teachers elsewhere in the state had to press for equality in their own districts.

Virginia State College historian Luther Porter Jackson, who researched and wrote pioneering books on African American history, urged fellow African Americans to engage in politics. In 1934 he founded the Petersburg League of Negro Voters, which became the Virginia Voters League, the only statewide organization of black voters. Jackson worked to persuade men and women to register and vote. For a time during the 1940s he wrote a weekly column entitled "Rights and Duties in a Democracy" for the Norfolk *Journal and Guide* to educate people about African American history and to encourage black voting. State laws gave voter registrars wide latitude to refuse to register people who did not fill out registration forms properly or who did not accurately answer questions registrars posed concerning their eligibility. In a May 1948 newspaper column Jackson quoted voter registrars he had polled about black voters in their districts. In answer to the question, "How many Negroes registered with you in your precinct during 1947?" one of them replied: "I have 3 men and 2 wimming." Another replied, "Their wosent any."[1] Jackson used the replies to condemn the state's electoral system for permitting such obviously unsuitable registrars to be allowed to decide who could vote. Jackson believed that with proper preparation, accurate knowledge, and courage black men and women could register to vote.

The stirring rhetoric of national unity during World War II and the terrible example of Japanese and Nazi racism and the Holocaust added a sense of moral power and urgency to the long struggle for civil rights for African Americans. They won an early legal victory in 1946 in the case *Morgan v. Commonwealth of Virginia*. Irene Morgan filed suit in federal court after she was arrested for refusing to sit in the back of the bus as she rode home to Baltimore from her mother's house in Gloucester County. The Supreme Court ruled that state laws that required segregated seating on interstate bus lines were excessive state burdens on interstate commerce and therefore unconstitutional.

Black veterans returned home from the war and were determined to win full citizenship rights. They and community leaders led campaigns to register black voters in several places during the 1940s. For the first time since the 1890s, African American candidates won election to local governing bodies. William Lawrence won election to the Nansemond County board of supervisors in 1947, and civil rights attorney Oliver W. Hill won election to the Richmond City Council in 1948. Four black men conducted unsuccessful campaigns for the General Assembly in 1949. In 1950, using the federal courts, Gregory Swanson became the first African American student at the University of Virginia when he enrolled in the law school.

In 1948 the Democratic National Convention adopted a platform that promised federal action to reduce racial discrimination. President Harry S. Truman had issued orders to desegregate the armed forces and to ensure fair employment practices for racial minorities. Hostile legislative leaders in Virginia almost succeeded in keeping Truman's name off the presidential ballot that year. Enough of them supported the segregationist governor of South Carolina, Strom Thurmond, rather than Truman for president that the Democrats almost lost the state for only the second time since 1872. The state's small number of African American voters, having been abandoned by the Republican Party early in the twentieth century and favorably impressed by the policies of the Roosevelt and Truman administrations, may have provided Truman's margin of victory in Virginia in 1948.

The outbreak of war in Korea in the summer of 1950 brought about the activation of Virginia national guard and reserve units, several of which served overseas and were involved in the fighting. Nearly a thousand Virginians died during the three years of the Korean War. Because the armed services were then desegregated, the black and white Virginians who served in Korea had what was probably their first exposure to living and working in constant close contact with each other in an environment that required them to depend on each other and be treated more nearly equally than at any previous time. Desegregation of the armed services was one of the first demonstrations of the power of the federal government to make changes in American culture.

Public Schools

Schools became the focal point of civil rights litigation, in part because of the gross inequalities of schools for children of different races and also because students, parents, and teachers forced the issue. Nearly all schools for African Americans had buildings, books, libraries, and laboratories that were inferior to those in schools for white children. Teacher preparation was often inferior, and teacher pay in those schools was almost always below the standards for white schools. In some rural counties school boards provided buses to transport white children to school but provided none for black children. In at least one such county parents pooled their resources to purchase a bus for their children.

Percy Casino Corbin, of Pulaski County, filed suit in federal court to force the county to provide better facilities for his children and not require them to travel long distances to an inferior Jim Crow school. In 1949 a federal judge ordered the county to provide more-nearly equal educational opportunities for African American children. The judge refused to make the county end the racial segregation that the state's constitution required. Instead, he merely ordered the county to provide substantially equal educational facilities for children of both races. The federal court ruled that the "separate but equal" practice the Supreme Court endorsed in its 1896 ruling in *Plessy v. Ferguson* required approximate equality to justify separation.

In April 1951 African American students in Prince Edward County's Robert R. Moton High School forced a full-scale assault on the whole legal system of racial segregation. Under the leadership of sixteen-year-old Barbara Johns they went on strike to protest the poor quality of their badly overcrowded school. Johns and the other students enlisted the aid of Oliver Hill and Spottswood Robinson Jr., then partners in a Richmond law firm that specialized in civil rights litigation, to file a lawsuit in federal court to challenge the constitutionality of the state's policy of mandatory racial segregation in public schools. Hill's old law school classmate Thurgood Marshall, head of the legal defense office of the National Association for the Advancement of Colored People (NAACP), argued *Davis v. County School Board of Prince Edward County* together with similar cases from other states and the District of Columbia in the Supreme Court of the United States.

On May 17, 1954, the Supreme Court unanimously declared in the combined cases, styled *Brown v. Board of Education of Topeka, Kansas,* that mandatory racial segregation of public schools was unconstitutional. Chief Justice Earl Warren went beyond the separate-but-equal doctrine and posed the legal question: "does segregation of children in public schools solely on the basis of race, even though the physical facilities and other 'tangible' factors may be equal, deprive the children of the minority group of equal educational opportunities?" He answered, "We believe that it does. . . . We conclude that, in the field of public education, the doctrine of 'separate but equal' has no place. Separate educational facilities are inherently unequal."[2] The following year the court ordered that states begin desegregating schools "with all deliberate speed."[3]

Governor Thomas B. Stanley and most other state officials reacted cautiously to the unanticipated Supreme Court decisions. Senator Harry Flood Byrd insisted that the state's political leaders mobilize public opinion in the South to block implementation of the court orders. Byrd called for massive resistance, and James J. Kilpatrick, editor of the Richmond *News Leader,* proposed that the state interpose itself between the power of the federal government and the people of the state to obstruct desegregation. Interposition had been discredited as a legitimate constitutional doctrine since the 1830s, but Kilpatrick argued for it strenuously, and many white political leaders in Virginia used his arguments to devise laws and tactics to prohibit school desegregation.

Public debates became heated. Newspaper editors took sides, political leaders tried to amass support for various proposals, and the state government sought a legal strategy to block enforcement of the court orders. People also wrote letters to editors and even to the governor to demand that he take action in accord with their personal views. The governor, though, listened to Byrd more closely than he did to more moderate constituents. People who proposed some limited, or token, desegregation that might satisfy a southern federal judge found themselves ostracized.

Emboldened African Americans increased their criticism of Jim Crow in the wake of state resistance to desegregation and used some of the same language of citizenship rights freedmen had used after the Civil War. One such man, Robert Leon Baker, wrote bluntly to the governor, "Virginia is no place for a colored citizen like me to live in. I am denied many rights and privileges by law that I should have. Virginia is the home of presidents but it is not the home of democracy. It is the home of white supremacy. The colored people (most of them) can hardly live decently in the South. . . . The South certainly did lose the Civil War. Now is the time for us colored people to rise up and demand our rights and first class privileges as citizens should always have."[4]

The General Assembly passed laws to deny state aid to any public school that placed white and black pupils in the same classroom and to harass members of the NAACP who supported racial desegregation. When the school board in Arlington County, which was the only elected local school board in the state, decided to allow limited desegregation the assembly revoked the citizens' right to elect their school board. In 1958 the assembly empowered the governor to close any public school that desegregated.

Opponents of school desegregation called their policy "massive resistance." Later, after the tactic was discredited, some supporters of massive resistance stated they were merely buying time, not trying to deny African American students their rights. But that was not true; they called their policy massive resistance, not massive wait-a-minute. Massive resistance was initially popular with many white Virginians, but when implementing it threatened the public schools, support began to weaken. In several cities white people formed committees to urge schools to comply with the Supreme Court rulings in order to preserve public education. Their actions were not unlike those of the biracial Readjuster coalition in the 1870s and 1880s that sought to preserve funding for public schools. Business leaders in some communities, particularly in Norfolk, also organized to pressure the city to desegregate its schools so as not to drive away potential new businesses. And some communities discovered that the political controversy about desegregation made it difficult for them to borrow money for important projects, including erecting necessary new schools.

In September 1958, Governor James Lindsay Almond Jr. closed public schools in Front Royal, Charlottesville, and Norfolk that had admitted some African American students. That denied education to about thirteen thousand Virginians, most of them white. Closings in Richmond and northern Virginia appeared imminent when, in January 1959, the Virginia Supreme Court of Appeals and a United States District Court both ruled that the massive resistance laws were unconstitutional. After one last defiant speech Almond broke with the Byrd organization and called the General Assembly into special session to repeal the massive resistance laws. By a margin of one vote the Senate passed the repeal bill, and the House of Delegates also passed it. Many of Virginia's white political and educational leaders nevertheless engaged in a campaign of noncompliance or accepted some minor token desegregation in order to delay or limit wider desegregation.

The public schools Almond had closed reopened, but in Prince Edward County the local government in effect abolished the public school system by stopping all funding for public education. White parents created a system of private schools for white children only, and the county appropriated tax revenue collected from both white and black taxpayers for the private white schools. Some African American students attended makeshift classes in their neighborhood churches, and others left the county to go to school elsewhere, but most black children were entirely deprived of schooling until 1964. Even after the county, under another order from the Supreme Court of the United States, reopened the public schools, most of the county's white children attended racially segregated private schools. The poorly equipped, poorly funded, and overcrowded public schools were almost entirely black when they reopened. After losing several years of their education, the black students who returned to school in the mid-1960s were behind their grade levels and without the educational assistance they required to catch up. Some of them lost as much as a decade of schooling.

Almost all of Virginia's white daily and weekly newspapers supported the failed policy of massive resistance more or less vigorously until the school closings began. However, Reuben Edward Alley, editor of the state's influential Baptist periodical, the *Religious Herald,* and Aubrey Neblett Brown, editor of *Presbyterian Outlook,* urged calm acceptance of the Supreme Court's decisions. Most other white clergymen vacillated or reacted cautiously to the challenges they faced when they had to decide whether to endorse, denounce, or keep quiet about federal orders to desegregate, about how to comment on the moral issues that racial segregation posed, and what to do when members of their congregations urged them to take differing positions on the issue. Few of them openly favored an end to racial segregation. It is unclear whether, had a significant number of the state's clergymen done so publicly and from their pulpits, the process of racial desegregation in Virginia might have been different.

Catholic schools in the state demonstrated that desegregation was not necessarily difficult or divisive. A few days before the first *Brown* decision, the Diocese of Richmond ordered that all the parochial schools in the state be desegregated. The priest who directed the parochial schools in Norfolk had already quietly and peacefully desegregated an elementary school.

Lenoir Chambers, then editor of the Norfolk *Virginian-Pilot* and author of an admiring biography of Stonewall Jackson, earned a Pulitzer Prize for two 1959 editorials that condemned massive resistance and the school closings. He was one of the few white journalists in Virginia to be so bold and critical. "So far as the future histories of this state can be anticipated now," Chambers wrote in the first of his celebrated editorials, "the year 1958 will be best known as the year Virginia closed the public schools. . . . The punishment of innocent children is too severe. The desertion of a doctrine of education on which democracy itself rests runs too much against basic American convictions and beliefs, many of which originated or first found nobility of expression in Virginia. The damage in prestige is too grave. The loss in business, in commerce,

in industry—in a state that just begins to realize that it has lagged in new efforts in these respects—is too costly even in prospect and in early results. It
would be disastrous in the long run."[5]

Chambers had seen some other consequences in Norfolk, which had been
attempting to change its raucous wartime image. Using federal urban redevelopment money the city began to rebuild itself but without regard to the
consequences for African Americans. Project Number One of the Norfolk
Redevelopment and Housing Authority cleared nearly fifty acres of African
American housing. Project Number Two began after the Supreme Court's
1954 ruling against mandatory racial segregation in public schools. Mayor
Fred Duckworth arranged for the housing authority to demolish a wartime
housing development called Broad Creek Village and more than two hundred
acres of bars, flophouses, and burlesque theaters that had given the city a bad
reputation. Before Project Two was completed eighteen months later the city
had cleared more than eight hundred acres of land and destroyed the homes
of about 20,000 people. The city and its housing authority provided no replacements for the residences destroyed, and many of the city blocks remained
vacant for decades. Duckworth had ordered the mass demolition of the neighborhoods to destroy two communities in which black and white families lived
in close proximity to prevent federal courts from forcing the people who lived
there to send their students to desegregated schools. After Project Two was
completed, there were no neighborhoods, there were no students, and there
were no schools to desegregate.

Most of the Byrd organization's leaders continued to fight against federal
enforcement of desegregation. Rather than improve the state's few small colleges for African Americans and make separate education equal or allow African Americans into the state's all-white universities, they offered scholarships
to black Virginians to attend integrated universities outside the state. In the
short term, the state avoided federal court orders to desegregate its universities, but the policy had an ironic and unintended consequence. Many African
Americans took advantage of the scholarships to attend graduate programs
and obtain advanced degrees at northern universities that offered graduate
education superior to what the state's better-paid white teachers could obtain
in Virginia's all-white colleges and universities.

Despite the court rulings and congressional legislation, school desegregation proceeded slowly in Virginia and elsewhere in the South. Officials
in some localities successfully ignored court orders for years. In Amherst
County, where Monacan Indians had always been excluded from the white
public schools and refused to attend the inferior schools provided for black
children, public school officials did not allow Monacan students into the
public schools for several more years. After the school board relented, white

school bus drivers still sometimes refused to stop and pick up Monacan students. The children had to walk several miles each way to and from school or miss school entirely.

In 1968 the Supreme Court in another Virginia case, *Green v. County School Board of New Kent County,* required that localities demonstrate actual progress in desegregation. The pace of change then quickened. Under court orders school systems in some cities began busing students out of their neighborhoods in order to desegregate the schools in the district. Busing was very unpopular with white parents in many parts of Virginia, and they organized private academies and schools and withdrew their children from the public schools. Busing also accelerated the movement of white families away from the cities and into the county suburbs, in effect resegregating the city schools they left behind. In 1973 the Supreme Court rejected a plan to bus students from adjacent counties into Richmond's city schools, and the resegregation of urban schools continued, as in most of parts of the country. Despite the hot rhetoric and anger of many white parents, actual desegregation in most parts of Virginia occurred with relatively little disruption. That is not to say that white students always openly welcomed black students. They sometimes subjected them to harassment or made them feel unwelcome; but the widespread violence some advocates of racial segregation predicted did not take place.

Demanding Civil Rights

For the most part, perhaps because many of the issues the civil rights movement raised became courtroom dramas in Virginia, the state avoided violence on the scale that some other states experienced, but some serious confrontations took place. In February 1960 African American students at Virginia Union University organized sit-ins at some of Richmond's downtown lunch counters. The arrest of thirty-four of the students was an important event and eventually led to the desegregation of the lunch counters. Several African American women then picketed two fashionable downtown Richmond department stores. Police broke up the demonstration and arrested the women. A photograph of policemen and their dog dragging Ruth E. Tinsley through the street appeared in newspapers throughout the nation and in the widely read *Life* magazine. Tinsley's husband was a member of the board of the NAACP, and she was an advisor to its youth group. About the same time students at white Randolph-Macon Woman's College and black Virginia Theological College, both in Lynchburg, jointly conducted sit-ins at local drugstores and were arrested. Sit-ins African Americans conducted in Greensboro, North Carolina, at about the same time attracted much more national attention.

Arrest of Ruth Tinsley in Richmond, February 1960; photograph by Malcolm O. Carpenter

The most violent event of the movement in Virginia occurred in June 1963 in Danville following student protests at city hall against segregation and discrimination. Police beat some of the students and arrested them for violating a 1960 law (based in part on laws from slavery times) that made it a criminal offense "to incite the colored population of the state in acts of violence and war against the white population."[6] The demonstrators had clearly done nothing of the sort. A few days later, on June 10, police used firehouses to disperse demonstrators and beat both black demonstrators and some white women who supported the protestors. Many of them required hospital care or spent time in jail. Trials of demonstrators continued for months and drew to Danville some of the most talented civil rights attorneys in the state to assist local defense attorney Ruth Harvey, who was better known later by her married name, Ruth Harvey Charity.

In most cities and towns African American men and women formed local organizations or joined state or national organizations like the NAACP to improve neighborhoods and schools or to lobby local government for better sanitation or public services. Evelyn Thomas Butts became active in Norfolk community affairs during the 1950s. In 1963 she enlisted local African American attorney Joseph A. Jordan to challenge the constitutionality of the section of the state constitution that required payment of a poll tax as a prerequisite for voting. On her behalf, Jordan argued, "Deprivation of the right to vote, of whomsoever, by whatsoever means, including the imposition of a poll tax penalty, is inherently repulsive to democracy, and has been too long tolerated by the citizens of Virginia."[7] It was an engine of racial discrimination, he continued, and therefore violated the equal protection clause of the Fourteenth Amendment. He lost the case in federal district court, but with the assistance of civil rights attorneys from Michigan and the District of Columbia Butts and Jordan appealed to the Supreme Court of the United States.

Arrest of demonstrators in Danville, June 1963

In the meantime, Annie E. Harper, of Fairfax County, and three other African Americans challenged the constitutionality of the Virginia poll tax in state court and also lost. They filed their appeal to the Supreme Court before Butts and Jordan filed theirs. The court combined the two cases and heard oral arguments of counsel in January 1964. The attorney general of the United States supported their cases by arguing that the poll tax was illegal under the new Voting Rights Act of 1965. On March 24, 1966, the Supreme Court ruled in *Harper v. Virginia Board of Elections* that the poll tax as a prerequisite for voting was unconstitutional. That decision, the Voting Rights Act of 1965, and the Twenty-fourth Amendment to the Constitution of the United States, ratified in 1964, that banned the poll tax in federal elections, together abolished one of the most effective means by which southern states had disfranchised African Americans—and in Virginia, under the Constitution of 1902, a great many poor white Americans, too.

In 1967 the Supreme Court declared that state laws that prohibited inter-racial marriage were unconstitutional. As with many other landmark cases, this one also arose in Virginia. Mildred Jeter, of mixed European, African, and Rappahannock ancestry (and therefore "colored" according to the 1924 Act

After barriers to registration and voting were eliminated, African Americans eagerly took the opportunity to register and vote, as in this scene in Portsmouth.

to Preserve Racial Integrity) had married a white man, Richard Loving. They were married in Washington, D.C., because the Racial Integrity Act prohibited marriage between white and "colored" people in Virginia. The law also prohibited mixed-race couples from living together in Virginia as wife and husband even if they had married in a place where mixed-race marriages were legal. They were arrested in their Caroline County home and convicted of violating the law. The presiding judge suspended their jail sentence on condition that they never live together in Virginia. In effect, he banished them from the state.

The Lovings resided for a time in Washington, D.C., but eventually they quietly returned to Virginia. Arrested a second time and with legal assistance they appealed the conviction. The Virginia Supreme Court of Appeals refused to overturn the circuit judge's order, and they appealed to the Supreme Court of the United States. In *Loving v. Virginia* the court ruled in 1967 that in spite of a very long tradition of allowing states to regulate conditions of marriage, the right to marry was a fundamental human right that the Constitution of

Mildred and Richard Loving

the United States protected. The decision made laws against interracial marriage invalid throughout the country.

Those important court decisions as well as actions of Congress provoked much controversy in Virginia, as elsewhere. Such white supremacist organizations as the Defenders of State Sovereignty and Individual Liberty—the Virginia counterpart of the more violent White Citizens Councils in other states—mobilized public opinion to delay or obstruct implementation of federal laws and court orders. Many of the most influential political leaders in the state condemned actions of Congress and the federal courts. Senator Harry Flood Byrd and almost all the southern members of both houses of Congress signed the Southern Manifesto against desegregation. Like opponents of desegregation elsewhere, they blamed outsiders (members of Congress, federal judges, and national civil rights organizations such as the NAACP) for the federal government's intrusion into what they regarded as matters within the sole control of the states. In truth, though, the court cases that arose in Virginia were the work of Virginians who challenged Jim Crow laws; and the strong opposition to the civil rights movement in the South, including much revolting violence, ultimately generated political support for stronger congressional action.

Opponents of desegregation also attempted to prevent supporters of civil rights from exercising political power. They even authorized voter registrars to issue blank registration forms to African Americans and to people of uncertain political loyalty. The state constitution and voting laws required applicants to fill out the form in their own handwriting and without assistance. By issuing a blank piece of paper the registrar in effect required each applicant to know in detail what information to supply and what to omit, which effectively prevented a great many people from registering and voting. Blank forms were not new. In 1945 a white professor at Virginia Union University in Richmond recalled his first encounter with the blank form and how the registrar told him what to write on the blank form, which was a violation of the law. Later, the professor wrote, "an African American professor asked me what was required to qualify one to participate in elections. I told him to go to the office of the city registrar, as I had done. He did so and came back to give me this story of what happened: He asked to register and was given a plain slip of paper as I had been. He was not told what to do with it. He asked the clerk what information was desired and was told, 'If you know enough to vote, you know enough to register.' He did the only thing he could do. He walked out."[8]

Byrd and Representative Howard W. Smith, of Alexandria, chair of the House Committee on Rules and the most powerful member of Congress from Virginia, tried to delay but were unable to prevent passage of the Civil Rights Act of 1964 and the Voting Rights Act of 1965. The Civil Rights Act derived its constitutional authority in large part from the Fourteenth Amendment and Congress's wide power to regulate interstate commerce. The law required places of business to serve customers regardless of race and placed many restrictions on the ability of private people as well as state and local governments to discriminate on the basis of race. In another of the ironies of Virginia history, Smith offered an amendment to the Civil Rights bill to outlaw unequal treatment of women as well as of African Americans. He believed that congressmen from outside the South who favored equal treatment of white and black men would never agree to equal treatment of men and women and would therefore vote against the bill. To his astonishment the amendment passed. Its language had precisely the opposite effect he intended. Smith accidentally advanced women's rights without wishing to do so.

The 1965 Voting Rights Act outlawed the poll tax and placed under federal supervision states with histories of racially discriminatory electoral practices. The law prohibited states from changing electoral districts or election laws in ways that could work to the disadvantage of minorities and granted the Department of Justice broad powers of enforcement. Together, the court decisions and the acts of Congress gradually eroded rigid segregation in housing, education, employment, and public services. After about three quarters of a century without political influence black Virginians were again able to register and vote in large numbers. Evelyn Butts, for example, who had filed one of the suits against the poll tax, founded the Concerned Citizens for Political Education and helped African Americans register to vote in Norfolk. In 1968 she supported the successful campaign of her former attorney, Joseph Jordan, for the city council. Butts later served on the Norfolk Redevelopment and Housing Authority and on the State Board of Housing and Community Development.

Jim Crow died hard. Generations of habits and prejudices durably outlasted changes in laws. In the field of public education, for instance, long-established patterns of mandatory residential segregation left individual schools racially segregated. White families who disapproved of desegregated schools often sent their children to more-expensive private schools. From the 1950s to the 1970s the number of private or church-sponsored private academies increased in and near urban areas. That and what was usually referred to as "white flight" of people from cities to suburbs left city schools largely black. One result of the creation of white academies and white flight was that fewer citizens had a strong personal motivation to support improvements in public education.

In August 1971, Governor A. Linwood Holton and his wife Virginia "Jinks" Holton decided to send their four children to the racially desegregated Richmond public schools rather than to a private school or an all-white county school. A photograph of the governor escorting one of his daughters to school was on the front pages of newspapers nationwide. More than fifteen years after the Supreme Court's decision the Holton family's actions showed how slowly desegregation of public education had proceeded, largely because of white resistance.

Holton was the first Virginia governor to serve under a new state consti-

Governor A. Linwood Holton escorting Tayloe Holton
to school in Richmond, August 1971

tution voters ratified in 1970. Some of its provisions brought Virginia law into alignment with reforms of the civil rights era. The new constitution omitted the clause that required racial segregation in public schools. It declared that all children in the state had a right to a high-quality education in the public schools. It omitted the poll tax as a prerequisite for voting, and it also declared, "the right to be free from any governmental discrimination upon the basis of religious conviction, race, color, sex, or national origin shall not be abridged, except, that the mere separation of the sexes shall not be considered discrimination."[9]

Gains and Losses

African Americans made important gains in politics following passage of the Voting Rights Act of 1965. They registered to vote and won election to office throughout the state. As elected members of city councils and county boards of supervisors and as appointed members of school boards and planning commissions, African Americans became important actors in local and state politics for the first time in three quarters of a century. In 1967 William Ferguson Reid, a Richmond-area dentist, won election to the first of three consecutive two-year terms in the House of Delegates. He was the first African American member of the General Assembly since the 1890s. The first African American member of a governor's cabinet, and also the first woman cabinet officer in Virginia, was Dr. Jean L. Harris, secretary of Human Resources from 1978 to 1981 during the administration of John Nichols Dalton. Thereafter, every governor's cabinet included both African Americans and women.

African Americans slowly increased their membership in the General Assembly. In 1991 two black men and one black woman sat in the Senate of Virginia and five black men and two black women in the House of Delegates. Following the 2019 legislative elections fourteen African Americans served in the hundred-member House of Delegates and four in the forty-member Senate of Virginia. In 1992, after a major realignment of the state's congressional districts, Robert Cortez "Bobby" Scott, of Newport News, won election to the House of Representatives. He was the second African American congressman from Virginia and the only one in the twentieth century. The first black member of the Senate of Virginia in the twentieth century, Lawrence Douglas Wilder, of Richmond, won election as lieutenant governor in 1985. In 1989, Wilder became the first African American in the United States elected governor of any state. He took the oath of office and began his four-year term on January 13, 1990.

On the other hand, after people began enforcing the public accommodations section of the Civil Rights Act of 1964 some African American business owners lost customers to white-owned businesses that had previously refused to serve or hire black men and women. Several of the historically black commercial districts in the state's cities and towns consequently declined in importance. Moreover, even though African American involvement in municipal government increased, African American communities remained vulnerable to destructive public policies. What happened in Norfolk when the city razed black neighborhoods to prevent desegregation was unique, but in other cities urban renewal projects altered the landscapes of Virginia cities with ill consequences for African American neighborhoods. In Newport News early in the 1960s city officials and the board of the new Christopher Newport College selected a downtown site for the campus that required the demolition of a small African American neighborhood. That forced its residents to relocate and doomed plans of a local black developer to enlarge the neighborhood with construction of more middle-class residences for blacks.

Later when the government constructed a spur of Interstate Highway 81 to link Roanoke's city center to the main highway in the Valley the road cut a swath through Gainsboro, the city's oldest African American neighborhood. Similarly, the 1950s design for Interstate Highway 95, which passed north and south through Richmond, and the 1960s design for Interstate Highway 64, which passed east and west through Richmond, merged the two high-speed highways for several miles through the heart of Jackson Ward, the oldest and largest African American neighborhood in the state. The highways bisected the remnants of a once-thriving community and hastened the decay of the whole area. In the 1970s Richmond added a downtown expressway that cut through, divided, and partially destroyed other working-class black and white neighborhoods. It also bulldozed a poor black neighborhood called Fulton without providing replacement housing for the people forced to leave and also without rebuilding the community. Little wonder that in many American cities African Americans understood the words "urban renewal" to mean "Negro removal."

Resistance to the end of Jim Crow segregation affected nearly every community in the state, sometime in large and conspicuous ways and sometime in small and petty ways. The city of Petersburg, for instance, closed Willcox Lake in Lee Memorial Park to swimming rather than have to allow black people to swim there with white people. Danville refused to allow black people to use the public library, which was in the former residence of a tobacco baron that Jefferson Davis occupied for a short time in the spring of 1865 as the last government building of the Confederacy. The city threatened to close the library but left it open after a court stipulated that the city had to allow African Americans to use the library but could forbid them from sitting down in it.

The civil rights movement was both a democratic and a democratizing event in Virginia. It was democratic in that students, teachers, and parents initiated many important lawsuits and organized demonstrations and boycotts. They organized local protest marches, conducted sit-ins to gain access to places of business that had denied them service, and campaigned to mobilize public opinion. In the beginning, they pushed further and faster against racial segregation than the state's principal civil rights organization, the NAACP, wished to move. The civil rights movement was also democratizing in that it brought into the political process many people who had been disfranchised or excluded from participation in public life.

In addition to the many courageous but otherwise ordinary people who moved civil rights to the center of the political stage, a number of leaders emerged whose talents, energies, and achievements made them, together, some of the most successful reformers in Virginia's history. W. Lester Banks, for example, executive secretary of the state's NAACP from 1947 to 1976, challenged racial segregation in public transportation and public education and boldly drove around the state in pursuit of equality and justice with the letters NAACP as conspicuous as a bull's-eye on the rear window of his automobile. Clergyman L. Francis Griffin, of Farmville, provided critical leadership to African Americans during the Prince Edward County school closings. Virginian Wyatt Tee Walker was a longtime close adviser of Martin Luther King Jr. and the Southern Christian Leadership Conference.

Civil rights attorneys braved opposition and often worked pro bono. Samuel W. Tucker, Spottswood W. Robinson Jr., Henry Marsh, Leonard Holt, Oliver W. Hill, Joseph Jordan, Roland J. Ealey, Edward Dawley, Ruth Harvey Charity, and Victor J. Ashe were the best known of the attorneys. Robinson, a Richmond native who taught at Howard University's law school in Washington, D.C., became the first African American federal judge in the United States in 1964. Charity, who practiced in Danville, became the first African American woman from Virginia to serve on the national committee of the Democratic Party. Hill was the dean of civil rights attorneys in Virginia. He grew up in Roanoke but had to move to Washington to attend high school because there was no public high school open to African Americans in Roanoke. A law school classmate of Thurgood Marshall, Hill was one of the first black men elected to public office in twentieth-century Virginia. He and Robinson led the legal team that prepared *Davis v. Prince Edward County* for argument in the Supreme Court of the United States, one of the cases decided in 1954 as *Brown v. Board of Education*. Hill practiced law into the 1990s and outlived all the other Virginia civil rights attorneys.

On July 21, 2008, the state unveiled a monument in Capitol Square to honor the men, women, and children of the civil rights movement. Lisa Collis, wife of Virginia governor Mark Warner, organized the fundraising for the

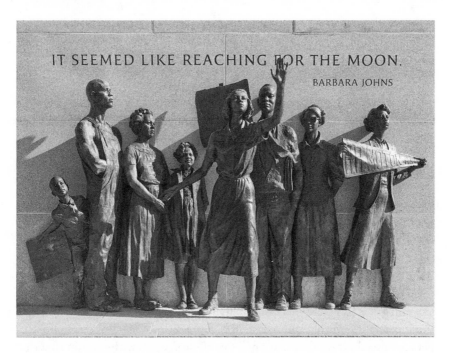

IT SEEMED LIKE REACHING FOR THE MOON.
BARBARA JOHNS

Civil Rights Monument in Capitol Square, Richmond

monument after her daughter asked why the statues around the Virginia Capitol did not include Rosa Parks, whom she had studied in school. Parks was a resident of Alabama, not Virginia, but the question gave Collis the idea of a memorial to the people of the civil rights movement in the state. It features likenesses of Barbara Johns, who organized the student strike in Prince Edward County in 1951, and of Oliver Hill and Spottswood Robinson, the attorneys the students recruited to represent them.

20

SUBURBAN STATE

I N 1949 THE FEDERAL government created an analytical model called the Standard Metropolitan Statistical Area for compiling and studying data on urban areas with densely populated suburbs. The new concept reflected a new reality. By the middle of the twentieth century the people of the United States were increasingly living in cities or their suburbs. Life in those places was visibly and measurably different in many ways from life earlier and elsewhere on farms, in small towns, or in cities without suburbs. That was the case in Virginia, too. The urban cores of the cities of Virginia at mid-century were comparatively small by the standards of most North American cities, and most Virginia cities already possessed spreading suburbs. The 1950 census showed that the population of Virginia was about 3.3 million people, and thereafter suburban areas exhibited by far the greatest population growth. During the 1950s the number of Virginians who lived in cities and suburban areas first surpassed the number who lived in small towns and rural areas. Virginia skipped from being a predominantly rural and small town state to being a predominantly suburban state.

World War II accelerated the pace of change in Virginia, in particular with the spread of suburban developments around the state capital in Richmond, near the naval and shipbuilding areas of Hampton Roads, and in the rapidly growing residential communities near Washington, D.C. The G.I. Bill of Rights, which supported returning service members who wished to continue their educations after the war, also allowed them to obtain low-interest loans to buy houses. An increase in private home ownership and automobiles made it possible for many more Americans families to have their own suburban houses and yards and to drive to their jobs in the city centers or in manufacturing or office complexes. Businessmen and real estate developers created suburban shopping centers that featured clusters of supermarkets, department stores, and other retail outlets. They were more convenient to residents of the suburbs than the remaining neighborhood markets or downtown retail districts that had been central commercial features of cities in the nineteenth century and first decades of the twentieth. Those changes began in the larger population centers of Virginia and spread during the decades after World War II to all the state's cities and larger towns.

Municipal Government

Several Virginia cities responded to the population changes that took place after World War II by annexing entire neighboring counties to allow more efficient provision of essential government services. The process began in Hampton Roads, where the city of Hampton merged with, or absorbed, Elizabeth City County and the town of Phoebus in 1952. The city of Newport News merged with Warwick County in 1958. In 1963 the city of South Norfolk and Norfolk County merged to form the new city of Chesapeake, and in the same year the city of Virginia Beach absorbed Princess Anne County. The rural county of Nansemond received a city charter in 1972 and merged with the small city of Suffolk in 1974. Each of the named counties became extinct with the merger. Other Virginia cities annexed densely populated portions of neighboring counties during the same years.

The capital city of Richmond annexed a large portion of suburban Chesterfield County in 1970 through a judicial process that did not allow residents of either jurisdiction an opportunity by referendum to approve or disapprove the annexation. A group of the city's African Americans filed suit in federal court alleging that the annexation violated the Voting Rights Act of 1965. The law had placed states with histories of racial discrimination in voting under federal supervision and prohibited alterations in voting laws and jurisdictional boundaries injurious to minorities that had been victims of discrimination. The Richmond suit charged that the annexation was illegal because its purpose was to add about 47,000 white people to the population to prevent Richmond from becoming a majority-black city. During the course of the trial it became obvious that at least some of the white city council members who negotiated the annexation had in fact intended it as a technique to preserve a white voting majority in the city.

The court ordered a moratorium on elections in Richmond until all the legal issues could be settled. Between 1970 and 1977 the city held no municipal elections. Despite the white council members' intentions, in 1977 African Americans won a majority of seats on the Richmond city council, and it elected Henry L. Marsh the city's first black mayor. Marsh was a civil rights attorney and a partner in the law firm of Oliver W. Hill and Samuel W. Tucker. Marsh later served in both houses of the General Assembly. The first African American mayor of a major Virginia city had been Hermanze Fauntleroy, who became mayor of Petersburg in 1973.

Richmond retained the annexed area because its attorneys convinced federal judges that the resulting increase in the city's tax base was by itself a sound justification for the annexation. A long-term consequence was that in 1979 the General Assembly granted the city's neighboring counties of Chesterfield and Henrico immunity from annexation, which froze the city's boundaries in place and eliminated the possibility that the city and its neighboring jurisdictions could emulate the examples of the cities and counties that had joined their resources for the overall benefit of the metropolitan area.

The physical appearance as well as the geographical size of the state's cities also changed after World War II. With money made available in part under the federal Housing Act of 1949, several cities implemented urban renewal projects. In their initial phases the projects destroyed dilapidated houses and places of business to make way for the construction of improved buildings and the development of better neighborhoods. Norfolk used some of that federal money in the 1950s to destroy neighborhoods without replacing housing rather than permit racial integration of public schools. Most of the state's cities, however, used federal money to construct low-rent housing projects to provide homes for poor working people and people without jobs. Unfortunately for many of the residents of those projects, concentrating poverty in certain areas concentrated crime and violence there as well.

Fairfax County grew into the most-populous jurisdiction in the state. Home of numerous large consulting firms and defense contractors, the county evolved differently from other Virginia suburbs. Instead of being largely a bedroom community whose residents commuted into the city, by the end of the twentieth century Fairfax County had several centers of office buildings among the residential areas throughout the county. Urban planners dubbed these "edge cities." In some respects Fairfax County physically resembled some cities in the western United States, which spread out over the landscape rather than built upward into the sky, as older cities such as New York and Chicago had done.

The Politics of Change

In those and many other ways, post–World War II Virginians lived in an increasingly interconnected national culture. They may have shared more with people in other states than they realized, but changing ideas created regional divisions within American society about race and racial segregation. In Virginia racial segregation had been both a legal mandate and a longstanding social and economic reality. Through the poll tax and complicated voter registration procedures put into place at the beginning of the twentieth century, the state's Democratic Party leadership maintained its control over the state government and most of the local governments in Virginia and enforced the state's racial segregation laws.

A few Democrats, who were called the Young Turks, together with some Republicans and African Americans, saw the restrictions on the suffrage as unjust or as an embarrassment to Virginia and tried without success during the 1940s to have the poll tax abolished. The Young Turks never defeated the political organization Senator Harry Flood Byrd controlled, but between the mid-1940s and the end of the 1950s they mounted several serious challenges to the organization. Democrats who resented Byrd's domination of the party or who sympathized with the Young Turks unified behind formidable challengers when he sought renomination in 1946 and 1952. They also opposed the organization's preferred candidates in the gubernatorial primaries of 1949 and 1953. By the mid-1950s the Republican Party was finally able to mount serious challenges to the organization's nominees for governor. Roanoke attorney and state senator Theodore Roosevelt "Ted" Dalton ran strong campaigns for governor in 1953 and 1957 by offering an alternative to Byrd's party rule and policies. In spite of the challenges, though, Byrd's organization never lost an

Storming the Bastille

On July 14, 1949, *Richmond Times-Dispatch* editorial cartoonist Fred Siebel depicted the Young Turks' campaign against the Byrd organization as an assault on a well-defended castle.

election for statewide office and maintained its overwhelming majorities in both houses of the General Assembly well into the 1960s.

The federal Voting Rights Act of 1965 and the abolition of the poll tax led to the demise of the Byrd organization. Some of the consequences of those changes quickly became obvious in the House of Delegates. Throughout the years 1950 to 1966 when Byrd's near neighbor and close political ally, Edgar Blackburn "Blackie" Moore, was Speaker of the House, he controlled the chamber with ruthless efficiently. He treated Young Turks and independent-minded Democrats as badly as he treated Republicans. Moore sometimes left them off committees entirely or appointed them to committees that seldom or never met or that met without their receiving any notification. Committees often killed their bills without giving the sponsors an opportunity to explain them. Following Moore's retirement, his successor, John Warren Cooke, relaxed the leadership's grip on the members. To the dismay of some veteran Democratic legislators Cooke appointed every delegate, including Republicans, to at least one important standing committee. Cooke's gradual reforms made the House of Delegates function more democratically but less efficiently. The legislative record beginning in the 1970s was of more contention and confrontation than before, a reflection of the divided opinions of the people of the state on major economic and social issues and the changing nature of the two political parties nationally.

One political leader more than any other exemplified the changes and continuities that characterized the state's political culture in the aftermath of the demise of the Byrd organization. Mills Edwin Godwin Jr. had been a leader of the massive resistance movement when he was a member of the Senate of Virginia in the 1950s, even though he had not been one of the organization's insiders. In 1961 he won nomination and election as lieutenant governor. Godwin recognized that the Byrd organization would not control state politics forever and that the failure of massive resistance indicated that racial segregation was not a sound platform on which to build the political future. He embraced a different political agenda. Godwin endorsed and campaigned for Democratic Party presidential nominee Lyndon B. Johnson in 1964. A large number of Byrd loyalists endorsed Johnson's Republican opponent, Arizona Senator Barry Goldwater, but Johnson won the state's electoral votes in 1964 and Godwin won the election for governor in 1965.

In Godwin's first message to the General Assembly in January 1966, he broke sharply with the Byrd organization's past orthodoxy and proposed a sales tax to support increased spending for public schools and other state programs. During his administration the state created a community college system that for the first time provided relatively inexpensive introductory college-level courses and professional occupational training to people

Mills Edwin Godwin Jr., governor of
Virginia 1966–70, 1974–78

throughout Virginia. The state also created several new colleges and universities to meet the needs of the rapidly increasing population. The Norfolk affiliate of the College of William and Mary, which opened in 1930, became an independent four-year college in 1962. Renamed Old Dominion University in 1970, it became the largest institution of higher education in southeastern Virginia and enrolled many more students than its parent, William and Mary, or the latter's new neighbor, Christopher Newport University, in Newport News. The Richmond Professional Institute, also once an affiliate of William and Mary, merged with the Medical College of Virginia in 1968 to become Virginia Commonwealth University. By the twenty-first century it was by far the largest university in central Virginia. The University of Virginia's separate campus in Fairfax County, created in 1948, gained independent status as George Mason University in 1972 and became the largest public university in northern Virginia. Older colleges also experienced significant growth during the latter decades of the twentieth century, most notably James Madison University, in Harrisonburg, and Virginia Tech, in Blacksburg.

Godwin recommended that the General Assembly establish a commission, with former governor Albertis S. Harrison as chair, to revise the Constitution of 1902. The bipartisan commission included civil rights attorney Oliver W. Hill. The commission submitted a detailed report to the assembly, which during the sessions of 1969 and 1970 rewrote the old constitution and submitted a revised constitution to the voters in a form known in parliamentary procedure as an amendment in the form of a substitute. Approved by a 72 percent majority of the voters on November 3, 1970, the constitution became effective

on January 1, 1971. It permitted the issuance of general obligation bonds if
voters approved them by referendum, increased the legislature's discretionary
powers, enlarged the governor's authority to direct the programs of state agencies, and explicitly guaranteed every Virginia child the right to a high-quality
public education. The new constitution also prohibited the poll tax and the
voter registration practices that had given the Byrd organization legal authority to dominate state politics. By then federal laws and courts had already made
illegal those and other techniques by which the political leaders of the state
had successfully discouraged voting.

The report of the constitutional revision commission included a long section on city and county government structure and responsibilities. The growth
of suburbs during the second half of the twentieth century imposed many new
responsibilities on county governments. The commission recommended and
the General Assembly added a new section to the constitution to authorize
the formation of regional governmental authorities that federal grant legislation made popular during the 1960s. That enabled groups of adjacent local
governments to cooperate effectively and efficiently in matters of regional importance. The legislators accepted most of the commission's recommendations
about regional governmental authorities.

Assembly members rejected the commission's suggestion that the new constitution modify the relationship between the state government and the localities by abolishing or significantly reducing reliance on a legal doctrine known
as the Dillon Rule. Named for a nineteenth-century federal judge who from
the bench and in a treatise on municipal government expounded the doctrine,
it stated the reality that institutions of local government had no inherent powers of their own but derived their powers from state constitutions and state
laws. From the earliest days of the colony, the General Assembly had created
counties and towns, granted or denied them authority to exercise specific responsibilities, and afterward overseen county and city governments closely.
As twentieth-century legislators and courts applied the rule, no county or
city government in Virginia could exercise any responsibility not specifically
granted to it in the constitution, a city charter, or by state law. That meant, in
effect, that the limited city charters and the similarly restrictive language of
statutes gave the General Assembly ultimate authority over a great many aspects of local government.

Virginia was one of only a few states that applied the Dillon Rule strictly.
The majority of the members of the constitutional revision commission believed that application of the rule inhibited local initiative and thwarted
democracy at the community level. The members of the General Assembly
refused to relinquish state control over local governments and did not incorporate into the new constitution any language that required change in the

way in which the state's legislators and judges applied the Dillon Rule. At every legislative session nearly every county and city lobbied the assembly for authority to change local laws and practices. Some of their requests were remarkably minor, which illustrate how little independent authority the Dillon rule allowed local governments. In 2003, for instance, the assembly passed a law at the request of several school districts to allow the districts to display on their school buses decals of American flags "no larger than 100 square inches."[1]

For all of the innovations in government and politics that occurred during Godwin's administration from 1966 to 1970, he was a man deeply committed to many traditional Virginia practices and policies. He accommodated himself to changed circumstances but never became a progressive reformer comfortable with the beliefs of the men and women who assumed national leadership of the Democratic Party in the 1960s and 1970s. A significant portion of Virginia Democrats shared Godwin's perspective and had become accustomed by then to voting for Republicans for president and for Congress but continuing to elect to the General Assembly Democrats who shared their opinions. That allowed the state's Republican Party, which had revived under the leadership of Dalton during the 1950s, to seize the initiative and win local and legislative elections by emphasizing the party's state and national opposition to the national leadership of the Democratic Party. From 1952 through 2004 Republican candidates won every presidential election in Virginia but one. Republicans profited from the disintegration of the old Byrd organization and the unpopularity among many Democrats of the liberal leaders of the national party. Augmented by those conservative Democrats, Republicans won a majority of the state's seats in the House of Representatives during the 1970s, and in 1972 Republican William Lloyd Scott won election to the United States Senate, making him the first Republican senator from Virginia since William Mahone in the 1880s.

After President Dwight Eisenhower appointed Dalton a federal judge, leadership of the Republicans fell to another southwestern Virginian, A. Linwood Holton. Dalton had made the party a strong and progressive alternative to Byrd's Democrats, but in spite of Dalton's opposition to massive resistance, on the whole he favored the racially segregated society in which he lived all of his life. Holton was not only much more progressive than Byrd's Democrats, he was more progressive than Dalton and favored desegregation and actively sought African American support in his campaigns for the General Assembly and when he ran for governor in 1965 and 1969.

In 1969 Holton won election as governor, the first Republican in a century. In 1972 he pushed through the General Assembly an act that established the state's first formal cabinet system. It placed state agencies and programs under the administrative control of cabinet secretaries appointed by and responsible

to the governor. Holton extended the reforms begun during Godwin's administration and attracted nationwide attention when he and his wife enrolled
their children in Richmond's racially desegregated public schools. Holton's
four-year administration represented as sharp a break with the state's political
past as had Godwin's. His open and unaffected acceptance of African Americans into his party and administration set a notable example in the South
when the struggles of the civil rights movement were still taking place. Partisan
opposition to Holton from Democratic remnants of the Byrd organization in
the General Assembly and differences of opinion within the Republican Party
about whether the future of the party was to be a progressive or a conservative one prevented Holton from as thoroughly reshaping Virginia politics as
he had hoped. Nevertheless, his election and administration were among the
most important in the second half of the twentieth century.

When Holton was elected governor, Democratic candidates won election
as lieutenant governor and attorney general. Thereafter both Democratic and
Republican candidates won election to the three statewide offices. Voters exhibited an increased willingness to split tickets, and on some occasions they
voted for Republicans in presidential elections and for Democrats in ensuing
legislative and gubernatorial elections. Republicans usually won a majority of
the state's congressional elections and during the 1980s began to make serious
inroads on the Democratic Party's overwhelming majorities in the two houses
of the General Assembly, even though they were at a severe disadvantage in
legislative elections because of Democrats' partisan gerrymandering of legislative districts.

The state's Republican Party gradually became more conservative, and the
state's Democratic Party gradually became more progressive. Within five years
of Byrd's death in 1966, reform-minded Democrats, including even some former Byrd loyalists, transformed the party and accepted the newly enfranchised
African American voters. Henry E. Howell, of Norfolk, an attorney and one
of the most progressive Democrats in the state, won a special election in 1971
to succeed Lieutenant Governor J. Sargeant Reynolds who had died in office. Howell had been one of the few white political leaders in southeastern
Virginia who defended the rights of African Americans during the 1950s and
1960s. He was unusual in twentieth-century Virginia politics, the opposite
of Godwin in nearly every way. Godwin projected a solemn, dignified, reserved demeanor, as if imitating a traditional nineteenth-century Virginia
gentleman. Howell spoke loudly and plainly; he challenged political practices
that he thought unfair; and he denounced many of the state's leading business
corporations because he believed that they exploited working people or, in
the case of public utilities, overcharged them. In 1973, Howell ran for governor and lost to Godwin, who recognized again and correctly anticipated the

changes that were taking place in the state. Godwin joined the Republicans in 1973 and won a second term as governor. Politically, the state was more closely divided than at any time since the Funder-Readjuster contests of the 1870s and 1880s.

Social and Cultural Changes

The 1960s and 1970s were decades of rapid social change and much unrest. In addition to the civil rights movement, the nation's involvement in the war in Vietnam that began early in the 1960s and lasted until 1975 contributed to the turmoil. The increasing unpopularity of the war during the second half of the 1960s, particularly among college students and young men who were vulnerable to conscription, produced violence and student strikes on some university campuses and an alienation, called the generation gap, between young protestors and older Americans who had difficulty understanding the skepticism and hostility toward national political leaders that many students embraced.

A large number of University of Virginia students participated in an antiwar moratorium (staying away from class) in October 1969. Edgar Finley Shannon, the president of the university, displeased the protesting students by trying to limit the event, but he also displeased members of the board of visitors and political leaders by not cracking down on them harder. In May 1970 when even more students went on strike to protest the deaths of students during an antiwar rally at Kent State University in Ohio, Shannon outraged conservatives and pleasantly surprised many of the students by speaking at their rally and condemning the way the president of the United States conducted the war. Nearly 1,500 Virginians were killed during the war.

Changing roles of women in American society also changed Virginia. In 1950 the General Assembly allowed women for the first time to serve on trial juries and in 1952 on grand juries. Three years after the end of World War II, six women in the Dickinson County mining town of Clintwood ran against the six men on the town council. Charging that the men paid scant attention to the needs of the town's residents, the women won the election, astonishing nearly everybody and gaining them a brief national notoriety. They were not the first women to win local elective office in Virginia, but they were pioneers in a trend that slowly spread during the ensuing decades. The process was slow. In 1955 the mayor of Suffolk resigned after a woman won election to the city council. He declared insultingly that he would "not serve on the same City Council with a woman."[2] Slowly, though, and in the face of considerable opposition, much of it blatantly hostile, from white men who regarded politics and government as their exclusive domain, women entered public life in increasing numbers. The first Virginia woman to serve as mayor of a major city was Eleanor P. Sheppard, who was mayor of Richmond from 1962 to 1964. She later served in the House of Delegates.

Kathryn H. Stone won election to the House of Delegates in 1953, the first woman elected to the assembly since 1931. Following her victory, numerous women of both parties sought election to public office at all levels of government. Many of them became involved in politics attempting to keep public schools open during massive resistance. Others entered politics as a consequence of the women's movement of the 1970s and 1980s that, hard on the heels of the civil rights movement, produced both controversy and change. All of those women faced resistance of various kinds. Even after half a dozen women won election to the House of Delegates in the 1960s and 1970s, the men who retained large majorities in both houses of the assembly delayed installing a restroom for women in the Capitol. Some of them treated the women legislators condescendingly or rudely or subjected them to sexual innuendoes or demeaning insults. Early in 1980 the Speaker of the House of Delegates kissed a lobbyist in the privacy of an elevator, following which several other women, including some members of the assembly, complained publicly about a wide range of insulting and abusive behavior. "The legislators treat you much nicer when you go visit their homes or home district offices," another woman lobbyist stated. "But boy, you get them in Richmond, and it's like one big fraternity party or locker room. . . . And juvenile, they are *SO* juvenile."[3]

In increasing numbers women sought higher education during the twentieth century, and in 1970, after more than half a century of intermittent pressure, the state first allowed women to enter the undergraduate programs of the University of Virginia. They, too, sometimes faced discrimination or harassment. Even before women entered the undergraduate classes at the university, some of the professors and many of the male students treated the few women in their graduate classes rudely or contemptuously or ignored them completely. The men's resistance to the inclusion of women in academic and other roles formerly reserved exclusively for males indicated how firmly entrenched traditional gender roles remained in Virginia during the second half of the twentieth century.

The women's movement gained momentum in the 1960s and became increasingly important during the 1970s. Like the woman suffrage movement fifty years earlier, the women's movement in Virginia was at first largely a white, urban, middle- or upper-class movement. The National Organization for Women, founded in 1966, was one of the most formidable advocates of women's rights in the workplace and in politics. As was the case with the civil rights movement, many of the most significant changes in the lives of Virginians that took place as a consequence of the women's movement came about as a result of acts of Congress and rulings of the federal courts.

One aspect of the women's movement that attracted wide attention and created much controversy arose from innovations in birth control technology. With relatively safe and convenient measures of birth control available, many women postponed having children, entered business and the professions, and worked hard to advance their careers. The birth control pill, first made legally available in 1960, was part of a larger cultural change within American society that enabled women to exercise more control over their personal lives. In addition, women made new demands on traditional health insurance providers, and some of them filed lawsuits to assert or defend their legal rights. Alice C. Cook, for instance, a married lieutenant commander in the Navy Nurse Corps in Norfolk, was forced to resign her commission after she became pregnant in 1966. She sued for reinstatement and back pay in hopes of procuring a court decision that her dismissal was unconstitutional. She eventually settled with the navy, but her case and others like it forced the Department of Defense to stop involuntary discharges of pregnant women.

The Equal Rights Amendment, which Congress submitted to the states for ratification or rejection in 1972, provided the focal point for the women's movement in Virginia. Several women's organizations united in a protracted, sometimes bitter, and ultimately unsuccessful campaign to win ratification in Virginia. Conservative men held most of the seats and all the leadership positions in the General Assembly. In the House of Delegates they refused to bring the ERA out of committee for a vote on the floor, and in the Senate they employed parliamentary maneuvers to prevent it from passing. Opposition to fully equal treatment of women was deeply entrenched in the state. Some Virginia women also opposed the ERA and argued that earlier reform legisla-

Members of the National Organization for Women were arrested in Capitol Square on February 10, 1978, when they protested the General Assembly's refusal to ratify the Equal Rights Amendment.

tion that benefited women could be jeopardized if the amendment were ratified. In January 2020 the assembly ratified the ERA.

A clause in the Virginia Constitution of 1970 that resembled the ERA
in substance, though not in wording, was never allowed to take full effect.
The Supreme Court of Virginia ruled in *Archer and Johnson v. Mayes et al.* in
1973 that the clause in the constitution of Virginia could not be interpreted
to permit women more rights in Virginia than the Constitution of the United
States, which had no such clause, permitted all American women. In effect,
the twentieth-century state court turned on its head the nineteenth-century
court's reliance on traditional states' rights doctrine. Instead of insisting that
Virginia courts should interpret Virginia constitutions and laws irrespective
of what federal courts decided, the Supreme Court of Appeals allowed federal
court decisions to set limits on the state's court and denied Virginia women
full legal equality with men. The judges who issued that unanimous ruling
were all men. Elizabeth Lacy, the first woman to serve on the court, took office
in 1989, sixteen years later.

It is perhaps both ironic and symbolic of the traditional conservatism of
Virginia's political leadership that the first woman to win election to the Senate of Virginia was an opponent of the ERA. Eva F. Scott, a small-business
executive from Amelia County, who had served in the House of Delegates,
won election to the Senate as a Republican in 1979. In 1985 Delegate Mary
Sue Terry, of Patrick County, was elected to the first of two consecutive four-
year terms as attorney general, the first woman to win election to a statewide
office in Virginia. She was the unsuccessful Democratic Party candidate for
governor in 1993. In 1992 Delegate Leslie Byrne, of Falls Church, was elected
to the House of Representatives, the first woman member of Congress from
Virginia and the only Virginia woman to win a seat in Congress during the
twentieth century. Following the legislative elections of 2019, thirty women
served in the hundred-member House of Delegates and eleven in the forty-
member Senate of Virginia. Even with an increase in the number of women
elected to the House of Delegates that year, the number and percentage of
women legislators remained, as it had been throughout the previous decades,
below the national average.

The women's movement changed society in many ways that did not require changes in the law or personal participation in politics. Among many
examples, through cooperative community action, women were able during
the final decades of the twentieth century to establish secure safe houses for
battered women in many places. Some city governments eventually provided
support for shelters, but not always initially. Prior to the late twentieth century spousal abuse and marital rape had almost never been prosecuted or even
regarded as crimes. At the same time, as more women entered the paid work-

force, they and their families and neighbors created new nursery schools and child-care centers. For the most part, women made changes in society and culture long before laws and public policies caught up with the new social realities.

One of the most conspicuous achievements of the women's movement in the twentieth century was a successful challenge in federal court to the state's policy of admitting only men to Virginia Military Institute. The Supreme Court of the United States in its 1996 decision in *United States v. Virginia* ordered that women must be allowed to enroll as cadets because VMI was a public university and under federal law could not discriminate on the basis of sex. The decision provided dramatic evidence of how much Virginia changed during the twentieth century and of how much that change was a result of, or part of, national changes and actions of the federal government. Admission of the first women to VMI was generally smooth and peaceful without any of the problems that occurred in similar circumstances elsewhere, as at the Citadel in South Carolina.

One other issue of continuing public controversy, linked in many people's eyes to the women's movement, had political, moral, and religious dimensions. Abortion had been illegal in many parts of the United States until the Supreme Court's 1973 decision in *Roe v. Wade* declared the medical procedure a constitutionally protected personal right. Many activists in the women's movement believed in a woman's right to chose whether to continue or terminate a pregnancy, and they applauded the decision and mobilized in order to defend access to abortion in Virginia and elsewhere. The practice of aborting fetuses was morally unacceptable to a large portion of Virginia's population, and political leaders in the state repeatedly made access to abortion a political issue in campaigns and introduced bills in the General Assembly to regulate or reduce the practice. The right-to-life movement, of which those efforts were a part, was a national phenomenon, and it directly linked state and national political campaigns and produced heated public debates and many intense legislative struggles. Geline Bowman Williams was chair of the board of directors of the National Right to Life Committee for many years and was also mayor of Richmond from 1988 to 1990.

Abortion became one of the defining political issues of the 1970s and 1980s, and it continued to be a hot political topic well into the twenty-first century. Church leaders of several denominations opposed abortion for religious reasons. Two Virginia religious leaders gained enlarged national attention and followings in part as a result of their opposition to abortion. Jerry Falwell, a Baptist minister in Lynchburg, and Marion G. "Pat" Robertson, an evangelical minister in Virginia Beach, had already become perhaps the most famous Virginians of their time as a result of their pioneering radio and television ministries. Robertson produced and syndicated his own television show, *The 700 Club,* and Falwell was reported at one time to enjoy the largest national audience of any clergyman for his televised sermons from Thomas Road Baptist Church. Both men spoke out against abortion and on many other moral and cultural issues, helping frame the public debate on a number of fundamentally important state and national issues. They both also created new universities—Liberty University in Lynchburg and Regent University in Virginia Beach—that offered religiously based higher education. Falwell formed a national political organization, the Moral Majority, in 1979, and Robertson campaigned unsuccessfully for the Republican presidential nomination in 1988.

Era of Big Government

Few aspects of Virginians' lives were insulated from the economic and social changes that took place elsewhere in the United States and the world. The expansion of the role of the federal government in the lives of all Americans that began in the 1930s and expanded during the 1950s and 1960s affected public education, health care, retirement planning, workplace safety and fairness, and transportation, to name but a few. Enormous and enormously expensive public welfare and healthcare programs such as Medicare and Medicaid, for example, changed the relationships between elderly or infirm people and their families and made possible the large retirement and nursing home complexes that by the end of the twentieth century were to be found in nearly every Virginia community. Federally mandated programs that led to the establishment of those facilities at the same time placed new financial responsibilities on state and local governments, which shared in the cost and administration. An increasingly large part of the state's budget was devoted to the care of the elderly and infirm and of people of all ages with health problems and inadequate income or insurance coverage. The involvement of public agencies and the expense required completely dwarfed the comparatively meager public health and welfare agencies that ministered to a small proportion of the state's population early in the twentieth century.

The benefits of those and similar social service agencies were of great importance to thousands of Virginia families, but the expense of supporting them was large, and it progressively increased. The federal government imposed additional requirements on the states in those areas as well as in education, requirements for which the states rather than the federal government often bore much of the financial burden. When federal subsidies fell or the national economy slowed and reduced state revenue, the effects on the state's budget were in some instances very dramatic and painful. Recessions that began in 1990, in 2000, and in 2008 reduced services on which many thousands of Virginians depended, and forced the state government to reduce or eliminate other programs in order to pay for those that federal law required it to administer. The state budget being in large measure dependent on revenue from income and sales taxes, economic hard times hit the state budget, the state's public employees, and the state's poor people hard.

It may be that the success that the conservative Republican Party had in Virginia in the 1980s and 1990s could be attributed in part to a reaction to the combined effects of all those pressures. In Virginia, as elsewhere, Republican candidates often blamed the federal government and its budget deficits and regulations for society's problems and for placing expensive responsibilities on state and local governments without compensating them adequately— commonly called unfunded mandates. Beginning in the 1970s, the state's Republican Party developed a superior organization to recruit candidates for local offices and the General Assembly, raise money, and mount effective campaigns. Richard Obenshain, one of the party's conservative leaders and a superb political organizer, earned widespread credit and praise for that organizational work. In 1978 he won the party's nomination for the United States Senate but died a few weeks later in an airplane crash while on a campaign trip.

Effective organization, adequate funding, and the popularity of such national conservative Republican leaders as Ronald Reagan all combined to enable Virginia Republicans to win an increasingly large number of elections. In 1997, for the first time ever, Republicans won election to all three major statewide offices—governor, lieutenant governor, and attorney general—and two years later for the first time won majorities in both houses of the General Assembly.

The centerpiece of the successful Republican campaign in 1997 was a promise to repeal the unpopular personal property tax on automobiles. Since the 1920s local governments, not the state, taxed personal property and real estate to raise money to support city and county governments and schools. Elimination of the tax on automobiles severely reduced the money available to local governments and required the General Assembly to compensate cities and counties for the lost revenue. Just as the gradual elimination of the car tax was being phased in, a serious slowdown in the national economy sharply reduced state revenue, which required deep cuts in many state programs to replace the revenue localities lost. Funding the tax cut cost much more than predicted, and the simultaneous reduction in revenue precipitated a major financial crisis in the state's budget in 2000. Even though the governor and the majority in both houses of the assembly were all Republicans, they struggled

Traffic in Northern Virginia, 2007

for months in an effort to balance the budget. An unanticipated consequence of reducing that tax on automobiles was an increased dependence of cities and counties on the state government for revenue.

Virginia's growing population and the concentration of people in the suburbs of Washington, D.C., around Richmond, and in Hampton Roads required construction of new roads and highways in addition to the interstate highway network the federal government constructed between the 1950s and 1970s. The Interstate system relieved congestion on the old routes based on the plan the General Assembly devised in the 1910s, but population increases and freight-hauling trucks later required widening of the highways between Richmond and Washington and between Richmond and Norfolk. Northern Virginia had the most congested roadways in the state. A multilane bypass, around the District of Columbia, part of Interstate Highway 95 and known as the Beltway, became famous by the 1970s for the traffic jams of commuters and long-distance drivers. A 2017 study by a West Coast consulting firm concluded that highway congestion in Northern Virginia was among the worst in the country and that commuters there wasted more time per capita in traffic jams than anywhere else.

Politicians of both political parties, however, were generally unwilling to raise taxes sufficiently to meet the transportation needs of the most densely populated portions of the state. One of the country's most famous road proj-

The Chesapeake Bay Bridge-Tunnel opened in 1964.

ects was constructed with an unusual means of financing. The 17.6-mile Chesapeake Bay Bridge-Tunnel opened in 1964. The bridge and its two tunnels under the sea-lanes provided for the first time a land transportation connection between Norfolk and the southern tip of the Delmarva Peninsula. A separate state corporation constructed and operated the bridge-tunnel and issued bonds and charged a toll to pay for construction and maintenance of the expensive traffic artery. Early in the twenty-first century the corporation had to construct a parallel set of lanes, bridges, and tunnels to carry the increasing traffic.

During the 1970s the city of Washington and the states of Maryland and Virginia formed a corporation to construct a commuter rail system for the national capital with feeder arteries into each state. The Metro system initially relieved traffic congestion inside the city, but because the lines into Virginia were not long they did not correspondingly improve commuter traffic problems in Virginia. In 1988 the state created the Virginia Railway Express to operate commuter trains into Washington along two lines, one from Manassas and the other from Fredericksburg. Trains began running in 1992 and within twenty-five years transported more than seventeen thousand people each day. Hampton Roads Transit opened a light rail commuter train along a 7.4-mile line from downtown Norfolk to the eastern portion of the city in 2011. The number of riders exceeded projections and appeared to justify high construction costs that many skeptics had believed unwarranted.

The Arts

The pervasive presence of music through radio, television, and the internet involved nearly all Virginians in the same cultural experiences available to other Americans. Some Virginians became famous recording artists or nationally known performers. Patsy Cline, of Winchester, performed throughout the country and recorded more than a hundred songs before her death at age thirty in an airplane crash in March 1963. She began singing in the same country music tradition as the Carter family but mastered other popular styles and became one of the country's most successful performing and recording artists. Cline's best-selling titles were "Walkin' after Midnight," "I Fall to Pieces," and "Crazy." Her fame endured after her death. Cline was the first solo performer inducted into the national Country Music Hall of Fame in 1973. The National Academy of Recording Arts and Sciences voted her a lifetime achievement award in 1995, and "I Fall to Pieces" and "Crazy" both later received Grammy Hall of Fame awards.

In Norfolk in the 1960s Frank Guida adapted calypso music, which he had performed while stationed in the West Indies during World War II, with propulsive horn flourishes, gospel-inflected vocal lines, and innovative recording techniques to create the ambience of a crowded party. Guida made a name for himself in rock and roll history with the Norfolk Sound. On his Legrand record label he released songs such as "Quarter to Three," "New Orleans," and "If You Wanna Be Happy" with talented local singers Jimmy Soul and Gary Anderson (Gary U.S. Bonds), saxophonist Gene "Daddy G" Barge, and the Church Street Five band.

In cities and towns with large universities, people had access to cultural amenities such as plays, art exhibitions, and classical music not readily available elsewhere. All the state's large universities had music and theater departments that presented performances of a very wide variety of productions. Other urban cultural organizations that rose to distinction during the second half of the twentieth century were the Richmond Symphony Orchestra and the Virginia Symphony, the latter founded in Norfolk and for many years known as the Norfolk Symphony. The Virginia Opera, founded in Norfolk in 1975, grew by the beginning of the next century into one of the largest regional opera companies in the United States. It presented full-scale opera seasons in Norfolk, Richmond, and at George Mason University in Fairfax County. Distinguished chamber music series in Richmond and Norfolk offered venues for some of the finest musicians in the world, and chamber music series in Fredericksburg and at Hampden-Sydney College provided residents of those smaller communities some of the same musical experiences. The Richmond Ballet evolved during the 1990s into a widely recognized ensemble that performed to high praise in New York several times as well as in London and China.

The national performing arts park, Wolf Trap, in Northern Virginia, presented jazz, country, blues, folk, and symphonic and operatic performances. The latter two genres were usually regarded as amusements of prosperous white people, but the two Virginia composers who received the most national attention for their symphonic and choral works during the latter years of the twentieth century were both African American: Adolphus Hailstork, who taught at Norfolk State University, and Undine Smith Moore, who taught at Virginia State University and was also an influential figure in American jazz.

The Virginia Museum of Fine Arts, in Richmond, created in the 1930s to house an art collection donated to the state, evolved into a large and distinguished institution with an eclectic collection. The museum also had its own theater program for many years and sponsored an art-mobile that toured the state to exhibit original works of art and to help adults and children develop their artistic talents. Enlarged several times during the ensuing decades, beginning in the twenty-first century the museum hosted the largest, most varied, and most important traveling exhibitions of art the state's people ever had opportunities to enjoy.

The Chrysler Museum, in Norfolk, developed from a local art gallery into a showcase for the art collection of Norfolk collector Jean Esther Outland Chrysler and her husband, Walter Chrysler. The Mariners' Museum in Newport News acquired an extremely distinguished collection of marine art, ship models, artifacts, maps, and charts that depicted and preserved records of maritime history. When the turret of the Civil War vessel *Monitor* was recovered from the floor of the Atlantic Ocean it went to the Mariners' Museum for restoration, preservation, and display. The Smithsonian Institution's vast Steven F. Udvar-Hazy air and space museum in Northern Virginia is the largest of its kind in the world and draws visitors from many countries. Those museums are among the state's cultural jewels.

Many commercially successful and critically acclaimed artists and writers worked in Virginia. Some of the state's writers and poets drew deeply on Virginia's land and people for their inspiration. William Styron, who grew up in Newport News, set several of his novels in southeastern Virginia, most notably his controversial *Confessions of Nat Turner,* a fictionalized narrative of the 1831 slave insurrection in Southampton County. Styron received the Pulitzer Prize for literature for that book in 1968. At Hollins College, the class of 1967 included the talented writers and literary critics Anne Goodwyn Jones and Lucinda Hardwick MacKethan and writers Annie Dillard and Lee Smith. They studied writing under Louis D. Rubin Jr., a prominent scholar

Poet Laureate of the United States in 1993–95, Rita Dove taught English at the University of Virginia.

of southern literature. While in college and during their subsequent careers, the Hollins group competed with and encouraged one another. Dillard won a Pulitzer Prize in 1975 for *Pilgrim at Tinker Creek,* a book set along a creek that runs near the campus. Rita Dove, who taught at the University of Virginia, became the first African American woman poet laureate of the United States in 1993.

Lee Smith's writing vividly embraced and described Appalachian Virginia. Raised in the southwestern town of Grundy and graduated from a Richmond high school, she published her first novel, *The Last Day the Dogbushes Bloomed,* in 1967. Her novels featured strong female characters who discovered ways to break free from some of the limitations southern society placed on women. Several of Smith's books were set in the mountains of southwestern Virginia and contained strikingly real depictions of Appalachian culture. Another writer who successfully created realistic Appalachian characters was Sharyn McCrumb, who moved to Virginia from North Carolina early in the 1980s to study writing at Virginia Polytechnic Institute and State University. She published her first novel, *Sick of Shadows,* in 1984. A prolific author, McCrumb refuted stereotypes of Appalachian people in her novels, especially in her Ballad Series.

21

COSMOPOLITAN STATE

THE WORD *cosmopolitan* came into widespread use in the nineteenth century and usually suggests to twenty-first-century readers a large measure of worldly sophistication. However, its original and more accurate meaning was that a person or phenomenon possessed characteristics of many parts of the world. The increasingly interconnected national and international economies of which Virginia was a part in the twentieth and twenty-first centuries together with demographic and cultural changes introduced many new cosmopolitan elements into Virginia's culture.

The National and World Economies

The federal government, with its thousands of employees in Northern Virginia and at naval and military bases elsewhere, became the largest single employer in Virginia by the end of World War II. State government employment thereafter increased more rapidly than the overall population as the General Assembly created or expanded programs in public health, education, air and water pollution control, and public safety. The pace of national and international economic integration increased during the final decades of the twentieth century and the first years of the twenty-first. An increase in the size and number of large retail outlet chains and a corresponding reduction in the number and variety of small, local retail businesses offered Virginia customers access to merchandise not previously available everywhere but restricted the ability of small manufacturing enterprises to market products to local shops or to sell to local customers through the large chains. The major urban banks in Virginia purchased controlling interests in smaller banks, and in turn even larger banks with headquarters outside Virginia purchased the large Virginia banks. Credit card companies also had their headquarters outside Virginia, meaning that for many of their purchases Virginians daily became involved in national and international economic transactions, many of them by virtually instantaneous electronic fund transfers.

As a result of the many federal installations in Virginia the state's economy became more dependent on government spending than in any other state. Federal spending provided jobs in the state, but occasional federal budget cuts consequently had unusually large negative consequences for Virginians. For decades the Central Intelligence Agency operated a training facility near Hampton, known as "the farm." The federal government's nearby Langley Research Center continued important aeronautical research begun during World War I. Very large wind tunnels allowed aircraft designers to test and refine their plans before beginning expensive production. During the 1950s and 1960s the National Aeronautics and Space Administration developed some key components of the manned spaceflight program there. The women who continued to work there after World War II included a large number of African Americans who were absolutely critical for computing the many variables necessary for manned spaceflight. A small rocket launching facility on Wallop's Island, on the Eastern Shore, grew in size and importance at the end of the twentieth century, and by the second decade of the twenty-first was able to launch large rockets that carried supplies to the International Space Station.

Newport News Shipbuilding and Dry Dock Company, which throughout the twentieth century was one of the state's largest private industrial employers, was more than once purchased by and then sold by an international conglomerate. Each purchase altered the relationship between the company and its employees and the Hampton Roads region. European and Asian firms cornered most of the world's market for building passenger and freight vessels during the final decades of the twentieth century, and the number of merchant ships flying the American flag radically declined. As a result, the company became for the most part a defense contractor that specialized in naval vessels.

By the end of the twentieth century in all of Virginia's cities and in most of its smaller communities national chain stores offered brand-name merchandise, sold prepared food, and provided people with essentially the same services and options Americans elsewhere had. Commercial advertising became a major factor in the creation and stimulation of markets for the products of national and international manufacturers. Some of the most profitable businesses in Virginia during the last years of the twentieth century were marketing and advertising firms that produced campaign materials in print, broadcast, and online formats for national and international firms. One consequence of the national integration of markets and of chain stores was the demise in Virginia of the Sunday-closing laws, or blue laws. Originally intended to prevent employers from forcing people to work seven days a week and in some instances to write one of the ten commandments into law, the Sunday-closing laws gradually fell victim to the forces and pressures of twentieth-century economic change.

The fast pace of change in electronic communications altered the ways in which Virginians lived and linked them more closely than ever to national and international markets and media sources. Electronic commerce became commonplace early in the twenty-first century and further involved Virginians in national and international transactions. From 1995 to 2007 the internet service provider AOL had its headquarters in Northern Virginia, and as a result a substantial portion of electronic mail and commercial transactions flowed through that Virginia nexus. Online commerce grew rapidly and drove many small firms out of business and endangered the large suburban malls that in the twentieth century had already put many small local shops out of business. Because of the reluctance of politicians to tax electronic commerce the same as governments for generations had taxed traditional buying and selling, the new mode of doing business online reduced sales tax revenue the state raised and relied on.

The governor and General Assembly recognized the emerging importance of technological innovation and in 1984 created the Center for Innovative Technology, a not-for-profit, semi-public institution with headquarters in Herndon. It assisted companies and institutions of higher education take advantage of emerging technologies in order to give Virginia a competitive edge in new markets. Initially hampered by an inadequate budget and inconsistent leadership, the center found its way in the 1990s under the leadership of Ronald Carrier, who was acting director while on leave from the presidency of James Madison University, and former governor Linwood Holton. The center encouraged research and promoted the economic development of Virginia through research grants and technology development centers at Virginia universities. It gradually increased the number and proportion of its grants to new businesses and also lured businesses from other states to Virginia.

The Virginia Department of Agriculture announced in 2004 that tobacco, which had been the most valuable cash crop in Virginia since John Rolfe introduced a West Indian variety to the colony 390 years earlier, was no longer the most valuable cash crop for the state's farmers. Soybeans took tobacco's place, followed by a mix of crops that well illustrated the varied commercial agriculture in Virginia at the beginning of the twenty-first century: tomatoes, small grains, hay, cotton, winter wheat, apples, peanuts, and summer potatoes. A slow but steady long-term decline in tobacco smoking and chewing in the United States after decades of public health warnings and the passage of laws to prohibit smoking in public places reduced demand for tobacco products in the country. At the same time, the largest tobacco manufacturing companies purchased more of their tobacco from less-expensive foreign sources. In

2004 the federal government began phasing out the tobacco allotment and price support systems put in place in the 1930s to stabilize the market for leaf tobacco. The last public tobacco auction in Virginia took place in Farmville in January 2005.

Another significant and symbolic event took place in 2005. Gujarat Heavy Chemicals Ltd. purchased Dan River Incorporated, the parent company of the once-thriving Dan River Mills, the largest of the textile mills in Danville, and announced that it would move production of textiles to India. The company had employed about 15,000 people in the Danville area at the time of World War II, but the loss of textile manufacturing jobs throughout the United States to factories in other countries reduced the number of textile workers in Danville to about 1,250 by the end of the twentieth century. Dan River Mills, once one of the largest and most successful industrial complexes in Virginia, filed for bankruptcy before the Indian company purchased it and was another casualty of international economic changes over which the firm's owners, managers, and employees had little or no influence. Most of the once-large and profitable furniture manufacturers in the Martinsville vicinity closed or moved out of state during the final years of the twentieth century, also the victims of changing international conditions. The regional economy fell into a deep and prolonged recession

Coal mining, too, declined in importance and employed fewer people at the end of the twentieth century than at the beginning, partly as a result of automation in the mines and increased, less-expensive production from mines in western states. Surface, or strip mining left large permanent scars on the face of the earth and contributed to pollution of the watercourses of southwestern Virginia. The United Mine Workers of America maintained a strong presence in the southwestern Virginia coalfields but could not exert as much leverage during contract negotiations on mining companies as in previous decades. Federal courts restricted the abilities of unions to maintain picket lines and use economic pressure tactics. Perhaps as a result of the inability of unions to be as effective, miners' frustration increased, and mine owners and operators sometimes reacted with force. In April 1989 violence erupted during a strike against the Pittston Coal Company at its mines on both sides of the Virginia-Kentucky border. The strike lasted nearly a year and was the most violent strike in Virginia in decades. The miners ultimately failed to achieve most of their objectives.

The chemical industry, in the meantime, grew into a major component of the state's industrial economy, with the largest facilities in Hopewell, Radford, and Richmond. Profitable though many of those businesses were, they exposed Virginians to new dangers. In 1975 the governor closed most of the James River between Hopewell and Hampton Roads to commercial and recreational fishing following disclosure that a decade of discharges of the powerful pesticide kepone (the commercial name of the chemical chlordecone) from a chemical plant in Hopewell endangered public health. The river remained closed to fishing for several years, and the toxic chemicals remained buried in the river's bottom sediment. A federal judge worked out a settlement between the chemical companies, workers whose health kepone had damaged, and the state whereby the parent company compensated the workers and contributed several million dollars to establish the Virginia Environmental Endowment. The endowment undertook research into air, water, and ground pollution and made important contributions to cleaning up contaminated sites and preventing pollution.

Other chemical and manufacturing plants elsewhere in Virginia also released toxic substances that poisoned rivers, polluted the air, and in some instances seriously endangered the public health. A huge pile of discarded automobile tires near Winchester caught fire in November 1983 and burned for months, which filled the air with acrid smoke and released toxic substances that melted out of the burning tires. In 1990 the state Department of Waste Management revoked the permit for a landfill in Alleghany County that leaked a mixture of rainwater and chemicals from decomposing garbage into the Jackson River. In 1999 the federal government declared it a Superfund site and began remediation in 2005. Virginia contained about one hundred Superfund sites. Periodic fish kills, perhaps caused by industrial discharges, in the Shenandoah River watershed became a serious concern after several consecutive massive kills beginning in 2004. If the fish died as the consequence of pollutants, their source or sources were not readily evident. If rising water temperature, runoff from farms, bacteria, or viruses were responsible alone or in combination, the remedy was not evident, either.

In the General Assembly and in the state courts, as in Congress and the federal courts, controversies about air and water pollution generated continuing public debate about interrelated issues involving economic development, public health, private property rights, and a host of environmental issues. Very large problems affected the Chesapeake Bay, the country's largest estuary and for centuries a bountiful food source for human beings. It suffered under pressure from increased marine traffic, runoff from farms and residential developments, and a rapidly increasing human population along the rivers that fed into the bay. One of the most serious problems was an increase in nitrogen and phosphorous in the water, probably from agricultural runoff. That produced algae blooms that depleted dissolved oxygen.

The most conspicuous evidence of deterioration of the bay was the rapid decline in the population of the bay's oysters. Oysters almost vanished late in the twentieth century as a consequence of poor water quality, disease, and

View of Chesapeake Bay from a satellite; U.S. Geological Survey

heavy harvesting. Virginia watermen had harvested as many as six or seven million bushels of oysters annually at the beginning of the twentieth century, and during the first half of the century between two and four million bushels. Late in the 1950s scientists first detected the parasitic diseases Dermo and MSX in the Chesapeake Bay. The commercial oyster harvest plummeted from 3,252,695 bushels in the 1959–60 season to an all-time low in 1995–96 of a mere 16,891 bushels. The economic consequences were disastrous for families who made their living from the water. The loss had other serious consequences, as well, because oysters are natural water filterers, and the disappearance of most of the oyster population aggravated water-quality problems in the bay and left vacant many oyster reefs that had provided important habitat for fish and crabs.

The Chesapeake Bay's blue crab population supported another important commercial and recreational fishery that was not as immediately vulnerable as the oyster. Nevertheless, scientists documented a large reduction in underwater grasses that were a critical habitat for part of the crabs' life cycle. The bay's crab population dropped drastically during the final decade of the twentieth century. The annual commercial harvest fell from more than 49 million pounds in 1990 to less than 26 million in 2000, but the population of crabs slowly increased thereafter. Several species of fish popular with recreational anglers and profitable for commercial fishermen also suffered population declines during the latter years of the twentieth century. That endangered commercial fisheries in the bay and throughout Virginia and put many Virginians out of work.

The Chesapeake Bay Foundation coordinated a bay recovery plan that relied on cooperation among the federal government, all the states in the bay's watershed (New York, Pennsylvania, Maryland, West Virginia, and Virginia) and the District of Columbia. Since 2000 the recovery led to a rebound in oyster and crab populations as well as in the underwater grasses on which many species of fish, shellfish, and waterfowl relied. Atlantic sturgeon had almost disappeared from the James River as a result of pollution, but early in the twenty-first century scientists discovered evidence of a breeding population, which indicated that the water had again become clean enough to nurture those specialized fish.

For much of the twentieth century the state government had regulated hunting and both freshwater and saltwater fishing. The great waves of ducks, geese, and swans that annually migrated from the north to spend the winter in the coastal regions of Maryland, Virginia, and North Carolina created an important local industry late in the nineteenth century. Commercial hunters harvested waterfowl for sale in local markets and to the cities of the north, and numerous residents of the coast and bay guided sport hunters and fishermen. Both commercial and sport hunting in Virginia became quite famous, and several lavish resorts catered to wealthy northerners, especially on the barrier islands of the Eastern Shore and at Back Bay in the southeastern corner of the state. In the 1910s, the General Assembly created a department to oversee wildlife in the state and eventually combined it with another that oversaw freshwater fisheries. The original departments and the later Department of Game and Inland Fisheries regulated hunting and fishing to preserve wildlife and fish populations, provide recreational opportunities for Virginians, and prevent commercial exploitation of freshwater fisheries that could endanger valuable fish populations.

The landscape of coastal Virginia graphically showed how much the area changed as the human population in the bay's watershed increased. Back during the colonial period ocean-going ships had anchored in protected bays and coves of the major rivers to unload immigrants and merchandise, to take on fresh food and water, and to load cargoes of tobacco. Erosive land-use practices changed Virginia's rivers and streams profoundly. By the beginning of the twentieth century deep-draft vessels could no longer ascend the Appomattox River to Petersburg, which had once been a busy seaport. The Pamunkey River at the site of the eighteenth-century port town of Columbia, in New Kent County, to which the General Assembly considered moving the capital of the colony in 1748, silted up so much that the town completely disappeared after commercial navigation became impossible. By the end of the twentieth century the water was so shallow at some of the old ports that even shallow-draft vessels could not reach them.

Beginning in the 1960s and 1970s the state government gave higher priority to air and water conservation, outdoor recreation, and protection of critical habitats. Private conservation efforts and federal projects undertaken under the Endangered Species Act led to the restoration of habitats for animal and plant communities. By the end of the twentieth century breeding populations of such highly visible species as bald eagles, osprey, and peregrine falcons had significantly rebounded. The new state constitution ratified in 1970 committed the state government "to conserve, develop and utilize its natural resources, its public lands, and its historical sites and buildings. Further, it shall be the Commonwealth's policy to protect its atmosphere, lands, and waters from pollution, impairment, or destruction, for the benefit, enjoyment, and general welfare of the people of the Commonwealth."[1]

The role of big government in environmental protection and the regulation of many other economic practices was always controversial. The schools of economics and law at George Mason University became nationally recognized centers of libertarian, free-market research and publication. Economist James McGill Buchanan published and spoke widely against the prevalent economic doctrines of John Maynard Keynes and other people who favored government intervention in the economy. Buchanan received the 1986 Nobel Prize for economics. Kansas billionaire Charles G. Koch provided funding for expanding the economics program at the university and well as for the law school and several other institutions and foundations, such as the Cato Institute, the Heritage Foundation, the Mercatus Center, and the American Legislative Exchange Council, that coordinated national opposition to and attempted to undermine the rationales and programs that throughout the twentieth century revolutionized American society and law. Koch's contributions become controversial because many of them were initially secret and also because members of organizations he funded sometimes had unusual opportunities to influence hiring practices and research agendas at the public university.

Terror

The twenty-first century began ominously for Virginians. The long economic boom of the 1990s collapsed into a recession. Disagreements in 2000 and 2001 among members of the General Assembly and between the governor and the assembly about taxes and spending priorities required reductions in public spending and cost many people their jobs. The state's budget problems increased after September 11, 2001. Terrorists that day crashed two hijacked passenger airliners into the World Trade Center buildings in New York City and another into the Pentagon across the Potomac River from Washington. A fourth airliner, probably also en route to Washington, crashed into a field in Pennsylvania. It was the first foreign attack on the soil of the United States since early in World War II. As a consequence, the national economy entered a brief recession, which seriously aggravated Virginia's existing economic problems.

Washington Post journalist Mary Beth Sheridan viewed the Pentagon a few hours after the airliner crashed into it and wrote, "The jet ripped a giant hole in the west side of the building near Washington Boulevard that stretched from the ground to the roof five floors up. At least four floors pancaked upon each other. Workers and neighbors stood staring in shock at the charred, smoke-wreathed building; one described it as looking like a doughnut with a large bite taken out."[2] The attack killed the 5 hijackers, 64 passengers and crewmembers, and 125 people in the Pentagon.

Like Americans elsewhere, Virginians were shocked and reacted with patriotic vigor. The day after the attack *Washington Post* reporter Marc Fisher noticed that American flags suddenly appeared nearly everywhere. Curious, he visited the headquarters of Alamo Flags in Falls Church. President Fawaz Ismail, a Palestinian who immigrated to the United States from Jordan as a child, told the reporter, "I'm a more proud American than I am a Palestinian."[3] Hearing that a local businessman had declined to pay $825 to purchase three hundred American flag pins to distribute to victims of the Pentagon terror, he provided them free of charge. Some other Virginians, like some other Americans, voiced resentment at people from the Islamic world after it became evident that the men who hijacked the airplanes and crashed them into iconic American buildings were all from the Middle East.

Another form of terror from a completely different source gripped the Blacksburg campus of Virginia Tech on April 16, 2007. A student with serious untreated mental health problems procured firearms and ammunition and killed thirty-two students and faculty members and wounded many more before he killed himself. At the time it was the largest death toll of any school shooting in United States history. Governor Timothy Kaine immediately returned from a trade mission to Japan and took part with President George W. Bush and poet Nikki Giovanni in a moving memorial service on the university campus a few days later. As with other mass killings elsewhere in the country, the tragedy at Virginia Tech called attention to the ease with which people of unsound minds could obtain lethal firearms; but also as with those other incidents neither the state government nor the federal government made any significant changes in laws respecting firearms, mental health, or campus safety.

Cosmopolitan Virginians

The inauguration of state officials in January 1986 and again in 1990 appeared to symbolize a new era of diversity in Virginia. In 1986 Gerald L. Baliles became governor, L. Douglas Wilder became lieutenant governor, and Mary Sue Terry became attorney. Wilder was the first African American elected to statewide office in Virginia, and Terry was the first woman. Four years later Wilder became the first African American governor of any state, Terry began her second term as attorney general, and Donald S. Beyer became lieutenant governor. At both inauguration ceremonies two men and one woman took office, and two white people and one black person. Until 2017 when Justin Fairfax won election as attorney general, however, no other African American won election to statewide office, and no woman did. The number of women and of African Americans in the General Assembly rose and fell. Following the 2019 election, Democrats had majorities in both houses of the General Assembly. Eileen Filler-Corn, of Fairfax County, became the first woman Speaker of the House of Delegates and the first Jewish Speaker. Charniele Herring, of Prince William County, became the first African American and the first woman to be majority leader of the House. Well before then, Leroy Rountree Hassell, the second African American to serve on the Supreme Court of Virginia, was the first black chief justice from 2003 to 2011; Cynthia Fannon Kinser was the first woman chief justice from 2011 to 2014.

Federal census figures for 1990, 2000, and 2010 documented major changes in Virginia's population. Immigrants from other states and countries became a large and important component of Virginia's population, more so than at any other time in its history. The change was swift. The 1970 census recorded that only about 1 percent of Virginia's residents were foreign born, but in 2010 the proportion was about 11 percent. And unlike the immigrant populations from earlier in the colony's and state's history, large numbers of the new residents came to the United States from Mexico, Central America, and Asia, especially the Philippines, Korea, and Vietnam. The state's population became more diverse culturally, ethnically, religiously, politically, and economically than it had ever before been.

The immigration was visible in most communities, often in the form of ethnic markets, grocery stores, and restaurants. Immigrants concentrated in Northern Virginia, where by 2012 an estimated 23 percent of all the residents had been born in another country. Immigrants from other states also continued to crowd into Virginia, often to work for the federal government or for

On January 13, 1990, L. Douglas Wilder, Donald S. Beyer, and Mary Sue Terry took the oaths of office as governor, lieutenant governor, and attorney general.

any of the many defense contractors and consulting firms that proliferated in Hampton Roads and especially in Northern Virginia. Census enumerators probably underestimated the number of people who resided temporarily in Virginia throughout the twentieth century and into the twenty-first. Migrant laborers were essential to the profitable agricultural economy in many parts of the state, particularly in the fruit orchards in the northwestern counties and in the vegetable-growing regions in eastern Virginia and on the Eastern Shore. A large proportion of migrant workers and of immigrants who entered the United States illegally—often referred to as undocumented aliens—were probably of Hispanic origin, which suggests that in some seasons Hispanics made up a larger proportion of the state's total population than official figures indicated. Spanish-language signs appeared throughout the state beginning in the 1990s, a recognition of the size and importance of the state's Hispanic population. But population estimates made in 2007 indicated that for the first time immigrants from Asia were probably more numerous in Virginia than Hispanics and Latinos.

Another conspicuous evidence of the cultural diversity of Virginia early in the twenty-first century could be seen in the increasing variety of places of worship, the many synagogues, mosques, temples, and churches in nearly every community. Dar Al Hijrah, in Falls Church, was one of the largest mosques in the United States when it was completed in 1991 to serve the many thousands of Muslims in Northern Virginia. Fifteen years later, approximately 40,000 Muslims resided in the area that it served. In some cities, church buildings originally erected for Catholic or Protestant congregations became mosques or centers of worship for one of the many Pentecostal Christian congregations that dramatically increased in number in the latter years of the twentieth century and the early years of the twenty-first.

Suburbs throughout the state grew, some very rapidly during the final decades of the twentieth century. Some old urban areas lost population, and the state's rural and small town populations declined in most regions. The most conspicuous changes in the state's population were in its diversity and the concentration of people in the suburban communities around Richmond, in Hampton Roads, and especially in Northern Virginia.

The characteristics of the population of Virginia changed dramatically beginning in the final decades of the twentieth century. The culture consequently changed, too. In many respects those changes paralleled changes elsewhere in the country. One of those changes—one of the most controversial—was open acceptance in some places of people whose sexual preferences did not conform to traditional heterosexual norms. Gay men, lesbian women, bisexual people, and transgender people (born with the body of one sex but with the gender identity of the other) emerged out of self-protective secrecy and into the open. LGBT communities in cities, in particular, provided comfort and security in a social culture that did not always or immediately accept their lifestyles.

A series of 1990s lawsuits brought issues relating to gender and sexuality into sharp relief. Sharon Lynne Bottoms lost custody of her own son to her mother, who filed for sole custody of the boy on the grounds that Bottoms's sexual relationship with another woman, April Wade, made her an unfit mother. The Virginia Supreme Court overturned a lower court's ruling. Another judge, for other reasons, later removed custody of the boy from Bottoms and returned him to the child's grandmother.

Critics of the changes in sexual mores persuaded the General Assembly to propose an amendment to the state constitution to make same-sex marriages unconstitutional. In 2006 the General Assembly proposed and the voters ratified an amendment to the Virginia constitution that prohibited same-sex marriage and all civil unions that approximated marriage or gave the parties the same legal rights and privileges as married people. One of several nationally important lawsuits involving same-sex marriage arose in Virginia as a consequence of that amendment. In 2014 a federal judge ruled in *Bostic v. Schaefer* that the amendment violated the Constitution of the United States, which since the 1967 Virginia case *Loving v. Virginia* had declared marriage a constitutionally protected human right that states could not infringe. She stated that marriage was a personal, human right that states may not infringe without showing a compelling reason. The state had not done that, she declared. Indeed, the attorney general refused to defend the state's laws and policies. The federal Court of Appeals upheld the decision, and the Supreme Court of the United States declined to reconsider. Even though the amendment remains in the Virginia constitution, it cannot be legally enforced.

People who lived in the different regions of Virginia shared in most of the changes that took place during the decades after World War II, but economic changes affected each region differently. In southwestern Virginia, the loss of jobs in the coal industry led to a long period of economic hardship and high unemployment. Large numbers of the people lived on public relief in the early decades of the twenty-first century because they could not afford to leave or did not wish to leave, and few businesses offered alternative employment. So, too, with the collapse of the furniture manufacturing and textile industries in the southern Piedmont. A traveler who visited the different regions of the state early in the twenty-first century could see some of the same landscape features that the first people saw thousands of years earlier, but in some places mining, lumbering, or intensive agriculture had significantly reshaped the landscape.

In other places, suburban sprawl had obliterated or so significantly modified the landscape that it could no longer be recognized. Because each place had its own unique history and changed in its own way, each town and county, each city, and each region had its own character. Living in southwestern Virginia was a very different experience than living in the Shenandoah Valley, which was different than living near the North Carolina border or near the Chesapeake Bay. The same might be said about almost any place in Virginia and especially about the heavily suburbanized appendages of Washington, D.C. Residents there uniquely described themselves as living in Northern Virginia, a region so unlike any other part of Virginia during the latter decades of the twentieth century that they awarded it capital letters, as Virginians had done for the Valley of Virginia earlier. People in Northern Virginia did not routinely identify themselves as residents of a particular city or county as people did elsewhere in the state. Instead, they used the phrase *Northern Virginia* to distinguish the distinctive region in which they all lived.

From the 1980s through the first decade of the twenty-first century the total population of Virginia increased at a rate of about 13 percent per decade. Much of that increase was a consequence of immigration from other states and countries. However, during the 2010s the rate of population increase began to decline. Economic and social changes operated then in different ways in the different regions of Virginia. In many rural communities, especially in south-western Virginia where good-paying jobs were hard to find, young people moved away, and the population aged with a consequent reduction in the proportion of tax-paying working people. The total cost of educating children in such places may have declined because of a drop in the number of school-aged children, but without good jobs, tax revenue also declined. In other places, such as in some urban areas, young people settled in city centers, which revived economic activity there and led to increased tax revenue. Some other areas, such as Albemarle County, near the University of Virginia, and some Valley counties and cities became popular retirement localities. Such changes in demographics meant that the consequences of economic change for different counties, cities, and towns were as diverse as their populations. One set of public policies could not meet all the needs for jobs, schools, health care, public welfare, and geriatric care.

It is possible that the deepened state budget crisis early in the twenty-first century that resulted from the combined effects of a recession, political stalemate in Richmond, and the terrorist attack contributed to Democratic candidates for governor and lieutenant governor winning election in November 2001. Many other factors were at work as well, including economic changes and the demographic revolution that was then transforming Virginia and making it less like other southern states and more like American states in other regions. In several ways those changes contributed to Democratic Party victories in congressional and senatorial races, and Democratic candidates for governor won four of the first five elections in the twenty-first century. Republicans, however, maintained control of the House of Delegates, in large part through gerrymandering district lines, as Democrats had done during the twentieth century; and more often than not Republicans maintained a narrow majority in the state Senate.

In 2008 Democratic Party presidential candidate Barack Obama won the electoral vote of Virginia, the first Democrat to do so since Lyndon Johnson in 1964 and only the second since Harry Truman in 1948. Obama won Virginia again in 2012, and in 2016 former Secretary of State Hillary Clinton and her running mate Timothy Kaine, who then represented Virginia in the United States Senate, also won Virginia, even though they carried no other southern state. Not since the 1940s had the Democratic Party's national candidates done so well in Virginia.

Another evidence of change within the state appeared in a continuing series of contentious public debates about the state's many monuments to Confederates and the Confederacy. Many newcomers and most African Americans found them disconcerting or offensive, but thousands of other Virginians and Americans viewed them as important reminders of one version of the past.

For the most part, people with differing views talked past or shouted at each other rather than discussed how to remember the Civil War. Those shouting matches and discussions always involved issues relating to race as well as to historical facts and memories. And they have not been confined to Virginia and Virginians. Men and women throughout the state watched and formed their own opinions as Confederate monuments came down in such distant cities as Baltimore and New Orleans, or the state government of South Carolina removed the Confederate battle flag from its state flag. Raucous public discussions took place in Richmond about what, if anything, to do about the statues on Monument Avenue. In August 2017 Virginians and people from other states descended on Charlottesville, where the city council planned to remove statues of Robert E. Lee and Stonewall Jackson from a public square. Some people came armed, and all people came with strongly held opinions. In a tragic conclusion, a man drove an automobile into a crowd and killed a woman. Two members of the Virginia State Police en route to the scene also died when their helicopter crashed.

Removal of Confederate iconography was not always so controversial. After circuit court judge Martin F. Clark Jr. ordered that a portrait of Confederate General J.E.B. Stuart be removed from the county courthouse in Patrick County in 2015, he received little public criticism. "The courtroom should be a place every litigant and spectator finds fair and utterly neutral," the judge explained. "In my estimation, the portrait of a uniformed Confederate general—and a slave owner himself—does not comport with that essential standard. . . . Still, it is my goal—and my duty as a judge—to provide a trial setting that is perceived by all participants as fair, neutral and without so much as a hint of prejudice. Confederate symbols are, simply, put, offensive to African-Americans, and this reaction is based on fact and clear, straightforward history."[4]

The Changing World

The land of Virginia occupies a very small proportion of the Earth's surface, and the state's approximately 8.5 million inhabitants comprise only a small fraction of the world's whole population. Forces and events outside Virginia and over which Virginians have had little or no influence have affected Virginians of all ages and classes. Some of those forces were economic, some political, some cultural, and some environmental. The environmental ones were not always conspicuous, but many of them were extremely important.

The most deadly modern natural disaster to strike the state was a powerful remnant of Hurricane Camille, which hit the Gulf Coast in August 1969 and traveled northeast along the mountains before it turned east and passed into the Atlantic Ocean. The storm dropped torrential rain all along the way and killed about 259 people, 123 of them in Virginia. Parts of the central Piedmont received from twelve to twenty inches of rain in a short time, and communities in Nelson and Amherst Counties that were the hardest hit received as much as twenty-seven inches. The floods washed out roads, bridges, and railroad lines, destroyed houses and places of business, and knocked out water and electric service in many communities. As the water swept downstream it flooded Richmond in what was probably the largest flood to hit that city since the flood of 1771.

Unlike sudden storms that come and go quickly, the climate changes very slowly and can sometimes be hard to perceive. The climate of the Earth has been very gradually warming for thousands of years. The earliest evidence of that was the melting of the ice sheets of the last Ice Age, which began about 17,000 BC, or about the same time people entered what became Virginia. Slow, minor changes in the climate across centuries and millennia, as distinguished from faster changes in weather from day to day or year to year, gradually wiped out most of the fir and spruce forests that covered the land when that warming began. That allowed pines and a variety of hardwood species to replace the fir and spruce forests, and animals that adapted to the changed climate replaced those that could not. A few remnants of the ancient forests survived into the twenty-first century at the highest elevations in Virginia where temperatures had not yet reached levels those species could not tolerate. On Mount Rogers, the highest mountain in Virginia, both fir and spruce trees live clustered on a small area at the very top. A small population of northern flying squirrels resides there, too, and nowhere else in the state. If the warming trend of the last several thousand years continues, those trees and squirrels will disappear from the landscape. So, too, some other species, such as rare salamanders that live in only a few streams in western and southwestern mountains and some species of trout that cannot live in water that is warmer than it was in the twentieth century.

An important consequence of the melting of the ice sheets was a slow rise in sea level. When the ice sheets began to thaw sea level was about 360 feet below what it was at the beginning of the twenty-first century. Virginia's Atlantic coastline was sixty or more miles east of where it was when the English invaded Tsenacomoco. Sea level has been rising at an almost invisible rate of about a foot a century. Scientists became alarmed late in the twentieth century that the accelerating rise of sea levels would inundate large portions of the state's ten thousand miles of coastal, bay, and tidal shorelines. That could destroy shallow wetlands that serve as nurseries of both fish and shellfish species as well as flood houses and coastal recreation facilities. By the early years of the twenty-first century scientists determined that the rate of increase of air temperature was accelerating, which made coastal areas even more vulnerable to storm flooding.

As the ocean rose, so did the temperature of its water. And so did the water in Chesapeake Bay, with the result that some species of fish and shellfish could not survive or were increasingly vulnerable to diseases or to the loss of microscopic plants and animals on which they fed. Warm water is inhospitable to some underwater grasses those occupants of the bay require for feeding, breeding, and shelter. The drastic declines in the bay's oyster and crab populations as well as some fish species important to commercial fishermen could be attributed in part to rising water temperature and to an accompanying rise in water acidity. The economic consequences of all those changes pose serious challenges for eastern Virginians. Predictions of continued warming of the atmosphere and of the state's coastal waters combined with rising sea level directly threaten millions of Virginians who live close to the bay or ocean. In the populous Hampton Road area the danger of permanent flooding has increased even more because the land has been slowly subsiding while the sea level was rising. The causes of the subsidence are complex, but the two factors pose unprecedented new regional problems in the twenty-first century.

The worldwide transportation of people, animals, and plant material in and out of Virginia began with the introduction of European, South American, and African plants and animals into North American agriculture in the seventeenth century. Sedimentation of shallow coastal bays was only one of many manifestations those changes produced. Malaria was another. It probably arrived in Tsenacomoco early in the seventeenth century. West Nile virus, Lyme disease, the Zika virus, and the infectious virus that caused acquired immune deficiency syndrome (AIDS) arrived late in the twentieth and early in the twenty-first centuries. Inadvertent or purposeful introductions of other plants and animals seriously disrupted the natural world. Thick clumps of phragmites, an Old World marsh grass, crowded out native wetland species and destroyed large areas of wetland habitat that native plant and animal species depended on. Dense mats of hydrilla blanketed some inland lakes and waterways and prevented sport fishermen and people seeking recreation in their boats from using those places. Kudzu became the most notorious introduced plant in the southeastern states because of its rapid growth and the difficulty of eradicating it. References to the kudzu that ate North Carolina became a joke noir by the end of the twentieth century, but some areas of Virginia were just as badly affected.

Foreign pests such as the gypsy moth devastated large areas of hardwood forest after Dutch elm disease and another parasite had virtually wiped out large populations of American elm and American chestnut in Virginia. The southern pine bark beetle killed pine forests in coastal Virginia, and other pests almost destroyed the hemlocks that were once numerous in the mountain forests of Virginia. Pigeons descended from imported birds soiled buildings, automobiles, and sidewalks in every town in the state, and introduced European starlings drove down populations of such popular native birds as red-headed woodpeckers and eastern bluebirds.

The Very First Families of Virginia

At the end of the twentieth century when Virginians filled out their 2000 census returns, 21,172 people identified themselves as American Indians. The census of 1900 had collected detailed information about the state's Indians, but it is probable that for much of the remainder of the century the census seriously undercounted the number of Indians in the state. Independent of the civil rights movement, Indians in Virginia gradually became disentangled from the racial discrimination that the 1924 Act to Preserve Racial Integrity and the racial purity campaign of Walter A. Plecker imposed on them. As wards of the state, Indians could not vote until the federal government's Office of Indian Affairs ruled in 1948 that they could vote in federal elections. The General Assembly amended the Racial Integrity Act in 1954 to acknowledge the Indians' legal existence and allow them to register and vote without having to pay the poll tax, which would have violated their seventeenth-century treaty rights.

The reservation lands of the Pamunkey and the Mattaponi were not under threat of encroachment from neighboring populations during the twentieth century as had been the case several times during the seventeenth, eighteenth, and nineteenth centuries. The very land itself, however, appeared threatened when in the 1980s the City of Newport News (named for Christopher Newport, commander of the 1607 invasion fleet) announced plans to build a dam on the Mattaponi River and create a reservoir to provide water for the city's growing population. The planned reservoir would have flooded a buffer area adjacent to the reservation and threatened vital fishing and important cultural sites. For twenty years the tribe, in conjunction with several environmental organizations and Indian advocacy groups, fought to prevent the city from creating the reservoir. A lawsuit the Mattaponi filed in 1998 dragged on for more than a decade as Indians sought to protect their land and traditional rights, and the city sought to provide basic services for all its residents. In 2009 a federal court ruled, largely on environmental grounds, against granting a permit to allow the Army Corps of Engineers to construct the dam. That terminated the city's plan that appeared the threaten Mattaponi land.

Throughout much of the twentieth century, chiefs of the Mattaponi and Pamunkey, both of which retained reservation land set aside during the sev-

Governor Charles S. Robb receiving the annual tribute
of game from representatives of the Mattaponi and Pamunkey tribes in the 1980s.

enteenth century, strove to convince other Virginians that they and the other
tribes were entitled to respect and official recognition. They called added attention to provisions of the 1646 and 1677 treaties that exempted residents of
the reservations from taxation if they annually presented the governor with
game instead. Early in the twentieth century, chiefs moved the ceremony from
the spring to November in order to attract maximum attention during the
Thanksgiving season.

Chief Otha T. Custalow opened a museum on the Mattaponi reservation
in King William County to educate visitors about the history and culture
of Virginia's Indians. During the latter years of the century as the American
Indian movement became consolidated, first in the western states and then in
the eastern, Virginians joined forces with them and with one another to revise public perceptions and encourage state and federal government action for
their benefit. Curtis L. Custalow and his cousin and successor Daniel Webster
Custalow served as chiefs of the Mattaponi from 1969 to 2003 and earned national recognition for their leadership and achievements.

Early in the four hundredth anniversary year 2007, the General Assembly
conducted a spirited debate about a proposal that the legislature apologize for
the enslavement of African Americans and the racial discrimination that was
associated with and followed slavery. The resolution the legislators adopted in
February acknowledged that Virginia's colonial and state governments were
fully responsible partners in the enslavement of hundreds of thousands of

Chickahominy chief Steve Adkins addressing the Virginia Forum, the annual Virginia history conference, at the Library of Virginia on April 13, 2007.

people and the mistreatment of African Americans during the long decades of Jim Crow segregation. Less controversially, the resolution also acknowledged centuries of official and unofficial mistreatment of Virginia's Indians, but it commended the tribes that beginning in 1607 enabled the first English settlers to survive in Virginia. The state dedicated a monument to Virginia's Indians on the grounds of the state Capitol in 2018, and in 2019 it dedicated a monument to honor Virginia's women of all centuries and races.

Virginia's Indians seized the opportunity the 2007 four hundredth anniversary of the first English settlement furnished to obtain a greater appreciation of their roles throughout Virginia's history. The public commemorations of 1807, 1857, 1907, and 1957 had all been celebrations of the achievements of Anglo-Americans in the New World. Those events left Indians and African Americans out of the historical narrative and ignored the many important ways in which the cultural and social history of Virginia and the United States were the result of amalgamations of American, European, and African beliefs and practices. When the General Assembly established the commission to plan for the 2007 anniversary, Indian leaders insisted that because of the many losses native peoples had suffered as a consequence of the European settlement of North America, the state commemorate but not celebrate the event.

The three museums the state and federal governments and the Jamestown Rediscovery Project opened at Jamestown in 2007 were consequently much more broadly based than had been the case at the previous large-scale anniversaries. The public commemorations and interpretive programs were also. The cultural heritages of American Indian and African American Virginians were effectively integrated into the anniversary events. Leaders of Virginia tribes made a well-publicized diplomatic trip to England in 2006 and before, during, and throughout the anniversary year spoke, wrote, and publicized the roles that their ancestors played throughout Virginia's history. They reminded people who may have forgotten or paid little attention that Indians were alive and well in Virginia in the twenty-first century.

Beginning in the fourth quarter of the twentieth century the state government paid more attention to Virginia's Indians than it had before. Early in the 1980s the government created the Virginia Council on Indians. The council established criteria for extending official state recognition to tribes with continuous organizational and cultural heritages, and reversed one of the consequences of the eugenics and racial integrity movements of the 1920s that had shaped the state's public policies so as to deny legal recognition of the existence of Virginia's Indians. The state officially recognized the Chickahominy, Chickahominy Eastern Division, Rappahannock, and Upper Mattaponi in 1983, the Nansemond in 1985, the Monacan in 1989, and the Cheroenhaka (Nottoway), Nottoway, and Patawomeck tribes in 2010. The Mattaponi and Pamunkey, because they had reservation land on which members had lived continuously since the seventeenth century, did not need to seek state recognition.

In 1999 the General Assembly requested federal recognition of all state-recognized tribes. Federal recognition would entitle them to the same status as tribes with which the federal government had concluded treaties. Under the 1990 Native American Graves Protection and Repatriation Act, federal recognition would facilitate return of aboriginal remains of several thousand Virginia Indians that had been deposited in public museums following archaeological investigations. Because the tribes lacked the continuous documentary records required for federal recognition by administrative action—another of the consequences of the eugenics movement and the Racial Integrity Act—the Virginia tribes sought direct congressional action. In 2016 the Pamunkey received federal recognition, almost thirty-five years after making the first request, and in January 2018 Congress recognized the Chickahominy, Eastern Chickahominy, Upper Mattaponi, Rappahannock, Nansemond, and Monacan tribes. For members of those tribes that finally closed a long and sad chapter in Virginia Indian history.

NOTES

2 The English Invasion of Tsenacomoco

1. "Observations gathered out of a Discourse of the Plantation of the Southerne Colonie in Virginia by the English, 1606, Written by that Honorable Gentleman Master George Percy," printed in *Purchas His Pilgrimes...*, ed. Samuel Purchas, 4 vols. (London, 1625), 4:1686.

2. [Gabriel Archer], "A relayton of the discovery of our River, from James Forte into the Maine," 21 May–21 June 1607, Public Record Office, Colonial Office 1/1, fol. 49, National Archives of the United Kingdom.

3. "Observations gathered out of a Discourse of the Plantation of the Southerne Colonie in Virginia," 4:1689.

4. Ibid., 4:1690.

5. Philip L. Barbour, ed. *The Complete Works of Captain John Smith, 1580–1631*, 3 vols. (Chapel Hill: University of North Carolina Press, 1986), 2:208.

6. Mark Nicholls, ed., "George Percy's 'Trewe Relacyon': A Primary Source for the Jamestown Settlement," *Virginia Magazine of History and Biography* 113 (2005): 248–49.

7. Ibid., 254.

8. "A Reporte of the Manner of Proceeding in the General Assembly convened at James citty in Virginia, July 30, 1619," National Archives of Great Britain, PRO CO 1/1, 15, printed in William J. Van Schreeven and George H. Reese, eds., *Proceedings of the General Assembly of Virginia, July 3–August 4, 1619* (Jamestown, Va.: Jamestown Foundation, 1969).

9. Printed from Smyth of Nibley Papers, New York Public Library, in *Bulletin of the New York Public Library, Astor, Lenox and Tilden Foundations* 3 (1899): 208, and in *The Records of the Virginia Company of London*, ed. Susan Myra Kingsbury, 4 vols. (Washington, D.C.: U.S. Government Printing Office, 1906–35): 3:207.

10. Virginia Company Records, July 16, 1621, Ferrar Papers, Magdalene College, Cambridge University.

11. *A Declaration of the State of the Colony and Affaires in Virginia* (London, 1620), 6.

12. John Rolfe to Sir Edwyn Sandys, Jan. 1619/20, Ferrar Papers.

13. Compare, William Thorndale, "A Passenger List of the 1619 Bona Nova," *Magazine of Virginia Genealogy* 33 (1995): 3–11, with Martha W. McCartney, "An Early Virginia Census Reprised," *Quarterly Bulletin of the Archaeological Society of Virginia* 54 (1999): 178–96; see also Engel Sluiter, "New Light on the '20. and Odd Negroes' Arriving in Virginia, August, 1619," *William and Mary Quarterly*, 3d ser., 54 (1997): 395–98, and

John Thornton, "The African Experience of the '20. and Odd Negroes' Arriving in Virginia in 1619," *William and Mary Quarterly*, 3d ser., 55 (1998): 421–34.

14. William Capps to Doctor Wynston, ca. 1623, PRO 30/15/2, no. 323.

3 Royal Colony

1. William Waller Hening, ed., *The Statutes at Large of Virginia*, 13 vols. (Richmond, New York, and Philadelphia, 1809–23), 1:323.

2. Ibid., 1:372, 428, 431.

3. Ibid,. 1:530.

4. York Co. Deeds, Orders, Wills, Etc., 3 (1657–1662), folio 96.

5. Warren M. Billings, with the assistance of Maria Kimberly, eds., *The Papers of Sir William Berkeley, 1605–1677* (Richmond: Library of Virginia, 2007), 184–85.

6. Hening, *Statutes at Large*, 3:181.

7. L.G., *Public Good without Private Interest; or, a Compendious Remonstrance of the Present Sad State and Condition of the English Colonie in Virginea. With a Modest Declaration of the Several Causes Why It Hath Not Prospered Better Hitherto; as also, a Submissive Suggestion to the Most Prudentiall Probable Wayes, and Means, Both Divine and Civill for its Happyer Improvement* (London, 1657), 23.

8. Thomas Mathew, "The Beginning Progress and Conclusion of Bacons Rebellion in Virginia in the Years 1675 & 1676" (1705), Thomas Jefferson Papers, series 8, volume 1:1–3, Library of Congress.

9. *Papers of Sir William Berkeley*, 486–87.

10. Ibid., 537.

11. PRO CO 1/37, fol. 129, National Archives of Great Britain.

12. Occahannock, Nansemond, and Nottaway Indians, to Governor Sir Francis Nicholson, and Nicholson's reply, April–May 1699, Colonial Papers, folder 12, no. 18, Record Group 1, Library of Virginia.

13. Petition of Queen Ann and the Great Men of the Pamunkey Indians to Governor Edward Nott, docketed "Between 15th of August 1705 & Aug 1706," ibid.

14. Benjamin Harrison to President Edmund Jenings, July 14, 1709, ibid.

4 Life in the Seventeenth Century

1. Thomas Yong to Worthy Sir, July 13, 1634, Personal Papers Collection, Library of Virginia; also printed in *Documents Connected with the History of South Carolina,* ed. Plowden Charles Jennett Weston (London, 1856), 29–44, *Collections of the Massachusetts Historical Society*, 4th ser., 9 (1871): 81–115, and in part in *Original Narratives of Early American History: Narratives of Early Maryland, 1633–1684,* ed. Clayton Colman Hall (New York, 1910), 53–61.

2. [John Cotton], Narrative of Bacon's Rebellion, MSS2 C8295 a1, (unnumbered page 24), Virginia Historical Society.

3. Accomack Co. Wills, Deeds, Orders (1672–1682), 160.

5   Tobacco and Slavery

1. William Waller Hening, ed., *The Statutes at Large of Virginia,* 13 vols. (Richmond, New York, and Philadelphia, 1809–23), 1:146.
2. Ibid., 1:226.
3. Ibid., 2:26.
4. Ibid., 2:170.
5. Ibid., 2:280–81.
6. Ibid., 2:270.
7. H. R. McIlwaine et al., eds., *Executive Journals of the Council of Colonial Virginia,* 6 vols. (Richmond: Virginia State Library, 1925–66), 1:86–87.
8. Middlesex Co. Order Book 5 (1710–1721), 40.
9. *Executive Journals of the Council,* 3:242–43.
10. Goochland Co. Free Negro and Slave Records, Aug. 16, 1739.
11. Williamsburg *Virginia Gazette,* Nov. 2, 1739.

6   Life in the Eighteenth Century

1. Robert Beverley, *The History and Present State of Virginia,* ed. Susan Scott Parrish (Chapel Hill: University of North Carolina Press, 2013), 8.
2. Ibid., 230.
3. Gilbert Chinard, trans. and ed., *A Huguenot Exile in Virginia; or, Voyages of a Frenchman exiled for His Religion with a Description of Virginia and Maryland* (New York: Press of the Pioneers, 1934), 142.
4. Julian P. Boyd et al., eds., *Papers of Thomas Jefferson* (Princeton, N.J.: Princeton University Press, 1950–), 10:27.
5. John Wayles to Sir (probably a partner in the Bristol, England, tobacco trading firm of Ferrell and Jones), Aug. 30, 1766, P.R.O., T. 79/30.
6. *Maryland Gazette* (Annapolis), Oct. 18, 1749.
7. Alexander Purdie and John Dixon's *Virginia Gazette,* June 6, 1771.

7   Mid-Century Challenges

1. William Byrd to Charles Boyce, earl of Orrery, July 5, 1726, in *The Correspondence of the Three William Byrds of Westover, Virginia, 1684–1776,* ed. Marion Tinling, 2 vols. (Charlottesville: University Press of Virginia, 1977), 1:355.
2. H. R. McIlwaine et al., eds., *Executive Journals of the Council of Colonial Virginia,* 6 vols. (Richmond: Virginia State Library, 1925–66), 5:490.
3. Alexander Purdie and John Dixon's *Virginia Gazette,* Feb. 20, 1772.
4. Petition of Arthur Dent, n.d., received May 11, 1774, Colonial Papers, Petitions, Record Group 1, Library of Virginia.
5. Petition of Timothy Conway, n.d., received May 17, 1774, Colonial Papers, Petitions, Record Group 1, Library of Virginia.

6. Petition of Jane Fraser, n.d., received May 25, 1774, Colonial Papers, Petitions, Record Group 1, Library of Virginia.

7. Quoted in William Stith to bishop of London, Apr. 21, 1753, and John Blair to bishop of London, Aug. 15, 1754, both in Fulham Palace Papers, Lambeth Palace Library, London.

8. *American Historical Review* 26 (1922): 745. When this account was first published the unnamed author of the journal was presumed to be a French spy, but early twenty-first-century scholarship identified him as Scotsman Charles Murray. See Jon Kukla, *Patrick Henry, Champion of Liberty* (New York: Simon and Schuster, 2017), 428n70.

9. Alexander Purdie and John Dixon's *Virginia Gazette,* Mar. 21, 1766.

10. 6 George III, ch. 12.

8 Independence and Revolution

1. George Washington to Bryan Fairfax, July 20, 1774, Virginia Historical Society, and printed in W. W. Abbot et al., eds., *The Papers of George Washington, Colonial Series,* 10 vols. (Charlottesville: University Press of Virginia, 1983–95), 10:130–31.

2. William Pinkney's *Virginia Gazette,* Aug. 24, 1775.

3. William Wirt, *Sketches of the Life and Character of Patrick Henry* (Philadelphia, 1817), 119–23, was the first publication of Henry's speech as compiled from memories of eyewitnesses.

4. Petition of Mary Webley, n.d., presented Oct. 11, 1776, Legislative Petitions, Norfolk Borough, Record Group 78, Library of Virginia.

5. Worthington C. Ford et al., eds., *Journals of the Continental Congress,* 34 vols. (Washington, D.C.: U.S. Government Printing Office, 1904–37), 5:507.

6. *Ordinances Passed at a General Convention* (Williamsburg, 1776), 5.

7. William J. Van Schreeven, Robert L. Scribner, and Brent Tarter, eds., *Revolutionary Virginia, The Road to Independence: A Documentary Record,* 7 vols. (Charlottesville: University Press of Virginia, 1973–83), 7:302, 449.

8. Petition of Inhabitants of Prince Edward Co., Sept. 24, 1776, presented Oct. 11, 1776, Legislative Petitions, Prince Edward Co., Record Group 78, Library of Virginia.

9. Enrolled Bills, Legislative Department, Record Group 78, Library of Virginia.

10. William Waller Hening, ed., *The Statutes at Large of Virginia,* 13 vols. (Richmond, New York, and Philadelphia, 1809–23), 9:351.

11. Richard Henry Lee to Hannah Lee Corbin, Mar. 17, 1778, in *The Letters of Richard Henry Lee,* ed. James Curtis Ballagh, 2 vols. (New York: Macmillan, 1911–14), 1:392–94, quotation on 393.

12. Accomack Co. Deed Book 6:448–50.

13. Gov. William H. Cabell to the Speaker of the House of Delegates, Jan. 28, 1808, Executive Communications, Record Group 79, Library of Virginia.

14. James Cleveland quoted in Lund Washington to George Washington, Feb. 29, 1776, Philander D. Chase et al., eds., *The Papers of George Washington: Revolutionary War Series* (Charlottesville: University Press of Virginia, 1985–), 3:396.

15. Petition of the "freeholders & Sundry of the Inhabitants of the County of Lunenburg," n.d., received May 11, 1776, Records of the Convention of 1776, Record Group 89, Library of Virginia, printed in *Revolutionary Virginia, the Road to Independence,* ed. Van Schreeven, Scribner, and Tarter, 6:474–77.

16. Petition of Martha Hodges, n.d., presented to the House of Delegates on Nov. 8, 1777, Legislative Petitions, York Co., Record Group 78, Library of Virginia.

17. "Autograph Letters," *American Historical Record* 2 (1873): 468. Also published in Julian P. Boyd et al., eds., *Papers of Thomas Jefferson* (Princeton, N.J.: Princeton University Press, 1950–), 4:691.

18. Petition of James, n.d., presented to the House of Delegates on Nov. 30, 1786, Legislative Petitions, New Kent Co., Library of Virginia.

19. Undated petition, ca. 1783, of Peter Anderson, PRO WO 1/1018, 13.

20. Undated petition, with Oct. 1, 1787, attestation and mark of Shadrack Furman, to William Pitt the Younger, PRO AO 13/29, Folder D.

21. Edward C. Carter II et al., eds., *The Virginia Journals of Benjamin Henry Latrobe, 1795–1798,* 2 vols. (New Haven, Conn.: Yale University Press, 1977), 1:83.

9 Virginians and the New Nation

1. Merrill Jensen, John P. Kaminsky, and Gaspare J. Saladino, eds., *Documentary History of the Ratification of the Constitution* (Madison: Wisconsin Historical Society Press, 1976–), 10:1537.

2. Richmond *Virginia Independent Chronicle,* July 9, 1788.

3. John Adams to Abigail Adams, Jan. 9, 1793, Adams Family Papers, Massachusetts Historical Society.

4. *Acts Passed at a General Assembly of the Commonwealth of Virginia* (Richmond, 1810), 9.

10 Life in the First Half of the Nineteenth Century

1. "Mend Your Ways," *Richmond Enquirer,* Feb. 6, 1817.

2. *Norfolk and Portsmouth Herald and General Advertiser,* May 13, 1835.

3. *Norfolk and Portsmouth Herald,* Mar. 16, 18, 1829.

4. Arthur Singleton (pseud. of Henry Cogswell Knight), *Letters from the South and West* (Boston, 1824), 57.

5. [Rebecca Blaine Harding], "Life in the Iron-Mills," *Atlantic Monthly: A Magazine of Literature, Art, and Politics* 7 (1861): 430.

6. *Herald, and Norfolk and Portsmouth Advertiser,* Jan. 31, 1795.

7. Legislative Petitions, Norfolk Borough, n.d. (received Dec. 9, 1800), Record Group 78, Library of Virginia.

8. *The Memorial of Sundry Citizens of the County of Halifax, to the Virginia Legislature, Praying for the Establishment of Free Schools in the State* (Richmond, 1854), 3–4.

11 Slave State

1. David Barrow, *Circular Letter, Southampton County, Virginia; February 14, 1798* (Norfolk, 1798).
2. Trial Record, Oct. 6, 1800, Executive Papers of Governor James Monroe, Record Group 3, Library of Virginia.
3. Petition of Nancy, Legislative Petitions, Loudoun Co., n.d., received Dec. 6, 1815, Record Group 78, Library of Virginia.
4. Petition of Lucinda, Nov. 27, 1815, King George Co., received Dec. 20, 1815, ibid.
5. Mary Jo Bratton, ed., "Fields's Observations: The Slave Narrative of a Nineteenth-Century Virginian," *Virginia Magazine of History and Biography* 88 (1980): 93.
6. *Norfolk and Portsmouth Herald,* Sep. 28, 1827.
7. Richmond City Hustings Court Minute Book, 20:401.
8. G. W. Featherstonhaugh, *Excursion through the Slave States,* 2 vols. (London, 1844), 1:119–21.
9. H. C. Bruce, *The New Man. Twenty-nine Years a Slave. Twenty-nine Years a Free Man* (York, Pa., 1895), 47–48.
10. Fredrika Bremer, *The Homes of the New World; Impressions of America,* trans. Mary Howitt, 2 vols. (New York, 1853), 2:533–36.

12 Divided State in a Divided Nation

1. *Proceedings and Debates of the Virginia State Convention, of 1829–30* (Richmond, 1830), 25–31; *Daily Richmond Whig,* Oct. 15, 1829, reported that Robertson drafted the petition at the request of the assembled petitioners.
2. Virginia Freewoman, "The Rights of Women," *Richmond Enquirer,* Oct 20, 1829.
3. Robert Johnston to John Letcher, May 9, 1861, Executive Papers of Governor John Letcher, Record Group 3, Library of Virginia.
4. John Thomas O'Brien, "'The People's Favorite': The Rise and Fall of Martin Meredith Lipscomb," *Virginia Cavalcade* 31 (1982): 216–23, quotation on 218.
5. George H. Reese, ed., *Proceedings of the Virginia State Convention of 1861,* 4 vols. (Richmond: Virginia State Library, 1965), 2: 2:142, 184–85.
6. *Acts of the General Assembly of Virginia* (1848), 117.
7. John Letcher to editor, June 25, 1858, in *Daily Richmond Enquirer,* June 30, 1858.
8. John M. Smith to Governor John Letcher, Sept. 23, 1860, Executive Office, Letters Received.

13 Civil War and Emancipation

1. *Abingdon Democrat,* Feb. 8, 1861.
2. George H. Reese, ed., *Proceedings of the Virginia State Convention of 1861,* 4 vols. (Richmond: Virginia State Library, 1965), 1:505.
3. Ibid., 3:92.

4. Address of the Women of Essex Co., *Daily Richmond Examiner,* Mar. 18, 1861.

5. *Lynchburg Daily Virginian,* May 2, 1861.

6. *Wellsburg Herald,* May 31, 1861.

7. Wheeling *Daily Intelligencer,* May 21, 1861.

8. Wheeling *Daily Intelligencer,* June 21, 1861.

9. Testimony of Terrill Bradby, Aug. 30, 1871, Southern Claims Commission, Approved Claims, 1871–1880, Virginia, Record Group 217, National Archives and Records Administration.

10. Testimony of Edward Whitehurst, July 31, 1877, Southern Claims Commission, Approved Claims, 1871–1880, Virginia, ibid.

11. *Constitution of the State of Virginia, and the Ordinances Adopted by the Convention Which Assembled at Alexandria, on the 13th Day of February, 1864* (1864), quotations on 14, 8.

12. Edward B. Williams, ed., *Rebel Brothers: The Civil War Letters of the Trueharts* (College Station, Tex.: Texas A&M University Press, 1995), 102.

14 Constructing a New Virginia

1. *Equal Suffrage. Address from the Colored Citizens of Norfolk Va., to the People of the United States* (New Bedford, Mass., 1865), 10.

2. Ibid., 1.

3. Philip S. Foner and George E. Walker, eds., *Proceedings of the Black State Conventions, 1840–1865,* 2 vols. (Philadelphia: Temple University Press, 1979–80), 2:258–76, quotation on 262.

4. *Daily Richmond Whig,* July 6, 1865.

5. Stephen Flemming to Governor Francis H. Pierpont, May 21, 1865, Executive Papers of Governor Francis H. Pierpont, Record Group 3, Library of Virginia.

6. *Daily Richmond Whig,* Jan. 26, 1866.

7. Circular No. 4, Conservative State Committee, Feb. 12, 1868, broadside, Library of Virginia.

8. *Journal of the Senate of Virginia,* 1870 sess., index separately paginated, 18.

9. *Constitution of Virginia, Framed by the Convention Which Met in Richmond, the Third Day of December, Eighteen Hundred and Sixty-eight* (Richmond, [1868]), 7.

10. *The Debates and Proceedings of the Constitutional Convention of the State of Virginia* (Richmond, 1868), 524–25.

11. *First Annual Report of the Superintendent of Public Instruction, for the Year Ending August 31, 1871* (Richmond, 1871), 54–55.

12. *Southern Planter and Farmer,* new ser., 3 (1869): 323–24.

13. *Roanoke Daily Times,* May 6, 1890.

14. Richmond *Daily Dispatch,* Mar. 14, 1884.

15 Three Lost Causes

1. *Lynchburg Daily Virginian,* Nov. 20, 1872.

2. Sarah Ann Brock, *Richmond during the War; Four Years of Personal Observation, by a Richmond Lady* (New York, 1867), 272–74.

3. *Richmond Daily Whig,* Jan. 30, 1878; confirmed in Richmond *Daily Dispatch,* Sept. 24, 1879.

4. *Journal of the House of Delegates of the State of Virginia, for the Session of 1877–8* (Richmond, 1877 [i.e., 1878]), 428–29.

5. *Journal of the House of Delegates of the State of Virginia for the Session of 1883–4* (Richmond, 1883 [i.e., 1884]), 20.

6. William Mahone to John D. Long, Feb. 11, 1882, reprinted in *Richmond Daily Whig,* Mar. 15, 1882.

7. Bathurst Browne Bagby, *Recollections* (West Point, Va.: Tidewater Review, 1950), 64–65.

8. *Acts of Assembly* (Richmond, 1894), 862–67, quotation on 865.

9. Richmond *Times,* Aug. 22, 1890.

10. *Richmond Dispatch,* Aug. 11, 1891.

11. Richmond *Virginia Sun,* June 1, 1892.

16 Jim Crow Virginia

1. Thomas Calhoun Walker, *The Honey-Pod Tree: The Life Story of Thomas Calhoun Walker* (New York: John Day, 1958), 160.

2. *Report of the Proceedings and Debates of the Constitutional Convention,* 2 vols. (Richmond, 1906), 2:2972–73.

3. Ibid., 2:3014.

4. Ibid., 2:3077.

5. William C. Pendleton, *Political History of Appalachian Virginia, 1776–1927* (Dayton, Va.: Shenandoah Press, 1927), 459.

6. *Taylor v. Commonwealth,* 101 Va (1903) 829–832; *Jones v. Montague* and *Selden v. Montague,* 194 US 147–153 (1904).

7. *Richmond Times-Dispatch,* July 22, 1923.

8. *Acts of Assembly,* 1910 sess., 581.

9. *Acts of Assembly,* 1924 sess., 534–35.

10. *Richmond Planet,* Feb. 11, 1928.

11. Richmond *News Leader,* July 8, 1925.

12. Norfolk *Virginian-Pilot,* July 22, 1927.

13. *Richmond Times-Dispatch,* Feb. 10, 1986.

17 Progressive Virginians

1. *City of Hampton v. Watson,* 119 Va (1916): 95–102, quotation on 96–97.
2. Report of Caryetta L. Davis, St. Peter's-in-the-Mountains, Calloway, June 29, 1926, *Southwestern Episcopalian* 6 (Aug. 1926): 17–18.
3. *Richmond Times-Dispatch,* Feb. 5, 1943.
4. *Washington Post,* Dec. 28, 1921.
5. *Buck v. Bell,* 274 US 200 (1927): 207.

18 Two World Wars and the Great Depression

1. Medal of Honor Citation for Sergeant Earl D. Gregory, Oct. 8, 1918.
2. *Annual Report of the State Board of Health and the State Health Commissioner* (Richmond, 1920), 6.
3. New York Bureau of Municipal Research, *County Government in Virginia: Report on a Survey Made for the Governor and His Committee on Consolidation and Simplification* (Richmond, 1928), 6.
4. Bathurst Browne Bagby, "If Truth be Told, the 'Good Old Days' Weren't," Richmond *News Leader,* Apr. 28, 1927.
5. Leila Blance Bess, interview with George Saunders, n.d., ca. 1940, W.P.A. Virginia Writers' Project Life Histories, Library of Virginia.

19 Civil Rights

1. Norfolk *Journal and Guide,* May 1, 1948.
2. *Brown v. Board of Education of Topeka, Kansas,* 347 US 483–496 (1954), quotations on 493, 494.
3. *Brown v. Board of Education of Topeka, Kansas,* 349 US 294–301 (1955), quotation on 301.
4. Robert Leon Bacon, to Governor Thomas B. Stanley, Dec. 2, 1955, Governor's Office, Letters Received, Record Group 3, Library of Virginia.
5. Norfolk *Virginian-Pilot,* Jan. 1, 1959.
6. *Acts and Joint Resolutions of the General Assembly of the Commonwealth of Virginia, Extra Session 1959, Regular Session 1960* (Richmond, 1960), 491.
7. Norfolk *Journal and Guide,* Dec. 7, 1963.
8. Emmet M. Frazer, "How Does It Feel to Be Colored?" *Commonwealth* 12 (June 1945): 10–13, quotation on 10.
9. 1970 Constitution of Virginia, Article I, Section 11.

20 Suburban State

1. *Acts of the General Assembly of the Commonwealth of Virginia, 2003 Regular Session* (Richmond, 2003), 1:181–82.

2. *Suffolk News-Herald,* June 15, 1955.
3. *Washington Post,* Feb. 24, 1980.

21 Cosmopolitan State

1. 1970 Constitution of Virginia, Article XI, Section 1.
2. *Washington Post,* Sept. 12, 2001.
3. *Washington Post,* Sept. 13, 2001.
4. *Martinsville Bulletin,* Sept. 3, 2015.

FURTHER READING

In the pages that follow, I list a few of the most important books and in some instances scholarly journal articles on important topics for which nobody has published a book or which present alternative interpretations, grouped by chapter. These are sources that focus on Virginia. A much larger body of scholarship on women, race, religion, economic history, and other important subjects on American and southern history also informs the interpretive narrative. Books that treat large themes through long periods of Virginia's history and two extended journal articles that survey that scholarship and provide insights on the writing of Virginia history include the following:

Ausband, Stephen Conrad. *Byrd's Line, A Natural History.* Charlottesville: University of Virginia Press, 2002.

Billings, Warren M., John E. Selby, and Thad W. Tate. *Colonial Virginia: A History.* White Plains, N.Y.: KTO Press, 1986.

Buckley, Thomas E., SJ. *Establishing Religious Freedom: Jefferson's Statute in Virginia.* Charlottesville: University of Virginia Press, 2013.

Coleman, Arica L. *That the Blood Stay Pure: African Americans, Native Americans, and the Predicament of Race and Identity in Virginia.* Bloomington: Indiana University Press, 2013.

Hall, Randal L. *Mountains on the Market: Industry, the Environment, and the South.* Lexington: University Press of Kentucky, 2013.

Kierner, Cynthia A., Jennifer R. Loux, and Megan Taylor Shockley. *Changing History: Virginia Women through Four Centuries.* Richmond: Library of Virginia, 2013.

Kierner, Cynthia A., and Sandra G. Treadway, eds. *Virginia Women: Their Lives and Times.* 2 vols. Athens: University of Georgia Press, 2015–16.

Kirby, Jack Temple. *Poquosin: A Study of Rural Landscape and Society.* Chapel Hill: University of North Carolina Press, 1995.

Peters, John O. *From Marshall to Moussaoui: Federal Justice in the Eastern District of Virginia.* Petersburg, Va.: Dietz Press, 2013.

Lebsock, Suzanne, and Kym S. Rice. *"A Share of Honour": Virginia Women, 1600–1945.* Richmond: Virginia Museum of Fine Arts, 1984. Rev. ed., Lebsock, Suzanne D. *Virginia Women, 1600–1945: "A Share of Honor."* Richmond: Virginia State Library, 1987.

Rountree, Helen C. *Pocahontas's People: The Powhatan Indians of Virginia through Four Centuries.* Norman: University of Oklahoma Press, 1990.

Sawyer, Roy T. *America's Wetland: An Environmental and Cultural History of Tidewater Virginia and North Carolina.* Charlottesville: University of Virginia Press, 2010.

Tarter, Brent. *The Grandees of Government: The Origins and Persistence of Undemocratic Politics in Virginia.* Charlottesville: University of Virginia Press, 2013.

———. "Making History in Virginia." *Virginia Magazine of History and Biography* 115 (2007): 2–55.

———. "The New Virginia Bookshelf." *Virginia Magazine of History and Biography* 104 (1996): 7–102.

Williams, John Alexander. *Appalachia: A History.* Chapel Hill: University of North Carolina Press, 2002.

1 The View from Cumberland Gap

Beck, Robin A. "From Joara to Chiaha: Spanish Exploration of the Appalachian Summit Area, 1540–1568." *Southeastern Archaeology* 16 (1997): 162–69.

Egloff, Keith, and Deborah Woodward. *First People: The Early Indians of Virginia.* 2d ed. Charlottesville: University of Virginia Press, 2006.

Gallivan, Martin D. *James River Chiefdoms: The Rise of Social Inequality in the Chesapeake.* Lincoln: University of Nebraska Press, 2003.

———. *The Powhatan Landscape: An Archaeological History of the Algonquian Chesapeake.* Gainesville: University Press of Florida, 2016.

Glanville, Jim. "Conquistadors at Saltville in 1567? A Review of the Archaeological and Documentary Evidence." *Smithfield Review* 8 (2004): 70–108.

———. "Conquistadors at Saltville in 1567 Revisited." *Smithfield Review* 18 (2014): 97–134.

Gleach, Frederic W. *Powhatan's World and Colonial Virginia: A Conflict of Cultures.* Lincoln: University of Nebraska Press, 1997.

Hantman, Jeffrey L. *Monacan Millennium: A Collaborative Archaeology and History of a Virginia Indian People.* Charlottesville: University of Virginia Press, 2018.

Potter, Stephen R. *Commoners, Tribute, and Chiefs: The Development of Algonquian Culture in the Potomac Valley.* Charlottesville: University Press of Virginia, 1993.

Rice, James D. *Nature and History in the Potomac Country: From Hunter-Gatherers to the Age of Jefferson.* Baltimore, Md.: Johns Hopkins University Press, 2009.

Rountree, Helen C. *The Powhatan Indians of Virginia: Their Traditional Culture.* Norman: University of Oklahoma Press, 1989.

Rountree, Helen C., and Thomas E. Davidson, *Eastern Shore Indians of Virginia and Maryland.* Charlottesville: University Press of Virginia, 1997.

Rountree, Helen C., and E. Randolph Turner III. *Before and After Jamestown: Virginia's Powhatans and Their Predecessors.* Gainesville: University Press of Florida, 2002.

Schmidt, Ethan A. *The Divided Dominion: Social Conflict and Indian Hatred in Early Virginia.* Boulder: University Press of Colorado, 2015.

Williamson, Margaret Holmes. *Powhatan Lords of Life and Death: Command and Consent in Seventeenth-Century Virginia.* Lincoln: University of Nebraska Press, 2003.

2 The English Invasion of Tsenacomoco

Anderson, Virginia DeJohn. *Creatures of Empire: How Domestic Animals Transformed Early America.* New York: Oxford University Press, 2004.

Bernhard, Virginia. *A Tale of Two Colonies: What Really Happened in Virginia and Bermuda?* Columbia: University of Missouri Press, 2011.

Coombs, John C. "'Others Not Christians in the Service of the English': Interpreting the Status of Africans and African Americans in Early Virginia." *Virginia Magazine of History and Biography* 127 (2019): 213–38.

Fausz, J. Frederick. "An 'Abundance of Blood Shed on Both Sides': England's First Indian War, 1609–1614." *Virginia Magazine of History and Biography* 98 (1990): 3–56.

———. "The Invasion of Virginia: Indians, Colonialism, and the Conquest of Cant: A Review Essay on Anglo-Indian Relations in the Chesapeake." *Virginia Magazine of History and Biography* 95 (1987): 133–56.

Guasco, Michael. *Slaves and Englishmen: Human Bondage in the Early Modern Atlantic World.* Philadelphia: University of Pennsylvania Press, 2014.

Hantman, Jeffrey L. *Monacan Millennium: A Collaborative Archaeology and History of a Virginia Indian People.* Charlottesville: University of Virginia Press, 2018.

Horn, James. *A Land as God Made It: Jamestown and the Birth of America.* New York: Basic Books, 2005.

———. *1619: Jamestown and the Forging of American Democracy.* New York: Basic Books, 2018.

Kelso, William M. *Jamestown: The Buried Truth.* 2d ed., rev. Charlottesville: University of Virginia Press, 2017.

Kupperman, Karen Ordahl. *The Jamestown Project.* Cambridge, Mass.: Belknap Press of Harvard University Press, 2007.

Mancall, Peter C., ed. *The Atlantic World and Virginia, 1550–1624.* Chapel Hill: University of North Carolina Press, 2007.

Musselwhite, Paul, Peter C. Mancall, and James Horn, eds. *Virginia 1619: Slavery and Freedom in the Making of English America.* Chapel Hill: University of North Carolina Press, 2019.

Potter, Jennifer. *The Jamestown Brides: The Story of England's "Maids for Virginia."* New York: Oxford University Press, 2019.

Rountree, Helen C. *Pocahontas, Powhatan, Opechancanough: Three Indian Lives Changed by Jamestown.* Charlottesville: University of Virginia Press, 2005.

Townsend, Camilla. *Pocahontas and the Powhatan Dilemma: An American Portrait.* New York: Hill and Wang, 2004.

Vaughan, Alden T. *Transatlantic Encounters: American Indians in Britain, 1500–1776.* Cambridge: Cambridge University Press, 2006.

White, Sam. *A Cold Welcome: The Little Ice Age and Europe's Encounter with North America.* Cambridge, Mass.: Harvard University Press, 2017.

3 Royal Colony

Billings, Warren M. *A Little Parliament: The Virginia General Assembly in the Seventeenth Century.* Richmond: Library of Virginia, 2004.

——. *Sir William Berkeley and the Forging of Colonial Virginia.* Baton Rouge: Louisiana State University Press, 2004.

Briceland, Alan Vance. *Westward from Virginia: The Exploration of the Virginia-Carolina Frontier, 1650–1710.* Charlottesville: University Press of Virginia, 1987.

Browne, Eric E. *The Westo: Slave Traders of the Early Colonial South.* Tuscaloosa: University of Alabama Press, 2005.

Gallay, Alan. *The Indian Slave Trade: The Rise of the English Empire in the American South, 1670–1717.* New Haven, Conn.: Yale University Press, 2002.

——, ed. *Indian Slavery in Colonial America.* Lincoln: University of Nebraska Press, 2009.

Hatfield, April Lee. *Atlantic Virginia: Intercolonial Relations in the Seventeenth Century.* Philadelphia: University of Pennsylvania Press, 2004.

Kukla, Jon. "Order and Chaos in Early America: Political and Social Stability in Pre-Restoration Virginia." *American Historical Review* 90 (1985): 275–98.

——. *Political Institutions in Virginia, 1619–1660.* New York: Garland, 1989.

Morgan, Edmund S. *American Slavery, American Freedom: The Ordeal of Colonial Virginia.* New York: Norton, 1975.

Rice, James D. *Tales from a Revolution: Bacon's Rebellion and the Transformation of Early America.* New York: Oxford University Press, 2012.

Tarter, Brent. "Bacon's Rebellion, the Grievances of the People, and the Political Culture of Seventeenth-Century Virginia." *Virginia Magazine of History and Biography* 119 (2011): 3–41.

Washburn, Wilcomb Edward. *The Governor and the Rebel: A History of Bacon's Rebellion in Virginia.* Chapel Hill: University of North Carolina Press, 1957.

Webb, Stephen Saunders. *1676: The End of American Independence.* New York: Knopf, 1984.

4 Life in the Seventeenth Century

Bailyn, Bernard. "Politics and Social Structure in Virginia." In *Seventeenth-Century America: Essays in Colonial History,* ed. James Morton Smith, 90–115. Chapel Hill: University of North Carolina Press, 1959.

Billings, Warren M. *A Little Parliament: The Virginia General Assembly in the Seventeenth Century.* Richmond: Library of Virginia, 2004.

——. *Sir William Berkeley and the Forging of Colonial Virginia.* Baton Rouge: Louisiana State University Press, 2004.

Bond, Edward L. *Damned Souls in a Tobacco Colony: Religion in Seventeenth-Century Virginia.* Macon, Ga.: Mercer University Press, 2000.

Bradburn, Douglas, and John C. Coombs, eds. *Early Modern Virginia: Reconsidering the Old Dominion.* Charlottesville: University of Virginia Press, 2011.

Breen, T. H. "Looking Out for Number One." In *Puritans and Adventurers: Change and Persistence in Early America,* 106–26. New York: Oxford University Press, 1980.

Carson, Cary, Joanne Bowen, Willie Graham, Martha McCartney, and Lorena Walsh. "New World, Real World: Improvising English Culture in Seventeenth-Century Virginia." *Journal of Southern History* (2008): 31–88.

Deal, Joseph Douglas. *Race and Class in Colonial Virginia: Indians, Englishmen, and Africans on the Eastern Shore during the Seventeenth Century.* New York: Garland, 1993.

Graham, Willie, Carter L. Hudgins, Carl R. Lounsbury, Fraser D. Neiman, and James P. Whittenburg. "Adaptation and Innovation: Archaeological and Architectural Perspectives on the Seventeenth-Century Chesapeake." *William and Mary Quarterly,* 3d ser., 64 (2007): 451–521.

Horn, James P. P. *Adapting to a New World: English Society in the Seventeenth-Century Chesapeake.* Chapel Hill: University of North Carolina Press, 1994.

Koot, Christian J. *A Biography of a Map in Motion: Augustine Herrman's Chesapeake.* New York: NYU Press, 2018.

Kukla, Jon. "Order and Chaos in Early America: Political and Social Stability in Pre-Restoration Virginia." *American Historical Review* 90 (1985): 275–98.

———. *Political Institutions in Virginia, 1619–1660.* New York: Garland, 1989.

Morgan, Edmund S. *American Slavery, American Freedom: The Ordeal of Colonial Virginia.* New York: Norton, 1975.

Pagan, John Ruston. *Anne Orthwood's Bastard: Sex and Law in Early Virginia.* New York: Oxford University Press, 2003.

Perry, James R. *The Formation of a Society on Virginia's Eastern Shore, 1615–1655.* Chapel Hill: University of North Carolina Press, 1990.

Rutman, Darrett Bruce, and Anita H. Rutman. *A Place in Time: Middlesex County, Virginia, 1650–1750.* 2 vols. New York: Norton, 1984.

Tate, Thad W., and David L. Ammerman, eds. *The Chesapeake in the Seventeenth Century: Essays on Anglo-American Society.* Chapel Hill: University of North Carolina Press, 1979.

5 Tobacco and Slavery

Billings, Warren M. "The Law of Servants and Slaves in Seventeenth-Century Virginia." *Virginia Magazine of History and Biography* 99 (1991): 45–62.

Breen, T. H., and Stephen Innes, *"Myne owne ground": Race and Freedom on Virginia's Eastern Shore, 1640–1676.* New York: Oxford University Press, 1980.

Coombs, John C. "'Others Not Christians in the Service of the English': Interpreting the Status of Africans and African Americans in Early Virginia." *Virginia Magazine of History and Biography* 127 (2019): 213–38.

Deal, Joseph Douglas. *Race and Class in Colonial Virginia: Indians, Englishmen, and Africans on the Eastern Shore during the Seventeenth Century.* New York: Garland, 1993.

Goetz, Rebecca. *The Baptism of Virginia: How Christianity Created Race.* Baltimore, Md.: Johns Hopkins University Press, 2012.

Kulikoff, Allan. *Tobacco and Slaves: The Development of Southern Cultures in the Chesapeake, 1680–1800.* Chapel Hill: University of North Carolina Press, 1986.

Morgan, Edmund S. *American Slavery, American Freedom: The Ordeal of Colonial Virginia.* New York: Norton, 1975.

Morgan, Philip. *Slave Counterpoint: Black Culture in the Eighteenth-Century Chesapeake and Lowcountry.* Chapel Hill: University of North Carolina Press, 1998.

Parent, Anthony S. Jr. *Foul Means: The Formation of a Slave Society in Virginia, 1660–1740.* Chapel Hill: University of North Carolina Press, 2003.

Rainbolt, John Corbin. *From Prescription to Persuasion: Manipulation of Eighteenth-Century Virginia Economy.* Port Washington, N.Y.: Kennikat Press, 1974. (Posthumously published with an incorrect title; it concerns economic diversification in the seventeenth century.)

Stubbs, Tristan. *Masters of Violence: The Plantation Overseers of Eighteenth-Century Virginia, South Carolina, and Georgia.* Columbia: University of South Carolina Press, 2018.

Vaughan, Alden T. "The Origins Debate: Slavery and Racism in Seventeenth-Century Virginia." *Virginia Magazine of History and Biography* 97 (1989): 311–54.

Walsh, Lorena S. "The Chesapeake Slave Trade: Regional Patterns, African Origins, and Some Implications." *William and Mary Quarterly,* 3d ser., 58 (2001): 139–70.

———. *From Calabar to Carter's Grove: The History of a Virginia Slave Community.* Charlottesville: University Press of Virginia, 1997.

———. *Motives of Honor, Pleasure, and Profit: Plantation Management in the Colonial Chesapeake, 1607–1763.* Chapel Hill: University of North Carolina Press, 2010.

6 Life in the Eighteenth Century

Billings, Warren M., and Brent Tarter, eds. *"Esteemed Bookes of Lawe" and the Legal Culture of Early Virginia.* Charlottesville: University of Virginia Press, 2017.

Brown, Kathleen M. *Good Wives, Nasty Wenches, and Anxious Patriarchs: Gender, Race, and Power in Colonial Virginia.* Chapel Hill: University of North Carolina Press, 1996.

Davis, Richard Beale. *Intellectual Life in the Colonial South, 1585–1763.* 3 vols. Knoxville: University of Tennessee Press, 1978.

Farmer, Charles J. *In the Absence of Towns: Settlement and Country Trade in Southside Virginia, 1730–1800.* Lanham, Md.: Rowman and Littlefield, 1993.

Fischer, David Hackett. *Albion's Seed: Four British Folkways in America.* New York: Oxford University Press, 1989.

Hofstra, Warren. *The Planting of New Virginia: Settlement and Landscape in the Shenandoah Valley.* Baltimore, Md.: Johns Hopkins University Press, 2004.

Kamoie, Laura Croghan. *Irons in the Fire: The Business History of the Tayloe Family and Virginia's Gentry, 1700–1860.* Charlottesville: University of Virginia Press, 2007.

Kolp, John Gilman. *Gentlemen and Freeholders: Electoral Politics in Colonial Virginia.* Baltimore, Md.: Johns Hopkins University Press, 1998.

Lounsbury, Carl. *The Courthouses of Early Virginia: An Architectural History.* Charlottesville: University of Virginia Press, 2005.

Martin, Ann Smart. *Buying into the World of Goods: Early Consumers in Backcountry Virginia.* Baltimore, Md.: Johns Hopkins University Press, 2008.

McCleskey, Turk. *The Road to Black Ned's Forge: A Story of Race, Sex, and Trade on the Colonial American Frontier.* Charlottesville: University of Virginia Press, 2014.

Middleton, Arthur Pierce. *Tobacco Coast: A Maritime History of Chesapeake Bay in the Colonial Era.* Newport News, Va.: Mariner's Museum, 1953.

Mitchell, Robert D. *Commercialism and Frontier: Perspectives on the Early Shenandoah Valley.* Charlottesville: University Press of Virginia, 1977.

———, ed. *Appalachian Frontiers: Settlement, Society, and Development in the Preindustrial Era.* Lexington: University Press of Kentucky, 1991.

Mooney, Barbara Burlison. *Prodigy Houses of Virginia: Architecture and the Native Elite.* Charlottesville: University of Virginia Press, 2008.

Musselwhite, Paul. *Urban Dreams, Rural Communities: The Rise of Plantation Society in the Chesapeake.* Chicago: University of Chicago Press, 2019.

Puglisi, Michael J., ed. *Diversity and Accommodation: Essays on the Cultural Composition of the Virginia Frontier.* Knoxville: University of Tennessee Press, 1997.

Rozbicki, Michal J. *The Complete Colonial Gentleman: Cultural Legitimacy in Plantation America.* Charlottesville: University Press of Virginia, 1998.

Smith, Daniel Blake. *Inside the Great House: Family Life in Eighteenth-Century Chesapeake Society.* Ithaca, N.Y.: Cornell University Press, 1980.

Snyder, Terri L. *Brabbling Women: Disorderly Speech and the Law in Early Virginia.* Ithaca, N.Y.: Cornell University Press, 2003.

Sobel, Mechal. *The World They Made Together: Black and White Values in Eighteenth-Century Virginia.* Princeton, N.J.: Princeton University Press, 1987.

Sturtz, Linda L. *Within Her Power: Propertied Women in Colonial Virginia.* New York: Routledge, 2002.

Sydnor, Charles S. *Gentlemen Freeholders: Political Practices in Washington's Virginia.* Chapel Hill: University of North Carolina Press, 1952. Reprinted as *American Revolutionaries in the Making: Political Practices in Washington's Virginia.* New York: Free Press, 1965.

Tillson, Albert H. Jr. *Gentry and Common Folk: Political Culture on a Virginia Frontier, 1740–1789.* Lexington: University Press of Kentucky, 1991.

Upton, Dell. *Holy Things and Profane: Anglican Parish Churches in Colonial Virginia.* New York: Architectural History Foundation and Cambridge, Mass.: MIT Press, 1986; 2d ed., New Haven, Conn.: Yale University Press, 1997.

Wells, Camille. *Material Witnesses: Domestic Architecture and Plantation Landscapes in Early Virginia.* Charlottesville: University of Virginia Press, 2018.

Winner, Lauren F. *A Cheerful and Comfortable Faith: Anglican Religious Practice in the*

Elite Households of Eighteenth-Century Virginia. New Haven, Conn.: Yale University Press, 2010.

Wust, Klaus. *The Virginia Germans.* Charlottesville: University Press of Virginia, 1969.

7 Mid-Century Challenges

Anderson, Fred. *Crucible of War: The Seven Years' War and the Fate of Empire in British North America, 1754–1766.* New York: Knopf, 2000.

Breen, T. H. *Tobacco Culture: The Mentality of the Great Tidewater Planters on the Eve of Revolution.* Princeton, N.J.: Princeton University Press, 1985. Reprinted with new preface, 2001.

Hofstra, Warren R., ed. *Cultures in Conflict: The Seven Years' War in North America.* Lanham, Md.: Rowman and Littlefield, 2007.

Isaac, Rhys. *The Transformation of Virginia, 1740–1790.* Chapel Hill: University of North Carolina Press, 1982.

Nelson, John K. *A Blessed Company: Parishes, Parsons, and Parishioners in Anglican Virginia, 1690–1776.* Chapel Hill: University of North Carolina Press, 2001.

Spangler, Jewel L. *Virginians Reborn: Anglican Monopoly, Evangelical Dissent, and the Rise of Baptists in the Late Eighteenth Century.* Charlottesville: University of Virginia Press, 2008.

Tillson, Albert H. Jr. *Gentry and Common Folk: Political Culture on a Virginia Frontier, 1740–1789.* Lexington: University Press of Kentucky, 1991.

Ward, Matthew C. *Breaking the Backcountry: The Seven Years' War in Virginia and Pennsylvania, 1754–1765.* Pittsburgh, Pa.: University of Pittsburgh Press, 2003.

8 Independence and Revolution

Brewer, Holly. "Entailing Aristocracy in Colonial Virginia: 'Ancient Feudal Restraints' and Revolutionary Reform." *William and Mary Quarterly,* 3d ser., 54 (1997): 307–46.

Buckley, Thomas E., SJ. *Church and State in Revolutionary Virginia, 1776–1787.* Charlottesville: University Press of Virginia, 1977.

———. *Establishing Religious Freedom: Jefferson's Statute in Virginia.* Charlottesville: University of Virginia Press, 2013.

David, James Corbett. *Dunmore's New World: The Extraordinary Life of a Royal Governor in Revolutionary America, with Jacobites, Counterfeiters, Land Schemes, Shipwrecks, Scalping, Indian Politics, Runaway Slaves, and Two Illegal Royal Weddings.* Charlottesville: University of Virginia Press, 2013.

Holton, Woody. *Forced Founders: Indians, Debtors, Slaves, and the Making of the American Revolution in Virginia.* Chapel Hill: University of North Carolina Press, 1999.

Isaac, Rhys. *The Transformation of Virginia, 1740–1790.* Chapel Hill: University of North Carolina Press, 1982.

Lindman, Janet Moore. *Bodies of Belief: Baptist Community in Early America.* Philadelphia: University of Pennsylvania Press, 2008.

Lowe, Jessica K. *Murder in the Shenandoah: Making Law Sovereign in Revolutionary Virginia.* Cambridge: Cambridge University Press, 2019.

McDonnell, Michael A. *The Politics of War, Race, Class, and Conflict in Revolutionary Virginia.* Chapel Hill: University of North Carolina Press, 2007.

Ragosta, John A. *Wellspring of Liberty: How Virginia's Religious Dissenters Helped Win the American Revolution and Secured Religious Liberty.* New York: Oxford University Press, 2010.

Rozbicki, Michal. *Culture and Liberty in the Age of the American Revolution.* Charlottesville: University of Virginia Press, 2011.

Selby, John E. *The Revolution in Virginia, 1775–1783.* Williamsburg, Va.: Colonial Williamsburg Foundation, 1988.

Spangler, Jewel L. *Virginians Reborn: Anglican Monopoly, Evangelical Dissent, and the Rise of Baptists in the Late Eighteenth Century.* Charlottesville: University of Virginia Press, 2008.

Tate, Thad W. "The Coming of the Revolution in Virginia: Britain's Challenge to Virginia's Ruling Class, 1763–1776." *William and Mary Quarterly,* 3d ser., 19 (1962): 323–43.

Taylor, Alan. *The Internal Enemy: Slavery and War in Virginia, 1772–1832.* New York: Norton, 2013.

Tillson, Albert H. Jr. *Accommodating Revolutions: Virginia's Northern Neck in an Era of Transformations, 1760–1810.* Charlottesville: University of Virginia Press, 2010.

———. *Gentry and Common Folk: Political Culture on a Virginia Frontier, 1740–1789.* Lexington: University Press of Kentucky, 1991.

9   Virginians and the New Nation

Baker, Meredith Henne. *The Richmond Theater Fire: Early America's First Great Disaster.* Baton Rouge: Louisiana State University Press, 2011.

Beeman, Richard R. *The Old Dominion and the New Nation, 1788–1801.* Lexington: University Press of Kentucky, 1972.

Buckley, Thomas E., SJ. *Establishing Religious Freedom: Jefferson's Statute in Virginia.* Charlottesville: University of Virginia Press, 2013.

———. *The Great Catastrophe of My Life: Divorce in the Old Dominion.* Chapel Hill: University of North Carolina Press, 2002.

Butler, Stuart Lee. *Defending the Old Dominion: Virginia and Its Militia in the War of 1812.* Lanham, Md.: University Press of America, 2013.

Jordan, Daniel P. *Political Leadership in Jefferson's Virginia.* Charlottesville: University Press of Virginia, 1983.

Lewis, Jan. *The Pursuit of Happiness: Family and Values in Jefferson's Virginia.* Cambridge: Cambridge University Press, 1983.

Risjord, Norman. *Chesapeake Politic, 1781–1800.* New York: Columbia University Press, 1978.

Taylor, Alan. *The Internal Enemy: Slavery and War in Virginia, 1772–1832.* New York: Norton, 2013.

Tillson, Albert H. Jr. *Accommodating Revolutions: Virginia's Northern Neck in an Era of Transformations, 1760–1810.* Charlottesville: University of Virginia Press, 2010.

10 Life in the First Half of the Nineteenth Century

Adams, Sean Patrick. *Old Dominion; Industrial Commonwealth: Coal, Politics, and Economy in Antebellum America.* Baltimore, Md.: Johns Hopkins University Press, 2004.

Barnes, L. Diane. *Artisan Workers in the Upper South: Petersburg, Virginia, 1820–1865.* Baton Rouge: Louisiana State University Press, 2008.

Cohen, Benjamin R. *Notes from the Ground: Science, Soil, and Society in the American Countryside.* New Haven, Conn.: Yale University Press, 2009.

Goldfield, David R. *Urban Growth in the Age of Sectionalism: Virginia, 1847–1861.* Baton Rouge: Louisiana State University Press, 1977.

Kimball, Gregg D. *American City, Southern Place: A Cultural History of Antebellum Richmond.* Athens: University of Georgia Press, 2000.

Jabour, Anya. *Marriage in the Early Republic: Elizabeth and William Wirt and the Companionate Ideal.* Baltimore, Md.: Johns Hopkins University Press, 1998.

Lebsock, Suzanne. *The Free Women of Petersburg: Status and Culture in a Southern Town, 1784–1860.* New York: Norton, 1984.

Lewis, Jan. *The Pursuit of Happiness: Family and Values in Jefferson's Virginia.* Cambridge: Cambridge University Press, 1983.

Majewski, John. *A House Dividing: Economic Development in Pennsylvania and Virginia before the Civil War.* New York: Cambridge University Press, 2000.

Pflugrad-Jackisch, Ami. *Brothers of a Vow: Secret Fraternal Orders and the Transformation of White Male Culture in Antebellum Virginia.* Athens: University of Georgia Press, 2010.

Schweiger, Beth Barton. *The Gospel Working Up: Progress and the Pulpit in Nineteenth-Century Virginia.* New York: Oxford University Press, 2000.

Siegel, Frederick F. *The Roots of Southern Distinctiveness: Tobacco and Society in Danville, Virginia, 1780–1865.* Chapel Hill: University of North Carolina Press, 1987.

Stealey, John E. III. *The Antebellum Kanawha Salt Business and Western Markets.* Lexington: University Press of Kentucky, 1993.

11 Slave State

Boger, Tommy. *Free Blacks in Norfolk, Virginia, 1790–1860.* Charlottesville: University Press of Virginia, 1997.

Breen, Patrick H. *The Land Shall Be Deluged in Blood: A New History of the Nat Turner Revolt.* New York: Oxford University Press, 2015.

Campbell, James M. *Slavery on Trial: Race, Class, and Criminal Justice in Antebellum Richmond, Virginia.* Gainesville: University Press of Florida, 2007.

Coates, Eyler Robert, ed. *The Jefferson-Hemings Myth: An American Travesty.* Charlottesville, Va.: Jefferson Editions, 2001.

Dew, Charles B. *Bond of Iron: Master and Slave at Buffalo Forge.* New York: Norton, 1994.

Deyle, Stephen. *Carry Me Back: The Domestic Slave Trade in American Life.* New York: Oxford University Press, 2005.

Egerton, Douglas R. *Gabriel's Rebellion: The Virginia Slave Conspiracies of 1800 and 1802.* Chapel Hill: University of North Carolina Press, 1993.

Ely, Melvin Patrick. *Israel on the Appomattox: A Southern Experiment in Black Freedom from the 1790s through the Civil War.* New York: Knopf, 2004.

Freehling, Alison Goodyear. *Drift toward Dissolution: The Virginia Slavery Debate of 1831–1832.* Baton Rouge: Louisiana State University Press, 1982.

French, Scot. *The Rebellious Slave: Nat Turner in American Memory.* Boston: Houghton Mifflin, 2004.

Gordon-Reed, Annette. *The Hemingses of Monticello: An American Family.* New York: Norton, 2008.

———. *Thomas Jefferson and Sally Hemings: An American Controversy.* Charlottesville: University Press of Virginia, 1997.

Greenberg, Kenneth S., ed. *Nat Turner: A Slave Rebellion in History and Memory.* New York: Oxford University Press, 2003.

Hadden, Sally E. *Slave Patrols: Law and Violence in Virginia and the Carolinas.* Cambridge, Mass.: Harvard University Press, 2001.

Irons, Charles F. *The Origins of Proslavery Christianity: White and Black Evangelicals in Colonial and Antebellum Virginia.* Chapel Hill: University of North Carolina Press, 2008.

Mariner, Kirk. *Slave and Free on Virginia's Eastern Shore.* Onancock, Va.: Milona Publications, 2014.

Maris-Wolfe, Ted. *Family Bonds: Free Blacks and Re-enslavement Law in Antebellum Virginia.* Chapel Hill: University of North Carolina Press, 2015.

McInnis, Maurie Dee. *Slaves Waiting for Sale: Abolitionist Art and the American Slave Trade.* Chicago: University of Chicago Press, 2011.

Miller, John Chester. *Wolf by the Ears: Thomas Jefferson and Slavery.* New York: Free Press, 1977.

Nicholls, Michael L. *Whispers of Rebellion: Narrating Gabriel's Conspiracy.* Charlottesville: University of Virginia Press, 2012.

Oast, Jennifer. *Institutional Slavery: Slaveholding Churches, Schools, Colleges, and Businesses in Virginia, 1680–1860.* New York: Cambridge University Press, 2015.

Pargas, Damian Alan. *The Quarters and the Fields: Slave Families in the Non-Cotton South.* New York: Cambridge University Press, 2010.

Root, Erick S. *All Honor to Jefferson? The Virginia Slavery Debates and the Positive Good Thesis.* Lanham, Md.: Lexington Books, 2008.

Rothman, Joshua D. *Notorious in the Neighborhood: Sex and Families across the Color Line in Virginia, 1787–1861.* Chapel Hill: University of North Carolina Press, 2003.

Schermerhorn, Calvin. *Money over Mastery, Family over Freedom: Slavery in the Antebellum Upper South.* Baltimore, Md.: Johns Hopkins University Press, 2011.

Schwartz, Marie Jenkins. *Ties That Bound: Founding First Ladies and Slaves.* Chicago: University of Chicago Press, 2017.

Schwarz, Philip J. *Migrants against Slavery: Virginians and the Nation.* Charlottesville: University of Virginia Press, 2001.

———. *Slave Laws in Virginia.* Athens: University of Georgia Press, 1996.

———. *Twice Condemned: Slaves and the Criminal Laws of Virginia, 1705–1865.* Baton Rouge: Louisiana State University Press, 1988.

Scully, Randolph Ferguson. *Religion and the Making of Nat Turner's Virginia: Baptist Community and Conflict, 1740–1840.* Charlottesville: University of Virginia Press, 2008.

Sidbury, James. *Plowshares into Swords: Race, Rebellion, and Identity in Gabriel's Virginia, 1730–1810.* New York: Cambridge University Press, 1997.

Stanton, Lucia. *"Those Who Labor for My Happiness": Slavery at Thomas Jefferson's Monticello.* Charlottesville: University of Virginia Press, 2012.

Stealey, John E. III. *The Antebellum Kanawha Salt Business and Western Markets.* Lexington: University Press of Kentucky, 1993.

Stevenson, Brenda E. *Life in Black and White: Family and Community in the Slave South.* New York: Oxford University Press, 1996.

Takagi, Midori. *Rearing Wolves to Our Own Destruction: Slavery in Richmond, Virginia, 1782–1865.* Charlottesville: University Press of Virginia, 1999.

Tyler-McGraw, Marie. *An African Republic: Black and White Virginians in the Making of Liberia.* Chapel Hill: University of North Carolina Press, 2007.

von Daacke, Kirt. *Freedom Has a Face: Race, Identity, and Community in Jefferson's Virginia.* Charlottesville: University of Virginia Press, 2012.

Wiencek, Henry. *Master of the Mountain: Thomas Jefferson and His Slaves.* New York: Farrar, Straus, and Giroux, 2012.

Winter, Kari J. *The American Dreams of John B. Prentis, Slave Trader.* Athens: University of Georgia Press, 2011.

Wolf, Eva Sheppard. *Almost Free: A Story about Family and Race in Antebellum Virginia.* Athens: University of Georgia Press, 2012.

———. *Race and Liberty in the New Nation: Emancipation in Virginia from the Revolution to Nat Turner's Rebellion.* Baton Rouge: Louisiana State University Press, 2006.

Zaborney, John J. *Slaves for Hire: Renting Enslaved Laborers in Antebellum Virginia.* Baton Rouge: Louisiana State University Press, 2012.

12 Divided State in a Divided Nation

Ambler, Charles Henry. *Sectionalism in Virginia from 1776 to 1861.* Chicago: University of Chicago Press, 1910; 2d ed., with introduction by Barbara Rasmussen, Morgantown: West Virginia University Press, 2008.

Brugger, Robert J. *Beverley Tucker: Heart over Head in the Old South.* Baltimore, Md.: Johns Hopkins University Press, 1978.

Crofts, Daniel W. *Old Southampton: Politics and Society in a Virginia County, 1834–1869.* Charlottesville: University Press of Virginia, 1992.

Curtis, Christopher Michael. *Jefferson's Freeholders and the Politics of Ownership in the Old Dominion.* New York: Cambridge University Press, 2012.

Freehling, Alison Goodyear. *Drift toward Dissolution: The Virginia Slavery Debate of 1831–1832.* Baton Rouge: Louisiana State University Press, 1982.

Link, William A. *Roots of Secession: Slavery and Politics in Antebellum Virginia.* Chapel Hill: University of North Carolina Press, 2003.

Noe, Kenneth W. *Southwest Virginia's Railroad: Modernization and the Sectional Crisis.* Urbana: University of Illinois Press, 1994.

Shade, William G. *Democratizing the Old Dominion: Virginia and the Second Party System, 1824–1861.* Charlottesville: University Press of Virginia, 1996.

Sutton, Robert P. *Revolution to Secession: Constitution Making in the Old Dominion.* Charlottesville: University Press of Virginia, 1989.

Tarter, Brent. *Gerrymanders: How Redistricting Has Protected Slavery, White Supremacy, and Partisan Minorities in Virginia.* Charlottesville: University of Virginia Press, 2019.

Varon, Elizabeth R. *We Mean to Be Counted: White Women and Politics in Antebellum Virginia.* Chapel Hill: University of North Carolina Press, 1998.

13 Civil War and Emancipation

Ash, Steven V. *Rebel Richmond: Life and Death in the Confederate Capital.* Chapel Hill: University of North Carolina Press, 2019.

Ayers, Edward L. *In the Presence of Mine Enemies: War in the Heart of America, 1859–1863.* New York: Norton, 2003.

———. *The Thin Light of Freedom: The Civil War and Emancipation in the Heart of America.* New York: Norton, 2017.

Bearss, Sara B. "'Restored and Vindicated': The Virginia Constitutional Convention of 1864." *Virginia Magazine of History and Biography* 122 (2014): 156–81.

Blair, William A. *Virginia's Private War: Feeding Body and Soul in the Confederacy, 1861–1865.* New York: Oxford University Press, 1998.

Brasher, Glenn David. *The Peninsula Campaign and the Necessity of Emancipation: African Americans and the Fight for Freedom.* Chapel Hill: University of North Carolina Press, 2012.

Brewer, James H. *The Confederate Negro: Virginia's Craftsmen and Military Laborers, 1861–1865.* Durham, N.C.: Duke University Press, 1969.

Carmichael, Peter S. *The Last Generation: Young Virginians in Peace, War, and Reunion.* Chapel Hill: University of North Carolina Press, 2005.

Chesson, Michael B. "Harlots or Heroines? A New Look at the Richmond Bread Riot." *Virginia Magazine of History and Biography* 92 (1984): 131–75.

Crofts, Daniel W. *Reluctant Confederates: Upper South Unionists in the Secession Crisis.* Chapel Hill: University of North Carolina Press, 1989.

Curry, Richard Orr. *A House Divided: A Study of the Statehood Politics and the Copperhead Movement in West Virginia.* Pittsburgh, Pa.: University of Pittsburgh Press, 1964.

DeCredico, Mary. *Confederate Citadel: Richmond and Its People at War.* Lexington: University Press of Kentucky, 2020.

Dew, Charles B. *Ironmaker to the Confederacy: Joseph R. Anderson and the Tredegar Iron Works.* New Haven, Conn.: Yale University Press, 1966; 2d ed., Richmond: Library of Virginia, 1999.

Dubbs, Carol Kettenburg. *Defend This Old Town: Williamsburg during the Civil War.* Baton Rouge: Louisiana State University Press, 2002.

Duncan, Richard R. *Beleaguered Winchester: A Virginia Community at War, 1861–1865.* Baton Rouge: Louisiana State University Press, 2007.

Freehling, William W. *The South vs. the South: How Anti-Confederate Southerners Shaped the Course of the Civil War.* New York: Oxford University Press, 2001.

Greene, A. Wilson. *Civil War Petersburg: Confederate City in the Crucible of War.* Charlottesville: University of Virginia Press, 2006.

Jordan, Ervin L. *Black Confederates and Afro-Yankees in Civil War Virginia.* Charlottesville: University Press of Virginia, 1995.

Levine, Bruce C. *Confederate Emancipation: Southern Plans to Free and Arm Slaves during the Civil War.* Oxford: Oxford University Press, 2006.

Link, William A. *Roots of Secession: Slavery and Politics in Antebellum Virginia.* Chapel Hill: University of North Carolina Press, 2003.

Lowe, Richard G. *Republicans and Reconstruction in Virginia, 1856–70.* Charlottesville: University Press of Virginia, 1991.

Martinez, Jaime Amanda. *Confederate Slave Impressment in the Upper South.* Chapel Hill: University of North Carolina Press, 2014.

Neely, Mark E. *Southern Rights: Political Prisoners and the Myth of Confederate Constitutionalism.* Charlottesville: University Press of Virginia, 1999.

Noe, Kenneth W. *Southwest Virginia's Railroad: Modernization and the Sectional Crisis.* Urbana: University of Illinois Press, 1994.

Shanks, Henry Thomas. *The Secession Movement in Virginia, 1847–1861.* Richmond, Va.: Garrett and Massie, 1934.

Sheehan-Dean, Aaron. *Why Confederates Fought: Family and Nation in Civil War Virginia.* Chapel Hill: University of North Carolina Press, 2007.

Stealey, John E. III. *West Virginia's Civil War–Era Constitution: Loyal Revolution, Confederate Counter-Revolution, and the Convention of 1872.* Kent, Ohio: Kent State University Press, 2013.

Sutherland, Daniel E. *Seasons of War: The Ordeal of a Confederate Community, 1861–1865.* New York: Free Press, 1995.

Tarter, Brent. *Daydreams and Nightmares: A Virginia Family Faces Secession and War.* Charlottesville: University of Virginia Press, 2015.

Thomas, Emory M. *The Confederate State of Richmond: A Biography of the Capital.* Austin: University of Texas Press, 1971.

Tripp, Steven Elliott. *Yankee Town, Southern City: Race and Class Relations in Civil War Lynchburg.* New York: NYU Press, 1996.

14 Constructing a New Virginia

Ayers, Edward L., and Scott Nesbit. "Seeing Emancipation: Scale and Freedom in the American South." *Journal of the Civil War Era* 1 (2011): 3–24.

Carmichael, Peter S. *The Last Generation: Young Virginians in Peace, War, and Reunion.* Chapel Hill: University of North Carolina Press, 2005.

Engs, Robert Francis. *Freedom's First Generation: Black Hampton, Virginia, 1861–1890.* Philadelphia: University of Pennsylvania Press, 1979.

Jones, Catherine A. *Intimate Reconstructions: Children in Postemancipation Virginia.* Charlottesville: University of Virginia Press, 2015.

Kerr-Ritchie, Jeffrey R. *Freedpeople in the Tobacco South: Virginia, 1860–1900.* Chapel Hill: University of North Carolina Press, 1999.

Lowe, Richard G. *Republicans and Reconstruction in Virginia, 1856–70.* Charlottesville: University Press of Virginia, 1991.

Maddex, Jack P. Jr. *The Virginia Conservatives, 1867–1879: A Study in Reconstruction Politics.* Chapel Hill: University of North Carolina Press, 1970.

Moger, Allen W. *Virginia: Bourbonism to Byrd, 1870–1925.* Charlottesville: University Press of Virginia, 1968.

Morgan, Lynda J. *Emancipation in Virginia's Tobacco Belt, 1850–1870.* Athens: University of Georgia Press, 1992.

O'Brien, John Thomas. *From Bondage to Citizenship: The Richmond Black Community, 1865–1867.* New York: Garland, 1990.

Rachleff, Peter J. *Black Labor in the South: Richmond, Virginia, 1865–1890.* Philadelphia: Temple University Press, 1984.

Shifflet, Crandall A. *Coal Towns: Life, Work, and Culture in Company Towns of Southern Appalachia, 1880–1960.* Knoxville: University of Tennessee Press, 1991.

———. *Patronage and Poverty in the Tobacco South: Louisa County, Virginia, 1860–1890.* Knoxville: University of Tennessee Press, 1982.

Thorp, Daniel B. *Facing Freedom: An African American Community in Virginia from Reconstruction to Jim Crow.* Charlottesville: University of Virginia Press, 2017.

15 Three Lost Causes

Blair, William A. *Cities of the Dead: Contesting the Memory of the Civil War in the South, 1865–1914.* Chapel Hill: University of North Carolina Press, 2004.

Brundage, W. Fitzhugh. *The Southern Past: A Clash of Race and Memory.* Cambridge, Mass.: Belknap Press of Harvard University Press, 2005.

Censer, Jane Turner. *The Reconstruction of White Southern Womanhood, 1865–1895.* Baton Rouge: Louisiana State University Press, 2003.

Chesson, Michael B. *Richmond after the War, 1865–1890*. Richmond: Virginia State Library, 1981.

Dailey, Jane. *Before Jim Crow: The Politics of Race in Postemancipation Virginia*. Chapel Hill: University of North Carolina Press, 2000.

Janney, Caroline E. *Burying the Dead but Not the Past: Ladies' Memorial Associations and the Lost Cause*. Chapel Hill: University of North Carolina Press, 2008.

Jones, Catherine A. *Intimate Reconstructions: Children in Postemancipation Virginia*. Charlottesville: University of Virginia Press, 2015.

Link, William A. *A Hard Country and a Lonely Place: Schooling, Society, and Reform in Rural Virginia, 1870–1920*. Chapel Hill: University of North Carolina Press, 1986.

Maddex, Jack P. Jr. *The Virginia Conservatives, 1867–1879: A Study in Reconstruction Politics*. Chapel Hill: University of North Carolina Press, 1970.

Moger, Allen W. *Virginia: Bourbonism to Byrd, 1870–1925*. Charlottesville: University Press of Virginia, 1968.

Moore, James Tice. *Two Paths to the New South: The Virginia Debt Controversy, 1870–1883*. Lexington: University of Kentucky Press, 1974.

Morsman, Amy Feely. *The Big House after Slavery: Virginia Plantation Families and Their Postbellum Domestic Experiment*. Charlottesville: University of Virginia Press, 2010.

Pulley, Raymond H. *Old Virginia Restored: An Interpretation of the Progressive Impulse, 1870–1930*. Charlottesville: University Press of Virginia, 1968.

Spriggs, William Edward. "The Virginia Colored Farmers' Alliance: A Case Study of Race and Class Identity." *Journal of Negro History* 64 (1979): 79–81.

Tarter, Brent. *A Saga of the New South: Race, Law, and Pubic Debt in Virginia*. Charlottesville: University of Virginia Press, 2016.

16 Jim Crow Virginia

Alexander, Ann Field. *Race Man: The Rise and Fall of the "Fighting Editor," John Mitchell Jr.* Charlottesville: University of Virginia Press, 2002.

Brundage, W. Fitzhugh. *Lynching in the New South: Georgia and Virginia, 1880–1930*. Urbana: University of Illinois Press, 1993.

Bunie, Andrew. *The Negro in Virginia Politics, 1902–1965*. Charlottesville: University Press of Virginia, 1967.

Gavins, Raymond. *The Perils and Prospects of Southern Black Leadership: Gordon Blaine Hancock, 1884–1970*. Durham, N.C.: Duke University Press, 1977.

Holt, Wythe. *Virginia's Constitutional Convention of 1901–1902*. New York: Garland, 1990.

Lebsock, Suzanne. *A Murder in Virginia: Southern Justice on Trial*. New York: Norton, 2003.

Moger, Allen W. *Virginia: Bourbonism to Byrd, 1870–1925*. Charlottesville: University Press of Virginia, 1968.

Pulley, Raymond H. *Old Virginia Restored: An Interpretation of the Progressive Impulse, 1870–1930.* Charlottesville: University Press of Virginia, 1968.

Sherman, Richard B. *The Case of Odell Waller and Virginia Justice, 1940–1942.* Knoxville: University of Tennessee Press, 1992.

———. "'The Last Stand': The Fight for Racial Integrity in Virginia in the 1920s." *Journal of Southern History* 54 (1988): 69–92.

———. "The 'Teachings at Hampton Institute': Social Equality, Racial Integrity, and the Virginia Public Assemblage Act of 1926." *Virginia Magazine of History and Biography* 95 (1987): 275–300.

Smith, J. Douglas. *Managing White Supremacy: Race, Politics, and Citizenship in Jim Crow Virginia.* Chapel Hill: University of North Carolina Press, 2002.

Sommerville, Diane Miller. *Rape and Race in the Nineteenth-Century South.* Chapel Hill: University of North Carolina Press, 2004.

Woodward, C. Vann. *The Strange Career of Jim Crow.* New York: Oxford University Press, 1955; 3d ed., rev., 1974.

Wynes, Charles Eldridge. *Race Relations in Virginia, 1870–1902.* Charlottesville: University Press of Virginia, 1961.

17 Progressive Virginians

Bain, Chester W. *A Body Incorporate: The Evolution of City-County Separation in Virginia.* Charlottesville: University Press of Virginia, 1967.

Brooks, Clayton McClure. *The Uplift Generation: Cooperation across the Color Line in Early Twentieth-Century Virginia.* Charlottesville: University of Virginia Press, 2017.

Dorr, Gregory Michael. *Segregation's Science: Eugenics and Society in Virginia.* Charlottesville: University of Virginia Press, 2008.

Dorr, Lisa Lindquist. *White Women, Rape, and the Power of Race in Virginia, 1900–1960.* Chapel Hill: University of North Carolina Press, 2004.

Dotson, Rand. *Roanoke, Virginia, 1882–1912: Magic City of the New South.* Knoxville: University of Tennessee Press, 2007.

Gilliam, George H. "Making Virginia Progressive: Courts and Parties, Railroads and Regulators, 1890–1910." *Virginia Magazine of History and Biography* 107 (1999): 189–222.

Green, Elna C. *This Business of Relief: Confronting Poverty in a Southern City, 1740–1940.* Athens: University of Georgia Press, 2003.

Hohner, Robert A. *Prohibition and Politics: The Life of Bishop James Cannon Jr.* Columbia: University of South Carolina Press, 1999.

Holloway, Pippa. *Sexuality, Politics, and Social Control in Virginia, 1920–1945.* Chapel Hill: University of North Carolina Press, 2006.

Holt, Wythe. *Virginia's Constitutional Convention of 1901–1902.* New York: Garland, 1990.

Lindgren, James M. *Preserving the Old Dominion: Historic Preservation and Virginia Traditionalism.* Charlottesville: University Press of Virginia, 1993.

Lombardo, Paul A. *Three Generations, No Imbeciles: Eugenics, the Supreme Court, and Buck v. Bell.* Baltimore, Md.: Johns Hopkins University Press, 2008.

Moger, Allen W. *Virginia: Bourbonism to Byrd, 1870–1925.* Charlottesville: University Press of Virginia, 1968.

Ooten, Melissa. *Race, Gender, and Film Censorship in Virginia, 1922–1965.* Lanham, Md.: Lexington Books, 2015.

Pulley, Raymond H. *Old Virginia Restored: An Interpretation of the Progressive Impulse, 1870–1930.* Charlottesville: University Press of Virginia, 1968.

Schuyler, Lorraine Gates. *The Weight of Their Votes: Southern Women and Political Leverage in the 1920s.* Chapel Hill: University of North Carolina Press, 2006.

Shepherd, Samuel C. Jr. *Avenues of Faith: Shaping the Urban Religious Culture of Richmond, Virginia, 1900–1929.* Tuscaloosa: University of Alabama Press, 2001.

Smith, J. Douglas. *Managing White Supremacy: Race, Politics, and Citizenship in Jim Crow Virginia.* Chapel Hill: University of North Carolina Press, 2002.

Tarter, Brent, Marianne E. Julienne, and Barbara C. Batson. *The Campaign for Woman Suffrage in Virginia.* Charleston, S.C.: History Press, 2020.

18 Two World Wars and the Great Depression

Gregg, Sara M. *Managing the Mountains: Land Use Planning, the New Deal, and the Creation of a Federal Landscape in Appalachia.* New Haven, Conn.: Yale University Press, 2010.

Heinemann, Ronald L. *Depression and New Deal in Virginia: The Enduring Dominion.* Charlottesville: University Press of Virginia, 1983.

———. *Harry Byrd of Virginia.* Charlottesville: University Press of Virginia, 1996.

Mundy, Liza. *Code Girls: The Untold Story of the American Women Code Breakers of World War II.* New York: Hachette Books, 2017.

Murray, Paul Thom. "Who Is an Indian? Who Is a Negro? Virginia Indians in the World War II Draft." *Virginia Magazine of History and Biography* 95 (1987): 215–31.

Rainville, Lynn. *Virginia and the Great War: Mobilization, Supply, and Combat.* Jefferson, N.C.: McFarland, 2018.

Shetterly, Margot Lee. *Hidden Figures: The American Dream and the Untold Story of the Black Women Mathematicians Who Helped Win the Space Race.* New York: William Morrow, 2016.

Shockley, Megan Taylor. *"We, Too, Are Americans": African American Women in Detroit and Richmond, 1940–54.* Urbana: University of Illinois Press, 2004.

Smith, J. Douglas. *Managing White Supremacy: Race, Politics, and Citizenship in Jim Crow Virginia.* Chapel Hill: University of North Carolina Press, 2002.

Tarter, Brent. *Gerrymanders: How Redistricting Has Protected Slavery, White Supremacy, and Partisan Minorities in Virginia.* Charlottesville: University of Virginia Press, 2019.

Whisnant, Anne Mitchell. *Super-Scenic Motorway: A Blue Ridge Parkway History.* Chapel Hill: University of North Carolina Press, 2006.

19 Civil Rights

Bonastia, Christopher. *Southern Stalemate: Five Years without Public Education in Prince Edward County, Virginia.* Chicago: University of Chicago Press, 2012.

Coleman, Arica L. *That the Blood Stay Pure: African Americans, Native Americans, and the Predicament of Race and Identity in Virginia.* Bloomington: Indiana University Press, 2013.

Daugherity, Brian J. *Keep on Keeping On: The NAACP and the Implementation of Brown v. Board of Education in Virginia.* Charlottesville: University of Virginia Press, 2016.

Edds, Margaret. *We Face the Dawn: Oliver Hill, Spottswood Robinson, and the Legal Team That Dismantled Jim Crow.* Charlottesville: University of Virginia Press, 2018.

Green, Kristen. *Something Must Be Done about Prince Edward County: A Family, a Virginia Town, a Civil Rights Battle.* New York: Harper, 2015.

Hayter, Julian Maxwell. *The Dream Is Lost: Voting Rights and the Politics of Race in Richmond, Virginia.* Lexington: University Press of Kentucky, 2017.

Hustwit, William P. *James J. Kilpatrick: Salesman for Segregation.* Chapel Hill: University of North Carolina Press, 2013.

Lewis, Earl. *In Their Own Interests: Race, Class, and Power in Twentieth-Century Norfolk, Virginia.* Berkeley: University of California Press, 1991.

Littlejohn, Jeffrey L., and Charles H. Ford. *Elusive Equality: Desegregation and Resegregation in Norfolk's Public Schools.* Charlottesville: University of Virginia Press, 2012.

Pratt, Robert A. *The Color of Their Skin: Education and Race in Richmond, Virginia, 1954–89.* Charlottesville: University Press of Virginia, 1992.

Ryan, James E. *Five Miles Away and a World Apart: One City, Two Schools, and the Story of Educational Opportunity in Modern America.* New York: Oxford University Press, 2010.

Tarter, Brent. *Gerrymanders: How Redistricting Has Protected Slavery, White Supremacy, and Partisan Minorities in Virginia.* Charlottesville: University of Virginia Press, 2019.

Titus, Jill Ogline. *Brown's Battleground: Students, Segregationists, and the Struggle for Justice in Prince Edward County, Virginia.* Chapel Hill: University of North Carolina Press, 2011.

Wallenstein, Peter. *Blue Laws and Black Codes: Conflict, Courts, and Change in Twentieth-Century Virginia.* Charlottesville: University of Virginia Press, 2004

———. *Tell the Court I Love My Wife: Race, Marriage, and Law—An American History.* New York: Palgrave Macmillan, 2002.

Wilkinson, J. Harvie III. *Harry Byrd and the Changing Face of Virginia Politics, 1945–1966.* Charlottesville: University Press of Virginia, 1968.

20 Suburban State

Atkinson, Frank B. *The Dynamic Dominion: Realignment and the Rise of Two-Party Politics in Virginia, 1945–1980.* 2d. ed., rev. Lanham, Md.: Rowman and Littlefield, 2006.

————. *Virginia in the Vanguard: Political Leadership in the 400-Year-Old Cradle of American Democracy, 1981–2006.* Lanham, Md.: Rowman and Littlefield, 2006.

Bain, Chester W. *Annexation in Virginia: The Use of the Judicial Process for Readjusting City-County Boundaries.* Charlottesville: University Press of Virginia, 1966.

Banham, Russ. *The Fight for Fairfax: A Struggle for a Great American County.* Fairfax, Va.: GMU Press, 2009.

Dennis, Michael. *The New Economy and the Modern South.* Gainesville: University Press of Florida, 2009.

Edds, Margaret. *Claiming the Dream: The Victorious Campaign of Douglas Wilder of Virginia.* Chapel Hill: Algonquin Books of Chapel Hill, 1990.

Morris, Thomas R., and Larry J. Sabato, eds. *Virginia Government and Politics: Readings and Comments.* 4th ed., rev. Charlottesville: Weldon Cooper Center for Public Service, University of Virginia, 1998.

Sabato, Larry J. *The Democratic Party Primary in Virginia: Tantamount to Election No Longer.* Charlottesville: University Press of Virginia, 1977.

Shockley, Megan Taylor. *Creating a Progressive Commonwealth: Women Activists, Feminism, and the Politics of Social Change in Virginia, 1970s–2000s.* Baton Rouge: Louisiana State University Press, 2018.

Silver, Christopher. *Twentieth-Century Richmond: Planning, Politics, and Race.* Knoxville: University of Tennessee Press, 1984.

Silver, Christopher, and John V. Moeser. *The Separate City: Black Communities in the Urban South, 1940–1968.* Lexington: University Press of Kentucky, 1995.

Thomas, Jeff. *Virginia Politics and Government in a New Century: The Price of Power.* Charleston, S.C.: History Press, 2016.

————. *The Virginia Way: Democracy and Power after 2016.* Charleston, S.C.: History Press, 2019.

Wilkinson, J. Harvie III. *Harry Byrd and the Changing Face of Virginia Politics, 1945–1966.* Charlottesville: University Press of Virginia, 1968.

21 Cosmopolitan State

Baker, Andrew C. *Bulldozer Revolutions: A Rural History of the Metropolitan South.* Athens: University of Georgia Press, 2018.

Boon, John D., John M. Brubaker, and David R. Forrest. *Chesapeake Bay Land Subsidence and Sea Level Change: An Evaluation of Past and Present Trends and Future Outlook.* A Report to the U.S. Army Corps of Engineers Norfolk District. Virginia Institute of Marine Science, Special Report no. 425 in Applied Marine Science and Ocean Engineering, November 2010.

Brisbin, Richard A. *A Strike Like No Other Strike: Law and Resistance during the Pittston Coal Strike of 1989–1990.* Baltimore, Md.: Johns Hopkins University Press, 2002.

Davison, Steven G. *Chesapeake Waters: Four Centuries of Controversy, Concern, and Legislation.* 2d ed., rev. Centerville, Md.: Tidewater Publishers, 1997.

Dennis, Michael. *The New Economy and the Modern South.* Gainesville: University Press of Florida, 2009.

Ford, Charles Howard, and Jeffrey L. Littlejohn. *LGBT Hampton Roads.* Charleston, S.C.: Arcadia, 2016.

Kapsidelis, Tom. *After Virginia Tech: Guns, Safety, and Healing in the Era of Mass Shootings.* Charlottesville: University of Virginia Press, 2019.

Keiner, Christine. *The Oyster Question: Scientists, Watermen, and the Maryland Chesapeake Bay since 1880.* Athens: University of Georgia Press, 2009.

MacLean, Nancy. *Democracy in Chains: The Deep History of the Radical Right's Stealth Plan for America.* New York: Viking, 2017.

Maurantonio, Nicole. *Confederate Exceptionalism: Civil War Myth and Memory in the Twenty-First Century.* Lawrence: University Press of Kansas, 2019.

Nash, Stephen. *Virginia Climate Fever: How Global Warming Will Transform Our Cities, Shorelines, and Forests.* Charlottesville: University of Virginia Press, 2014.

Peters, Margaret T. *Conserving the Commonwealth: The Early Years of the Environmental Movement in Virginia.* Charlottesville: University of Virginia Press, 2008.

Sarvis, Will. *The Jefferson National Forest: An Appalachian Environmental History.* Knoxville: University of Tennessee Press, 2011.

Shetterly, Margot Lee. *Hidden Figures: The American Dream and the Untold Story of the Black Women Mathematicians Who Helped Win the Space Race.* New York: William Morrow, 2016.

Spiers, John H. *Smarter Growth: Activism and Environmental Policy in Metropolitan Washington.* Philadelphia: University of Pennsylvania Press, 2018.

Teles, Steven M. *The Rise of the Conservative Legal Movement: The Battle for Control of the Law.* Princeton, N.J.: Princeton University Press, 2008.

Wallenstein, Peter. *Blue Laws and Black Codes: Conflict, Courts, and Change in Twentieth-Century Virginia.* Charlottesville: University of Virginia Press, 2004.

ILLUSTRATION CREDITS

Illustrations not otherwise credited are from the collections of the Library of Virginia.

Berkeley Will Trust, Berkeley Castle, Gloucestershire, U.K., and Virginia Historical Society: *page 45*

John Carter Brown Library, Brown University: *page 83*

Colonial Williamsburg Foundation, Williamsburg, Virginia: *pages 85 (gift of the Bodleian Library, Oxford University), 199 (Museum Purchase)*

Jamestown Rediscovery (Preservation Virginia): *pages 22, 23*

Library of Congress, Washington, DC: *pages 92, 105 (Historic American Buildings Survey), 132, 202, 224, 249, 251, 260, 262, 355, 390 (Prints & Photographic Division, NYWT&S Collection)*

Maryland Historical Society: *page 71 (1960.108.1.3.21)*

National Archives and Records Administration, Special Media Archives Service Division, College Park, Maryland: *page 370 (Harmon Foundation, Collection H, 1922–1967)*

National Museum of American History, Smithsonian Institution: *page 124 (Division of Cultural and Community Life, 2006.0229.01ab)*

National Portrait Gallery, Smithsonian Institution: *pages 31, 98*

Old Salem Museums & Gardens, Museum of Early Southern Decorative Arts: *page 55 (s-5958)*

Richmond Times-Dispatch: *pages 395, 403, 411*

William Smith Morton Library Archives, Union Presbyterian Seminary: *page 111*

Valentine Museum, Richmond: *page 256*

Virginia Commonwealth University: *page 346 (Adèle Clark Papers)*

Virginia Department of Transportation: *page 416*

Virginia Museum of Fine Arts: *page 30 (52.8)*

Virginia Museum of History and Culture: *page 216 (1957.39)*

INDEX

Italicized page numbers refer to illustrations.